S0-CBU-864

INTERTEC BOOKS

President and CEO Raymond E. Maloney
Vice President, Book Group Ted Marcus

The following books and guides are published by Intertec Publishing.

CLYMER SHOP MANUALS
Boat Motors and Drives
Motorcycles and ATVs
Snowmobiles
Personal Watercraft

ABOS/INTERTEC/CLYMER BLUE BOOKS AND TRADE-IN GUIDES
Recreational Vehicles
Outdoor Power Equipment
Agricultural Tractors
Lawn and Garden Tractors
Motorcycles and ATVs
Snowmobiles and Personal Watercraft
Boats and Motors

AIRCRAFT BLUEBOOK-PRICE DIGEST
Airplanes
Helicopters

AC-U-KWIK DIRECTORIES
The Corporate Pilot's Airport/FBO Directory
International Manager's Edition
Jet Book

I&T SHOP SERVICE MANUALS
Tractors

INTERTEC SERVICE MANUALS
Snowmobiles
Outdoor Power Equipment
Personal Watercraft
Gasoline and Diesel Engines
Recreational Vehicles
Boat Motors and Drives
Motorcycles
Lawn and Garden Tractors

YAMAHA

O   ANUAL
2-250 HP 2-   cludes Jet Drives)

The World's Finest Publisher of Mechanical How-To Manuals

INTERTEC PUBLISHING

P.O. Box 12901, Overland Park, Kansas 66282-2901

Copyright ©1996 Intertec Publishing Corporation

FIRST EDITION
First Printing April, 1996
Second Printing January, 1998

Printed in U.S.A.

ISBN: 0-89287-650-6

Library of Congress: 95-75310

Tools shown in Chapter Two courtesy of Thorsen Tool, Dallas, Texas. Test equipment shown in Chapter Two courtesy of Dixson, Inc., Grand Junction, Colorado.

COVER: Photo courtesy of Yamaha Motor Corporation, U.S.A., 35655 Katella Avenue, Cypress, CA, 90630

Contents

CHAPTER FIVE

TIMING, SYNCHRONIZATION AND ADJUSTMENT 121

CHAPTER SIX

FUEL SYSTEM 197

CHAPTER SEVEN

IGNITION AND ELECTRICAL SYSTEMS. 272

CHAPTER EIGHT

POWER HEAD 304

Quick Reference Data

MAINTENANCE SCHEDULE*

After each use	Check for loose nuts, bolts and spark plug(s)
	Check propeller, shear pin and cotter pin condition
	Make sure cooling water runs out of exhaust ports while cruising
	Grease jet drive bearing(s)
Initial 10 hours or 1 month	Check throttle operation
	Check shift mechanism operation
	Check tightness of all bolts and nuts
	Check PTT operation*
	Check throttle grip/housing
	Check choke lever
	Check and adjust idle speed
	Check swivel bracket
	Check condition of anode
	Check fuel filter(s), fuel line(s), fuel tank(s)
	Check idle speed
	Check spark plug(s)
	Check oil injection pump operation*
	Check water drain (on engine oil tank)
	Electrical wiring and connections
	Check for exhaust leakage
	Check for water leakage
	Check gear oil level and condition
	Check condition and charge of battery
	Check carburetor(s)
	Inspect propeller for tightness and damage
	Check compression pressure
Initial 50 hours or 3 months	Check and adjust carburetor(s)
	Check carburetor link length*
	Check fuel filter(s)
	Check spark plug(s) adjust if necessary
	Check ignition timing
	Check oil pump operation*
	Check water drain (on engine oil tank)
	Check electrical wiring and connections
	Check for exhaust leakage
	Check for water leakage
	Check water pump impeller
	Check tightness of all bolts and nuts
	Check condition of anode(s)
	Inspect propeller for tightness and damage
	Check propeller cotter pin*
	Check compression pressure
Every 100 hours or 6 months	Check and adjust the carburetor(s)
	Check fuel filter(s), fuel line(s), fuel tank(s)
	Check and adjust idle speed

(continued)

MAINTENANCE SCHEDULE* (continued)

Every 100 hours **or 6 months (continued)**	Check carburetor link length* Check swivel bracket Check carburetor-to-ignition synchronization Check prime start operation* Check spark plug(s) adjust if necessary Check PTT operation* Check and adjust idle speed Check condition of anode Check oil injection pump* Check water drain (on engine oil tank) Check electrical wiring and connections Check for exhaust leakage Check for water leakage Gear oil level and condition Check condition and charge of battery Inspect propeller for tightness and damage Check compression pressure
Every 200 hours **or 1 year**	Inspect fuel tank(s) for rust or corrosion Check entire fuel system for leaks Electrical wiring and connections Check throttle sensor* Check fuel enrichment line filter* Inspect the PTT system operation* Check cowling locking and release mechanism

* Not all items apply to all engines. Perform only those pertaining to your engine.

RECOMMENDED SPARK PLUGS

	NGK No.	Champion No.	Gap mm (In.)
2 hp	B5HS	L90	0.6 (0.024)
3 hp	B6HS-10	L86C	1.0 (0.039)
4, 5 hp	B7HS	L82C	0.6 (0.024)
6, 8, 9.9, 15, 25 hp	B7HS-10	L82C	1.0 (0.039)
C25	B7HS	L82C	0.6 (0.024)
30, 40 hp	B7HS	L82C	1.0 (0.039)
C40	B8HS	L78C	0.6 (0.024)
C30, 50 hp, Pro 50, C55, Pro 60, 70 hp, C75, C85, 90 hp	B8HS-10	L78C	1.0 (0.039)
115 hp, C115, 150 hp	B8HS-10	L78C	1.0 (0.039)
Pro 150, L150, 175 hp, Pro 175, 200 hp, L200			
1990-1993	B8HS-10	L78C	1.0 (0.039)
1994-on	BR8HS-10	QL78C	1.0 (0.039)
130 hp, L130, Pro V 200			
1990-1993	B9HS-10	L77J4	1.0 (0.039)
1994-on	BR9HS-10	QL77CJ4	1.0 (0.039)
225 hp (90° V6)	BR9HS-10	QL77CJ4	1.0 (0.039)
225 hp, L225, 250 hp, L250 (76° V6)	BR8HS-10	QL78C	1.0 (0.039)

TEST PROPELLER RECOMMENDATIONS

Engine	Part No.
2, 3 hp	*
4, 5 hp	90890-01630
6, 8 hp	90890-01625
9.9, 15 hp	YB-1619
C25, 25 hp, 30 hp	YB-1621
C40, C55	YB-1611
C30	YB-1629
40 hp, 50 hp, Pro 50, Pro 60, 70 hp, 90 hp	YB-1611
C75, C85	YB-1620
115 hp, C115, 130 hp	YB-1624
150 hp, Pro V 150, 175 hp,	YB-1626
200 hp, Pro V 200, 225 hp	
(90° V6)	*
225 hp, L225, 250 hp, L250	
(76° V6)	*

* Information not available.

BATTERY CAPACITY (HOURS)

Accessory draw	80 amp-hour battery provides continuous power for:	Approximate recharge time
5 amps	13.5 hours	16 hours
15 amps	3.5 hours	13 hours
25 amps	1.8 hours	12 hours

Accessory draw	105 amp-hour battery provides continuous power for:	Approximate recharge time
5 amps	15.8 hours	16 hours
15 amps	4.2 hours	13 hours
25 amps	2.4 hours	12 hours

STATE OF BATTERY CHARGE

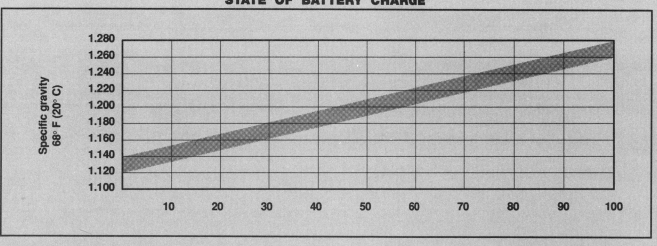

CLYMER™

YAMAHA

OUTBOARD SHOP MANUAL
2-250 HP 2-STROKE · 1990-1995 (Includes Jet Drives)

Introduction

This detailed, comprehensive manual covers Yamaha 2 hp single cylinder through 250 hp V6 outboard motors from 1990-on.

The expert text gives complete information on maintenance, tune-up, repair and overhaul. Hundreds of illustrations guide you through every step. The book includes all you will need to know to keep your Yamaha running right.

A shop manual is a reference. You want to be able to find information fast. As in all Clymer books, this one is designed with you in mind. All chapters are thumb tabbed. Important items are extensively indexed at the rear of the book. All procedures, tables, photos and illustrations in this manual are intended for the reader who may be working on the outboard motor for the first time or using this manual for the first time. Frequently used specifications are summarized in the *Quick Reference Data* pages at the front of the book.

Having a well-maintained outboard will increase your enjoyment of your boat as well as ensure your safety when offshore. Keep the book handy in your tool box. It will help you better understand how your outboard motor runs, lower repair costs and make yours a reliable, top-performing boat.

Chapter One

General Information

This detailed, comprehensive manual contains complete information on maintenance, tune-up, repair and overhaul. Hundreds of photos and drawings guide you through every step-by-step procedure.

Troubleshooting, tune-up, maintenance and repair are not difficult if you know what tools and equipment to use and what to do. Anyone not afraid to get their hands dirty, of average intelligence and with some mechanical ability, can perform most of the procedures in this book. See Chapter Two for more information on tools and techniques.

A shop manual is a reference. You want to be able to find information fast. Clymer books are designed with you in mind. All chapters are thumb tabbed and important items are indexed at the end of the book. All procedures, tables, photos, etc., in this manual assume that the reader may be working on the machine or using this manual for the first time.

Keep this book handy in your tool box. It will help you to better understand how your machine runs, lower repair and maintenance costs and generally increase your enjoyment of your marine equipment.

MANUAL ORGANIZATION

This chapter provides general information useful to marine owners and mechanics.

Chapter Two discusses the tools and techniques for preventive maintenance, troubleshooting and repair.

Chapter Three describes typical equipment problems and provides logical troubleshooting procedures.

Following chapters describe specific systems, providing disassembly, repair, assembly and adjustment procedures in simple step-by-step form. Specifications concerning a specific system are included at the end of the appropriate chapter.

NOTES, CAUTIONS AND WARNINGS

The terms NOTE, CAUTION and WARNING have specific meanings in this manual. A NOTE provides additional information to make a step or procedure easier or clearer. Disregarding a NOTE could cause inconvenience, but would not cause damage or personal injury.

A CAUTION emphasizes areas where equipment damage could result. Disregarding a CAUTION could cause permanent mechanical damage; however, personal injury is unlikely.

A WARNING emphasizes areas where personal injury or even death could result from negligence. Mechanical damage may also occur. WARNINGS *are to be taken seriously.* In some cases, serious injury or death has resulted from disregarding similar warnings.

TORQUE SPECIFICATIONS

Torque specifications throughout this manual are given in foot-pounds (ft.-lb.) and either Newton meters (N.m) or meter-kilograms (mkg). Newton meters are being adopted in place of meter-kilograms in accordance with the International Modernized Metric System. Existing torque wrenches calibrated in meter-kilograms can be used by performing a simple conversion: move the decimal point one place to the right. For example, 4.7 mkg = 47 N.m. This conversion is accurate enough for mechanics' use even though the exact mathematical conversion is 3.5 mkg = 34.3 N.m.

ENGINE OPERATION

All marine engines, whether 2- or 4-stroke, gasoline or diesel, operate on the Otto cycle of intake, compression, power and exhaust phases.

4-stroke Cycle

A 4-stroke engine requires two crankshaft revolutions (4 strokes of the piston) to complete the Otto cycle. **Figure 1** shows gasoline 4-stroke engine operation. **Figure 2** shows diesel 4-stroke engine operation.

2-stroke Cycle

A 2-stroke engine requires only 1 crankshaft revolution (2 strokes of the piston) to complete the Otto cycle. **Figure 3** shows gasoline 2-stroke engine operation. Although diesel 2-strokes exist, they are not commonly used in light marine applications.

FASTENERS

The material and design of the various fasteners used on marine equipment are not arrived at by chance or accident. Fastener design determines the type of tool required to work with the fastener. Fastener material is carefully selected to decrease the possibility of physical failure or corrosion. See *Galvanic Corrosion* in this chapter for more information on marine materials.

Threads

Nuts, bolts and screws are manufactured in a wide range of thread patterns. To join a nut and bolt, the diameter of the bolt and the diameter of the hole in the nut must be the same. It is just as important that the threads on both be properly matched.

The best way to determine if the threads on two fasteners are matched is to turn the nut on the bolt (or the bolt into the threaded hole in a piece of equipment) with fingers only. Be sure both pieces are clean. If much force is required, check the thread condition on each fastener. If the thread condition is good but the fasteners jam, the threads are not compatible.

Four important specifications describe every thread:

   a. Diameter.
   b. Threads per inch.
   c. Thread pattern.
   d. Thread direction.

Figure 4 shows the first two specifications. Thread pattern is more subtle. Italian and British

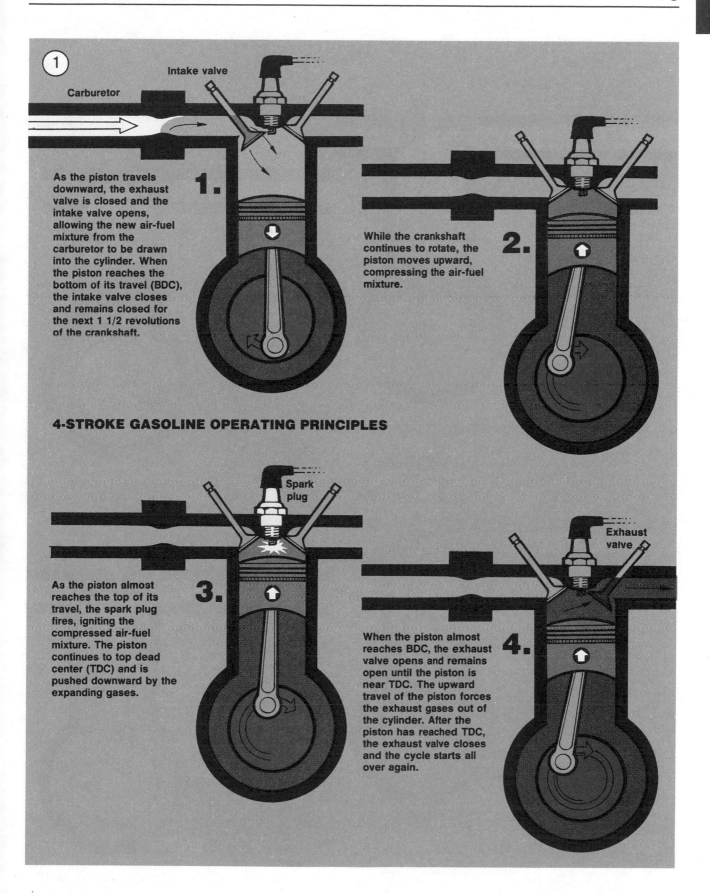

4-STROKE GASOLINE OPERATING PRINCIPLES

1. As the piston travels downward, the exhaust valve is closed and the intake valve opens, allowing the new air-fuel mixture from the carburetor to be drawn into the cylinder. When the piston reaches the bottom of its travel (BDC), the intake valve closes and remains closed for the next 1 1/2 revolutions of the crankshaft.

2. While the crankshaft continues to rotate, the piston moves upward, compressing the air-fuel mixture.

3. As the piston almost reaches the top of its travel, the spark plug fires, igniting the compressed air-fuel mixture. The piston continues to top dead center (TDC) and is pushed downward by the expanding gases.

4. When the piston almost reaches BDC, the exhaust valve opens and remains open until the piston is near TDC. The upward travel of the piston forces the exhaust gases out of the cylinder. After the piston has reached TDC, the exhaust valve closes and the cycle starts all over again.

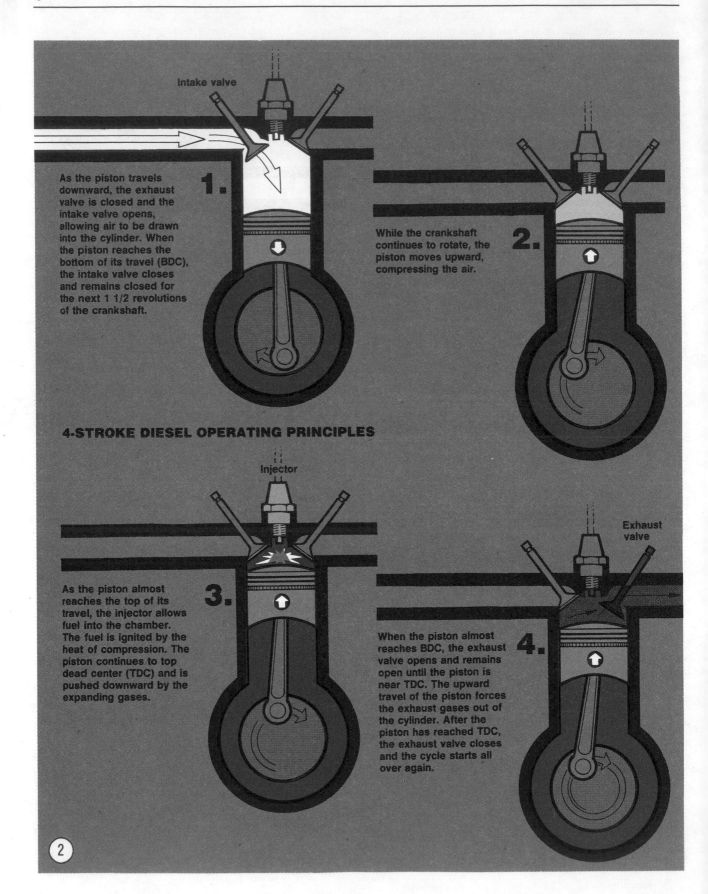

Intake valve

1. As the piston travels downward, the exhaust valve is closed and the intake valve opens, allowing air to be drawn into the cylinder. When the piston reaches the bottom of its travel (BDC), the intake valve closes and remains closed for the next 1 1/2 revolutions of the crankshaft.

2. While the crankshaft continues to rotate, the piston moves upward, compressing the air.

4-STROKE DIESEL OPERATING PRINCIPLES

Injector

3. As the piston almost reaches the top of its travel, the injector allows fuel into the chamber. The fuel is ignited by the heat of compression. The piston continues to top dead center (TDC) and is pushed downward by the expanding gases.

Exhaust valve

4. When the piston almost reaches BDC, the exhaust valve opens and remains open until the piston is near TDC. The upward travel of the piston forces the exhaust gases out of the cylinder. After the piston has reached TDC, the exhaust valve closes and the cycle starts all over again.

As the piston travels downward, it uncovers the exhaust port (A) allowing the exhaust gases to leave the cylinder. A fresh air-fuel charge, which has been compressed slightly in the crankcase, enters the cylinder through the transfer port (B). Since this charge enters under pressure, it also helps to push out the exhaust gases.

While the crankshaft continues to rotate, the piston moves upward, covering the transfer (B) and exhaust (A) ports. The piston compresses the new air-fuel mixture and creates a low-pressure area in the crankcase at the same time. As the piston continues to travel, it uncovers the intake port (C). A fresh air-fuel charge from the carburetor (D) is drawn into the crankcase through the intake port.

2-STROKE OPERATING PRINCIPLES

As the piston almost reaches the top of its travel, the spark plug fires, igniting the compressed air-fuel mixture. The piston continues to top dead center (TDC) and is pushed downward by the expanding gases.

As the piston travels down, the exhaust gases leave the cylinder and the complete cycle starts all over again.

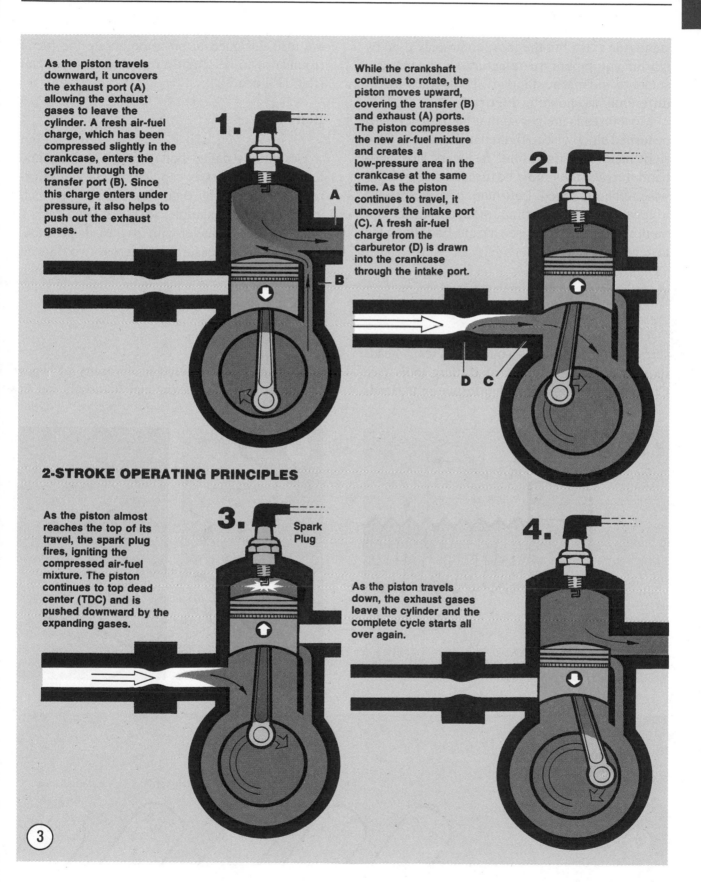

standards exist, but the most commonly used by marine equipment manufacturers are American standard and metric standard. The threads are cut differently as shown in **Figure 5**.

Most threads are cut so that the fastener must be turned clockwise to tighten it. These are called right-hand threads. Some fasteners have left-hand threads; they must be turned counterclockwise to be tightened. Left-hand threads are used in locations where normal rotation of the equipment would tend to loosen a right-hand threaded fastener.

Machine Screws

There are many different types of machine screws. **Figure 6** shows a number of screw heads requiring different types of turning tools (see Chapter Two for detailed information). Heads are also designed to protrude above the metal (round) or to be slightly recessed in the metal (flat) (**Figure 7**).

Bolts

Commonly called bolts, the technical name for these fasteners is cap screw. They are normally described by diameter, threads per inch and length. For example, 1/4-20 × 1 indicates a bolt 1/4 in. diameter with 20 threads per inch, 1 in. long. The measurement across two flats on the head of the bolt indicates the proper wrench size to be used.

Nuts

Nuts are manufactured in a variety of types and sizes. Most are hexagonal (6-sided) and fit

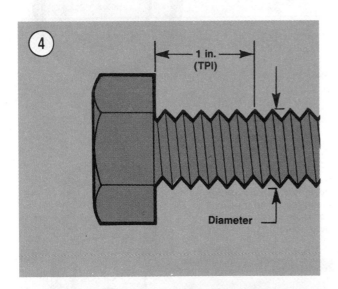

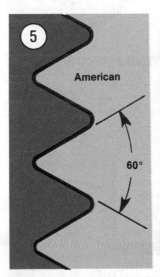
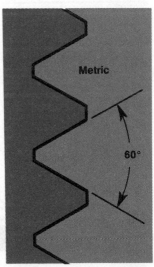

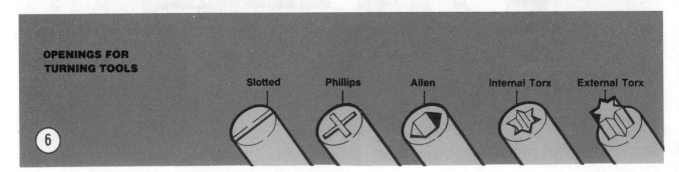

OPENINGS FOR
TURNING TOOLS

Slotted   Phillips   Allen   Internal Torx   External Torx

on bolts, screws and studs with the same diameter and threads per inch.

Figure 8 shows several types of nuts. The common nut is usually used with a lockwasher. Self-locking nuts have a nylon insert that prevents the nut from loosening; no lockwasher is required. Wing nuts are designed for fast removal by hand. Wing nuts are used for convenience in non-critical locations.

To indicate the size of a nut, manufacturers specify the diameter of the opening and the threads per inch. This is similar to bolt specification, but without the length dimension. The measurement across two flats on the nut indicates the proper wrench size to be used.

Washers

There are two basic types of washers: flat washers and lockwashers. Flat washers are simple discs with a hole to fit a screw or bolt. Lockwashers are designed to prevent a fastener from working loose due to vibration, expansion and contraction. **Figure 9** shows several types of lockwashers. Note that flat washers are often used between a lockwasher and a fastener to provide a smooth bearing surface. This allows the fastener to be turned easily with a tool.

Cotter Pins

Cotter pins (**Figure 10**) are used to secure special kinds of fasteners. The threaded stud

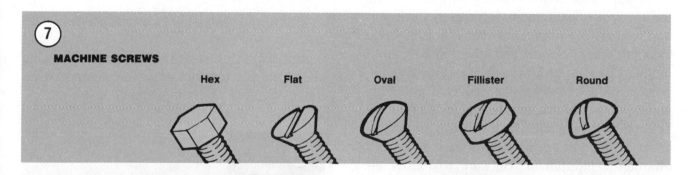

⑦ **MACHINE SCREWS**

Hex   Flat   Oval   Fillister   Round

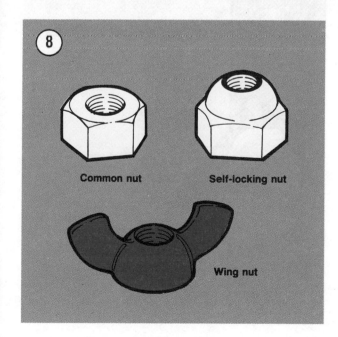

⑧

Common nut   Self-locking nut

Wing nut

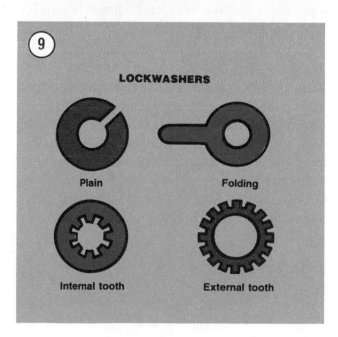

⑨ **LOCKWASHERS**

Plain   Folding

Internal tooth   External tooth

must have a hole in it; the nut or nut lock piece has projections that the cotter pin fits between. This type of nut is called a "Castellated nut." Cotter pins should not be reused after removal.

Snap Rings

Snap rings can be of an internal or external design. They are used to retain items on shafts (external type) or within tubes (internal type). Snap rings can be reused if they are not distorted during removal. In some applications, snap rings of varying thickness can be selected to control the end play of parts assemblies.

LUBRICANTS

Periodic lubrication ensures long service life for any type of equipment. It is especially important to marine equipment because it is exposed to salt or brackish water and other harsh environments. The *type* of lubricant used is just as important as the lubrication service itself; although, in an emergency, the wrong type of lubricant is better than none at all. The following paragraphs describe the types of lubricants most often used on marine equipment. Be sure to follow the equipment manufacturer's recommendations for lubricant types.

Generally, all liquid lubricants are called "oil." They may be mineral-based (including petroleum bases), natural-based (vegetable and animal bases), synthetic-based or emulsions (mixtures). "Grease" is an oil which is thickened with a metallic "soap." The resulting material is then usually enhanced with anticorrosion, antioxidant and extreme pressure (EP) additives. Grease is often classified by the type of thickener added; lithium and calcium soap are commonly used.

4-stroke Engine Oil

Oil for 4-stroke engines is graded by the American Petroleum Institute (API) and the So-

ciety of Automotive Engineers (SAE) in several categories. Oil containers display these ratings on the top or label (**Figure 11**).

API oil grade is indicated by letters, oils for gasoline engines are identified by an "S" and oils for diesel engines are identified by a "C." Most modern gasoline engines require SF or SG graded oil. Automotive and marine diesel engines use CC or CD graded oil.

Viscosity is an indication of the oil's thickness, or resistance to flow. The SAE uses numbers to indicate viscosity; thin oils have low numbers and thick oils have high numbers. A "W" after the number indicates that the viscosity testing was done at low temperature to simulate cold weather operation. Engine oils fall into the 5W-20W and 20-50 range.

Multi-grade oils (for example, 10W-40) are less viscous (thinner) at low temperatures and more viscous (thicker) at high temperatures. This allows the oil to perform efficiently across a wide range of engine operating temperatures.

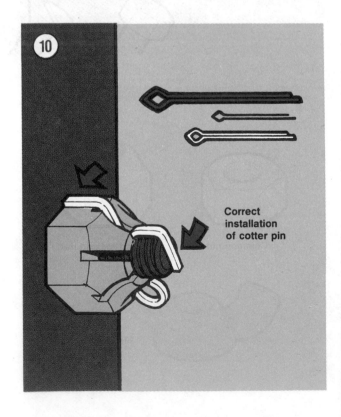

Correct installation of cotter pin

2-stroke Engine Oil

Lubrication for a 2-stroke engine is provided by oil mixed with the incoming fuel-air mixture. Some of the oil mist settles out in the crankcase, lubricating the crankshaft and lower end of the connecting rods. The rest of the oil enters the combustion chamber to lubricate the piston, rings and cylinder wall. This oil is then burned along with the fuel-air mixture during the combustion process.

Engine oil must have several special qualities to work well in a 2-stroke engine. It must mix easily and stay in suspension in gasoline. When burned, it can't leave behind excessive deposits. It must also be able to withstand the high temperatures associated with 2-stroke engines.

The National Marine Manufacturer's Association (NMMA) has set standards for oil used in 2-stroke, water-cooled engines. This is the NMMA TC-W (two-cycle, water-cooled) grade (**Figure 12**). The oil's performance in the following areas is evaluated:

   a. Lubrication (prevention of wear and scuffing).
   b. Spark plug fouling.
   c. Preignition.
   d. Piston ring sticking.
   e. Piston varnish.
   f. General engine condition (including deposits).
   g. Exhaust port blockage.
   h. Rust prevention.
   i. Mixing ability with gasoline.

In addition to oil grade, manufacturers specify the ratio of gasoline to oil required during break-in and normal engine operation.

Gear Oil

Gear lubricants are assigned SAE viscosity numbers under the same system as 4-stroke engine oil. Gear lubricant falls into the SAE 72-250 range (**Figure 13**). Some gear lubricants are multi-grade; for example, SAE 85W-90.

Three types of marine gear lubricant are generally available: SAE 90 hypoid gear lubricant is designed for older manual-shift units; Type C gear lubricant contains additives designed for electric shift mechanisms; High viscosity gear lubricant is a heavier oil designed to withstand the shock loading of high-performance engines or units subjected to severe duty use. Always use a gear lubricant of the type specified by the unit's manufacturer.

Grease

Greases are graded by the National Lubricating Grease Institute (NLGI). Greases are graded by number according to the consistency of the grease; these ratings range from No. 000 to No. 6, with No. 6 being the most solid. A typical multipurpose grease is NLGI No. 2 (**Figure 14**). For specific applications, equipment manufacturers may require grease with an additive such as molybdenum disulfide (MOS^2).

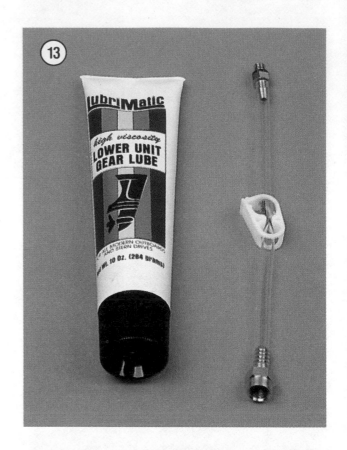

GASKET SEALANT

Gasket sealant is used instead of pre-formed gaskets on some applications, or as a gasket dressing on others. Two types of gasket sealant are commonly used: room temperature vulcanizing (RTV) and anaerobic. Because these two materials have different sealing properties, they cannot be used interchangeably.

RTV Sealant

This is a silicone gel supplied in tubes (**Figure 15**). Moisture in the air causes RTV to cure. Always place the cap on the tube as soon as possible when using RTV. RTV has a shelf life of one year and will not cure properly when the shelf life has expired. Check the expiration date

on RTV tubes before using and keep partially used tubes tightly sealed. RTV sealant can generally fill gaps up to 1/4 in. (6.3 mm) and works well on slightly flexible surfaces.

Applying RTV Sealant

Clean all gasket residue from mating surfaces. Surfaces should be clean and free of oil and dirt. Remove all RTV gasket material from blind attaching holes because it can create a "hydraulic" effect and affect bolt torque.

Apply RTV sealant in a continuous bead 2-3 mm (0.08-0.12 in.) thick. Circle all mounting holes unless otherwise specified. Torque mating parts within 10 minutes after application.

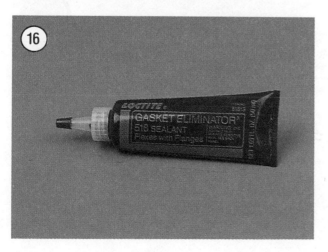

Anaerobic Sealant

This is a gel supplied in tubes (**Figure 16**). It cures only in the absence of air, as when squeezed tightly between two machined mating surfaces. For this reason, it will not spoil if the cap is left off the tube. It should not be used if one mating surface is flexible. Anaerobic sealant is able to fill gaps up to 0.030 in. (0.8 mm) and generally works best on rigid, machined flanges or surfaces.

Applying Anaerobic Sealant

Clean all gasket residue from mating surfaces. Surfaces must be clean and free of oil and dirt. Remove all gasket material from blind attaching holes, as it can cause a "hydraulic" effect and affect bolt torque.

Apply anaerobic sealant in a 1 mm or less (0.04 in.) bead to one sealing surface. Circle all mounting holes. Torque mating parts within 15 minutes after application.

GALVANIC CORROSION

A chemical reaction occurs whenever two different types of metal are joined by an electrical conductor and immersed in an electrolyte. Electrons transfer from one metal to the other through the electrolyte and return through the conductor.

The hardware on a boat is made of many different types of metal. The boat hull acts as a conductor between the metals. Even if the hull is wooden or fiberglass, the slightest film of water (electrolyte) within the hull provides conductivity. This combination creates a good environment for electron flow (**Figure 17**). Unfortunately, this electron flow results in galvanic corrosion of the metal involved, causing one of the metals to be corroded or eaten away by the process. The amount of electron flow (and, therefore, the amount of corrosion) depends on several factors:

    a. The types of metal involved.

    b. The efficiency of the conductor.

    c. The strength of the electrolyte.

Metals

The chemical composition of the metals used in marine equipment has a significant effect on the amount and speed of galvanic corrosion. Certain metals are more resistant to corrosion than others. These electrically negative metals are commonly called "noble;" they act as the cathode in any reaction. Metals that are more subject to corrosion are electrically positive; they act as the anode in a reaction. The more noble metals include titanium, 18-8 stainless steel and nickel. Less noble metals include zinc, aluminum and magnesium. Galvanic corrosion becomes more severe as the difference in electrical potential between the two metals increases.

In some cases, galvanic corrosion can occur within a single piece of metal. Common brass is a mixture of zinc and copper, and, when immersed in an electrolyte, the zinc portion of the mixture will corrode away as reaction occurs between the zinc and the copper particles.

Conductors

The hull of the boat often acts as the conductor between different types of metal. Marine equipment, such as an outboard motor or stern drive unit, can also act as the conductor. Large masses of metal, firmly connected together, are more efficient conductors than water. Rubber mountings and vinyl-based paint can act as insulators between pieces of metal.

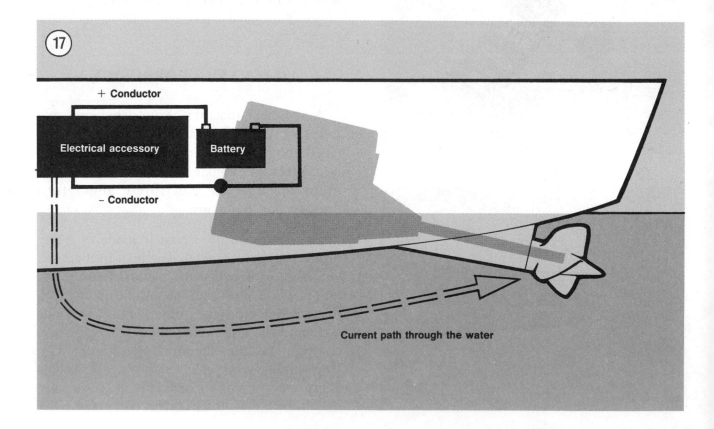

Electrolyte

The water in which a boat operates acts as the electrolyte for the galvanic corrosion process. The better a conductor the electrolyte is, the more severe and rapid the corrosion.

Cold, clean freshwater is the poorest electrolyte. As water temperature increases, its conductivity increases. Pollutants will increase conductivity; brackish or saltwater is also an efficient electrolyte. This is one of the reasons that most manufacturers recommend a freshwater flush for marine equipment after operation in saltwater, polluted or brackish water.

PROTECTION FROM GALVANIC CORROSION

Because of the environment in which marine equipment must operate, it is practically impossible to totally prevent galvanic corrosion. There are several ways by which the process can be slowed. After taking these precautions, the next step is to "fool" the process into occurring only where *you* want it to occur. This is the role of sacrificial anodes and impressed current systems.

Slowing Corrosion

Some simple precautions can help reduce the amount of corrosion taking place outside the hull. These are *not* a substitute for the corrosion protection methods discussed under *Sacrificial Anodes* and *Impressed Current Systems* in this chapter, but they can help these protection methods do their job.

Use fasteners of a metal more noble than the part they are fastening. If corrosion occurs, the larger equipment will suffer but the fastener will be protected. Because fasteners are usually very small in comparison to the equipment being fastened, the equipment can survive the loss of material. If the fastener were to corrode instead of the equipment, major problems could arise.

Keep all painted surfaces in good condition. If paint is scraped off and bare metal exposed, corrosion will rapidly increase. Use a vinyl- or plastic-based paint, which acts as an electrical insulator.

Be careful when using metal-based antifouling paints. These should not be applied to metal parts of the boat, outboard motor or stern drive unit or they will actually react with the equipment, causing corrosion between the equipment and the layer of paint. Organic-based paints are available for use on metal surfaces.

Where a corrosion protection device is used, remember that it must be immersed in the electrolyte along with the rest of the boat to have any effect. If you raise the power unit out of the water when the boat is docked, any anodes on the power unit will be removed from the corrosion cycle and will not protect the rest of the equipment that is still immersed. Also, such corrosion protection devices must not be painted because this would insulate them from the corrosion process.

Any change in the boat's equipment, such as the installation of a new stainless steel propeller, will change the electrical potential and could cause increased corrosion. Keep in mind that when you add new equipment or change materials, you should review your corrosion protection system to be sure it is up to the job.

Sacrificial Anodes

Anodes are usually made of zinc, a far from noble metal. Sacrificial anodes are specially designed to do nothing but corrode. Properly fastening such pieces to the boat will cause them to act as the anode in *any* galvanic reaction that occurs; any other metal present will act as the cathode and will not be damaged.

Anodes must be used properly to be effective. Simply fastening pieces of zinc to your boat in random locations won't do the job.

You must determine how much anode surface area is required to adequately protect the equipment's surface area. A good starting point is provided by Military Specification MIL-A-818001, which states that one square inch of new anode will protect either:

a. 800 square inches of freshly painted steel.
b. 250 square inches of bare steel or bare aluminum alloy.
c. 100 square inches of copper or copper alloy.

This rule is for a boat at rest. When underway, more anode area is required to protect the same equipment surface area.

The anode must be fastened so that it has good electrical contact with the metal to be protected. If possible, the anode can be attached directly to the other metal. If that is not possible, the entire network of metal parts in the boat should be electrically bonded together so that all pieces are protected.

Good quality anodes have inserts of some other metal around the fastener holes. Otherwise, the anode could erode away around the fastener. The anode can then become loose or even fall off, removing all protection.

Another Military Specification (MIL-A-18001) defines the type of alloy preferred that will corrode at a uniform rate without forming a crust that could reduce its efficiency after a time.

Impressed Current Systems

An impressed current system can be installed on any boat that has a battery. The system consists of an anode, a control box and a sensor. The anode in this system is coated with a very noble metal, such as platinum, so that it is almost corrosion-free and will last indefinitely. The sensor, under the boat's waterline, monitors the potential for corrosion. When it senses that

corrosion could be occurring, it transmits this information to the control box.

The control box connects the boat's battery to the anode. When the sensor signals the need, the control box applies positive battery voltage to the anode. Current from the battery flows from the anode to all other metal parts of the boat, no matter how noble or non-noble these parts may be. This battery current takes the place of any galvanic current flow.

Only a very small amount of battery current is needed to counteract galvanic corrosion. Manufacturers estimate that it would take two or three months of constant use to drain a typical marine battery, assuming the battery is never recharged.

An impressed current system is more expensive to install than simple anodes but, considering its low maintenance requirements and the excellent protection it provides, the long-term cost may actually be lower.

PROPELLERS

The propeller is the final link between the boat's drive system and the water. A perfectly

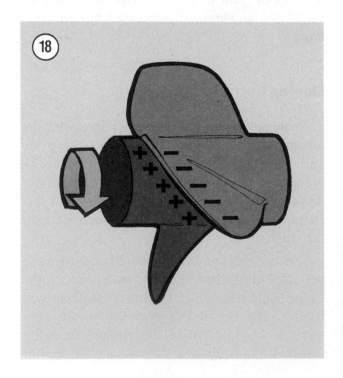

maintained engine and hull are useless if the propeller is the wrong type or has been allowed to deteriorate. Although propeller selection for a specific situation is beyond the scope of this book, the following information on propeller construction and design will allow you to discuss the subject intelligently with your marine dealer.

How a Propeller Works

As the curved blades of a propeller rotate through the water, a high-pressure area is created on one side of the blade and a low-pressure area exists on the other side of the blade (**Figure 18**). The propeller moves toward the low-pressure area, carrying the boat with it.

Propeller Parts

Although a propeller may be a one-piece unit, it is made up of several different parts (**Figure 19**). Variations in the design of these parts make different propellers suitable for different jobs.

The blade tip is the point on the blade farthest from the center of the propeller hub. The blade tip separates the leading edge from the trailing edge.

The leading edge is the edge of the blade nearest to the boat. During normal rotation, this is the area of the blade that first cuts through the water.

The trailing edge is the edge of the blade farthest from the boat.

The blade face is the surface of the blade that faces away from the boat. During normal rotation, high pressure exists on this side of the blade.

The blade back is the surface of the blade that faces toward the boat. During normal rotation, low pressure exists on this side of the blade.

The cup is a small curve or lip on the trailing edge of the blade.

The hub is the central portion of the propeller. It connects the blades to the propeller shaft (part of the boat's drive system). On some drive systems, engine exhaust is routed through the hub; in this case, the hub is made up of an outer and an inner portion, connected by ribs.

The diffuser ring is used on through-hub exhaust models to prevent exhaust gases from entering the blade area.

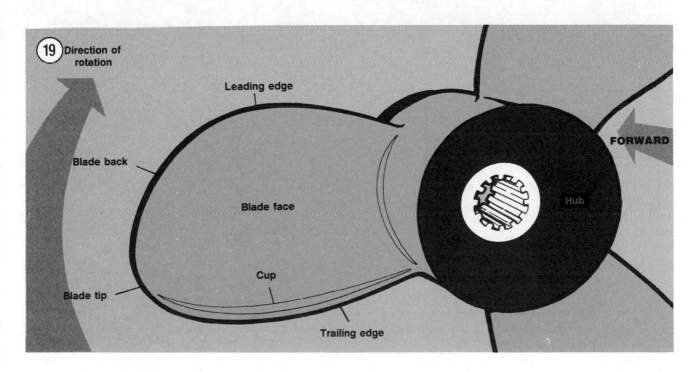

(19) Direction of rotation

Leading edge

Blade back

Blade face

FORWARD

Hub

Cup

Blade tip

Trailing edge

Propeller Design

Changes in length, angle, thickness and material of propeller parts make different propellers suitable for different situations.

Diameter

Propeller diameter is the distance from the center of the hub to the blade tip, multiplied by 2. That is, it is the diameter of the circle formed by the blade tips during propeller rotation (**Figure 20**).

Pitch and rake

Propeller pitch and rake describe the placement of the blade in relation to the hub (**Figure 21**).

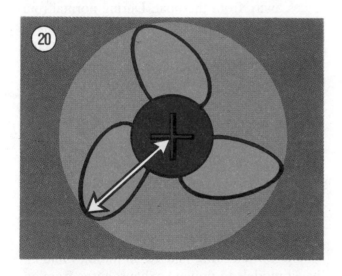

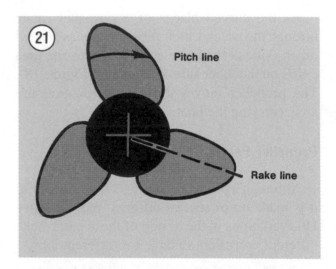

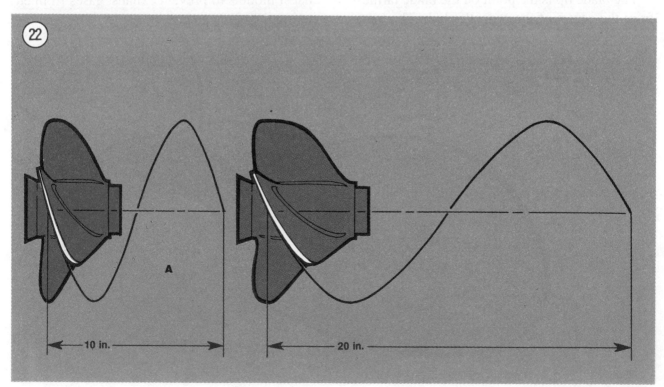

Pitch is expressed by the theoretical distance that the propeller would travel in one revolution. In A, **Figure 22**, the propeller would travel 10 inches in one revolution. In B, **Figure 22**, the propeller would travel 20 inches in one revolution. This distance is only theoretical; during actual operation, the propeller achieves about 80% of its rated travel.

Propeller blades can be constructed with constant pitch (**Figure 23**) or progressive pitch (**Figure 24**). Progressive pitch starts low at the leading edge and increases toward to trailing edge. The propeller pitch specification is the average of the pitch across the entire blade.

Blade rake is specified in degrees and is measured along a line from the center of the hub to the blade tip. A blade that is perpendicular to the hub (A, **Figure 25**) has 0° of rake. A blade that is angled from perpendicular (B, **Figure 25**) has a rake expressed by its difference from perpen-

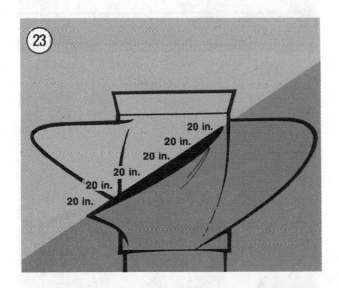

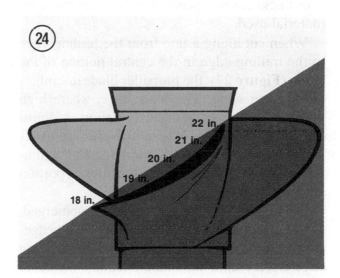

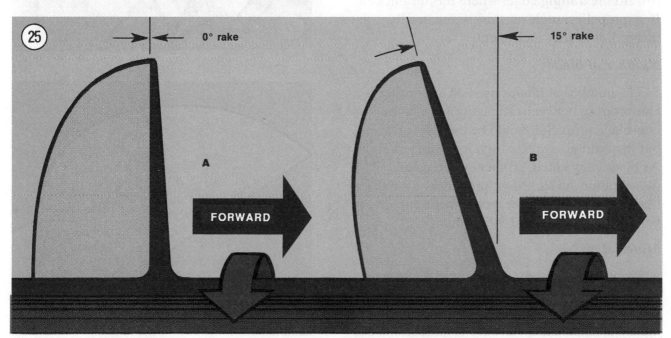

dicular. Most propellers have rakes ranging from 0-20°.

Blade thickness

Blade thickness is not uniform at all points along the blade. For efficiency, blades should be as thin as possible at all points while retaining enough strength to move the boat. Blades tend to be thicker where they meet the hub and thinner at the blade tip (**Figure 26**). This is to support the heavier loads at the hub section of the blade. This thickness is dependent on the strength of the material used.

When cut along a line from the leading edge to the trailing edge in the central portion of the blade (**Figure 27**), the propeller blade resembles an airplane wing. The blade face, where high pressure exists during normal rotation, is almost flat. The blade back, where low pressure exists during normal rotation, is curved, with the thinnest portions at the edges and the thickest portion at the center.

Propellers that run only partially submerged, as in racing applications, may have a wedge-shaped cross-section (**Figure 28**). The leading edge is very thin; the blade thickness increases toward the trailing edge, where it is the thickest. If a propeller such as this is run totally submerged, it is very inefficient.

Number of blades

The number of blades used on a propeller is a compromise between efficiency and vibration. A one-blade propeller would be the most efficient, but it would also create high levels of vibration. As blades are added, efficiency decreases, but so do vibration levels. Most propellers have three blades, representing the most practical trade-off between efficiency and vibration.

Material

Propeller materials are chosen for strength, corrosion resistance and economy. Stainless steel, aluminum and bronze are the most commonly used materials. Bronze is quite strong but

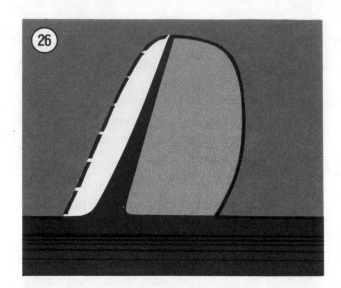

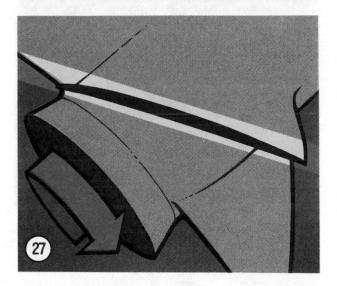

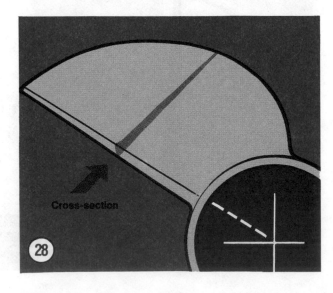

Cross-section

rather expensive. Stainless steel is more common than bronze because of its combination of strength and lower cost. Aluminum alloys are the least expensive but usually lack the strength of steel. Plastic propellers may be used in some low horsepower applications.

Direction of rotation

Propellers are made for both right-hand and left-hand rotation although right-hand is the most commonly used. When seen from behind the boat in forward motion, a right-hand propeller turns clockwise and a left-hand propeller turns counterclockwise. Off the boat, you can tell the difference by observing the angle of the blades (**Figure 29**). A right-hand propeller's blades slant from the upper left to the lower right; a left-hand propeller's blades are the opposite.

Cavitation and Ventilation

Cavitation and ventilation are *not* interchangeable terms; they refer to two distinct problems encountered during propeller operation.

To understand cavitation, you must first understand the relationship between pressure and the boiling point of water. At sea level, water will boil at 212° F. As pressure increases, such as within an engine's closed cooling system, the boiling point of water increases—it will boil at some temperature higher than 212° F. The opposite is also true. As pressure decreases, water will boil at a temperature lower than 212° F. If pressure drops low enough, water will boil at typical ambient temperatures of 50-60° F.

We have said that, during normal propeller operation, low-pressure exists on the blade back. Normally, the pressure does not drop low enough for boiling to occur. However, poor blade design

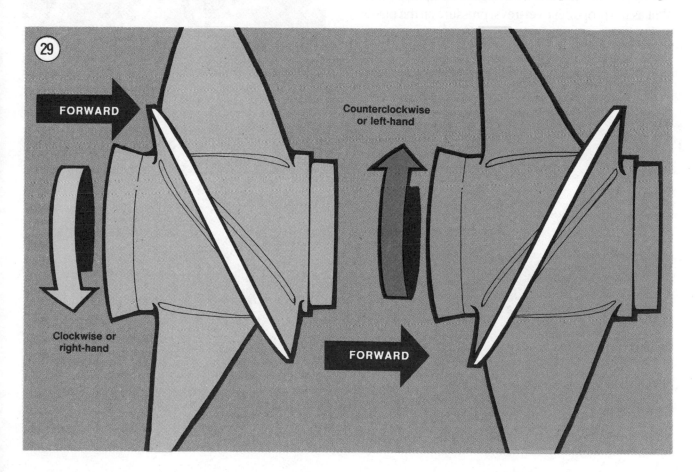

or selection, or blade damage can cause an unusual pressure drop on a small area of the blade (**Figure 30**). Boiling can occur in this small area. As the water boils, air bubbles form. As the boiling water passes to a higher pressure area of the blade, the boiling stops and the bubbles collapse. The collapsing bubbles release enough energy to erode the surface of the blade.

This entire process of pressure drop, boiling and bubble collapse is called "cavitation." The damage caused by the collapsing bubbles is called a "cavitation burn." It is important to remember that cavitation is caused by a decrease in pressure, *not* an increase in temperature.

Ventilation is not as complex a process as cavitation. Ventilation refers to air entering the blade area, either from above the surface of the water or from a through-hub exhaust system. As the blades meet the air, the propeller momentarily over-revs, losing most of its thrust. An added complication is that as the propeller over-revs, pressure on the blade back decreases and massive cavitation can occur.

Most pieces of marine equipment have a plate above the propeller area designed to keep surface air from entering the blade area (**Figure 31**). This plate is correctly called an "antiventilation plate," although you will often *see* it called an "anticavitation plate." Through hub exhaust systems also have specially designed hubs to keep exhaust gases from entering the blade area.

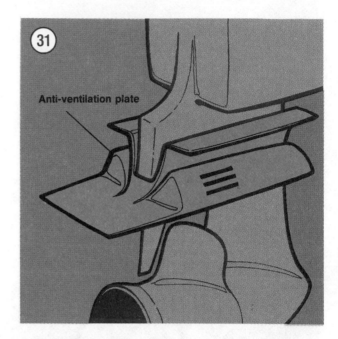

Anti-ventilation plate

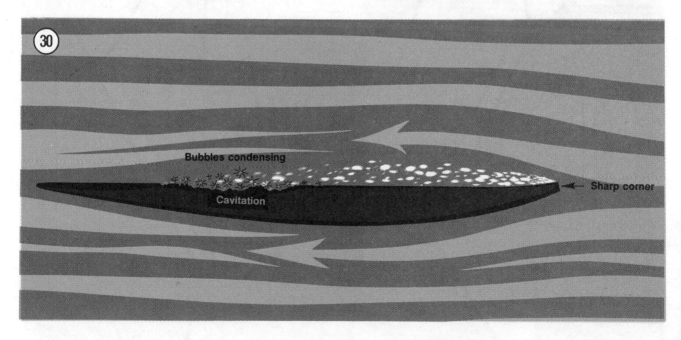

Bubbles condensing

Cavitation

Sharp corner

Chapter Two

Tools and Techniques

This chapter describes the common tools required for marine equipment repairs and troubleshooting. Techniques that will make your work easier and more effective are also described. Some of the procedures in this book require special skills or expertise; in some cases, you are better off entrusting the job to a dealer or qualified specialist.

SAFETY FIRST

Professional mechanics can work for years and never suffer a serious injury. If you follow a few rules of common sense and safety, you too can enjoy many safe hours servicing your marine equipment. If you ignore these rules, you can hurt yourself or damage the equipment.

1. Never use gasoline as a cleaning solvent.
2. Never smoke or use a torch near flammable liquids, such as cleaning solvent. If you are working in your home garage, remember that your home gas appliances have pilot lights.
3. Never smoke or use a torch in an area where batteries are being charged. Highly explosive hydrogen gas is formed during the charging process.

4. Use the proper size wrenches to avoid damage to fasteners and injury to yourself.
5. When loosening a tight or stuck fastener, think of what would happen if the wrench should slip. Protect yourself accordingly.
6. Keep your work area clean, uncluttered and well lighted.
7. Wear safety goggles during all operations involving drilling, grinding or the use of a cold chisel.
8. Never use worn tools.
9. Keep a Coast Guard approved fire extinguisher handy. Be sure it is rated for gasoline (Class B) and electrical (Class C) fires.

BASIC HAND TOOLS

A number of tools are required to maintain marine equipment. You may already have some of these tools for home or car repairs. There are also tools made especially for marine equipment repairs; these you will have to purchase. In any case, a wide variety of quality tools will make repairs easier and more effective.

Keep your tools clean and in a tool box. Keep them organized with the sockets and related drives together, the open end and box wrenches together, etc. After using a tool, wipe off dirt and grease with a clean cloth and place the tool in its correct place.

The following tools are required to perform virtually any repair job. Each tool is described and the recommended size given for starting a tool collection. Additional tools and some duplications may be added as you become more familiar with the equipment. You may need all standard U.S. size tools, all metric size tools or a mixture of both.

Screwdrivers

The screwdriver is a very basic tool, but if used improperly, it will do more damage than good. The slot on a screw has a definite dimension and shape. A screwdriver must be selected to conform with that shape. Use a small screwdriver for small screws and a large one for large screws or the screw head will be damaged.

Two types of screwdriver are commonly required: a common (flat-blade) screwdriver (**Figure 1**) and Phillips screwdrivers (**Figure 2**).

Screwdrivers are available in sets, which often include an assortment of common and Phillips blades. If you buy them individually, buy at least the following:

    a. Common screwdriver—5/16 × 6 in. blade.
    b. Common screwdriver—3/8 × 12 in. blade
    c. Phillips screwdriver—size 2 tip, 6 in. blade.

Use screwdrivers only for driving screws. Never use a screwdriver for prying or chiseling. Do not try to remove a Phillips or Allen head screw with a common screwdriver; you can damage the head so that the proper tool will be unable to remove it.

Keep screwdrivers in the proper condition and they will last longer and perform better. Always keep the tip of a common screwdriver in good condition. **Figure 3** shows how to grind the tip to the proper shape if it becomes damaged. Note the parallel sides of the tip.

Pliers

Pliers come in a wide range of types and sizes. Pliers are useful for cutting, bending and crimping. They should never be used to cut hardened objects or to turn bolts or nuts. **Figure 4** shows several types of pliers.

Each type of pliers has a specialized function. General purpose pliers are used mainly for holding things and for bending. Locking pliers are used as pliers or to hold objects very tightly, like a vise. Needlenose pliers are used to hold or bend small objects. Adjustable or slip-joint pliers can

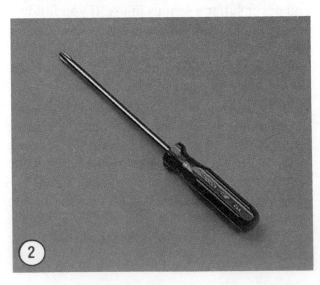

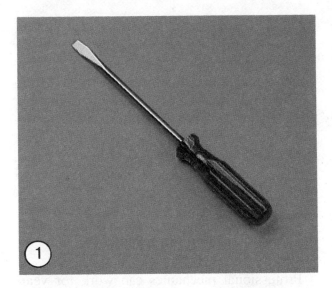

be adjusted to hold various sizes of objects; the jaws remain parallel to grip around objects such as pipe or tubing. There are many more types of pliers. The ones described here are the most commonly used.

Box and Open-end Wrenches

Box and open-end wrenches are available in sets or separately in a variety of sizes. See **Figure 5** and **Figure 6**. The number stamped near the end refers to the distance between two parallel flats on the hex head bolt or nut.

Box wrenches are usually superior to open-end wrenches. An open-end wrench grips the nut on only two flats. Unless it fits well, it may slip and round off the points on the nut. The box wrench grips all 6 flats. Both 6-point and 12-point openings on box wrenches are available. The 6-point gives superior holding power; the 12-point allows a shorter swing.

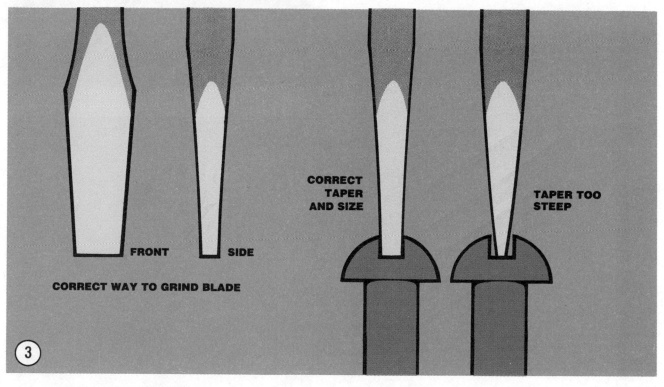

FRONT SIDE

CORRECT WAY TO GRIND BLADE

CORRECT TAPER AND SIZE

TAPER TOO STEEP

Combination wrenches, which are open on one side and boxed on the other, are also available. Both ends are the same size.

Adjustable Wrenches

An adjustable wrench can be adjusted to fit nearly any nut or bolt head. See **Figure 7**. However, it can loosen and slip, causing damage to the nut and maybe to your knuckles. Use an adjustable wrench only when other wrenches are not available.

Adjustable wrenches come in sizes ranging from 4-18 in. overall. A 6 or 8 in. wrench is recommended as an all-purpose wrench.

Socket Wrenches

This type is undoubtedly the fastest, safest and most convenient to use. See **Figure 8**. Sockets, which attach to a suitable handle, are available with 6-point or 12-point openings and use 1/4, 3/8 and 3/4 inch drives. The drive size indicates

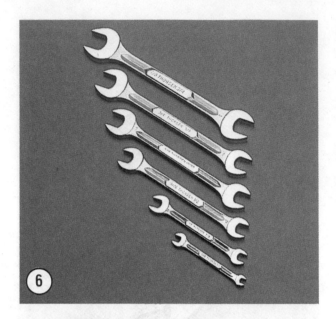

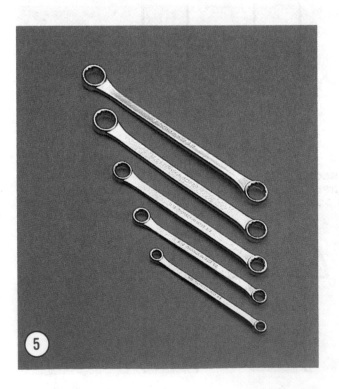

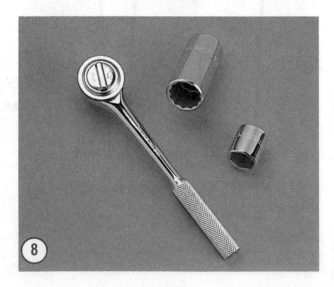

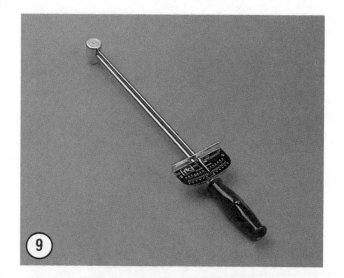

the size of the square hole that mates with the ratchet or flex handle.

Torque Wrench

A torque wrench (**Figure 9**) is used with a socket to measure how tight a nut or bolt is installed. They come in a wide price range and with either 3/8 or 1/2 in. square drive. The drive size indicates the size of the square drive that mates with the socket. Purchase one that measures up to 150 ft.-lb. (203 N·m).

Impact Driver

This tool (**Figure 10**) makes removal of tight fasteners easy and eliminates damage to bolts and screw slots. Impact drivers and interchangeable bits are available at most large hardware and auto parts stores.

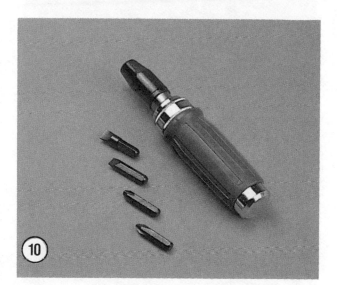

Circlip Pliers

Circlip pliers (sometimes referred to as snapring pliers) are necessary to remove circlips. See **Figure 11**. Circlip pliers usually come with several different size tips; many designs can be switched from internal type to external type.

Hammers

The correct hammer is necessary for repairs. Use only a hammer with a face (or head) of rubber or plastic or the soft-faced type that is filled with buckshot (**Figure 12**). These are sometimes necessary in engine tear-downs. *Never* use a metal-faced hammer as severe damage will result in most cases. You can always produce the same amount of force with a soft-faced hammer.

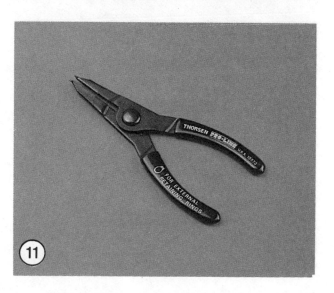

Feeler Gauge

This tool has either flat or wire measuring gauges (**Figure 13**). Wire gauges are used to measure spark plug gap; flat gauges are used for all other measurements. A non-magnetic (brass) gauge may be specified when working around magnetized parts.

Other Special Tools

Some procedures require special tools; these are identified in the appropriate chapter. Unless otherwise specified, the part number used in this book to identify a special tool is the marine equipment manufacturer's part number.

Special tools can usually be purchased through your marine equipment dealer. Some can be made locally by a machinist, often at a much lower price. You may find certain special tools at tool rental dealers. Don't use makeshift tools if you can't locate the correct special tool; you will probably cause more damage than good.

TEST EQUIPMENT

Multimeter

This instrument (**Figure 14**) is invaluable for electrical system troubleshooting and service. It combines a voltmeter, an ohmmeter and an ammeter into one unit, so it is often called a VOM.

Two types of multimeter are available, analog and digital. Analog meters have a moving needle with marked bands indicating the volt, ohm and amperage scales. The digital meter (DVOM) is ideally suited for troubleshooting because it is easy to read, more accurate than analog, contains internal overload protection, is auto-ranging (analog meters must be recalibrated each time the scale is changed) and has automatic polarity compensation.

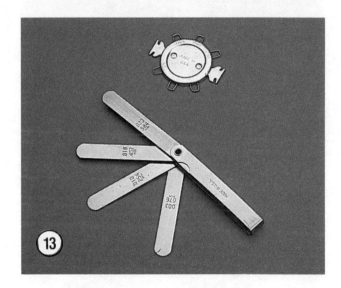

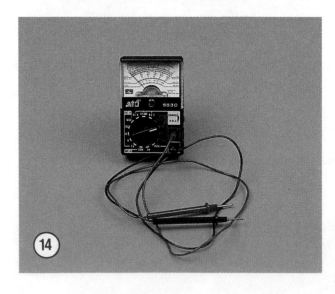

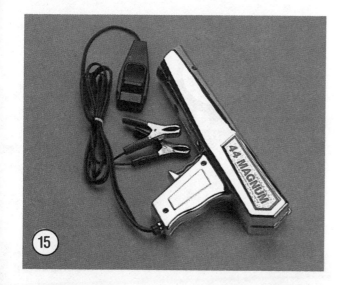

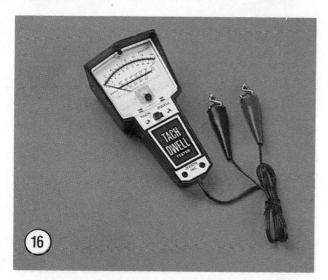

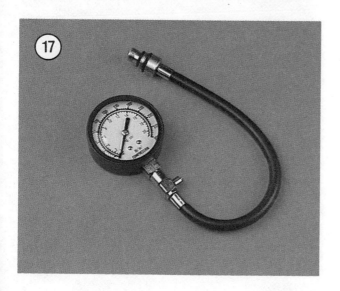

Strobe Timing Light

This instrument is necessary for dynamic tuning (setting ignition timing while the engine is running). By flashing a light at the precise instant the spark plug fires, the position of the timing mark can be seen. The flashing light makes a moving mark appear to stand still opposite a stationary mark.

Suitable lights range from inexpensive neon bulb types to powerful xenon strobe lights. See **Figure 15**. A light with an inductive pickup is best because it eliminates any possible damage to ignition wiring.

Tachometer/Dwell Meter

A portable tachometer is necessary for tuning. See **Figure 16**. Ignition timing and carburetor adjustments must be performed at the specified idle speed. The best instrument for this purpose is one with a low range of 0-1000 or 0-2000 rpm and a high range of 0-6000 rpm. Extended range (0-6000 or 0-8000 rpm) instruments lack accuracy at lower speeds. The instrument should be capable of detecting changes of 25 rpm on the low range.

A dwell meter is often combined with a tachometer. Dwell meters are used with breaker point ignition systems to measure the amount of time the points remain closed during engine operation.

Compression Gauge

This tool (**Figure 17**) measures the amount of pressure present in the engine's combustion chamber during the compression stroke. This indicates general engine condition. Compression readings can be interpreted along with vacuum gauge readings to pinpoint specific engine mechanical problems.

The easiest type to use has screw-in adapters that fit into the spark plug holes. Press-in rubber-tipped types are also available.

Vacuum Gauge

The vacuum gauge (**Figure 18**) measures the intake manifold vacuum created by the engine's intake stroke. Manifold and valve problems (on 4-stroke engines) can be identified by interpreting the readings. When combined with compression gauge readings, other engine problems can be diagnosed.

Some vacuum gauges can also be used as fuel pressure gauges to trace fuel system problems.

Hydrometer

Battery electrolyte specific gravity is measured with a hydrometer (**Figure 19**). The specific gravity of the electrolyte indicates the battery's state of charge. The best type has automatic temperature compensation; otherwise, you must calculate the compensation yourself.

Precision Measuring Tools

Various tools are needed to make precision measurements. A dial indicator (**Figure 20**), for example, is used to determine run-out of rotating parts and end play of parts assemblies. A dial indicator can also be used to precisely measure piston position in relation to top dead center; some engines require this measurement for ignition timing adjustment.

Vernier calipers (**Figure 21**) and micrometers (**Figure 22**) are other precision measuring tools used to determine the size of parts (such as piston diameter).

Precision measuring equipment must be stored, handled and used carefully or it will not remain accurate.

SERVICE HINTS

Most of the service procedures covered in this manual are straightforward and can be performed by anyone reasonably handy with tools.

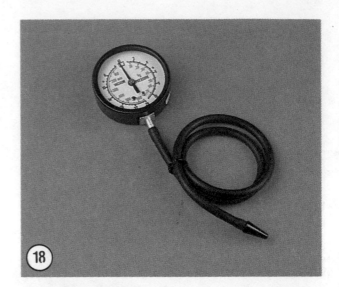

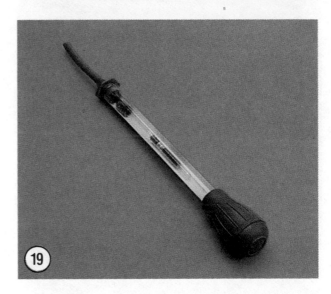

It is suggested, however, that you consider your own skills and toolbox carefully before attempting any operation involving major disassembly of the engine or gearcase.

Some operations, for example, require the use of a press. It would be wiser to have these performed by a shop equipped for such work, rather than trying to do the job yourself with makeshift equipment. Other procedures require precise measurements. Unless you have the skills and

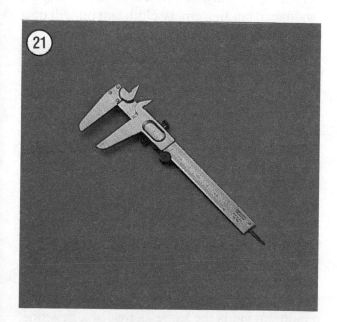

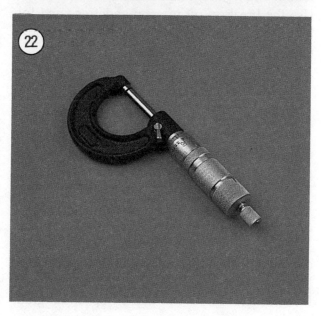

equipment required, it would be better to have a qualified repair shop make the measurements for you.

Preparation for Disassembly

Repairs go much faster and easier if the equipment is clean before you begin work. There are special cleaners, such as Gunk or Bel-Ray Degreaser, for washing the engine and related parts. Just spray or brush on the cleaning solution, let it stand, then rinse away with a garden hose. Clean all oily or greasy parts with cleaning solvent as you remove them.

> *WARNING*
> *Never use gasoline as a cleaning agent. It presents an extreme fire hazard. Be sure to work in a well-ventilated area when using cleaning solvent. Keep a Coast Guard approved fire extinguisher, rated for gasoline fires, handy in any case.*

Much of the labor charged for repairs made by dealers is for the removal and disassembly of other parts to reach the defective unit. It is frequently possible to perform the preliminary operations yourself and then take the defective unit in to the dealer for repair.

If you decide to tackle the job yourself, read the entire section in this manual that pertains to it, making sure you have identified the proper one. Study the illustrations and text until you have a good idea of what is involved in completing the job satisfactorily. If special tools or replacement parts are required, make arrangements to get them before you start. It is frustrating and time-consuming to get partly into a job and then be unable to complete it.

Disassembly Precautions

During disassembly of parts, keep a few general precautions in mind. Force is rarely needed to get things apart. If parts are a tight fit, such as a bearing in a case, there is usually a tool designed to separate them. Never use a screwdriver to pry apart parts with machined surfaces (such as cylinder heads and crankcases). You will mar the surfaces and end up with leaks.

Make diagrams (or take an instant picture) wherever similar-appearing parts are found. For example, head and crankcase bolts are often not the same length. You may think you can remember where everything came from, but mistakes are costly. There is also the possibility you may be sidetracked and not return to work for days or even weeks. In the interval, carefully laid out parts may have been disturbed.

Cover all openings after removing parts to keep small parts, dirt or other contamination from entering.

Tag all similar internal parts for location and direction. All internal components should be reinstalled in the same location and direction from which removed. Record the number and thickness of any shims as they are removed. Small parts, such as bolts, can be identified by placing them in plastic sandwich bags. Seal and label them with masking tape.

Wiring should be tagged with masking tape and marked as each wire is removed. Again, do not rely on memory alone.

Protect finished surfaces from physical damage or corrosion. Keep gasoline off painted surfaces.

Assembly Precautions

No parts, except those assembled with a press fit, require unusual force during assembly. If a part is hard to remove or install, find out why before proceeding.

When assembling two parts, start all fasteners, then tighten evenly in an alternating or crossing pattern if no specific tightening sequence is given.

When assembling parts, be sure all shims and washers are installed exactly as they came out.

Whenever a rotating part butts against a stationary part, look for a shim or washer. Use new gaskets if there is any doubt about the condition of the old ones. Unless otherwise specified, a thin coat of oil on gaskets may help them seal effectively.

Heavy grease can be used to hold small parts in place if they tend to fall out during assembly. However, keep grease and oil away from electrical components.

High spots may be sanded off a piston with sandpaper, but fine emery cloth and oil will do a much more professional job.

Carbon can be removed from the cylinder head, the piston crown and the exhaust port with a dull screwdriver. *Do not* scratch either surface. Wipe off the surface with a clean cloth when finished.

The carburetor is best cleaned by disassembling it and soaking the parts in a commercial carburetor cleaner. Never soak gaskets and rubber parts in these cleaners. Never use wire to clean out jets and air passages; they are easily damaged. Use compressed air to blow out the carburetor *after* the float has been removed.

Take your time and do the job right. Do not forget that the break-in procedure on a newly rebuilt engine is the same as that of a new one. Use the break-in oil recommendations and follow other instructions given in your owner's manual.

SPECIAL TIPS

Because of the extreme demands placed on marine equipment, several points should be kept in mind when performing service and repair. The following items are general suggestions that may improve the overall life of the machine and help avoid costly failures.

1. Unless otherwise specified, use a locking compound, such as Loctite Threadlocker, on all bolts and nuts, even if they are secured with lockwashers. Be sure to use the specified grade

of thread locking compound. A screw or bolt lost from an engine cover or bearing retainer could easily cause serious and expensive damage before its loss is noticed.

When applying thread locking compound, use a small amount. If too much is used, it can work its way down the threads and stick parts together that were not meant to be stuck together.

Keep a tube of thread locking compound in your tool box; when used properly, it is cheap insurance.

2. Use a hammer-driven impact tool to remove and install screws and bolts. These tools help prevent the rounding off of bolt heads and screw slots and ensure a tight installation.

3. When straightening the fold-over type lockwasher, use a wide-blade chisel, such as an old and dull wood chisel. Such a tool provides a better purchase on the folded tab, making straightening easier.

4. When installing the fold-over type lockwasher, always use a new washer if possible. If a new washer is not available, always fold over a part of the washer that has not been previously folded. Reusing the same fold may cause the washer to break, resulting in the loss of its locking ability and a loose piece of metal adrift in the engine.

When folding the washer, start the fold with a screwdriver and finish it with a pair of pliers. If a punch is used to make the fold, the fold may be too sharp, thereby increasing the chances of the washer breaking under stress.

These washers are relatively inexpensive and it is suggested that you keep several of each size in your tool box for repairs.

5. When replacing missing or broken fasteners (bolts, nuts and screws), always use authorized replacement parts. They are specially hardened for each application. The wrong 50-cent bolt could easily cause serious and expensive damage.

6. When installing gaskets, always use authorized replacement gaskets *without* sealer, unless designated. Many gaskets are designed to swell when they come in contact with oil. Gasket sealer will prevent the gaskets from swelling as intended and can result in oil leaks. Authorized replacement gaskets are cut from material of the precise thickness needed. Installation of a too thick or too thin gasket in a critical area could cause equipment damage.

MECHANIC'S TECHNIQUES

Removing Frozen Fasteners

When a fastener rusts and cannot be removed, several methods may be used to loosen it. First, apply penetrating oil, such as Liquid Wrench or WD-40 (available at any hardware or auto supply store). Apply it liberally and allow it penetrate for 10-15 minutes. Tap the fastener several times with a small hammer; do not hit it hard enough to cause damage. Reapply the penetrating oil if necessary.

For frozen screws, apply penetrating oil as described, then insert a screwdriver in the slot and tap the top of the screwdriver with a hammer. This loosens the rust so the screw can be removed in the normal way. If the screw head is too chewed up to use a screwdriver, grip the head with locking pliers and twist the screw out.

Avoid applying heat unless specifically instructed because it may melt, warp or remove the temper from parts.

Remedying Stripped Threads

Occasionally, threads are stripped through carelessness or impact damage. Often the threads can be cleaned up by running a tap (for internal threads on nuts) or die (for external threads on bolts) through threads. See **Figure 23**.

Removing Broken Screws or Bolts

When the head breaks off a screw or bolt, several methods are available for removing the remaining portion.

If a large portion of the remainder projects out, try gripping it with vise-grip pliers. If the projecting portion is too small, file it to fit a wrench or cut a slot in it to fit a screwdriver. See **Figure 24**.

If the head breaks off flush, use a screw extractor. To do this, centerpunch the remaining portion of the screw or bolt. Drill a small hole in the screw and tap the extractor into the hole. Back the screw out with a wrench on the extractor. See **Figure 25**.

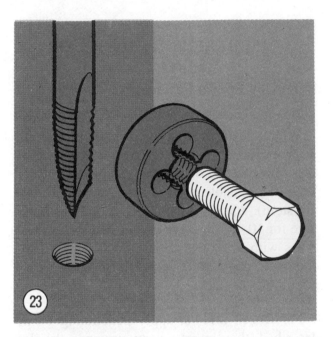

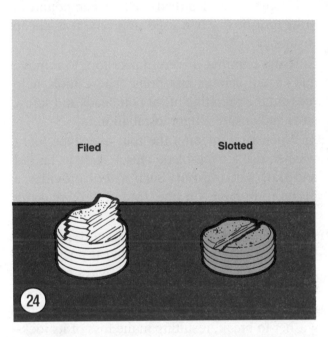

Filed   Slotted

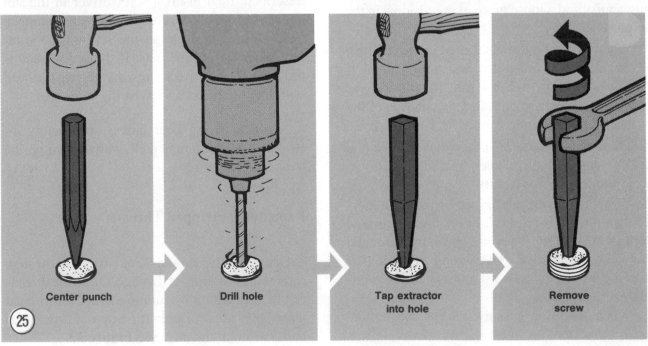

Center punch   Drill hole   Tap extractor into hole   Remove screw

Chapter Three

Troubleshooting

Troubleshooting is a relatively simple matter when it is done logically. The first step in any troubleshooting procedure is to define the symptoms as closely as possible and then localize the problem. Subsequent steps involve testing and analyzing those areas which could cause the symptoms. A haphazard approach may eventually solve the problem, but it can be very costly in terms of wasted time and unnecessary parts replacement.

Proper lubrication, maintenance and periodic tune-ups as described in Chapter Four will reduce the necessity for troubleshooting. Even with the best of care, however, an outboard motor is prone to problems which will require troubleshooting.

> *NOTE*
> *Some of the procedures or service specifications listed in this manual may not be applicable if your Yamaha outboard has been modified or if it is equipped with aftermarket equipment. When modifying or installing aftermarket equipment, file all printed instructions or technical information regarding the new equipment in a folder or notebook for future reference. If your Yamaha was purchased sec-*

> *ond hand, the previous owner may have installed aftermarket parts. If necessary, consult your dealer or the accessory manufacturer regarding components that may affect tuning or repair procedures.*

This chapter contains brief descriptions of each operating system and troubleshooting procedures to be used. **Tables 1-3** present typical starting, ignition and fuel system problems with their probable causes and solutions. **Tables 1-7** are at the end of the chapter.

> *NOTE*
> *The "L" series outboards (counter rotation models) are included in all procedures. Unless there is a separate procedure designated for the L130, L150, etc., refer to the procedure that relates to the same horsepower rating. If the outboard motor you are working on is the L200, then refer to the 200 hp procedure.*

Troubleshooting Test Equipment

For accurate test results, Yamaha recommends using a digital type ohmmeter when testing circuits where the component being tested has a minimal resistance value (10 ohms or less).

If the ohmmeter is powered by a dry-cell battery, make sure the battery is new and fully charged. If the ohmmeter battery is old (partially discharged), the readings may be false which could lead to the wrong diagnosis and unnecessary replacement of a good component.

OPERATING REQUIREMENTS

Every outboard power head requires 3 basic things to run properly: an uninterrupted supply of fuel and air in the correct proportions, adequate compression and proper ignition at the right time (**Figure 1**). If any of these are lacking, the engine will not run.

The electrical system is the weakest link in the chain. More problems result from electrical malfunctions than from any other source. Keep this in mind before you blame the fuel system and start making unnecessary carburetor adjustments.

If an outboard motor has been sitting for any length of time and refuses to start, check the condition of the battery first to make sure it has an adequate charge, then look to the fuel delivery system. This includes the gas tank(s), fuel pump, fuel lines and carburetor(s). Rust may have formed in the tank, obstructing fuel flow. Gasoline deposits may have gummed up carburetor jets and air passages. Gasoline tends to lose its potency after standing for long periods. Condensation may contaminate it with water. Drain the old gas and try starting with a fresh tankful.

Always use major a premium grade of gasoline produced by a national brand refinery. Premium grade gasolines contain a high concentration of detergent and dispersant additives that prevent carbon deposits on the pistons, rings and combustion chamber.

STARTING SYSTEM

Description

Yamaha 6 hp and larger outboard motors whose model description contains the letter "E" following the model number (Yamaha 40EN) use an electric starter motor (**Figure 2**).

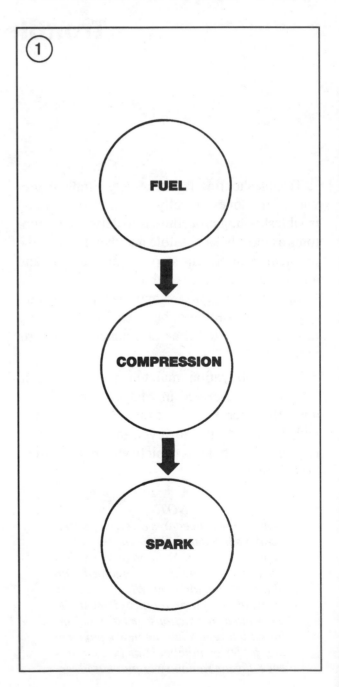

The starter motor is mounted vertically on the engine. When battery current is supplied to the starter motor, its pinion gear is thrust upward to engage the teeth on the flywheel. Once the engine starts, the pinion gear disengages from the flywheel. This is similar to the method used in cranking an automotive engine.

The electric starting system requires a fully charged battery to provide the large amount of current required to operate the starter motor. The battery may be charged externally or by a charging coil on the magneto base (7-70 hp) or alternator stator (90-250 hp) which will keep the battery charged while the engine is running.

The starting circuit on all outboard motors covered in this manual is equipped with an electric starting system which consists of the battery, a key ignition or push-button starter switch, an interlock or neutral start switch, a stop switch, the starter motor, a starter relay (**Figure 3**) (to carry the heavy electrical current to the motor),

a choke solenoid and the connecting electrical wiring.

Depressing the starter button or turning the key switch to the START position allows current to flow from the battery through the relay coil. The relay contacts close and allow current to flow from the battery through the relay to the starter motor.

An interlock or neutral safety switch in the remote control box prevents current flow to the starter motor if the shift mechanism is not in NEUTRAL. Most Yamaha models without a remote control box have a mechanical interlock in the rewind starter. This device is connected to the interlock switch by a cable.

The stop switch shorts out the magneto base or stator charge coil(s). The choke solenoid electrically moves the choke linkage to open and close the choke.

Figure 4 is a schematic of a typical Yamaha electrical system showing the starting and stop circuits.

> *CAUTION*
> *Do not operate an electric starter motor continuously for more than 10 seconds. Allow the motor to cool for at least 2 minutes between attempts to start the engine.*

Starting Difficulties

Older outboard motors, especially motors with high hours, are sometimes plagued by hard starting and generally poor performance, for which there is no readily apparent reason. The fuel and ignition systems are operating correctly and a compression test indicates the cylinder(s), piston(s) and rings are in acceptable condition.

What a compression test does not show, however, is a possible lack of primary compression. On a 2-stroke engine, the crankcase must be alternately under pressure and vacuum. After the piston closes the intake port, further downward movement of the piston causes the fuel/air mix-

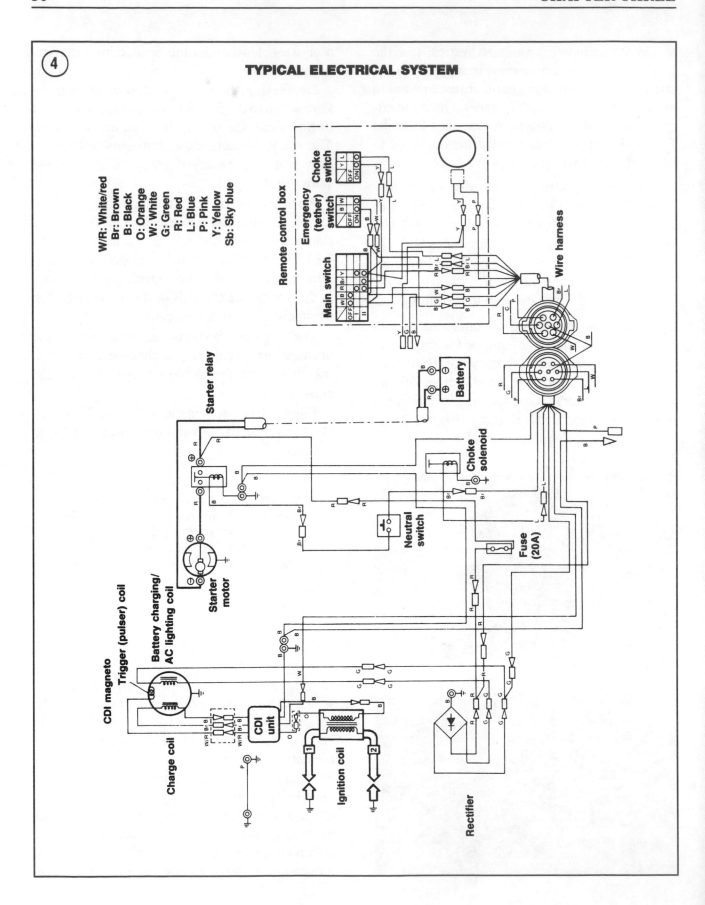

TYPICAL ELECTRICAL SYSTEM

ture in the crankcase to be pressurized, so it can move quickly into the cylinder when the exhaust ports are opened. Then, the upward movement of the piston creates a vacuum in the crankcase, which draws a new fuel/air mixture into the crankcase from the carburetor(s).

If the crankcase seals or case gasket leaks, the crankcase cannot hold pressure or vacuum and proper engine operation becomes impossible. Any other source of leakage, such as a defective cylinder base gasket or a porous or cracked crankcase casting will result in the same condition.

Such engines suffering from hard starting should be checked for pressure leaks with a small brush and a solution of soap suds. The following is a list of possible leakage points in the engine:

a. Crankshaft seals.
b. Spark plug threads.
c. Cylinder head joint.
d. Cylinder base joint.
e. Carburetor mounting flange(s).
f. Crankcase joint.

Troubleshooting Preparation

If the following procedures do not locate the cause of the problem, refer to **Table 1** for more extensive testing. Before troubleshooting the starting circuit, make sure that:

a. The battery is fully charged.
b. The battery cables are the proper size and length. Replace cables that are undersize or relocate the battery to shorten the distance between battery and the starter relay.
c. The shift mechanism is in NEUTRAL and the emergency switch lock plate or lanyard is properly installed on remote control models.
d. All electrical connections are clean, free of corrosion and are tight.
e. The wiring harness is in good condition, with no worn or frayed insulation or loose harness sockets.

f. The electrical circuit fuse (if so equipped) is in good condition.
g. The fuel system is filled with an adequate supply of fresh gasoline that has been properly mixed with Yamaha TC-W3 Outboard Oil. See Chapter Four.
h. The spark plug(s) is in good condition and properly gapped.
i. The ignition system is correctly timed, synchronized and adjusted. See Chapter Five.

Troubleshooting is intended only to isolate a malfunction to a certain component. If further bench testing is necessary, remove the suspected component and have it tested by an authorized service center. Refer to Chapter Seven for component removal and installation procedures.

Starter Relay Resistance Check

See Chapter Four

Push Button Start Switch Continuity Test

1. Disconnect the starter button red and black leads.
2. Connect an ohmmeter between the disconnected push button leads. There should be no continuity (infinite resistance).
3. Depress the start button while watching the meter needle. The meter should show continuity (low resistance). If the needle does not deflect (indicating continuity) when the button is depressed and returned to its original position when released, replace the starter push-button switch.

Engine Stop Switch Continuity Test

1. Disconnect the black and white leads from the stop switch.

2. Connect an ohmmeter between the disconnected stop switch leads. There should be no continuity (infinite resistance).

3. Depress the engine stop switch while watching the meter needle. The meter should show continuity (low resistance). If the needle does not deflect (indicating continuity) when the button is depressed and return to its original position when released, replace the stop switch.

Neutral Start Switch Continuity Test (25-50 hp Engine)

1. Make sure the shift lever is in NEUTRAL.

2. Disconnect the neutral start switch leads at the starter relay and wiring harness.

3. Connect an ohmmeter between the disconnected start switch leads. There should be continuity (low resistance).

4. Move the shift lever from NEUTRAL to FORWARD, then back to NEUTRAL and into REVERSE while watching the meter needle. The meter should show continuity only in NEUTRAL. If continuity is shown in FORWARD or REVERSE, or no continuity is shown in NEUTRAL, replace the neutral start switch.

Choke Solenoid Resistance Check

See Chapter Four.

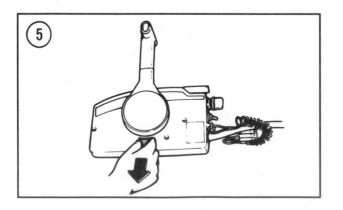

Carburetor Electrothermal Valve Resistance Check (1992-on 40 hp, 50 hp, Pro 60, 70 hp and 90 hp Engines)

1. Disconnect the black and blue leads from the electrothermal valve on the carburetor.

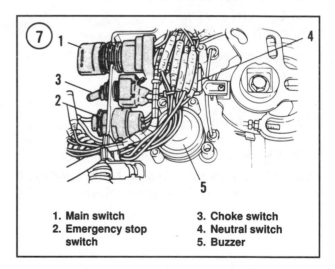

1. Main switch
2. Emergency stop switch
3. Choke switch
4. Neutral switch
5. Buzzer

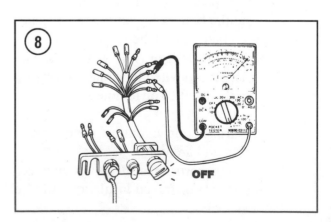

2. Connect an ohmmeter between the disconnected electrothermal leads. The electrothermal valve resistance should be low, typically within 2.3-3.5 ohms at 68° (20° C).

3. Replace the electrothermal valve if its resistance is not as specified.

4. Repeat this procedure for all remaining electrothermal valves.

Remote Control Box Switches (Models So Equipped)

The warning buzzer, ignition, choke, emergency stop, neutral start and power trim/tilt switches are located in the remote control box on models so equipped.

1. Remove the remote control box from its mounting bracket.

2. Remove the cover from the lower side of the box (**Figure 5**).

3. Loosen the back plate screws (arrows, **Figure 6**). Remove the back plates.

4. Loosen the fasteners holding the switch(es) to be tested. Remove the switch(es) or warning buzzer (**Figure 7**).

5. To test the ignition switch, perform the following:

   a. Connect an ohmmeter between the switch white and black electrical leads (**Figure 8**). There should be continuity (low resistance) when the switch is in the OFF position.

   b. Connect an ohmmeter between the switch red and yellow electrical leads (**Figure 9**). Turn the ignition switch first to the ON and then the START position. There should be continuity (low resistance) on both positions.

   c. Connect an ohmmeter between the switch red and brown electrical leads (**Figure 10**). There should be continuity (low resistance) when the switch is in the START position.

6. To test the emergency stop switch, connect an ohmmeter between the stop switch electrical leads. The meter should show continuity (low resistance) with the lock plate removed and no continuity (infinity) when the lock plate is properly installed (**Figure 11**).

7. To test the choke switch, connect an ohmmeter between the choke switch electrical leads. The meter should show continuity (low resistance) with the switch in the ON position no

3

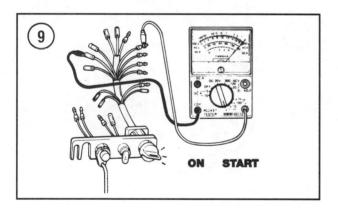

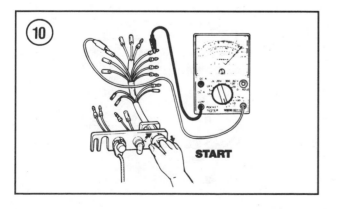

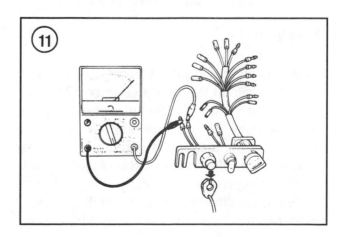

continuity (infinity) when the switch is in the OFF position (**Figure 12**).

8. To test the neutral start switch, connect an ohmmeter between the neutral switch electrical leads. The meter should show continuity (low resistance) with the switch plunger depressed and no continuity (infinity) when the switch plunger is released (**Figure 13**).

9. To test the power trim/tilt switch, perform the following:

   a. Connect an ohmmeter between the switch red and sky blue electrical leads (**Figure 14**). There should be continuity (low resistance) when the switch is pushed upward and no continuity when it is released.

   b. Connect an ohmmeter between the switch red and light green electrical leads (**Figure 15**). There should be continuity (low resistance) when the switch is pushed downward and no continuity when it is released.

10. To test the warning buzzer, connect the buzzer electrical leads to a 12-volt battery with jumper leads (**Figure 16**). Replace the buzzer if it does not emit a steady sound.

11. Replace any switch that does not perform as specified in this procedure.

12. Install all removed switch(es) and reassemble the remote control box by reversing Steps 1-4.

CHARGING SYSTEM

Description

The standard charging system consists of a magneto base on 9.9-70 hp (**Figure 17**) or an alternator stator on 75-250 hp engines (**Figure 18**) containing one or more coils wound on a laminated core, a series of permanent magnets located within the flywheel rim (**Figure 19**), a rectifier (**Figure 20**) or rectifier/regulator to change alternating current (AC) to direct (DC), the starter relay, battery and connecting wiring.

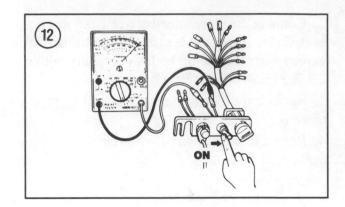

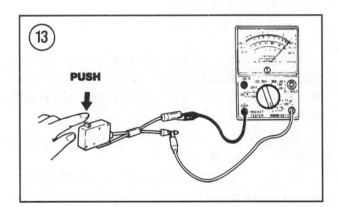

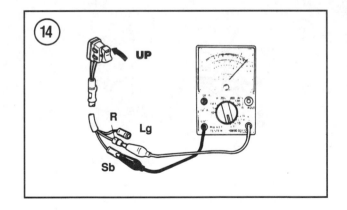

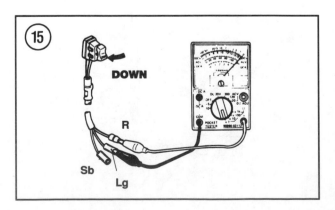

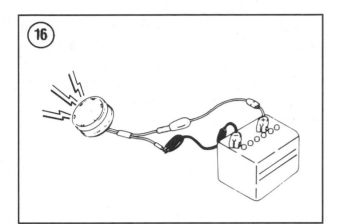

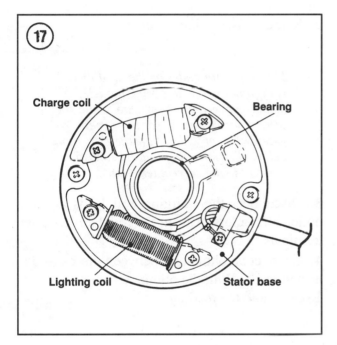

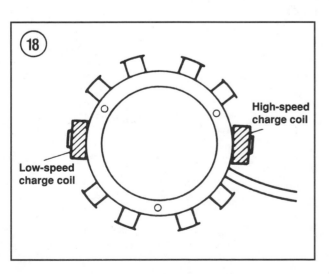

Figure 4 is a schematic of a typical Yamaha electrical system showing the charging circuit.

NOTE
The AC lighting coil system used on 6-25 hp manual start engines consists of a coil mounted on the magneto base and a flywheel with permanent magnets in the rim. The AC current produced is sent directly to the AC accessories. An AC lighting coil can be tested with the same procedures specified for a battery charging coil.

A malfunction in the charging system generally causes the battery to remain undercharged. Since the magneto base or stator is located underneath the flywheel and is thus protected, it is more likely that the battery, rectifier (or rectifier/regulator), starter relay or connecting wiring

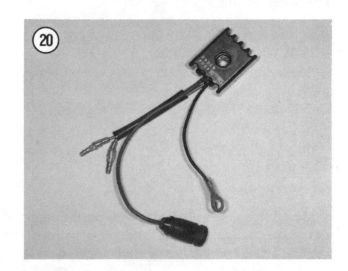

3

will cause problems. The following conditions will cause rectifier (or rectifier/regulator) damage:

  a. The battery leads reversed.
  b. Running the engine with the battery leads disconnected.
  c. A broken wire or loose connection resulting in an open circuit.

Loose Main Fuse
(1990 115 hp and 200 hp Engines)

Yamaha has determined that there could be a problem with a loose main fuse within the holder on these models. If all 3 oil warning lights flash and the engine rpm reduction is activated, but there doesn't seem to be a problem, a loose main fuse within the holder may cause this false indication. These models are equipped with a loose battery cable warning system and this system can also be activated by a loose connection within the main fuse holder.

If this problem does occur, and the main fuse appears to be loose, remove the main fuse from the holder, carefully squeeze the fuse holder with a pair of pliers to tighten the contact on the fuse. Reinstall the fuse and restart the engine to make sure the problem has been solved.

Troubleshooting

Before performing any charging circuit tests, visually check the following.

1. Make sure the battery cables are properly connected. If battery polarity is reversed, check for a damaged rectifier or rectifier/regulator.

NOTE
A damaged rectifier (or rectifier/regulator) will generally have a discolored or a burned appearance.

2. Carefully inspect all wiring between the magneto base, or stator, and battery for worn or cracked insulation. Makes sure all electrical connectors are free of corrosion and are pushed together tight. Replace any defective wiring and/or clean and tighten connections as required.

3. Check the battery condition. Clean and recharge as required as described in Chapter Seven.

Battery Charging (Lighting)
Coil Resistance Test

1. Disconnect the negative battery cable, if so equipped.
2. Remove the engine cover.

NOTE
The wire color codes on the lighting coil vary among the different models. All models have one green wire while the other wire may also be green, or green/white or white. Note their position before disconnecting and be sure to reconnect to the correct terminals.

3. Disconnect the charging coil leads at their bullet connectors or from the regulator/rectifier terminals.
4. Connect an ohmmeter between the 2 disconnected leads. With the ohmmeter set on the R × 1 scale, note the reading.

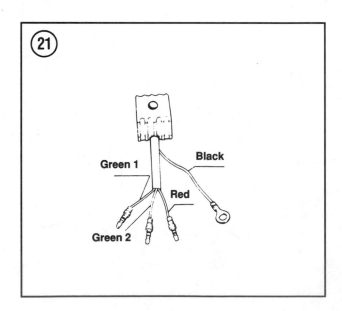

(21)

Green 1   Black

Red

Green 2

5. Compare the reading to the specification given in **Table 4**. If not within specification, replace the battery charging (lighting) coil. See Chapter Seven.

Rectifier or Rectifier/ Regulator Test

1. Disconnect the negative battery cables from the battery.
2. Remove the engine cover.

NOTE
If the rectifier or rectifier/regulator is installed on the CDI unit bracket, the CDI unit cover must be removed to provide access for testing.

3A. On models equipped with a rectifier, separate the 2 green leads at their bullet connectors. Disconnect the black ground lead (**Figure 21**).
3B. On models equipped with a rectifier/regulator; disconnect the red, black and 2 green leads (or 1 green and 1 green/white) from their rectifier/regulator terminals (**Figure 22**).
4. Set the ohmmeter on the R × 1 scale.
5. Connect the red ohmmeter test lead to the rectifier black electrical lead or terminal. Con-

nect the red ohmmeter test lead alternately to the red and 2 green leads or terminals. The ohmmeter should show continuity (low resistance).
6. Connect the black ohmmeter test lead to the black rectifier lead or terminal. Connect the red ohmmeter test lead alternately to the red and 2 green leads or terminals. The ohmmeter should show no continuity (infinity).
7. Connect the black ohmmeter test lead to the red rectifier lead or terminal. Connect the black ohmmeter test lead alternately to the red and 2 green leads or terminals. The ohmmeter should show no continuity (infinity).

NOTE
The ohmmeter's internal battery polarity may cause the test results to turnout exactly opposite of those specified. If this occurs, the rectifier or rectifier/regulator is good and does not require replacement.

8. Replace the rectifier or rectifier/regulator if the ohmmeter readings are not as specified in Steps 4-7.

Voltage Regulator Test

CAUTION
*The outboard motor must be provided with an adequate supply of water while performing this procedure. The use of a flushing device is **not** recommended. Place the engine in a test tank or perform the test with the boat in the water.*

1. Install the outboard motor in a test tank, or place the boat in the water. Connect a remote tank to the fuel inlet.
2. Make sure the battery is fully charged. Refer to Chapter Seven.
3. Remove the engine cover.
4. Connect a tachometer according to its manufacturer's instructions.
5. Start the engine and warm it to normal operating temperature.

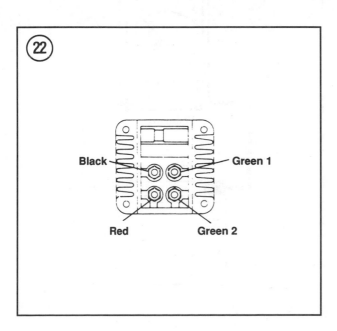
Black   Green 1
Red   Green 2

6. Connect a voltmeter across the battery terminals (**Figure 23**).

7. Gradually increase engine speed to approximately 5,000 rpm and note the voltmeter reading. If it is not 14-15 volts, replace the voltage regulator.

IGNITION SYSTEM

The wiring harness used between the ignition switch and engine is adequate to handle the electrical needs of the outboard motor. It will *not* handle the electrical needs of accessories. If an accessory is added, install *new wiring* between the battery and the new accessory. Also be sure to install a separate fuse panel to the instrument panel.

If the ignition switch requires replacement, *never* install an automotive-type switch. A marine-type switch must always be used.

Description

Variations of different ignition systems are used on Yamaha outboards and a full description of each system is covered in Chapter Seven. For the purposes of troubleshooting, the ignition systems can be divided into 2 basic types:

1. A flywheel magneto breaker-point ignition (1990-1994 2 hp only).

2. A magneto- or alternator-driven capacitor discharge (breakerless) ignition (CDI).

General troubleshooting procedures are provided in **Table 2**.

Precautions

Several precautions should be strictly observed to avoid damage to the ignition system.

1. Do not reverse the battery connections. This reverses polarity and will damage the rectifier, rectifier/regulator or CDI unit on CDI ignition systems.

2. Do not "spark" the battery terminals with the battery cable connections to check polarity.

3. Do not disconnect the battery cables while the engine is running.

4. Do not crank the outboard if the CDI unit is not grounded to the engine.

5. Do not touch or disconnect any ignition components while the engine is running, while the ignition switch is ON or while the battery cables are connected.

6. If a CDI equipped outboard motor must be run while the battery is disconnected, disconnect the stator wires from the rectifier. Tape the wires separately to prevent them from contacting the ground.

Troubleshooting Preparation (All Ignition Systems)

NOTE
To test the wiring harness for poor solder connections in Step 1, bend the molded

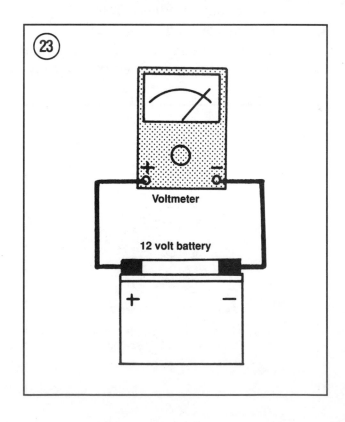

Voltmeter

12 volt battery

rubber connector while checking each wire for excessive resistance.

1. Check the wiring harness and all plug-in connectors to make sure that all terminals are free of corrosion, all connectors are tight and the wiring insulation is in good condition.

2. Check all electrical components that are grounded to the engine for a good ground connection. Disconnect, thoroughly clean and reconnect all grounds.

3. Make sure that all ground wires are properly connected and the connections are clean and tight. Disconnect them, thoroughly clean and then reconnect.

4. Check the remainder of the wiring for disconnected wires and for short or open circuits.

5. Check the fuse (if so equipped) to make sure it is not defective.

6. Make sure there is an adequate supply of fresh and properly mixed fuel available to the engine.

7. Check the battery condition (if so equipped). The battery must be fully charged. If necessary, clean the terminals and recharge the battery, as described in Chapter Seven.

8. Check the spark plug cable routing. Make sure the cables are properly connected to their respective spark plugs.

9. Remove all spark plugs, keeping them in order. Check the condition of each plug as described in Chapter Four.

WARNING
If it is necessary to hold the spark plug cable during the next step, do so with an insulated pair of pliers. The high voltage generated within the CDI unit could produce serious or fatal shocks.

10. Install a spark tester between the spark plug wire and a good ground to check for spark at each cylinder. If a spark tester is not available, reconnect the proper plug cable to one plug. Lay the plug against the cylinder head so its base makes a good connection and crank the engine. If there is no spark or only a weak one, check for loose connections at the ignition coil and battery. Repeat the check with each remaining plug. If all external wiring connections are good, the problem is most likely in the ignition system.

BREAKER POINT IGNITION TESTING (1990-1994 2 HP ENGINE)

Breaker Point Test

NOTE
A suitable ignition analyzer is necessary to perform the following test. One such analyzer is the Merc-O-Tronic Model 9800 Ignition Analyzer. The Model 9800 is available from: Merc-O-Tronic Instruments Corporation, 215 Branch Street, Almont, Michigan 48003.

1. Remove the engine cowling.

2. Remove the flywheel. See Chapter Eight.

3. Disconnect the breaker point leads from the magneto base.

NOTE
Prior to the test, clean the points with rubbing alcohol and make sure the analyzer test lead connections are tight. The low current present in this test makes clean points and proper connections very important.

4. Connect one analyzer test lead to the breaker arm. Connect the other test lead to the breaker point screw terminal.

5. Make sure the breaker points are fully closed. Turn the crankshaft as necessary to close the points.

6. Set the analyzer controls according to its manufacturer's instructions.

7. If the breaker points are good, the analyzer needle will rest in the OK segment.

8. If the analyzer needle does not fall within the specified segment on the scale, reclean the points with alcohol and recheck the analyzer test leads

to make sure that the connections are tight before discarding the point set.

Condenser Tests

1. Remove the engine cowling.
2. Remove the flywheel. See Chapter Eight.
3. Disconnect the condenser lead from the breaker point set.
4. Connect one analyzer test lead to condenser lead. Connect the other test lead to the magneto base.

> *WARNING*
> *High voltage is involved in a condenser leak test. Handle the analyzer leads carefully and turn the analyzer switch to DISCHARGE before disconnecting the leads from the condenser.*

5. Set the analyzer controls according to its manufacturer's instructions. Check the condenser for leakage, resistance and capacity.
6. Condenser capacity is 0.25 microfarads ±10 percent. Condenser resistance should be 5,000 ohms. Replace the condenser if it does not perform as specified.

Ignition Coil Test

This test checks the primary and secondary coil windings for circuit continuity.
1. Remove the engine cowling.
2. Disconnect the white primary coil lead (**Figure 24**) from the coil.
3. Disconnect the secondary coil lead from the spark plug.
4. Remove the flywheel. See Chapter Eight.
5. Set the ohmmeter on the R × 1 scale. Connect the ohmmeter between the primary coil lead and the ignition coil body. Note the reading.
6. Set the ohmmeter on the R × 1,000 scale. Connect the ohmmeter between the secondary coil lead and the ignition coil body. Note the reading.

7. Compare the readings obtained in Step 5 and Step 6 with the specifications listed in **Table 5**.
8. If the resistance values are not as specified, replace the ignition coil. See Chapter Seven.

CDI IGNITION TESTING

Charge Coil Resistance Test

1. Disconnect the negative battery cable, if so equipped.
2. Remove the engine cover.
3. Remove the CDI cover as required. Disconnect the charge coil leads from the CDI unit or connector. Refer to **Table 6** for wire color for each specific model.
4. Connect the ohmmeter test leads to the specific wire color connectors listed in **Table 6**.
5. Replace the charge coil if the readings are not within the specifications listed in **Table 6**. See Chapter Seven.
6. On 115-250 hp models, take the reading and repeat this step to test the other set of leads. Replace the alternator stator if either reading is not within the specifications listed in **Table 6**. See Chapter Seven.

Pulser Coil Resistance Test

> *NOTE*
> *The pulser coil may also be referred to as the trigger coil.*

1. Disconnect the negative battery cable from the battery, if so equipped.

2. Remove the engine cover.

3. Remove the CDI cover as required. Disconnect the pulser coil leads from the CDI unit or connector. Refer to **Table 7** for wire color for each specific model.

> *NOTE*
> *On models with multiple pulser coils, be sure to test all pulser coils. **Table 7** lists all combinations of test lead locations required to test the coil(s).*

4. Connect the ohmmeter test leads to the specific wire color connectors listed in **Table 7**.

5. Replace the pulser coil(s) if the readings are not within the specification listed in **Table 7**. See Chapter Seven.

Ignition Coil Resistance Test

1. Disconnect the negative battery cable from the battery, if so equipped.

2. Remove the engine cover.

3. Remove the coil(s) to be tested from the engine. See Chapter Seven.

4. Disconnect the secondary coil lead from the spark plug.

5. Set the ohmmeter on the R × 1 scale. Connect an ohmmeter between the primary coil lead and the ignition coil body. Note the reading.

6. Set the ohmmeter on the R × 1,000 scale.

7A. On single spark plug lead coils, connect an ohmmeter between the ground lead and the spark plug lead. Note the reading.

7B. On dual spark plug lead coils, connect an ohmmeter between the spark plug leads. Note the reading.

8. On multicoil models, repeat Steps 5-7 for all remaining coils.

9. Compare the readings obtained in Step 5 and Step 7 with the specifications listed in **Table 5**.

10. If the resistance values are not as specified in Step 5 and Step 6, replace the ignition coil(s). See Chapter Seven.

CDI Unit Resistance Test

The test procedure in this section requires the use of a special Yamaha Pocket Tester (part No. YU-3112). Do *not* use the Yamaha Digital Tester as it will give a false reading when testing CDI units. If another type of ohmmeter is used, the readings obtained may not agree with those specified due to the different internal resistance of the ohmmeter. During the test, when switching between ohmmeter scales, always touch both test leads together and adjust the meter to zero the meter needle.

> *NOTE*
> *If the CDI unit fails the following test using the Pocket Tester, take the CDI unit to a Yamaha dealer and have them test it using the Yamaha Ignition Tester (part No. YU-91022-A). This piece of test equipment is too expensive for the home mechanic but is currently the most accurate tester available to troubleshoot the CDI system. If the CDI unit fails this test, then purchase a new CDI unit.*

Refer to the following illustrations for this procedure:
   a. 2 hp: **Figure 25**.
   b. 3 hp: **Figure 26**.
   c. 4 hp, 5 hp: **Figure 27**.

25 **CDI UNIT TEST (2 HP)**

Unit: kΩ

		Positive test lead			
		W	B	Br	O
Negative test lead	W		•	∞	•
	B	2.2~9.5		2.2~9.5	•
	Br	∞	•		•
	O	7~30	2~9	7~30	

d. 6-15 hp: **Figure 28**.
e. C25: **Figure 29**.
f. 25 hp: **Figure 30**.
g. 30 hp (3-cylinder): **Figure 31**.
h. C30 (2-cylinder): **Figure 32**.
i. C40: **Figure 33**.
j. 40 hp, Pro 50: **Figure 34**.
k. C55: **Figure 35**.
l. Pro 60, 70 hp: **Figure 36**.
m. 90 hp: **Figure 37**.
n. C75, C85: **Figure 38**.
o. C115: **Figure 39**.

p. 115-130 hp: **Figure 40**.
q. 150-200 hp, Pro V 200 **Figure 41**.
r. 225 hp 90° V6: **Figure 42**.
s. 225 hp 76° V6 (1990-1994): **Figure 43**.
t. 250 hp 76° V6 (1990-1994): **Figure 44**.
u. 225-250 hp 76° V6 (1995): **Figure 45**.

1. Remove the CDI unit. See Chapter Seven.
2. Set the Yamaha Pocket Tester to the appropriate range as indicated by the specified resistance values in each illustration.
3. Refer to the appropriate illustration for test lead connections and specified resistance values.

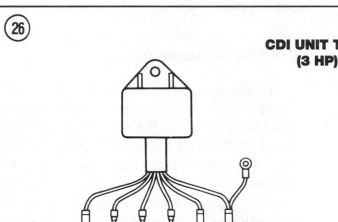

26

**CDI UNIT TEST
(3 HP)**

O : Orange
R/W : Red/white
G/W : Green/white
Br : Brown
W : White
B : Black

O   R/W   G/W   Br   W   B

Unit: kΩ

		Positive test lead				
		Stop	Charge	Pulser		Ground	Ignition
		W	Br	G/W	R/W	B	O
Negative test lead	W		0	∞	∞	∞	∞*
	Br	0		∞	∞	∞	∞*
	G/W	23	23		25	9	∞
	R/W	20	20	∞		12	∞
	B	4	4	∞	12		∞*
	O	∞	∞	∞	∞	∞	

∞ : No continuity.

 * : Needle swings once and returns to home position (∞).

CDI UNIT TEST
(4 AND 5 HP)

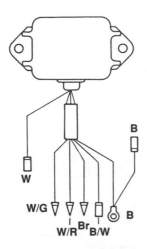

B : Black
Br : Brown
W : White
B/W : Black/white
W/G : White/green
W/R : White/red

Unit: kΩ

			Positive test lead				
			Stop	**Charge**	**Pulser 2 Low speed**	**Pulser 1 High speed**	**Ground**	**Ignition**
			W	Br	W/G	W/R	B	B/W
Negative test lead	**Stop**	W		0	∞	∞	∞	∞*
	Charge	Br	0		∞	∞	∞	∞*
	Pulser 2 Low speed	W/G	18.4~27.6	18.4~27.6		20~30	7.2~10.8	∞
	Pulser 1 High speed	W/R	16~24	16~24	∞		9.6~14.4	∞
	Ground	B	3.2~4.8	3.2~4.8	∞	9.6~14.4		∞*
	Ignition	B/W	∞	∞	∞	∞	∞	

∞ : No continuity.

* : Needle swings once and returns to home position (∞).

CDI UNIT TEST
(6-15 HP)

W : White
B : Black
Br : Brown
W/R : White/red
O : Orange

Unit: kΩ

		Positive test lead				
		W	B	Br	W/R	O
Negative test lead	W		∞	∞	∞	∞
	B	∞		7.5~11.3	∞	•
	Br	∞	63.2~94.8		∞	•
	W/R	8.8~13.2	14.4~21.6	30.4~45.6		•
	O	∞	∞	∞	∞	

∞ : No continuity.

* : Needle swings once and returns to home position (∞).

**CDI UNIT TEST
(C25)**

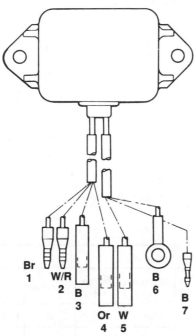

Br : Brown
W/R : White/red
B : Black
O : Orange
W : White

3

Unit: kΩ

		Positive test lead						
		1 Charge	2 Pulser	3 Ground	4 Ignition	5 Stop	6 Ground	7 Ground
		Br	W/R	B	O	W	B	B
Negative test lead	Br		∞	79	•	∞	79	79
	W/R	38		18	•	11	18	18
	B	9.4	∞		•	∞	0	0
	O	∞	∞	∞		∞	∞	∞
	W	∞	∞	∞	∞		∞	∞
	B	9.4	∞	0	•	∞		0
	B	9.4	∞	0	•	∞	0	

∞ : No continuity.

* : Needle swings once and returns to home position (∞).

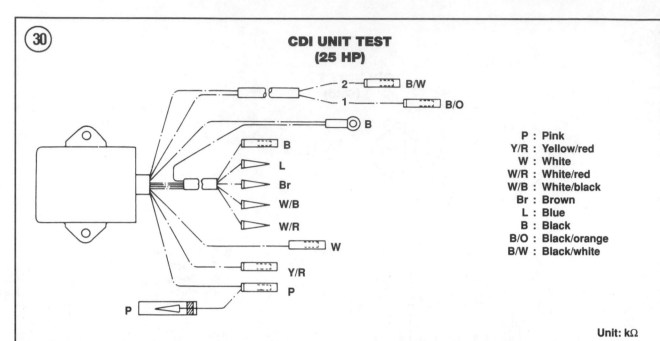

(30) **CDI UNIT TEST
(25 HP)**

P : Pink
Y/R : Yellow/red
W : White
W/R : White/red
W/B : White/black
Br : Brown
L : Blue
B : Black
B/O : Black/orange
B/W : Black/white

Unit: kΩ

		Positive test lead									
		Thermo-switch	Over-heat	Stop	Pulser		Charge (+)	Charge (−)	Ground	Ignition	
		P	Y/R	W	W/R	W/B	Br	L	B	B/O	B/W
Negative test lead	P		∞	∞	∞	∞	∞	∞	∞	∞	∞
	Y/R	∞		∞	∞	∞	∞	∞	∞	∞	∞
	W	∞	∞		∞	∞	∞	∞	∞	∞	∞
	W/R	∞	∞	∞		∞	∞	∞	∞	∞	∞
	W/B	∞	∞	∞	∞		∞	∞	∞	∞	∞
	Br	100K - 1M	100K - 1M	80K - 1M	100K - 1M	∞		80K - 300K	80K - 300K	80K - 1M	80K - 1M
	L	9K - 30K	3K - 10K	40K - ∞	10K - 30K	∞	3K - 10K		0	2K - 8K	2K - 8K
	B	9K - 30K	3K - 10K	40K - ∞	10K - 30K	∞	3K - 10K	0		2K - 8K	2K - 8K
	B/O	∞	∞	∞	∞	∞	∞	∞	∞		∞
	B/W	∞	∞	∞	∞	∞	∞	∞	∞	∞	

∞ : No continuity.

31

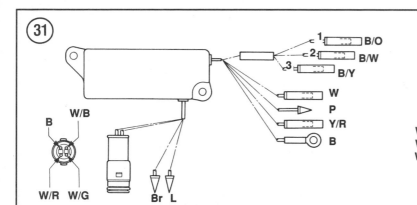

CDI UNIT TEST (30 HP 3-CYLINDER)

Br : Brown	Y/R : Yellow/red
L : Blue	P : Pink
W/R : White/red	W : White
W/B : White/black	B/O : Black/orange
W/G : White/green	B/W : Black/white
B : Black	B/Y : Black/yellow

Unit: kΩ

Negative test lead	Positive test lead											
	Charge		Pulser			Ground	Over-heat	Thermo-switch	Ignition			
	Br	L	W/R	W/B	W/G	B	Y/R	P	W	B/O (1)	B/W (2)	B/Y (3)
Br		+400 *400 −200	+∞ *1000 −500	←	←	+400 *400 −200	+∞ *1000 −500	←	+100 *140 −40	+∞ *1000 −500	←	←
L	4±2		16±6	←	←	0	4.3±2	13±6	62 +60 −30	4±2	←	←
W/R	∞	∞		∞	∞	∞	∞	∞	∞	34 +30 −15	∞	∞
W/B	↑	↑	∞		↑	↑	↑	↑	↑	∞	34 +30 −15	∞
W/G	↑	↑	↑	∞		↑	↑	↑	↑	↑	∞	34 +30 −15
B	4±2	0	16±6	←	←		4.3±2	13±6	62 +60 −30	4±2	←	←
Y/R	∞	∞	∞	∞	∞	∞		∞	∞	∞	∞	∞
P	↑	↑	↑	↑	↑	↑	∞		↑	↑	↑	↑
W	↑	↑	↑	↑	↑	↑	↑	∞		↑	↑	↑
B/O (1)	↑	↑	↑	↑	↑	↑	↑	↑	∞		↑	↑
B/W (2)	↑	↑	↑	↑	↑	↑	↑	↑	↑	∞		↑
B/Y (3)	↑	↑	↑	↑	↑	↑	↑	↑	↑	↑	∞	

∞ : No continuity.

* : Indicates the needle of the tester should swing towards "0" and then slowly swing back to indicate the specified value.

CDI UNIT TEST
(C30 2-CYLINDER)

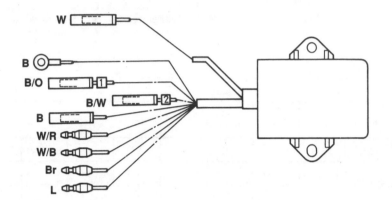

W : White
B : Black
B/O : Black/orange
B/W : Black/white
W/R : White/red
W/B : White/black
Br : Brown
L : Blue

Unit: kΩ

			Positive test lead								
			Stop	Ground	Ignition		Ground	Pulser		Charge	
			W	B	B/O	B/W	B	W/R	W/B	Br	L
Negative test lead	Stop	W		∞	∞	∞	∞	∞	∞	∞	∞
	Ground	B	3.5~7.0		2.7~6.2	2.7~6.2	0	∞	∞	3.0~7.0	3.0~7.0
	Ignition	B/O	∞	∞		∞	∞	∞	∞	∞	∞
		B/W	∞	∞	∞		∞	∞	∞	∞	∞
	Ground	B	3.5~7.0	0	2.7~6.2	2.7~6.2		∞	∞	3.0~7.0	3.0~7.0
	Pulser	W/R	∞	∞	18~36	∞	∞		∞	∞	∞
		W/B	∞	∞	∞	18~36	∞	∞		∞	∞
	Charge	Br	70~160	53~88	75~145	75~145	53~88	∞	∞		75~145
		L	70~160	53~88	75~145	75~145	53~88	∞	∞	75~145	

∞ : No continuity.

CDI UNIT TEST
(C40)

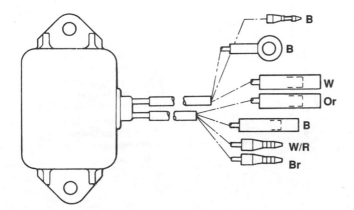

W : White
B : Black
Br : Brown
W/R : White/red
Or : Orange

Unit: kΩ

			Positive test lead				
			Stop	Ground	Charge	Pulser	Ignition
			W	B	Br	W/R	O
Negative test lead	Stop	W		∞	∞	∞	∞
	Ground	B	9~19		2~6	∞	∞
	Charge	Br	80~160	70~150		∞	•
	Pulser	W/R	33~63	7~17	15~35		•
	Ignition	O	∞	∞	∞	∞	

∞ : No continuity.
• : Needle swings once and returns to home position.

Note : The test indicated by "•" should be made with the condenser completely discharged, and therefore, the needle will not deflect again. If any charge remains in the condenser, the needle will not swing at all.

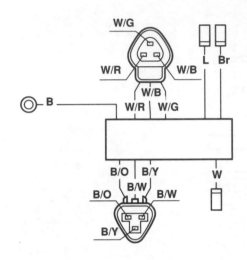

CDI UNIT TEST
(40 HP AND PRO 50)

Br : Brown
L : Blue
W/R : White/red
W/B : White/black
W/G : White/green
B/O : Black/orange
B/W : Black/white
B/Y : Black/yellow
W : White
B : Black

Unit: kΩ

		Positive test lead									
		Br	L	W/R	W/B	W/G	B/O	B/W	B/Y	W	B
Negative test lead	Br		50~110	30~120	30~120	30~120	40~160	40~160	40~160	50~300	25~75
	L	*50~200		*30~120	*30~120	*30~120	*50~200	*50~200	*50~200	500~∞	*20~80
	W/R	9~25	9~25		9~27	9~27	7~19	9~25	9~25	200~∞	4~12
	W/B	9~25	9~25	9~27		9~27	9~25	7~19	9~25	200~∞	4~12
	W/G	9~25	9~25	9~27	9~27		9~25	9~25	7~19	200~∞	4~12
	B/O	∞	∞	∞	∞	∞		∞	∞	∞	∞
	B/W	∞	∞	∞	∞	∞	∞		∞	∞	∞
	B/Y	∞	∞	∞	∞	∞	∞	∞		∞	∞
	W	∞	∞	∞	∞	∞	∞	∞	∞		∞
	B	2~6	2~6	4.5~12.5	4.5~12.5	4.5~12.5	2~6	2~6	2~6	200~∞	

∞ : No continuity.
* : Indicates that the pointer deflects once and returns to specification.

CDI UNIT TEST
(C55)

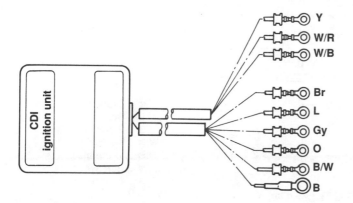

B/W : Black/white
B : Black
Br : Brown
L : Blue
W/R : White/red
W/B : White/black
Y : Yellow
Gy : Gray
O : Orange

3

Unit: kΩ

			Positive test lead								
			Stop (engine)	Ground	Charge		Pulser		Trigger	Ignition	
			B/W	B	Br	L	W/R	W/B	Y	Gy	O
Negative test lead	Stop (engine)	B/W		∞	∞	∞	∞	∞	∞	∞	∞
	Ground	B	9 ± 3		6 ± 2	6 ± 2	∞	∞	4 ± 2	•	•
	Charge	Br	300 ± 100	180 ± 50		300 ± 100	∞	∞	200 ± 50	•	•
		L	300 ± 100	180 ± 50	300 ± 100		∞	∞	200 ± 50	•	•
	Pulser	W/R	40 ± 10	20 ± 5	40 ± 10	40 ± 10		∞	25 ± 10	•	•
		W/B	40 ± 10	20 ± 5	40 ± 10	40 ± 10	∞		25 ± 10	•	•
	Trigger	Y	10 ± 5	4 ± 2	13 ± 5	13 ± 5	∞	∞		•	•
	Ignition	Gy	22 ± 5	6 ± 2	18 ± 6	18 ± 6	∞	∞	13 ± 5		•
		O	22 ± 5	6 ± 2	18 ± 6	18 ± 6	∞	∞	13 ± 5	•	

∞ : No continuity.
• : Needle swings once and returns to home position.

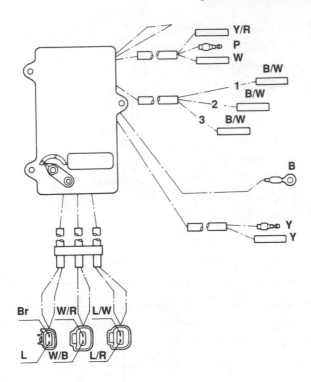

CDI UNIT TEST
(PRO 60 AND 70 HP)

Br : Brown
L : Blue
B : Black
W/R : White/red
W/B : White/black
L/W : Blue/white
L/R : Blue/red

CHARGE COIL

Unit: kΩ

		Positive test lead		
		Br	L	B
Negative test lead	Br		12~29	8~18
	L	15~40		9.5~22
	B	2.5~6.7	2.7~7.0	

PULSER COIL

Unit: kΩ

		Positive test lead		
		W/R	W/B	B
Negative test lead	W/R		35~500	37.5~1000
	W/B	37.5~1000		28~175
	B	2.7~7.0	2.7~7.0	

IGNITION COIL

B/W — B: 2.5~6.7 kΩ

CRANKSHAFT POSITION SENSOR

Unit: kΩ

		Positive test lead		
		L/W	L/R	B
Negative test lead	L/W		∞	∞
	L/R	8.9~20		0
	B	2.7~7.0	8.9~20	

∞ : No continuity.

CDI UNIT TEST
(90 HP)

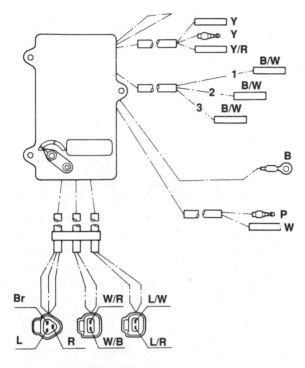

Br : Brown
R : Red
L : Blue
B : Black
W/R : White/red
W/B : White/black
L/W : Blue/white
L/R : Blue/red

3

CHARGE COIL

Unit: kΩ

		Positive test lead			
		Br	R	L	B
Negative test lead	Br		13~37	13~37	8~17
	R	∞		∞	∞
	L	15~40	15~40		9.5~22
	B	2.4~6.3	2.8~7.4	2.5~6.7	

IGNITION COIL

B/W — B: 2.5~6.7 kΩ

PULSER COIL

Unit: kΩ

		Positive test lead		
		W/R	W/B	B
Negative test lead	W/R		35~400	23~90
	W/B	37.5~1000		28~140
	B	3~7	3~7	

CRANKSHAFT POSITION
SENSOR

Unit: kΩ

		Positive test lead		
		L/W	L/R	B
Negative test lead	L/W		∞	∞
	L/R	10~24		0
	B	10~24	0	

∞ : No continuity.

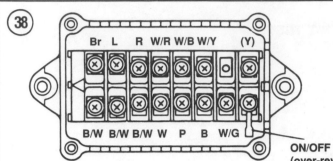

38

Br L R W/R W/B W/Y (Y)

B/W B/W B/W W P B W/G

ON/OFF
(over-rev protection)

CDI UNIT TEST
(C75 AND C85)

W : White	W/B : White/black
B : Black	W/Y : White/yellow
Br : Brown	W/G : White/green
L : Blue	B/W : Black/white
R : Red	P : Pink
W/R : White/red	Y : Yellow

Unit: kΩ ± 20%

		Positive test lead														
		Stop	Ground	Charge			Pulser				Ignition			Overheat		Over-rev
		W	B	Br	L	R	W/R	W/B	W/Y	W/G	Coil 1 B/W	Coil 2 B/W	Coil 3 B/W	P	Y	ON	OFF
Negative test lead	W		52	75	∞	120	75	∞	75	52	75	75	75	180	130	55	150
	B	12		4.2	∞	13	4.2	∞	4.2	0	4.2	4.2	4.2	75	28	1.7	25
	Br	350	250		∞	500	400	∞	400	250	350	350	350	500	14.5	260	500
	L	450	350	4.2		1000	500	∞	500	350	500	500	500	1000	28	350	1000
	R	160	45	120	∞		120	∞	120	45	110	110	110	500	500	50	60
	W/R	4.2	75	120	∞	200		∞	120	75	28	120	120	300	220	80	280
	W/B	4.2	75	120	∞	200	120		120	75	120	28	120	300	220	80	280
	W/Y	4.2	75	120	∞	200	120	∞		75	120	120	28	300	220	80	280
	W/G	12	0	4.2	∞	13	4.2	∞	4.2		4.2	4.2	4.2	75	28	1.7	25
	Coil 1 B/W	∞	∞	∞	∞	∞	∞	∞	∞	∞		∞	∞	∞	∞	∞	∞
	Coil 2 B/W	∞	∞	∞	∞	∞	∞	∞	∞	∞	∞		∞	∞	∞	∞	∞
	Coil 3 B/W	∞	∞	∞	∞	∞	∞	∞	∞	∞	∞	∞		∞	∞	∞	∞
	P	∞	∞	∞	∞	∞	∞	∞	∞	∞	∞	∞	∞		∞	∞	∞
	Y	∞	∞	∞	∞	∞	∞	∞	∞	∞	∞	∞	∞	∞		∞	∞
	ON	14.5	1.7	6.5	∞	16.5	6.5	∞	6.5	1.7	6.5	6.5	6.5	80	31		29
	OFF	∞	∞	∞	∞	∞	∞	∞	∞	∞	∞	∞	∞	∞	∞	∞	

∞ : No continuity.
Note : When working this resistance test, disconnect the lead from the over-rev terminal.

CDI TEST UNIT (C115)

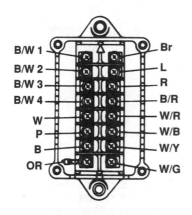

Br : Brown
L : Blue
R : Red
B/R : Black/red
W/R : White/red
W/B : White/black
W/Y : White/yellow
W/G : White/green

B/W 1 : Coil 1 black/white
B/W 2 : Coil 2 black/white
B/W 3 : Coil 3 black/white
B/W 4 : Coil 4 black/white
W : White
P : Pink
B : Black
OR : Over-rev

3

		Negative test lead															
		Charge				Trigger				Ignition				Stop	Ground		Over-rev	
		Br	L	R	B/R	W/R	W/B	W/Y	W/G	Coil 1 B/W	Coil 2 B/W	Coil 3 B/W	Coil 4 B/W	W	P	B	OR	OR LE104
Positive test lead	Br		77~143	105~195	77~143	77~143	77~143	77~143	77~143	77~143	77~143	77~143	77~143	112~208	140~260	68~102	105~195	∞
	L	3.6~5.4		*98~182	*64~96	*64~96	*64~96	*60~90	*64~96	*64~96	*64~96	*64~96	*64~96	*105~195	60~90	*37~57	48~72	∞
	R	105~195	77~143		77~143	77~143	77~143	77~143	84~156	77~143	77~143	77~143	77~143	112~208	140~260	68~102	140~260	∞
	B/R	*91~169	*64~96	3.6~5.4		*64~96	*64~96	*64~96	*64~96	*64~96	*64~96	*64~96	*64~96	98~182	60~90	*37~57	48~72	∞
	W/R	91~169	60~90	91~169	60~90		60~90	64~96	60~90	29~43	56~84	56~84	56~84	12~18	122~227	36~54	112~208	∞
	W/B	98~182	64~96	98~182	64~96	64~96		60~90	64~96	60~90	29~44	60~90	60~90	12~18	140~260	37~57	110~221	∞
	W/Y	98~182	64~96	98~182	64~96	64~96	64~96		64~96	60~90	60~90	29~44	56~84	12~18	140~260	37~57	119~221	∞
	W/G	98~182	64~96	98~182	64~96	64~96	64~96	60~90		60~90	60~90	60~90	29~44	12~18	140~260	37~57	119~221	∞
	Coil 1 B/W	∞	∞	∞	∞	∞	∞	∞	∞		∞	∞	∞	∞	∞	∞	∞	∞
	Coil 2 B/W	∞	∞	∞	∞	∞	∞	∞	∞	∞		∞	∞	∞	∞	∞	∞	∞
	Coil 3 B/W	∞	∞	∞	∞	∞	∞	∞	∞	∞	∞		∞	∞	∞	∞	∞	∞
	Coil 4 B/W	∞	∞	∞	∞	∞	∞	∞	∞	∞	∞	∞		∞	∞	∞	∞	∞
	W	∞	∞	∞	∞	∞	∞	∞	∞	∞	∞	∞	∞		∞	∞	∞	∞
	P	∞	∞	∞	∞	∞	∞	∞	∞	∞	∞	∞	∞	∞		∞	∞	∞
	B	11.8~17.8	3.7~5.5	11.8~17.8	3.6~5.5	3.7~5.5	3.7~5.5	3.2~4.9	3.7~5.5	3.0~4.6	3.2~4.8	3.0~4.6	3.1~4.7	24~36	28~42		17~26	∞
	OR	∞	∞	∞	∞	∞	∞	∞	∞	∞	∞	∞	∞	∞	∞	∞		∞
	OR LE104	∞	∞	∞	∞	∞	∞	∞	∞	∞	∞	∞	∞	∞	∞	∞	∞	

* : The meter needle will swing toward 0 and slowly return to the specified value if tested component is functioning properly.

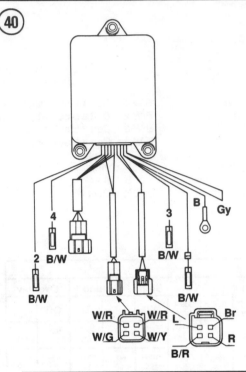

CDI UNIT TEST
(115-130 HP)

Br : Brown
L : Blue
R : Red
B/R : Black/red
B : Black
W/R : White/red
W/B : White/black
W/Y : White/yellow
W/G : White/green
Gy : Gray

CHARGE COIL

Unit: kΩ

	Br	L	R	B/R	B
Br		30~300	40~∞	30~300	19~60
L	50~∞		50~∞	50~∞	35~1000
R	50~∞	35~1000		35~1000	19~60
B/R	60~∞	50~∞	2.6~7.0		35~1000
B	9.0~20	2.6~7.0	8.5~19	2.4~6.5	

PULSER COIL

Unit: kΩ

	W/R	W/B	W/Y	W/G	B
W/R		22~80	22~80	22~80	13~35
W/B	22~80		22~80	22~80	13~35
W/Y	22~80	22~80		22~80	13~35
W/G	22~80	22~80	22~80		13~35
B	2.6~7.0	2.6~7.0	2.6~7.0	2.6~7.0	

IGNITION COIL

B/W — B: 2.4~6.5 kΩ

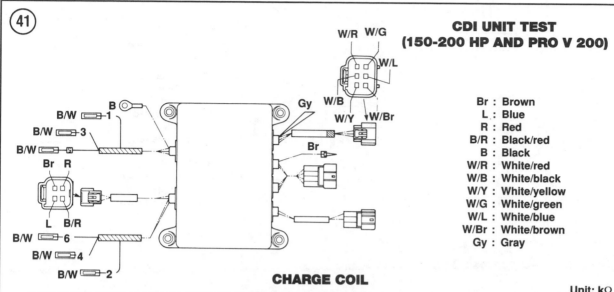

41

CDI UNIT TEST (150-200 HP AND PRO V 200)

Br : Brown
L : Blue
R : Red
B/R : Black/red
B : Black
W/R : White/red
W/B : White/black
W/Y : White/yellow
W/G : White/green
W/L : White/blue
W/Br : White/brown
Gy : Gray

3

CHARGE COIL

Unit: kΩ

	Br	L	R	B/R	B
Br		28~150	40~∞	28~150	17~45
L	2.2~6.0		50~∞	40~∞	28~150
R	45~∞	28~150		28~150	17~45
B/R	60~∞	45~∞	2.2~6.0		28~150
B	8.0~17	2.2~6.0	7.5~17	2.2~6.0	

PULSER COIL

Unit: kΩ

	W/R	W/B	W/Y	W/G	W/L	W/Br	B
W/R		45~∞	45~∞	45~∞	45~∞	45~∞	40~∞
W/B	∞		∞	∞	∞	∞	∞
W/Y	45~∞	45~∞		45~∞	45~∞	45~∞	40~∞
W/G	∞	∞	∞		∞	∞	∞
W/L	45~∞	45~∞	45~∞	45~∞		45~∞	40~∞
W/Br	∞	∞	∞	∞	∞		∞
B	2.4~6.5	2.4~6.5	2.4~6.5	2.6~7.0	2.6~7.0	2.6~7.0	

IGNITION COIL

B/W — B: 2.4~6.5 kΩ

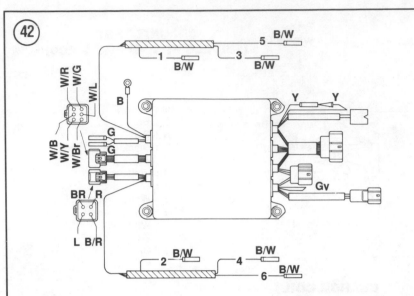

**CDI UNIT TEST
(225 HP 90° V6)**

Br : Brown
L : Blue
R : Red
B/R : Black/red
B : Black
W/R : White/red
W/B : White/black
W/Y : White/yellow
W/G : White/green
W/L : White/blue
W/Br : White/brown
Gy : Gray
Y : Yellow

CHARGE COIL

Unit: kΩ

	Br	L	R	B/R	B
Br		40~∞	52~∞	40~∞	32~200
L	2.6~6.8		65~∞	52~∞	42~∞
R	52~∞	40~∞		40~∞	32~200
B/R	65~∞	52~∞	2.6~6.8		42~∞
B	9.3~22	2.6~6.8	9.3~22	2.6~6.8	

PULSER COIL

Unit: kΩ

	W/R	W/B	W/Y	W/G	W/L	W/Br	B
W/R		65~∞	65~∞	65~∞	65~∞	65~∞	58~∞
W/B	65~∞		65~∞	65~∞	65~∞	65~∞	58~∞
W/Y	30~170	30~170		30~170	30~170	30~170	20~65
W/G	30~170	30~170	30~170		30~170	30~170	20~65
W/L	65~∞	65~∞	65~∞	65~∞		65~∞	58~∞
W/Br	65~∞	65~∞	65~∞	65~∞	65~∞		58~∞
B	2.8~7.2	2.8~7.2	2.8~7.2	2.8~7.2	2.8~7.2	2.8~7.2	

IGNITION COIL

B/W — B: 2.4~6.5 kΩ

CRANKSHAFT POSITION SENSOR

Unit: kΩ

	G1	G2	B
G1		13.5~35	5~11.5
G2	13.5~35		5~11.5
B	2.6~6.8	2.6~6.8	

(43)

CDI UNIT TEST
(225 HP 76° V6 [1990-1994])

Br : Brown	W/Y : White/yellow
L : Blue	W/G : White/green
R : Red	W/L : White/blue
B/R : Black/red	W/Br : White/brown
B : Black	G1 : Green
W/R : White/red	G2 : Green
W/B : White/black	

3

CHARGE COIL

Unit: kΩ

	Br	L	R	B/R	B
Br		40~∞	52~∞	40~∞	32~200
L	2.6~6.8		65~∞	52~∞	42~∞
R	52~∞	40~∞		40~∞	32~260
B/R	65~∞	52~∞	2.6~6.8		42~∞
B	9.3~22	2.6~6.8	9.3~22	2.6~6.8	

PULSER COIL

Unit: kΩ

	W/R	W/B	W/Y	W/G	W/L	W/Br	B
W/R		65~∞	65~∞	65~∞	65~∞	65~∞	58~∞
W/B	65~∞		65~∞	65~∞	65~∞	65~∞	58~∞
W/Y	30~170	30~170		30~170	30~170	30~170	20~65
W/G	30~170	30~170	30~170		30~170	30~170	20~65
W/L	65~∞	65~∞	65~∞	65~∞		65~∞	58~∞
W/Br	65~∞	65~∞	65~∞	65~∞	65~∞		58~∞
B	2.8~7.2	2.8~7.2	2.8~7.2	2.8~7.2	2.8~7.2	2.8~7.2	

IGNITION COIL

B/W — B: 2.2~6.5 kΩ

CRANKSHAFT POSITION SENSOR

Unit: kΩ

	G1	G2	B
G1		13.5~35	5~11.5
G2	13.5~35		5~11.5
B	2.6~6.8	2.6~6.8	

CDI UNIT TEST
(250 HP 76° V6 [1990-1994])

Br : Brown
L : Blue
R : Red
B/R : Black/red
B : Black
W/R : White/red
W/B : White/black
W/Y : White/yellow
W/G : White/green
W/L : White/blue
W/Br : White/brown
G/W : Green/white
G/L : Green/blue

CHARGE COIL
Unit: kΩ

	Br	L	R	B/R	B
Br		100~400	100~400	100~400	25~100
L	100~400		500~2000	500~2000	10~40
R	75~300	75~300		75~300	25~250
B/R	100~400	100~400	100~400		
B	2~6	2~6	2~6	2~6	

PULSER COIL
Unit: kΩ

	W/R	W/B	W/Y	W/G	W/L	W/Br	B
W/R		9~36	9~36	9~36	9~36	9~36	4~18
W/B	9~36		9~36	9~36	9~36	9~36	4~18
W/Y	9~36	9~36		9~36	9~36	9~36	4~18
W/G	9~36	9~36	9~36		9~36	9~36	4~18
W/L	9~36	9~36	9~36	9~36		9~36	4~18
W/Br	9~36	9~36	9~36	9~36	9~36		4~18
B	5~20	5~20	5~20	5~20	5~20	5~20	

IGNITION COIL

B/W — B: 2.0~6.0 kΩ

CRANKSHAFT POSITION SENSOR
Unit: kΩ

	G1	G2	B
G1		4~12	2~6
G2	4~12		2~6
B	2~6	2~6	

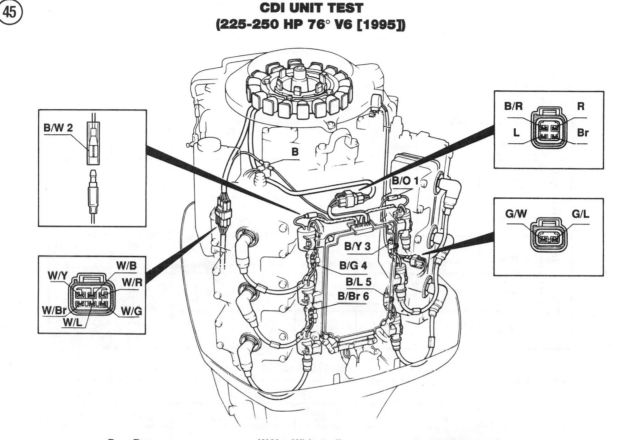

④⑤

CDI UNIT TEST
(225-250 HP 76° V6 [1995])

3

Br : Brown	W/Y : White/yellow	B/W : Black/white
L : Blue	W/G : White/green	B/O : Black/orange
R : Red	W/L : White/blue	B/Y : Black/yellow
B/R : Black/red	W/Br : White/brown	B/G : Black/green
B : Black	G/W : Green/white	B/L : Black/blue
W/R : White/red	G/L : Green/blue	B/Br : Black/brown
W/B : White/black		

CHARGE COIL

Unit: kΩ

		Positive test lead				
		Br	**L**	**R**	**B/R**	**B**
Negative test lead	**Br**		$200 \begin{array}{c}+200\\-200\end{array}$	$200 \begin{array}{c}+200\\-200\end{array}$	$200 \begin{array}{c}+200\\-200\end{array}$	$50 \begin{array}{c}+50\\-25\end{array}$
	L	$200 \begin{array}{c}+200\\-200\end{array}$		$1000 \begin{array}{c}+1000\\-500\end{array}$	$1000 \begin{array}{c}+1000\\-500\end{array}$	$20 \begin{array}{c}+20\\-10\end{array}$
	R	$150 \begin{array}{c}+150\\-75\end{array}$	$150 \begin{array}{c}+150\\-75\end{array}$		$150 \begin{array}{c}+150\\-75\end{array}$	$200 \begin{array}{c}+100\\-50\end{array}$
	B/R	$200 \begin{array}{c}+200\\-100\end{array}$	$200 \begin{array}{c}+200\\-100\end{array}$	$200 \begin{array}{c}+200\\-100\end{array}$		$150 \begin{array}{c}+150\\-75\end{array}$
	B	4 ± 2	4 ± 2	4 ± 2	4 ± 2	

(continued)

45 (continued)

PULSER COIL

Unit: kΩ

		Positive test lead						
		W/R	W/B	W/Y	W/G	W/L	W/Br	B
Negative test lead	W/R		18 +18 −9	18 +18 −9	18 +18 −9	18 +18 −9	18 +18 −9	9 +9 −5
	W/B	18 +18 −9		18 +18 −9	18 +18 −9	18 +18 −9	18 +18 −9	9 +9 −5
	W/Y	18 +18 −9	18 +18 −9		18 +18 −9	18 +18 −9	18 +18 −9	9 +9 −5
	W/G	18 +18 −9	18 +18 −9	18 +18 −9		18 +18 −9	18 +18 −9	9 +9 −5
	W/L	18 +18 −9	18 +18 −9	18 +18 −9	18 +18 −9		18 +18 −9	9 +9 −5
	W/Br	18 +18 −9	18 +18 −9	18 +18 −9	18 +18 −9	18 +18 −9		9 +9 −5
	B	10 +10 −5	10 +10 −5	10 +10 −5	10 +10 −5	10 +10 −5	10 +10 −5	

IGNITION COIL

Unit: kΩ

		Positive test lead						
		B/W1	B/W2	B/W3	B/W4	B/W5	B/W6	B
Negative test lead	B/O1		∞	∞	∞	∞	∞	∞
	B/W2	∞		∞	∞	∞	∞	∞
	B/Y3	∞	∞		∞	∞	∞	∞
	B/G4	∞	∞	∞		∞	∞	∞
	B/L5	∞	∞	∞	∞		∞	∞
	B/Br6	∞	∞	∞	∞	∞		∞
	B	4 ± 2	4 ± 2	4 ± 2	4 ± 2	4 ± 2	4 ± 2	

CRANSHAFT POSITION SENSOR

Unit: kΩ

		Positive test lead		
		G/W	G/L	B
Negative test lead	G/W		8 ± 4	4 ± 2
	G/L	8 ± 4		4 ± 2
	B	4 ± 2	4 ± 2	

Make each connection and compare the meter readings to the specified value.

4. If any of the meter readings differ from the specified resistance values, replace the CDI.

Oil Pump Control Unit Resistance Test (115-200 hp Engines)

The test procedure in this section requires the use of a special Yamaha Pocket Tester (part No. YU-3112). If another type of ohmmeter is used, the readings obtained may not agree with those specified due to the different internal resistance of the ohmmeter. During the test, when switching between ohmmeter scales, always touch both test leads together and adjust the meter to zero the meter needle.

NOTE
These models are the only ones with an oil pump control unit with the exception of the 225 and 250 hp models. On these models, the microcomputer controls the oil pump and requires no inspection.

Refer to the following illustrations for this procedure:

a. 115-130 hp: **Figure 46**.

b. 150-200 hp, Pro V 200: **Figure 47**.

1. Disconnect the oil pump control unit leads.

2. Set the Yamaha Pocket Tester to the appropriate range as indicated by the specified resistance values in each illustration.

3. Refer to the appropriate illustration for test lead connections and specified resistance values. Make each connection and compare the meter readings to the specified value.

4. If any of the meter readings differ from the specified resistance values, replace the oil pump control unit.

Thermoswitch Continuity Test

The test procedure in this section requires the use of a special Yamaha Pocket Tester (part No. YU-3112).

1. Remove the engine cover.

2. Disconnect and remove the thermoswitch(es) from the power head (**Figure 48**, typical).

3. Pour some water in a container that can be heated. Suspend a thermometer in the container.

4. Connect the Pocket Tester to the thermoswitch leads and suspend the tip of the thermoswitch in the water as it is being heated (**Figure 49**). Do not submerge the thermoswitch in the water as the readings will be incorrect.

5. No continuity should be shown until the water temperature reaches the following:

a. 25 hp and 30 hp: 199° F (93° C).

b. C30: 230° F (110° C).

c. C40: 212° F (100° C).

d. 40 hp and 50 hp: Pink-black—199° F (93° C) and orange-orange/green—100-125° F (38-52° C).

e. C55: 143° F (62° C).

f. Pro 60, 70-250 hp: 183-194° F (84-90° C).

6. When the water reaches the temperature specified in Step 5, the ohmmeter should read continuity (low resistance). Allow the water to reach the boiling point and allow it to cool down. The meter should continue to show continuity (low resistance) until the water cools to:

a. 25 hp and 30 hp: 181° F (83° C).

b. C30: 203° F (95° C).

c. C40: 176° F (80° C).

d. 40 hp and 50 hp: Pink-black—181° F (83° C) and orange-orange/green—78-93° F (26-34° C).

e. C55: 136° F (58° C).

f. Pro 60, 70-250 hp: 140-165° F (60-74° C).

7. When the water cools to the temperature specified in Step 6, the ohmmeter should show no continuity (infinity).

3

OIL PUMP CONTROL UNIT TEST
(115-130 HP)

Y : Yellow
Br : Brown
L : Blue
B : Black
G/R : Green/red
G : Green
Y/R : Yellow red
W : White
R : Red

Unit: kΩ

		Positive test lead										
		Y	Y*1	Br1	L	L*2	B	G/R	G	Y/R	W	Br2	R
Negative test lead	Y			3.2~4.8	12~18	4.8~7.2	4.8~7.2	16~24	16~24	16~24	16~24	16~24	16~24
	Br1	∞	∞		4.8~7.2	1.6~2.4	1.6~2.4	8~12	6.4~9.6	4.8~7.2	8~12	8~12	8~12
	L	∞	∞	3.2~4.8			4.8~7.2	16~24	16~24	16~24	16~24	16~24	16~24
	B	∞	∞	1.6~2.4	3.2~4.8	0		8~12	8~12	3.2~4.8	8~12	8~12	8~12
	G/R	∞	∞	∞	∞	∞	∞		∞	∞	∞	∞	0
	G	∞	∞	∞	∞	∞	∞	∞		∞	∞	∞	∞
	Y/R	∞	∞	∞	∞	∞	∞	∞	∞		∞	∞	∞
	W	∞	∞	8~12	16~24	8~12	8~12	16~24	16~24	16~24		16~24	16~24
	Br2	∞	∞	8~12	16~24	8~12	8~12	16~24	16~24	16~24	16~24		16~24
	R	∞	∞	∞	∞		∞	0	∞	∞	∞	∞	

*1 : Tilt up position.
*2 : Emergency switch "ON."

OIL PUMP CONTROL UNIT TEST
(150-200 HP AND PRO V 200)

L/W : Blue/ white
L/G : Blue/green
L/R : Blue/red
B : Black
Br : Brown
Y/R : Yellow/red
G/B : Green/black
G/R : Green/red
Y : Yellow
L : Blue

Unit: kΩ

		Positive test lead									
		L/W	L/G	L/R	B	Br	Y/R	G/B	G/R	Y	L
Negative test lead	L/W		6~14	3.6~9	1.4~4.8	7~16	3.8~9.5	2~5.5	4.2~10	9.5~22	5.5~12
	L/G	∞		∞	∞	∞	∞	∞	∞	∞	∞
	L/R	6.5~15	11~26		5.5~12	12~30	10~24	6~14	9~20	2.4~6.5	10~24
	B	1.4~4.8	5.5~12	2.6~7		3.8~9.5	2.2~6	1.4~4.8	2.2~6	8.519	2.2~6
	Br	50~∞	60~∞	50~∞	50~∞		60~∞	50~∞	60~∞	60~∞	60~∞
	Y/R	∞	∞	∞	∞	∞		∞	∞	∞	∞
	G/B	2~6	6~14	3.6~9	1.4~4.8	6.5~15	3.8~9.5		3.8~9.5	9.5~22	5.5~12
	G/R	∞	∞	∞	∞	∞	∞	∞		∞	∞
	Y	4.2~10	11~26	7~16	3.6~9	13~35	8~18	4.2~10	8~18		10~24
	L	28~150	45~∞	30~200	28~150	50~∞	45~∞	28~150	45~∞	50~∞	

3

8. If the thermoswitch does not indicate the readings as specified in Step 5 and Step 6, replace the thermoswitch.

9. Install the thermoswitch(es) in the power head and reconnect the electrical leads. Install the engine cover.

YMIS Component Testing

The YMIS uses a microprocessor that analyzes signals sent from several sensors and switches to control ignition timing. This system "custom fits" the ignition timing to meet the needs of the engine in any given situation.

The 1992-on Pro 60, 70-90 hp and all 225-250 V6 engines are equipped with two separate versions of the YMIS ignition system. The system used on 1992-on Pro 60 and 70-90 hp incorporates only the crankshaft position sensor. All 225-250 hp V6 engines incorporate the thermosensor, crankshaft position sensor, throttle position sensor and knock sensor. These sensors are not found on other CDI ignition systems used among the various models covered in this book. The following procedures will determine whether or not the sensors are functioning properly.

NOTE
The most common failure on 225-250 hp models is the throttle position sensor. If the throttle position sensor fails, it gen-

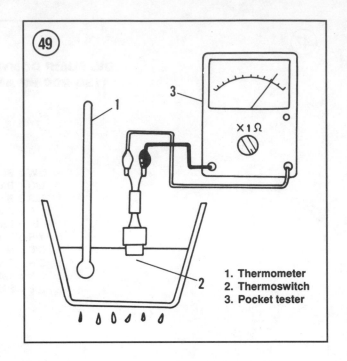

1. Thermometer
2. Thermoswitch
3. Pocket tester

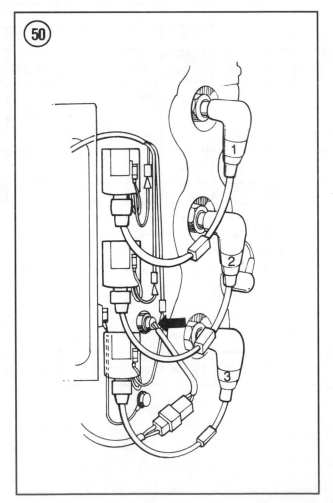

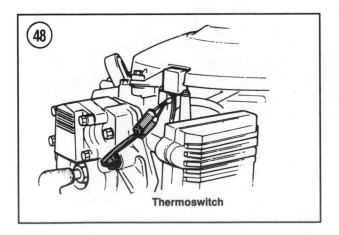

Thermoswitch

erally results in erratic timing fluctuation.

The test procedure in this section requires the use of a special Yamaha Digital Multimeter (part No. YU-34899-A). If another type of ohmmeter is used, the readings obtained may not agree with those specified due to the different internal resistance of the ohmmeter.

Thermosensor (225-250 hp V6)

1. Remove the engine cover.

> *NOTE*
> *Do not confuse the thermosensor with the thermoswitch installed in each cylinder head. The thermosensor is located on the starboard rear side of the power head between the 2 lower coils. The ther-*

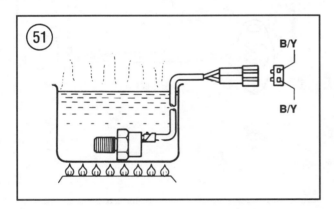

mosensor connects to the YMIS box, and the thermoswitch connects to the CDI unit.

2. Disconnect and remove the thermosensor from the engine (**Figure 50**, typical).

3. Pour some water in a container that can be heated. Suspend a thermometer in the container. The water temperature should be 68° F (20° C).

4. Connect the digital meter to the thermosensor lead. Suspend the tip of the thermosensor in the water for more than one minute and note the reading.

    a. 225 hp 90° V6: 2,100-2,900 ohms.

    b. 225-250 hp 76° V6: 54,200-69,000 ohms.

5A. On 225 hp 90° V6 models, gradually heat the water to 122° F (50° C). Do not submerge the thermoswitch in the water as the readings will be incorrect. At this point note the reading (**Figure 51**). The specified resistance is 680-1,000 ohms.

5B. On 225-250 hp 76° V6 models, gradually heat the water to 212° F (100° C). Do not submerge the thermoswitch in the water as the readings will be incorrect. At this point note the reading (**Figure 51**). The specified resistance is 3,120-3,480 ohms.

6. If the thermosensor resistance is not as specified in Step 4 and Step 5, replace the thermosensor.

7. Install the thermosensor and reconnect the electrical leads. Install the engine cover.

Crankshaft Position Sensor (All Models)

1. Remove the engine cover.

2. Disconnect the crankshaft position sensor connector from the CDI unit terminals. See **Figure 52** for typical sensor location.

3. Connect the digital meter to the crankshaft position sensor terminals and note the reading. The specified resistance is as follows:

    a. Pro 60, 70-90 hp: 158-236 ohms.

    b. 225 hp 90° V6: 158-236 ohms.

    c. 225-250 hp 76° V6: 179-242 ohms.

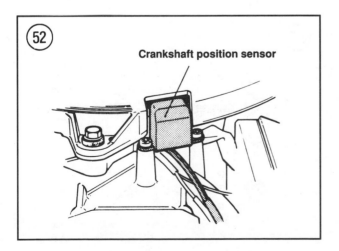

Crankshaft position sensor

4. If the crankshaft position sensor resistance is not as as specified in Step 3, replace the crankshaft position sensor.

5. Install the crankshaft position sensor and reconnect the electrical leads. Install the engine cover.

Throttle Position Sensor (225-250 hp V6)

1. Remove the engine cover.

2. Disconnect the throttle position sensor connector from the CDI unit terminals. See **Figure 53** for typical sensor location.

3. Connect the digital meter to the crankshaft position sensor pink and orange terminals. Rotate the shaft clockwise to the limit and note the reading (**Figure 54**). The specified resistance is 4,000-6,000 ohms.

4. Move the meter test leads to the sensor pink and red wire terminals. Rotate the shaft counterclockwise to the limit and note the reading (**Figure 55**). The specified resistance is 4,000-6,000 ohms.

5. If the throttle position sensor resistance is not as specified in Step 3 and Step 4, replace the throttle position sensor.

6. Install the throttle position sensor and reconnect the electrical leads. Install the engine cover.

Knock Sensor (225-250 hp V6)

1. Remove the engine cover.

2. Disconnect the knock sensor connector from the knock sensor located on the cylinder head (**Figure 56**).

> *NOTE*
> *Set the digital meter to the AC voltage test mode.*

3. Connect one of the digital meter test leads to the knock sensor single terminal. Connect the other test lead to the sensor body.

4. Lightly tap the sensor and check the meter reading. It should indicate that several millivolts were generated. If not, replace the knock sensor.

5. Reconnect the electrical lead to the sensor. Install the engine cover.

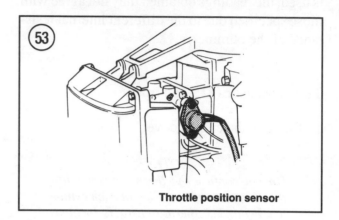

Throttle position sensor

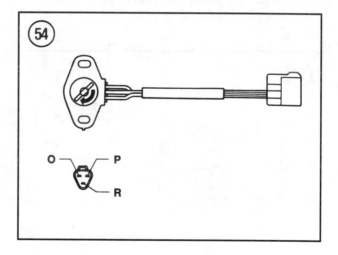

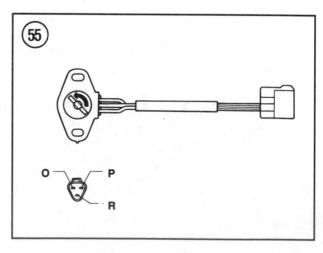

FUEL ENRICHMENT SYSTEM

The fuel enrichment system is used on some electric start models to aid in cold starting.

1. Remove the engine cover.

2. Disconnect the electrical leads from the fuel enrichment solenoid located on the carburetor assembly (**Figure 57**, typical).

3. Connect the digital meter test leads to the fuel enrichment solenoid blue and black terminals and note the reading. The specified resistance is as follows:

    a. 9.9, 15 hp, C30: 6.39-7.81 ohms.

    b. C25: 7.2-8.8 ohms.

    c. 25 hp: 3.6-4.4 ohms.

    d. 30 hp: 3.4-4.0 ohms.

    e. 40 hp, 50 hp, Pro 50, Pro 60, 70 hp, 90 hp: 2.3-3.5 ohms.

4. If the fuel enrichment solenoid resistance is not as specified in Step 3, replace the fuel enrichment solenoid.

5. Reconnect the electrical leads. Install the engine cover.

FUEL SYSTEM

Many outboard owners automatically assume that the carburetor(s) is at fault if the engine does not run properly. While fuel system problems are not uncommon, carburetor adjustment is seldom the answer. In many cases, adjusting the carburetor only compounds the problem by making the engine run worse.

Fuel system troubleshooting should start at the gas tank and work all the way through the system, reserving the carburetor(s) as the last item to check. The majority of fuel system problems result from an empty fuel tank, sour fuel, a plugged fuel filter or a malfunctioning fuel

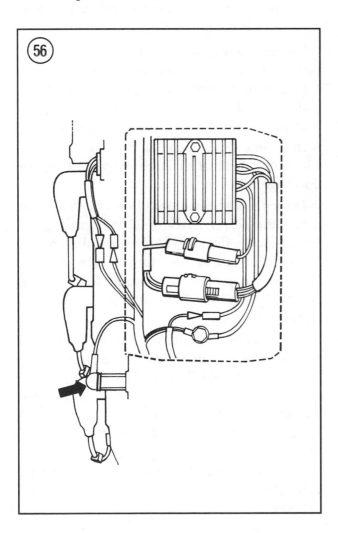

56

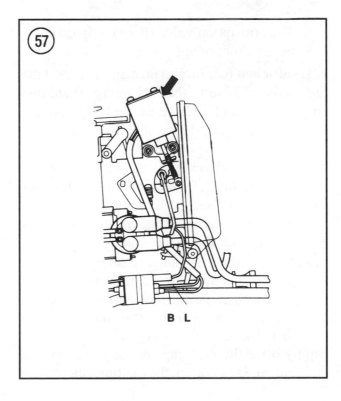

57

B L

pump. **Table 3** provides a series of symptoms and causes that can be useful in localizing fuel system problems. Chapter Six contains inspection and overhaul procedures for the fuel system components. Chapter Thirteen contains inspection and service procedures for oil injection system components.

Troubleshooting

As a first step, check the fuel flow. Remove the fuel tank cap and look into the tank. If there is fuel present, disconnect and ground the spark plug lead(s) as a safety precaution. Disconnect the fuel line from the fuel pump and place it in a suitable container to catch any discharged fuel. See if fuel flows freely from the line when the primer bulb is squeezed.

If there is no fuel flow from the line:

a. The fuel petcock may be shut off or blocked by rust or foreign matter.

b. The fuel line may be plugged or kinked.

c. A primer bulb check valve may be defective.

d. The antisiphon valve (if so equipped) may be malfunctioning.

If sufficient fuel flow is present, reconnect the fuel delivery hose to the fuel pump. Then, disconnect the fuel line from the carburetor(s) and crank the engine 10-12 revolutions to check fuel pump operation. A pump that is operating satisfactorily will deliver a good, constant flow of fuel from the line. If the amount of flow varies from pulse to pulse, the fuel pump is probably failing. Discard the spent fuel properly—do not throw it overboard into the water.

In accordance with industry safety standards, all late-model boats with a built-in fuel tank are equipped with some form of antisiphon device installed between the tank outlet and the engine fuel inlet. This devise is designed to shut the fuel supply off if the boat capsizes or is involved in an accident. Quite often, the malfunction of such

devices leads the owner to replace the fuel pump in the belief that it is the defective component.

Antisiphon devices can malfunction in one of the following ways:

a. Antisiphon valve: orifice in valve is too small and plugs easily; valve sticks in closed or partially closed position; valve fluctuates between open and closed position; thread sealer, metal filing or other debris plugs the orifice or lodges in the relief spring.

b. Solenoid-operated fuel shut-off valve: solenoid fails with the valve in the closed position; solenoid malfunctions, leaving valve in partially closed position.

c. Manually-operated fuel shut-off valve: valve is left in completely closed position; valve is not fully opened.

The easiest way to determine if the antisiphon valve is defective is to bypass it by operating the engine with a remote fuel supply such as an outboard fuel tank.

Carburetor chokes can also present problems. A choke that sticks open will cause hard starting when cold; one that sticks closed will result in a flooding condition.

During a hot engine shut-down, the fuel bowl temperature can rise above 200° F, causing the fuel inside the float bowl to boil. While carburetors used on outboard motors are vented to atmosphere to prevent this problem, there is a possibility that some fuel will percolate over the high-speed nozzle.

A leaking inlet needle and seat or a defective float will allow an excessive amount of fuel into the intake manifold. Pressure in the fuel line after the engine is shut down forces fuel past the leaking needle and seat. This raises the fuel bowl level, allowing fuel to overflow into the manifold.

A defective bleed line or bleed line check valve may cause fuel starvation in one or more cylinders.

Excessive fuel consumption may not necessarily mean an engine or fuel system problem. Marine growth on the boat's hull, a bent or otherwise damaged propeller or a fuel line leak can cause an increase in fuel consumption. These areas should all be checked *before* blaming the carburetor(s).

ENGINE TEMPERATURE AND OVERHEATING

Proper engine temperature is critical to good engine operation. An engine that runs too hot will be damaged internally. One that operates too cool will not run smoothly or efficiently, resulting in poor fuel economy.

A variety of problems can cause engine overheating. Some of the most commonly encountered are a defective thermostat, defective water pump, damaged or mispositioned water passage restrictors or plugged cooling water passages.

Troubleshooting

> *NOTE*
> *Never attempt to troubleshoot a cooling system problem by running the engine on a flushing attachment. Always put the engine in the water or in a test tank.*

Engine temperature can be checked using Markal Thermomelt Stiks available at your local marine dealer. This heat-sensitive stick looks

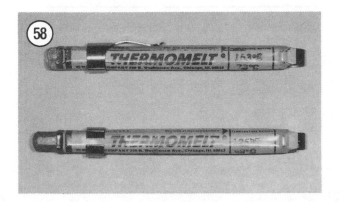

like a large crayon (**Figure 58**) and will melt at the specific temperature indicated on the stick label.

Two thermomelt sticks are required to check a Yamaha outboard properly: a 125° F (52° C) stick and a 163° F (73° C) stick. The stick should *not* be applied to the center of the cylinder head, as this area may normally run hotter than 163° F (73° C).

The test is most efficient when performed on an outboard motor operating on a boat in the water. If necessary to perform the test using a test tank, run the engine at 3,000 rpm for a minimum of 5 minutes to ensure that it is at operating temperature. Make sure inlet water temperature is below 80° F (26° C) and perform the test as follows.

1. Mark the cylinder water jacket with each thermomelt stick. The mark will appear similar to a chalk mark. Make sure sufficient material is applied to the metal surface.

2. With the engine at operating temperature and running at idle in FORWARD gear, the 125° F stick mark should melt. If it does not melt on thermostat-equipped models, the thermostat is stuck open and the engine is running too cold.

3. With the engine at operating temperature and running at full throttle in FORWARD gear, the 163° F stick mark should not melt. If it does, the power head is overheating. Look for a defective water pump or a clogged or leaking cooling system. On thermostat-equipped models, the thermostat may be stuck closed.

POWER HEAD

Power head problems are generally symptoms of something wrong in another system, such as ignition, fuel or starting. If properly maintained and serviced, the engine should experience no problems other than those caused by age and normal wear.

Overheating and Lack of Lubrication

Overheating and lack of lubrication cause the majority of engine mechanical problems. Outboard motors create a great deal of heat and are not designed to operate at a standstill for any length of time. Using a spark plug of the wrong heat range can burn a piston. Incorrect ignition timing, a defective water pump or thermostat, a propeller that is too large (over-propping) or an excessively lean fuel mixture can also cause the engine to overheat.

Preignition

Preignition is the premature burning of fuel and is caused by hot carbon spots in the combustion chamber (**Figure 59**). The fuel actually ignites before it is supposed to. Glowing deposits in the combustion chamber, inadequate cooling or overheated spark plugs can all cause preignition. This is first noticed in the form of a power loss but will eventually result in extensive damage to the internal parts of the engine because of higher combustion chamber temperatures.

Detonation

Commonly called "spark knock" or "fuel knock," detonation is the violent explosion of fuel in the combustion chamber instead of the controlled burn that occurs during normal combustion (**Figure 60**). Severe damage can result. The use of low octane gasoline is a common cause of detonation.

Other causes are over-advanced ignition timing, lean fuel mixture at or near full throttle, inadequate engine cooling, cross-firing of spark plugs, spark plug(s) of the wrong heat range, excessive accumulation of deposits on piston(s) and combustion chamber(s) or the use of a propeller that is too large (over-propping).

Since outboard engines are noisy, engine knock or detonation is likely to go unnoticed by owners, especially at high engine rpm when wind noise is also present. Such inaudible detonation, as it is called, is usually the cause when engine damage occurs for no apparent reason.

Poor Idling

A poor idle can be caused by improper carburetor adjustment, incorrect timing or ignition

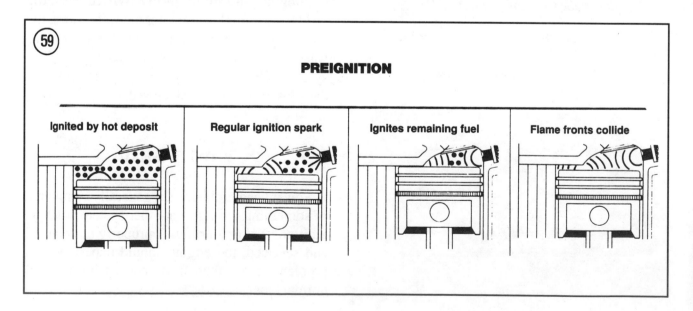

(59)

PREIGNITION

| Ignited by hot deposit | Regular ignition spark | Ignites remaining fuel | Flame fronts collide |

system malfunctions. Check the fuel tank vent for an obstruction.

Misfiring

Misfiring can result from a weak spark or an excessively worn or fouled spark plug(s). Check for fuel contamination. If misfiring occurs only under heavy load, as when accelerating, it is usually caused by a defective spark plug(s). Run the engine at night or use a spark leak tester to check for spark leakage along the plug wire(s) and under spark plug cap(s).

> *WARNING*
> *Do not run the outboard in a dark garage, or enclosure, to check for spark leak. There is considerable danger of carbon monoxide poisoning.*

Water Leakage in Cylinder

The fastest and easiest method to check for water leakage into a cylinder is to inspect the spark plugs. Water inside the combustion chamber during combustion will turn to steam and thoroughly clean the spark plug and combustion chamber. If one spark plug on a multicylinder engine is very clean, and the other plugs show normal deposits, water ingestion is possibly taking place in the cylinder with the clean plug.

Water ingestion can be verified by installing used spark plugs with normal deposits into each cylinder. Run the engine in a test tank or on a boat in the water for 5-10 minutes. Stop the engine and allow it to cool. Then remove and inspect the spark plugs. If one or more spark plugs are thoroughly clean, water leakage is probably occurring.

Flat Spots

If the engine seems to die momentarily when the throttle is opened and then recovers, check for a restricted main jet in the carburetor(s), water in the fuel or an excessively lean mixture.

Power Loss

Several factors can cause a lack of power and speed. Look for air leaks in the fuel line or fuel pump, a clogged fuel filter or a choke/throttle

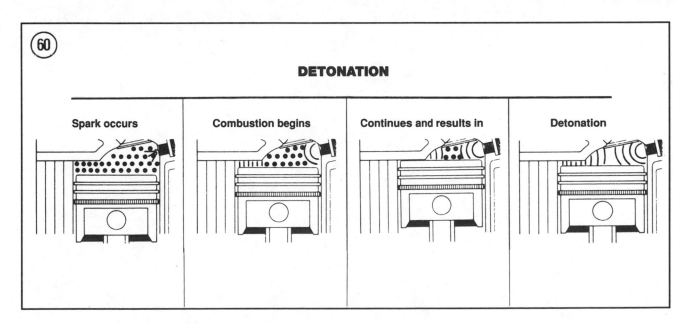

60

DETONATION

| Spark occurs | Combustion begins | Continues and results in | Detonation |

valve that does not operate properly. Check ignition timing.

A piston or cylinder that is galling, incorrect piston clearance or a worn/sticky piston ring may be responsible. Look for loose bolts, defective gaskets or leaking machined mating surfaces on the cylinder head, cylinder or crankcase. Also check the crankcase seals for leakage.

Piston Seizure

This is caused by one or more pistons with incorrect bore clearances, piston rings with an improper end gap, the use of a fuel/oil mixture containing less than 1 part oil to 50 parts of gasoline or an oil of poor quality, a spark plug of the wrong heat range or incorrect ignition timing. Overheating from any cause may result in piston seizure.

Excessive Vibration

Excessive vibration may be caused by a damaged propeller, loose engine mounts, worn bearings or a generally poor running engine.

Engine Noises

Experience is needed to diagnose accurately in this area. Noises are difficult to differentiate and even harder to describe. Deep knocking noises usually mean main bearing failure. A slapping noise generally comes from a loose piston. A light knocking noise during acceleration may be an excessively worn connecting rod bearing. Pinging should be corrected immediately or damage to the piston will result. A compression leak at the head-to-cylinder joint will sound like a rapid on-off squeal.

Table 1 STARTER TROUBLESHOOTING

Trouble	Cause	Remedy
Pinion does not move when starter is turned on	Blown fuse	Replace fuse.
	Pinion rusted to armature shaft	Remove, clean or replace as required.
	Series coil or shunt broken or shorted	Replace coil or shunt.
	Loose switch connections	Tighten connections.
	Rusted or dirty plunger	Clean plunger.
Pinion meshes with ring gear but starter does not run	Worn brushes or brush springs touching armature	Replace brushes or brush springs.
	Dirty or burned commutator	Clean or replace as required.
	Defective armature field coil	Replace armature.
	Worn or rusted armature shaft bearing	Replace bearing.
Starter motor runs at full speed before pinion meshes with ring gear	Worn pinion sleeve	Replace sleeve.
	Pinion does not stop in correct position	Replace pinion.
Pinion meshes with gear and motor starts but does not crank	Defective overrunning clutch	Replace overrunning clutch.
Starter motor does not stop when turned off after engine has started	Rusted or dirty plunger	Clean or replace plunger.
Starter motor has low no-load speed and high current draw	Armature may be dragging on pole shoes from bent shaft, worn bearings or loose pole shoes	Replace shaft or bearings and/or tighten pole shoes.
	Tight or dirty bearings	Loosen or clean bearings.
High current draw with no armature rotation	A direct ground switch, at terminal or at brushes or field connections	Replace defective parts.
	Frozen shaft bearings which prevent armature from rotating	Loosen, clean or replace bearings.
Starter motor has grounded armature or field winding	Current passes through armature first, then to ground field windings	Disconnect grounded leads, then locate any abnormal grounds in starter motor.
Starter motor fails to operate and draws no current and/or high resistance	Open circuit in fields or armature, at connections or brushes or between brushes and commutator	Repair or adjust broken or weak brush springs, worn brushes, high insulation between commutator bars or a dirty, gummy or oily commutator.

(continued)

Table 1 STARTER TROUBLESHOOTING (continued)

Trouble	Cause	Remedy
Low no-load and a low current draw and low developed torque	High resistance in starter motor	Close "open" field windings on unit which has 2 or 3 circuits in starter motor (unit in which current divides as it enters, taking 2 or 3 parallel paths).
High free speed and high current draw	Shorted fields in starter starter motor	Install new fields and check for improved performance (fields normally have very low resistance, thus it is difficult to detect shorted fields, since difference in current draw between normal starter motor field windings would not be very great).
Excessive voltage drop	Cables too small	Install larger cables to accomodate high current draw.
High circuit resistance	Dirty connections	Clean connections.
Field and/or armature is burned or lead is thrown out of commutator due to excess leakage	Starter motor has grounded armature or field winding	Raise grounded brushes from commutator and insulate them with cardboard. Use Magneto Analyzer (part No. C-91-25213) (Selector No. 3) and test points to check between insulated terminal or starter motor and starter motor frame (remove ground connection of shunt coils on motors with this feature). If analyzer shows resistance (meter needle moves to the right), there is a ground. Raise other brushes from armature and check armature and fields separately to locate ground.
Starter does not operate	Run-down battery	Check battery with hydrometer. If reading is below 1.230, recharge or replace battery.
	Poor contact at terminals	Remove terminal clamps. Scrape terminals and clamps clean and tighten bolts securely.
	Wiring or key switch	Coat with sealer to protect against further corrosion.
	Starter solenoid	Check for resistance between: (a) positive (+) terminal of battery and large input terminal of starter solenoid, (b) large wire at top of starter motor and negative (–) terminal of battery and (c) small terminal of starter solenoid and positive battery terminal. Key switch must be in START position. Repair all defective parts.

(continued)

Table 1 STARTER TROUBLESHOOTING (continued)

Trouble	Cause	Remedy
Starter does not operate (continued)	Starter motor	With a fully charged battery, connect a negative (-) jumper wire to upper terminal on side of starter motor and a positive jumper to large lower terminal of starter motor. If motor still does not operate, remove for overhaul or replacement.
Starter turns over too slowly	Low battery or poor contact at battery terminal	See "Starter does not operate."
	Poor contact at starter solenoid or starter motor	Check all terminals for looseness and tighten all nuts securely.
	Starter mechanism	Disconnect positive (+) battery terminal. Rotate pinion gear in disengaged position. Pinion gear motor should run freely by hand. If motor does not turn over easily, clean starter and replace all defective parts.
	Starter motor	See "Starter does not operate."
Starter spins freely but does not engage engine	Low battery or poor contact at battery terminal	See "Starter does not operate."
	Poor contact at starter solenoid or starter motor	See "Starter does not operate."
	Dirty or corroded pinion drive	Clean thoroughly and lubricate the spline underneath the pinion with water-resistant grease
Starter does not engage freely	Pinion or flywheel gear	Inspect mating gears for excessive wear. Replace all defective parts.
	Small anti-drift spring	If drive pinion interferes with flywheel gear after engine has started, inspect anti-drift spring located under pinion gear. Replace all defective parts. NOTE: If drive pinion tends to stay engaged in flywheel gear when starter motor is in idle position, start motor at 1/4 throttle to allow starter pinion gear to release flywheel ring gear instantly.
Starter keeps on spinning after key is turned ON	Key not fully returned	Check that key has returned to normal ON position from START position. Replace switch if key constantly stays in START position.

(continued)

3

Table 1 STARTER TROUBLESHOOTING (continued)

Trouble	Cause	Remedy
Starter keeps on spinning after key is turned ON (continued)	Starter solenoid	Inspect starter solenoid to see if contacts have become stuck in closed position. If starter does not stop running with small yellow lead disconnected from starter solenoid, replace starter solenoid.
	Wiring or key switch	Inspect all wires for defects. Open remote control box and inspect wiring at switches. Repair or replace all defective parts.
Wires overheat	Battery terminals improperly connected	Check that negative marking on harness matches that of battery. If battery is connected improperly, red wire to rectifier will overheat.
	Short circuit in wiring system	Inspect all connections and wires for looseness or defects. Open remote control box and inspect wiring at switches.
	Short circuit in choke solenoid	Repair or replace all defective parts. Check for high resistance. If blue choke wire heats rapidly when choke is used, choke solenoid may have internal short. Replace if defective.
	Short circuit in starter relay	If starter relay lead overheats, there may be internal short (resistance) in starter relay. Replace if defective.
	Low battery voltage	Battery voltage is checked with an ampere-volt tester when battery is under a starting load. Battery must be recharged if it registers under 9.5 volts. If battery is below specified hydrometer reading of 1.230, it will not turn engine fast enough to start it.

Table 2 IGNITION TROUBLESHOOTING

Symptom	Probable cause
Engine won't start, but fuel and spark are good	Defective or dirty spark plugs Spark plug gap set too wide Improper spark timing Shorted stop button Air leaks into fuel pump

(continued)

Table 2 IGNITION TROUBLESHOOTING (continued)

Symptom	Probable cause
Engine won't start, but fuel and spark are good (continued)	Broken piston ring(s) Cylinder head, crankcase or cylinder sealing faulty Worn crankcase oil seal
Engine misfires at idle	Incorrect spark plug gap Defective, dirty or loose spark plugs Spark plugs of incorrect heat range Cracked distributor cap Leaking or broken high tension wires Weak armature magnets Defective coil or condenser Defective ignition switch Spark timing out of adjustment
Engine misfires at high speed	See "Engine misfires at idle" Coil breaks down Coil shorts through insulation Spark plug gap too wide Wrong type spark plugs Too much spark advance
Engine backfires through exhaust	Cracked spark plug insulator Carbon path in distributor cap Improper timing Crossed spark plug wires
Engine backfires through carburetor	Improper ignition timing
Engine preignition	Spark advanced too far Incorrect type spark plug Burned spark plug electrodes
Engine noises (knocking at power head)	Spark advance too far
Ignition coil fails	Extremely high voltage Moisture formation Excessive heat from engine
Spark plugs burn and foul	Incorrect type plug Fuel mixture too rich Inferior grade of gasoline Overheated engine Excessive carbon in combustion chambers
Ignition causing high fuel consumption	Incorrect spark timing Leaking high tension wires Incorrect spark plug gap Fouled spark plugs Incorrect spark advance Weak ignition coil Preignition

3

Table 3 FUEL SYSTEM TROUBLESHOOTING

No fuel at carburetor	No gas in tank
	Air vent in gas cap not open
	Air vent in gas cap clogged
	Fuel tank sitting on fuel line
	Fuel line fittings not properly connected to engine or fuel tank
	Air leak at fuel connection
	Fuel pickup clogged
	Defective fuel pump
Flooding at carburetor	Choke out of adjustment
	High float level
	Float stuck
	Excessive fuel pump pressure
	Float saturated beyond bouyancy
Rough operation	Dirt or water in fuel
	Reed valve open or broken
	Incorrect fuel level in carburetor bowl
	Carburetor loose at mounting flange
	Throttle shutter not closing completely
	Throttle shutter valve installed incorrectly
	Carburetor backdraft jets plugged (if so equipped)
Carburetor spit back at idle	Chipped or broken reed valve(s)
Engine misfires at high speed	Dirty carburetor
	Lean carburetor adjustment
	Restriction in fuel system
	Low fuel pump pressure
Engine backfires	Poor quality fuel
	Air-fuel mixture too rich or too lean
	Improperly adjusted carburetor
Engine preignition	Excessive oil in fuel
	Inferior grade of gasoline
	Lean carburetor mixture
Spark plugs burn and foul	Fuel mixture too rich
	Inferior grade of gasoline
	Lean carburetor mixture
High gas consumption: Flooding and leaking	Cracked carburetor casting
	Leaks at line connections
	Defective carburetor bowl gasket
	High float level
	Plugged vent hole in cover
	Loose needle and seat
	Defective needle valve seat gasket
	Worn needle valve and seat

(continued)

Table 3 FUEL SYSTEM TROUBLESHOOTING (continued)

High gas consumption:	
Flooding and leaking (continued)	Foreign matter clogging needle valve
	Worn float pin or bracket
	Float binding in bowl
	High fuel pump pressure
Overrich mixture	Choke lever stuck
	High float level
	High fuel pump pressure
Abnormal speeds	Carburetor out of adjustment
	Too much oil in fuel

3

Table 4 BATTERY CHARGING (LIGHTING) COIL RESISTANCE SPECIFICATIONS*

Model	Ohms
2-5 hp	N/A
6, 8, 9.9, 15 hp	0.36-0.44
C25	0.38-0.46
25 hp	0.30-0.36
30 hp	0.23-0.34
C30	0.31-0.37
C40	0.23-0.29
40, 40 hp, Pro 50	0.56-0.84
C55	0.26-0.32
Pro 60, 70 hp	0.57-0.85
C75, C85	0.54-0.66
90 hp	0.40-0.60
C115	0.48-0.72
115, 130 hp, Pro 115, L130	0.29-0.43
150, 175, 200, 225 hp, Pro V 150, Pro V 175, Pro V 200, L150, L200	0.27-0.40
225, 250 hp, L225, L250	0.23-0.28

* Tests to be made with the coil temperature at a minimum of 20° C (68° F).
N/A—Not applicable. These models not equipped with this coil.

Table 5 IGNITION COIL RESISTANCE SPECIFICATIONS*

Model	Primary (ohms)	Secondary (ohms)
2 hp		
1990-1994	0.96-1.16	5,990-6,655
1995	0.18-0.24	2,720-3,680
3 hp	0.08-0.12	2,080-3,120
4, 5 hp	0.17-0.25	2,500-3,700
6, 8, 9.9, 15 hp	0.12-0.18	4,300-6,500
C25	0.12-0.18	4,320-6,480
25 hp	0.18-0.24	2,720-3,680
30 hp	0.46-0.62	5,360-7,250
C30	0.18-0.24	2,700-3,700

(continued)

Table 5 IGNITION COIL RESISTANCE SPECIFICATIONS* (continued)

Model	Primary (ohms)	Secondary (ohms)
C40	0.076-0.104	2,970-4,030
40, 50 hp, Pro 50	0.18-0.24	2,720-3,680
C55	0.20-0.30	2,000-3,000
Pro 60, 70, 90 hp	0.18-0.24	3,260-4,880
C75, C85	0.176-0.264	3,840-5,760
C115	0.20-0.30	2,000-3,000
115 hp, Pro 115, 130 hp, L130, 150 hp, Pro V 150, L150, 175 hp, Pro V 175, 200, Pro V 200, L200, 225 hp (90° V6)	0.15-0.21	3,000-4,600
225, 250 hp, L225, L250 (76° V6)	0.18-0.24	2,700-3,700

* Tests to be made with the coil temperature at a minimum of 20° C (68° F).

Table 6 CHARGE COIL RESISTANCE SPECIFICATIONS*

Model	Ohms
2 hp	
1990-1994	N/A
1995	316.8-387.2
3 hp	247.5-302.5
4, 5 hp	248-303
6, 8, 9.9, 15 hp	81-99
C25	211.5-258.5
25 hp	342-418
30 hp	164-296
C30	401-490
C40	120.6-147.4
40, 50 hp, Pro 50	368-552
C55	210-256
Pro 60, 70 hp	136-204
C75, C85	
Brown and blue	765-935
Brown and red	108-132
90 hp	191-288
C115	
Brown and red	840-1,260
Black/red and blue	102-153
115 hp, Pro 115, 130 hp, L130, 150 hp, Pro V 150, L150, 175 hp, Pro V 175, 200, Pro V 200, L200, 225 hp (90° V6)	
Brown and red	592-888
Black/red and blue	55-83
225, 250 hp, L225, L250 (76° V6)	
Brown and red	224-336
Black/red and blue	224-336

* Tests to be made with the coil temperature at a minimum of 20° C (68° F).
N/A—Not applicable. These models are not equipped with this coil.

Table 7 PULSER COIL RESISTANCE SPECIFICATIONS*

Model	Ohms
2 hp	N/A
3 hp	247.5-302.5
Black to red/white	29.7-36.2
Black to green/white	279-341
4, 5 hp	
White/red to black	30-36
White/green to black	279-341
6, 8, 9.9, 15 hp	92-112
C25	94.5-115.5
25 hp	311-318
30 hp	276-415
C30	311-381
C40	12.6-15.4
40, 50 hp, Pro 50	168-252
C55	70-86
Pro 60, 70 hp	240-360
C75, C85	342-418
90 hp	241-362
C115	288-432
115 hp, Pro 115, 130 hp, L130	264-396
150 hp, Pro V 150, L150, 175 hp	256-384
Pro V 175, 200 hp, Pro V 200, L200, 225 hp (90° V6)	
225, 250 hp, L225, L250 (76° V6)	294-398

* Tests to be made with the coil temperature at a minimum of 20° C (68° F).
N/A—Not applicable. These models are not equipped with this coil.

3

Chapter Four

Lubrication, Maintenance
and Tune-up

The modern 2-stroke outboard motor delivers more power and performance than ever before, with higher compression ratios, new and improved electrical systems and other design advances. Proper lubrication, maintenance and tune-ups have thus become increasingly important as ways in which you can maintain a high level of performance, extend engine life and extract the maximum economy of operation.

You can do your own lubrication, maintenance and tune-ups if you follow the correct procedures and use common sense. You should read and follow the information provided by Yamaha in the Owner's Manual accompanying your outboard motor. This booklet is a good source of operating and maintenance information pertaining to your particular model. If you have lost or misplaced your Owner's Manual, or if you have purchased the outboard used, purchase a replacement manual from your Yamaha dealer.

The following information is based on recommendations from Yamaha that will help you keep your outboard motor operating at its peak performance level.

Tables 1-3 are at the end of the chapter.

NOTE
The "L" series outboards (counter rotation models) are included in all procedures. Unless there is a separate procedure designated for the "L" series model, refer to the procedure that relates to the same horsepower rating. If you are working on an L200 model, then refer to the 200 hp procedure.

LUBRICATION

Proper Fuel Selection

Two-stroke engines are lubricated by mixing oil with the fuel. The various components of the engine are lubricated as the fuel/oil mixture passes through the crankcase and cylinders. Since outboard fuel serves the dual function of producing ignition and distributing the lubrication, the use of low-octane marine white gasoline should be avoided. Such gasoline also has a tendency to cause ring sticking and port plugging.

Yamaha recommends the use of any gasoline with a minimum posted pump octane rating of 84 for use in its 2-50 hp models. A minimum posted pump octane of 86 is recommended for 70-220 models. The 225 and 250 hp models, however, require an octane rating of 89 to prevent engine knock and assure proper operation.

When possible, use a premium grade gasoline produced by a national brand refinery. Premium grade gasoline contains a high concentration of detergent and dispersant additives that prevent carbon deposits on the pistons, rings and combustion chamber.

Sour Fuel

Fuel should *not* be stored for more than 60 days even under ideal conditions. Gasoline forms gum and varnish deposits as it ages. Gasoline tends to lose its potency after standing for long periods and condensation may contaminate it with water. Among other problems, such fuel will cause hard starting and poor performance. A good grade of gasoline stabilizer and conditioner additive may be used to prevent gum and varnish formation during storage or prolonged periods of non-use but it is always better to drain the tank in such cases. Always use *fresh* gasoline when mixing fuel for your outboard. This will help keep you from getting stranded in the middle of a lake with no power.

Fuel Additives

The gasoline available today is formulated mainly for use in the 4-stroke automobile engine to comply with regulations for lower exhaust emissions. Such fuel can create deposits, especially in 2-stroke engines, that can potentially cause problems with outboard motor performance. To counteract this problem, Yamaha has developed 2 products; the Yamalube TC-W3 2-stroke Outboard Motor Oil and the Ring Free Fuel Additive. The use of these products helps reduce these deposits for optimum engine performance and reliability in your outboard motor.

Yamaha recommends the use of the Ring Free Fuel Additive even though Yamalube TC-W3 outboard motor oil is used. The recommended amount to be added on a constant basis is 1 oz. of additive to every 15 gallons of fuel.

Water Separator Filter

Water will eventually find its way into the fuel system and into the engine. Small amounts of water may not affect engine power, but the water will wash away oil from moving parts and the cylinder walls. If internal engine parts are left unprotected from corrosion, engine failure can occur after even a short period of storage. A large amount of water in the fuel system can cause problems after a storage period of as little as two days.

To protect against water in the fuel system, Yamaha suggests the installation of a water separator filter. Install the Yamaha Fuel/Water/Separator/Filter (ABA-SEPAR-AT-OR) in the fuel system and change the filter element on a regular basis. A boat with a large fuel tank(s) operating in high-humidity areas will need to replace the filter element more often than a boat with a smaller tank(s) operating in dryer areas.

Alcohol Extended Gasoline

Some gasoline sold for marine use contains alcohol, even though it may not be advertised as containing alcohol. Although the manufacturer does not recommend using alcohol extended

4

gasoline, testing to date has found that it causes no major deterioration of fuel system components when consumed *immediately* after purchase.

Gasoline with alcohol slowly absorbs moisture from the atmosphere. When the moisture content of the fuel reaches approximately one half of one percent, it combines with the alcohol and separates (phase separation) from the gasoline. This separation does not normally occur in an automobile, as the fuel is generally consumed within a few days after purchase; however, because boats often remain idle for days or even weeks, the problem does occur in marine use.

Moisture and alcohol become very corrosive when mixed and will cause corrosion of metal components and deterioration of rubber and plastic fuel system components. In addition, the alcohol and water mixture will settle to the bottom of the fuel tank. If this mixture enters the engine, it can wash the oil film off the cylinder walls and other internal components, resulting in excessive wear and corrosion. If a large amount of alcohol and water enters the engine, it may become necessary to drain the fuel tank, flush out the fuel system and, possibly, remove and clean the spark plugs before the outboard motor can be started.

The following is an accepted and widely used field procedure for detecting alcohol in gasoline. Note that the gasoline should be tested prior to mixing with the oil. Use any small transparent bottle or tube that can be capped and can be provided with graduations or a mark at approximately 1/3 full. A pencil mark on a piece of adhesive tape is sufficient.

1. Fill the container with water to the 1/3 full mark.

2. Add gasoline until the container is almost full. Leave a small air space at the top.

3. Shake the container vigorously, then allow it to set for 3-5 minutes. If the volume of water appears to have increased, alcohol is present in the gasoline. If the dividing line between the water and gasoline becomes cloudy, reference from the center of the cloudy band.

This procedure cannot differentiate between types of alcohol (ethanol or methanol), nor is it considered absolutely accurate from a scientific standpoint, but it is accurate enough to determine if sufficient alcohol is present to cause the operator to take precautions.

Although plain tap water is used in this test, it may not show the presence of alcohol if cosolvents were used as a suspension agent when the alcohol was blended with the gasoline. If cosolvents are present, use ethylene glycol (automotive antifreeze) instead of water. To ensure accurate results, test the gasoline twice, once using plain tap water, then with antifreeze.

Recommended Fuel Mixture

The Yamaha Precision Blend oil injection system (**Figure 1**) is used on 25-250 hp engines with

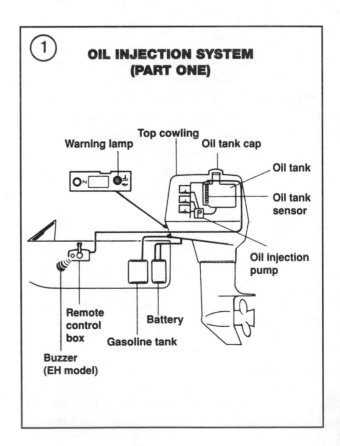

① OIL INJECTION SYSTEM (PART ONE)

Warning lamp
Top cowling
Oil tank cap
Oil tank
Oil tank sensor
Oil injection pump
Remote control box
Battery
Gasoline tank
Buzzer (EH model)

the exception of the "C" series engines (C25 C30, C40, C55, C75, C85 and C115). A crankshaft-driven injection pump automatically injects oil into the intake manifold at a variable ratio from approximately 200:1 at idle to 100:1 on 25-50 hp models at full throttle or 50:1 at full throttle on 70-250 hp models. **Figure 2** shows the typical engine-mounted components of the oil injection system.

A sensor monitoring the injection system sounds a buzzer and illuminates a gauge warning lamp when the oil tank requires replenishment. Engine rpm is also reduced at this time on some models. The engines should be run with a 50:1

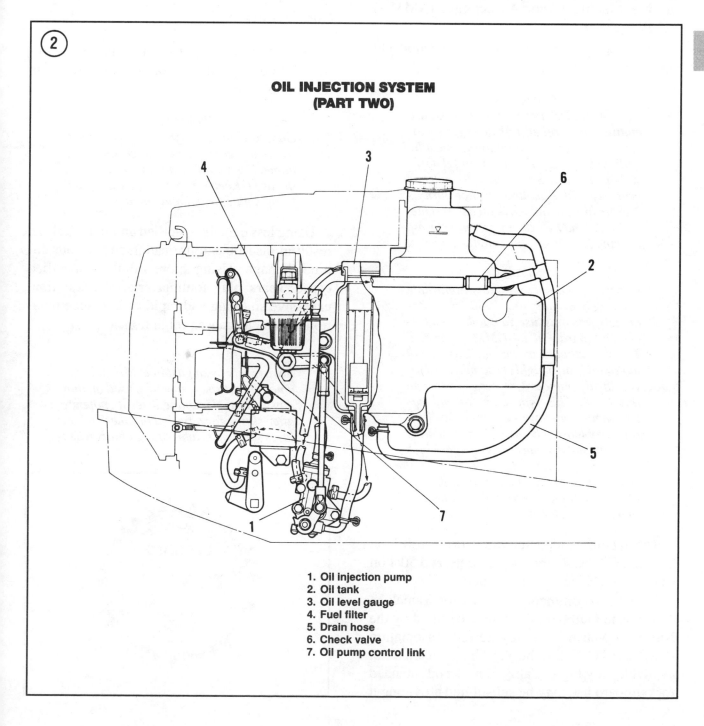

② OIL INJECTION SYSTEM
(PART TWO)

1. Oil injection pump
2. Oil tank
3. Oil level gauge
4. Fuel filter
5. Drain hose
6. Check valve
7. Oil pump control link

premix during the break-in period or after a long period of storage as specified in your owner's manual.

To replenish the system, lift the lid on the engine cover. Remove the oil tank cap and pour in the required amount of Yamalube Two-Cycle Outboard Oil that is certified by the National Marine Manufacturers Association (NMMA) TC-W3 (**Figure 3**).

See Chapter Twelve for system operation and service procedures.

CAUTION
Do not, under any circumstances, use multigrade or other high detergent automotive oils or oils containing metallic additives. Such oils are harmful to 2-stroke engines. Since they do not mix properly with gasoline, do not burn as 2-cycle oils do and leave an ash residue, their use may result in piston scoring, bearing failure or other engine damage.

NOTE
In order to comply with any applicable Yamaha warranty on 1990 and later models, you must use Yamalube Two-Cycle Outboard Oil or NMMA Certified TC-W3 outboard motor oil. This type of motor oil is also highly recommended for use in all outboard motors covered in this book. This type of motor oil has shown no tendency to gel or cause filtration problems. The use of the normally recommended ashless oils can gel which will lead to filter blockage in the oil injection system. This blockage can cause insufficient lubrication to the cylinders and can result in engine seizure.

The recommended fuel/oil ratio is 100:1 on 2-20 hp, C25, C30 and C40 models, and 50:1 on C60, C75, C85 and C115 models.

Yamaha recommends the use of Yamalube Two-Cycle Outboard Oil that is certified by the National Marine Manufacturers Association (NMMA) TC-W3. If the Yamaha lubricant is not available, any high-quality 2-stroke oil intended for outboard use may be substituted providing it

meets the NMMA TC-W3 rating and specifies so on the container. Follow the manufacturer's instructions on the container but do not exceed a 100:1 ratio on 2-20 hp, C25, C30 and C40 models, or a 50:1 ratio on C60, C75, C85 and C115 models.(after break-in).

Correct Fuel Mixing

Mix the fuel and oil outdoors or in a well-ventilated indoor location. Mix the fuel directly in the portable tank.

WARNING
Gasoline is an extreme fire hazard. Never use gasoline near heat, sparks or flame. Do not allow anyone to smoke in the area. Keep a fire extinguisher, rated for gasoline fires, handy in any case.

Using less than the specified amount of oil can result in insufficient lubrication and serious engine damage. Using more oil than specified causes spark plug fouling, erratic carburetion, excessive smoking and rapid carbon accumulation which can cause preignition.

NOTE
Always mix fresh gasoline. Mix only the amount that you feel will be used on that day's outing. Gasoline loses its potency after sitting for a period of time. The oil loses some of its lubricating ability when

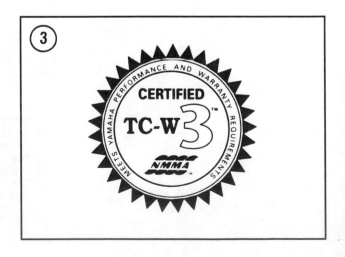

*mixed with the gasoline then not used for
a period of time.*

Cleanliness is of prime importance. Even a
very small particle of dirt can cause carburetion
problems. Always use fresh gasoline. Gum and
varnish deposits tend to form in gasoline stored
in a tank for any length of time. Use of sour fuel
can result in carburetor problems and spark plug
fouling.

Above 32° F (10° C)

Measure the required amounts of gasoline and
Yamalube Two-Cycle Outboard Oil accurately.
Pour the specified amount of oil into the portable
tank and add one-half of the gasoline to be
mixed. Install the tank filler cap and mix the fuel
by tipping the tank on its side and back to an
upright position several times (**Figure 4**). Re-

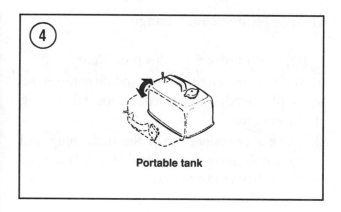

Portable tank

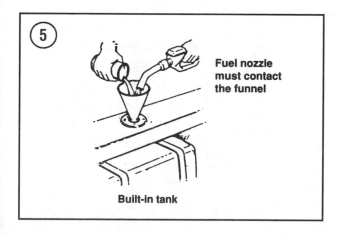

**Fuel nozzle
must contact
the funnel**

Built-in tank

move the tank cap and add the balance of the
gasoline, then thoroughly mix again.

If a built-in tank is used, insert a large metal
filter funnel in the tank filler neck. Slowly pour
the Yamalube Two-Cycle Outboard Oil into the
funnel at the same time the tank is being filled
with gasoline (**Figure 5**).

Below 32° F (0° C)

Measure the required amounts of gasoline and
Yamalube Two-Cycle Outboard Oil accurately.
Pour about one gallon of gasoline in the tank and
then add the required amount of oil. Install the
tank filler cap and shake the tank to mix the fuel
and oil thoroughly. Remove the cap and add the
balance of the gasoline, then thoroughly mix
again.

If a built-in tank is used, insert a large metal
filter funnel in the tank filler neck. Mix the
required amount of Yamalube Two-Cycle Outboard Oil with one gallon of gasoline in a separate container. Slowly pour the mixture into the
funnel at the same time the tank is being filled
with gasoline.

Consistent Fuel Mixtures

The carburetor idle adjustment is sensitive to
fuel mixture variations which result from the use
of different oils and gasolines or from inaccurate
measuring and mixing. This may require readjustment of the idle needle. To prevent the necessity for constant readjustment of the carburetor
from one batch of fuel to the next, always be
consistent. Prepare each batch of fuel exactly the
same as previous ones.

Premixed fuel sold at some marinas is not
recommended for use in Yamaha outboards,
since the quality and consistency can vary
greatly. The possibility of power head damage
resulting from use of an incorrect fuel mixture

outweighs the convenience offered by premixed fuel.

Gearcase Lubrication

Change the gearcase lubricant after the first 10 hours of operation. Replace the lubricant at 50 hour intervals or once per season. Use Yamaha Gearcase Lube.

> *CAUTION*
> *Do not use regular automotive grease in the gearcase. Its expansion and foam characteristics are not suitable for marine use.*

Gearcase Lubricant Check

To ensure a correct level check, the outboard motor must be in the upright position and not run for at least 2 hours before performing this procedure. Refer to **Figure 6** for this procedure.

1. Remove the engine cover and disconnect the spark plug lead(s) to prevent accidental starting of the engine.

2. Locate and loosen the gearcase drain plug on the right side of the gear housing (just above the skeg). Allow a small amount of lubricant to drain. If there is water in the gearcase, it will drain out before the lubricant. Retighten the drain plug securely.

3. If water is noted in Step 2, retighten the plug securely and pressure test the gearcase to determine if a seal has failed or if the water is simply condensation in the gearcase. See Chapter Nine.

4. Remove the oil level plug above the antiventilation plate. Do not lose the accompanying washer. The lubricant should be level with the bottom rim of the plug hole.

> *CAUTION*
> *Never lubricate the gearcase without first removing the vent plug, as the injected lubricant displaces air which must be allowed to escape. The gearcase cannot be completely filled otherwise.*

5. If the lubricant level is low, place a suitable size container under gearcase and remove the drain plug.

6. Inject lubricant into the drain hole until excess fluid flows out the oil level plug hole.

7. Install the oil level plug then the oil drain plug. Be sure the washers are in place under the head of each plug, so that water will not leak past the threads into the housing.

8. Wipe any excess lubricant off the gearcase exterior. Let gearcase stand upright for a minimum of 1/2 hour, then recheck the lubricant level. Top up if necessary, then reinstall oil level plug and washer.

> *NOTE*
> *If the gearcase has been disassembled, recheck the lubricant level after 2-3 hours of operation. Top up if necessary.*

Gearcase Lubricant Change

Refer to **Figure 6** for this procedure.

1. Remove the engine cover and disconnect the spark plug lead(s) to prevent accidental starting of the engine.

2. Place a container under the drain plug and remove it. Remove the oil level plug. Drain the lubricant from the gearcase.

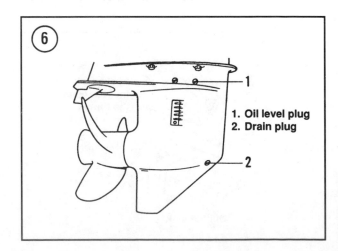

6

1. Oil level plug
2. Drain plug

NOTE
If the lubricant is creamy in color or metallic particles are found in Step 3, remove and disassemble the gearcase to determine and correct the cause of the problem.

3. Wipe a small amount of lubricant on a finger and rub the finger and thumb together. Check for the presence of metallic particles in the lubricant. Note the color of the lubricant. A white or creamy

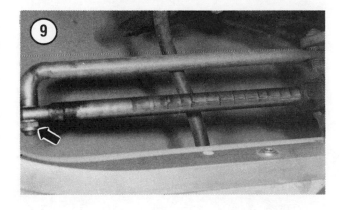

color indicates water in the lubricant. Check the drain container for signs of water separation from the lubricant. If water is present, it will rise to the top of the lubricant.

4. Perform Steps 6-9 of *Gearcase Lubricant Check* in this chapter.

Jet Drive Bearing Lubrication

The jet drive bearings should be lubricated after *each* operating period, after every 10 hours of operation and prior to storage. In addition, after every 50 hours of operation, additional grease should be pumped into the bearings to purge any moisture. The bearings are lubricated by first removing the cap on the end of the excess grease hose from the grease fitting on the side of the jet drive (**Figure 7**). Use a grease gun and inject grease into the fitting until grease exits from the capped end of the excess grease hose. Use only Yamalube All-purpose Marine grease or a NLGI No. 1 rated grease to lubricate the bearings.

Note the color of the grease being expelled from the excess grease hose. During the break-in period some discoloration of the grease is normal. After the break-in period, if the grease starts to turn dark or dirty gray, the jet drive assembly should be disassembled as outlined under *Jet Drive* in Chapter Ten. The seals and bearings should then be inspected and replaced as needed. If you detect moisture being expelled from the excess grease hose, the jet drive should be disassembled and the seals replaced and the bearing(s) inspected and replaced if needed.

Other Lubrication Points

Refer to **Figures 8-14**, typical and **Table 1** for other lubrication points. Also provided are frequency of lubrication and type of lubricant to use.

In addition to these lubrication points, some outboards may also have grease fittings provided at critical points where bearing surfaces are not externally exposed (**Figure 15**, typical). Remove the protective rubber cap from the fittings (A, **Figure 15**) and lubricate at least once each season with Yamalube All-purpose Marine grease until grease can be seen at an external point (B, **Figure 15**).

CAUTION
When lubricating the steering cable on models so equipped, make sure its core is fully retracted into the cable housing. Lubricating the cable while extended can cause a hydraulic lock to occur.

Saltwater Corrosion of Gearcase Bearing Housing or Cap

Saltwater corrosion that is allowed to build up unchecked can eventually split the gearcase and destroy the lower unit. If the outboard is used in saltwater, remove the propeller shaft bearing housing at least once per. Clean all corrosive deposits and dried-up lubricant from each end of the housing.

Install *new* O-rings on the bearing housing and wipe the outer diameter of the housing at A and B, **Figure 16** with Yamalube All-purpose Marine grease. Install the housing or cap and tighten the bolts to specification (Chapter Nine). Lubricate the propeller shaft splines with the same grease and reinstall the propeller.

STORAGE

The major consideration in preparing an outboard motor for storage is to protect it from rust, corrosion and dirt. Use the following procedure to prepare your outboard motor for storage.

1. Remove the engine cover.

2A. On propeller models, operate the outboard in a test tank or attach a flush device (**Figure 17**). Start the engine and run at fast idle until warmed up.

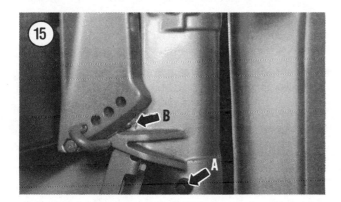

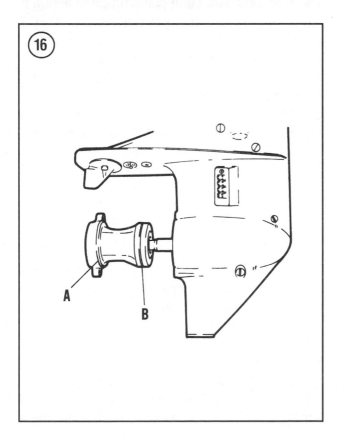

2B. On jet drive models, operate the outboard with a cooling system flush device attached as outlined in Chapter Ten. Start the engine and run at fast idle until warmed up.

3. On propeller-driven models, shift the engine into NEUTRAL.

4. Disconnect the fuel line and run the outboard at fast idle while pouring about 2 oz.(59 ml) of Yamalube Two-Cycle Outboard Oil into each carburetor throat until the engine stalls out.

5. Remove spark plug(s) as described in this chapter. Pour about 1 oz.(30 ml) of Yamalube Two-Cycle Outboard Oil into each spark plug hole. Slowly rotate the flywheel by hand several times to distribute the oil throughout the cylinder(s). Reinstall the spark plug(s).

6. Service the portable fuel tank filter (strainer) as follows:

    a. Disconnect the fuel line from the fuel meter housing on the tank. Remove the attaching screws and pull the housing assembly from the tank.

    b. Clean the fine wire mesh filter (strainer) at the bottom of the housing assembly suction pipe by rinsing it in clean benzine.

    c. Pour approximately 1 qt.(0.9 l) of clean benzine in the tank and slosh it about to clean the tank interior. Pour out the benzine and discard it safely.

    d. Reinstall the fuel meter housing to the fuel tank and connect the fuel line.

7. Service the engine fuel filter as described in this chapter.

8A. On propeller-driven models, drain and refill the gearcase as described in this chapter. Check the condition of the oil level and drain plug gaskets. Replace as required.

8B. On jet drive models, lubricate the jet drive bearings as described in this chapter.

9. Refer to **Figures 9-14** and **Table 1** as appropriate and lubricate the outboard motor at all specified points.

10. Clean the entire outboard motor, including all accessible power head parts. Remove all dirt, grease and scum with a good quality marine cleaner. Coat all surfaces with a good marine-type wax. Install the engine cover and wipe a thin film of clean engine oil on all painted surfaces.

11. On propeller-driven models, remove the propeller and lubricate the propeller shaft splines with Yamalube All-purpose Marine grease. Re-install the propeller.

CAUTION
Make certain that all water drain holes in the gearcase are free and open to allow water to drain out. Water expands as it freezes and can crack the gearcase or water pump.

12. Drain the system completely to prevent damage from freezing.

13. Store the outboard motor upright in a dry and well-ventilated area.

14. Service the battery (if so equipped) as follows:

   a. Disconnect the negative battery cable, then the positive battery cable.

   b. Remove all grease, corrosion and dirt from the battery surface.

   c. Check the electrolyte level in each battery cell and top up with distilled water, if necessary. Fluid level in each cell should not be higher than 3/16 in.(4.8 mm) above the perforated baffles. Gently shake the battery to mix the water with the electrolyte.

   d. Lubricate the cable terminal bolts with grease or petroleum jelly.

CAUTION
A discharged battery can be damaged by freezing.

   e. With the battery in a fully charged condition (specific gravity 1.260-1.275), store in a dry place where the temperature will not drop below freezing.

   f. Recharge the battery every 45 days or whenever the specific gravity drops below 1.230. Before charging, add sufficient distilled water to cover the top of the plates, but not more than 3/16 in.(4.8 mm) above the perforated baffles. The charge rate should not exceed 6 amps. Stop charging when the specific gravity reaches 1.260 at 80° F (27° C).

   g. Before placing the battery back into service after storage, remove the excess grease from the terminals, leaving on a small amount. Install the battery in the boat in a fully charged state.

15. If an outboard equipped with oil injection is stored for more than one season, use a 50:1 premix to start the engine and follow the *Break-in Procedure* provided in Chapter Thirteen.

16. Cover the outboard motor with a tarp, blanket or heavy plastic drop cloth. Place this cover over the outboard mainly as a dust cover—do not wrap it tightly, especially if using plastic material, as it may trap condensation. Leave room for air to circulate around the outboard.

ANTI-CORROSION MAINTENANCE

1. Flush the cooling system with freshwater as described in this chapter after each time outboard is used in saltwater. Completely wash the exterior with freshwater.

2. Dry the exterior of the outboard with compressed air to remove all moisture from all crevices. Apply Yamaha zinc primer (part No. LUB-84-PNT-PR-MR) over any paint nicks and scratches. Use only Yamaha touch-up paint

available at your dealer. If Yamaha paint is not available, use a suitable antifouling paint. Do not use paints containing mercury or copper. Do *not* paint sacrificial anodes.

3. Spray the power head and all electrical connections with a good quality corrosion and rust preventive.

4. Check the condition of sacrificial anodes and the trim tab. Replace any anodes that are less than half their original size. Replace the trim tab, if damaged.

5. Lubricate more frequently than specified in **Table 1**. If used consistently in saltwater, reduce lubrication intervals (**Table 1**) by one-half.

COMPLETE SUBMERSION

An outboard motor which has been lost overboard should be recovered as quickly as possible. If the engine was running when submerged, disassemble and clean it immediately—any delay will result in rust and corrosion of internal components once it has been removed from the water. If the engine was not running and appears to be undamaged mechanically with no abrasive dirt or silt inside, take the following emergency steps immediately.

1. Wash the outside of the outboard with clean water to remove weeds, mud and other debris.

2. Remove the engine cover.

3. If recovered from saltwater, flush the engine completely with freshwater. If compressed air is available, blow off all water from exterior surfaces.

4. Remove the spark plug(s) as described in this chapter.

CAUTION
Do not force the engine if it does not turn over freely by hand in Step 5. This may be an indication of internal damage such as a bent connecting rod or broken piston.

5. Drain as much water as possible from the power head by placing the outboard in a horizontal position. Manually rotate the flywheel with the spark plug hole(s) facing downward to expel the water within the cylinder(s).

6. Pour rubbing alcohol into the carburetor throat(s) to displace the water. Manually rotate the flywheel at least one full turn, then position the engine so you can pour alcohol into the spark plug hole(s). Manually rotate the flywheel another full turn.

7. Completely dry and reinstall the spark plug(s).

8. Dry all ignition components, use compressed air if available. Spray all components with an aerosol electrical contact cleaner. This will help evaporate any remaining moisture.

9. Drain the fuel lines and carburetor(s). Discard spent fuel safely.

10. On models with an integral fuel tank, drain the tank and flush with fresh gasoline until all water has been removed. Discard spent fuel safely.

CAUTION
If there is a possibility that sand may have entered the power head, do not try to start the engine or severe internal damage may occur.

11. Place the engine in a test tank. Try starting the engine with a tank of fresh fuel. If the engine will start, let it run at least 1 hour to eliminate any water remaining inside.

CAUTION
If it is not possible to disassemble and clean the engine immediately in Step 12, resubmerge the power head in freshwater to prevent rust and corrosion formation until it can be properly serviced.

12. If the engine will not start in Step 11, try to diagnose the cause as fuel, electrical or mechanical and correct the problem. If the engine cannot be started within 2 hours, disassemble, clean and oil all parts thoroughly as soon as possible.

ENGINE FLUSHING

Propeller-driven models

Periodic engine flushing will prevent salt or silt deposits from accumulating within the engine's water passageways. This procedure should also be performed whenever an outboard engine is operated in saltwater or polluted water.

Keep the engine in an upright position during and after flushing. This prevents water from passing into the power head through the drive shaft housing and exhaust ports during the flushing procedure. This also eliminates the possibility of residual water being trapped in the drive shaft housing or other passageways.

Some Yamaha outboard engines have the water intake located on the underside of the antiventilation plate (**Figure 18**). These models require the use of flushing devices other than the flush-test unit. See your Yamaha dealer for the proper flushing device.

1. Attach a flushing device onto the front of the gearcase according to its manufacturer's instructions (**Figure 17**).

2. Connect a garden hose between a water tap and the flushing device.

3. Open the water tap partially—do not use full pressure.

4. Shift into NEUTRAL, then start engine. Keep engine speed at idle speed—do not run above idle speed.

5. Adjust the water flow so there is a slight loss of water around the rubber cups of the flushing device.

6. Check the engine to make sure that water is being discharged from the pilot or the "tell-tale" nozzle. If it is not, stop the engine immediately and determine the cause of the problem.

> ### CAUTION
> *Flush the engine for at least 5 minutes if used in saltwater.*

7. Flush the engine until the discharged water is clear. Stop the engine.

8. Close the water tap and remove the flushing device from the gearcase.

Jet drive models

The cooling system can become blocked by sand and salt deposits if it not flushed occasionally. Clean the cooling system after each use in saltwater.

1. Remove the plug and gasket from the port side of the jet drive housing to gain access to the flush passage.

2. Install the adapter (part No. 6EO-28193-00-94) into the flush passage.

3. Connect a garden hose to the adapter and turn the water tap to full pressure (maximum output).

> ### CAUTION
> *When the outboard motor is running, make sure a stream of water is being discharged from the engine's tell-tale outlet. If not, stop the motor immediately and diagnose the problem.*

> ### CAUTION
> *Do not operate the outboard motor at high speed when connected to the flush adapter.*

4. Start the engine and allow the freshwater to circulate for approximately 15 minutes. Keep engine speed at idle speed—do not run above idle speed.

5. Stop the engine, turn off the auxiliary water supply and disconnect the water supply from the adapter.

6. Remove the adapter.

7. Replace the gasket if damage is noted, then install it on the plug.

8. Install the plug and gasket onto the jet drive housing flush passage and securely tighten.

NOTE
To flush the jet drive impeller and intake housing, direct a freshwater supply into the intake housing area.

TUNE-UP

A tune-up consists of a series of inspections, adjustments and parts replacements to compensate for normal wear and deterioration of outboard engine components. A regular tune-up is important for power, performance and economy. Yamaha recommends that its outboards be serviced every 6 months or 100 hours of operation (whichever comes first). See **Table 1**. If subjected to limited use, the outboard should be tuned at least once a year.

Since proper outboard engine operation depends upon a number of interrelated system functions, a tune-up consisting of only one or two corrections will seldom give lasting results. For best results, a thorough and systematic procedure of analysis and correction is necessary.

Prior to performing a tune-up, it is a good idea to flush the engine as described in this chapter and check for satisfactory water pump operation.

NOTE
Start the outboard after each tune-up procedure is completed and make sure it runs okay. If for some reason, the procedure was not done correctly or a faulty new part(s) was installed, you can then concentrate on that specific procedure and part(s) and correct the problem. If you wait until all of the tune-up procedures are completed and the engine runs worse or does not start at all, then you have to narrow it down to which procedure or part is causing the problem.

The tune-up sequence recommended by Yamaha includes the following:

a. Compression check.
b. Spark plug service.
c. Gearcase and water pump check.
d. Fuel system service.
e. Ignition system service.
f. Battery, starter and relay/solenoid check (if so equipped).
g. Wiring harness check.
h. Timing, synchronization and adjustment.
i. Performance test (on boat).

Anytime the fuel or ignition systems are adjusted or defective parts replaced, the engine timing, synchronization and adjustment *must* be checked. These procedures are described in Chapter Five. Perform the timing, synchronization and adjustment procedure for your engine *before* running the performance test.

Compression Check

An accurate cylinder compression check gives a good idea of the condition of the basic working parts of the engine. It is also an important first step in any tune-up, as an engine with low or unequal compression between cylinders *cannot* be satisfactorily tuned. Any compression problem discovered during this check must be corrected before continuing with the tune-up procedure.

1. With the engine warm, disconnect the spark plug wire(s) and remove the spark plug(s) as described in this chapter.

2. Ground the spark plug wire(s) to the engine to disable the ignition system.

NOTE
The top cylinder is the No. 1 cylinder on inline engines. On V4 or V6 engines, the top cylinder on the starboard bank is the No. 1 cylinder.

3. Connect the compression tester to the top spark plug hole according to its manufacturer's instructions (**Figure 19**).

4. With the throttle set to the wide-open position, crank the engine through at least 4 compression strokes. Record the gauge reading.

5. Repeat Step 3 and Step 4 on each remaining cylinder.

NOTE
To maintain proper cylinder temperature on 3-cylinder and V6 engines, Yamaha varies the cylinder head volume on some models. A V6 will normally show the highest compression on cylinders No. 1 and No. 2, with cylinders No. 5 and No. 6 giving lowest reading. Always compare cylinder No. 1 to No. 2, cylinder No. 3 to No. 4 and cylinder No. 5 to No. 6. Do not compare compression top to bottom. Three-cylinder engines follow the same progression, with the highest reading in No. 1 cylinder and the lowest in the No. 3 cylinder.

The actual readings are not as important as the differences in readings when interpreting the results. A variation of more than 10-15 psi (69-103 kPa) between 2 cylinders indicates a problem with the lower reading cylinder, such as worn or sticking piston rings or scored pistons or cylinders. In such cases, pour a tablespoon of engine oil into the suspect cylinder and repeat Step 3 and Step 4. If the compression is raised significantly (by 10 psi [69 kPa] in an older engine), the rings are worn and should be replaced.

Older outboard motors, especially motors with high hours, are sometimes plagued by hard starting and generally poor performance, for which there is no readily apparent reason. The fuel and ignition systems are operating correctly and a compression test indicates the cylinder(s), piston(s) and rings are in acceptable condition.

What a compression test does not show, however, is a possible lack of primary compression. On a 2-stroke engine, the crankcase must be alternately under pressure, then vacuum. If the crankshaft seals or crankcase gaskets leak, and the crankcase is unable to contain pressure and/or vacuum, proper engine operation becomes impossible. Any other source of leakage, such as a defective cylinder base gasket or a porous or cracked crankcase casting will result in the same condition.

If the power head shows signs of overheating (discolored or scorched paint) but the compression test turns up nothing abnormal, check the cylinder(s) visually through the transfer ports for possible scoring. A cylinder can be slightly scored and still deliver a relatively good compression reading. In such a case, it is also a good idea to double-check the water pump operation as a possible cause of overheating.

Correct Spark Plug Heat Range

Yamaha outboards are equipped with NGK spark plugs selected for average use conditions. Under adverse use conditions, the recommended spark plug may foul or overheat. In such cases, check the ignition and fuel systems to make sure they are operating correctly. If no defect is found, replace the spark plug with one of a hotter or colder heat range as required.

NOTE
*Spark plug gap specifications are listed in **Table 2**.*

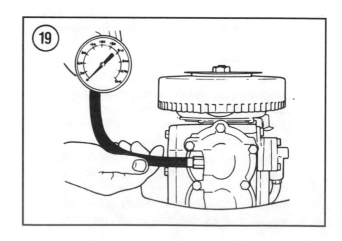

The proper spark plug is important in obtaining maximum performance and reliability. The condition of a used spark plug can tell a trained mechanic a lot about engine condition and carburetion.

Select a plug of the heat range designed for the loads and conditions under which the engine will be run. Using the incorrect heat range can cause a seized piston, scored cylinder wall, or damaged piston crown.

In general, use a hot plug when operating at low speeds and low temperatures. Use a cold plug for high speed, high engine load and high temperature operation. The plug should operate hot enough to burn off unwanted deposits, but not so hot that they burn themselves or cause preignition. A spark plug of the correct heat range will show a light tan color on the portion of the insulator inside the cylinder after the plug has been in service (**Figure 20**).

The reach (length) of a plug is also important. A longer than specified plug could interfere with the piston, causing permanent and severe damage (**Figure 21**).

Table 2 contains the recommended spark plugs for all models covered in this book.

Spark Plug Removal

CAUTION
Whenever a spark plug is removed, dirt around it can fall into the plug hole and into the cylinder resulting in expensive engine damage. This can cause engine damage that is expensive to repair.

1. Blow out any foreign matter from around the spark plug(s) with compressed air. Use a compressor if you have one. If you do not, use a can of compressed inert gas, available from photo stores.

2. Disconnect the spark plug wire(s) by twisting the wire boot back and forth on the plug insulator while pulling outward (**Figure 22**). Pulling on the wire instead of the boot may cause internal damage to the wire.

NOTE
If the plug is difficult to remove, apply penetrating oil, like WD-40 or Liquid Wrench, around the base of the plug and let it soak in about 10-20 minutes.

3. Remove the plug(s) with an appropriate size spark plug socket or box-end wrench. Keep the plugs in order so you know which cylinder they came from.

4. Inspect the plug carefully. Look for a broken center porcelain, excessively eroded electrodes, and excessive carbon or oil fouling. Compare its condition with **Figure 20**. Spark plug condition indicates engine condition and can warn of developing trouble.

5. Check each plug for make and heat range. All should be of the same make and number or heat range.

6. Yamaha recommends the plugs be cleaned and reused if in good condition; however, such plugs seldom last very long. New plugs are inexpensive and far more reliable.

Spark Plug Gap Adjustment

New or used plugs must be carefully gapped to ensure a reliable, consistent spark. Use a special spark plug tool with a wire gauge.

1. Remove the plugs and gaskets from the boxes. Install the gaskets.

NOTE
Some plug brands may have small end pieces that must be screwed on before the plugs can be used.

2. Insert the appropriate size wire gauge (**Figure 23**) between the electrodes, refer to **Table 2**. If the gap is correct, there will be a slight drag as the wire is pulled through. If there is no drag or if the wire will not pull through, bend the side

⓴ **SPARK PLUG ANALYSIS**

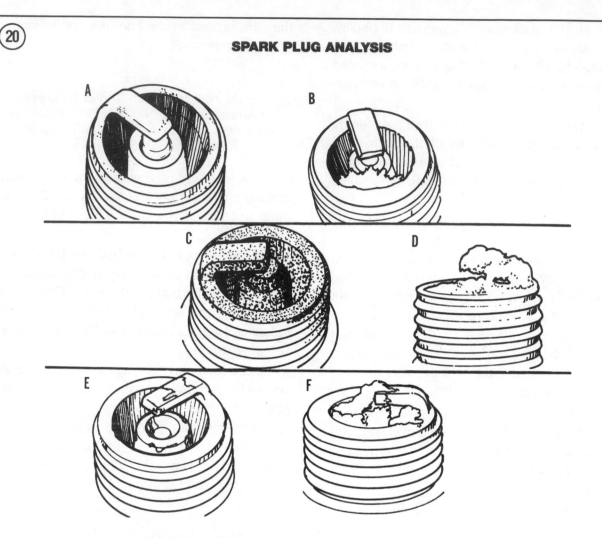

A. **Normal**—Light to tan gray color of insulator indicates correct heat range. Few deposits are present and the electrodes are not burned.

B. **Core bridging**—These defects are caused by excessive combustion chamber deposits striking and adhering to the firing end of the plug. In this case, they wedge or fuse between the electrode and core nose. They originate from the piston and cylinder head surfaces. Deposits are formed by one or more of the following:
    a. Excessive carbon in cylinder.
    b. Use of non-recommended oils.
    c. Immediate high-speed operation after prolonged trolling.
    d. Improper fuel-oil ratio.

C. **Wet fouling**—Damp or wet, black carbon coating over entire firing end of plug. Forms sludge in some engines. Caused by one or more of the following:
    a. Spark plug heat range too cold.
    b. Prolonged trolling.
    c. Low-speed carburetor adjustment too rich.

    d. Improper fuel-fuel oil ratio.
    e. Induction manifold bleed-off passage obstructed.
    f. Worn or defective breaker points.

D. **Gap bridging**—Similar to core bridging, except the combustion particles are wedged or fused between the electrodes. Causes are the same.

E. **Overheating**—Badly worn electrodes and premature gap wear are indicative of this problem, along with a gray or white "blistered" appearance on the insulator. Caused by one or more of the following:
    a. Spark plug heat range too hot.
    b. Incorrect propeller usage, causing engine to lug.
    c. Worn or defective water pump.
    d. Restricted water intake or restriction somewhere in the cooling system.

F. **Ash deposits or lead fouling**—Ash deposits are light brown to white in color and result from use of fuel or oil additives. Lead fouling produces a yellowish brown discoloration and can be avoided by using unleaded fuels.

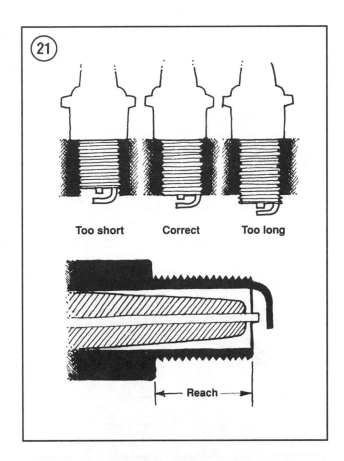

Too short   Correct   Too long

Reach

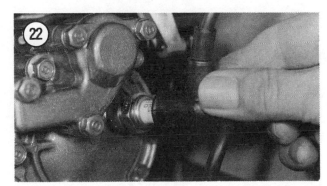

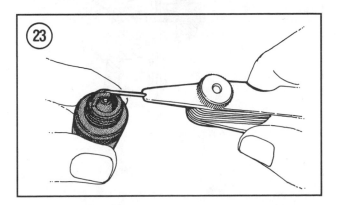

electrode with the gapping tool (**Figure 24**) to change the gap. Remeasure with the wire gauge.

CAUTION
Never try to close the electrode gap by tapping the spark plug on a solid surface. This can damage the plug internally. Always use the gapping tool to open or close the gap.

3. Check the spark plug hole threads and clean with an appropriate size spark plug chaser (**Figure 25**), if necessary, before installing the plug.

4

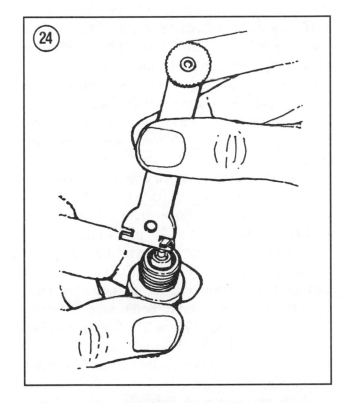

This will remove any corrosion, carbon buildup or minor flaws from the threads. Coat the chaser threads with grease to catch chips or foreign matter. Use care to avoid cross-threading. Wipe the cylinder head seats clean before installing the new plugs.

4. Apply a thin film of antiseize compound to the spark plug threads.

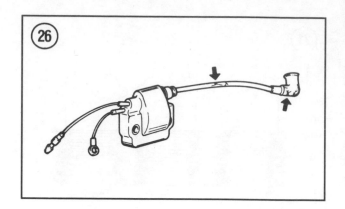

Spark Plug Installation

Improper installation of spark plugs is one of the most common causes of poor spark plug performance in outboard engines. The gasket on the plug must be fully compressed against a clean plug seat for heat transfer to take place effectively. This requires close attention to proper tightening during installation.

1. Screw each plug in by hand until it seats. Very little effort is required. If force is necessary, the plug is cross-threaded. Unscrew it and try again.

2. Tighten the spark plugs. If you have a torque wrench, tighten to 10-15 ft.-lb (13.6-20.0 N•m). If not, seat the plug finger-tight on the gasket, then tighten an additional 1/4 turn with a wrench.

3. Inspect each spark plug wire before reconnecting it to its plug (**Figure 26**). If insulation is damaged or deteriorated, install a new plug wire.

4. If the cap is cracked or deteriorated, remove it from the coil lead (**Figure 27**). Wipe the spring on the end of the coil lead with a light coat of Yamalube All-purpose Marine Grease and install a new cap.

5. Push the wire boot onto plug terminal and make sure it seats fully.

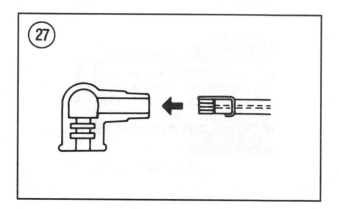

Water Pump Check

A faulty water pump can result in extensive engine damage. Thus, it is a good idea to replace the water pump impeller, seals and gaskets once per year or whenever the gearcase (see Chapter Nine) or jet drive (see Chapter Ten) is removed for service.

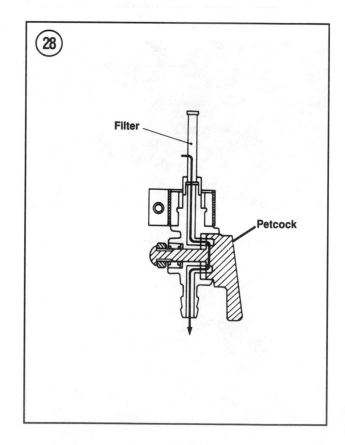

Filter

Petcock

Normally, proper cooling system operation on an outboard motor is verified by watching the water stream discharged from the "tell-tale" hole. However, a far more effective indicator of cooling system performance is to install a water pressure gauge. A water pressure gauge kit is available from the manufacturer for installation on 30 hp and larger outboards. The kit includes a sending unit that is permanently installed in the cylinder head and a gauge designed for installation in the boat.

After installing a pressure meter, note the gauge reading the first time the engine is run. If the pressure reading falls off during subsequent engine use, service the water pump as soon as possible. See Chapter Nine or Chapter Ten.

Fuel System Service

The clearance between the carburetor and choke shutter should not be greater than 0.38 mm

(0.015 in.) when the choke is closed or a hard starting condition will result.

When changing from one brand of gasoline to another, it may be necessary to readjust the carburetor idle mixture needle slightly (1/4 turn) to accommodate the variations in volatility.

Fuel Lines

1. Visually check all fuel lines for kinks, leaks, deterioration or other damage.
2. Disconnect fuel lines and blow out with compressed air to dislodge any contamination or foreign material.
3. Coat fuel line fittings sparingly with Type 2 Permatex and reconnect the fuel lines. Make sure they are on tight.

Engine Fuel Filter Service

The 2-5 hp engines have an integral fuel tank and use gravity fuel feed instead of a fuel pump (see Chapter Six). A filter screen (**Figure 28**) is installed in the fuel tank petcock (**Figure 29** shows the 4 hp engine; the 2, 3 hp and 5 hp engines are similar).

Other models may use one of the following:
   a. An inline filter (**Figure 30**).
   b. A canister filter (**Figure 31**).

Integral tank filter

Refer to **Figure 32** for this procedure.

1. Remove the fuel tank, if necessary, to provide working room. See Chapter Six.

2. Loosen the fuel petcock clamp screw or nut. Remove the petcock from the clamp and tank, then disconnect the hose.

3. Clean the filter assembly in solvent and blow dry with compressed air. If excessively dirty or contaminated with water, replace the filter.

4. Installation is the reverse of removal.

Inline filter

1. Place a clean cloth under the inline filter to absorb spilled fuel.

2. Slide the hose retaining clips off the filter nipple with a pair of pliers and disconnect the hoses from the filter (**Figure 33**).

3. Clean the filter assembly in solvent to remove any particles. If excessively dirty or contaminated with water, discard and install a new filter.

4. Reinstall the hoses on the filter nipples. Make sure the embossed arrow on the filter points in the direction of fuel flow (**Figure 34**).

5. Slide the retaining clips on each hose over the filter nipples to ensure a leak-free connection.

6. Check the fuel filter installation for leakage by priming the fuel system with the fuel line primer bulb.

Canister filter—except 76° V6 engine

> *NOTE*
> *On some models, it may be possible to service the filter element without removing the entire canister assembly from the engine. If this is the case, only perform Steps 3-9 and Step 13.*

1A. On models with metal clips, slide each hose retaining clip off the filter assembly cover nipples with a pair of pliers. Disconnect the hoses

from the cover and plug the hoses to prevent fuel leakage.

1B. On models with plastic clips, unsnap the plastic clips holding the hoses to the filter assembly cover. Disconnect the hoses from the cover and plug the hoses with golf tees to prevent fuel leakage.

2. Remove the nut securing the filter cover to its mounting bracket (**Figure 35**). Remove the cover and canister assembly.

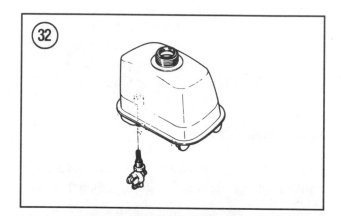

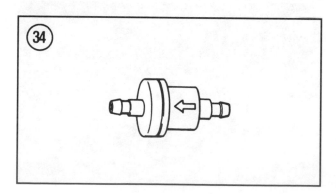

3. Unscrew the canister from the filter assembly cover. Remove the filter element from the canister (**Figure 36**).

4. Drain the canister and wipe the inside dry with a clean lint-free cloth or paper towel.

5. Remove and discard the cover O-ring and gasket (if used).

6. Clean the filter screen with solvent to remove any particles (**Figure 37**). If the filter screen is severely clogged or dirty, replace it.

7. Inspect the filter screen for damage, replace if necessary.

8. Install a new O-ring seal and gasket (if used) in the filter canister.

9. Install the filter and the filter canister. Tighten the canister securely.

10. If removed, connect the inlet and outlet hoses to the canister cover.

11. Install the nut securing the filter cover to its mounting bracket and tighten securely.

12A. On models with metal clips, slide each hose retaining clip onto the filter assembly cover nipples with a pair of pliers.

12B. On models with plastic clips, snap the plastic clips holding the hoses to the filter assembly cover.

13. Check the fuel filter installation for leakage by priming the fuel system with the fuel line primer bulb.

Canister filter—76° V6 engine

1. Unscrew the ring nut securing the canister to the filter assembly cover.

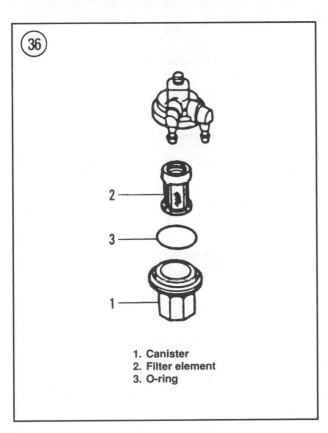

1. Canister
2. Filter element
3. O-ring

4

2. Remove the canister and filter element from the cover (**Figure 38**).

3. Remove the filter element and spring from the canister.

4. Drain the canister and wipe the inside dry with a clean lint-free cloth or paper towel.

5. Remove and discard the cover O-ring and gasket.

6. Clean the filter screen with solvent to remove any particles (**Figure 37**). If the filter screen is severely clogged or dirty, replace it.

7. Inspect the filter screen for damage and replace if necessary.

8. Install a new O-ring seal and gasket in the filter canister.

9. Install the spring and filter into the filter canister.

10. Install the canister assembly onto the filter assembly cover and screw on the ring nut. Tighten the ring nut securely.

11. Check the fuel filter installation for leakage by priming the fuel system with the fuel line primer bulb.

Fuel Pump

The fuel pump does not generally require service during a tune-up. However, if the engine has more than 100 hours on it since the fuel pump was last serviced, it is a good idea to remove and disassemble the pump, inspect each part carefully for wear or damage and reassemble it with a new diaphragm. See Chapter Six.

Fuel pump diaphragms are fragile and one that is defective often produces symptoms that are diagnosed as an ignition system problem. A common malfunction results from a tiny pinhole or crack in the diaphragm caused by an engine backfire. This defect allows gasoline to enter the crankcase and wet-foul the spark plug(s) at idle speed, causing hard starting and stalling at low rpm. The problem disappears at higher speeds, because fuel demand is greater. Since the plug(s)

is not fouled by excess fuel at higher speeds, it fires normally.

Pressure test—115-250 hp engine

> *NOTE*
> *Yamaha does not provide service information for fuel pumps on smaller horsepower engines.*

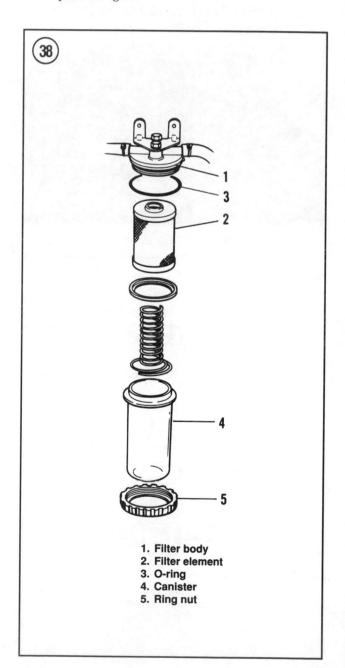

1. Filter body
2. Filter element
3. O-ring
4. Canister
5. Ring nut

NOTE
The fuel pump must be "wet" with gasoline to perform this test correctly. A dry (new or newly rebuilt) fuel pump cannot be tested. The internal diaphragms and gaskets must be moist from having gasoline passed through them.

1. Drain as much gasoline from the fuel pump as possible.

2. Close off the carburetor side of the fuel pump with your finger.

3. Connect a Mityvac hand-held pump (part No. 35956, or equivalent) to the other side of the fuel pump (**Figure 39**). Apply positive pressure at 49.5 kPa (7.1 psi). The pump should maintain

this pressure. If the pump will not maintain this pressure, the pump is faulty.

4. Switch the hose to the vacuum side of the Mityvac.

5. Connect the Mityvac to the same fitting of the fuel pump (**Figure 40**). Apply negative pressure (vacuum) at 49.5 kPa (7.1 psi). The pump should release the vacuum gradually. If the vacuum is released quickly, the pump is faulty.

6. Connect the hose to the pressure side of the Mityvac.

7. Connect the Mityvac to the carburetor side of the fuel pump (**Figure 41**). Apply positive pressure at 7.1 psi. The pump should release this positive pressure gradually. If the pressure is released quickly, the pump is faulty.

8. If the fuel pump fails any of these tests, disassemble, clean and replace any faulty parts. See Chapter Six.

Breaker Point Ignition System Service (1990-1994 2 hp Engine)

The 1990-1994 2 hp outboards are equipped with breaker-point ignitions; the 1995 2 hp and all other models covered in this manual are equipped with a CDI ignition system.

The condition and gap of the breaker points greatly affect engine operation. Burned or badly

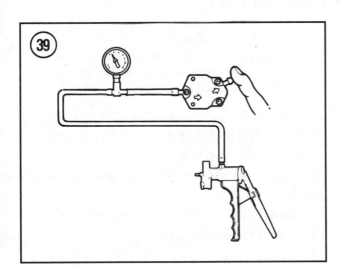

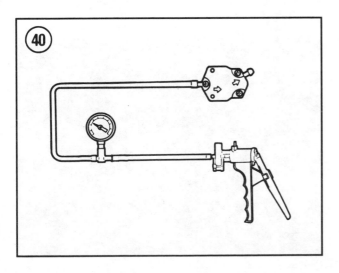

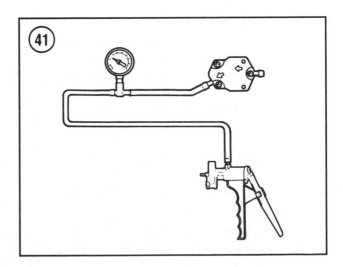

oxidized points allow little or no current to pass. A gap that is too narrow will not allow the coil to build up sufficient voltage and results in a weak spark. An excessive point gap allows the points to open before the primary current reaches its maximum.

While slightly pitted points can be dressed with a file, this should be done only as a temporary measure, as the points may arc after filing. Oxidized, dirty or oily points can be cleaned with alcohol but new points are inexpensive and always preferable for efficient engine operation.

The condenser absorbs the surge of high voltage from the coil and prevents current from arcing across the points as they open. Condensers can be tested with a condenser tester but are also inexpensive and it should be replaced as a matter of course whenever a new breaker point set is installed.

NOTE
Breaker points must be adjusted correctly. An error in gap of 0.038 mm (0.0015 in.) will change engine timing by as much as one degree.

The breaker point set is installed on the stator base under the flywheel and are set to 0.35-0.41 mm (0.014-0.016 in.). After establishing the breaker point gap, ignition timing should be checked. See Chapter Five.

CAUTION
*Always rotate the crankshaft in a **clockwise** direction in the following procedures. If rotated more than 180° in a counterclockwise direction, the water pump impeller may be damaged.*

Breaker Point Replacement

1. Disconnect the negative battery cable, if so equipped.
2. Remove the engine cover.
3. Remove the flywheel. See Chapter Eight.

4. Remove the screw holding the breaker point set to the stator base (A, **Figure 42**).
5. Disconnect the coil and condenser leads (B, **Figure 42**) from the breaker point set. Remove the breaker point set.
6. Remove the screw holding the condenser (C, **Figure 42**) to the stator base. Remove the condenser.
7. Install a new breaker point set on the stator base. Make sure the pivot point on the bottom of the point set engages the hole in the stator base. Install but do not tighten the hold-down screw.
8. Install a new condenser on the stator base and tighten the attaching screw securely, then connect the coil and the condenser leads to the breaker point set.

CAUTION
Do not over-lubricate the breaker cam in Step 9. Excessive lubrication will cause premature point set failure.

9. Squeeze the felt lubrication wick (D, **Figure 42**) to see if it is dry. If dry, lubricate it with 1-2 drops of 30W motor oil.
10. Adjust the breaker point gap as described in this chapter.
11. Install the flywheel. See Chapter Eight.
12. Install the engine cover.
13. Connect the negative battery cable, if so equipped.

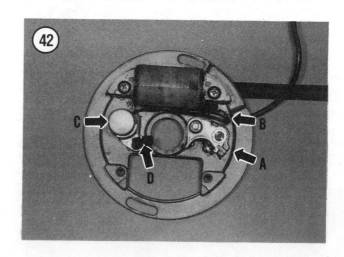

Breaker Point Adjustment

The following procedure is used when new breaker points have been installed. Slots are provided in the flywheel rotor for checking and adjusting the point gap without flywheel rotor removal.

> *CAUTION*
> *Always rotate the crankshaft in a **clockwise** direction in the following procedures. If rotated more than 180° in a counterclockwise direction, the water pump impeller may be damaged.*

1. Install the flywheel nut on the crankshaft. Rotate the stator base to the wide-open throttle position.

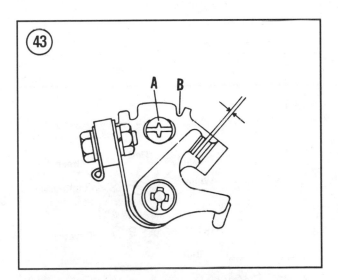

2. Place a wrench on the flywheel nut and rotate the crankshaft clockwise until the breaker point rubbing block rests on a high point on the cam (the points will be fully open).

3. Loosen the point set hold-down screw (A, **Figure 43**). Insert a screwdriver in the adjusting notch (B, **Figure 43**) and move the point set base to obtain a gap of 0.35-0.41 mm (0.014-0.016 in.) when measured with a flat feeler gauge. The gap is correct when the feeler gauge offers a slight drag as it is slipped between the points. When the gap is correct, tighten the hold-down screw securely and recheck the point gap.

Battery and Starter Motor Check (Electric Start Models Only)

1. Check the battery's state of charge and charge the battery, if necessary, prior to performing this test. See Chapter Seven.

2. Connect a voltmeter between the starter motor positive terminal (**Figure 44**) and ground.

3. Turn the ignition switch to START and check the voltmeter scale.

4A. If the voltage exceeds 9.5 volts but the starter motor does not operate, replace the motor.

4B. If the voltage is less than 9.5 volts, recheck the battery and all electrical connections for corrosion and tightness. Charge the battery, if necessary, and repeat this procedure.

Starter Relay Test (Electric Start Models Only)

1. Remove the starter relay as described in Chapter Seven.

2. Connect the test leads of an ohmmeter to the large terminals on top of the starter relay. There should be no continuity (infinite resistance).

3. Connect the starter relay black electrical lead to the negative terminal and the brown electrical lead to the positive terminal of a fully-charged 12-volt battery.

4. Connect the ohmmeter test leads to the large terminals on top of the starter relay (**Figure 45**). There should be continuity (low resistance).

5. Disconnect the electrical leads from the battery.

6. If the starter relay fails either of these tests, the relay is faulty and must be replaced.

Choke Solenoid, or Fuel Enrichment Solenoid Resistance Checker (Electric Start Models Only)

The choke solenoid, or fuel enrichment solenoid, may be located on the port or starboard side of the engine.

1. Disconnect the electrical lead(s) from the solenoid at the bullet connector(s).

2. Connect an ohmmeter between single connector and ground or between the 2 leads.

3. If the resistance reading obtained in Step 2 is not with the specifications listed in Table 3, replace the solenoid.

Wiring Harness Check

1. Check the wiring harness for signs of frayed or chafed insulation.

2. Check for loose connections between the wires and terminal ends (**Figure 46**).

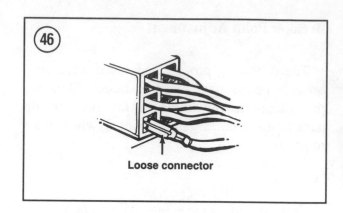

Loose connector

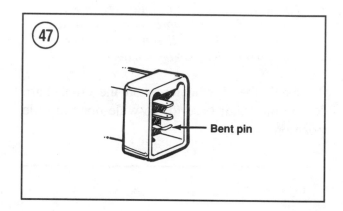

Bent pin

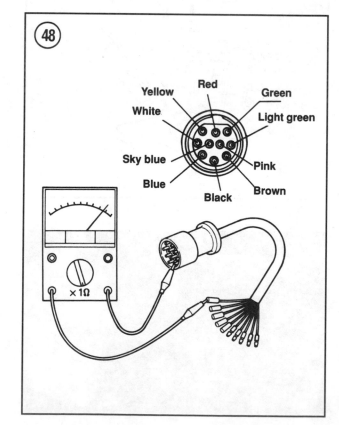

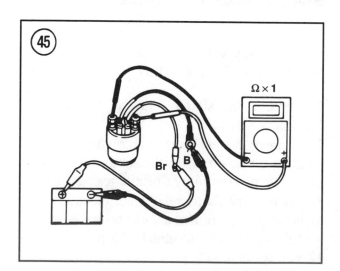

3. Check all harness connectors for bent electrical prongs (**Figure 47**).

4. Check all harness connectors and prongs for corrosion. Clean as required.

5. If the harness is suspected of contributing to electrical malfunctions, disconnect the harness at the motor and switch panel. Check all wires within the harness for continuity and resistance between harness connection and terminal end (**Figure 48**, typical). Repair the harness if any wire shows no continuity (infinite resistance).

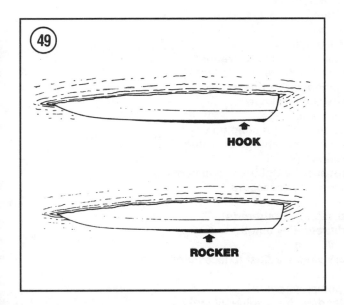

Engine Synchronization and Adjustment

See Chapter Five.

Performance Test (On Boat)

Before performance testing the engine, make sure the boat bottom is cleaned of all marine growth and there is no evidence of a "hook" or "rocker" (**Figure 49**) on the bottom. Any of these conditions will reduce performance considerably.

Performance test the boat with an average load and with the outboard tilted at an angle that allows the boat to ride on an even keel. If equipped with an adjustable trim tab, adjust it to allow the boat to steer in either direction with equal ease.

Check the engine rpm at full throttle. If not within the maximum rpm range for the engine as specified in Chapter Five, check the propeller pitch. A higher-pitch propeller will reduce rpm while a lower pitch prop will increase it.

Readjust the idle mixture and speed under actual operating conditions as required to obtain the best low-speed engine performance.

Tables 1-3 are on the following pages.

Table 1 MAINTENANCE SCHEDULE*

After each use	Check for loose nuts, bolts and spark plug(s)
	Check propeller, shear pin and cotter pin condition
	Make sure cooling water runs out of exhaust ports while cruising
	Grease jet drive bearing(s)
Initial 10 hours or 1 month	Check throttle operation
	Check shift mechanism operation
	Check tightness of all bolts and nuts
	Check PTT operation*
	Check throttle grip/housing
	Check choke lever
	Check and adjust idle speed
	Check swivel bracket
	Check condition of anode
	Check fuel filter(s), fuel line(s), fuel tank(s)
	Check idle speed
	Check spark plug(s)
	Check oil injection pump operation*
	Check water drain (on engine oil tank)
	Electrical wiring and connections
	Check for exhaust leakage
	Check for water leakage
	Check gear oil level and condition
	Check condition and charge of battery
	Check carburetor(s)
	Inspect propeller for tightness and damage
	Check compression pressure
Initial 50 hours or 3 months	Check and adjust carburetor(s)
	Check carburetor link length*
	Check fuel filter(s)
	Check spark plug(s) adjust if necessary
	Check ignition timing
	Check oil pump operation*
	Check water drain (on engine oil tank)
	Check electrical wiring and connections
	Check for exhaust leakage
	Check for water leakage
	Check water pump impeller
	Check tightness of all bolts and nuts
	Check condition of anode(s)
	Inspect propeller for tightness and damage
	Check propeller cotter pin*
	Check compression pressure
Every 100 hours or 6 months	Check and adjust the carburetor(s)
	Check fuel filter(s), fuel line(s), fuel tank(s)
	Check and adjust idle speed
	Check carburetor link length*
	Check carburetor-to-ignition synchronization
	Check prime start operation*
	Check spark plug(s) adjust if necessary
	Check PTT operation*
	Check and adjust idle speed

(continued)

Table 1 MAINTENANCE SCHEDULE* (continued)

Every 100 hours or 6 months (continued)	Check swivel bracket
	Check condition of anode
	Check oil injection pump*
	Check water drain (on engine oil tank)
	Check electrical wiring and connections
	Check for exhaust leakage
	Check for water leakage
	Gear oil level and condition
	Check condition and charge of battery
	Inspect propeller for tightness and damage
	Check compression pressure
Every 200 hours or 1 year	Inspect fuel tank(s) for rust or corrosion
	Check entire fuel system for leaks
	Electrical wiring and connections
	Check throttle sensor*
	Check fuel enrichment line filter*
	Inspect the PTT system operation*
	Check cowling locking and release mechanism

* Not all items apply to all engines. Perform only those pertaining to your engine.

Table 2 RECOMMENDED SPARK PLUGS

	NGK No.	Champion No.	Gap mm (in.)
2 hp	B5HS	L90	0.6 (0.024)
3 hp	B6HS-10	L86C	1.0 (0.039)
4, 5 hp	B7HS	L82C	0.6 (0.024)
6, 8, 9.9, 15, 25 hp	B7HS-10	L82C	1.0 (0.039)
C25	B7HS	L82C	0.6 (0.024)
30, 40 hp	B7HS	L82C	1.0 (0.039)
C40	B8HS	L78C	0.6 (0.024)
C30, 50 hp, Pro 50, C55, Pro 60, 70 hp, C75, C85, 90 hp	B8HS-10	L78C	1.0 (0.039)
115 hp, C115, 150 hp	B8HS-10	L78C	1.0 (0.039)
Pro 150, L150, 175 hp, Pro 175, 200 hp, L200			
1990-1993	B8HS-10	L78C	1.0 (0.039)
1994-on	BR8HS-10	QL78C	1.0 (0.039)
130 hp, L130, Pro V 200			
1990-1993	B9HS-10	L77J4	1.0 (0.039)
1994-on	BR9HS-10	QL77CJ4	1.0 (0.039)
225 hp (90° V6)	BR9HS-10	QL77CJ4	1.0 (0.039)
225 hp, L225, 250 hp, L250 (76° V6)	BR8HS-10	QL78C	1.0 (0.039)

Table 3 CHOKE, OR FUEL ENRICHMENT, SOLENOID RESISTANCE SPECIFICATIONS*

Model	Ohms
2-8 hp	N/A
9.9, 15 hp	6.39-7.81
C25	7.2-8.8
25 hp	3.6-4.4
	(continued)

Table 3 CHOKE, OR FUEL ENRICHMENT, SOLENOID RESISTANCE SPECIFICATIONS* (continued)

Model	Ohms
30 hp	3.4-4.0
C30	6.39-7.81
C40	3.6-4.4
40, 50 hp, Pro 50	2.32-3.48
C55	3.33-4.07
Pro 60, 70, 90 hp	2.3-3.5
C75, C85, C115, 115, 130 hp, L130, 150 hp, L150, Pro 150, 175 hp, Pro 175, 200 hp, L200, Pro V 200, 225 (90° V6)	3.4-4.0
225 hp, L225, 250 hp, L250 (76° V6)	32-48

*Tests to be made with the coil temperature at approximately 20° C (68° F).
N/A—Not applicable. These models are not equipped with this solenoid.

Chapter Five

Timing, Synchronization and Adjustment

If an outboard motor is to deliver its maximum efficiency and peak performance, the ignition system must be properly timed and the carburetor operation synchronized with the ignition. The engine must be timed and synchronized as the final step of a tune-up or whenever the fuel or ignition systems are serviced or adjusted.

Procedures for timing, synchronization and adjustment on Yamaha outboards differ according to model and type of ignition system. This chapter is divided into self-contained sections dealing with particular models/ignition systems for fast and easy reference. Each section specifies the appropriate procedure and sequence to be followed and provides the necessary tune-up data. Read the general information at the beginning of the chapter and then select the section pertaining to your specific model and year.

Tables 1-28 are at the end of the chapter.

NOTE
The "L" series outboards (counter rotation models), are included in all procedures. Unless there is a separate procedure designated for "L" series models, refer to the procedure that relates to the same horsepower rating. If you are working on an L200, refer to the 200 hp procedure.

ENGINE TIMING AND SYNCHRONIZATION

Ignition timing advance and throttle opening must be synchronized to occur at the correct time for the engine to perform properly. Synchronization is the process of timing the carburetor operation to the ignition spark advance.

The 1990-1994 2 hp models are equipped with a breaker point ignition and is static-timed by measuring the amount of piston travel relative to breaker point opening and closing. Therefore, correct timing depends on the correct breaker point gap setting. All other models covered in this manual are equipped with a CDI ignition system.

Required Equipment

Static timing of an engine requires the use of an accurate dial indicator to determine top dead center (TDC) of the piston before making any timing adjustment. TDC is determined by removing the spark plug and installing the dial indicator in the spark plug opening (**Figure 1**).

> *NOTE*
> *Most Yamaha cylinder heads use offset spark plug holes. Therefore, the spark plug holes are **not** perpendicular to the piston. For a true reading, the dial indicator must be installed so that the indicator plunger **is** perpendicular to the piston. When properly installed, the indicator plunger will be off-center in the spark plug hole.*

Dynamic engine timing uses a stroboscopic timing light connected to the No. 1 spark plug wire (**Figure 2**). As the engine is cranked or operated, the light flashes each time the spark plug fires. When the light is pointed at the mov-

ing flywheel, the mark on the flywheel appears to stand still. The flywheel mark should align with the stationary timing pointer or decal on the power head.

A portable tachometer connected to the engine is used to determine engine speed during idle and high-speed adjustments.

> *CAUTION*
> *Never operate the outboard without water circulating through the gearcase to the power head. If the outboard is run in a dry condition, it will damage the water pump and gearcase and can cause severe engine damage.*

Some form of water supply is required whenever the engine is operated during the procedure. The use of a test tank and test wheel is the most convenient method. While the procedure may be carried out with the boat in the water, checking ignition timing while speeding across open water is neither easy nor safe. The use of a flushing

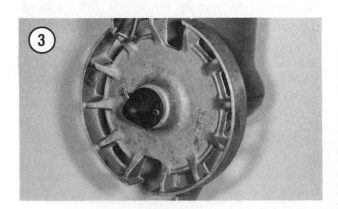

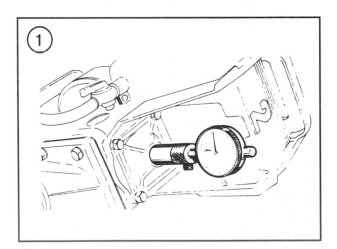

device is not recommended if the engine must be run above idle speed.

Yamaha recommends that a test wheel (**Figure 3**) be substituted for the propeller to put a load on the engine and prevent engine damage from excessive rpm. Yamaha test wheel recommendations and part numbers are given in **Table 1** and installation is covered in Chapter Nine.

1990-1994 2 HP MODELS

Timing Adjustment

The breaker point flywheel magneto ignition on this model is designed to provide automatic spark advance. Timing adjustments are made by accurately setting the breaker point gap to the correct specification.

1. Remove the engine cover.
2. Remove the flywheel. See Chapter Eight.
3. Remove the spark plug. See Chapter Four.
4. Disconnect the white magneto lead from the connector (**Figure 4**).
5. Check and adjust the breaker point gap as required. See Chapter Four.
6. Install a dial indicator in the spark plug hole (**Figure 1**).
7. Disconnect the black stator lead at the bullet connector.

8. Rotate the flywheel *clockwise* until the dial indicator gauge shows that the piston has reached top dead center (TDC). This is the point at which the dial indicator needle reverses its direction of movement as the flywheel is rotated.

9. At this point, reset the dial indicator to zero.

NOTE
Use an ohmmeter, self-powered test lamp or the Yamaha Point Checker in the following steps.

10. Connect the ohmmeter or point checker positive (red) lead to the white magneto primary wire. Connect the negative (black) ohmmeter or point checker lead to a good engine ground (**Figure 5**).

NOTE
If using an ohmmeter instead of the point checker, the ohmmeter will indicate continuity when the breaker points close. If using a test lamp, the lamp will light when the points close.

11. Slowly turn the flywheel *clockwise* until the point checker needle moves from OPEN to CLOSE, the ohmmeter indicates continuity or the test lamp lights. When the breaker points just close, the dial indicator should show 0.99-1.23 mm (0.039-0.048 in.) BTDC. Loosen the

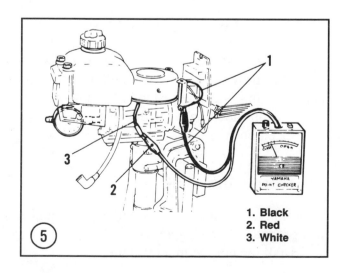

1. Black
2. Red
3. White

breaker point hold-down screw (**Figure 6**) and adjust the point gap as necessary.

12. If the correct timing cannot be obtained by adjusting the breaker point gap, replace the point set. See Chapter Four.

13. Remove the dial indicator and reinstall the spark plug.

14. Disconnect the point check, ohmmeter or test lamp, then reconnect the magneto wires.

NOTE
If the engine is installed in a test tank, remove the standard propeller and install the test wheel as described in Chapter Nine.

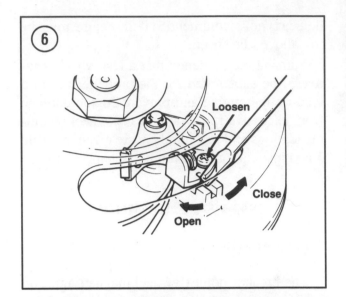

15. With the outboard motor in a test tank or on the boat in the water, turn the idle adjust screw (**Figure 7**) clockwise until it lightly seats, then back it out 3 full turns.

16. Connect a portable tachometer to the engine according to its manufacturer's instructions.

17. Start the engine, place in FORWARD gear and warm it to the normal operating temperature.

18. Adjust the idle speed screw as required to bring idle speed within the specification listed in **Table 2**.

19. Shut the engine off, remove the tachometer and install the engine cover. Remove the test wheel and reinstall the propeller. Refer to Chapter Nine.

1995 2 HP MODELS

The CDI system used on these models is designed to provide automatic spark advance. Ignition timing is not adjustable. For this model, Yamaha provides an adjustment procedure for idle speed only.

Idle Speed Adjustment

1. Remove the standard propeller and install a test propeller. See Chapter Nine.

2. Install the engine in a test tank.

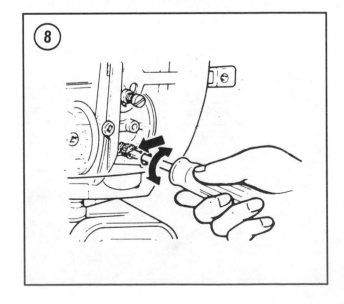

3. Remove the engine cover.

4. Connect a portable tachometer according to its manufacturer's instructions.

5. Start the engine, place it in FORWARD gear and warm it to normal operating temperature.

6. Observe the engine speed on the tachometer and compare to the specification listed in **Table 2**. If out of specification, perform Step 7.

7. Adjust the idle speed screw (**Figure 8**) in or out until the specified idle speed is obtained.

8. Shut the engine off and disconnect the portable tachometer.

9. Install the engine cover. Remove the test wheel and install the propeller. See Chapter Nine.

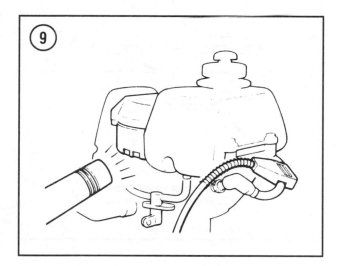

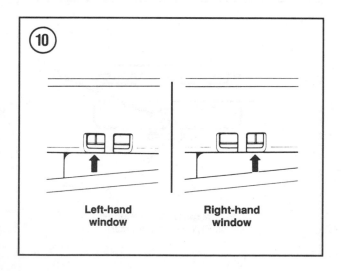

Left-hand window   Right-hand window

3 HP MODELS

The CDI system used on 3 hp models is designed to provide automatic spark advance. Ignition timing is not adjustable, but should be checked periodically to ensure proper ignition system operation.

Ignition Timing

1. Remove the standard propeller and install a test propeller. See Chapter Nine.

2. Install the outboard in a test tank.

3. Remove the engine cover.

4. Connect a portable tachometer and timing light to the spark plug lead (**Figure 9**) according to its manufacturer's instructions.

5. Start the engine, place it in FORWARD gear and warm it to normal operating temperature.

6. Check idle speed and adjust if necessary.

7. Aim the timing light at the timing windows.

8. If the timing mark on the flywheel can be seen through the left-hand timing window (**Figure 10**), the idle timing is correct.

9. Increase engine speed to full throttle. If the timing mark on the flywheel can be seen through the right-hand timing window (**Figure 10**), the full-speed timing is correct.

10. Shut the engine off and disconnect the timing light and portable tachometer. Remove the test propeller and reinstall the propeller. See Chapter Nine.

11. Ignition timing cannot be adjusted. If the ignition timing is incorrect, inspect the CDI components as shown in Chapter Three. Refer to Chapter Seven for replacement procedures.

Idle Speed Adjustment

1. Remove the standard propeller and install a test propeller. See Chapter Nine.

2. Install the outboard in a test tank.

3. Remove the engine cover.

5

4. Connect a portable tachometer according to its manufacturer's instructions.

5. Turn the pilot screw in until it *lightly* seats, then back it out 1-1 1/2 turns (**Figure 11**).

6. Start the engine, place it in FORWARD gear and warm it to the normal operating temperature.

7. Observe the engine speed on the tachometer and compare to the specification listed in **Table 3**. If out of specification, perform Step 8.

8. Adjust the idle speed screw in or out until the specified idle speed is obtained (**Figure 12**).

9. Shut the engine off and disconnect the portable tachometer. Remove the test propeller and install the propeller. See Chapter Nine.

10. Install the engine cover unless the ignition timing is going to be checked as previously described.

4 HP AND 5 HP MODELS

The CDI system used on 4 and 5 hp models is designed to provide automatic spark advance. Ignition timing is not adjustable, but should be checked periodically to ensure proper ignition system operation.

Low Speed Ignition Timing
(Between Idle and 1,700 rpm)

1. Remove the standard propeller and install a test propeller. See Chapter Nine.

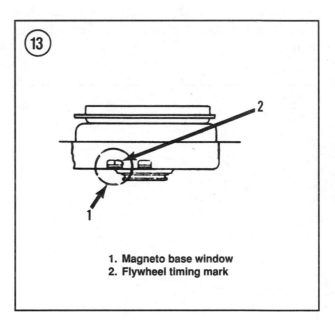

1. Magneto base window
2. Flywheel timing mark

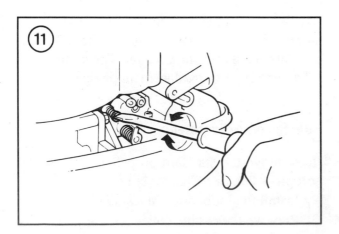

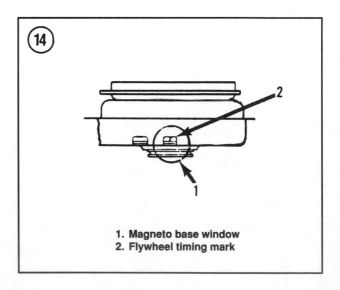

1. Magneto base window
2. Flywheel timing mark

2. Install the outboard in a test tank.

3. Remove the engine cover.

4. Connect a portable tachometer and timing light according to their manufacturer's instructions.

5. Start the engine, place it in NEUTRAL and let it run until it reaches normal operating temperature.

6. Maintain engine speed between 1,000-1,700 rpm.

7. Aim the timing light at the timing windows.

8. If the timing mark on the flywheel can be seen through the left-hand timing window (**Figure 13**), the idle timing is correct.

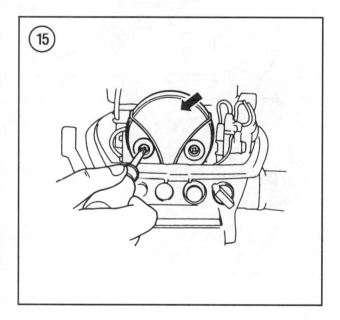

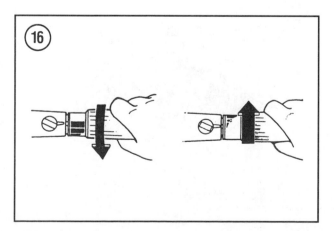

9. Shut the engine off and disconnect the timing light and portable tachometer.

10. Ignition timing cannot be adjusted. If the ignition timing is incorrect, inspect the CDI components as shown in Chapter Three and refer to Chapter Seven for replacement procedures.

Full Throttle Ignition Timing (Between 4,500 and 5,500 rpm)

1. Remove the standard propeller and install a test propeller. See Chapter Nine.

2. Install the outboard in a test tank.

3. Remove the engine cover.

4. Connect a portable tachometer and timing light according to their manufacturer's instructions.

5. Start the engine, place it in NEUTRAL and warm it to the normal operating temperature.

6. Increase engine speed to 4,500-5,500 rpm.

7. Aim the timing light at the timing windows.

8. If the timing mark on the flywheel can be seen through the right-hand timing window (**Figure 14**), the full throttle timing is correct.

9. Shut the engine off and disconnect the timing light and portable tachometer.

10. Ignition timing cannot be adjusted. If the ignition timing is incorrect, inspect the CDI components as shown in Chapter Three and refer to Chapter Seven for replacement procedures.

Throttle Wire Adjustment

> *NOTE*
> *Prior to adjusting the throttle wire, adjust the engine idle speed as previously described in this chapter.*

1. Place the outboard in an upright position and remove the engine cover.

2. Remove the screws and washers securing silencer cover (**Figure 15**), remove the cover.

3. Turn the throttle control from FAST to SLOW 2-3 times (**Figure 16**).

4. Turn the throttle control to the FAST position (A, **Figure 17**), and check if the full open side stopper (B, **Figure 17**) for the throttle valve (C, **Figure 17**) is contacting the stopper on the carburetor.

5. If this does not occur or if it contacts the stopper before the throttle grip comes to the FAST position, adjust the throttle wire.

6. Loosen the throttle wire retaining screw (A, **Figure 18**) and pull out the wire (B, **Figure 18**).

7. Set the throttle grip to the SLOW position (A, **Figure 19**).

8. Insert the inner wire (B, **Figure 19**) into the hole in the throttle lever (C, **Figure 19**) and lock it in place with the screw (D, **Figure 19**). The end of wire should project out from the throttle lever by 3-4 mm (0.12-0.16 in.)(E, **Figure 19**).

9. Pull out the outer wire (F, **Figure 19**) and hook it onto the wire hook (G, **Figure 19**) on the carburetor.

10. Turn the throttle control from FAST to SLOW 2-3 times.

11. Turn the throttle control to the FAST position (A, **Figure 17**), and make sure the full open side stopper (B, **Figure 17**) for the throttle valve (C, **Figure 17**) is contacting the stopper on the carburetor.

12. After proper adjustment is completed, start the engine and move the steering tiller from complete port to complete starboard several times and make sure engine idle does not increase during tiller movement.

13. Install the screws and washers securing the silencer cover and tighten securely.

14. Install the engine cover.

Idle Speed Adjustment

1. Remove the standard propeller and install a test propeller. See Chapter Nine.

2. Install the outboard in a test tank.

3. Remove the engine cover.

4. Connect a portable tachometer according to its manufacturer's instructions.

5. Start the engine, place it in NEUTRAL and warm it to the normal operating temperature.

6. Turn the throttle grip to the fully closed position.

7. Observe the engine speed on the tachometer and compare to the specification listed in **Table 4**. If out of specification, continue at Step 8.

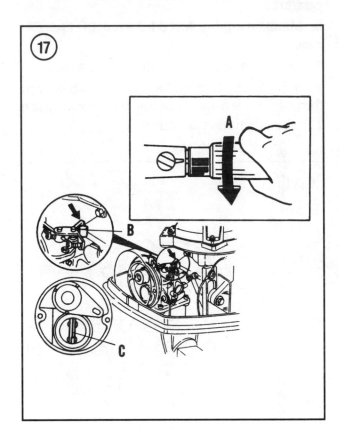

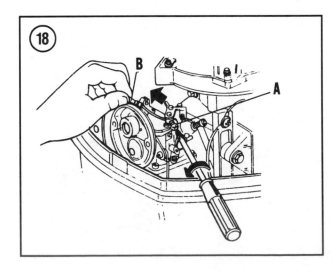

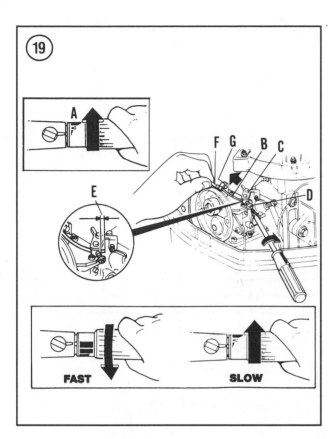

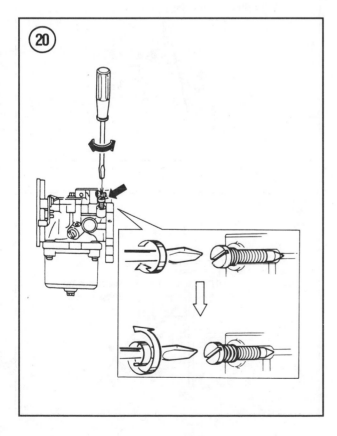

8. Turn the pilot screw (**Figure 20**) in until it *lightly* seats, then back it out 1 1/2-2 turns.

9. Start the engine and observe the engine speed on the tachometer.

10. Adjust the idle speed screw (**Figure 21**) in or out until the specified idle speed is obtained.

11. Shut the engine off and disconnect the portable tachometer.

12. Adjust the throttle wire as described in this section.

13. Install the engine cover.

6 HP AND 8 HP MODELS

Timing Adjustment

1. Remove the engine cover.

2. Move the shift lever to the NEUTRAL position.

3. Disconnect the magneto base link rod from the control lever ball stud (**Figure 22**).

4. Slowly rotate the flywheel *clockwise* and align the timing plate with the 35° BTDC ± 1° mark on the flywheel indicator (**Figure 23**).

5. Align the marks on the magneto base and flywheel by turning the magneto base. Make sure the magneto base (A, **Figure 24**) contacts the stopper plate (B, **Figure 24**). If this does not occur, the timing must be adjusted as follows.

6. Remove both spark plugs. See Chapter Four.

7. Install a dial indicator in the top cylinder spark plug hole.

8. Slowly rotate flywheel *clockwise* and stop when the piston reaches top dead center (TDC).

9. Set the timing plate at TDC.

10. Slowly rotate the flywheel *clockwise* and align the timing plate with the 35° BTDC ± 1° mark on the flywheel indicator (**Figure 25**).

11. Loosen the magneto base stop screw (**Figure 26**).

12. Slowly rotate the magneto base until the marks on the magneto base (A, **Figure 27**) and flywheel align (B, **Figure 27**).

13. Adjust the stopper plate so it contacts the magneto base stopper (C, **Figure 27**). Press the

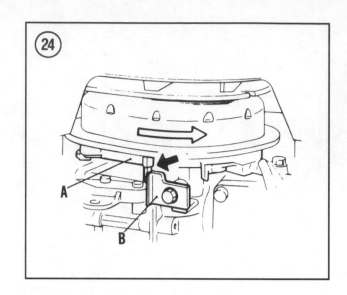

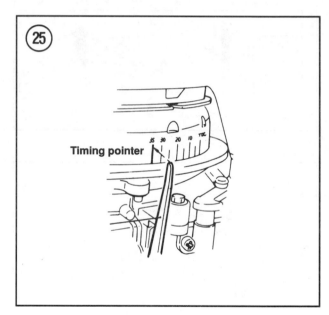

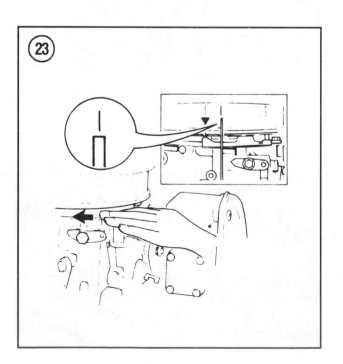

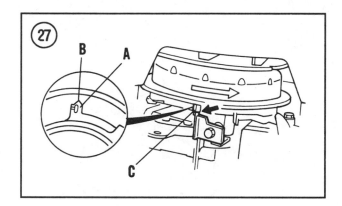

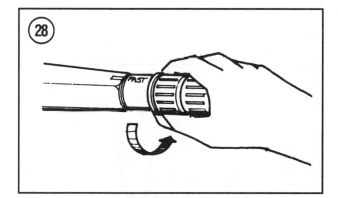

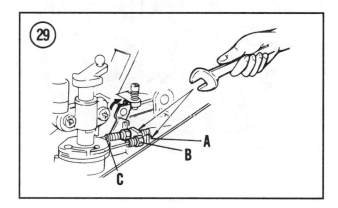

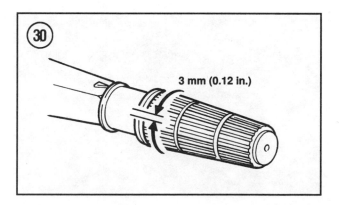

stopper plate against the full-advance side of the magneto base and tighten the bolt securely.

14. Reconnect the magneto base link rod onto the control lever ball stud.

15. Remove the dial indicator and install both spark plugs.

Throttle Linkage Adjustment

1. Remove the engine cover.

2. Disconnect the magneto base link rod from the control lever ball stud (**Figure 22**).

3. Rotate the magneto base until the full-advance side stop contacts the magneto base stop (C, **Figure 27**).

4. Rotate the throttle grip to the wide-open position (**Figure 28**).

5. Loosen the locknut on the "PULL" cable (A, **Figure 29**) and adjust it until it fully opens the carburetor throttle valve. Tighten the locknut (B, **Figure 29**).

6. Loosen the locknut on the "PUSH" cable and adjust the cable adjuster (C, **Figure 29**) until there is 3.0 mm (0.12 in.) of free play in the thottle grip (**Figure 30**). Tighten the locknut.

7. Adjust the plastic snap-on connector on the end of the link rod until it can be reconnected to the control lever ball stud without changing the position of the linkage or magneto base (**Figure 31**). Connect the link rod.

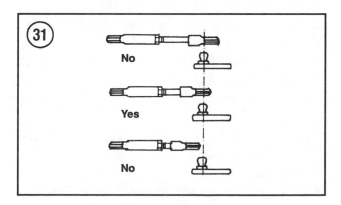

Idle Speed Adjustment

1. Remove the standard propeller and install a test propeller. See Chapter Nine.
2. Install the outboard in a test tank.
3. Remove the engine cover.
4. Connect a portable tachometer according to its manufacturer's instructions.
5. Turn the pilot screw in until it *lightly* seats, then back it out 7/8-1 3/8 turns (**Figure 32**). Repeat for the other carburetor.
6. Start the engine, place it in NEUTRAL and warm it to the normal operating temperature.
7. Observe the engine speed on the tachometer and compare to the specification listed in **Table 5**. If out of specification, perform Step 8.
8. Adjust the idle speed screw in or out until the specified idle speed is obtained (**Figure 33**).
9. Shut the engine off and disconnect the portable tachometer.
10. Adjust the throttle control link as described in the following procedure.
11. Install the engine cover. Remove the test propeller and reinstall the standard propeller.

9.9 HP AND 15 HP MODELS

Timing Adjustment

1. Remove the engine cover.
2. Move the shift lever to the NEUTRAL position.
3. Disconnect the magneto control rod from the control lever ball stud (**Figure 34**).
4. Slowly rotate the flywheel *clockwise* and align the left-side edge of the timing plate with the $30° \pm 1°$ BTDC timing mark on the flywheel.
5. Align the marks on the magneto base and flywheel by turning the magneto base (**Figure 35**).
6. Make sure the accelerator cam stopper (A, **Figure 36**) contacts the magneto base stopper (B, **Figure 36**).
7. If alignment is incorrect proceed to Step 8.

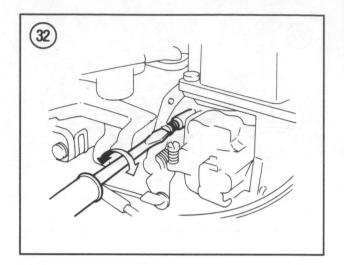

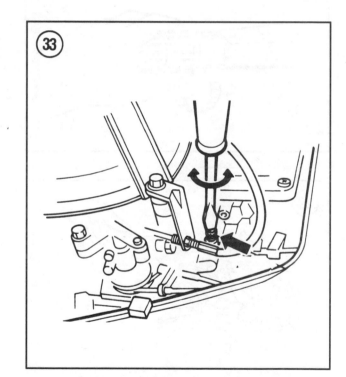

8. Remove the cylinder head. See Chapter Eight.

9. Attach a dial indicator and stand on the top cylinder (**Figure 37**).

10. Slowly rotate the flywheel *clockwise* and stop when the piston reaches top dead center (TDC). This is the point at which the dial indi-cator needle reverses its direction as the flywheel is rotated.

11. Slowly rotate the flywheel *clockwise* until the dial indicator reads 4.22 ± 0.27 mm (0.166 ± 0.011 in.) (equivalent to 30° ± 1° BTDC).

12. Loosen the accelerator cam set-bolt (**Figure 38**).

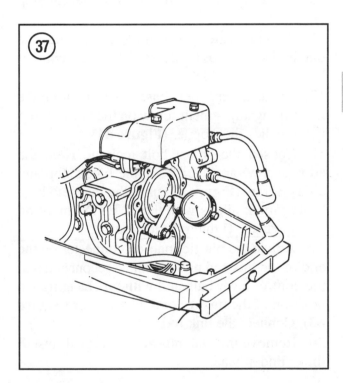

5

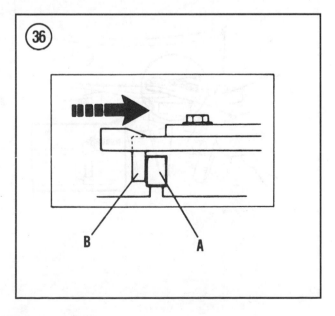

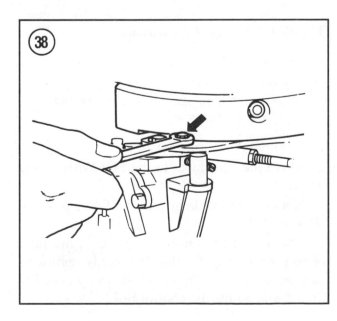

13. Align the marks on the magneto base and the flywheel by turning the magneto base (**Figure 39**).

14. Adjust the accelerator cam so that it makes contact with the magneto base stopper (**Figure 40**). Tighten the accelerator cam set-bolt securely.

15. Once full-advance timing is set, repeat Step 10.

16. Slowly rotate flywheel *clockwise* until the dial indicator reads 0.12 mm (0.005 in.) (equivalent to 5° ± 1° BTDC).

17. Rotate the magneto base *clockwise* until the idle timing adjustment screw on the bracket stop just touches the stopper (**Figure 41**).

18. Loosen the adjust bolt locknut. Hold the adjust screw against the engine block stop and adjust screw (**Figure 42**) until the magneto base timing mark aligns with the 5° BTDC mark on the flywheel. Tighten the locknut.

19. Adjust the plastic snap-on connector on the end of the link rod until it can be reconnected to the control lever ball stud without changing the position of the linkage or magneto base (**Figure 43**). Connect the link rod.

20. Remove the dial indicator and stand. Install the cylinder head.

Throttle Linkage Adjustment

> *NOTE*
> *Prior to adjusting the throttle linkage, ignition timing should be checked and adjusted if necessary.*

1. Remove the engine cover.

2. Move the shift lever to the FORWARD gear position.

3. Rotate the throttle grip to the FAST position (**Figure 44**).

4. Check that the throttle valve is in the fully open position and the thottle lever is against its stop as shown in **Figure 45**. If not, proceed to Step 5 and adjust the control link.

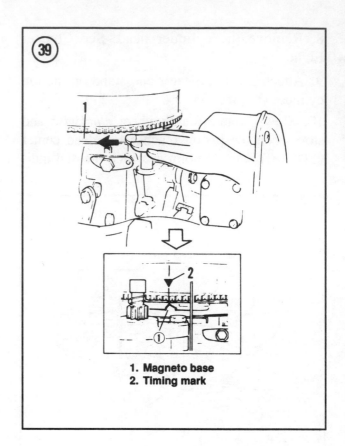

1. Magneto base
2. Timing mark

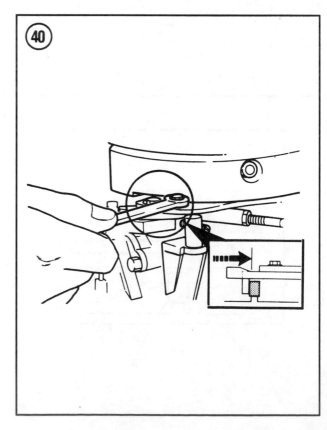

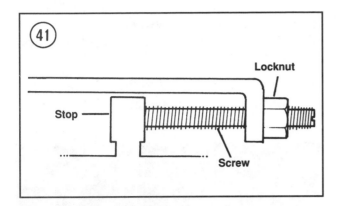

Locknut

Stop

Screw

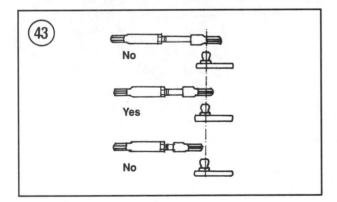

No

Yes

No

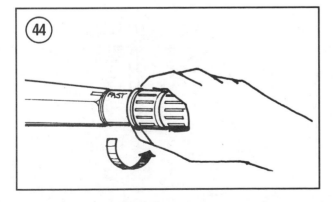

5. Disconnect the magneto base link rod from the control lever ball stud (**Figure 22**).

6. Rotate the magneto base until the full-advance side stop contacts the magneto base stop (**Figure 46**).

7. Rotate the throttle grip to the wide-open throttle position (**Figure 44**).

8. Adjust the plastic snap-on connector on the end of the link rod until it can be reconnected to the control lever ball stud without changing the position of the linkage or magneto base (**Figure 43**). Connect the control rod.

9. Adjust the throttle valve to the fully open position.

Idle Speed Adjustment

1. Remove the standard propeller and install a test propeller. See Chapter Nine.

2. Install the outboard in a test tank.

3. Remove the engine cover.

4. Connect a portable tachometer according to manufacturer's instructions.

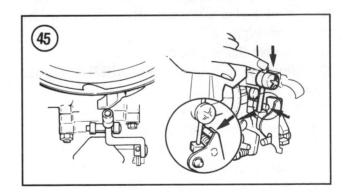

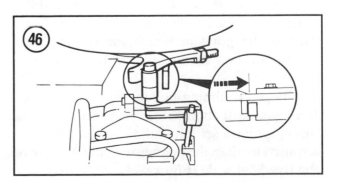

5

5. Turn the pilot screw (A, **Figure 47**) in until it *lightly* seats, then back it out 1-1 1/2 turns. Repeat for the other carburetor.

6. Start the engine, place it in NEUTRAL and warm it to normal the operating temperature.

7. Observe the engine speed on the tachometer and compare to the specification listed in **Table 6**. If out of specification, perform Step 8.

8. Adjust the idle speed screw (B, **Figure 47**) in or out until the specified idle speed is obtained.

9. Shut the engine off and disconnect the portable tachometer. Remove the test propeller and reinstall the standard propeller. See Chapter Nine.

10. Adjust the throttle control link as described in the following procedure.

11. Install the engine cover.

C25 MODELS

Timing Adjustment (At Full-advance)

Correctly adjusting the full-advance timing on this model also automatically adjusts the full retard timing.

1. Remove the engine cover.

2. Move the shift lever to the NEUTRAL position.

3. Disconnect the magneto control rod from the control lever ball stud (**Figure 48**).

4. Remove both spark plugs. See Chapter Four.

5. Install a dial indicator in top cylinder spark plug hole.

6. Slowly rotate the flywheel *clockwise* and stop when the piston reaches top dead center (TDC). This is the point at which the dial indicator needle reverses its direction as the flywheel is rotated.

7. Check the timing pointer with the flywheel timing scale. If alignment is incorrect, loosen the timing pointer set nut and move the pointer as required to align the pointer with the 0° mark on the flywheel scale (**Figure 49**).

8. Slowly rotate the flywheel *clockwise* and align the timing plate with the 24° ± 1° mark on the flywheel indicator.

9. Set the magneto base to the fully advanced position and set the stopper at BTDC.

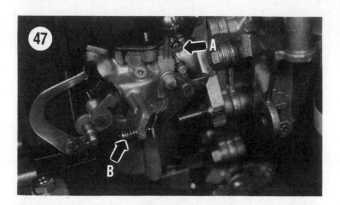

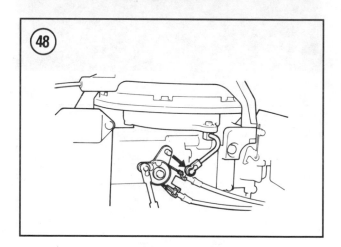

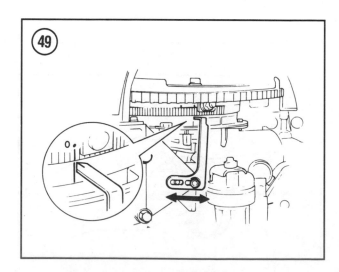

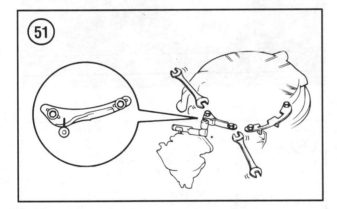

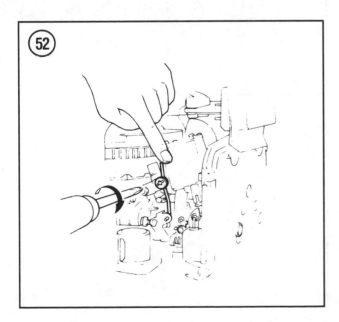

10. Adjust the magneto control rod length and reinstall it onto the control lever ball stud (**Figure 48**).

11. Remove the dial indicator. Install the spark plugs and engine cover.

Carburetor Control Linkage Adjustment

1. Remove the engine cover.

2. Loosen the carburetor control link set-screw (**Figure 50**).

3. Set the magneto control lever in the fully advanced position. Adjust the guide collar so that it is in the specified position on the accelerator cam as shown in **Figure 51**, then tighten the screw.

4. Hold down the control ring and tighten the set-screw securely (**Figure 52**).

Throttle Control Linkage Adjustment

1. Remove the engine cover.

2. Move the shift lever to the FORWARD gear position.

3. Make sure the accelerator cam and the guide collar are positioned as shown in **Figure 53**.

4. Adjust the accelerator control link length to 69 mm (2.72 in.) (A, **Figure 53**).

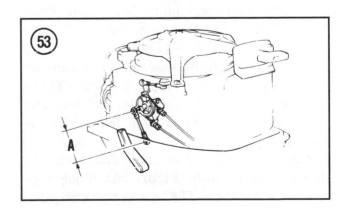

Idle Speed Adjustment

1. Remove the standard propeller and install a test propeller. See Chapter Nine.
2. Install the outboard in a test tank.
3. Remove the engine cover.
4. Connect a portable tachometer according to its manufacturer's instructions.
5. Turn the pilot screw (**Figure 54**) in until it *lightly* seats, then back it out 1 1/4-1 3/4 turns. Repeat for the other carburetor.
6. Start the engine, place it in NEUTRAL and warm it to normal operating temperature.
7. Observe the engine rpm on the tachometer and compare to the specification listed in **Table 7**. If out of specification, perform Step 7.
8. Adjust the idle speed screw in or out until the specified idle speed is obtained.
9. Shut the engine off and disconnect the portable tachometer. Remove the test propeller and reinstall the standard propeller. See Chapter Nine.
10. Adjust the throttle control link as described in the following procedure.
11. Install the engine cover.

25 HP MODELS

Timing Adjustment

1. Remove the engine cover.
2. Move the shift lever to the NEUTRAL position.
3. Remove both spark plugs. See Chapter Four.
4. Install a dial indicator in the No. 1 (top) cylinder spark plug hole (**Figure 55**).
5. Slowly rotate the flywheel *clockwise* and stop when the piston reaches top dead center (TDC). This is the point at which the dial indicator needle reverses its direction as the flywheel is rotated.
6. Check the timing pointer alignment with the flywheel timing scale (**Figure 56**). If not properly aligned with the TDC mark, repeat Step 5 to

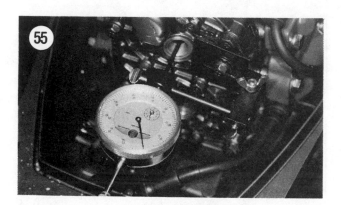

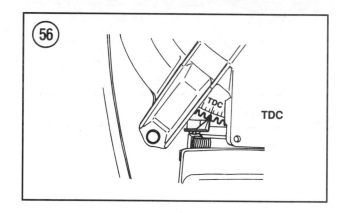

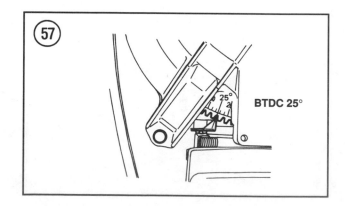

make sure the piston is at TDC. If the piston is at TDC, loosen the timing pointer set screw and move the pointer as required to align the timing pointer with the flywheel TDC mark, then tighten the set screw securely.

7. Remove the dial indicator.

8. Slowly rotate the flywheel *clockwise* and align the timing pointer with the 25° BTDC mark on the flywheel timing scale (**Figure 57**).

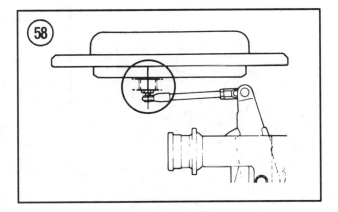

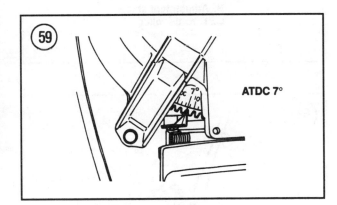

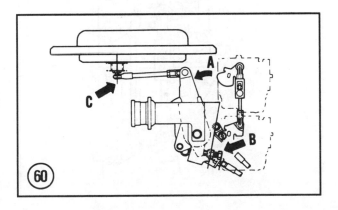

9. Move the magneto control lever to the right (full advance) until it touches the stopper.

10. If the timing marks on the magneto base plate and the flywheel do not align as shown in **Figure 58**, disconnect the link rod from the control lever ball stud. Loosen the locknut and adjust the plastic snap-on connector on the end of the link rod until it can be reconnected to the ball stud without changing the position of the linkage or timing marks. Reconnect the link rod to the ball stud and tighten the locknut.

11. Slowly rotate flywheel *clockwise* and align the timing pointer with the 7° ATDC mark on the flywheel timing scale (**Figure 59**).

12. Move the magneto control lever (A, **Figure 60**) to the full left (full retard) until it touches the stopper bolt (B, **Figure 60**).

13. If the timing marks do not align as shown in C, **Figure 60**, loosen the stopper bolt locknut and adjust the bolt length as required to align the marks, then tighten the locknut.

14. Install the spark plugs and engine cover.

Carburetor Linkage Adjustment

1. Loosen the throttle stop screw (**Figure 61**) until clearance is noted between the end of the screw and the throttle valve stop.

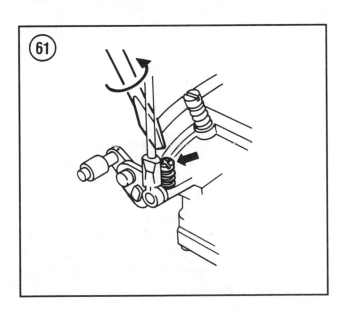

2. Close the throttle valves.

CAUTION
The throttle lever screws have left-hand
threads. Turn the screws clockwise to
loosen and counterclockwise to tighten.

3. If the throttle valves do not completely close, loosen the No. 1 cylinder (top) carburetor throttle lever screw (A, **Figure 62**).

4. Completely loosen the adjustment screw (B, **Figure 62**) on the accelerator lever rod.

5. Make sure the No. 1 cylinder (top) carburetor throttle valve is closed, then tighten the throttle lever screw (A, **Figure 62**).

6. Make sure the No. 1 cylinder (top) and the No. 2 cylinder (bottom) carburetor throttle valves are closed, then tighten the adjustment screw (B, **Figure 62**).

7. Adjust the idle speed as described in the following procedure.

Idle Speed Adjustment

1. Remove the standard propeller and install a test propeller. See Chapter Nine.

2. Install the outboard in a test tank.

3. Remove the engine cover.

4. Connect a portable tachometer according to its manufacturer's instructions.

5. Turn the pilot screw (**Figure 63**) in until it *lightly* seats, then back it out 1 1/4-2 3/4 turns. Repeat for the other carburetor.

6. Start the engine, place it in FORWARD gear and let it run until it reaches normal operating temperature.

7. Observe the engine speed on the tachometer and compare to the specification listed in **Table 8**. If out of specification, perform Step 8.

8. Adjust the idle speed screw in or out until the specified idle speed is obtained.

9. Shut the engine off and disconnect the portable tachometer. Remove the test propeller and install the standard propeller. See Chapter Nine.

10. Install the engine cover.

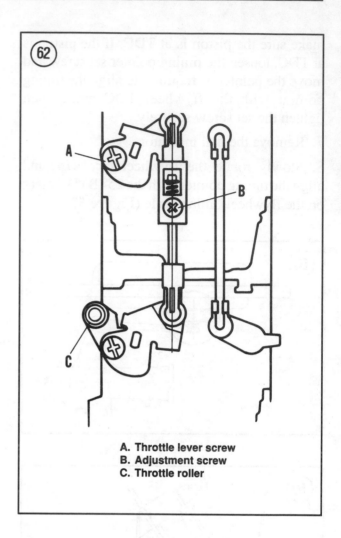

A. Throttle lever screw
B. Adjustment screw
C. Throttle roller

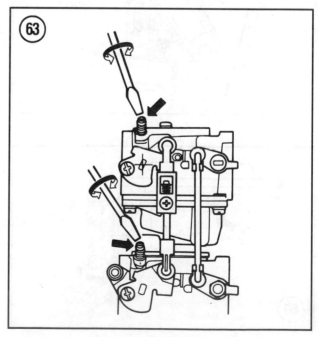

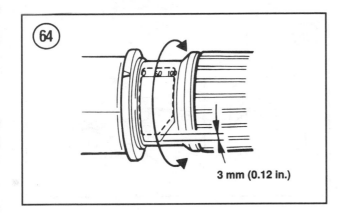

3 mm (0.12 in.)

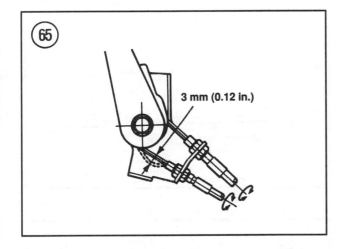

3 mm (0.12 in.)

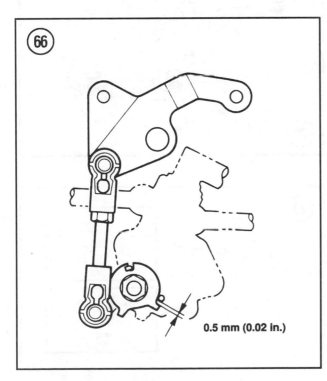

0.5 mm (0.02 in.)

Throttle Cable Adjustment

1. Shift into FORWARD gear.

2. Rotate the throttle grip to the wide-open throttle position. At this point, the center of the throttle roller should align with the wide-open throttle mark on the throttle cam (**Figure 64**).

3. If the marks do not align in Step 2, loosen the adjusting bolt locknut on the "pull" side of the throttle cable. Turn the adjusting bolt until all slack is removed, then tighten the locknut.

4. Loosen the adjusting bolt locknut on the "push" side of the throttle cable. Turn the adjusting bolt until the cable has approximately 3 mm (0.12 in.) slack, then tighten the locknut (**Figure 65**).

Oil Pump Link Adjustment

1. Rotate the throttle grip to the wide-open throttle position. At this point, the oil pump lever should be 0.5 mm (0.02 in.) off the full-open side stopper (**Figure 66**).

2. If adjustment is necessary, disconnect the link rod from the oil pump lever ball stud. Rotate the oil pump lever against the wide-open stop. Loosen the locknut and adjust the plastic snap-on connector on the end of the link rod until it can be reconnected to the ball stud without changing the throttle or oil pump lever position.

3. Reconnect the link rod to the ball stud and tighten the locknut.

4. Rotate the throttle grip toward the wide-open throttle position and recheck the adjustment.

C30 (2-CYLINDER) MODELS

Timing Adjustment

1. Remove the standard propeller and install a test propeller. See Chapter Nine.

2. Install the outboard in a test tank.

3. Remove the engine cover.

5

4. Connect a timing light and portable tachometer according to their manufacturer's instructions.

5. Shift into NEUTRAL.

6. Start the engine and allow it to warm up for approximately 5 minutes.

7. Increase engine speed to 4,500-5,500 rpm and point the timing light at the timing indicator on the rewind starter case. It should align with the 25° BTDC ± 2° mark (**Figure 67**).

8. If the timing pointer does not align as specified in Step 7, shut the engine off.

9. Shift into FORWARD gear.

10. Fully open the throttle grip.

11. Slowly rotate the flywheel *clockwise* and align the full-advance timing mark with the 25° BTDC ± 2° mark on the timing indicator (**Figure 68**).

12. Rotate the magneto base and align the timing mark with the ignition mark on the rotor (**Figure 69**).

13. If the magneto base stopper (A, **Figure 70**) is not in contact with the full-open stopper on the cylinder body (B, **Figure 70**), loosen the set bolts and adjust it until contact is correct.

14. Check that the full-open marking "T" on the accelerator cam aligns with the center of the cam roller (**Figure 71**). If alignment is incorrect, perform Step 15.

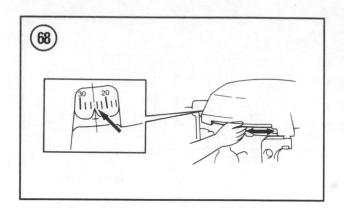

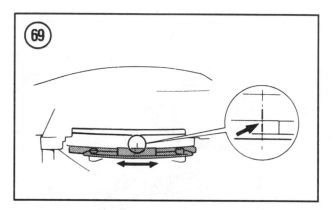

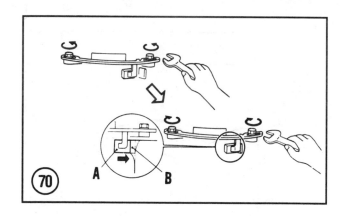

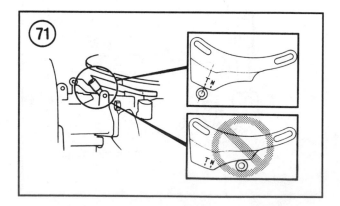

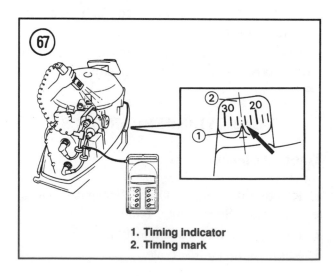

1. Timing indicator
2. Timing mark

15. Loosen the accelerator cam (A, **Figure 72**) bolts and align the full-open mark "T" with the center of the carburetor throttle roller (B, **Figure 72**) and tighten the set bolts.

16. Remove the rewind starter. See Chapter Eleven.

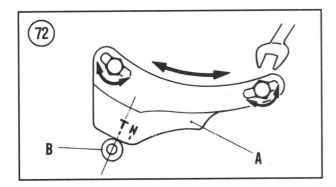

17. Loosen the rod tightening screw (A, **Figure 73**). Push the rod with your finger and tighten the screw so the throttle is fully open and the full-open stopper (B, **Figure 73**) is pushed up against the stopper. Tighten the screw.

18. Install the rewind starter.

19. Remove the timing light and portable tachometer.

20. Install the engine cover.

Idle Speed Adjustment

1. Remove the standard propeller and install a test propeller. See Chapter Ninc.

2. Install the outboard in a test tank.

3. Remove the engine cover.

4. Connect a portable tachometer according to its manufacturer's instructions.

5. Turn the pilot screw (**Figure 74**) in until it *lightly* seats, then back it out 1-1 1/2 turns. Repeat for the other carburetor.

6. Start the engine, place it in NEUTRAL and warm it to the normal operating temperature.

7. Observe the engine speed on the tachometer and compare to the specification listed in **Table 9**. If out of specification, perform Step 8.

8. Adjust the idle speed screw (**Figure 75**) in or out until the specified idle speed is obtained.

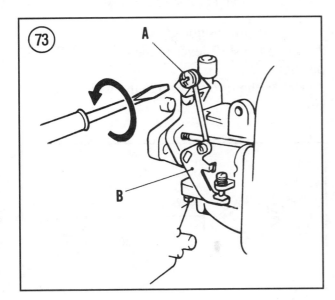

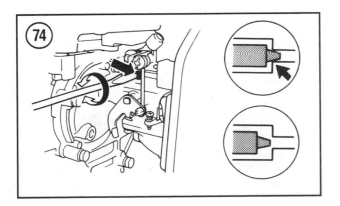

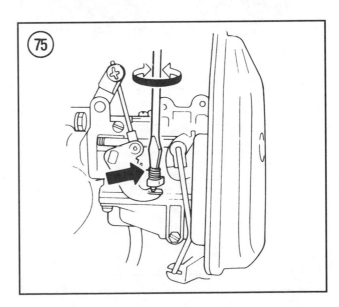

9. Shut the engine off and disconnect the portable tachometer. Remove the test propeller and install the standard propeller. See Chapter Nine.

10. Adjust the throttle control link as described in the one of the following procedures.

11. Install the engine cover.

Throttle Cable Adjustment

1. Shift into FORWARD gear.

2. Rotate the throttle grip to the wide-open throttle position. At this point, the magneto base stopper should contact the full-open stopper on the cylinder (**Figure 76**).

3. If adjustment is required, loosen the adjusting bolt locknut on the "pull" side of the throttle cable. Turn the adjusting bolt until all slack is removed, then tighten the locknut.

4. Loosen the adjusting bolt locknut on the "push" side of the throttle cable. Turn the adjusting bolt until the cable has approximately 3 mm (0.12 in.) slack with the throttle grip in the slow position (**Figure 77**). Then tighten the locknut.

5. Rotate the throttle grip to the wide-open throttle position. At this point, the throttle shaft full-open stopper (A, **Figure 78**) should contact the full-open stopper on the carburetor (B, **Figure 78**). If the throttle shaft full-open stopper is not up against the full-open stopper on the carburetor, loosen the throttle shaft rod locking screw and adjust it. Tighten the locking screw.

6. Adjust the throttle control link as described in the following procedure.

Throttle Control Link Adjustment

NOTE
Prior to adjusting the throttle control linkage, ignition timing should be checked and adjusted. Also, the throttle cable should be correctly adjusted.

1. Remove the engine cover.

2. Move the shift lever to the FORWARD gear position.

3. Rotate the throttle grip to the wide-open position.

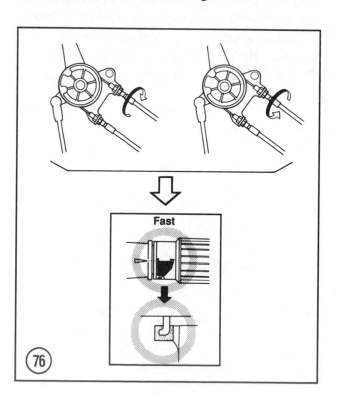

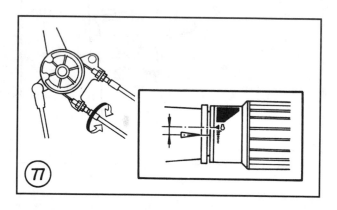

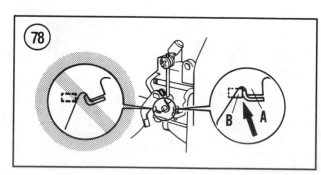

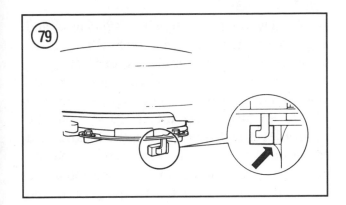

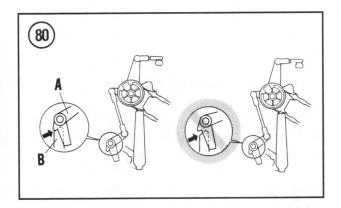

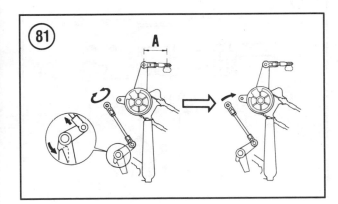

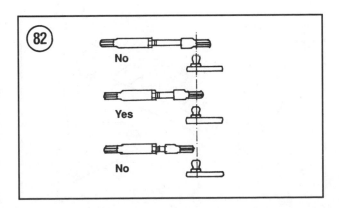

4. With the throttle grip in this position, check the following:

    a. Check that the magneto base stopper is in contact with the stopper on the cylinder (**Figure 79**).

    b. Check that the throttle control lever (A, **Figure 80**) is in contact with the stopper on the bottom cowling (B, **Figure 80**).

    c. If not, proceed to Step 5 and adjust the control link.

5. Disconnect the magneto base link rod from the control lever ball stud.

6. Rotate the magneto base until the stopper is in contact with the stopper on the cylinder.

7. Rotate the throttle grip to the wide-open throttle position.

8. Adjust the plastic snap-on connector on the end of the link rod to the length of 46 mm (1.81 in.)(A, **Figure 81**). Connect the link onto the control lever ball stud without changing the position of the linkage or magneto base (**Figure 82**).

30 HP
(3-CYLINDER) MODELS

Timing Adjustment

1. Remove the engine cover.

2. Move the shift lever to the NEUTRAL position.

3. Remove all 3 spark plugs. See Chapter Four.

4. Install a dial indicator in the No. 1 (top) cylinder spark plug hole (**Figure 83**).

5. Slowly rotate the flywheel *clockwise* and stop when the piston reaches top dead center (TDC). This is the point at which the indicator needle reverses its direction as the flywheel is rotated.

6. With the No. piston at TDC, the timing pointer should be aligned with the TDC mark on the flywheel (**Figure 84**). If not, first make sure the No. 1 piston is still exactly at TDC, then loosen the timing plate set screw and move the plate as required to align the pointer with the flywheel TDC mark. Tighten the timing plate screw securely.

7. Remove the dial indicator.

8. Slowly rotate the flywheel *clockwise* and align the timing pointer with the 25° BTDC mark on the flywheel timing scale (**Figure 85**).

9. Move the magneto control lever to the right (full advance) until it touches the stopper (**Figure 86**).

10. Slowly rotate the flywheel *clockwise* and align the timing pointer with the 5° ATDC mark on the flywheel timing scale (**Figure 87**).

11. If the timing marks on the magneto base plate and the flywheel do not align as shown in **Figure 88**, disconnect the link rod from the control lever ball stud. Loosen the locknut and adjust the plastic snap-on connector on the end of the link rod until it can be reconnected to the ball stud without changing the position of the linkage or timing marks. Reconnect the link rod to the ball stud and tighten the locknut.

12. Install the spark plugs and engine cover.

Carburetor Linkage Adjustment

1. Loosen the throttle stop screw (**Figure 89**) until clearance is noted between the end of the screw and the throttle valve stop.

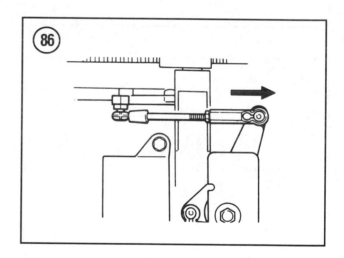

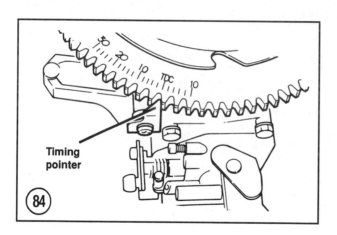

Timing pointer

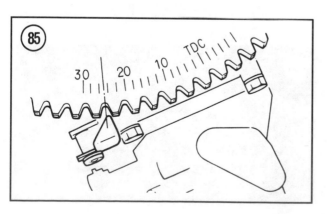

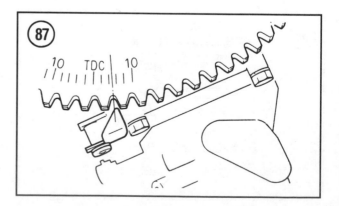

2. Close the throttle valves.

CAUTION
The throttle lever screws have left-hand threads. Turn the screws clockwise to loosen and counterclockwise to tighten.

3. Loosen the throttle lever screws for the No. 1 and No. 2 carburetors (**Figure 90**).

4. Make sure all carburetor throttle valves are closed, then lightly depress the No. 2 carburetor

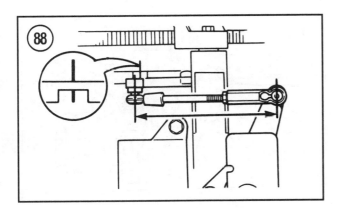

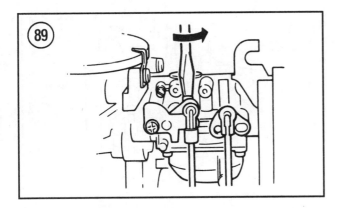

throttle roller (**Figure 91**) and tighten the No. 1 and No. 2 throttle lever screws.

5. Adjust the idle speed as described in the following procedure.

Pickup Timing Adjustment

1. Remove the standard propeller and install a test propeller. See Chapter Nine.

2. Install the outboard in a test tank.

3. Remove the engine cover.

4. Connect a portable tachometer and timing light according to their manufacturer's instructions.

5. Start the engine, place it in NEUTRAL and let it run until it reaches normal operating temperature.

6. Aim the timing light at the timing plate and manually move the magneto control lever to the

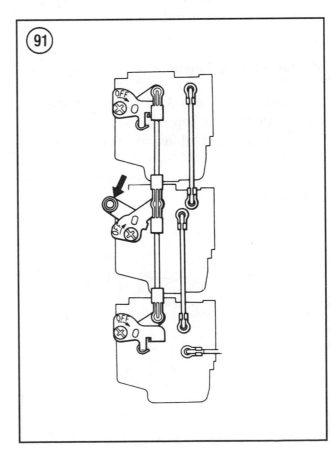

5

fully retarded position (**Figure 92**). The 2° ± 1° ATDC timing mark on the flywheel should align with the timing pointer.

7. If the timing mark and the pointer do not align as shown in **Figure 92**, shut off the engine. Disconnect the link rod from the control lever ball stud. Loosen the locknut and adjust the plastic snap-on connector on the end of the link rod until it can be reconnected to the ball stud without changing the position of the linkage or timing marks. Reconnect the link rod to the ball stud and tighten the locknut.

> *CAUTION*
> *The throttle lever screws have left-hand threads. Turn the screws clockwise to loosen and counterclockwise to tighten.*

8. Loosen the throttle lever screw for the No. 2 carburetor (**Figure 93**). Lightly depress the No. 2 carburetor throttle roller (**Figure 93**) and tighten the No. 2 throttle lever screw.

9. Disconnect the timing light.

Idle Speed Adjustment

1. Remove the standard propeller and install a test propeller. See Chapter Nine.
2. Install the outboard in a test tank.

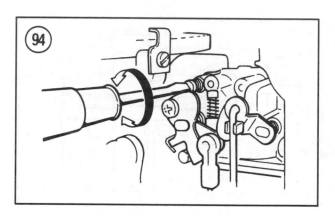

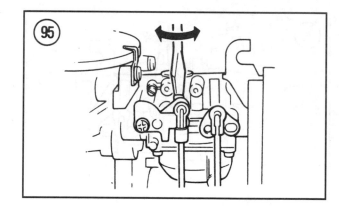

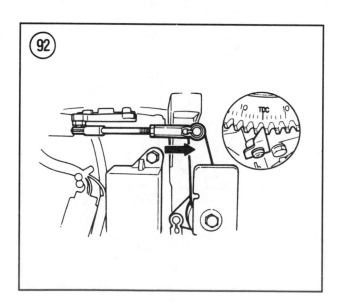

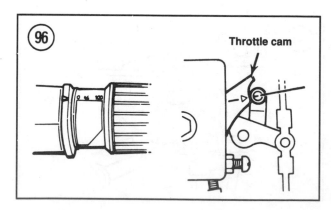

Throttle cam

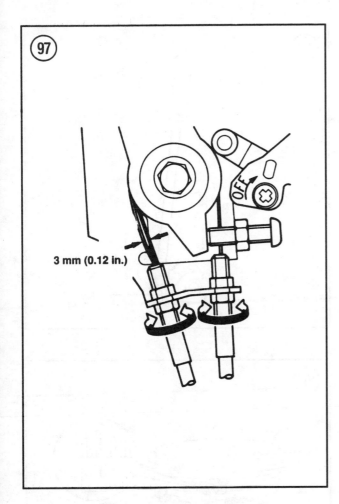

3 mm (0.12 in.)

3. Remove the engine cover.

4. Connect a portable tachometer according to its manufacturer's instructions.

5. Turn the pilot screw (**Figure 94**) in until it *lightly* seats, then back it out the following number of turns:

  a. Carburetor No. 1: 1/2-1 turns out.

  b. Carburetor No. 2: 1 1/2-2 turns out.

  c. Carburetor No. 3: 3/4-1 1/4 turns out.

6. Start the engine, place it in FORWARD gear and warm it to normal operating temperature.

7. Observe the engine speed on the tachometer and compare to the specification listed in **Table 10**. If out of specification, perform Step 9.

8. Adjust the idle speed screw (**Figure 95**) in or out until the specified idle speed is obtained.

9. Shut the engine off and disconnect the portable tachometer.

10. Install the engine cover.

**Throttle Cable Adjustment
(Manual Control Model)**

1. Shift into FORWARD gear.

2. Rotate the throttle grip to the wide-open throttle position. At this point, the center of the throttle roller should align with the wide-open throttle mark on the throttle cam (**Figure 96**).

3. If the marks do not align in Step 2, loosen the adjusting bolt locknut on the "pull" side of the throttle cable. Turn the adjusting bolt until all slack is removed, then tighten the locknut.

4. Loosen the adjusting bolt locknut on the "push" side of the throttle cable. Turn the adjusting bolt until the cable has approximately 3 mm (0.12 in.) slack, then tighten the locknut (**Figure 97**).

Oil Pump Link Adjustment

1. Rotate the throttle grip to the wide-open throttle position (**Figure 98**).

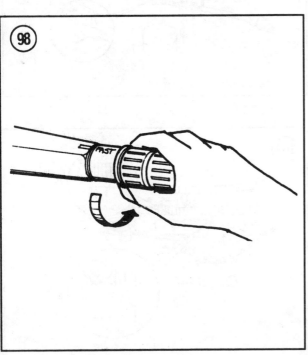

5

2. Turn the oil pump lever (A, **Figure 99**) toward the full-open position until it is against the wide-open stopper (B, **Figure 99**).

3. Loosen the locknut and adjust the plastic snap-on connector on the end of the link rod until it can be reconnected to the ball stud without changing the throttle or oil pump lever position.

4. Reconnect the link rod to the ball stud and tighten the locknut.

5. Rotate the throttle grip to the wide-open throttle position and make sure the throttle valve opens fully.

C40 (2-CYLINDER) MODELS

Timing Adjustment (Dynamic)

1. Remove the standard propeller and install a test propeller. See Chapter Nine.

2. Install the outboard in a test tank.

3. Remove the engine cover.

4. Connect a timing light and portable tachometer according to their manufacturer's instructions.

5. Shift into NEUTRAL.

6. Start the engine and allow it to warm up for approximately 5 minutes.

7. Manually move the magneto control lever to the closed throttle position (full-retard ignition).

8. Point the timing light at the timing indicator on the rewind starter case. It should align with the 2° BTDC marks.

9. If the timing pointer does not align as specified in Step 8, adjust the magneto base stopper screw until the magneto base contacts the stopper (**Figure 100**).

10. Manually move the magneto control lever to the wide-open throttle position (full-advanced ignition).

11. Increase engine speed to more than 4,500 rpm.

12. Point the timing light at the timing indicator on the rewind starter case. It should align with the 22° BTDC mark (A, **Figure 101**) or the

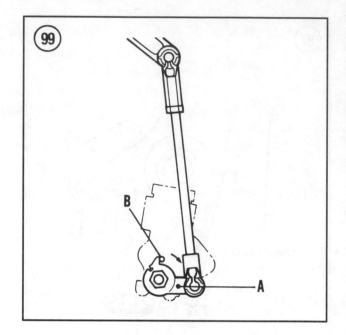

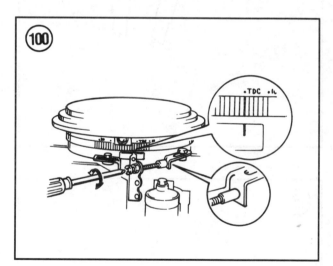

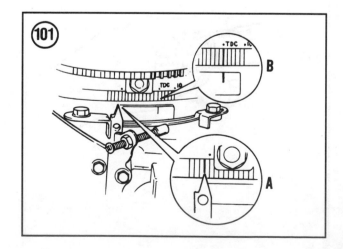

ignition mark on the magneto base should align with the TDC mark on the flywheel (B, **Figure 101**).

13. If the timing pointer does not align as specified in Step 12, adjust the timing plate as described in the following procedure.

Ignition Timing Adjustment (Static)

Full-advanced position

1. Remove the engine cover.

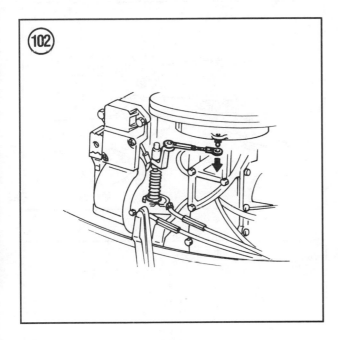

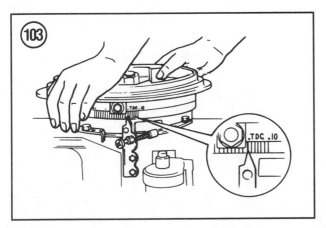

2. Disconnect the magneto control rod (**Figure 102**).

3. Remove all 3 spark plugs. See Chapter Four.

4. Install a dial indicator in the No. 1 (top) cylinder spark plug hole.

5. Slowly rotate the flywheel *clockwise* and stop when the piston reaches top dead center (TDC). This is the point at which the dial indicator needle reverses its direction as the flywheel is rotated.

6. Check the timing pointer alignment with the flywheel timing scale (**Figure 103**). If the end of the timing pointer is not aligned with the TDC mark on the CDI magneto rotor, loosen the timing pointer set screw, align the timing pointer end with the TDC mark, then tighten the screw (**Figure 104**).

7. Slowly rotate the magneto rotor *counter-clockwise* so the 22° ± 1° BTDC timing mark aligns with the timing pointer (**Figure 104**).

8. Loosen the 2 bolts securing the magneto base stopper No. 1. Move the stopper on the full-open side of the magneto base No. 1 stopper to contact

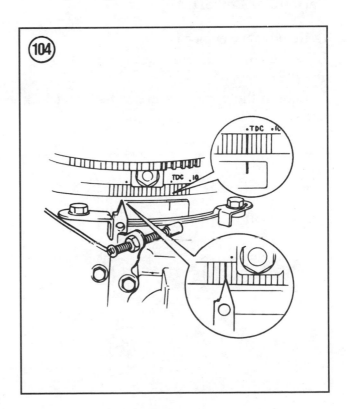

the left side of the cap on the magneto base stopper No. 2. (**Figure 105**), then tighten the 2 bolts to secure the magneto base stopper No. 1.

9. Remove the dial indicator.

10. Adjust the full-retarded position as described in the following procedure.

Full-retarded position

1. Slowly rotate the magneto rotor *clockwise* so that the 2 ± 1° BTDC timing mark aligns with the timing pointer (**Figure 106**).

2. Align the ignition mark on the flywheel magneto base with the TDC mark on the rotor (**Figure 107**). If the marks do not align, loosen the locknut, then adjust the magneto base stopper screw so the magneto base contacts the stopper. Tighten the locknut.

3. Connect the magneto control rod.

4. Install the spark plugs and engine cover.

Carburetor Linkage Adjustment

1. Remove the engine cover.

2. Loosen the carburetor idle adjust screw (**Figure 108**).

3. Loosen the upper carburetor ball joint lock screw.

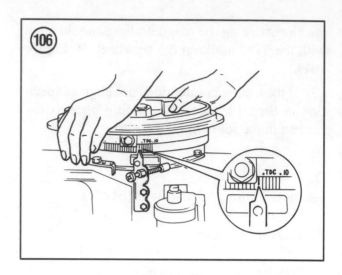

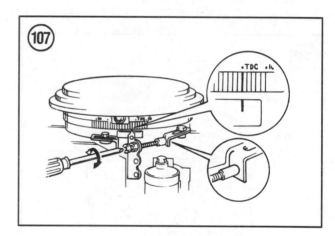

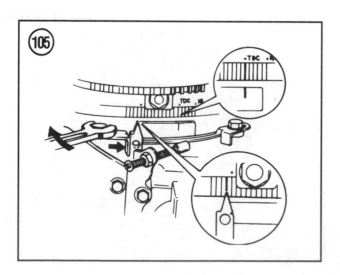

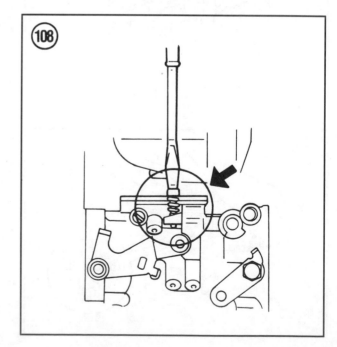

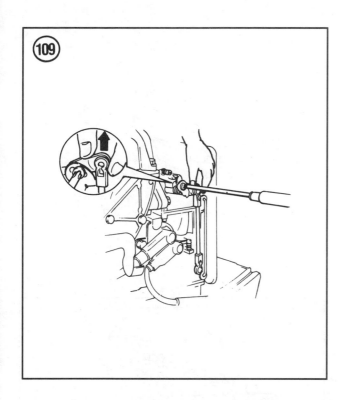

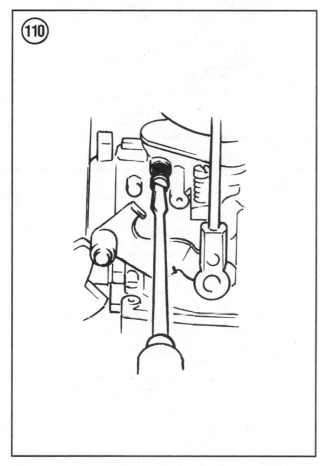

4. Pull up on the upper carburetor ball joint to remove play between the upper and lower carburetors, then tighten the upper lock screw (**Figure 109**).

5. Move the accelerator lever up and down several times to make sure the upper and lower carburetors open and close simultaneously.

6. Install the engine cover.

Idle Speed Adjustment

1. Remove the standard propeller and install a test propeller. See Chapter Nine.

2. Install the outboard in a test tank.

3. Remove the engine cover.

4. Connect a portable tachometer according to its manufacturer's instructions.

5. Turn the pilot screw (**Figure 110**) in until it *lightly* seats, then back it out 1 1/2-2 turns. Repeat for the other carburetor.

6. Start the engine, place it in NEUTRAL and warm it to normal operating temperature.

7. Observe the engine speed on the tachometer and compare to the specification listed in **Table 11**. If out of specification, perform Step 8.

8. Adjust the idle speed screw (**Figure 111**) in or out until the specified idle speed is obtained.

5

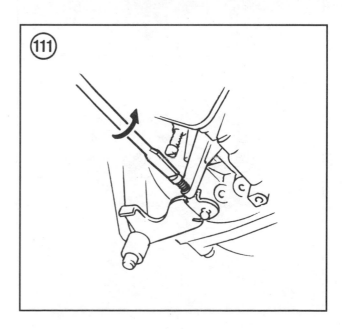

9. Shut the engine off and disconnect the portable tachometer. Remove the test propeller and install the standard propeller. See Chapter Nine.

10. Adjust the throttle link as described in the following procedure.

11. Install the engine cover.

Throttle Link Adjustment

> *NOTE*
> *Prior to adjusting the throttle linkage, ignition timing should be checked and adjusted, if necessary.*

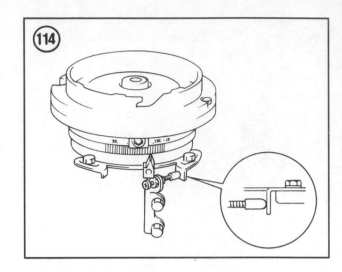

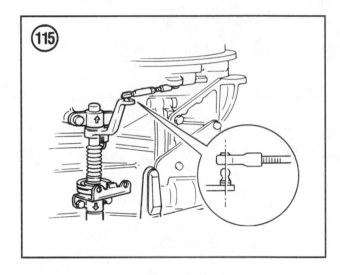

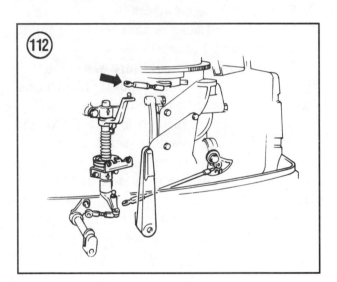

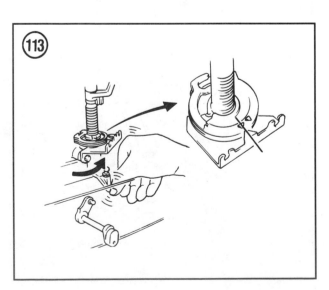

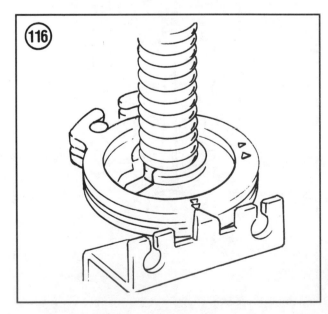

1. Remove the engine cover.

2. Disconnect the magneto control link (**Figure 112**).

3. Align the full-closed mark on the pulley with the mark on the bracket (**Figure 113**).

4. Rotate the magneto base *clockwise* until the full-closed side of the magneto base stopper No. 1 contacts the adjust bolt for the magneto base stopper No. 2 (**Figure 114**).

5. Adjust the plastic snap-on connector on the end of the link rod until it can be reconnected to the control lever ball stud without changing the position of the linkage or magneto base (**Figure 115**).

6. Align the full-open mark on the pulley with the mark on the throttle bracket (**Figure 116**).

7. Adjust the throttle link joint so the full-open mark on the throttle cam aligns with the center of the carburetor throttle roller (**Figure 117**).

8. Install the engine cover.

40 HP, 50 HP AND PRO 50 (3-CYLINDER) MODELS

These models are equipped with an electronic ignition advance mechanism in place of a mechanical ignition advance system. Adjustment of the throttle linkage sets the timing.

Throttle Linkage Adjustment

1. Remove the engine cover.

2. Turn the magneto control lever (A, **Figure 118**) so that the adjust screw contacts the full-retard stopper (B, **Figure 118**).

3. Check the CDI indicator to see if it aligns with the full-retard 7° ATDC mark on the plate (**Figure 119**). If alignment is incorrect, perform Step 6.

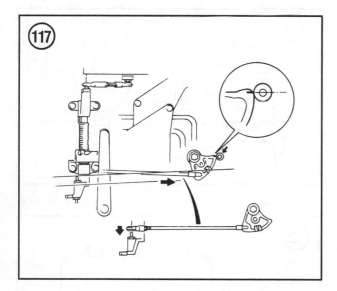

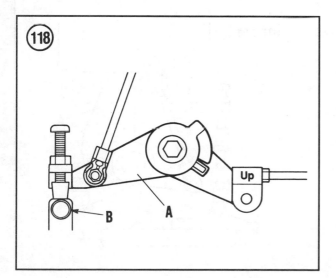

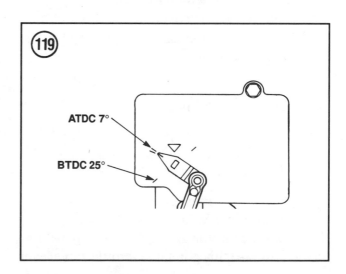

4. Turn the magneto control lever (A, **Figure 118**) so that the adjust screw contacts the full-advance adjusting screw (**Figure 120**).

5. Check the CDI indicator to see if it aligns with the full-advance 25° BTDC mark on the plate (**Figure 119**). If alignment is incorrect, perform Step 6.

6. To adjust full-retard and/or full advance, perform the following:

  a. Loosen the locknut and adjust the length (A, **Figure 121**) of the full-retard screw (B, **Figure 121**) to 20 mm (0.79 in.). Tighten the locknut.

  b. Loosen the control rod locknut (A, **Figure 122**) and disconnect the control rod (B, **Figure 122**) from the CDI unit.

  c. Turn the magneto control lever so its adjusting screw contacts the full-retard stopper (C, **Figure 122**).

  d. Adjust the control rod (B, **Figure 122**) length so the CDI unit indicator aligns with the 7° ATDC mark on the plate.

  e. Connect the magneto control rod to the CDI unit.

  f. Turn the magneto control lever so that it contacts the full-advance adjusting screw (D, **Figure 122**).

  g. Adjust the full-advance adjusting screw so that the CDI unit indicator aligns with the 25° BTDC mark on the plate.

7. Install the engine cover.

8. Adjust the throttle cable as described in the following procedure.

Throttle Cable Adjustment

NOTE
Adjust the throttle link prior to adjusting the throttle cable.

1. Remove the engine cover.

2. Shift into FORWARD gear.

3. Rotate the throttle grip to the wide-open throttle position. At this point, the throttle valve lever

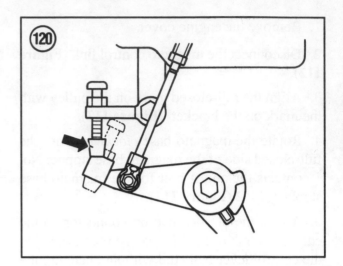

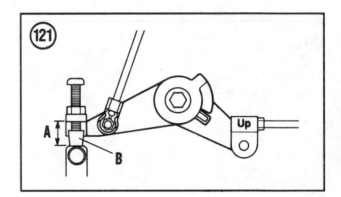

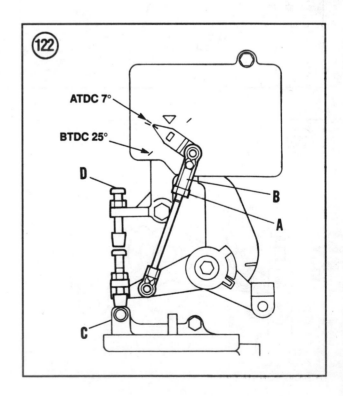

should contact the full-open stopper (**Figure 123**).

4. If it does not make contact, loosen the locknut (A, **Figure 124**) and remove the clip (B, **Figure 124**).

5. Disconnect the cable joint from the magneto control lever.

6. Rotate the throttle grip to the fully closed position.

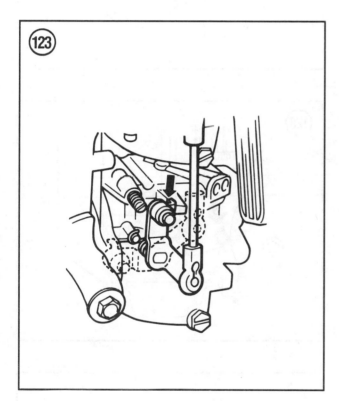

7. Turn the magneto control lever (A, **Figure 125**) so that its adjusting screw contacts the full-retard stopper (B, **Figure 125**).

WARNING
The cable joint should be screwed into the fitting by more than 8 mm (0.31 in.).

8. Adjust the position of the cable joint until its hole aligns with the set pin. Position the cable joint with the UP mark facing up and install it onto the set pin.

9. Install the clip (B, **Figure 124**) and tighten the locknut (A, **Figure 124**).

10. Install the engine cover.

5

Idle Speed Adjustment

NOTE
Adjust the throttle link prior to adjusting the idle speed.

1. Remove the standard propeller and install a test propeller. See Chapter Nine.

2. Install the outboard in a test tank.

3. Remove the engine cover.

4. Connect a portable tachometer to the No. 1 cylinder according to its manufacturer's instructions.

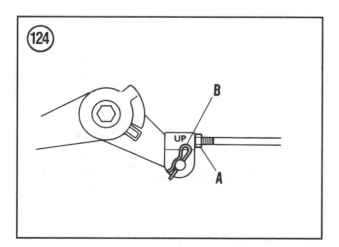

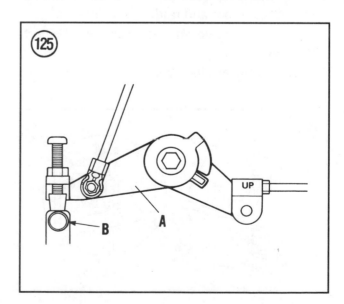

5. Loosen the idle adjust screw (A, **Figure 126**) and fully close the throttle valve.

> *CAUTION*
> *The throttle lever screws have left-hand threads. Turn the screws clockwise to loosen and counterclockwise to tighten.*

6. Loosen the throttle lever securing screws (B, **Figure 126**) for the upper and middle carburetors.

7. Turn the pilot screw (**Figure 127**) in until it *lightly* seats, then back it out the following number of turns:

    a. 40 hp: 1 1/4-1 3/4 turns out.

    b. 50 hp and Pro 50: 1 1/8-1 7/8 turns out.

    Repeat for all carburetors.

8. Start the engine, place it in FORWARD and warm it to normal operating temperature.

9. Observe the engine speed on the tachometer and compare to the specification listed in **Table 12** (40 hp) or **Table 13** (50 hp and Pro 50). If out of specification, perform Step 10.

10. Adjust the idle speed screw in or out until the specified idle speed is obtained.

11. Lightly push down on the throttle lever on the lower carburetor in the direction of the arrow in **Figure 128** to the full-closed position. Tighten the throttle lever securing screw *counterclockwise* on the upper and middle carburetors.

12. Shut the engine off and disconnect the portable tachometer.

13. Install the engine cover.

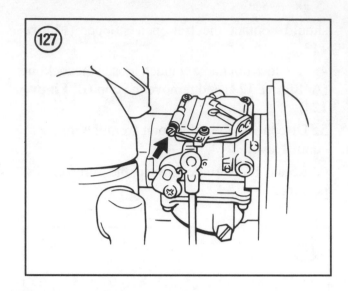

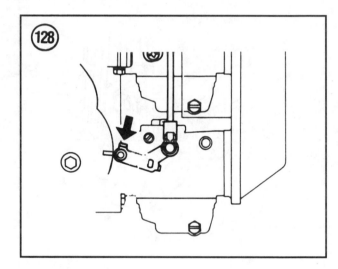

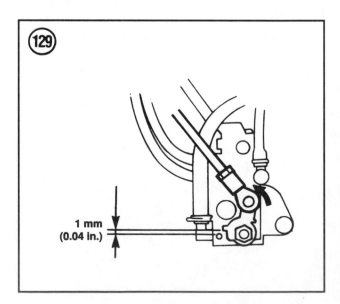

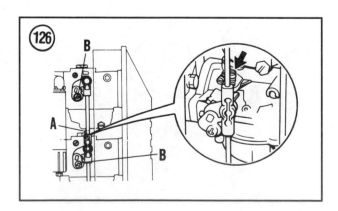

Oil Pump Link Adjustment

1. Rotate the throttle grip to the wide-open throttle position. At this point, the oil pump lever should be 1.0 mm (0.04 in.) off the full-open side stopper (**Figure 129**).

2. If adjustment is necessary, fully open the carburetor throttle valve. Set the oil pump lever 1 mm (0.04 in.) off the full open side stopper.

3. Loosen the locknut on the link joint, then disconnect the link rod from the oil pump lever ball stud. Adjust the plastic snap-on connector on the end of the link rod until its hole aligns with the oil pump set pin.

4. Connect the link joint and check that the throttle valve opens fully.

5. Reconnect the link rod to the ball stud and tighten the locknut.

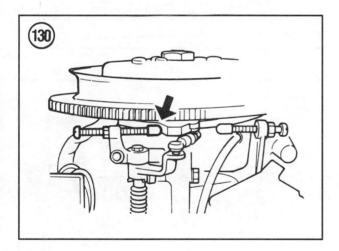

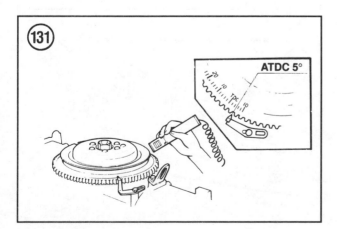

6. Rotate the throttle grip to the wide-open throttle position and recheck the clearance listed in Step 1.

C55 MODELS

Ignition Timing Adjustment

1. Remove the standard propeller and install a test propeller. See Chapter Nine.

2. Install the outboard in a test tank.

3. Remove the engine cover.

4. Connect a timing light and portable tachometer according to their manufacturer's instructions.

5. Shift into NEUTRAL.

6. Start the engine and allow it to warm up for approximately 5 minutes.

7. Manually full-retard the ignition (**Figure 130**).

8. Point the timing light at the timing pointer. The timing pointer should align with the $5° \pm 1°$ ATDC marks (**Figure 131**).

9. If the timing pointer does not align as specified in Step 8, turn the adjusting screw and adjust the timing as necessary (**Figure 132**).

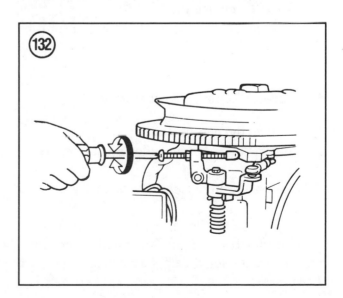

5

10. Manually move the magneto control lever to the wide-open throttle position (full-advanced ignition) (**Figure 133**).

11. Increase engine speed to more than 4,500 rpm.

12. Point the timing light at the timing pointer. It should align with the 26° ± 1° BTDC marks (**Figure 134**).

13. If the timing pointer does not align as specified in Step 12, loosen the locknut, turn the screw (**Figure 135**) and adjust the timing as necessary. Tighten the locknut.

14. To adjust the pick-up timing, perform the following:

    a. Manually full-retard the ignition (**Figure 130**).

    b. Allow the engine to idle at 1,050-1,150 rpm. If necessary, adjust the idle speed as described in this section.

    c. Bring the throttle cam to contact the throttle lever roller (**Figure 136**) lightly. The throttle valve should not open.

    d. Loosen the locknut on the link joint, then disconnect the link rod from the oil pump lever ball stud. Adjust the plastic snap-on connector on the end of the link rod until its hole aligns with the set pin. Install the link joint.

15. Turn the engine off.

16. Disconnect the timing light and install the engine cover.

Carburetor Linkage Adjustment

1. Remove the engine cover.

2. Loosen the carburetor idle adjust screw (**Figure 137**).

3. Loosen the upper carburetor ball joint lock screw.

4. Pull up on the upper carburetor ball joint to remove play between the upper and lower carburetors then tighten the upper lock screw (**Figure 138**).

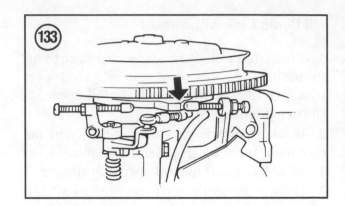

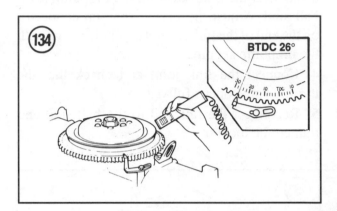

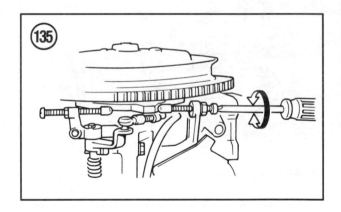

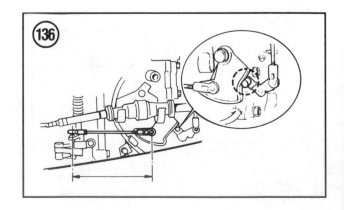

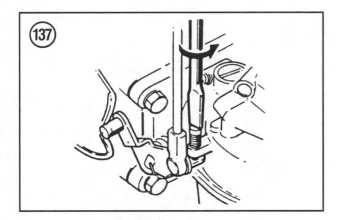

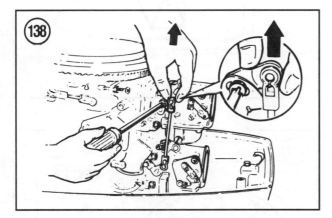

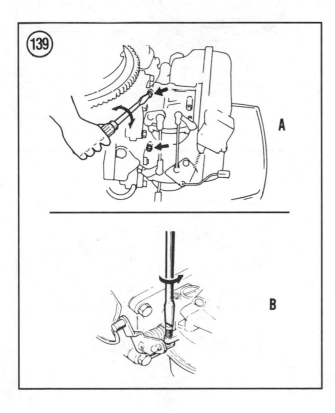

5. Move the accelerator lever up and down several times to make sure the upper and lower carburetors open and close simultaneously.

6. Install the engine cover.

Idle Speed Adjustment

1. Remove the standard propeller and install a test propeller. See Chapter Nine.

2. Install the outboard in a test tank.

3. Remove the engine cover.

4. Connect a portable tachometer according to its manufacturer's instructions.

5. Turn the pilot screw (A, **Figure 139**) in until it *lightly* seats, then back it out 1 3/4-2 1/4 turns. Repeat for the other carburetor.

6. Start the engine, place it in NEUTRAL and warm it to the normal operating temperature.

7. Observe the engine speed on the tachometer and compare to the specification listed in **Table 14**. If out of specification, perform Step 8.

8. Adjust the idle speed screw (B, **Figure 139**) in or out until the specified idle speed is obtained.

9. Shut the engine off and disconnect the portable tachometer. Remove the test propeller and install the standard propeller. See Chapter Nine.

10. Adjust the throttle link as described in the following procedure.

11. Install the engine cover.

PRO 60, 70 HP AND 90 HP MODELS

Timing Plate Position Adjustment

If the timing plate is moved even a little during inspection or repair procedures, it must be readjusted properly.

This procedure must be performed prior to adjusting the ignition timing.

1. Remove the engine cover.

2. Remove all 3 spark plugs. See Chapter Four.

3. Install a dial indicator in the No. 1 (top) cylinder spark plug hole.

4. Slowly rotate the flywheel *clockwise* and stop when the piston reaches top dead center (TDC). This is the point at which the indicator needle reverses its direction as the flywheel is rotated.

5. Check the timing plate alignment with the flywheel timing scale. Refer to **Figure 140** for Pro 60 and 70 hp models or **Figure 141** for 90 hp models.

6. If the end of the timing plate is not aligned with the TDC mark on the CDI magneto rotor, loosen the timing plate set screw, align the timing plate end with the TDC mark, then tighten the screw.

7. Remove the dial indicator. Install the spark plugs and the engine cover.

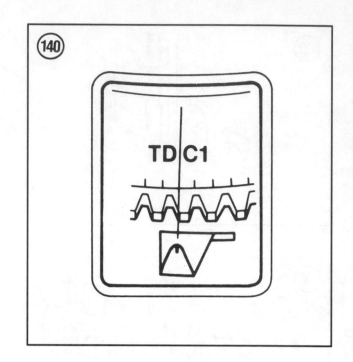

Timing Adjustment

> *NOTE*
> *Check and adjust, if necessary, the timing plate position prior to checking and adjusting the timing.*

1. Remove the standard propeller and install a test propeller. See Chapter Nine.

2. Install the outboard in a test tank.

3. Remove the engine cover.

4. Connect a timing light to the No. 1 cylinder and a portable tachometer according to the manufacturer's instructions.

5. Shift into NEUTRAL.

6. Start the engine and allow it to warm up for approximately 5 minutes. Let the engine idle at 750-850 rpm.

7. Manually full-retard the ignition (**Figure 142**).

8. Point the timing light at the timing pointer. It should align with the following marks (**Figure 143**):

    a. Pro 60 and 70 hp: 7° ± 1° ATDC marks.

    b. 90 hp: 8° ± 1° ATDC marks.

9. If the timing pointer does not align as specified in Step 8, adjust the screw and adjust the timing as necessary (**Figure 144**).

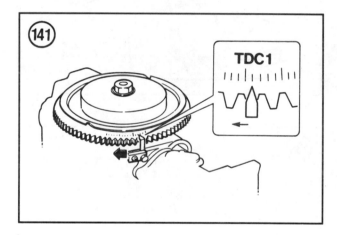

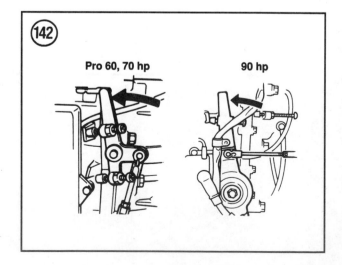

10. Manually move the magneto control lever to the wide-open throttle position (full-advanced ignition).

11. Increase engine speed to more than the following:

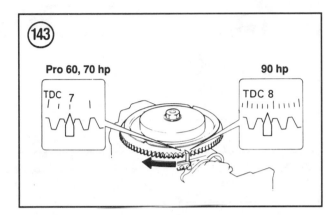

12. Point the timing light at the timing pointer. It should align with the following marks (**Figure 145**):

    a. Pro 60 and 70 hp: 22° ± 1° BTDC marks.

    b. 90 hp: 20° ± 1° BTDC marks.

a. Pro 60: 4,500-5,500 rpm.

b. 70 hp: 5,000-6,000 rpm.

c. 90 hp: 4,500-5,500 rpm.

13. If the timing pointer does not align as specified in Step 12, loosen the locknut, turn the screw (**Figure 146**) and adjust the timing as necessary. Tighten the locknut.

14. To adjust the pickup timing, perform the following:

    a. Manually full-retard the ignition (**Figure 142**).

    b. Bring the throttle cam to contact the throttle lever roller lightly. The throttle valve should not open.

    c. Loosen the locknut on the link joint, then disconnect the link rod from the oil pump lever ball stud. Adjust the plastic snap-on connector on the end of the link rod until its

5

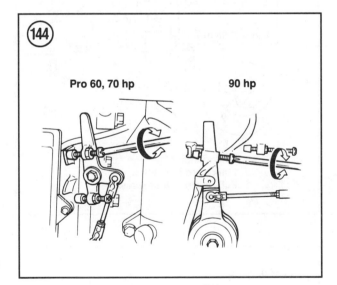

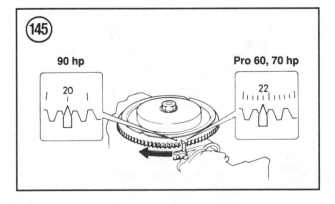

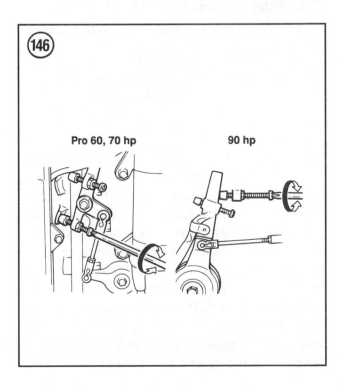

hole aligns with the set pin (**Figure 147**). Install the link joint.

15. Turn the engine off.

16. Disconnect the timing light and tachometer. Install the engine cover. Remove the test propeller and install the standard propeller. See Chapter Nine.

Throttle Sensor Control Link Adjustment

1. Loosen the locknut on the throttle sensor control link and the throttle cam link joint, then disconnect the link rods from the lever ball stud.

2. Adjust the plastic snap-on connector on the end of the throttle sensor control link rod to the following dimensions:

    a. Pro 60 and 70 hp: 128.5-129.5 mm (5.06-5.10 in.)

    b. 90 hp: 93-94 mm (3.66-3.70 in.)

3. Adjust the plastic snap-on connector on the end of the throttle cam link rod to the following dimensions:

    a. Pro 60 and 70 hp: 58 mm (2.28 in.).

    b. 90 hp: 120.5 mm (4.74 in.).

4. Install the link joints and tighten the locknuts.

NOTE
*The nut in the magneto control lever should be 2 mm (0.08 in.) from the end of the magneto control lever (**Figure 148**).*

5. Adjust the length of the full-retard adjusting screw so that when the full-retard adjusting screw contacts the stopper, the full-retard indication on the CDI unit aligns with the timing indicator. Refer to **Figure 149** for Pro 60 and 70 hp models or **Figure 148** for 90 hp models.

6. Adjust the length of the full-advance adjusting screw so that when the full-advance adjusting screw contacts the stopper, the full-advance indication on the CDI unit aligns with the timing indicator. Refer to **Figure 150** for Pro 60 and 70 hp models or **Figure 151** for 90 hp models.

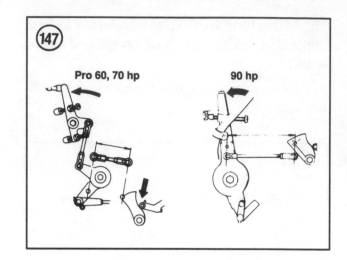

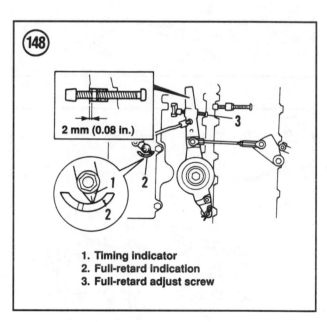

1. Timing indicator
2. Full-retard indication
3. Full-retard adjust screw

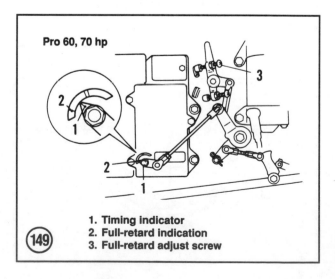

1. Timing indicator
2. Full-retard indication
3. Full-retard adjust screw

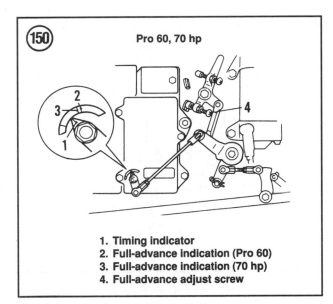

Pro 60, 70 hp

1. Timing indicator
2. Full-advance indication (Pro 60)
3. Full-advance indication (70 hp)
4. Full-advance adjust screw

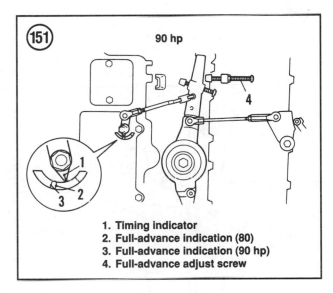

90 hp

1. Timing indicator
2. Full-advance indication (80)
3. Full-advance indication (90 hp)
4. Full-advance adjust screw

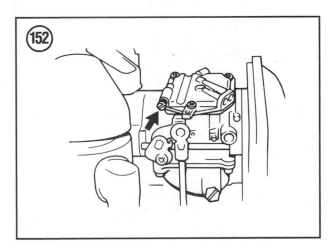

Idle Speed Adjustment

1. Remove the standard propeller and install a test propeller. See Chapter Nine.

2. Install the outboard in a test tank.

3. Remove the engine cover.

4. Connect a portable tachometer according to its manufacturer's instructions.

5. Turn the pilot screw (**Figure 152**) in until it *lightly* seats, then back it out the following number of turns:

     a. Pro 60: 1 1/4-1 3/4 turns.

     b. 70 hp and 90 hp: 1-1 1/2 turns.

     Repeat for the other carburetors.

6. Start the engine, place it in NEUTRAL and warm it to the normal operating temperature.

7. Observe the engine rpm on the tachometer and compare to the specification listed in the appropriate table at the end of this chapter. If out of specification, perform Step 8.

8. Adjust the idle speed screw in or out until the specified idle speed is obtained. Refer to **Figure 153** for Pro 60 and 70 hp models or **Figure 154** for 90 hp models.

5

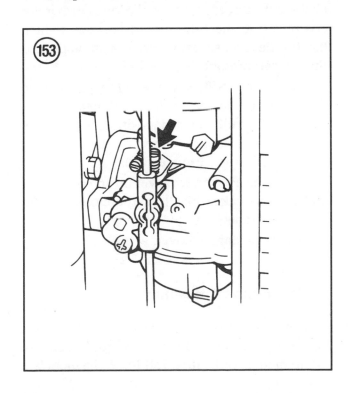

9. Shut the engine off and disconnect the portable tachometer.

10. Adjust the throttle link as described in the following procedure.

11. Install the engine cover.

Carburetor Linkage Adjustment

1. Remove the engine cover.

2. Loosen the carburetor idle adjust screw and close the throttle valve.

> *CAUTION*
> *The throttle lever screws have left-hand threads. Turn the screws clockwise to loosen and counterclockwise to tighten.*

3A. On Pro 60 and 70 hp models, loosen the throttle lever securing screws on the upper and middle carburetors.

3B. On 90 hp models, loosen the throttle lever securing screws on the upper and lower carburetors.

4A. On Pro 60 and 70 hp models, while lightly pushing the throttle lever on the lower carburetor downward to the fully closed position, tighten the throttle lever securing screw on the upper and middle carburetors (**Figure 155**).

4B. On 90 hp models, while lightly pushing the throttle lever on the middle carburetor downward to the fully closed position, tighten the throttle lever securing screw on the upper and lower carburetors (**Figure 156**).

5. Move the accelerator lever up and down several times to make sure all 3 carburetors open and close simultaneously.

6. Install the engine cover.

Oil Pump Link Adjustment

1. Rotate the throttle grip to the wide-open throttle position. Refer to **Figure 157** for Pro 60 and 70 hp models or **Figure 158** for 90 hp models.

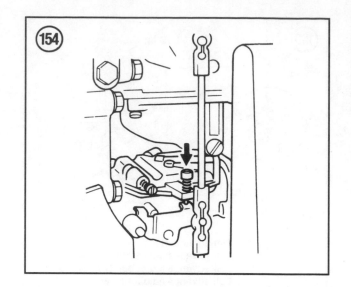

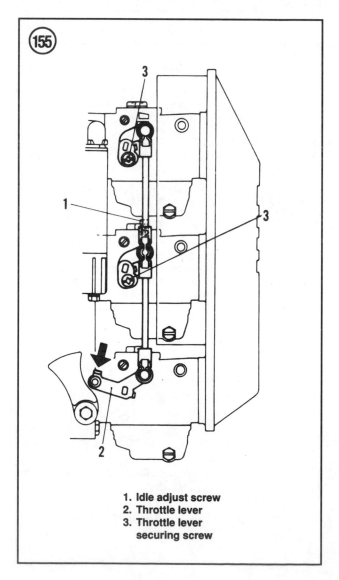

1. Idle adjust screw
2. Throttle lever
3. Throttle lever
   securing screw

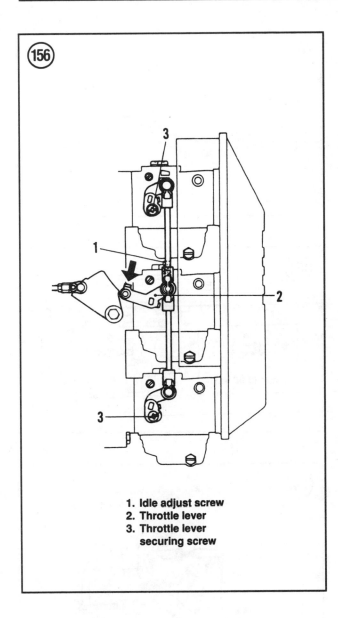

1. Idle adjust screw
2. Throttle lever
3. Throttle lever
   securing screw

2. At this point, the oil pump lever should be 1 mm (0.04 in.) off the full-open side stopper (**Figure 159**).

3. If adjustment is necessary, fully open the carburetor throttle valve. Set the oil pump lever 1 mm (0.04 in.) off the full-open side stopper.

4. Loosen the locknut on the link joint, then disconnect the link rod from the oil pump lever ball stud. Adjust the plastic snap-on connector on the end of the link rod until its hole aligns with the oil pump set pin.

5. Connect the link joint and check that the throttle valve opens fully.

6. Reconnect the link rod to the ball stud and tighten the locknut.

7. Rotate the throttle grip to the wide-open throttle position and recheck the clearance listed in Step 2.

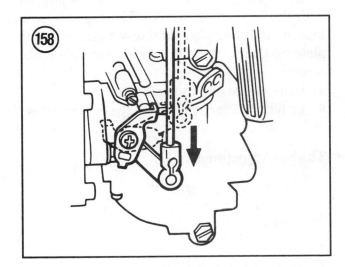

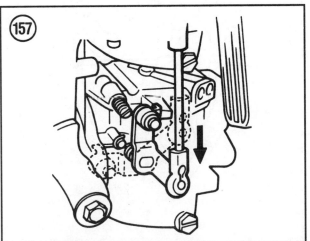

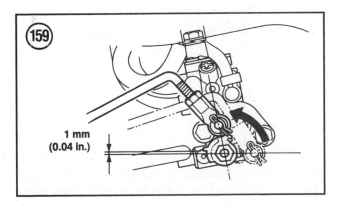

C75 HP AND C85 MODELS

Timing Plate Position Adjustment

If the timing plate is moved even a little during inspection or repair procedures, it must be readjusted properly.

This procedure must be performed prior to adjusting the ignition timing.

1. Remove the engine cover.
2. Remove all 3 spark plugs. See Chapter Four.
3. Install a dial indicator in the No. 1 (top) cylinder spark plug hole.
4. Slowly rotate the flywheel *clockwise* and stop when the piston reaches top dead center (TDC). This is the point at which the indicator needle reverses its direction as the flywheel is rotated.
5. Check the timing plate alignment with the flywheel timing scale. Refer to **Figure 160**.
6. If the end of the timing plate is not aligned with the TDC mark on the CDI magneto rotor, loosen the timing plate set screw, align the timing plate end with the TDC mark, then tighten the screw.
7. Remove the dial indicator.
8. Install the spark plugs and the engine cover.

Timing Adjustment

NOTE
Check and adjust, if necessary, the timing plate position prior to checking and adjusting the timing.

1. Remove the standard propeller and install a test propeller. See Chapter Nine.
2. Install the outboard in a test tank.
3. Remove the engine cover.

NOTE
The following dimensions are preliminary adjustments and will probably be changed to a different length during this procedure.

4. Perform a preliminary link length adjustment on all control links related to timing. Loosen the

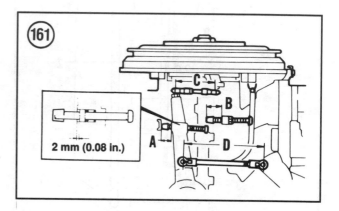

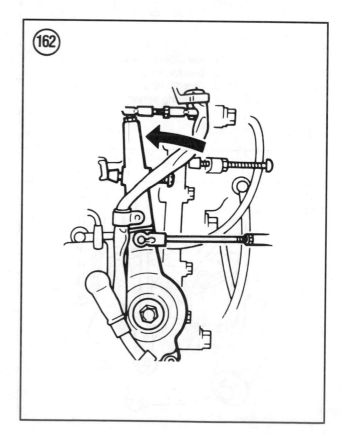

locknut on the links, then adjust the lengths (**Figure 161**) to the following dimension:

   a. A: 13 mm (0.51 in.).

   b. B: 35 mm (1.38 in.).

   c. C: 74 mm (2.91 in.).

   d. D: 124 mm (4.88 in.).

   Do not tighten the locknuts at this time.

5. Connect a timing light to the No. 1 cylinder and a portable tachometer according to their manufacturer's instructions.

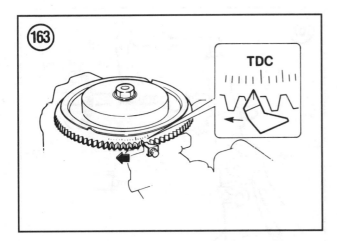

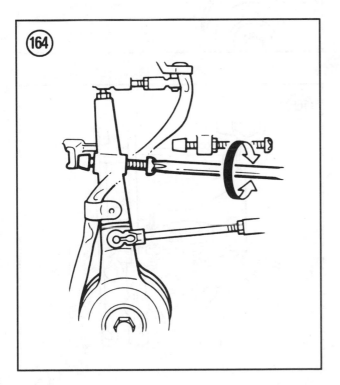

6. Shift into NEUTRAL.

7. Start the engine and allow it to warm up for approximately 5 minutes.

8. Increase engine speed to more than 4,500 rpm.

9. Manually full-retard the ignition (**Figure 162**).

10. Point the timing light at the timing pointer. It should align with the 2° ± 1° ATDC marks (**Figure 163**).

11. If the timing pointer does not align as specified in Step 10, turn the screw and adjust the timing as necessary (**Figure 164**).

12. Manually move the magneto control lever to the wide-open throttle position (full-advanced ignition) (**Figure 165**).

13. Maintain engine speed at more than 4,500 rpm.

5

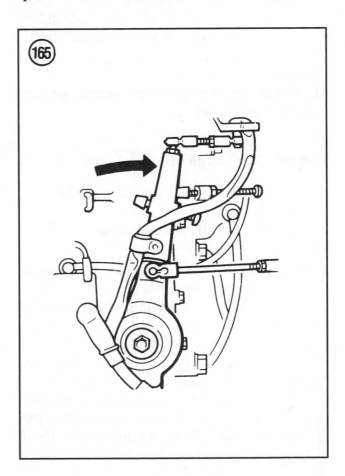

14. Point the timing light at the timing pointer. It should align with the 24° ± 1° BTDC marks (**Figure 166**).

15. If the timing pointer does not align as specified in Step 14, loosen the locknut, turn the screw (**Figure 167**) and adjust the timing as necessary. Tighten the locknut.

16. To adjust the pickup timing, perform the following:

    a. Manually full-retard the ignition (**Figure 162**).

    b. Set the idle speed to 750-850 rpm. Turn the throttle stop screw (**Figure 168**) as necessary.

    c. Bring the throttle cam to contact the throttle lever roller lightly. The throttle valve should not open.

    d. Loosen the locknut on the link joint, then disconnect the link rod from the oil pump lever ball stud. Adjust the plastic snap-on connector on the end of the link rod until its hole aligns with the set pin (**Figure 169**). Install the link joint.

17. Turn the engine off.

18. Disconnect the timing light and tachometer. Install the engine cover.

Idle Speed Adjustment

1. Remove the standard propeller and install a test propeller. See Chapter Nine.

2. Install the outboard in a test tank.

3. Remove the engine cover.

4. Connect a portable tachometer according to its manufacturer's instructions.

5. Turn the pilot screw (**Figure 170**) in until it *lightly* seats, then back it out 7/8-1 3/8 turns. Repeat for the other carburetors.

6. Start the engine, place it in NEUTRAL and warm it to normal operating temperature.

7. Observe the engine speed on the tachometer and compare to the specification listed in the appropriate table at the end of this chapter. If out of specification, perform Step 8.

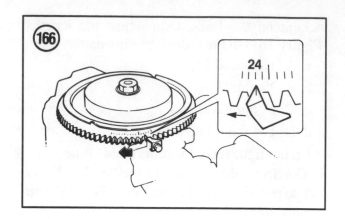

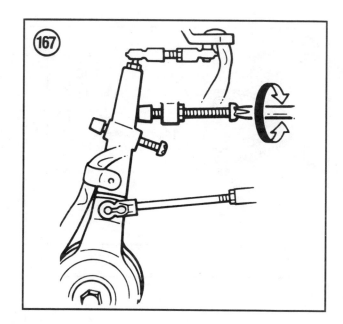

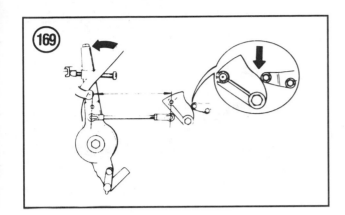

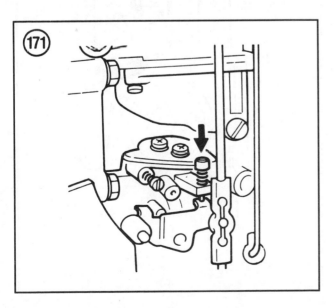

8. Adjust the idle speed screw (**Figure 171**) in or out until the specified idle speed is obtained.

9. Shut the engine off and disconnect the portable tachometer. Remove the test propeller and install the standard propeller. See Chapter Nine.

10. Adjust the throttle link as described in the following procedure.

11. Install the engine cover.

Carburetor Linkage Adjustment

Refer to **Figure 172** for this procedure.

1. Remove the engine cover.

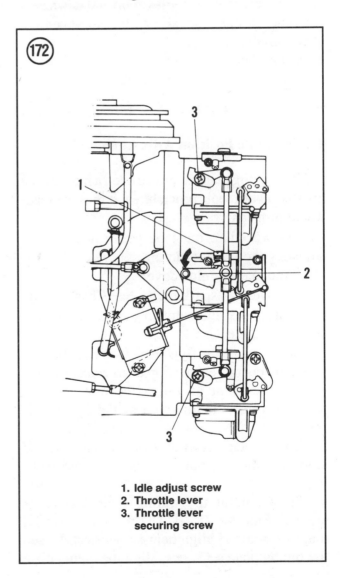

1. Idle adjust screw
2. Throttle lever
3. Throttle lever securing screw

2. Loosen the carburetor idle adjust screw (1, **Figure 172**) and close the throttle valve.

NOTE
The throttle lever screws have left-hand threads. Turn the screws clockwise to loosen and counterclockwise to tighten.

3. Loosen the throttle lever securing screws (3, **Figure 172**) on the upper and lower carburetors.

4. While lightly pushing the throttle lever (2, **Figure 172**) on the middle carburetor downward to the full-closed position, tighten the throttle lever securing screw on the upper and lower carburetors.

5. Move the accelerator lever up and down several times to make sure all 3 carburetors open and close simultaneously.

6. Install the engine cover.

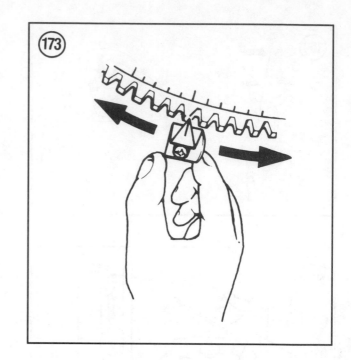

C115 MODELS

Timing Plate Position Adjustment

If the timing plate is moved even a little during inspection or repair procedures, it must be readjusted properly.

This procedure must be performed prior to adjusting the ignition timing.

1. Remove the engine cover.

2. Remove all 4 spark plugs. See Chapter Four.

3. Install a dial indicator in the No. 1 cylinder spark plug hole.

4. Slowly rotate the flywheel *clockwise* and stop when the piston reaches top dead center (TDC). This is the point at which the dial indicator needle reverses its direction as the flywheel is rotated.

5. Slowly rotate flywheel *counterclockwise* and stop when the dial indicator reads 3.91 mm (0.15 in.) BTDC.

6. At this point the timing plate should be aligned with the 25° BTDC mark on the CDI magneto rotor. If alignment is incorrect, loosen the timing plate set screw, align the timing plate

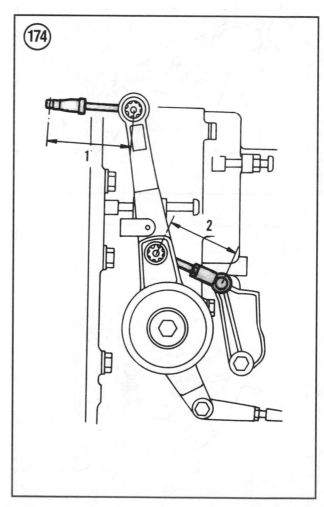

end with the 25° BTDC mark, then tighten the screw (**Figure 173**).

7. Remove the dial indicator. Install the spark plugs and the engine cover.

Timing Adjustment

NOTE
Check and adjust, if necessary, the timing plate position prior to checking and adjusting the timing.

1. Remove the standard propeller and install a test propeller. See Chapter Nine.

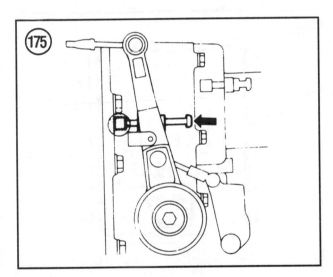

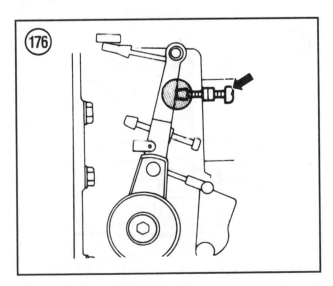

2. Install the outboard in a test tank.
3. Remove the engine cover.

NOTE
The following dimensions are preliminary adjustments and will probably be changed to a different length during this procedure.

4. Perform a preliminary link length adjustment on both the magneto control link and throttle cam control link. Loosen the locknut on the links and adjust the lengths (**Figure 174**) to the following dimension:
   a. Magneto control link length (1, **Figure 174**): 60 mm (2.36 in.).
   b. Throttle cam control link length (2, **Figure 174**): 53 mm (2.09 in.).

Do not tighten the locknuts at this time.
5. Connect a timing light to the No. 1 cylinder and a portable tachometer according to their manufacturer's instructions.
6. Shift into NEUTRAL.
7. Start the engine and allow it to warm up for approximately 5 minutes. Let the engine idle at 700-800 rpm.
8. Manually full-retard the ignition.
9. Point the timing light at the timing plate and the timing indicator. It should align with the 5° ATDC mark.
10. If the timing pointer does not align as specified in Step 9, loosen the locknut, turn the screw (**Figure 175**) and adjust the timing as necessary.
11. Manually move the magneto control lever to the wide-open throttle position (full-advanced ignition).
12. Increase engine speed to more than 4,500 rpm.
13. Point the timing light at the timing plate and the timing indicator. It should align with the 25° BTDC mark.
14. If the timing pointer does not align as specified in Step 13, loosen the locknut, turn the screw (**Figure 176**) and adjust the timing as necessary. Tighten the locknut.

15. Turn the engine off.

16. To adjust the pickup timing, perform the following:

    a. Disconnect the throttle cam control link (**Figure 177**).

    b. Slowly rotate flywheel *clockwise* and stop when the timing plate is aligned with the 4° BTDC mark (**Figure 178**).

    c. Align the mark on the pulser assembly arm with the timing mark on the flywheel rotor (**Figure 179**).

    d. Loosen the roller adjusting screw and adjust so the mark on the throttle cam is centered on the roller (**Figure 180**). The throttle valve should not open.

    e. Loosen the locknut on the throttle cam control link joint. Adjust the plastic snap-on connector on the end of the link rod until its hole aligns with the set pin. Install the link joint.

17. Disconnect the timing light and the tachometer. Remove the test propeller and install the standard propeller. See Chapter Nine. Install the engine cover.

Idle Speed Adjustment

> *NOTE*
> *Adjust timing prior to adjusting the idle speed.*

1. Remove the standard propeller and install a test propeller. See Chapter Nine.

2. Install the outboard in a test tank.

3. Remove the engine cover.

4. Connect a portable tachometer according to its manufacturer's instructions.

5. Turn the pilot screw (**Figure 181**) in until it *lightly* seats, then back it out 5/8 of a turn. Repeat for the other carburetors.

6. Adjust the idle speed screw (**Figure 182**) in 1-1 1/8 turns from the position where the throttle valve begins to move.

7. Start the engine, place it in NEUTRAL and warm it to the normal operating temperature.

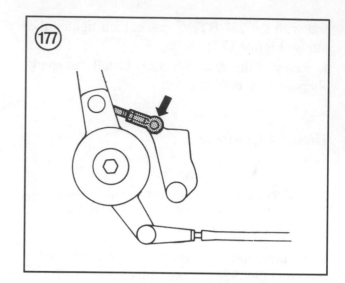

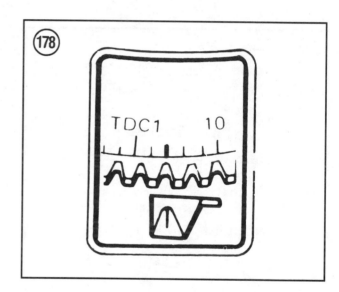

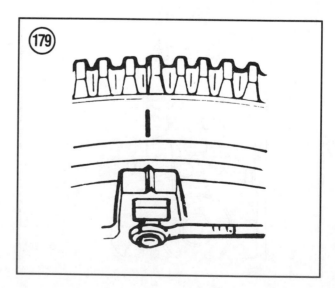

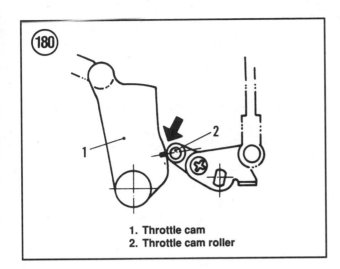

1. Throttle cam
2. Throttle cam roller

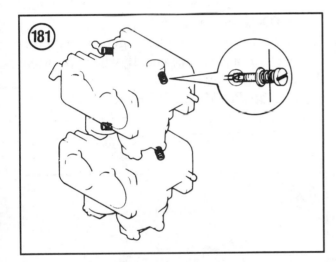

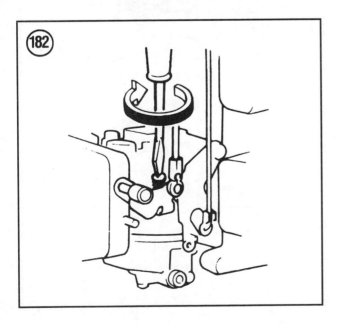

8. Observe the engine speed on the tachometer and compare to the specification listed in the appropriate table at the end of this chapter. If out of specification, perform Step 9.

9. Adjust the idle speed screw (**Figure 181**) in or out until the specified idle speed is obtained.

10. Shut the engine off and disconnect the portable tachometer. Remove the test propeller and install the standard propeller. See Chapter Nine.

11. Adjust the throttle link as described in the following procedure.

12. Install the engine cover.

Carburetor Linkage Adjustment

Refer to **Figure 183** for this procedure.

1. Remove the engine cover.

CAUTION
The throttle lever screws have left-hand threads. Turn the screws clockwise to loosen and counterclockwise to tighten.

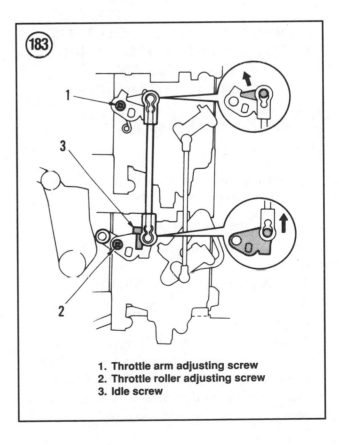

1. Throttle arm adjusting screw
2. Throttle roller adjusting screw
3. Idle screw

5

2. Loosen the roller adjusting screw (2, **Figure 183**) and the throttle arm adjusting screw (1, **Figure 183**).

3. Loosen the carburetor idle adjust screw (3, **Figure 183**) and completely close all throttle valves.

4. With the throttle valves on both carburetors fully closed, tighten the roller adjusting screw and the throttle arm adjusting screw.

5. Remove the play in the throttle link and throttle arm ball joint so that the upper and lower throttle valves open simultaneously.

6. Tighten the idle adjust screw into the original position.

7. Move the accelerator lever up and down several times to make sure all 3 carburetors open and close simultaneously.

8. Perform Step 16 (pick-up timing) of *Timing adjustment* in this chapter.

9. Install the engine cover.

115 HP, PRO V 115, 130 HP V4; 150 HP, PRO V 150, 175 HP, PRO V 175, 200 HP, PRO V 200 AND 225 HP 90° V6 MODELS

Timing Adjustment (Static)

NOTE
Yamaha does not provide a dynamic timing procedure for these models.

1. Remove the engine cover.

2. Move the shift lever to the NEUTRAL position.

3. Remove the spark plugs. See Chapter Four.

4. Install a dial indicator in the No. 1 cylinder spark plug hole.

5. Slowly rotate the flywheel *clockwise* and stop when the piston reaches top dead center (TDC). This is the point at which the dial indicator needle reverses its direction as the flywheel is rotated.

NOTE
Steps 6-11 are for the ignition timing at full-advance.

6. Slowly rotate flywheel *counterclockwise* and position the piston at the following BTDC dimension:

  a. 115 hp, Pro V 115: 3.91 mm (0.1539 in.) BTDC.

  b. 130 hp: 3.05 mm (0.1201 in.) BTDC.

  c. 150 hp: 3.61 mm (0.1421 in.) BTDC.

  d. Pro V 150: 2.05 mm (0.0807 in.) BTDC.

  e. 175, 200, 225 hp: 3.05 mm (0.1201 in.) BTDC.

  f. Pro V 175, Pro V 200: 2.53 mm (0.0996 in.) BTDC.

7. Check the timing pointer alignment with the flywheel timing scale. The flywheel position should be as follows:

  a. 115 hp, Pro V 115: 25° BTDC.

  b. 130 hp: 22° BTDC.

  c. 150 hp: 24° BTDC.

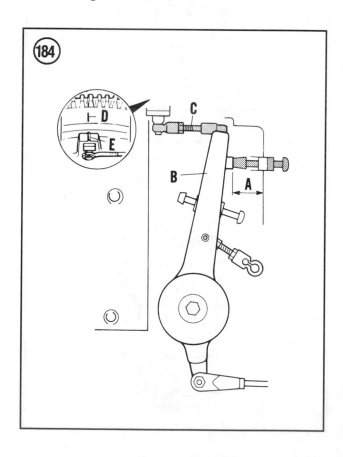

d. Pro V 150: 18° BTDC.

e. 175 hp, 200 hp, 225 hp: 22° BTDC.

f. Pro V 175, Pro V 200: 20° BTDC.

If not properly aligned, first repeat Step 6 to make sure the piston is at the correct BTDC location. Then loosen the timing plate set screw and move the plate as required to align the pointer with the flywheel BTDC mark (**Figure 173**), then tighten the set screw securely.

8. Loosen the locknut and adjust the length of the full-advance stopper (A, **Figure 184**) to the following specifications (dimension A):

a. 115 hp, Pro V 115: 26 mm (1.02 in.).

b. 130 hp: 29 mm (1.14 in.).

c. 150 hp: 17 mm (0.67 in.).

d. Pro V 150: 44.2 mm (1.74 in.).

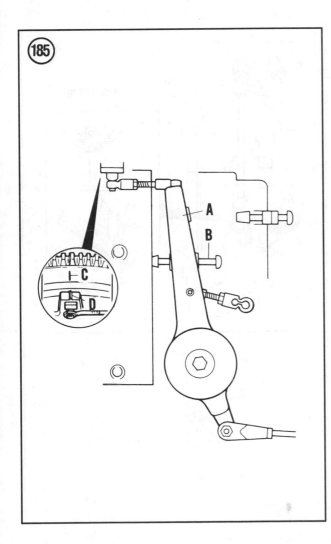

e. 175 hp, 200 hp: 20 mm (0.79 in.).

f. Pro V 175, Pro V 200: 41.5 mm (1.63 in.).

g. 225 hp: (information not available).

Tighten the locknut.

9. Disconnect the magneto control link from the base assembly.

10. Move the magneto control lever (B, **Figure 184**) to the full-advance position, until it touches the full-advance stopper.

11. Loosen the magneto control link locknut and adjust the length of the link (C, **Figure 184**) until the mark on the flywheel (D, **Figure 184**) aligns with the mark on the base assembly (E, **Figure 184**). Tighten the locknut and reinstall the control link.

NOTE
Steps 12-14 are for the ignition timing at full-retard.

12. Slowly rotate the flywheel *clockwise* and stop when the piston reaches the following ATDC dimension:

a. 115 hp, Pro V 115, 130 hp: 5° ATDC.

b. 150 hp, Pro V 150, 175 hp, Pro V 175, 200 hp, Pro V 200: 7° ATDC.

c. 225 hp: 6° ATDC.

13. Move the magneto control lever (A, **Figure 185**) to the full-retard position, until it touches the full-retard stopper (B, **Figure 185**).

14. Adjust the full-retard stopper so the mark on the flywheel (C, **Figure 185**) aligns with the mark on the base assembly (D, **Figure 185**).

15. Remove the dial indicator.

16. Install the spark plugs and engine cover.

Carburetor Linkage Adjustment

NOTE
Adjust the ignition timing prior to performing this procedure.

1. Remove the engine cover.

2. Remove the air silencer. See Chapter Six.

3. Move the throttle link up and down and observe the opening and closing of the throttle valves (**Figure 186**).

4. Loosen the idle adjust screw (A, **Figure 187**) and remove the screw from the throttle arm stopper (B, **Figure 187**).

> *CAUTION*
> *The throttle lever screws have left-hand threads. Turn the screws clockwise to loosen and counterclockwise to tighten.*

5. Loosen the throttle valve screw (C, **Figure 187**) and make sure the throttle valves are fully closed. Retighten the throttle valve screw.

6. Slowly tighten the idle adjust screw until it contacts the throttle arm stopper. From this position, further tighten the screw the following number of turns:

    a. 115 hp, Pro V 115, 130 hp, 225 hp: 1 1/8 turns.

    b. 150 hp, Pro V 150, 175 hp, Pro V 175, 200 hp, Pro V 200: 1 turn.

7. Move the throttle link up and down several times to make sure the carburetors open and close simultaneously.

8. Adjust the oil pump control link as described in one of the following procedures.

9. On 225 hp models, adjust the throttle sensor as described in one of the following procedures.

10. Install the silencer and the engine cover.

Carburetor Pickup Timing Adjustment

> *NOTE*
> *Adjust the ignition timing, carburetor linkage and idle speed prior to performing this procedure.*

1. Remove the engine cover.

2. Loosen the locknut and adjust the length of the throttle cam control link (A, **Figure 188**) to the following standard length (B, **Figure 188**):

    a. 115 hp, Pro V 115, 130 hp: 53.0 mm (2.09 in.).

    b. 150 hp, 175 hp, 200 hp: 42.5 mm (1.67 in.).

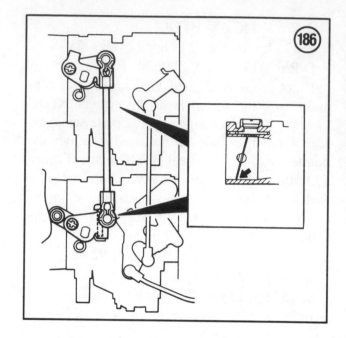

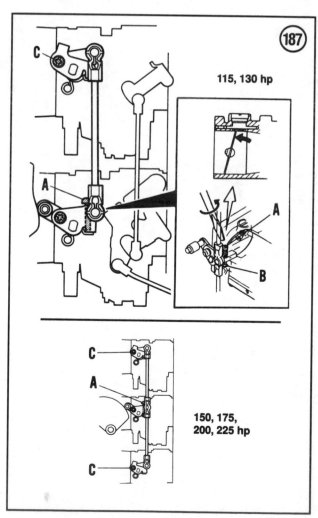

115, 130 hp

150, 175,
200, 225 hp

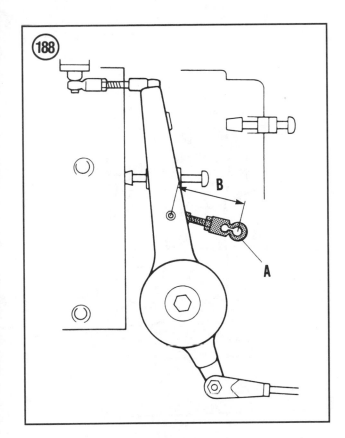

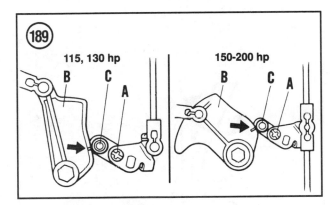

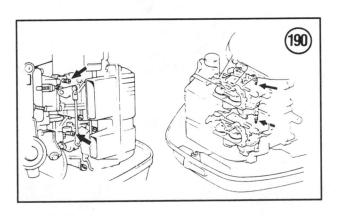

c. Pro V 150, Pro V 175, Pro V 200: 61.0 mm (2.40 in.).

d. 225 hp: 72.0 mm (2.83 in.).

Tighten the locknut.

3. Remove all spark plugs. See Chapter Four.

4. Slowly rotate the flywheel *clockwise* and stop when the timing plate is aligned with the following degree mark:

   a. 115 hp, Pro V 115, 130 hp: 4° ATDC.

   b. 150 hp, Pro V 150, 175 hp, Pro V 175, 200 hp, Pro V 200, 225 hp: 6° ATDC.

5. Align the magneto control lever so the mark on the flywheel aligns with the mark on the pulser assembly.

6. Loosen the throttle roller adjusting screw (A, **Figure 189**).

7. Align the mark on the throttle cam (B, **Figure 189**) with the center line on the throttle roller (C, **Figure 189**).

8. If alignment cannot be achieved in Step 7, loosen the locknut and adjust the length of the throttle cam control link (A, **Figure 188**). Tighten the locknut.

9. Tighten the throttle roller adjust screw.

10. Install the engine cover.

Idle Speed Adjustment

NOTE
Adjust ignition timing and carburetor linkage prior to adjusting the idle speed.

1. Remove the standard propeller and install a test propeller. See Chapter Nine.

2. Install the outboard in a test tank.

3. Remove the engine cover.

4. Connect a portable tachometer according to its manufacturer's instructions.

5. Turn the pilot screw (**Figure 190**) in until it *lightly* seats, then back it out the following number of turns:

   a. 115 hp, Pro V 115: 3/8-7/8 turns out.

   b. 130 hp: 5/8-1 1/8 turns out.

   c. 150 hp: 3/4-1 1/4 turns out.

d. Pro V 150, 175 hp, Pro V 200: 1 1/8-1 5/8 turns out.

e. Pro V 175: 1-1 1/2 turns out.

f. 200 hp, port side—1-1 1/2 turns out; starboard side—1/2-1 turns out.

g. 225 hp: 7/8-1 3/8 turns out.

Repeat for the other carburetors.

6. Loosen the throttle roller adjust screw (A, **Figure 191**).

7. Start the engine, place it in NEUTRAL and warm it to normal operating temperature.

8. Set the magneto control lever (B, **Figure 191**) to the full-retard position. Move it until it contacts the full-retard screw to the full-retard screw (C, **Figure 191**).

9. Observe the engine speed on the tachometer and compare to the specification listed in the appropriate table at the end of this chapter. If out of specification, perform Step 10.

10. Adjust the idle-speed screw (**Figure 192**) in or out until the specified idle speed is obtained.

11. Shut the engine off and disconnect the portable tachometer.

12. Install the engine cover.

**Throttle Sensor Adjustment
(225 hp Models Only)**

1. Remove the engine cover.

2. Loosen the idle adjust screw (**Figure 193**) to make sure the throttle valve is in the closed position.

3. Disconnect the 3-pin electrical connector (A, **Figure 194**) from the throttle sensor. Connect the test lead (part No. YB-6443) to each side of the disconnected 3-pin connector as shown in (B, **Figure 194**).

4. Connect the voltmeter (C, **Figure 194**) leads to the test lead as follows:

a. Voltmeter positive lead to the pink terminal connector.

b. Voltmeter negative lead to the orange terminal connector.

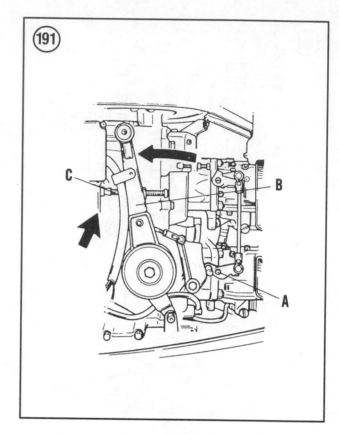

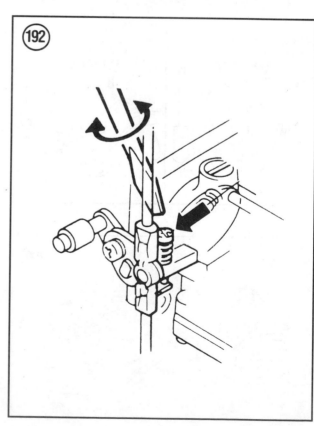

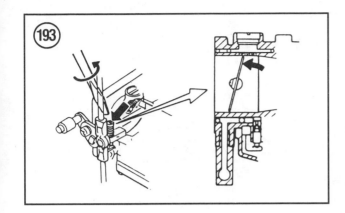

5. Turn the main switch to the ON position and measure the voltage. The correct voltage is 0.49-0.51 volts. If voltage is not as specified, perform Step 5.

6. Loosen the throttle sensor mounting screws and slowly turn the throttle sensor (**Figure 195**) until the specified voltage is obtained. Tighten the screws.

7. Disconnect the voltmeter and the test lead. Reconnect the 3-pin electrical connector.

8. Adjust the idle speed as described in this chapter.

9. Install the engine cover.

5

Oil Pump Link Adjustment

Refer to **Figure 196** for this procedure.

1. Remove the engine cover.

2. Remove the clip and washer and disconnect the control link (A, **Figure 196**) from the oil pump.

3. Loosen the idle adjust screw (B, **Figure 196**) and make sure the screw is not touching the

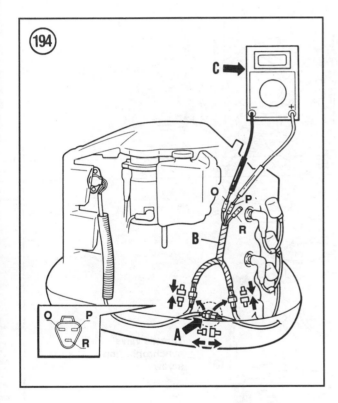

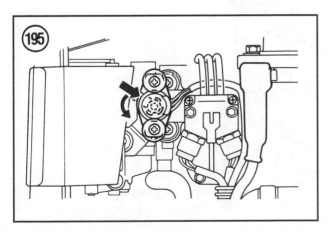

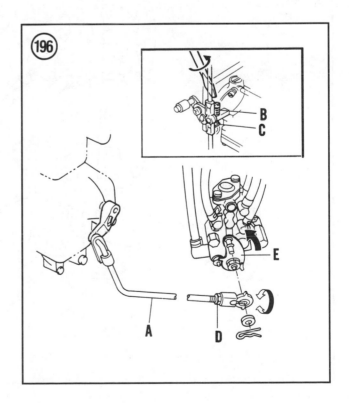

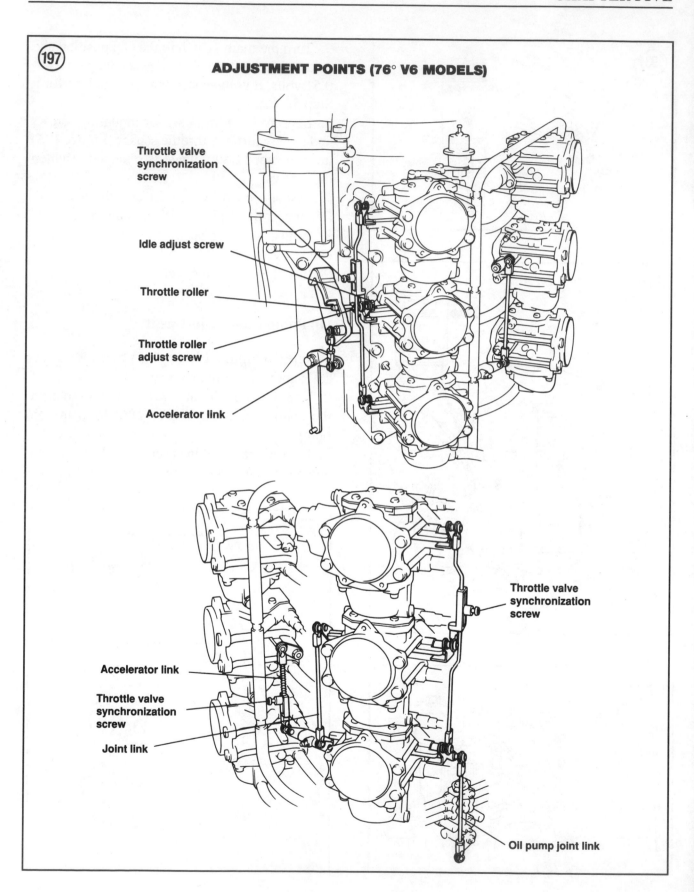

⑲⑦

ADJUSTMENT POINTS (76° V6 MODELS)

Throttle valve synchronization screw

Idle adjust screw

Throttle roller

Throttle roller adjust screw

Accelerator link

Throttle valve synchronization screw

Accelerator link

Throttle valve synchronization screw

Joint link

Oil pump joint link

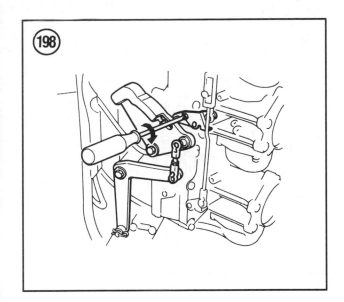

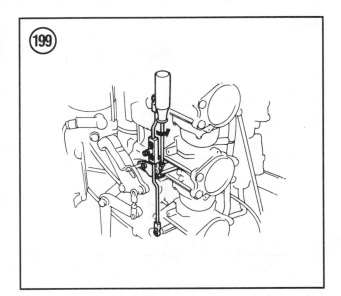

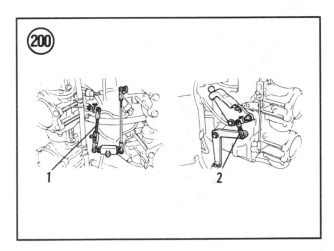

throttle arm stopper (C, **Figure 196**). Make sure the throttle valves are fully closed.

4. Loosen the oil control link locknut (D, **Figure 196**).

5. Hold the oil injection pump lever (E, **Figure 196**) in the fully closed position, then adjust the control link length and reinstall it onto the oil pump.

6. Tighten the locknut.

7. Adjust the carburetor linkage as described in this chapter.

225 HP, 250 HP 76° V6 MODELS

NOTE
The 225 hp and 250 hp 76° V6 models are equipped with the Yamaha Microcomputer Ignition System (YMIS) and do not require timing advance adjustment.

Carburetor Linkage Adjustment

Refer to **Figure 197** for this procedure.

1. Remove the engine cover.

2. Remove the air silencer. See Chapter Six.

3. Move the throttle link up and down and make sure the throttle valves are completely closed when the throttle valve control lever is in the fully closed position. If not, continue with this procedure.

NOTE
The throttle roller adjust screw has left-hand threads. Turn the screw clockwise to loosen and counterclockwise to tighten.

4. Loosen the throttle roller adjust screw (**Figure 198**).

5. Turn the starboard middle carburetor idle adjust screw *counterclockwise* until it does not touch the throttle linkage (**Figure 199**).

6. Disconnect the No. 1 and No. 2 accelerator links from the ball joints (**Figure 200**).

7. Disconnect the link joint, adjust the length to 141.5 mm (5.571 in.) from center-to-center and reconnect it (**Figure 201**).

8. Remove the oil pump joint link (**Figure 202**).

9. Loosen the throttle valve synchronization screw on each set of carburetors. Push on the throttle valve pivots with your fingers to make sure each of the throttle valves are completely closed. Refer to **Figure 203** and **Figure 204**. With the throttle valves in the closed position, tighten the screws.

10. Connect the accelerator link (A, **Figure 205**) to the ball joint.

11. Loosen the throttle valve synchronization screw. Keep pushing the point (B, **Figure 205**) until all play is removed, then tighten the screw.

12. Hold the oil pump lever and oil pump control arm at the fully open position. Adjust the length of the oil pump control link to the correct length and reconnect it (**Figure 206**).

13. Slowly turn the No. 4 carburetor idle adjust screw *clockwise* until the throttle valve just starts to move (**Figure 207**). From this point, turn the screw an additional 1 1/2 turn.

14. Adjust the throttle roller (A, **Figure 208**) so the roller contacts the accelerator cam at the alignment mark (B, **Figure 208**). Tighten the screw.

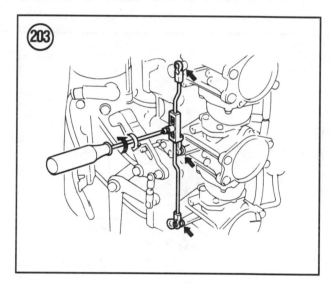

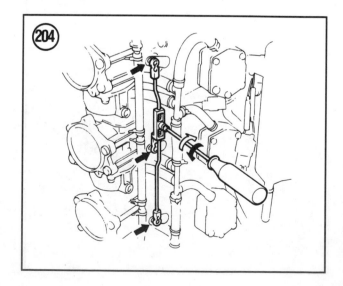

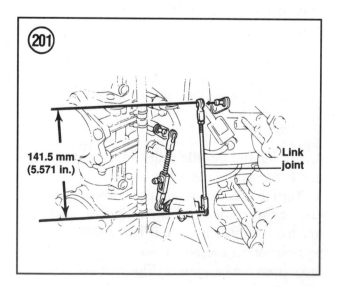

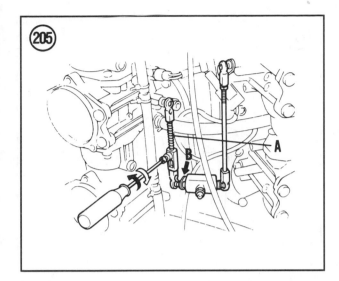

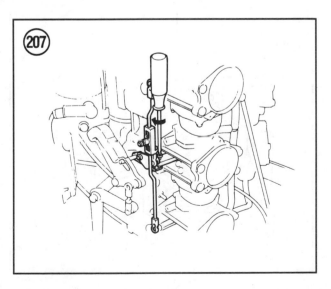

15. Adjust the length of the accelerator link (A, **Figure 209**) to 50 mm (1.97 in.) from center-to-center and reconnect it.

16. Move the throttle link up and down and make sure the throttle valves are completely closed when the throttle valve control lever is in the fully closed position.

17. Install the air silencer and the engine cover.

Carburetor Pickup Timing Adjustment

1. Remove the engine cover.

5

CAUTION
The throttle roller adjust screw has left-hand threads. Turn the screw clockwise

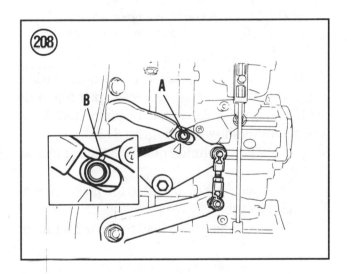

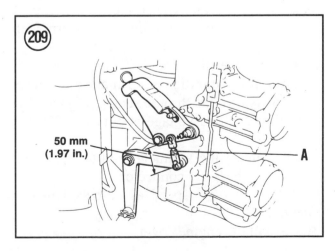

to loosen and counterclockwise to tighten.

2. Loosen the throttle roller adjust screw (**Figure 210**).

3. Adjust the throttle roller (A, **Figure 211**) so the roller contacts the accelerator cam at the alignment mark (B, **Figure 211**).

4. Tighten the throttle roller adjust screw.

5. Install the engine cover.

Throttle Sensor Adjustment

1. Remove the engine cover.

2. Remove the throttle lever rod (**Figure 212**) from the No. 1 carburetor.

CAUTION
Do not try to start the engine when this procedure and adjustments are in progress.

3. Disconnect the throttle sensor 3-pin electrical connector. Connect the test lead (part No. YB-6443) to each side of the disconnected 3-pin connector as shown in (**Figure 213**).

4. Connect the voltmeter leads to the test lead as follows:

    a. Voltmeter positive lead to the pink terminal connector.

    b. Voltmeter negative lead to the red terminal connector.

5. Turn the main switch to the ON position and measure the voltage. The correct voltage is 0.54 volts. If voltage is not as specified, perform Step 6.

6. Remove the silencer.

7. Loosen the throttle sensor mounting screws and slowly turn the throttle sensor (**Figure 214**) until the specified voltage is obtained. Tighten the screws.

8. Disconnect the voltmeter and the test lead. Reconnect the 3-pin connector.

9. Adjust the idle speed as described in this chapter.

10. Install the engine cover.

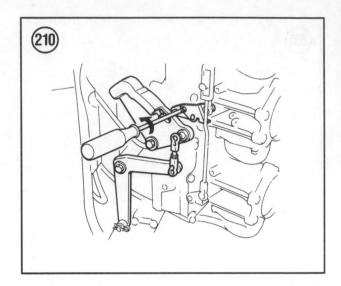

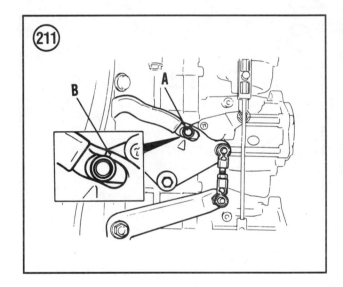

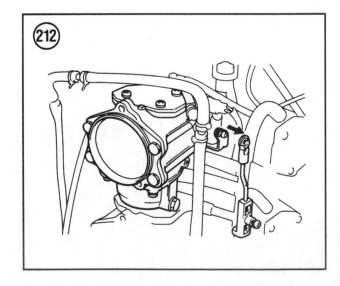

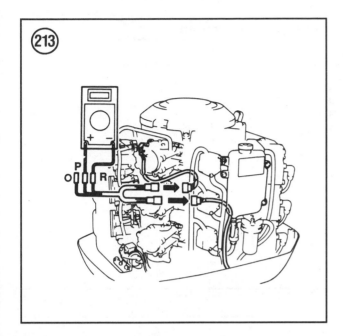

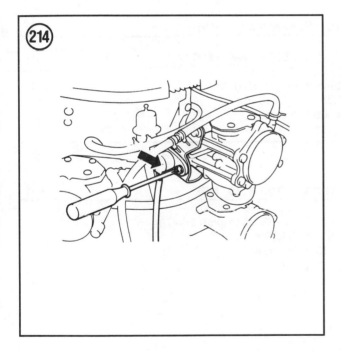

Idle Speed Adjustment

NOTE
Adjust the carburetor linkage prior to adjusting the idle speed.

1. Remove the standard propeller and install a test propeller. See Chapter Nine.
2. Install the outboard in a test tank.
3. Remove the engine cover.
4. Connect a portable tachometer according to its manufacturer's instructions.
5. Start the engine, place it in NEUTRAL and warm it to normal operating temperature.
6. Observe the engine speed on the tachometer and compare to the specification listed in the appropriate table at the end of this chapter. If out of specification, perform Step 7.

NOTE
The throttle roller adjust screw has left-hand threads. Turn the screw clockwise to loosen and counterclockwise to tighten.

7. Loosen the throttle roller adjust screw (**Figure 210**).
8. Turn the idle adjust screw on the No. 4 carburetor and adjust the throttle opening angle so that the idle speed stays within the specification listed in **Table 18**.
9. Adjust the carburetor pickup timing as described in this chapter.
10. Shut the engine off and disconnect the portable tachometer. Remove the test propeller and install the standard propeller. See Chapter Nine.
11. Install the engine cover.

Tables 1-28 are on the following pages.

5

Table 1 TEST PROPELLER RECOMMENDATIONS

Engine	Part No.
2, 3 hp	*
4, 5 hp	90890-01630
6, 8 hp	90890-01625
9.9, 15 hp	YB-1619
C25, 25 hp, 30 hp	YB-1621
C40, C55	YB-1611
C30	YB-1629
40 hp, 50 hp, Pro 50, Pro 60, 70 hp, 90 hp	YB-1611
C75, C85	YB-1620
115 hp, C115, 130 hp	YB-1624
150 hp, Pro V 150, 175 hp,	YB-1626
200 hp, Pro V 200, 225 hp	
(90 ° V6)	*
225 hp, L225, 250 hp, L250	
(76 ° V6)	*

* Information not available.

Table 2 TUNE-UP SPECIFICATIONS (2 HP)

Spark plug	
Type	NGK B5HS, Champion L90
Gap	0.6 mm (0.024 in.)
Torque	20-25 N•m (14-18 ft.-lb.)
Breaker point gap (1990-1994)	0.35 mm (0.014 in.)
Full throttle rpm	4,000-5,000 rpm
Idle rpm	1,150 ± 50 rpm

Table 3 TUNE-UP SPECIFICATIONS (3 HP)

Spark plug	
Type	NGK B6HS-10, Champion L86C
Gap	1.0 mm (0.039 in.)
Torque	25 N•m (18 ft.-lb.)
Idle timing	6 ± 2° BTDC
Maximum timing	21 ± 3° BTDC
Full throttle rpm	4,500-5,500 rpm
Idle rpm	
In neutral	1,200 rpm
In gear (trolling)	1,050 rpm
Carburetor pilot screw turns out	1 1/4 turns

Table 4 TUNE-UP SPECIFICATIONS (4 HP, 5 HP)

Spark plug	
Type	NGK B7HS, Champion L82C
Gap	0.6 mm (0.024 in.)
Torque	25 N•m (18 ft.-lb.)
Idle timing	6 ± 3° BTDC

(continued)

Table 4 TUNE-UP SPECIFICATIONS (4 HP, 5 HP) (continued)

Maximum timing	28 ± 3° BTDC
Full throttle rpm	4,500-5,500 rpm
Idle rpm	
In neutral	1,150 rpm
In gear (trolling)	1,000 rpm
Carburetor pilot screw turns out	
4 hp	1 3/4 turns
5 hp	1 5/8 turns

Table 5 TUNE-UP SPECIFICATIONS (6 HP, 8 HP)

Spark plug	
Type	NGK B7HS-10, Champion L82C
Gap	1.0 mm (0.039 in.)
Torque	25 N•m (18 ft.-lb.)
Idle timing	4 ± 1° BTDC
Maximum timing	35 ± 1° BTDC
Full throttle rpm	
6 hp	4,000-5,000 rpm
8 hp	4,500-5,500 rpm
Idle rpm	
In neutral	900 rpm
In gear (trolling)	800 rpm
Carburetor pilot screw turns out	1 1/8 turns

Table 6 TUNE-UP SPECIFICATIONS (9.9 HP, 15 HP)

Spark plug	
Type	NGK B7HS-10, Champion L82C
Gap	1.0 mm (0.039 in.)
Torque	25 N•m (18 ft.-lb.)
Idle timing	5 ± 1° BTDC
Maximum timing	30 ± 1° BTDC
Full throttle rpm	4,500-5,500 rpm
Idle rpm	
In neutral	900 rpm
In gear (trolling)	750 rpm
Carburetor pilot screw turns out	1 1/4 turns

Table 7 TUNE-UP SPECIFICATIONS (C25)

Spark plug	
Type	NGK B7HS, Champion L82C
Gap	0.6 mm (0.024 in.)
Torque	28 N•m (20 ft.-lb.)
Idle timing	2 ± 1° ATDC
Maximum timing	24 ± 1° BTDC
Full throttle rpm	4,500-5,500 rpm
Idle rpm	
In neutral	950 rpm
In gear (trolling)	850 rpm
Carburetor pilot screw turns out	1 1/2 turns

5

Table 8 TUNE-UP SPECIFICATIONS (25 HP)

Spark plug	
Type	NGK B7HS-10, Champion L82C
Gap	1.0 mm (0.039 in.)
Torque	25 N•m (18 ft.-lb.)
Idle timing	2 ± 1° ATDC
Maximum timing	24 ± 1° BTDC
Full throttle rpm	5,000-6,000 rpm
Idle rpm	
In neutral	750 rpm
In gear (trolling)	600 rpm
Carburetor pilot screw turns out	2 turns

Table 9 TUNE-UP SPECIFICATIONS (C30 HP)

Spark plug	
Type	NGK B8HS-10, Champion L78C
Gap	1.0 mm (0.039 in.)
Torque	28 N•m (20 ft.-lb.)
Idle timing	2 ± 1° ATDC
Maximum timing	25 ± 1° BTDC
Full throttle rpm	4,500-5,500 rpm
Idle rpm	
In neutral	1,150 rpm
In gear (trolling)	950 rpm
Carburetor pilot screw turns out	1 1/2 turns

Table 10 TUNE-UP SPECIFICATIONS (30 HP)

Spark plug	
Type	NGK B7HS-10, Champion L82C
Gap	1.0 mm (0.039 in.)
Torque	25 N•m (18 ft.-lb.)
Idle timing	5 ± 1° ATDC
Maximum timing	25 ± 1° BTDC
Full throttle rpm	4,500-5,500 rpm
Idle rpm	
In neutral	750 rpm
In gear (trolling)	650 rpm
Carburetor pilot screw turns out	
Top carburetor	3/4 turns
Center carburetor	
1990-1992	1 1/4 turns
1993-on	1 3/4 turns
Bottom carburetor	1 turn

Table 11 TUNE-UP SPECIFICATIONS (C40)

Spark plug	
Type	NGK B8HS, Champion L78C
Gap	0.6 mm (0.024 in.)
Torque	25 N•m (18 ft.-lb.)
(continued)	

Table 11 TUNE-UP SPECIFICATIONS (C40) (continued)

Idle timing	2 ± 1° BTDC
Maximum timing	22 ± 1° BTDC
Full throttle rpm	4,500-5,500 rpm
Idle rpm	
In neutral	1,150 rpm
In gear (trolling)	950 rpm
Carburetor pilot screw turns out	1 3/4 turns

Table 12 TUNE-UP SPECIFICATIONS (40 HP)

Spark plug	
Type	NGK B7HS-10, Champion L82C
Gap	1.0 mm (0.039 in.)
Torque	25 N•m (18 ft.-lb.)
Idle timing	
1990-1994	5 ± 1° ATDC
1995	7 ± 1° ATC
Maximum timing	
1990-1994	25 ± 1° BTDC
1995	25 + 3, – 2° ATC
Full throttle rpm	4,500-5,500 rpm
Idle rpm	
In neutral	800 rpm
In gear (trolling)	600 rpm
Carburetor pilot screw turns out	
1990-1994	1 1/8 turns
1995	1 1/2 turns

Table 13 TUNE-UP SPECIFICATIONS (50 HP, PRO 50)

Spark plug	
Type	NGK B8HS-10, Champion L78C
Gap	1.0 mm (0.039 in.)
Torque	25 N•m (18 ft.-lb.)
Idle timing	
1990-1994	5 ± 1° ATDC
1995	7 ± 1° ATC
Maximum timing	
1990-1994	25 ± 1° BTDC
1995	25 + 3, – 2° ATC
Full throttle rpm	4,500-5,500 rpm
Idle rpm	
In neutral	800 rpm
In gear (trolling)	600 rpm
Carburetor pilot screw turns out	
1990-1994	1 3/4 turns
1995	
Manual start	1 5/8 turns
Electric start	1 3/8 turns

5

Table 14 TUNE-UP SPECIFICATIONS (C55)

Spark plug	
Type	NGK B8HS-10, Champion L78C
Gap	1.0 mm (0.039 in.)
Torque	25 N•m (18 ft.-lb.)
Idle timing	5 ± 1° ATDC
Maximum timing	26 ± 1° BTDC
Full throttle rpm	4,500-5,500 rpm
Idle rpm	
In neutral	1,100 rpm
In gear (trolling)	800 rpm
Carburetor pilot screw turns out	
1990-1994	2 turns
1995	2 1/4 turns

Table 15 TUNE-UP SPECIFICATIONS (PRO 60)

Spark plug	
Type	NGK B8HS-10, Champion L78C
Gap	1.0 mm (0.039 in.)
Torque	25 N•m (18 ft.-lb.)
Idle timing	7 ± 1° ATDC
Maximum timing	22 ± 1° BTDC
Full throttle rpm	4,500-5,500 rpm
Idle rpm	
In neutral	800 rpm
In gear (trolling)	600 rpm
Carburetor pilot screw turns out	
1991	1 1/4 turns
1992-on	1 1/2 turns

Table 16 TUNE-UP SPECIFICATIONS (70 HP)

Spark plug	
Type	NGK B8HS-10, Champion L78C
Gap	1.0 mm (0.039 in.)
Torque	25 N•m (18 ft.-lb.)
Idle timing	7 ± 1° ATDC
Maximum timing	20 ± 1° BTDC
Full throttle rpm	
1990-1991	4,500-5,500 rpm
1992-on	5,000-6,000 rpm
Idle rpm	
In neutral	800 rpm
In gear (trolling)	600 rpm
Carburetor pilot screw turns out	
1990-1991	1 3/8 turns
1992-on	1 1/4 turns

Table 17 TUNE-UP SPECIFICATIONS (C75, C85)

Spark plug	
Type	NGK B8HS-10, Champion L78C
Gap	1.0 mm (0.039 in.)
Torque	25 N•m (18 ft.-lb.)
	(continued)

Table 17 TUNE-UP SPECIFICATIONS (C75, C85) (continued)

Idle timing	7 ± 1° BTDC
Maximum timing	
C75	22 ± 1° BTDC
C85	24 ± 1° BTDC
Full throttle rpm	4,500-5,500 rpm
Idle rpm	
In neutral	800 rpm
In gear (trolling)	600 rpm
Carburetor pilot screw turns out	
C75	1 1/4 turns
C85	1 1/8 turns

Table 18 TUNE-UP SPECIFICATIONS (90 HP)

Spark plug	
Type	NGK B8HS-10, Champion L78C
Gap	1.0 mm (0.039 in.)
Torque	25 N•m (18 ft.-lb.)
Idle timing	
1990-1991	10 ± 1° ATDC
1992-on	8 ± 1° ATDC
Maximum timing	22 ± 1° BTDC
Full throttle rpm	4,500-5,500 rpm
Idle rpm	
In neutral	800 rpm
In gear (trolling)	600 rpm
Carburetor pilot screw turns out	
1990-1991	1 1/2 turns
1992-on	1 1/4 turns

Table 19 TUNE-UP SPECIFICATIONS (115 HP, C115, PRO V 115)

Spark plug	
Type	NGK B8HS-10, Champion L78C
Gap	1.0 mm (0.039 in.)
Torque	25 N•m (18 ft.-lb.)
Idle timing	5 ± 1° ATDC
Maximum timing	25 ± 1° BTDC
Full throttle rpm	4,500-5,500 rpm
Idle rpm	
In neutral	750 rpm
In gear (trolling)	650 rpm
Carburetor pilot screw turns out	5/8 turn

Table 20 TUNE-UP SPECIFICATIONS (130 HP, L130)

Spark plug	
Type	
1990-1993	NGK B9HS-10, Champion L77J4
1994-on	NGK BR9HS-10, Champion QL77CJ4
Gap	1.0 mm (0.039 in.)
Torque	25 N•m (18 ft.-lb.)
(continued)	

5

Table 20 TUNE-UP SPECIFICATIONS (130 HP, L130) (continued)

Idle timing	5 ± 1° ATDC
Maximum timing	22 ± 1° BTDC
Full throttle rpm	5,000-6,000 rpm
Idle rpm	
In neutral	750 rpm
In gear (trolling)	650 rpm
Carburetor pilot screw turns out	7/8 turn

Table 21 TUNE-UP SPECIFICATIONS (150 HP, L150)

Spark plug	
Type	
1990-1993	NGK B8HS-10, Champion L78C
1994-on	NGK BR8HS-10, Champion QL78C
Gap	1.0 mm (0.039 in.)
Torque	25 N•m (18 ft.-lb.)
Idle timing	7 ± 1° ATDC
Maximum timing	24 ± 1° BTDC
Full throttle rpm	4,500-5,500 rpm
Idle rpm	
In neutral	700 rpm
In gear (trolling)	575 rpm
Carburetor pilot screw turns out	
1990-1991	1 1/4 turns
1992-on	1 turn

Table 22 TUNE-UP SPECIFICATIONS (PRO V 150)

Spark plug	
Type	
1990-1993	NGK B8HS-10, Champion L78C
1994-on	NGK BR8HS-10, Champion QL78C
Gap	1.0 mm (0.039 in.)
Torque	25 N•m (18 ft.-lb.)
Idle timing	7 ± 1° ATDC
Maximum timing	28 ± 1° BTDC
Full throttle rpm	4,500-5,500 rpm
Idle rpm	
In neutral	
1990-1993	700 rpm
1994-on	750 rpm
In gear (trolling)	575 rpm
Carburetor pilot screw turns out	
1990-1991	
Port	1 1/4 turns
Starboard	3/4 turn
1992-on	1 3/8 turns

Table 23 TUNE-UP SPECIFICATIONS (175 HP, PRO V 175)

Spark plug	
Type	
1990-1993	NGK B8HS-10, Champion L78C
1994-on	NGK BR8HS-10, Champion QL78C
Gap	1.0 mm (0.039 in.)
Torque	25 N•m (18 ft.-lb.)
Idle timing	7 ± 1° ATDC
Maximum timing	
175 hp	22 ± 1° BTDC
Pro V 175	20 ± 1° BTDC
Full throttle rpm	4,500-5,500 rpm
Idle rpm	
In neutral	700 rpm
In gear (trolling)	575 rpm
Carburetor pilot screw turns out	
175 hp	1 3/8 turns
Pro V 175	1 1/4 turns

5

Table 24 TUNE-UP SPECIFICATIONS (200 HP, L200)

Spark plug	
Type	
1990-1993	NGK B8HS-10, Champion L78C
1994-on	NGK BR8HS-10, Champion QL78C
Gap	1.0 mm (0.039 in.)
Torque	25 N•m (18 ft.-lb.)
Idle timing	7 ± 1° ATDC
Maximum timing	22 ± 1° BTDC
Full throttle rpm	4,500-5,500 rpm
Idle rpm	
In neutral	700 rpm
In gear (trolling)	575 rpm
Carburetor pilot screw turns out	
Port	1 1/4 turns
Starboard	3/4 turn

Table 25 TUNE-UP SPECIFICATIONS (PRO V 200)

Spark plug	
Type	
1991-1993	NGK B9HS-10, Champion L77JC
1994-on	NGK BR9HS-10, Champion QL77JC4
Gap	1.0 mm (0.039 in.)
Torque	25 N•m (18 ft.-lb.)
Idle timing	7 ± 1° ATDC
Maximum timing	20 ± 1° BTDC
Full throttle rpm	4,500-5,500 rpm
Idle rpm	
In neutral	700 rpm
In gear (trolling)	575 rpm
Carburetor pilot screw turns out	1 3/8 turns

Table 26 TUNE-UP SPECIFICATIONS (225 HP 90° V6)

Spark plug	
Type	NGK BR9HS-10, Champion L77CJ4
Gap	1.0 mm (0.039 in.)
Torque	25 N•m (18 ft.-lb.)
Idle timing	6 ± 1° ATDC*
Maximum timing	22 ± 1° BTDC*
Full throttle rpm	5,000-6,000 rpm
Idle rpm	
In neutral	750 rpm
In gear (trolling)	600 rpm
Carburetor pilot screw turns out	1 1/8 turns

* Computer controlled, timing non-adjustable.

Table 27 TUNE-UP SPECIFICATIONS (225 HP, L225 76° V6)

Spark plug	
Type	NGK BR8HS-10, Champion QL78C
Gap	1.0 mm (0.039 in.)
Torque	25 N•m (18 ft.-lb.)
Idle timing	10 ± 1° ATDC*
Maximum timing	
Cylinders Nos. 1, 2, 5, 6	18 ± 1° BTDC*
Cylinders Nos. 3, 4	20 ± 1° BTDC*
Full throttle rpm	4,500-5,500 rpm
Idle rpm	
In neutral	700 rpm
In gear (trolling)	625 rpm
Carburetor pilot screw turns out	5/8 turn

* Computer controlled, timing non-adjustable.

Table 28 TUNE-UP SPECIFICATIONS (250 HP, L250 76° V6)

Spark plug	
Type	NGK BR8HS-10, Champion QL78C
Gap	1.0 mm (0.039 in.)
Torque	25 N•m (18 ft.-lb.)
Idle timing	6 ± 1° ATDC*
Maximum timing	18 ± 1° BTDC*
Full throttle rpm	4,500-5,500 rpm
Idle rpm	
In neutral	700 rpm
In gear (trolling)	625 rpm
Carburetor pilot screw turns out	5/8 turn

* Computer controlled, timing non-adjustable.

Chapter Six

Fuel System

This chapter contains removal, overhaul, installation and adjustment procedures for fuel pump(s), carburetor(s), portable fuel tank(s) and connecting lines used with the Yamaha outboards covered in this book. Carburetor specifications are listed in **Table 1** and reed stop specifications are listed in **Table 2**. **Tables 1** and **2** are at the end of the chapter.

NOTE
The "L" series engines (counter rotation models), are included in all procedures. Unless there is a separate procedure designated for an "L" series outboard, refer to the procedure that relates to the same horsepower rating. If you are working on an L200, refer to the 200 hp procedure.

FUEL SYSTEM CONNECTIONS

Connections between fuel system components may be secured with wire spring clips, plastic clamp bands or molded plastic connectors.

To remove the wire clip type, squeeze the ends together with pliers and slide the clip off the fuel fitting (**Figure 1**). Installation is the reverse of removal. Wire clips should be replaced when they have lost tension.

Plastic band clamps are reusable if removed properly. This type of clamp depends upon tension maintained by serrated teeth when the clamp is pulled tight (**Figure 2**). To remove the clamp, insert the tip of a small flat-blade screwdriver into the ends of the band. Pry the ends apart, pushing the longer end of the band to loosen it sufficiently to slide the clamp off the fuel fitting. To reinstall the clamp, position it on the fuel fitting and insert the loose end into the band, then pull it tight with a pair of pliers. The teeth will engage and hold the tension applied (**Figure 3**). These clamps should be routinely replaced especially if they become brittle.

The molded plastic connectors are used on various models in different locations. To disconnect the connector, release the locking loop on the female connector from the male connector and carefully pull both connectors apart (**Figure 4**). Pull on the connectors—*not* on the fuel hoses. Inspect the O-ring seal on the connector and replace if necessary. To reinstall, push the connectors together and securely lock the loop onto the male connector.

Pressure test the male portion of the molded connector. Attach a hand held vacuum/pressure pump (MityVac, or equivalent) to the fuel hose fitting of the male connector. Apply 50 kPa (7.1 psi) of pressure to the fitting (**Figure 5**). The connector should maintain this pressure for 10 seconds. If the connector fails this test, replace the connector assembly.

FUEL PUMPS

Some Yamaha outboards equipped with an integral fuel tank use a gravity flow fuel system (**Figure 6**) that requires no fuel pump. The diaphragm-type fuel pump used on Yamaha outboards with an internal and external fuel tank operates by crankcase pulsations. Since this type of fuel pump cannot create sufficient pressure to draw fuel from the tank during cranking, fuel is transferred to the carburetor for starting by hand

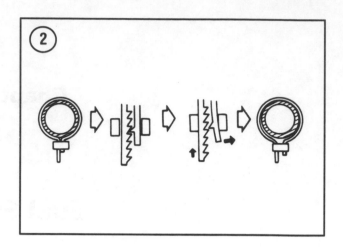

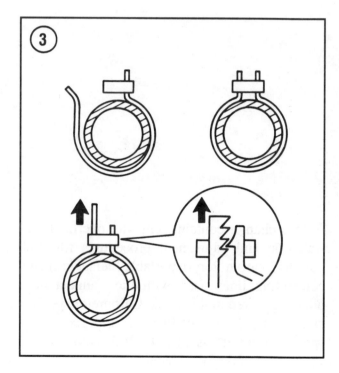

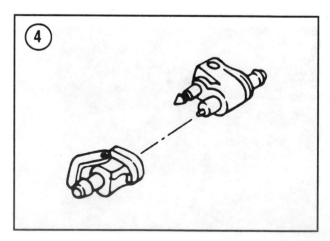

squeezing the primer bulb installed in the fuel line.

The carburetors on 40-90 hp (except "C" series) 3-cylinder models are equipped with a fuel enrichment pump that is built into the float bowl

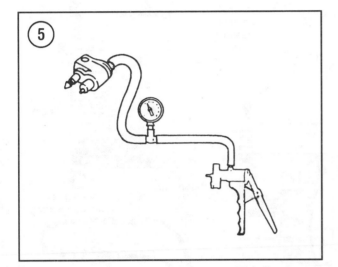

assembly. This fuel pump works along with the electrothermal valve to aid in cold starting.

Diaphragm Type Fuel Pump

Pressure pulsations created by movement of the pistons reach the fuel pump through a passageway between the crankcase and the pump.

Upward piston motion creates a low pressure on the pump diaphragm. This low pressure opens the inlet check valve in the pump, drawing fuel from the line into the pump. At the same time, the low pressure draws the air-fuel mixture from the carburetor into the crankcase.

Downward piston motion creates a high pressure on the pump diaphragm. This pressure closes the inlet check valve and opens the outlet check valve, forcing fuel into the carburetor and drawing the air-fuel mixture from the crankcase

6

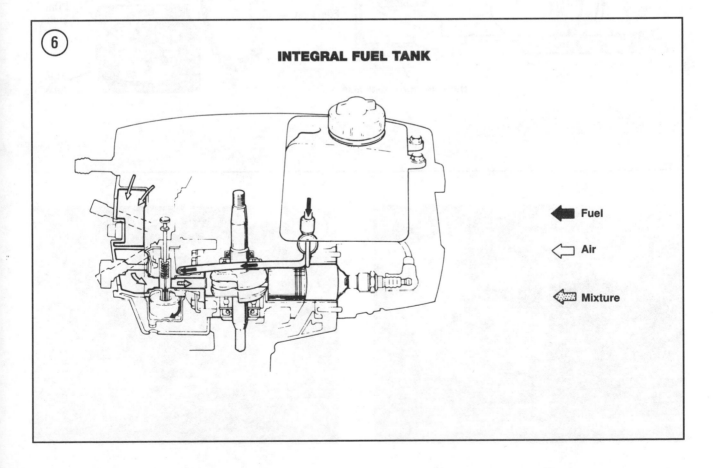

INTEGRAL FUEL TANK

➡ Fuel

⇦ Air

⬅ Mixture

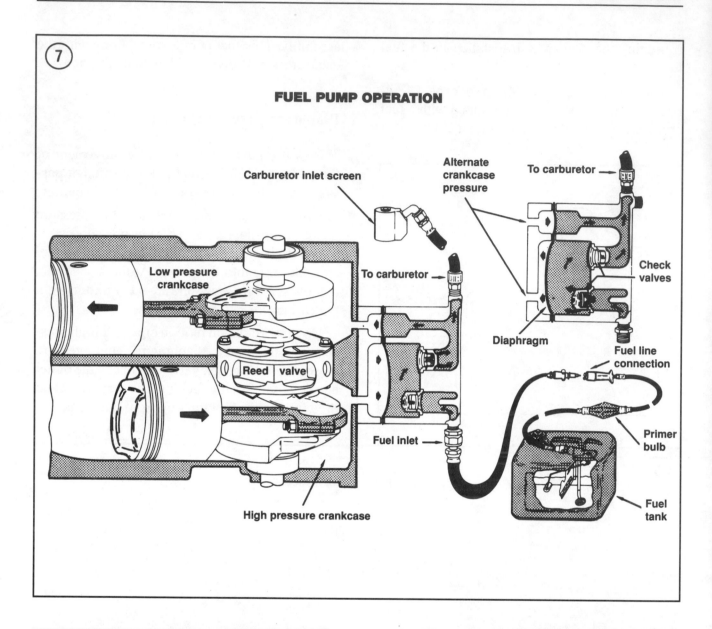

⑦

FUEL PUMP OPERATION

Carburetor inlet screen

Alternate crankcase pressure

To carburetor

Low pressure crankcase

To carburetor

Check valves

Reed valve

Diaphragm

Fuel line connection

Fuel inlet

High pressure crankcase

Primer bulb

Fuel tank

⑧

⑨

into the cylinder for combustion. **Figure 7** shows the operational sequence of a typical Yamaha fuel pump (high output models use two pumps). Outboard fuel pumps are extremely simple in design and are reliable in operation. Diaphragm failures are the most common problem, although the use of dirty or improper fuel/oil mixtures can cause check valve problems.

The fuel system is also equipped with a separate fuel filter.

Electric Fuel Pump

The 225 and 250 hp 76° V6 engines are equipped with an additional fuel feed pump that is connected to the fuel feed solenoid on each carburetor and is part of the prime start system.

Remote Diaphragm Fuel Pump Removal/Installation

1. Remove and discard any straps holding the carburetor fuel line to the fuel pump. Compress the fuel line fitting clamp with hose clamp pliers. Disconnect the fuel lines at from the pump (**Figure 8**, typical). Plug the fuel lines to prevent leakage.
2. Remove the screws holding the fuel pump assembly to the power head. Remove the fuel pump from the power head and discard the gasket.

3. Clean all gasket residue from the pump mounting pad. Work carefully to avoid gouging or damaging the mounting surface.
4. Installation is the reverse of removal, noting the following.
5. Use a new mounting gasket and install new clamp straps.

Integral Diaphragm Fuel Pump Removal/Installation

1. Remove the engine cover.
2. Disconnect the fuel line from the inlet cover (A, **Figure 9**). Plug the fuel line to prevent leakage.
3. Remove the 4 screws securing the fuel pump components to the side of the carburetor (B, **Figure 9**).
4. Remove the components.
5. Installation is the reverse of removal.

Remote Diaphragm Fuel Pump Inspection/Disassembly/Assembly

Refer to **Figure 10** or **Figure 11** as appropriate for this procedure.

> *WARNING*
> *In Step 1 and Step 2, do **not** suck on the fuel pump opening with your mouth as you may ingest any fuel remaining in the pump.*

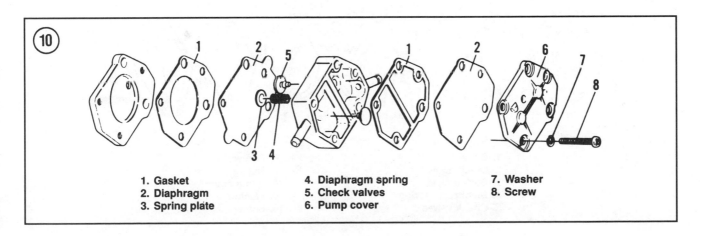

1. Gasket
2. Diaphragm
3. Spring plate
4. Diaphragm spring
5. Check valves
6. Pump cover
7. Washer
8. Screw

1. Test the pump *outlet* valve by pulling a vacuum or applying pressure through the outlet opening. Use a hand-held vacuum/pressure pump (MityVac, or equivalent) to perform the vacuum portion of the test. You should be able to draw air through it with the vacuum pump but not be able to blow air through the valve.

2. Test the pump *inlet* valve by pulling a vacuum or applying pressure through the outlet opening. Use a hand-held vacuum/pressure pump (Mity-Vac, or equivalent) to perform the vacuum portion of the test. You should be able to blow air through the valve but not be able to be able to draw air through it with the vacuum pump.

3. If the check valves do not operate as specified in Step 1 and Step 2, replace them as described in this chapter.

4. Remove the 3 screws securing the fuel pump assembly together (**Figure 12**). Separate the covers from the body.

5. Remove the diaphragms(s) and gaskets. Separate the diaphragms(s) from the gaskets. Discard all gaskets (**Figure 13**).

6. Note the position of the spring (5, **Figure 13**). Remove the spring and check valves. Some fuel pumps use a flat-type check valve diaphragm; others use metal reed valves secured by a small bolt and nut.

7. Clean and inspect the pump components as described in this chapter.

NOTE
Do not use any form of gasket sealer with the fuel pump gaskets.

8. Assembly is the reverse of disassembly. Note the following:

   a. Repeat Step 1 and Step 2 to test the check valve after installation. Install a new gasket and new diaphragms(s).

   b. Install the fuel pump as described in this chapter.

Integral Diaphragm Fuel Pump Disassembly/Assembly

There are several variations of the fuel pump design used on the different models. All operate essentially the same, but the parts within the fuel pump have slight variations. Note the location of the these parts and any spring location during disassembly.

Refer to **Figure 14**, typical, for this procedure:

1. Remove the screws and washers that hold the fuel pump assembly together.

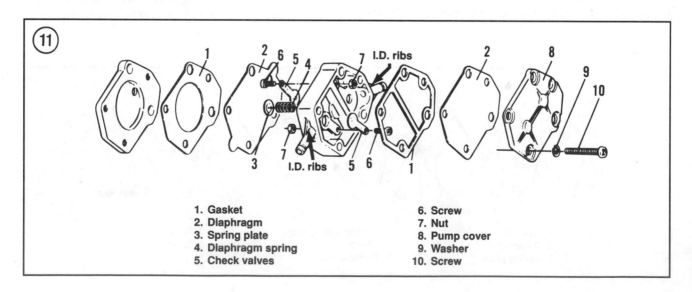

1. Gasket
2. Diaphragm
3. Spring plate
4. Diaphragm spring
5. Check valves
6. Screw
7. Nut
8. Pump cover
9. Washer
10. Screw

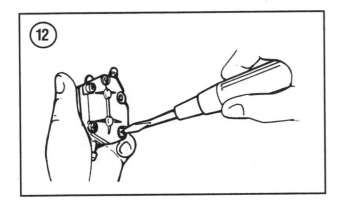

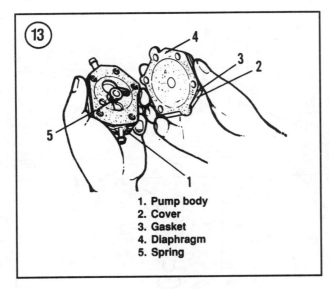

1. Pump body
2. Cover
3. Gasket
4. Diaphragm
5. Spring

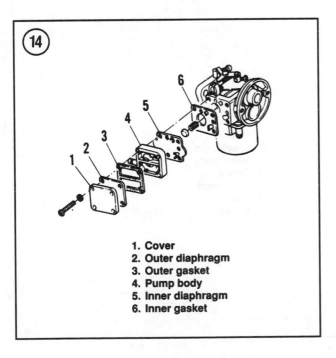

1. Cover
2. Outer diaphragm
3. Outer gasket
4. Pump body
5. Inner diaphragm
6. Inner gasket

2. Separate the pump covers, diaphragms, valve and strainer assembly and fuel pump body. Remove and discard all gaskets.

3. Clean and inspect the fuel pump components as described in this chapter.

4. Assembly is the reverse of disassembly. Install new gaskets.

Fuel Enrichment Fuel Pump Disassembly/Assembly

Refer to **Figure 15** for this procedure:

1. Remove the screws securing the fuel pump assembly to the float bowl.

2. Separate the pump cover, gaskets, diaphragm, valve body and valve seats. Discard all gaskets.

3. Clean and inspect the fuel pump components as described in this chapter.

4. Assembly is the reverse of disassembly. Install new gaskets.

Cleaning and Inspection (Remote Diaphragm Fuel Pump)

1. Clean all metal parts in solvent and blow dry with compressed air. Allow the check valves to air dry.

2. Inspect the check valves and replace any valve that is slightly warped, has weak tension or broken springs.

3. Inspect the pump body. Make sure the valve seats provide a flat contact area for the valve disc. Replace the pump body if cracks or rough gasket mating surfaces are found.

4. Check the body fitting. If loose or damaged, tighten or replace as required.

Cleaning and Inspection (Integral Diaphragm Fuel Pump)

1. Clean all metal parts in solvent and blow dry with compressed air.

6

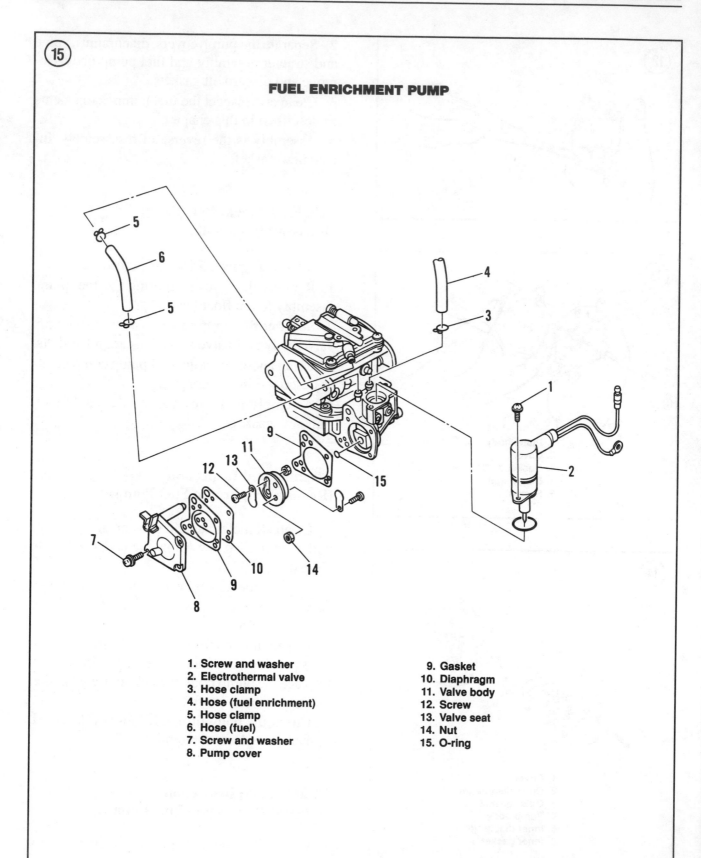

FUEL ENRICHMENT PUMP

1. Screw and washer
2. Electrothermal valve
3. Hose clamp
4. Hose (fuel enrichment)
5. Hose clamp
6. Hose (fuel)
7. Screw and washer
8. Pump cover

9. Gasket
10. Diaphragm
11. Valve body
12. Screw
13. Valve seat
14. Nut
15. O-ring

2. Inspect the check valve diaphragm for signs of warpage or other damage. Replace as required.

Cleaning and Inspection (Fuel Enrichment Fuel Pump)

1. Clean all metal parts in solvent and blow dry with compressed air.

2. Inspect the valve seats and the diaphragm for signs of warpage or other damage. Replace as required.

3. Make sure all valve body openings are clear.

Electric Fuel Pump Removal/Installation

NOTE
The electric fuel pump cannot be serviced. If defective, it must be replaced as a unit.

1. Remove the engine cover.

2. Turn the main switch to the OFF position.

3. Disconnect the electrical connector from the fuel pump.

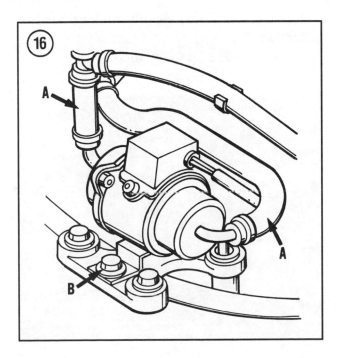

4. Disconnect both fuel lines (A, **Figure 16**) from the fuel pump. Plug the fuel lines to prevent leakage.

5. Remove the bolt (B, **Figure 16**) securing the fuel pump to the mounting bracket.

6. Remove the fuel pump.

7. Installation is the reverse of removal.

PRIME START SYSTEM

The 40-90 hp (except "C" series) 3-cylinder engines and all 225 hp and 250 hp V6 engines are equipped with the Prime Start system to aid in cold starting. Although the systems vary slightly among the different models, they all operate essentially the same. The Prime Start system basically allows additional fuel to be drawn into the engine during cold starts.

On 40-90 hp (except "C" series) 3-cylinder models, the amount of fuel enrichment is determined by the position of the metering rod connected to the electro-magnetic or electro-thermal valve mounted on one of the carburetor assemblies. The engine temperature is measured by a thermosensor mounted on the cylinder head.

The 225 hp 90° V6 models, are equipped with a fuel primer pump assembly that contains 2 electric solenoids and is controlled by the CDI unit. During cold starting, the CDI will open one or both of the solenoids (depending on engine temperature) to pump extra fuel to the primer ports on the intake manifold. The CDI unit also advances ignition timing from 7° ATDC to 7° BTDC. When the engine reaches normal operating temperature, the ignition timing will return to normal idle timing of 7° ATDC.

On 225 and 250 hp 76° V6 models, the electronically controlled carburetors and the CDI unit are controlled by the microprocessor. During cold starting, the computer will activate the solenoids on the carburetors depending on engine temperature. This allows the extra fuel supplied by the feed pump to pass into the intake manifold. The computer will also advance igni-

6

tion timing from 6° ATDC to 7° BTDC. When the engine reaches normal operating temperature, the ignition timing will return to the normal idle timing of 6° ATDC.

CARBURETORS

All carburetors used on Yamaha outboard motors use a fixed main jet and require no high-speed adjustment. A main jet with a smaller number should be substituted if the engine is used primarily at slow speeds or at high elevations. A larger number main jet should be substituted for use in extremely cold areas.

When installing a carburetor, make sure that the mounting nuts are securely tightened. A loose carburetor will cause a lean-running condition.

Before removing and disassembling any carburetor, be sure you have the correct overhaul kit, the proper tools and a sufficient quantity of fresh cleaning solvent.

Work slowly and carefully, follow the disassembly procedure and refer to the exploded drawing of your carburetor when necessary. When referring to the exploded drawing, note that not all carburetors will use all of the components shown.

Do not apply excessive force at any time.

It is not necessary to disassemble the carburetor linkage or remove the throttle cam or other external components. Remove the throttle or choke plate only if it is damaged or binds. Carburetor specifications are listed in **Table 1**.

THROTTLE PLUNGER CARBURETOR (2 HP)

Removal/Installation

1. Remove the screws securing the 2 halves of the engine cover. Remove the engine cover.
2. Loosen the screw holding the throttle lever knob (A, **Figure 17**). Remove the knob from the lever.

3. Loosen the screw holding the choke lever knob (A, **Figure 18**). Remove the knob from the lever.
4. Disconnect the white stop button lead from the magneto base connector (B, **Figure 17**).
5. Disconnect the black ground lead from the rewind starter bracket (C, **Figure 17**).
6. Remove the 2 screws holding the air intake silencer to the carburetor. Remove the air intake silencer.
7. Make sure the fuel line petcock is in the OFF position. Disconnect the fuel line at the carburetor (B, **Figure 18**). Plug the line to prevent leakage.
8. Loosen the clamp screw holding the carburetor to the reed valve housing (C, **Figure 18**). Remove the carburetor.
9. Remove and discard the O-ring inside the carburetor throat.
10. Installation is the reverse of removal. Note the following:
    a. Install a new O-ring in the carburetor throat.
    b. Tighten the clamp screw securely to prevent an air or fuel leak.

Disassembly

Refer to the following illustrations for this procedure:
    a. **Figure 19**: 2 hp (1990 models).

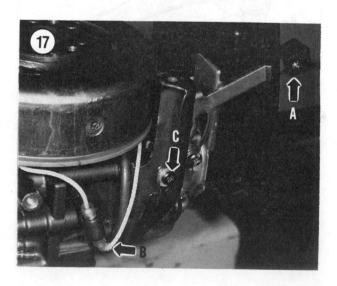

b. **Figure 20**: 2 hp (1991-on models).

1. Remove the throttle lever tension screw, spring and washer.

2. Remove the snap ring and pin holding the throttle lever to the bracket. Remove the throttle lever.

3. Remove the fuel bowl attaching screws. Separate the fuel bowl (A, **Figure 21**) from carburetor body. Remove and discard the fuel bowl gasket.

4A. On 1990 models, perform the following:

    a. Slide the float (B, **Figure 21**) off the main nozzle.

    b. Slide the float pivot pin from the float arm.

    c. Remove the float arm and needle valve (**Figure 22**).

4B. On 1991-on models, perform the following:

    a. Remove the float pivot pin.

    b. Remove the float and needle valve.

5. Remove the main nozzle (A, **Figure 23**) and the main jet assembly (B).

6. Unscrew the seat nut from the valve seat. Remove the fuel line connector and gaskets from the fuel seat (**Figure 24**).

7. Remove the valve seat (**Figure 25**).

8. Loosen the throttle stop screw and unscrew the retainer cap. Remove the cap with bracket and throttle valve assembly (**Figure 26**).

9. Disconnect the throttle plunger from the throttle needle. Remove the valve and spring plate. Make sure the tiny E-clip is intact on the throttle needle (**Figure 27**).

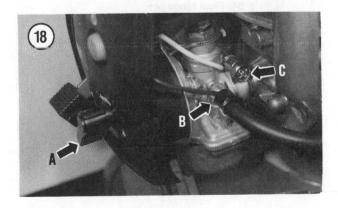

10. Lightly seat the pilot screw, counting the number of turns required for reinstallation reference. Back the screw out and remove from the carburetor (**Figure 28**).

11. Clean and inspect all parts as described under *Cleaning and Inspection (All Models)* in this chapter.

Assembly

Refer to the following illustrations for this procedure:

    a. **Figure 19**: 2 hp (1990 models).

    b. **Figure 20**: 2 hp (1991-on models).

1. Slide the spring onto the idle adjust screw and install the screw into the carburetor. Lightly seat the screw, then back it out the number of turns noted during *Disassembly* Step 10. This will result in approximately the correct idle speed when the engine is first started.

2. Make sure the E-clip is installed in the second notch from the top of the throttle needle. Fit the needle inside the throttle valve, then insert the spring plate.

3. Place the spring over the plunger cable. Compress the spring and connect the plunger to the throttle valve. Inserting the plunger cable through the slot in the side of the valve.

4. Install the throttle valve assembly into the carburetor. Position the slot in the valve over the idle mixture screw. Thread the retainer cap onto the carburetor body and tighten securely.

5. Install the inlet needle valve seat.

6. Install a gasket over the needle valve seat assembly, then thread the fuel line connector on the seat. Place the other gasket over the fuel line connector and install the needle valve nut.

7. Install the main nozzle into the carburetor body. The throttle needle must enter the nozzle.

8. Install the main jet into the main nozzle and tighten securely.

9A. On 1990 models, perform the following:

    a. Insert the needle valve into the float arm slot.

6

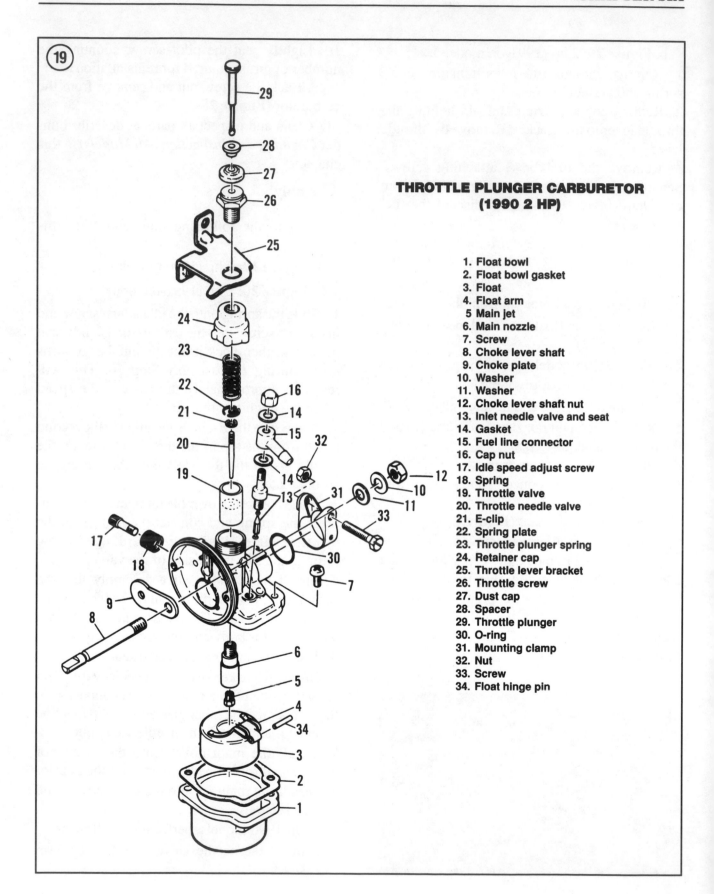

19

**THROTTLE PLUNGER CARBURETOR
(1990 2 HP)**

1. Float bowl
2. Float bowl gasket
3. Float
4. Float arm
5. Main jet
6. Main nozzle
7. Screw
8. Choke lever shaft
9. Choke plate
10. Washer
11. Washer
12. Choke lever shaft nut
13. Inlet needle valve and seat
14. Gasket
15. Fuel line connector
16. Cap nut
17. Idle speed adjust screw
18. Spring
19. Throttle valve
20. Throttle needle valve
21. E-clip
22. Spring plate
23. Throttle plunger spring
24. Retainer cap
25. Throttle lever bracket
26. Throttle screw
27. Dust cap
28. Spacer
29. Throttle plunger
30. O-ring
31. Mounting clamp
32. Nut
33. Screw
34. Float hinge pin

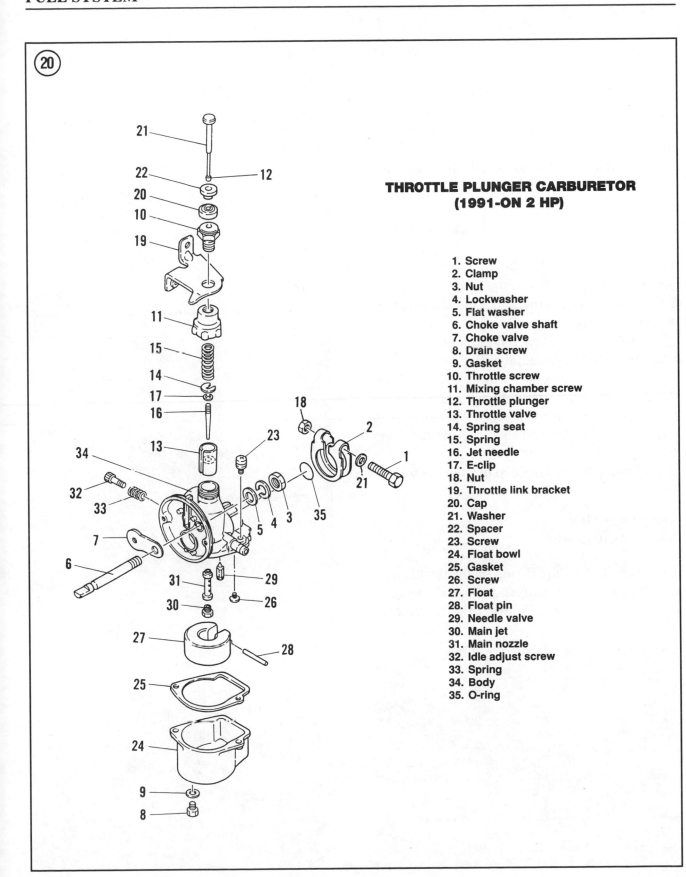

**THROTTLE PLUNGER CARBURETOR
(1991-ON 2 HP)**

1. Screw
2. Clamp
3. Nut
4. Lockwasher
5. Flat washer
6. Choke valve shaft
7. Choke valve
8. Drain screw
9. Gasket
10. Throttle screw
11. Mixing chamber screw
12. Throttle plunger
13. Throttle valve
14. Spring seat
15. Spring
16. Jet needle
17. E-clip
18. Nut
19. Throttle link bracket
20. Cap
21. Washer
22. Spacer
23. Screw
24. Float bowl
25. Gasket
26. Screw
27. Float
28. Float pin
29. Needle valve
30. Main jet
31. Main nozzle
32. Idle adjust screw
33. Spring
34. Body
35. O-ring

6

b. Install the float arm and needle valve, then install the float pivot pin.

c. Slide the float (B, **Figure 21**) onto the main nozzle.

9B. On 1991 and later models, perform the following:

a. Insert the needle valve in the float arm slot.

b. Install the float and needle valve.

c. Install the float pivot pin.

10. Install a new float bowl gasket on the carburetor body.

11. Check the float height and if necessary, adjust as described in this chapter.

12. Install the float bowl and screws. Tighten the screws securely.

13. Insert the mounting pin through the throttle lever and bracket. Install the snap ring.

14. Install the spring and washer over the throttle lever tensioner screw. Install the screw and tighten until the throttle lever can be moved with light force. This establishes the throttle lever bracket position.

15. Tighten the retainer cap throttle screw.

Mid-range Throttle
Needle Adjustment

The position of the E-ring on the throttle needle determines the proper low- and medium-speed range mixture (**Figure 29**). The standard

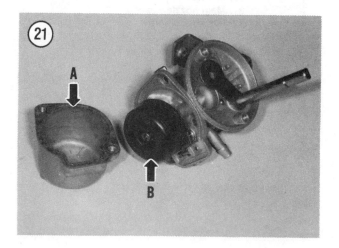

setting (the 2nd groove from the top) should be suitable for most operating conditions.

If a too-rich or too-lean condition results from extreme changes in elevation, temperature or humidity, the E-ring position can be changed. The closer the E-ring is installed to the top of the

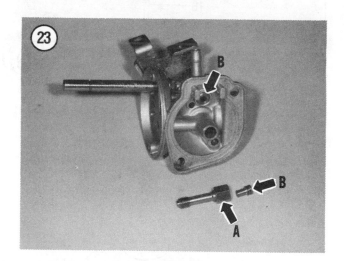

needle, the leaner the mixture. Remember, it is always preferable to run a slightly richer mixture than one that is too lean.

INTEGRAL FUEL PUMP CARBURETOR

An integral carburetor and fuel pump assembly is used on the 3-30 hp (except C25 and C30)

models. On 25 hp models, the fuel pump is located on the bottom carburetor and on 30 hp models, the fuel pump is located on the middle carburetor.

The fuel pump assembly on 3, 6, 8, 25 and 30 hp models is attached to the float bowl. On the 4, 5, 9.9 and 15 hp models, the fuel pump is attached to the carburetor body. Fuel pump location has no affect on the carburetor disassembly and assembly procedures.

Removal/Installation

1. Remove the engine cover.
2. On 9.9 and 15 hp models, perform the following:

6

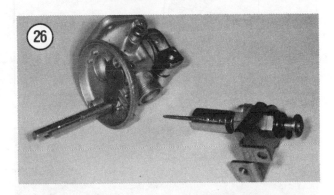

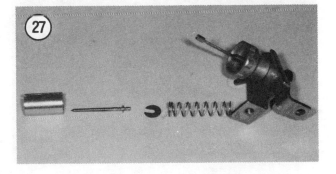

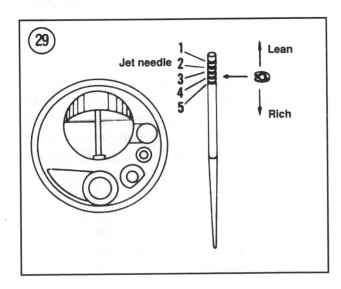

a. Fully open the choke valve, remove the O-ring (A, **Figure 30**) and disconnect the pull wire from the choke lever pin.

b. Remove the fuel enrichment valve (B, **Figure 30**).

3. On 6 and 8 hp models, perform the following:

a. Disconnect the choke joint link from the carburetor.

b. Remove the choke knob from the choke lever.

c. Remove the screws (A, **Figure 31**) securing the front panel and remove the panel (B, **Figure 31**).

4. Remove the air intake panel and gasket. **Figure 32** shows the cover on 4 and 5 hp models. On all other models, the covers are shaped differently but are removed in a similar manner (**Figure 33**).

5. On all models except 6 and 8 hp, disconnect the choke lever and bushing from the carburetor linkage (**Figure 34**, typical).

6. Disconnect the throttle cable or linkage from the carburetor. **Figure 35** shows a 4 and 5 hp model (3 hp similar). The 6 and 8 hp linkage is connected to the throttle lever on the port side of the carburetor (9.9 and 15 hp similar). On 25 and 30 hp models, disconnect the linkage from the carburetor being serviced or remove the carburetor assembly.

7. Disconnect the fuel line from the fuel pump. Plug the line to prevent leakage.

8. On models so equipped, disconnect the crankcase recirculation lines from the carburetor.

9. Remove the port side mounting nut and washer. Partially loosen the starboard nut, pull the carburetor forward and slide it to the port side. Remove the carburetor and gasket. Discard the gasket.

10. Installation is the reverse of removal. Install a new gasket and tighten the mounting nuts evenly and securely to prevent carburetor warpage and an air leak.

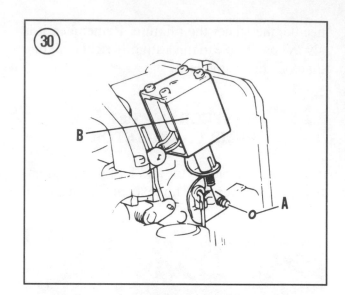

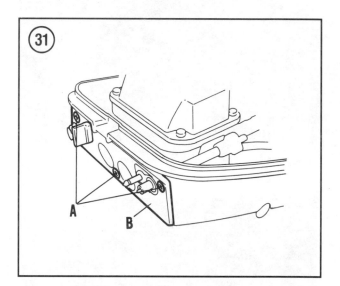

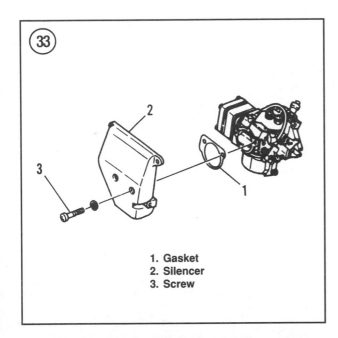

1. Gasket
2. Silencer
3. Screw

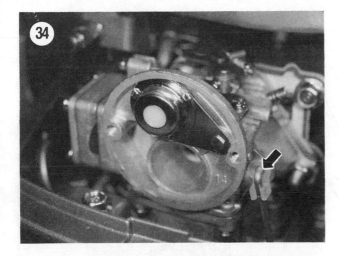

Disassembly

Refer to the following illustrations for this procedure:

    a. **Figure 36**: 3, 6 and 8 hp models.

    b. **Figure 37**: 4 and 5 hp models.

    c. **Figure 38**: 9.9 and 15 hp models.

    d. **Figure 39**: 25 hp models.

    e. **Figure 40**: 30 hp models.

1. Disassemble the fuel pump portion of the carburetor (**Figure 41**) as described in this chapter.

2. Remove the cover or mixing chamber cover and gasket (**Figure 42**). Discard the gasket.

3A. On 9.9 and 15 hp models, perform the following:

    a. Unscrew the main jet and gasket (A, **Figure 43**) from the bottom of the float bowl.

    b. Remove the float bowl (B, **Figure 43**) and gasket (C). Discard the gasket.

3B. On all other models, remove the screws and washer securing the float bowl. Remove the float bowl and gasket. Discard the gasket.

4A. On 6 and 8 hp models, perform the following:

    a. Remove the float pivot pin retaining screw (A, **Figure 44**).

    b. Remove the float pivot pin (B, **Figure 44**).

    c. Remove the float (C, **Figure 44**) and needle valve (D, **Figure 44**) as an assembly. Slide the valve off the float tang.

4B. On 9.9 and 15 hp models, perform the following:

    a. Carefully tap the float pivot pin out of the pivot pin bosses. Tap the pin out in the opposite direction as indicated by the raised arrow on the boss (**Figure 45**).

    b. Remove the float and needle valve as an assembly. Slide the valve off the float tang.

4C. On all other models, perform the following:

    a. Carefully tap the float pivot pin out of the pivot pin bosses.

    b. Remove the float and needle valve as an assembly. Slide the valve off the float tang.

6

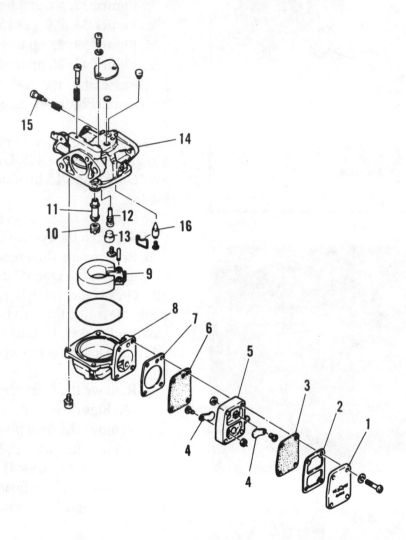

**INTEGRAL BOWL PUMP CARBURETOR
(3, 6 AND 8 HP)**

1. Pump cover
2. Gasket
3. Diaphragm
4. Check valve
5. Fuel pump body
6. Diaphragm
7. Gasket
8. Float chamber
9. Float
10. Main jet
11. Main nozzle
12. Idle jet
13. Seal
14. Mixing chamber
15. Idle mixture screw
16. Inlet needle valve

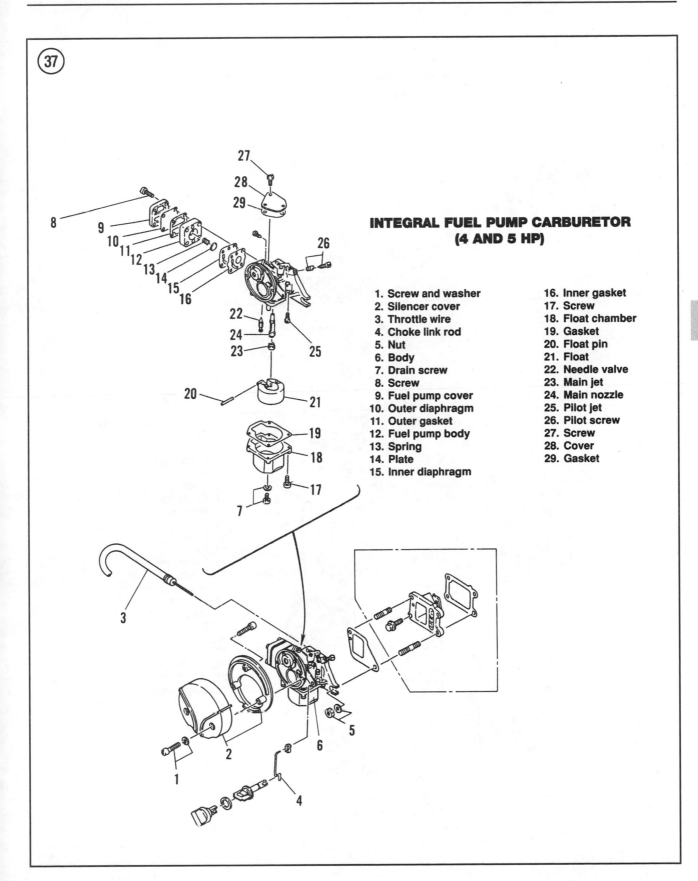

37

INTEGRAL FUEL PUMP CARBURETOR (4 AND 5 HP)

1. Screw and washer
2. Silencer cover
3. Throttle wire
4. Choke link rod
5. Nut
6. Body
7. Drain screw
8. Screw
9. Fuel pump cover
10. Outer diaphragm
11. Outer gasket
12. Fuel pump body
13. Spring
14. Plate
15. Inner diaphragm
16. Inner gasket
17. Screw
18. Float chamber
19. Gasket
20. Float pin
21. Float
22. Needle valve
23. Main jet
24. Main nozzle
25. Pilot jet
26. Pilot screw
27. Screw
28. Cover
29. Gasket

6

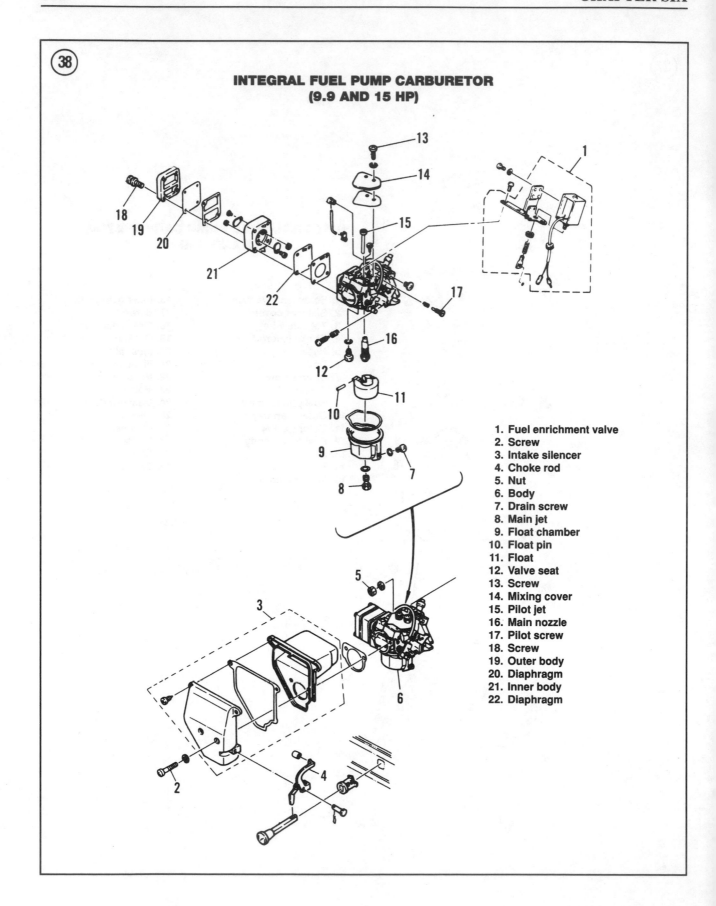

38

**INTEGRAL FUEL PUMP CARBURETOR
(9.9 AND 15 HP)**

1. Fuel enrichment valve
2. Screw
3. Intake silencer
4. Choke rod
5. Nut
6. Body
7. Drain screw
8. Main jet
9. Float chamber
10. Float pin
11. Float
12. Valve seat
13. Screw
14. Mixing cover
15. Pilot jet
16. Main nozzle
17. Pilot screw
18. Screw
19. Outer body
20. Diaphragm
21. Inner body
22. Diaphragm

**INTEGRAL FUEL PUMP CARBURETOR
(25 HP)**

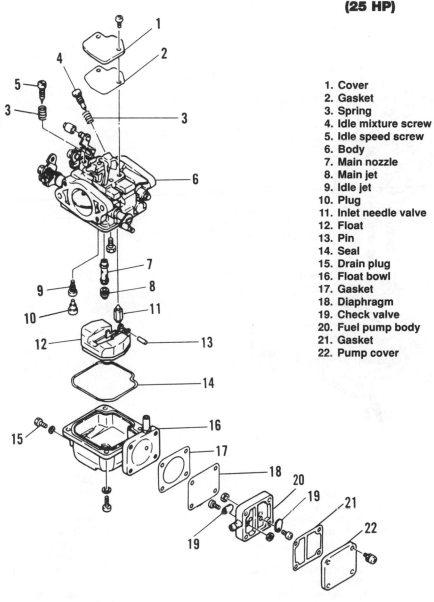

1. Cover
2. Gasket
3. Spring
4. Idle mixture screw
5. Idle speed screw
6. Body
7. Main nozzle
8. Main jet
9. Idle jet
10. Plug
11. Inlet needle valve
12. Float
13. Pin
14. Seal
15. Drain plug
16. Float bowl
17. Gasket
18. Diaphragm
19. Check valve
20. Fuel pump body
21. Gasket
22. Pump cover

6

**INTEGRAL FUEL PUMP CARBURETOR
(30 HP)**

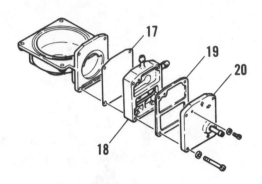

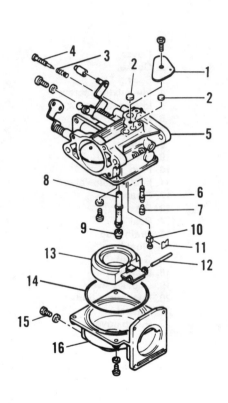

1. Cover
2. Gasket
3. Spring
4. Idle mixture screw
5. Body
6. Idle jet
7. Plug
8. Main nozzle
9. Main jet
10. Inlet needle valve

11. Clip
12. Pin
13. Float
14. Seal
15. Drain plug
16. Float bowl
17. Diaphragm
18. Fuel pump body
19. Gasket
20. Pump cover

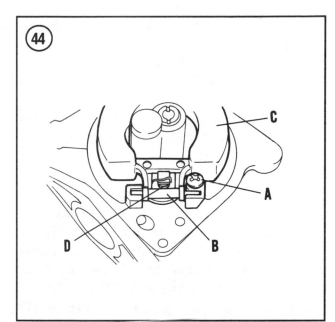

6

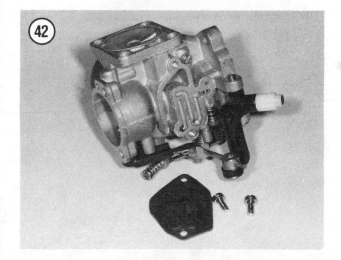

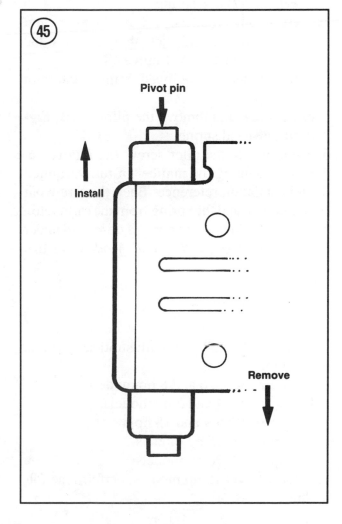

5A. On 9.9 and 15 hp models, perform the following:

a. Remove the pilot jet (A, **Figure 46**) and spring from the top surface of the carburetor.

b. Unscrew and remove the main nozzle and the valve seat from the bottom surface of the carburetor.

5B. On 6 and 8 hp models, perform the following:

a. Unscrew the main jet (A, **Figure 47**).

b. Unscrew the main jet nozzle (B, **Figure 47**). Note the direction of the main jet nozzle—the horizontal hole in the end faces out. Note this during installation.

c. Remove the pilot jet cap (C, **Figure 47**) then unscrew and remove the pilot jet (D, **Figure 47**) and spring .

5C. On all other models, perform the following:

a. Unscrew the main jet, then unscrew the main jet nozzle (A, **Figure 48**).

b. On models so equipped, remove the pilot jet cap.

c. Unscrew and remove the pilot jet (B, **Figure 48**) and spring.

6. Lightly seat the pilot screw (B, **Figure 46**, typical), counting the number of turns required for reinstallation reference. Back the screw out and remove it and the spring from the carburetor.

7. Clean and inspect all parts as described under *Cleaning and Inspection (All Models)* in this chapter.

Assembly

Refer to the following illustrations for this procedure:

a. **Figure 36**: 3, 6 and 8 hp models.

b. **Figure 37**: 4 and 5 hp models.

c. **Figure 38**: 9.9 and 15 hp models.

d. **Figure 39**: 25 hp models.

e. **Figure 40**: 30 hp models.

1A. On 9.9 and 15 hp models, perform the following:

a. Install the valve seat and the main nozzle into the bottom surface of the carburetor. Tighten both securely.

b. Slide the spring onto the pilot screw (B, **Figure 46**) and install into the carburetor. Lightly seat the screw, then back out the number of turns noted during *Disassembly*.

1B. On 6 and 8 hp models, perform the following:

a. Slide the spring onto the pilot screw and install into the carburetor. Lightly seat the screw, then back out the number of turns noted during *Disassembly*.

b. Install the pilot jet (D, **Figure 47**) and tighten securely. Install the cap onto the pilot jet (C, **Figure 47**).

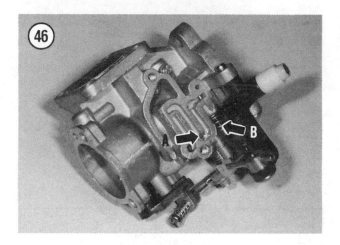

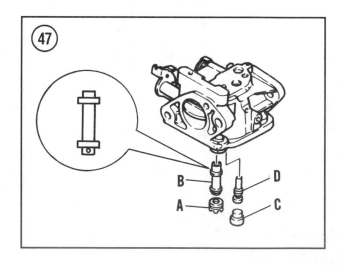

c. Position the main jet nozzle with the horizontal hole in the end facing out and install the main jet nozzle (B, **Figure 47**).

d. Install the main jet (A, **Figure 47**) and tighten securely.

1C. On all other models, perform the following:

a. Slide the spring onto the pilot screw, then install the screw into the carburetor. Lightly seat the screw, then back it out the number of turns noted during disassembly.

b. Install the pilot jet (B, **Figure 48**) into the carburetor body and tighten it securely. Install the cap onto the pilot jet.

c. Install the main jet nozzle in the direction shown in A, **Figure 48**.

d. Install the main jet and tighten securely.

2A. On 6 and 8 hp models, perform the following:

a. Slide the valve onto the float tang.

b. Install the float (C, **Figure 44**) and needle valve (C, **Figure 44**) as an assembly.

c. Install the float pivot pin (B, **Figure 44**) into the float pivot receptacles, then install the pin retaining screw (A, **Figure 44**).

2B. On 9.9 and 15 hp models, perform the following:

a. Slide the valve onto the float tang.

b. Install the float and needle valve as an assembly.

c. Carefully tap the float pivot pin into the pivot pin bosses in the direction indicated

by the raised arrow on the boss (**Figure 45**). Tap the pivot pin until it stops.

2C. On all other models, perform the following:

a. Slide the valve onto the float tang.

b. Install the float and needle valve as an assembly.

c. Carefully tap the float pivot pin into the pivot pin bosses. Tap the pivot pin until it stops.

3. Check the float height and if necessary adjust as described in this chapter.

4. Install a new float bowl gasket on the carburetor body.

5A. On 9.9 and 15 hp models, perform the following:

a. Install the float bowl (B, **Figure 43**) and gasket (C) and hold in place.

b. Install the main jet and gasket (A, **Figure 43**) through the bottom of the float bowl. Tighten securely.

5B. On all other models, install the float bowl and gasket and hold in place. Install the screws and washer securing the float bowl. Tighten the screws securely.

6. Install the mixing chamber cover and gasket (**Figure 42**).

7. Assemble the fuel pump portion of the carburetor (**Figure 41**) as described in this chapter.

CENTERBOWL CARBURETOR
(C25)

Removal/Installation

1. Remove the engine cover.

2. On electric start models, perform the following:

a. Disconnect the choke valve electrical connector.

b. Fully open the choke valve, remove the O-ring (A, **Figure 30**) and disconnect the pull wire from the choke lever pin.

c. Remove the screws securing the choke valve and remove the valve (B, **Figure 30**).

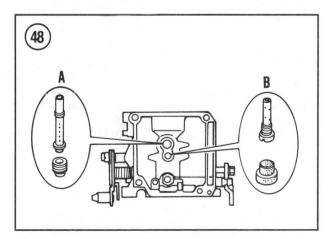

3. Disconnect the choke link rod from the choke lever.

4. Remove the screws securing the air silencer cover and choke lever to the carburetor (**Figure 49**). Remove the cover and gasket(s).

5. Disconnect the fuel line from the carburetor. Plug the line to prevent leakage.

6. Remove the nuts and washers securing the carburetor to the engine. Remove the carburetor and gasket. Discard the gasket.

7. Installation is the reverse of removal. Install a new gasket and tighten the mounting nuts evenly and securely to prevent carburetor warpage and an air leak.

Disassembly

Refer to **Figure 50** for this procedure.

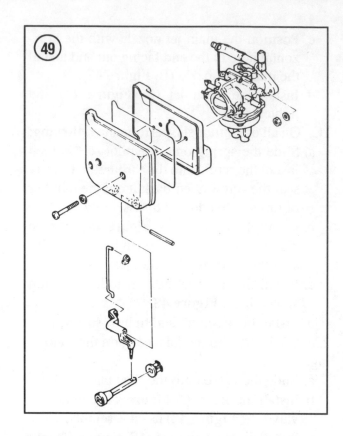

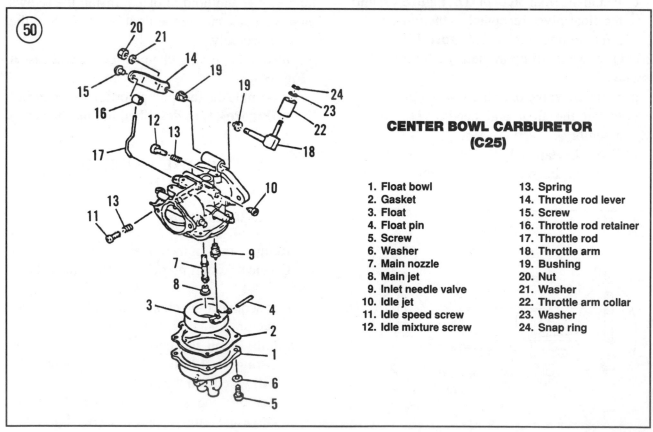

CENTER BOWL CARBURETOR (C25)

1. Float bowl
2. Gasket
3. Float
4. Float pin
5. Screw
6. Washer
7. Main nozzle
8. Main jet
9. Inlet needle valve
10. Idle jet
11. Idle speed screw
12. Idle mixture screw
13. Spring
14. Throttle rod lever
15. Screw
16. Throttle rod retainer
17. Throttle rod
18. Throttle arm
19. Bushing
20. Nut
21. Washer
22. Throttle arm collar
23. Washer
24. Snap ring

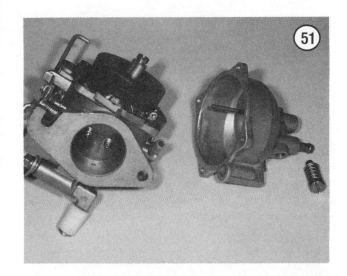

1. Remove the screws and washer securing the float bowl. Remove the float bowl and gasket (**Figure 51**). Discard the gasket (A, **Figure 52**).

2. Carefully tap the float pivot pin out of the pivot pin bosses. Tap the pin out in the direction indicated by the raised arrow on the boss.

3. Remove the float (B, **Figure 52**).

> **CAUTION**
> *The inlet needle is permanently installed in the valve seat. Do not try to remove the needle in Step 4. If replacement is required, the entire carburetor assembly must be replaced.*

4. Remove the inlet needle valve assembly (A, **Figure 53**). Discard the gasket.

6

> **CAUTION**
> *Use a jet remover tool or an appropriate size screwdriver to remove the components in Step 5. If the screwdriver used to remove the main jet nozzle is too large, the screwdriver may damage the housing threads and prevent proper installation of the main jet during assembly.*

5. Remove the main jet (B, **Figure 53**) and the main jet nozzle (C, **Figure 53**).

6. Remove the pilot jet (**Figure 54**).

7. Lightly seat the pilot screw, counting the number of turns required for reinstallation refer-

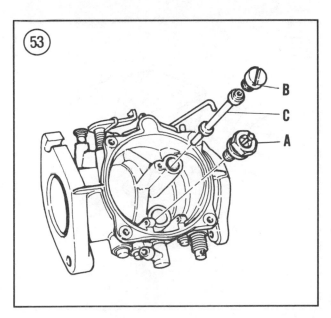

ence. Back the screw out and remove from the carburetor along with the spring (**Figure 55**).

8. Clean and inspect all parts as described under *Cleaning and Inspection (All Models)* in this chapter.

Assembly

Refer to the **Figure 50** for this procedure.

1. Slide the spring onto the pilot screw and install into the carburetor (**Figure 55**). Lightly seat the screw, then back it out the number of turns noted during *Disassembly* Step 7.

2. Install the pilot jet (**Figure 54**) and tighten securely.

> *CAUTION*
> *Use a jet remover tool or an appropriate size screwdriver to install the components in Step 3. If the screwdriver used to install the main jet nozzle is too large, the screwdriver may damage the housing threads and prevent proper installation of the main jet.*

3. Install the main jet nozzle (A, **Figure 56**). Screw it in until it bottoms out.

4. Install the main jet (B, **Figure 56**) and tighten securely.

5. Install the inlet needle valve assembly (A, **Figure 53**) with a new gasket.

6. Install the float (B, **Figure 52**).

7. Carefully tap the float pivot pin into one of the pivot pin bosses in the direction indicated by the raised arrow on the boss. Tap the pivot pin until it stops.

8. Check the float height and if necessary adjust as described in this chapter.

9. Install a new float bowl gasket into the float bowl groove. Make sure it is properly seated.

10. Install the float bowl, then install the screws and washers securing the float bowl. Tighten the screws securely.

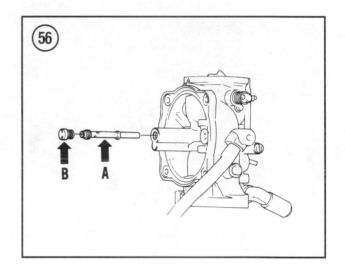

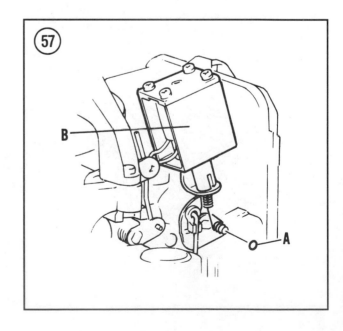

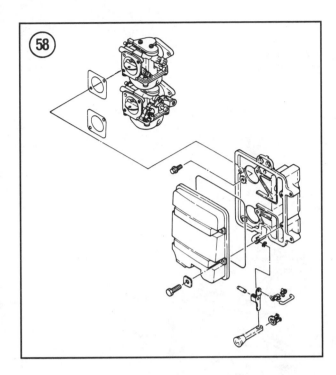

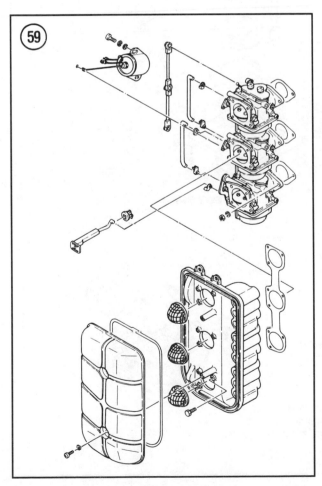

CENTER BOWL CARBURETOR
(C30, C40, C75 AND C85)

Removal/Installation

1. Remove the engine cover.

2. On C30 electric start models, perform the following:

    a. Disconnect the choke valve electrical connector.

    b. Fully open the choke valve, remove the O-ring (A, **Figure 57**) and disconnect the pull wire from the choke lever pin.

    c. Remove the screws securing the choke valve and remove the valve (B, **Figure 57**).

3. Disconnect the choke link rod from the choke lever.

4. Remove the screws securing the air silencer cover and choke lever to the carburetor. Refer to **Figure 58** for C30 and C40 models or **Figure 59** for C75 and C85 models. Remove the cover and gasket(s).

5. Disconnect the fuel line from the carburetor. Plug the line to prevent leakage.

6. Remove the nuts and washers securing the carburetors to the engine. Remove the carburetors and gaskets. Discard the gaskets.

7. Installation is the reverse of removal. Install new gaskets and tighten the mounting nuts evenly and securely to prevent carburetor warpage and an air leak.

Disassembly

Refer to the **Figure 60** for this procedure.

1. Remove the screws securing the top cover. Remove the top cover and the packing (**Figure 61**). On C30 models, remove the top cover gasket and discard it.

2. Remove the screws and washers securing the float bowl. Remove the float bowl and O-ring gasket (**Figure 62**). Discard the O-ring gasket.

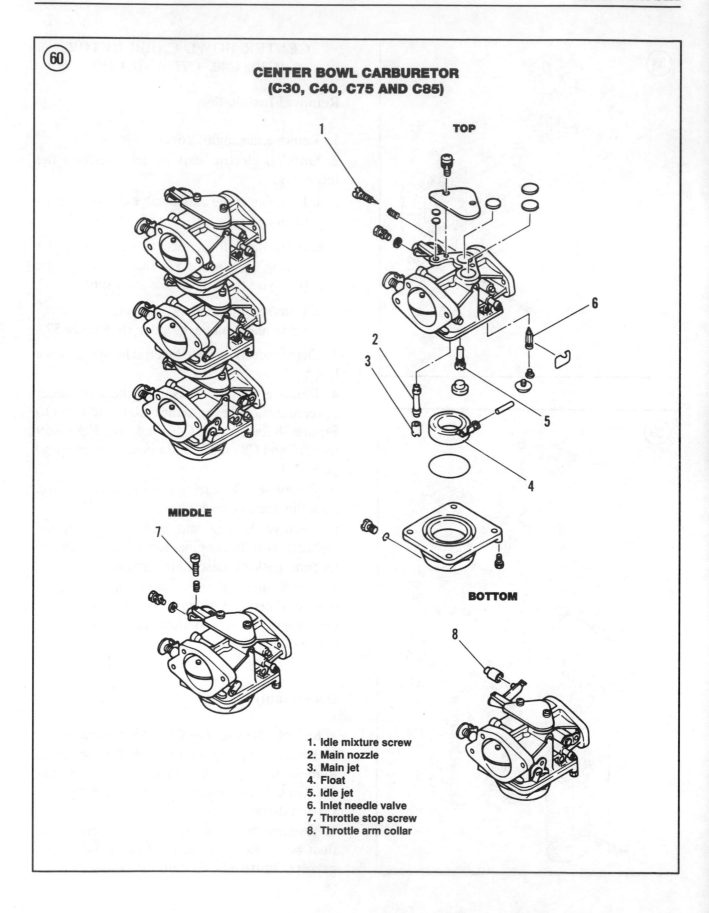

⑥⓪

**CENTER BOWL CARBURETOR
(C30, C40, C75 AND C85)**

TOP

MIDDLE

BOTTOM

1. Idle mixture screw
2. Main nozzle
3. Main jet
4. Float
5. Idle jet
6. Inlet needle valve
7. Throttle stop screw
8. Throttle arm collar

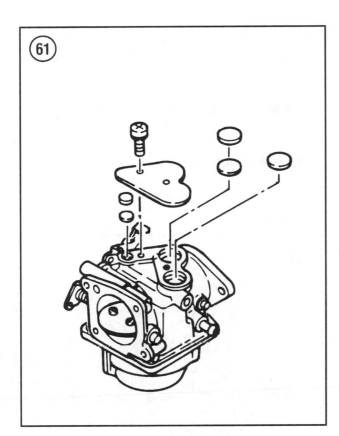

3. Carefully tap the float pivot pin out of the pivot pin bosses. Remove the float (A, **Figure 63**).

4. Remove the inlet needle valve assembly (B, **Figure 63**). Discard the O-ring seal.

> *CAUTION*
> *Use a jet remover tool or an appropriate size screwdriver to remove the components in Step 5. If the screwdriver used to remove the main jet nozzle is too large, the screwdriver may damage the housing threads and prevent proper installation of the main jet during assembly.*

5. Remove the main jet and the main jet nozzle (A, **Figure 64**).

6. Remove the plug above the pilot jet, then remove the pilot jet (B, **Figure 64**).

6

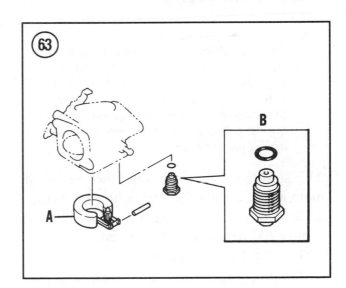

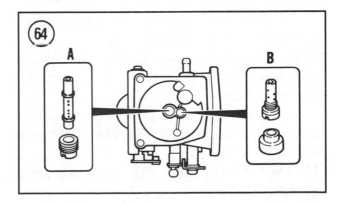

7. Lightly seat the pilot screw, counting the number of turns required for reinstallation reference. Back the screw out and remove it from the carburetor along with the spring (**Figure 65**).

8. Clean and inspect all parts as described under *Cleaning and Inspection (All Models)* in this chapter.

Assembly

Refer to the **Figure 60** for this procedure.

1. Slide the spring onto the pilot screw and install it into the carburetor (**Figure 65**). Lightly seat the screw, then back it out the number of turns noted during *Disassembly* Step 7.

2. Install the pilot jet (B, **Figure 64**) and tighten securely. Install the plug.

> *CAUTION*
> *Use a jet remover tool or an appropriate size screwdriver to install the components in Step 3. If the screwdriver used to install the main jet nozzle is too large, the screwdriver may damage the housing threads and prevent proper installation of the main jet.*

3. Install the main jet nozzle, then install the main jet (A, **Figure 64**) and tighten securely.

4. Install the inlet needle valve assembly (B, **Figure 63**) with a new O-ring seal.

5. Install the float (A, **Figure 63**).

6. Carefully tap the float pivot pin into the pivot pin bosses. Tap the pivot pin until it stops.

7. Check the float height and if necessary adjust as described in this chapter.

8. Install a new float bowl O-ring gasket into the float bowl groove (**Figure 62**). Make sure it is properly seated.

9. Install the float bowl, then install the screws and washers securing the float bowl. Tighten the screws securely.

10. On C30 models, install a new top cover gasket.

11. Install new packing in the cover plate recess. Install the top cover and screws. Tighten the screws securely.

CENTER BOWL CARBURETOR (C55)

Removal/Installation

1. Remove the engine cover.

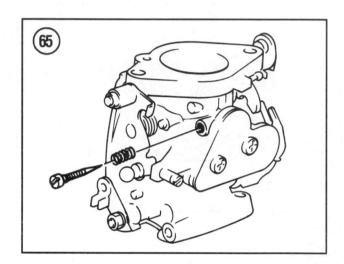

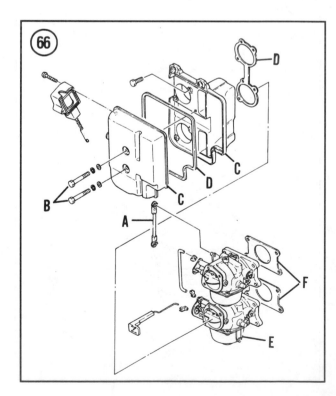

2. Disconnect the choke valve electrical connector.

3. Fully open the choke valve, remove the O-ring (A, **Figure 57**) and disconnect the pull wire from the choke lever pin.

4. Remove the screws securing the choke valve and remove the valve (B, **Figure 57**).

5. Disconnect the choke link rod (A, **Figure 66**) from the choke lever.

6. Remove the screws (B, **Figure 66**) securing the air silencer covers and choke lever to the carburetor. Remove the covers (C, **Figure 66**) and gasket(s) (D, **Figure 66**).

7. Disconnect the fuel line from the carburetor. Plug the line to prevent leakage.

8. Remove the nuts and washers securing the carburetor to the engine. Remove the carburetors (E, **Figure 66**) and gaskets (F, **Figure 66**), then discard the gaskets.

9. Installation is the reverse of removal. Install new gaskets and tighten the mounting nuts evenly and securely to prevent carburetor warpage and an air leak.

Disassembly

Refer to **Figure 67** for this procedure.

6

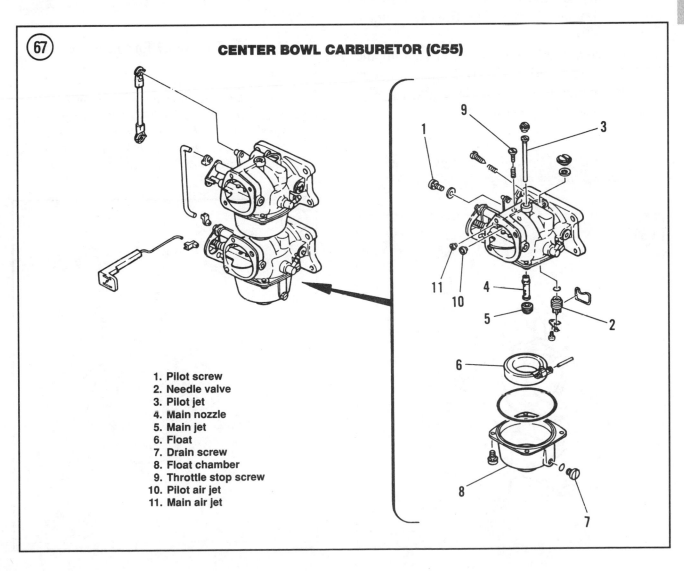

⑥⑦ **CENTER BOWL CARBURETOR (C55)**

1. Pilot screw
2. Needle valve
3. Pilot jet
4. Main nozzle
5. Main jet
6. Float
7. Drain screw
8. Float chamber
9. Throttle stop screw
10. Pilot air jet
11. Main air jet

1. Lightly seat the pilot screw, counting the number of turns required for reinstallation reference. Back the screw out and remove it from the carburetor along with the spring (**Figure 68**).

2. Remove the pilot air jet (A, **Figure 69**) and the main air jet (B, **Figure 69**).

3. Remove the idle adjust screw and spring (C, **Figure 69**) and the top plug and gasket (D, **Figure 69**).

4. Remove the screw and gasket (E, **Figure 69**) from the side of the carburetor.

5. Remove the screws and washer securing the float bowl. Remove the float bowl and O-ring gasket (**Figure 70**). Discard the O-ring gasket.

6. Carefully tap the float pivot pin out of the pivot pin bosses. Remove the float (A, **Figure 71**).

7. Remove the screws and retainer securing the inlet needle valve assembly (B, **Figure 71**), then remove the inlet needle valve assembly (C, **Figure 71**). Discard the O-ring seal.

CAUTION
Use a jet remover tool or an appropriate size screwdriver to remove the compo-

nents in Step 8. If the screwdriver used to remove the main jet is too large, the screwdriver may damage the housing threads and prevent proper installation of the main jet during assembly.

8. Remove the main jet and the main jet nozzle (A, **Figure 72**).

9. Remove the screw plug above the pilot jet, then remove the pilot jet (B, **Figure 72**) from the top surface of the carburetor.

10. Clean and inspect all parts as described under *Cleaning and Inspection (All Models)* in this chapter.

Assembly

Refer to the **Figure 67** for this procedure.

CAUTION
Use a jet remover tool or an appropriate size screwdriver to install the components in Step 1. If the screwdriver used to install the main jet is too large, the screwdriver may damage the housing

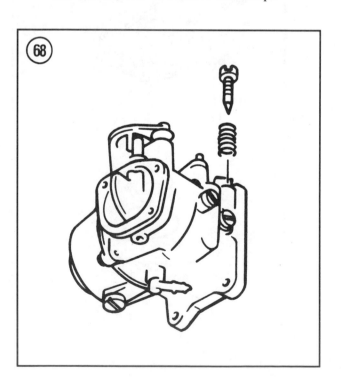

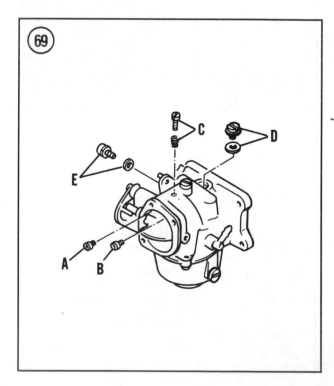

threads and prevent proper installation of the main jet.

1. Install the main jet nozzle, then install the main jet (A, **Figure 72**) and tighten securely.

2. Install the pilot jet (B, **Figure 72**) into the top surface of the carburetor. Install the plug above the pilot jet and tighten securely.

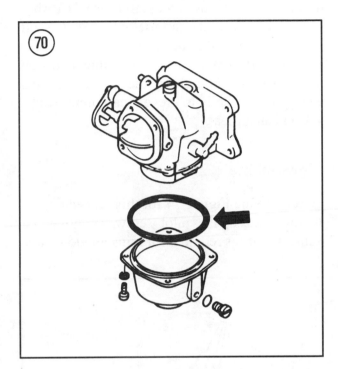

3. Install a new O-ring seal, then install the inlet needle valve assembly (C, **Figure 71**).

4. Install the inlet valve retainer and screws (B, **Figure 71**). Tighten the screws securely.

5. Install the float (A, **Figure 71**).

6. Carefully tap the float pivot pin into the pivot pin bosses. Tap the pivot pin until it stops.

7. Check the float height and if necessary adjust as described in this chapter.

8. Install a new float bowl O-ring gasket into the float bowl groove (**Figure 70**). Make sure it is properly seated.

9. Install the float bowl, then install the screws and washers securing the float bowl. Tighten the screws securely.

10. Install the screw and gasket (E, **Figure 69**) into the side of the carburetor. Tighten securely.

11. Install the idle adjust screw and spring (C, **Figure 69**) and the top plug and gasket (D, **Figure 69**).

12. Install the pilot air jet (A, **Figure 69**) and the main air jet (B, **Figure 69**). Tighten securely.

13. Slide the spring onto the pilot screw and install into the carburetor (**Figure 68**). Lightly seat screw, then back out the number of turns noted during *Disassembly* Step 1.

6

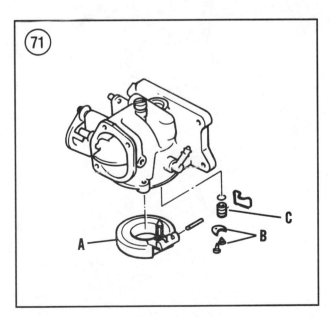

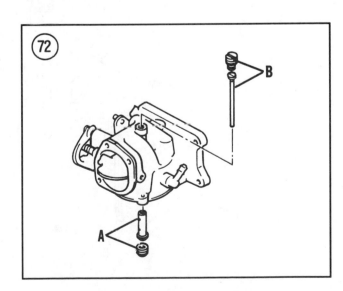

CENTER BOWL CARBURETOR
(40, 50, 70 AND 90 HP AND PRO 50 AND PRO 60)

Removal/Installation

Refer to **Figure 73**, typical for this procedure.

1. Remove the engine cover.

2. Remove the oil tank assembly.

3. Remove the screws (A, **Figure 73**) securing the air silencer cover to the carburetor. Remove the cover (B, **Figure 73**) and gaskets (C).

4. Disconnect the electrothermal electrical connectors (one black and one blue).

5. Disconnect the fuel lines from the carburetors. Plug the ends to prevent leakage.

6. Disconnect the pulser hose from the center carburetor.

7. Disconnect the fuel enrichment hose from the power head.

8. Disconnect the accelerator rod from the carburetor assembly.

9. Remove the oil pump link rod and link joint.

10. Remove the link joint.

11. On manual start models, disconnect the choke rod, link joint, choke lever joint and link joint.

12. Remove the bolts (D, **Figure 73**) securing the carburetors to the engine. Remove the carburetors (E, **Figure 73**), carburetor bracket (F) and gaskets (G). Discard the gaskets.

13. Installation is the reverse of removal. Install new gaskets and tighten the mounting nuts evenly and securely to prevent carburetor warpage and an air leak.

Disassembly

Refer to the **Figure 74** for this procedure.

1. Lightly seat the pilot screw, counting the number of turns required for reinstallation refer-

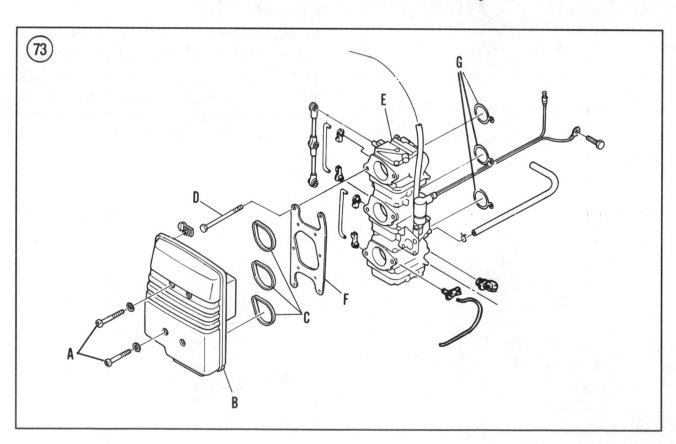

(74)

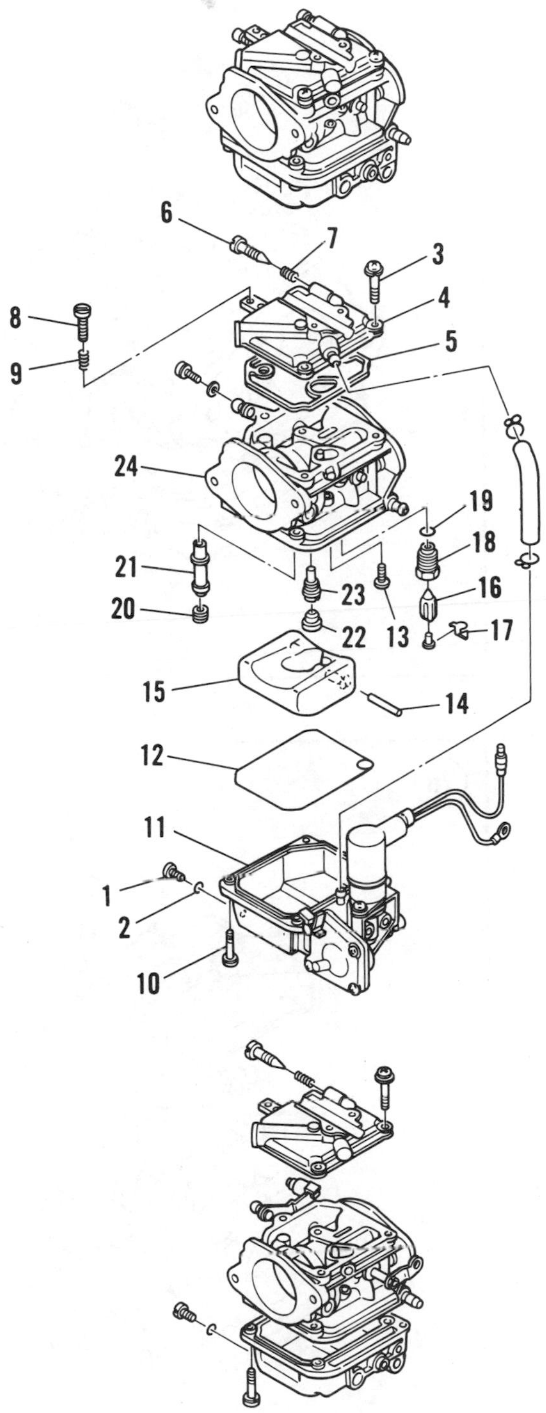

**CENTER BOWL CARBURETOR
(40, 50, 70, 90 HP PRO 50 AND PRO 60)**

1. Drain screw
2. O-ring
3. Screw/washer
4. Cover
5. Gasket
6. Pilot adjust screw
7. Spring
8. Stop screw
9. Spring
10. Screw/washer
11. Float chamber
12. Gasket
13. Screw
14. Pivot pin
15. Float
16. Needle valve
17. Clip
18. Valve seat
19. O-ring
20. Main jet
21. Main nozzle
22. Cap
23. Pilot jet
24. Body

6

ence. Back the screw out and remove it from the carburetor along with the spring (**Figure 75**).

2. Remove the screws securing the top cover. Remove the top cover and the gasket (**Figure 76**).

3. Remove the screws and washer securing the float bowl. Remove the float bowl and O-ring gasket. Discard the O-ring gasket.

4. Carefully tap the float pivot pin (A, **Figure 77**) out of the pivot pin bosses. Remove the float (B, **Figure 77**).

5. Remove the screw and retainer (D, **Figure 77**) securing the inlet needle valve assembly (C, **Figure 77**), then remove the inlet needle valve assembly. Discard the O-ring seal.

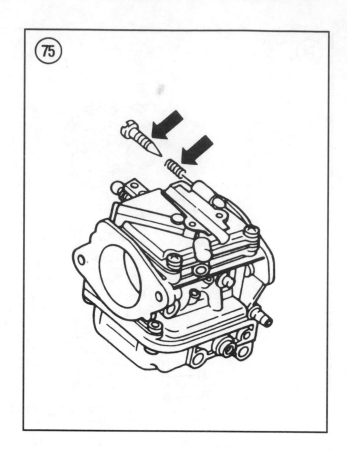

CAUTION
Use a jet remover tool or an appropriate size screwdriver to remove the components in Step 6. If the screwdriver used to remove the main jet nozzle is too large, the screwdriver may damage the housing threads and prevent proper installation of the main jet during assembly.

6. Remove the main jet and the main jet nozzle (A, **Figure 78**).

7. Remove the plug above the pilot jet, then remove the pilot jet (B, **Figure 78**).

8. If necessary, remove the screws securing the electrothermal valve to the center carburetor float bowl and remove the valve (A, **Figure 79**).

9. If necessary, remove and disassemble the fuel enrichment pump (B, **Figure 79**) from the center carburetor float bowl as described in this chapter.

10. Clean and inspect all parts as described under *Cleaning and Inspection (All Models)* in this chapter.

Assembly

Refer to the **Figure 74** for this procedure.

1. If removed and disassembled, assemble and install the fuel enrichment pump (B, **Figure 79**) onto the center carburetor float bowl as described in this chapter.

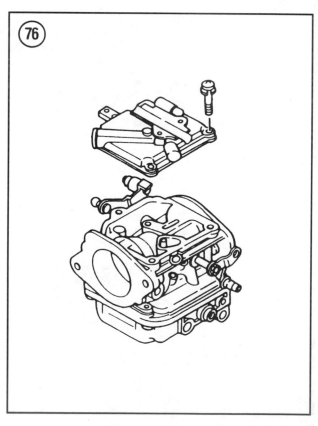

2. If removed, install the electrothermal valve to the center carburetor float bowl (A, **Figure 79**). Install the screws and tighten securely.

3. Install the pilot jet (B, **Figure 78**) and tighten securely. Install the plug.

CAUTION
Use a jet remover tool or an appropriate size screwdriver to install the components in Step 3. If the screwdriver used

to install the main jet nozzle is too large, the screwdriver may damage the housing threads and prevent proper installation of the main jet.

4. Install the main jet nozzle, then install the main jet (A, **Figure 78**) and tighten securely.

5. Install a new O-ring on the inlet needle. Install the inlet needle valve assembly (C, **Figure 77**) with a new O-ring seal. Install the retainer and screws (D, **Figure 77**) and tighten securely.

6. Install the float (B, **Figure 77**) and secure it with the pin (A).

7. Carefully tap the float pivot pin into the pivot pin bosses. Tap the pivot pin until it stops.

8. Check the float height and if necessary adjust as described in this chapter.

9. Install a new float bowl O-ring gasket into the float bowl groove. Make sure it is properly seated.

10. Install the float bowl, then install the screws and washers securing the float bowl. Tighten the screws securely.

11. Install a new top cover gasket.

12. Install the top cover and screws (**Figure 76**). Tighten the screws securely.

13. Slide the spring onto the pilot screw and install into the carburetor (**Figure 75**). Lightly seat the screw, then back it out the number of turns noted during *Disassembly* Step 1.

6

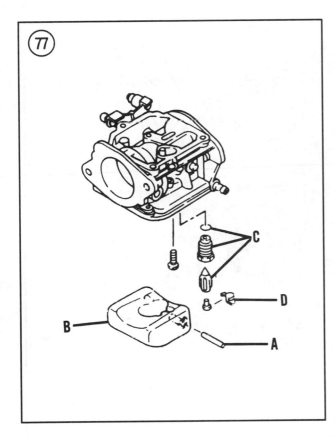

(77)

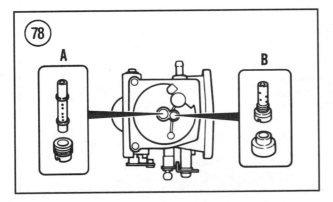

(78)

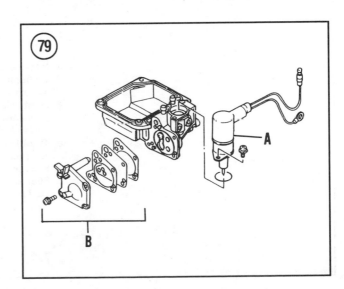

(79)

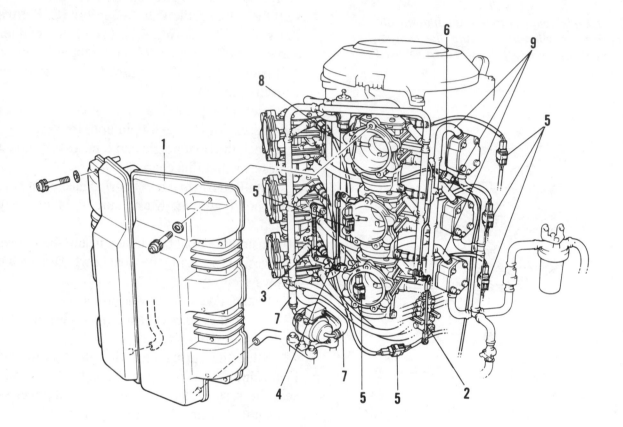

80

**AIR SILENCER AND RELATED FUEL SYSTEM COMPONENTS
(225 AND 250 HP 76° V6)**

1. Intake silencer
2. Oil pump joint link
3. Accelerator link
4. Joint link
5. Fuel enrichment
   valve electrical connector
6. Throttle sensor
   electrical connector
7. Feed pump fuel hose
8. Fuel regulator fuel hose
9. Fuel pump fuel hose

CENTER BOWL CARBURETOR
(225, 250 HP 76° V6)

Removal/Installation

Refer to **Figure 80** for this procedure.
1. Remove the engine cover.

NOTE
The 1992 and later 250 hp models are equipped a pair of air silencers, one for each set of carburetors. All other models are equipped with a single air silencer for both sets of carburetors.

2. Remove the screws and washers securing the air silencer cover(s) to the carburetors. Remove the cover(s) (1, **Figure 80**).
3. Disconnect the oil pump link rod (2, **Figure 80**) and link joint.
4. Disconnect the accelerator rod (3, **Figure 80**) from the carburetor assembly.
5. Disconnect the joint link (4, **Figure 80**) from the carburetor assembly.
6. Disconnect the fuel enrichment electrical connector (5, **Figure 80**).
7. Disconnect the throttle sensor electrical connector (6, **Figure 80**).

NOTE
In Steps 8-10, after disconnecting the different fuel hoses, plug the ends to prevent leakage.

8. Disconnect the fuel hose from the feed pump (7, **Figure 80**).
9. Disconnect the fuel hose from the fuel regulator (8, **Figure 80**).
10. Disconnect the fuel hose from the fuel pump (9, **Figure 80**).
11. Remove the bolts securing the carburetors to the engine. Remove the carburetors, carburetor bracket and gasket. Discard the gasket.

NOTE
Yamaha has determined that on some 250 hp models there may be a problem with fuel lines becoming kinked. If this

occurs, it will result in reduced fuel flow at top speed. Make sure the fuel hoses between the fuel filter, check valve, one-way check valve and center fuel pump are installed correctly and not kinked.

12. Installation is the reverse of removal. Note the following:
   a. Install new gaskets and tighten the mounting nuts evenly and securely to prevent carburetor warpage and an air leak.
   b. Refer to **Figure 81** for correct fuel hose routing.

Disassembly

Refer to **Figure 82** for this procedure.
1. Lightly seat the pilot screw, counting the number of turns required for reinstallation reference. Back the screw out and remove it from the carburetor along with the spring (A, **Figure 83**).
2. Remove the fuel enrichment assembly and O-ring from the carburetor (B, **Figure 83**).
3. Remove the screws securing the top cover. Remove the top cover and the gasket (**Figure 84**).
4. Remove the main air jet from the top of the carburetor.
5. Remove the screws and washer securing the float bowl. Remove the float bowl and O-ring gasket (A, **Figure 85**). Discard the O-ring gasket.
6. Carefully tap the float pivot pin out of the pivot pin bosses. Remove the float (B, **Figure 85**).

CAUTION
Use a jet remover tool or an appropriate size screwdriver to remove the components in Step 7. If the screwdriver used to remove the main jet is too large, the screwdriver may damage the housing threads and prevent proper installation of the main jet during assembly.

7. Remove the main jet and the main jet nozzle (A, **Figure 86**).

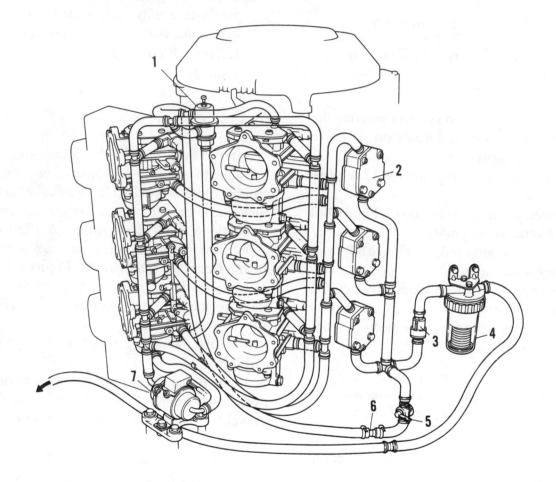

(81)

**HOSE ROUTING, CENTER BOWL CARBURETOR
(225 AND 250 HP 76° V6)**

1. Fuel regulator
2. Fuel pump
3. Fuel flow
   check valve
4. Fuel filter
5. Manual enrichment
   valve
6. Breather
7. Feed pump

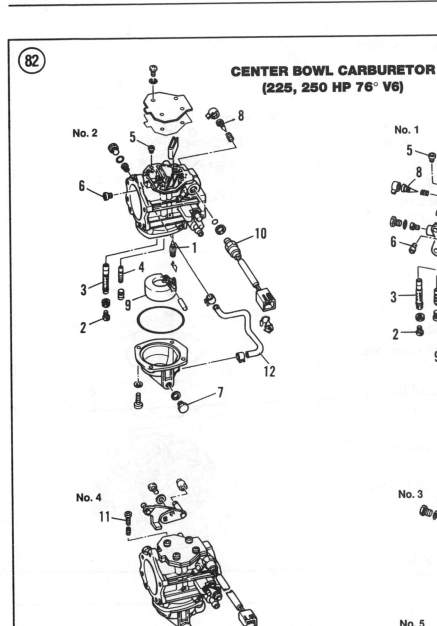
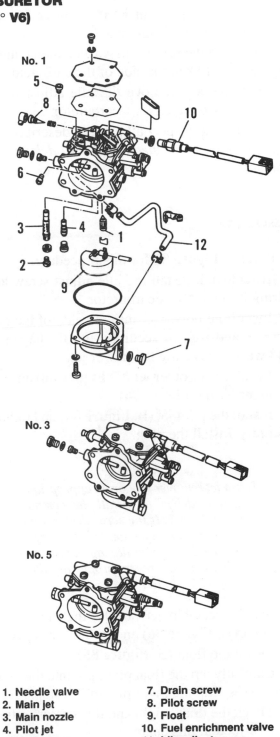

CENTER BOWL CARBURETOR
(225, 250 HP 76° V6)

No. 2

No. 1

No. 4

No. 3

No. 5

No. 6

1. Needle valve
2. Main jet
3. Main nozzle
4. Pilot jet
5. Main air jet
6. Pilot air jet
7. Drain screw
8. Pilot screw
9. Float
10. Fuel enrichment valve
11. Idle adjust screw
12. Fuel hose

82

6

8. Remove the plug above the pilot jet, then remove the pilot jet (B, **Figure 86**).

9. Remove the pilot air jet (C, **Figure 86**) and the main air jet (D, **Figure 86**).

10. Remove the screw and washer, then remove the power jet from the side of the carburetor.

11. If necessary, remove the idle adjust screw and spring from the No. 4 carburetor.

12. Clean and inspect all parts as described under *Cleaning and Inspection (All Models)* in this chapter.

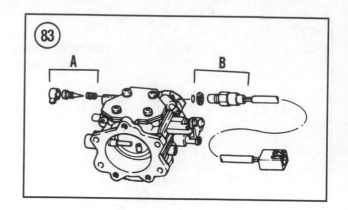

Assembly

Refer to **Figure 82** for this procedure.

1. If removed, install the idle adjust screw and spring into the No. 4 carburetor.

2. Install the power jet into the side of the carburetor and tighten securely. Install the screw and washer covering the power jet.

3. Install the pilot air jet (C, **Figure 86**) and the main air jet (D, **Figure 86**).

4. Install the pilot jet (B, **Figure 86**) and tighten securely. Install the plug.

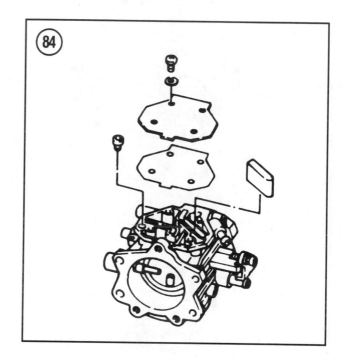

> *CAUTION*
> *Use a jet remover tool or an appropriate size screwdriver to install the components in Step 5. If the screwdriver used to install the main jet nozzle is too large, the screwdriver may damage the housing threads and prevent proper installation of the main jet.*

5. Install the main jet nozzle, then install the main jet (A, **Figure 86**) and tighten securely.

6. Install the float (B, **Figure 85**).

7. Carefully tap the float pivot pin into the pivot pin bosses. Tap the pivot pin until it stops.

8. Check the float height and if necessary adjust as described in this chapter.

9. Install a new float bowl O-ring gasket into the float bowl groove. Make sure it is properly seated.

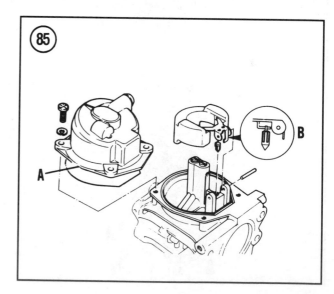

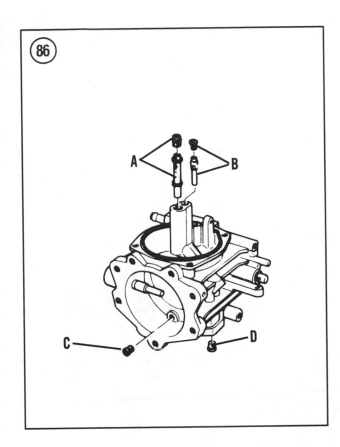

10. Install the float bowl, then install the screws and washers securing the float bowl (A, **Figure 85**). Tighten the screws securely.

11. Install the main air jet into the top of the carburetor. Tighten it securely.

12. Install a new top cover gasket.

13. Install the top cover and screws (**Figure 84**). Tighten the screws securely.

14. Install a new O-ring seal on the fuel enrichment assembly. Install the fuel enrichment assembly and O-ring (B, **Figure 83**) into the carburetor (**Figure 87**).

15. Slide the spring onto the pilot screw and install into the carburetor (A, **Figure 83**). Lightly seat the screw, then back it out the number of turns noted during *Disassembly* in Step 1.

TWIN-BARREL CARBURETOR (115-130 HP V4 AND 150-225 HP 90° V6)

Removal/Installation

Refer to the following illustrations for this procedure:

    a. **Figure 88**: 115-130 hp V4.

    b. **Figure 89**: 150-225 hp V6.

1. Remove the engine cover.

2A. On V4 models, refer to **Figure 88** and perform the following:

    a. Remove the bolts (1, **Figure 88**) and washers securing the air silencer outer cover (2) to the inner cover. Remove the outer cover and gasket (3, **Figure 88**).

    b. Remove the bolts and washers securing the air silencer inner cover (4, **Figure 88**) to the carburetor assembly. Remove the inner cover and gasket (5, **Figure 88**).

2B. On V6 models, refer to **Figure 89** and perform the following:

    a. Remove the screws (10, **Figure 89**) securing the air silencer cover (9) to the carburetor assembly.

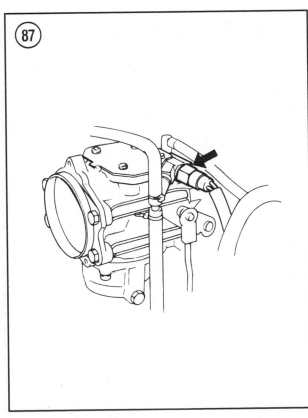

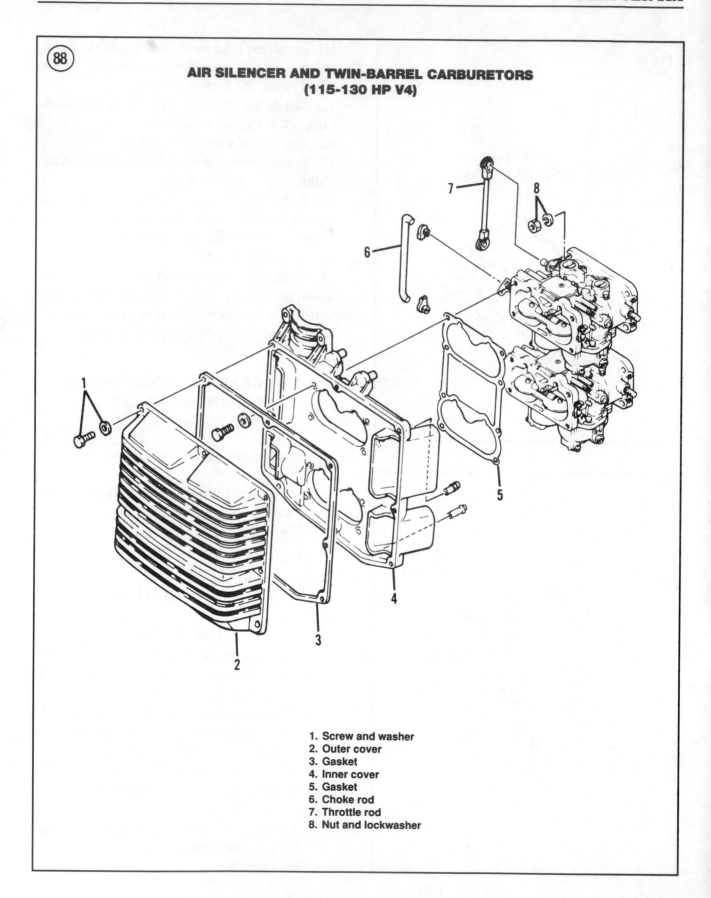

**AIR SILENCER AND TWIN-BARREL CARBURETORS
(115-130 HP V4)**

1. Screw and washer
2. Outer cover
3. Gasket
4. Inner cover
5. Gasket
6. Choke rod
7. Throttle rod
8. Nut and lockwasher

b. Remove the cover and gaskets (8, **Figure 89**).

3. Disconnect the choke rod(s) from the carburetor assembly.

4. Disconnect the throttle link from the carburetor assembly.

5. Disconnect the fuel hoses from the carburetor assembly, then plug the ends to prevent leakage.

6. On 225 hp V6 models, perform the following:

a. Disconnect the throttle sensor electrical connector.

b. Remove the screws and remove the throttle sensor from the starboard side of the top carburetor assembly (**Figure 90**).

7. Remove the bolts and washers securing the carburetors to the engine. Remove the carburetor assembly and gasket. Discard the gasket.

8. Installation is the reverse of removal. Note the following:

a. Install new gaskets and tighten the mounting nuts evenly and securely to prevent carburetor warpage and an air leak.

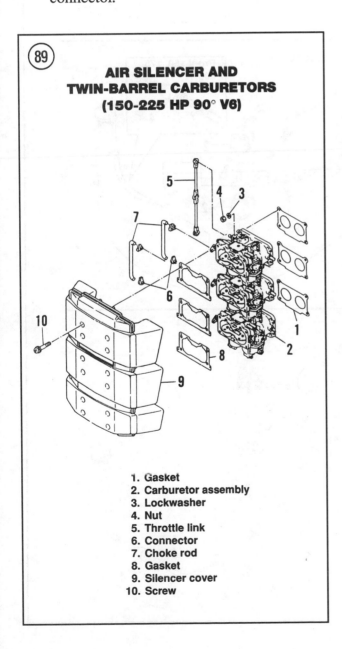

(89)

AIR SILENCER AND TWIN-BARREL CARBURETORS (150-225 HP 90° V6)

1. Gasket
2. Carburetor assembly
3. Lockwasher
4. Nut
5. Throttle link
6. Connector
7. Choke rod
8. Gasket
9. Silencer cover
10. Screw

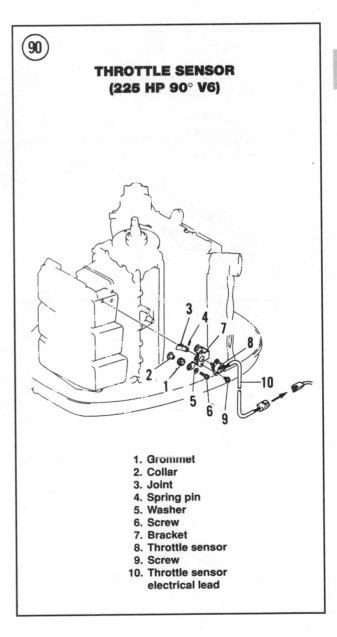

(90)

THROTTLE SENSOR (225 HP 90° V6)

1. Grommet
2. Collar
3. Joint
4. Spring pin
5. Washer
6. Screw
7. Bracket
8. Throttle sensor
9. Screw
10. Throttle sensor electrical lead

6

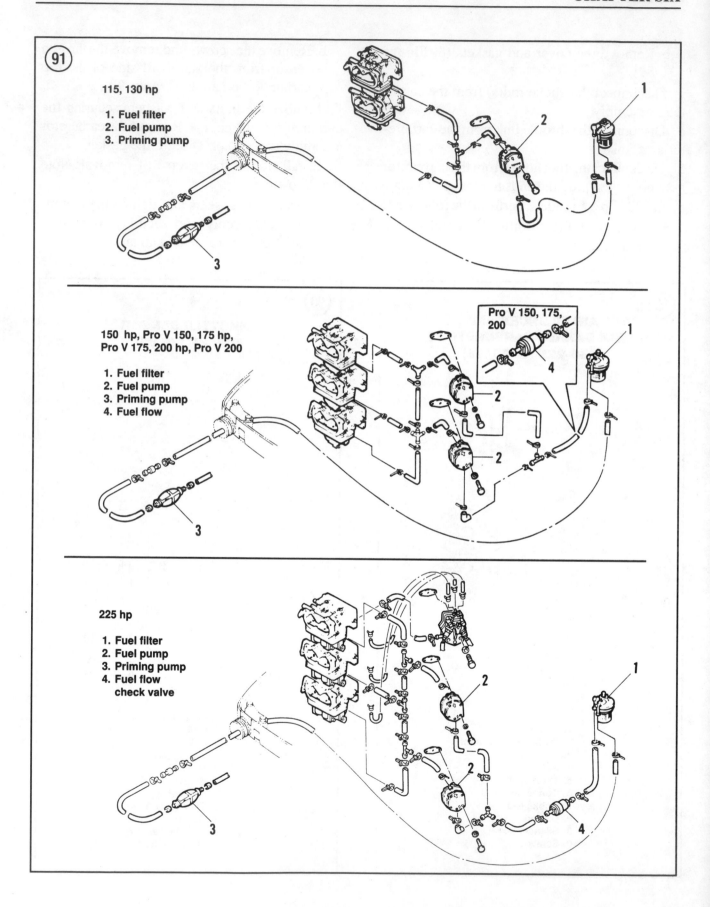

91

115, 130 hp

1. Fuel filter
2. Fuel pump
3. Priming pump

150 hp, Pro V 150, 175 hp, Pro V 175, 200 hp, Pro V 200

1. Fuel filter
2. Fuel pump
3. Priming pump
4. Fuel flow

Pro V 150, 175, 200

225 hp

1. Fuel filter
2. Fuel pump
3. Priming pump
4. Fuel flow check valve

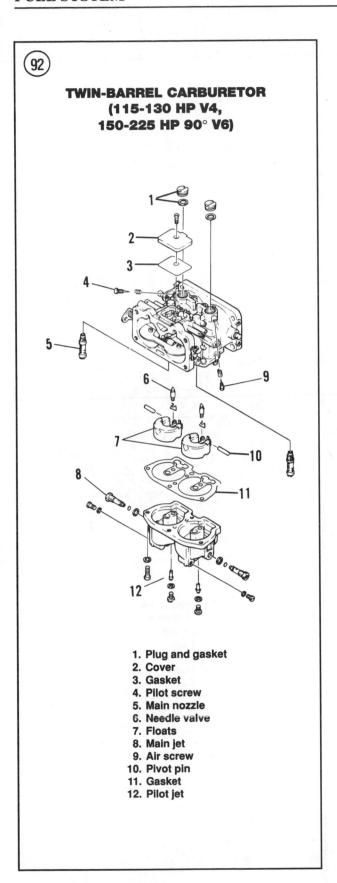

**TWIN-BARREL CARBURETOR
(115-130 HP V4,
150-225 HP 90° V6)**

1. Plug and gasket
2. Cover
3. Gasket
4. Pilot screw
5. Main nozzle
6. Needle valve
7. Floats
8. Main jet
9. Air screw
10. Pivot pin
11. Gasket
12. Pilot jet

b. Refer to **Figure 91** for correct fuel hose connections and routing.

c. Adjust the throttle position sensor. Refer to Chapter Five.

Disassembly

Refer to **Figure 92** for this procedure.

1. Remove the screws (1, **Figure 93**) and washer securing the float bowl. Remove the float

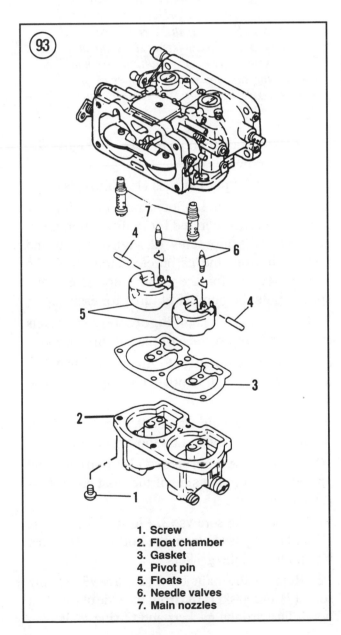

1. Screw
2. Float chamber
3. Gasket
4. Pivot pin
5. Floats
6. Needle valves
7. Main nozzles

6

bowl (2, **Figure 93**) and gasket (3). Discard the gasket.

2. Carefully tap the float pivot pin (4, **Figure 93**) out of the pivot pin bosses and remove the float (5). Repeat for the other float.

3. Remove the needle valves (6, **Figure 93**). The needle valves will either come out with the float(s) or stay in the carburetor body.

CAUTION
Use a jet remover tool or an appropriate size screwdriver to remove the components in Step 4. If the screwdriver used to remove the main jet nozzle is too large, the screwdriver may damage the housing threads and prevent proper installation of the main jet nozzle during assembly.

4. Remove both main jet nozzles (7, **Figure 93**) from the carburetor body.

5. Remove the pilot air jets (1, **Figure 94**).

6. Lightly seat the pilot screw, counting the number of turns required for reinstallation reference. Back the pilot screw (2, **Figure 94**) out and remove it from the carburetor along with the spring. Repeat for the other pilot screw and spring; note the number of turns for each screw.

7. Remove the plugs (4, **Figure 94**) and gaskets (5) from the top surface of the carburetor body.

8. Remove the screw (6, **Figure 94**) securing the top cover (7) and remove the top cover and gasket (8).

9. Remove the main air jets (9, **Figure 94**) from within the area covered by the top cover.

10. Remove the drain screws (1, **Figure 95**) and gaskets (2) from the side of the float bowl. Discard the gaskets.

11. Remove the screws (3, **Figure 95**), gaskets (4) and pilot jets (5) from the bottom of the float bowl. Discard the gaskets.

12. Remove the main jets (6, **Figure 95**), O-ring seals (7) and gaskets (8) from the side of the float bowl. Discard the gaskets and O-ring seals.

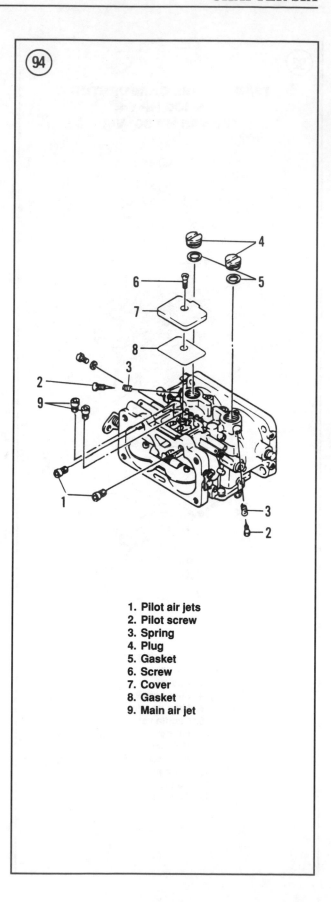

1. Pilot air jets
2. Pilot screw
3. Spring
4. Plug
5. Gasket
6. Screw
7. Cover
8. Gasket
9. Main air jet

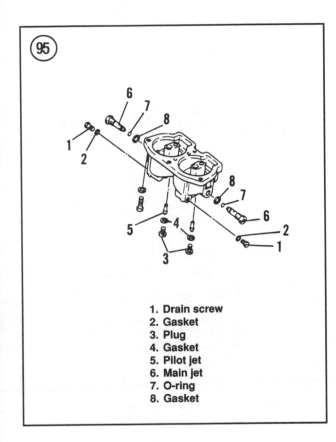

1. Drain screw
2. Gasket
3. Plug
4. Gasket
5. Pilot jet
6. Main jet
7. O-ring
8. Gasket

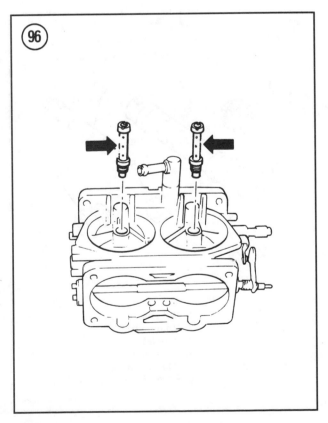

13. Clean and inspect all parts as described under *Cleaning and Inspection (All Models)* in this chapter.

Assembly

Refer to **Figure 92** for this procedure.

1. Install new O-ring seals (7, **Figure 95**) and gaskets (8) onto the main jets (6). Install the main jets into each side of float bowl. Tighten securely.

2. Install new gaskets (4, **Figure 95**) onto the plugs (3). Install the pilot jets (5, **Figure 95**) into the bottom of the float bowl and tighten them securely. Then install and securely tighten the plugs (3, **Figure 95**).

3. Install new gaskets (2, **Figure 95**) onto the drain screws (1) and install the drain screws (1) into the side of the float bowl. Tighten securely.

4. Install the main air jets (9, **Figure 94**) into the top surface of the carburetor body.

5. Install a new gasket (8, **Figure 94**) and top cover (7). Install the screw (6, **Figure 94**) securing the top cover and tighten securely.

6. Install new gaskets (5, **Figure 94**) and install the plugs (4) into the top surface of the carburetor body. Tighten securely.

7. Slide the spring onto the pilot screw (2, **Figure 94**) and install it into the carburetor. Lightly seat the screw, then back it out the number of turns noted during *Disassembly* Step 6. Repeat for the other pilot screw and spring.

8. Install the pilot air jets (1, **Figure 94**) and tighten securely.

CAUTION
Use a jet remover tool or an appropriate size screwdriver to install the components in Step 9. If the screwdriver used to remove the main jet nozzle is too large, the screwdriver may damage the housing threads and prevent proper installation of the main jet nozzle.

9. Install both main jet nozzles (7, **Figure 93**) into the carburetor body. Tighten securely (**Figure 96**).

10. Install the needle valves (6, **Figure 93**) onto the floats.

11. Install the floats (A, **Figure 97**).

12. Carefully tap the float pivot pin (4, **Figure 93**) into the pivot pin bosses. Tap the pivot pin until it stops. Repeat for the other float.

13. Install a new float bowl gasket (B, **Figure 97**), then install the float bowl (2, **Figure 93**) and screws (1). Tighten the screws securely.

CARBURETOR CLEANING AND INSPECTION (ALL MODELS)

CAUTION
A sealing compound is used to eliminate any porosity in the carburetor body and float bowl. Submersion of these components in a hot tank or soaking in a container of caustic carburetor cleaning solvent will remove this sealing compound. Use only a good grade of petroleum-based cleaning solvent and rinse in hot water for all cleaning purposes.

1. Clean all parts, except rubber or plastic parts, in a good grade of petroleum-based cleaning solvent and rinse in clean water.

2. Allow the carburetor parts to dry thoroughly before assembly.

CAUTION
If compressed air is not available, allow the parts to air dry or use a clean lint-free cloth. Do not use paper towels to dry carburetor parts, as small paper particles may plug openings in the carburetor body or jets.

NOTE
***Figure 98** is from a V6 engine and shows the maximum number of jets used among the various models. This is a representation of various jets as the number of jets, their size and configuration varies with the different models.*

3. Blow out the jets (**Figure 98**) with compressed air. Do *not* use a piece of wire to clean them as minor gouges in the jet can alter flow

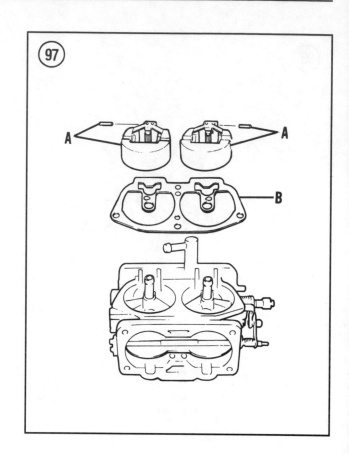

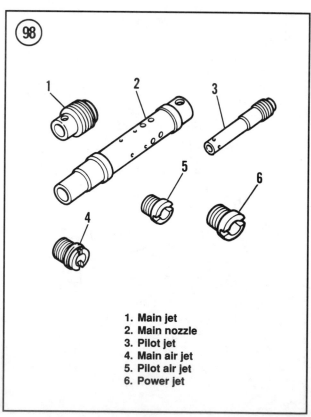

1. Main jet
2. Main nozzle
3. Pilot jet
4. Main air jet
5. Pilot air jet
6. Power jet

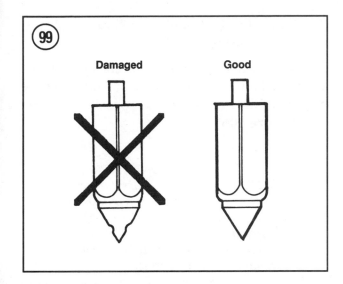

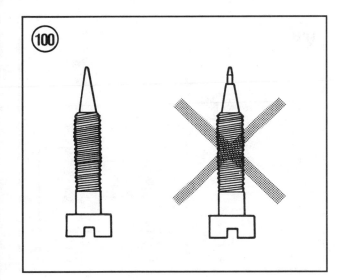

rate and upset the fuel/air mixture. If compressed air is not available, use a piece of straw from a broom to clean the jets. Make sure all openings are clear.

4. Inspect the tip of the needle valve (**Figure 99**) for wear or damage. Replace the valve and seat (if removable) as a set if damaged or worn.

5. Inspect the tip of the pilot screw (**Figure 100**) for wear or damage; replace the valve if damaged or worn.

6. O-ring seals and small gaskets tend to become hardened after prolonged use and exposure to heat and therefore lose their ability to seal properly. Inspect all O-rings and small gaskets and replace them unless they are relatively new.

7. On models so equipped, remove the O-ring gasket from the float bowl and install a new gasket.

8. Check the float (**Figure 101**) for leaks. Fill the float bowl with water, push the float down into it and hold it there. There should be no bubbles. If bubbles are evident, replace the float.

9. Check the throttle shaft(s) for excessive wear or play (**Figure 102**). The throttle valve(s) must move freely without binding. Replace the carburetor if any of these defects are noted. Make sure the screws securing the throttle valve are tight. Tighten securely if necessary.

6

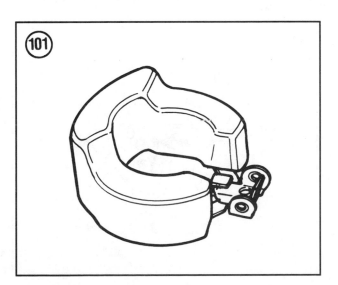

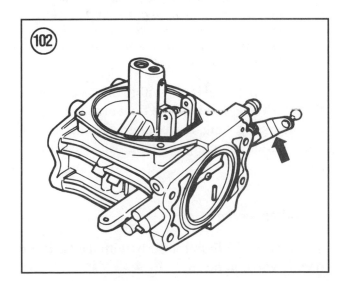

10. Blow out all jets and passages in the carburetor bodies with compressed air (**Figure 103**). Clean out if they are plugged in any way.

11. Inspect the float pivot pin bosses for cracks or damage. If any damage is noted, replace the carburetor assembly.

12. Inspect all interconnecting linkage for wear, looseness or damage; replace as necessary. Make sure all linkage moves smoothly with no binding or hesitation.

13. On models so equipped, inspect the collar (**Figure 104**) at the end of the accelerator arm for wear. Replace if necessary.

FLOAT ADJUSTMENT

1990 2 hp

1. Invert the carburetor body with the float arm and needle valve in place.

2. Lower the float arm until the adjusting tab just touches the needle valve.

3. Hold the float arm in this position and measure the distance between the carburetor body, with gasket in place, and the bottom of the float arm (**Figure 105**).

> *CAUTION*
> *Bend the float adjustment arm carefully when adjustment is required—do **not** press down on the float arm. Downward pressure on the float arm will press the inlet needle tip into its seat and can damage the tip surface.*

4. If the float level is not within the specification listed in **Table 1**, adjust the float arm by bending the adjusting tang as required. Recheck float height after adjusting the tang. Readjust if necessary.

All other models

1. Invert the carburetor body with the float and needle valve in place.

2. Lower the float until the adjusting tab just touches the needle valve.

3. Hold the float in this position and measure the distance between the carburetor body and the bottom of the float at the end opposite the hinge pin (**Figure 106**).

> *CAUTION*
> *Bend the float adjustment arm tang carefully when adjustment is required—do **not** press down on the float arm or float. Downward pressure on the float will press the inlet needle tip into its seat and can damage the tip surface.*

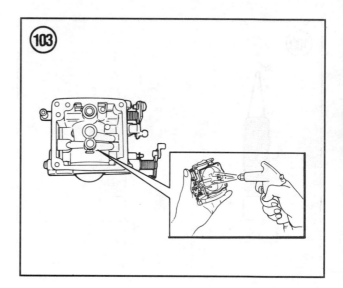

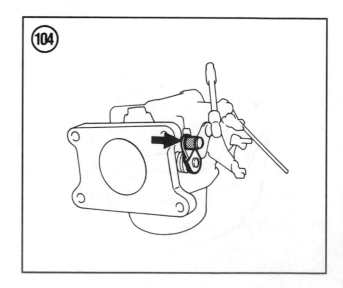

4. If the float level is not within the specification listed in **Table 1**, adjust the float arm tang by bending the adjusting tang as required. Recheck float height after adjusting the tang. Readjust if necessary

PRIMER ASSEMBLY
(225 HP 90° V6)

The 225 hp 90° V6 models, are equipped with a fuel primer pump assembly that contains 2 electric solenoids that are controlled by the CDI unit. During cold starting, the CDI will open one

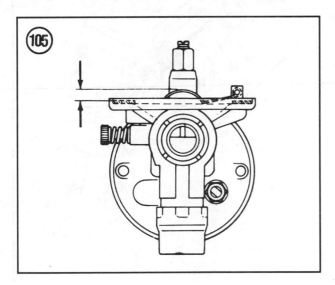

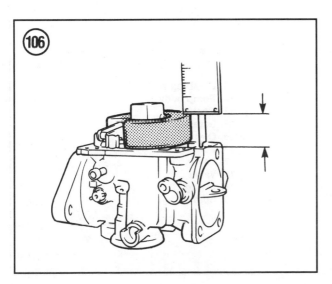

or both of the solenoids (depending on engine temperature) to pump extra fuel to the primer ports on the intake manifold.

The fuel primer pump assembly is mounted to the starboard side of the intake manifold.

Removal/Installation

Refer to **Figure 107** for this procedure.
1. Remove the engine cover.
2. Disconnect the vacuum hose (1, **Figure 107**) from the side of the primer pump. Plug the end to prevent contamination.
3. Disconnect the 3 fuel hoses (2, **Figure 107**) from the top of the primer pump. Plug the ends to prevent leakage.
4. Remove the bolts and washers (3, **Figure 107**) securing the primer pump to the intake manifold.
5. Remove the primer pump (5, **Figure 107**) and gasket (4) from the intake manifold.
6. Test the pump as described in the following procedure.
7. Installation is the reverse of removal. Note the following:

    a. Install a new gasket and tighten the mounting bolts evenly and securely to prevent warpage.

    b. Make sure all fuel hoses are properly secured to the primer pump.

Testing

1. Attach a hand held vacuum/pressure pump (MityVac, or equivalent) to the vacuum fitting on the primer pump.
2. Apply 100 kPa (14.2 psi) of pressure to the fitting (**Figure 108**). The primer pump should maintain this pressure for 10 seconds. If the primer pump fails this test, disassemble the primer pump and correct the problem.
3. Disconnect the vacuum/pressure pump.

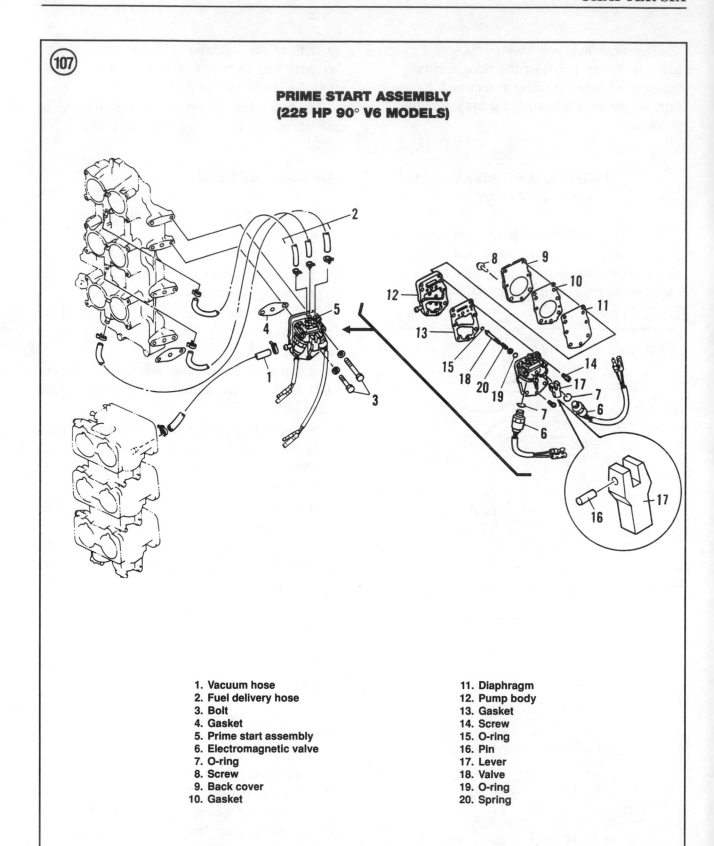

107

**PRIME START ASSEMBLY
(225 HP 90° V6 MODELS)**

1. Vacuum hose
2. Fuel delivery hose
3. Bolt
4. Gasket
5. Prime start assembly
6. Electromagnetic valve
7. O-ring
8. Screw
9. Back cover
10. Gasket
11. Diaphragm
12. Pump body
13. Gasket
14. Screw
15. O-ring
16. Pin
17. Lever
18. Valve
19. O-ring
20. Spring

Disassembly/Assembly

Refer to **Figure 107** for this procedure.

1. Remove the primer pump as described in this chapter.

2. Disconnect the electromagnetic valve (6, **Figure 107**) and O-ring seal (7) from the pump.

3. Remove the 2 screws (8, **Figure 107**) at the rear and the 3 screws (14) at the front securing the pump assembly together.

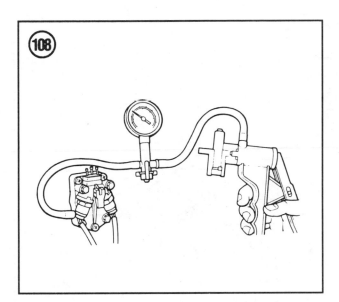

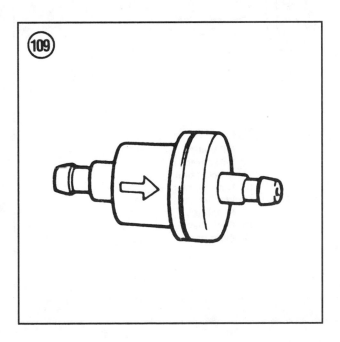

4. Remove the back cover (9, **Figure 107**), cover gasket (10), diaphragm (11), pump body (12) and body gasket(13) from the pump body.

5. Discard all gaskets.

6. Remove the O-ring (15, **Figure 107**) from the end of the valve (18).

7. Carefully tap the pin (16, **Figure 107**) from the lever (17) and remove the lever from the pump body.

8. Note the direction of the valve (18), then remove the valve (18), O-ring (19) and spring (20) from the valve.

9. Clean and inspect the pump components as described in this chapter.

NOTE
Do not use any form of gasket sealer with the fuel pump gaskets.

10. Assembly is the reverse of disassembly. Note the following:

    a. Using new gaskets and O-ring seals.

    b. Install the fuel pump as described in this chapter.

Cleaning and Inspection

1. Clean all metal parts in solvent and blow dry with compressed air.

2. Inspect the valve diaphragm for signs of warpage, or damage. Replace as required.

FUEL FILTER

Models equipped with an integral fuel tank contain a fuel filter screen in the petcock. Some 4-8 hp engines are equipped with a small in-line fuel filter installed in the fuel line between the fuel line and the carburetor. When installing a new in-line fuel filter, correctly position the fuel filter with the arrow pointing in the direction of fuel flow—toward the carburetor (**Figure 109**).

All other models are equipped with a water-separating filter canister positioned between the

6

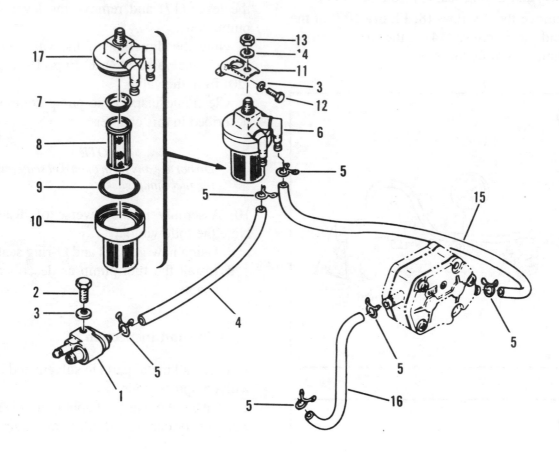

110

FUEL FILTER AND PUMP ASSEMBLY (TYPICAL)

1. Fuel line connector
2. Bolt
3. Washer
4. Inlet fuel hose
5. Hose clamp
6. Filter assembly
7. Gasket
8. Filter element
9. O-ring
10. Filter cup
11. Filter bracket
12. Bracket bolt
13. Nut
14. Washer
15. Fuel hose
16. Fuel hose
17. Filter base

fuel line connector and the fuel pump (**Figure 110**, typical). This canister traps moisture and prevents it from entering the carburetor(s) when the engine is in its normal operating position. The filter should be serviced if water can be seen in the bowl or at the intervals specified in Chapter Four.

REED VALVE ASSEMBLY

On 2 hp models, the reed valve assembly is attached directly to the intake manifold (**Figure**

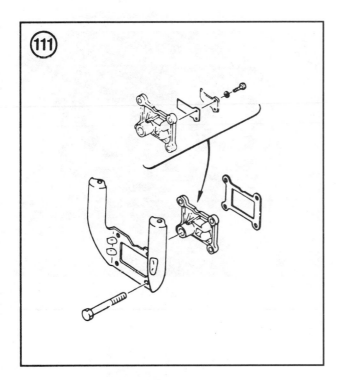

111). On all other models, the reed valve assembly is mounted between the intake manifold and the crankcase (**Figure 112**, typical).

Reed valves control the passage of air/fuel mixture into the crankcase by opening and closing as the crankcase pressure changes. When the crankcase pressure is high, the reeds maintain contact with the reed plate to which they are attached. As the crankcase pressure drops on the compression stroke, the reeds move away from the plate and allow air/fuel mixture to pass. Reed travel is limited by the reed stop. As the crankcase pressure increases, the reeds return to the reed plate.

Removal/Installation (All Models)

1. Remove the carburetor(s) as described in this chapter.
2. Label and disconnect any hoses connected to the intake manifold.

> *NOTE*
> *On some models, the reed valve assembly is secured to the crankcase by one or more separate fasteners. With this design, the intake manifold must be removed first, then the reed valve assembly fastener(s) removed before the assembly and gasket can be removed.*

3. Remove the fasteners holding the intake manifold(s) to the crankcase. Remove the intake manifold(s), gasket(s), reed valve assembly(ies) and gasket(s) from the crankcase. Discard the gaskets.
4. Clean all mating surfaces of old gasket or sealant residue.
5. Clean and inspect the reed valve assembly as described in this chapter.
6. Installation is the reverse of removal. Note the following:
   a. Use new gaskets.
   b. Make sure the reed assembly(ies) face the crankcase.

Cleaning and Inspection

1. Clean the reed valve assembly in solvent and blow dry with low pressure compressed air. Do *not* direct the air stream directly on or through the reed valve as it will be damaged.

2. Remove all old gasket or sealant residue from the reed block assembly.

3. Check the intake side of the assembly to make sure that the reeds are not sticking tightly to the valve face. They must be able to move freely.

4. Inspect the crankcase side of the assembly to make sure that the reeds are lying flat on the valve face with no preload. To check flatness, gently push each reed petal out. Constant resistance should be felt with no audible noise.

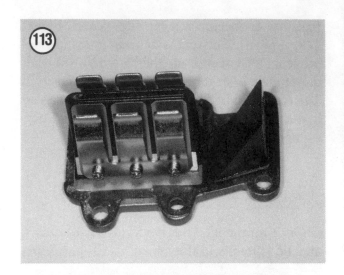

> *CAUTION*
> *Always replace reeds in sets. **Never** turn a reed over for reuse.*

5. Check for chipped, cracked or broken reeds. Replace if any defects are noted. Refer to **Figure 112**, **Figure 113** and **Figure 114** for typical reed valve layouts on models covered in this manual.

6. Check the clearance between the reed and the valve seat with a flat feeler gauge. Replace reeds if they are preloaded (adhere tightly to the reed block) or if the gap is excessive. Refer to specifications listed in **Table 2**.

7. Check each reed stop opening by measuring from the inside of the reed stop to the tip of the closed reed. Refer to **Figures 115-117** for typical reed block designs. If the reed stop is not within the specification listed in **Table 2**, carefully bend the reed valve stop to obtain the specified opening.

> *NOTE*
> *Make sure that all parts are clean and free of any small dirt particles or lint from a shop cloth as they may cause a small amount of distortion in the reed plate.*

8. Reinstall the reed valve assembly as described in this chapter.

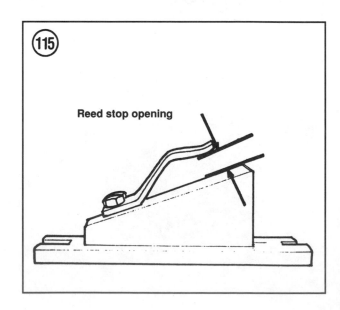

Reed stop opening

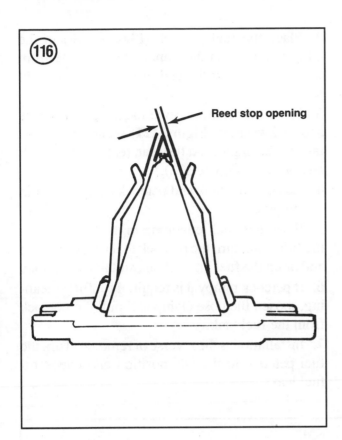

Reed stop opening

Reed and Reed Stop Replacement

1. Remove the screws holding the reed stop and reeds to the valve seat (**Figure 118**, typical).

2. Remove the reed stop and reeds.

3. Place a new reed on the valve seat and check for flatness.

4. Center the reed over the valve seat openings.

5. Apply red Loctite (No. 242) to the stop screw threads prior to installation. Install reed stop and screws, then gradually tighten the screws securely.

6. Check reed tension and opening. See *Cleaning and Inspection* in this chapter.

INTEGRAL FUEL TANK
(2-5 HP)

The 2-5 hp models have an integral fuel tank. Except for 3 hp engines, the fuel is transported from the tank to the carburetor by gravity feed

6

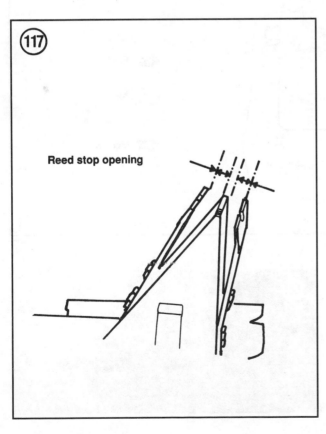

Reed stop opening

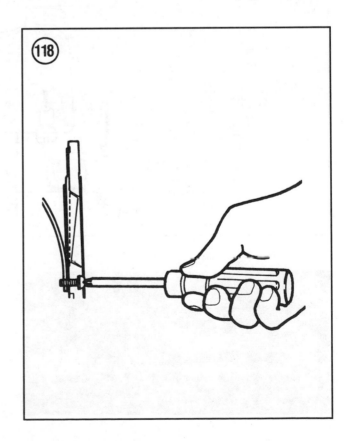

(**Figure 119**, typical). The 3 hp outboard is equipped with a fuel pump. A nonserviceable petcock controls the flow of fuel. If the petcock leaks or is faulty, it must be replaced as an assembly.

> *WARNING*
> *Some fuel may spill in the following procedure. Work in a well-ventilated area at least 50 ft. (15 m) from any sparks or flames, including gas appliance pilot lights. Do not allow anyone to smoke in the area. Keep a B:C-rated fire extinguisher handy.*

Removal/Installation (2 hp)

1. Remove the right and left engine covers.

2. Place the fuel petcock (**Figure 120**) in the OFF position and disconnect the fuel line from the petcock. Plug the end of the line to prevent leakage.

3. From the front, remove the 2 nuts, washers and lockwashers (**Figure 121**) securing the fuel tank to the engine. At the rear, remove the 1 bolt and washer (**Figure 122**).

4. Remove the tank and petcock assembly from the engine.

5. If there is fuel remaining in the tank, loosen the filler cap, turn the petcock to the ON position and drain the fuel into a clean, suitable container.

6. If petcock removal is required for filter cleaning, loosen the hose clamp and pull the petcock from the fuel tank.

7. Installation is the reverse of removal. Turn the fuel petcock to the ON position and check for fuel leaks.

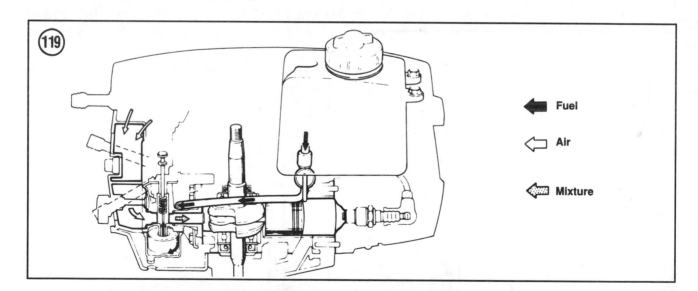

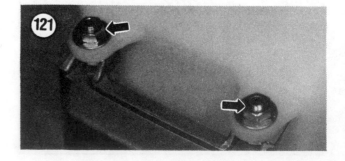

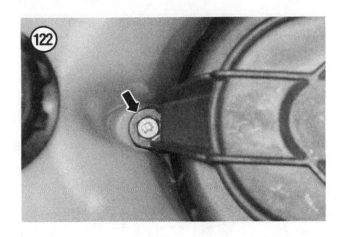

**Removal/Installation
(3 hp)**

Refer to **Figure 123** for this procedure.
1. Remove the engine cover.
2. Turn the fuel petcock (1, **Figure 123**) to the OFF position.

WARNING
*Do **not** disconnect the fuel line from the fuel tank side of the fuel petcock as the fuel will drain from the tank immediately.*

6

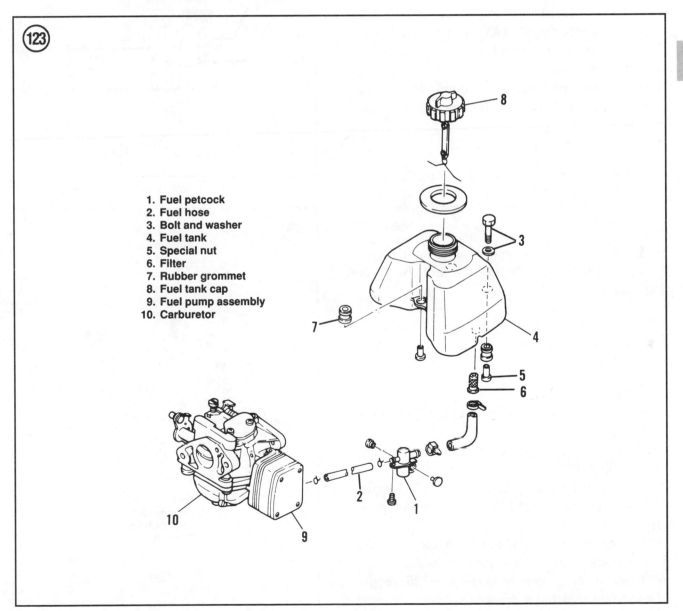

1. Fuel petcock
2. Fuel hose
3. Bolt and washer
4. Fuel tank
5. Special nut
6. Filter
7. Rubber grommet
8. Fuel tank cap
9. Fuel pump assembly
10. Carburetor

3. Disconnect the fuel hose (2, **Figure 123**) from the *fuel pump side* of the petcock. Plug the end of the line to prevent leakage.

4. Remove the bolt and washer (3, **Figure 123**) from the front and rear securing the fuel tank to the engine.

5. Remove the tank (4, **Figure 123**) and petcock assembly from the engine.

6. Don't lose the metal collars located within the rubber dampers (7, **Figure 123**) at the mounting tabs on the fuel tank. They may fall out during removal and must be reinstalled.

7. If there is fuel remaining in the tank, loosen the filler cap (8, **Figure 123**), turn the petcock to the ON position and drain the fuel into a clean, suitable container.

8. If petcock removal is required, loosen the hose clamps and remove the petcock from the fuel lines.

NOTE
The rubber dampers must be reinstalled in the fuel tank mounting tabs. These dampers absorb vibrations and must be used.

9. Installation is the reverse of removal. Turn the fuel petcock to the ON position and check for fuel leaks.

**Removal/Installation
(4 and 5 hp)**

1. Remove the engine cover.

2. Turn the fuel petcock lever to the OFF position (**Figure 124**).

3. Remove the bolt (1, **Figure 125**) securing the change shaft (2) to the engine cowling.

4. Carefully pull the change shaft (2, **Figure 125**) and change lever (3) out and disengage it from the petcock (4).

5. Disconnect the fuel line from the petcock. Plug the end of the line to prevent leakage.

6. Remove the 2 lower bolts (**Figure 126**) securing the fuel tank to the lower cowling.

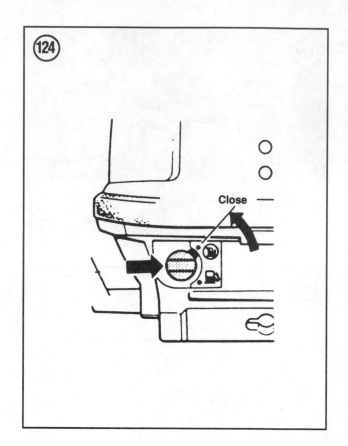

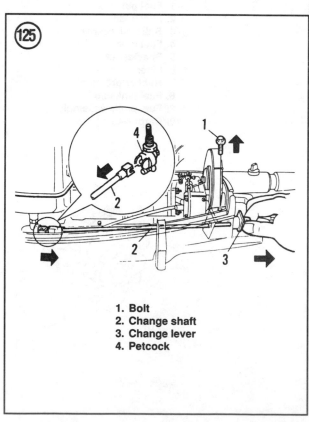

1. Bolt
2. Change shaft
3. Change lever
4. Petcock

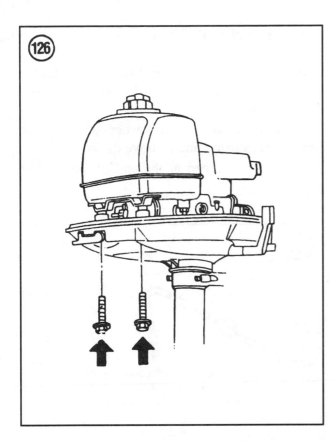

7. Remove the tank and petcock assembly from the engine.

8. Don't lose the metal collars located within the rubber dampers at the mounting tabs on the fuel tank. They may fall out during removal and must be reinstalled.

9. If there is fuel remaining in the tank, loosen the filler cap, turn the petcock to the ON position and drain the fuel into a clean, suitable container.

10. If petcock removal is required, loosen the petcock nut with an open-end wrench and remove the petcock from the fuel tank.

NOTE
The rubber dampers must be reinstalled in the fuel tank mounting tabs. These dampers absorb vibrations and must be used.

11. Installation is the reverse of removal. Note the following:

    a. If removed, make sure the petcock faces in the same direction as it was before removal (**Figure 127**). When properly installed, the petcock should align correctly with the change shaft (**Figure 128**).

    b. Turn the fuel petcock to the ON position and check for fuel leaks.

Cleaning and Inspection

1. Remove the fuel tank and drain the fuel from the tank as described in this chapter.

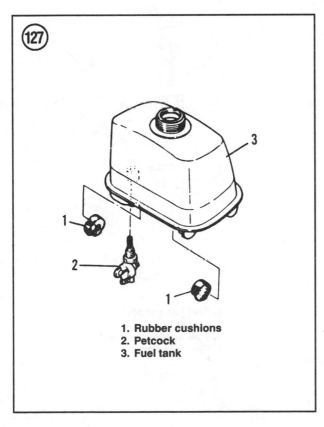

1. **Rubber cushions**
2. **Petcock**
3. **Fuel tank**

6

2. Pour several ounces of petroleum-based solvent into the fuel tank. Reinstall the tank filler cap and slosh the solvent around in the tank. Drain the solvent into a suitable container and dispose of properly. If the solvent is dirty, repeat this Step until the drained solvent is clean.

3. Check the fuel tank filler cap for a worn gasket or packing; replace as necessary to prevent the entry of moisture. Make sure the air vent is clear. Clean out if necessary.

4. Clean the petcock filter in solvent and blow dry with low pressure compressed air.

PORTABLE FUEL TANK
(7-250 HP)

Figure 129 shows the typical components of the portable fuel tank, including the fuel gauge sender, the in-tank filter housed in the fuel metering assembly and the primer bulb.

When some oils are mixed with gasoline and stored in a warm place, a bacterial substance will form. This colorless substance covers the fuel pickup, restricting flow through the fuel system. Bacterial formation can be prevented by using the additive, Yamalube Fuel Conditioner on a regular basis. If present, the bacteria can be removed with a good marine engine cleaner.

To remove any dirt or water that may have entered the tank during refilling and to prevent the build-up of gum and varnish, clean the inside of the tank once each season by flushing with clean, lead-free gasoline or kerosene. Properly dispose of the spent gasoline or kerosene

Check the inside and outside of the tank for signs of rust, leakage or corrosion. Replace the tank as required. Do not attempt to patch the tank with automotive fuel tank repair materials. Portable marine fuel tanks are subject to much greater vibration and other stresses.

Portable Fuel Tank Filter Cleaning

If you feel there is a restriction in the fuel flow, check the fuel tank adapter filter screen for possible contaminants.

1. Remove the bolts and washers securing the fuel meter housing and remove the housing.

2. Inspect the screen at the end of the suction pipe.

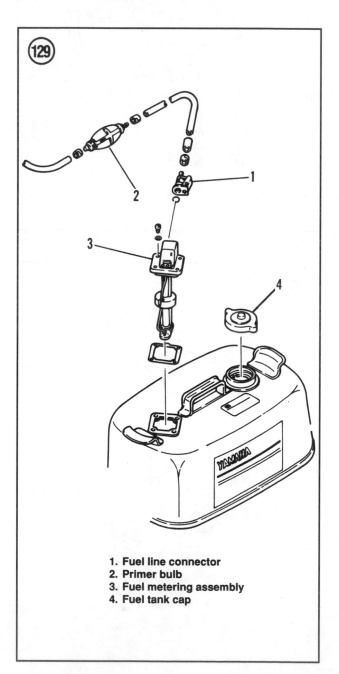

1. Fuel line connector
2. Primer bulb
3. Fuel metering assembly
4. Fuel tank cap

3. Clean the screen with solvent, then blow dry with low-pressure compressed air to remove any particles (**Figure 130**, typical).

4. Install all parts removed.

FUEL LINE AND PRIMER BULB

Figure 129 shows the primer bulb installation in the fuel line. **Figure 131** shows the inlet and outlet check valves inside the primer bulb. When priming the engine, the primer bulb should gradually become firm. If it does not become firm or if it stays firm even when disconnected, the check valve inside the primer bulb is malfunctioning.

> *WARNING*
> *Leaking gasoline presents a real fire danger that may lead to loss of life and damage or total destruction of the boat.*

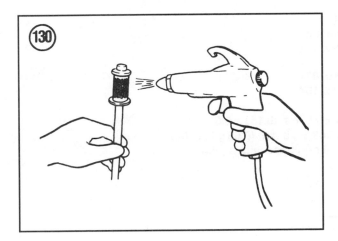

Always replace any fuel lines or connectors immediately after any fuel leakage is observed.

The fuel line and primer bulb should be checked periodically for cracks, breaks, restrictions and chafing. The bulb should be checked periodically for proper operation and make sure it is installed correctly within the fuel line with the fuel flow arrow pointing in the correct direction—toward the carburetor(s). Make sure all fuel line connections are tight and securely clamped.

ANTI-SIPHON DEVICES

In accordance with the Marine Industry Safety Standards, all late model boats equipped with a built-in fuel tank has some form of anti-siphon device installed between the fuel tank outlet and the outboard motor fuel. This device is designed to shut the fuel supply off if the boat capsizes or is involved in an accident. Quite often, the malfunction of such devices will lead the owner to replace the fuel pump in the belief that the pump is faulty.

Anti-siphon devices can malfunction in one of the following ways:

a. Anti-siphon valve: orifice in the valve is too small or clogs easily; valve sticks in closed or partially closed position; valve fluctuates between open and closed position; thread

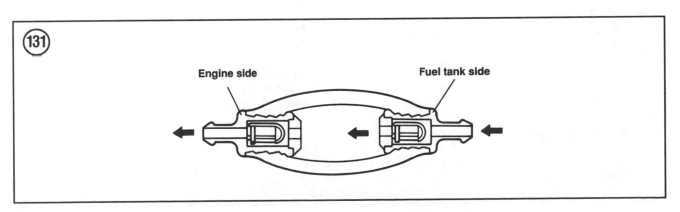

Engine side   Fuel tank side

sealer, metal filings or dirt/debris clogs the orifice or lodges in the relief spring.

b. Solenoid-operated fuel shut-off valve: solenoid fails with the valve in the closed position; solenoid malfunctions, leaving valve in the partially closed position.

c. Manually-operated fuel shut-off valve: valve is left in completely closed position; valve is not fully opened.

The easiest way to determine if an anti-siphon valve is defective is to bypass it with a remote fuel supply. If a fuel system problem is suspected, check the fuel filter first. See Chapter Four. If the filter is not clogged or dirty, bypass the anti-siphon device. If the engine runs properly with the anti-siphon device bypassed, contact the boat manufacturer for replacement of the anti-siphon device.

Table 1 CARBURETOR SPECIFICATIONS

Model	Specification
2 hp	
Carburetor stamped mark	
1990-1994	K
1995	6A103
Main jet	No. 96
Needle jet	
1990-1994	No. 071
1995	No. 167
Float level	
1990-1994	4 ± 0.5 mm (0.157 ± 0.02 in.)
1995	17.03 ± 0.5 mm (0.68 ± 0.02 in.)
Pilot screw turns out	Not equipped with a pilot screw
3 hp	
Carburetor stamped mark	6L503
Main jet	No. 68
Main air jet	No. 95
Pilot jet	No. 40
Pilot air jet	No. 70
Needle jet	
1990-1994	No. 071
1995	No. 167
Float level	
1990-1994	4 ± 0.5 mm (0.157 ± 0.02 in.)
1995	17.03 ± 0.5 mm (0.68 ± 0.02 in.)
Pilot screw turns out	Not equipped with a pilot screw
4, 5 hp	
Carburetor stamped mark	
4 hp	6E004
5 hp	6E304
Main jet	No. 80
(continued)	

Table 1 CARBURETOR SPECIFICATIONS (continued)

Model	Specification
4, 5 hp (continued)	
Main air jet	
4 hp	1.2 mm (0.047 in.)
5 hp	1.5 mm (0.059 in.)
Pilot jet	
4 hp	No. 46
5 hp	No. 52
Pilot air jet	70
4 hp	1.4 mm (0.055 in.)
5 hp	1.2 mm (0.047 in.)
Float level	22 ± 0.5 mm (0.87 ± 0.02 in.)
Pilot screw turns out	
4 hp	1 3/4 turns
5 hp	1 5/8 turns
6, 8 hp	
Carburetor stamped mark	
6 hp	6H601
8 hp	6G101
Main jet	No. 98
Pilot jet	No. 45
Float level	14 ± 2.0 mm (0.55 ± 0.08 in.)
Pilot screw turns out	1 1/8 turns
9.9, 15 hp	
Carburetor stamped mark	
9.9 hp	6E774
15 hp	6E805
Main jet	
9.9 hp	No. 104
15 hp	No. 135
Main nozzle	
9.9 hp	3.1 mm (0.122 in.)
15 hp	3 mm (0.118 in.)
Pilot jet	
9.9 hp	No. 58
15 hp	No. 56
Float level	20 ± 0.5 mm (0.79 ± 0.02 in.)
Pilot screw turns out	1 1/4 turns
25 hp	
Carburetor stamped mark	69L201
Main jet	No. 125
Main nozzle	3.2 mm (0.13 in.)
Pilot jet	No. 60
Float level	14.5 ± 0.5 mm (0.571 ± 0.02 in.)
Pilot screw turns out	2 turns out
C25	
Carburetor stamped mark	69501
Main jet	No. 145
Main air jet	1.0 mm (0.039 in.)
Pilot jet	No. 60
Pilot air jet	1.2 mm (0.047 in.)
Float level	18.0 ± 1.0 mm (0.71 ± 0.04 in.)
Pilot screw turns out	1 1/2 turns out

(continued)

6

Table 1 CARBURETOR SPECIFICATIONS (continued)

Model	Specification
30 hp	
Carburetor stamped mark	6J811
Main jet	No. 102
Main air jet	
Carb. No. 1, 2	No. 140
Carb. No. 3	No. 150
Pilot jet	No. 50
Pilot air jet	
Carb. No. 1, 2	No. 140
Carb. No. 3	No. 120
Float level	15.0 ± 0.5 mm (0.59 ± 0.02 in.)
Pilot screw turns out	
Top carburetor	3/4 turns
Center carburetor	
1990-1992	1 1/4 turns
1993-on	1 3/4 turns
Bottom carburetor	1 turn
C30	
Carburetor stamped mark	61T00
Main jet	No. 130
Main air jet	0.8 mm (0.031 in.)
Main nozzle	4.0 mm (0.16 in.)
Pilot jet	No. 64
Pilot air jet	0.8 mm (0.031 in.)
Float level	14.5 mm (0.571 in.)
Pilot screw turns out	1 1/2 turns out
40 hp	
Carburetor stamped mark	63B00
Main jet	
Carb. No. 1, 3	No. 115
Carb. No. 2	No. 118
Main air jet	No. 160
Main nozzle	3.0 mm (0.12 in.)
Pilot jet	No. 60
Pilot air jet	No. 75
Float level	15.0 ± 1.0 mm (0.59 ± 0.04 in.)
Pilot screw turns out	
1990-1994	1 1/8 turns
1995	1 1/2 turns
C40	
Carburetor stamped mark	6E902
Main jet	No. 170
Main air jet	No. 180
Pilot jet	No. 75
Pilot air jet	No. 100
Float level	19.5 ± 3 mm (0.77 ± 0.12 in.)
Pilot screw turns out	1 3/4 turns out
50 hp, Pro 50	
Carburetor stamped mark	62X00
Main jet	No. 130
Main air jet	No. 140
Main nozzle	4.0 mm (0.16 in.)

(continued)

Table 1 CARBURETOR SPECIFICATIONS (continued)

Model	Specification
50 hp, Pro 50 (continued)	
Pilot jet	No. 62
Pilot air jet	No. 80
Float level	15.0 ± 1.0 mm (0.59 ± 0.04 in.)
Pilot screw turns out	
1990-1994	1 3/4 turns
1995	
Manual start	1 5/8 turns
Electric start	1 3/8 turns
C55	
Carburetor stamped mark	69703
Main jet	No. 160
Main air jet	No. 125
Pilot jet	No. 80
Pilot air jet	No. 100
Float level	19.0 ± 1.0 mm (0.75 ± 0.04 in.)
Pilot screw turns out	
1990-1994	2 turns
1995	2 1/4 turns
Pro 60	
Carburetor stamped mark	6H20A
Main jet	No. 150
Main air jet	No. 160
Pilot jet	No. 75
Pilot air jet	No. 70
Float level	14.0 ± 1.0 mm (0.55 ± 0.04 in.)
Pilot screw turns out	
1991	1 1/4 turns
1992-on	1 1/2 turns
70 hp	
Carburetor stamped mark	6H30A
Main jet	No. 150
Main air jet	No. 160
Pilot jet	No. 75
Pilot alr jet	No. 70
Float level	14.0 ± 1.0 mm (0.55 ± 0.04 in.)
Pilot screw turns out	
1990-1991	1 3/8 turns
1992-on	1 1/4 turns
C75, C85	
Carburetor stamped mark	68806
Main jet	No. 165
Main air jet	No. 180
Pilot jet	No. 78
Pilot air jet	No. 100
Float level	19.5 ± 3.0 mm (0.77 ± 0.12 in.)
Pilot screw turns out	
C75	1 1/4 turns
C85	1 1/8 turns

(continued)

6

Table 1 CARBURETOR SPECIFICATIONS (continued)

Model	Specification
90 hp	
Carburetor stamped mark	6H107
Main jet	No. 160
Main air jet	No. 175
Pilot jet	No. 78
Pilot air jet	No. 70
Float level	14.0 ± 1.0 mm (0.55 ± 0.04 in.)
Pilot screw turns out	
1990-1991	1 1/2 turns
1992-on	1 1/4 turns
115 hp, C115, Pro 115	
Carburetor stamped mark	
115 hp, Pro 115	6E514
C115	6E512
Main jet	No. 180
Main air jet	No. 290
Main nozzle (115 hp, Pro 115)	3.6 mm (0.142 in.)
Pilot jet	No. 78
Pilot air jet	No. 60
Float level	16.0 ± 0.5 mm (0.63 ± 0.02 in.)
Pilot screw turns out	5/8 turn
130 hp, L130	
Carburetor stamped mark	6L102
Main jet	No. 180
Main air jet	No. 220
Main nozzle	3.6 mm (0.142 in.)
Pilot jet	No. 80
Pilot air jet	No. 60
Float level	16.0 ± 0.5 mm (0.63 ± 0.02 in.)
Pilot screw turns out	7/8 turn
150 hp, L150	
Carburetor stamped mark	6R902
Main jet	No. 124
Main air jet	No. 210
Main nozzle	3.8 mm (0.150 in.)
Pilot jet	No. 80
Pilot air jet	No. 60
Float level	16.0 ± 0.5 mm (0.63 ± 0.02 in.)
Pilot screw turns out	
1990-1991	1 1/4 turns
1992-on	1 turn
Pro V 150	
Carburetor stamped mark	6N902
Main jet	
Starboard	No. 126
Port lower	No. 136
All others	No. 130
Main air jet	No. 220
Main nozzle	3.8 mm (0.15 in.)
Pilot jet	No. 76
Pilot air jet	No. 60

(continued)

Table 1 CARBURETOR SPECIFICATIONS (continued)

Model	Specification
Pro V 150 (continued)	
Float level	16.0 ± 0.5 mm (0.63 ± 0.02 in.)
Pilot screw turns out	
1990-1991	
Port	1 1/4 turns
Starboard	3/4 turn
1992-on	1 3/8 turns
175 hp	
Carburetor stamped mark	6R301
Main jet	No. 126
Main air jet	No. 200
Main nozzle	3.8 mm (0.150 in.)
Pilot jet	No. 76
Pilot air jet	No. 60
Float level	16.0 ± 0.5 mm (0.63 ± 0.02 in.)
Pilot screw turns out	1 3/8 turns
Pro V 175	
Carburetor stamped mark	62H00
Main jet	
Lower	No. 158
All others	No. 154
Main air jet	No. 290
Main nozzle	4.5 mm (0.177 in.)
Pilot jet	No. 80
Pilot air jet	No. 60
Float level	16.0 ± 0.5 mm (0.63 ± 0.02 in.)
Pilot screw turns out	1 1/4 turns
200 hp, L200	
Carburetor stamped mark	6R401
Main jet	
Starboard middle	No. 158
All others	No. 154
Main air jet	No. 290
Main nozzle	4.5 mm (0.177 in.)
Pilot jet	No. 84
Pilot air jet	No. 60
Float level	16.0 ± 0.5 mm (0.63 ± 0.02 in.)
Pilot screw turns out	
Port	1 1/4 turns
Starboard	3/4 turn
Pro V 200	
Carburetor stamped mark	61H03
Main jet	No. 154
Main air jet	No. 240
Main nozzle	4.5 mm (0.177 in.)
Pilot jet	No. 76
Pilot air jet	No. 60
Float level	16.0 ± 0.50 mm (0.63 ± 0.02 in.)
Pilot screw turns out	1 3/8 turns

(continued)

6

Table 1 CARBURETOR SPECIFICATIONS (continued)

Model	Specification
225 hp 90° V6	
Carburetor stamped mark	6R501
Main jet	No. 154
Main air jet	No. 190
Main nozzle	4.5 mm (0.177 in.)
Pilot jet	No. 76
Pilot air jet	No. 60
Float level	16.0 ± 0.5 mm (0.63 ± 0.02 in.)
Pilot screw turns out	1 1/8 turns
225 hp, L225 76° V6	
Carburetor stamped mark	62J01
Main jet	
Cylinders No. 1, 2, 3, 4, 5	No. 150
Cylinder No. 6	No. 155
Main air jet	
Cylinders No. 1, 2	No. 230
Cylinders No. 3, 4, 5	No. 240
Cylinder No. 6	No. 200
Pilot jet	No. 94
Pilot air jet	No. 70
Float level	15.5 ± 0.5 mm (0.61 ± 0.02 in.)
Pilot screw turns out	5/8 turn
250 hp, L250 76° V6	
Carburetor stamped mark	61A04
Main jet	
Cylinders No. 1, 2, 3, 4	No. 155
Cylinders No. 5, 6	No. 165
Main air jet	
Cylinders No. 1, 2, 3, 5	No. 220
Cylinders No. 4, 6	No. 200
Pilot jet	No. 102
Pilot air jet	No. 60
Float level	15.5 ± 0.5 mm (0.61 ± 0.02 in.)
Pilot screw turns out	5/8 turn

Table 2 REED STOP SPECIFICATIONS

Model	Reed stop clearance mm (in.)	Warp limit mm (in.)
2 hp	6.0 ± 0.2 (0.24 ± 0.01)	0.3 (0.01)
3 hp	4.0 ± 0.2 (0.16 ± 0.008)	0.2 (0.008)
4, 5 hp	7.0 ± 0.2 (0.28 ± 0.008)	0.2 (0.008)
6, 8 hp	4.5 ± 0.2 (0.177 ± 0.008)	0.2 (0.008)
9.9 hp	1.6 ± 0.1 (0.063 ± 0.004)	0.2 (0.008)
15 hp	4.0 ± 0.1 (0.157 ± 0.004)	0.2 (0.008)
25 hp	6.0 ± 0.2 (0.236 ± 0.008)	0.2 (0.008)
C25, C30	5.0-5.5 (0.197-0.217)	0.2 (0.008)
30 hp	2.7 ± 0.2 (0.106 ± 0.008)	0.2 (0.008)
40 hp	6.0 ± 0.2 (0.24 ± 0.01)	0.2 (0.008)

(continued)

Table 2 REED STOP SPECIFICATIONS

Model	Reed stop clearance mm (in.)	Warp limit mm (in.)
C40	5.0 ± 0.2 (0.20 ± 0.01)	0.2 (0.008)
50 hp, Pro 50	6.0 ± 0.2 (0.24 ± 0.01)	0.2 (0.008)
C55, C75, C85	8.6 ± 0.2 (0.34 ± 0.01)	0.5 (0.020)
60 hp	3.0 ± 0.2 (0.118 ± 0.01)	0.2 (0.008)
90 hp	9.9 ± 0.2 (0.39 ± 0.01)	0.2 (0.008)
115 hp, Pro 115, 130 hp, Pro 130	6.5 ± 0.3 (0.256 ± 0.01)	0.2 (0.008)
150 hp, L150, Pro V 150, 175 hp	5.7 ± 0.2 (0.224 ± 0.01)	0.2 (0.008)
Pro V 175, 200 hp, L200, Pro V 200, 225 hp 90° V6	6.5 ± 0.3 (0.256 ± 0.01)	0.2 (0.008)
225 hp, L225, 250 hp, L250 76° V6	9.0 ± 0.3 (0.354 ± 0.01)	0.2 (0.008)

6

Chapter Seven

Ignition and Electrical Systems

This chapter provides service procedures for the battery, charging system, starter motor (if so equipped) and ignition system used on Yamaha outboard motors. Wiring diagrams are included at the end of the book.

Tables 1-5 are at the end of the chapter.

> *NOTE*
> *The "L" series engines (counter rotation models), are included in all procedures. Unless there is a separate procedure designated for the "L" series outboard motor, refer to the procedure that relates to the same horsepower rating. If you are working on an L200, then refer to the 200 hp procedure.*

ELECTRICAL CONNECTOR ADAPTERS

The 1994 and later 50-250 hp models are equipped with new self-locking wiring connectors. These electrical connectors are designed to work with a boat rigged for the 1994 and later models only. Difficulties may occur if trying to install a 1994 and later outboard motor on an older boat that is already wired with a rigging kit for a 1993 or earlier model, or when installing a previous model outboard motor in a boat pre-rigged for a 1994 and later model.

Because this problem may occur, Yamaha has developed wiring harness adapter kits to simplify either type of installation. The wiring har-

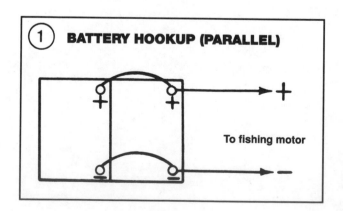

① **BATTERY HOOKUP (PARALLEL)**

To fishing motor

ness kits for the various engines are listed in **Table 1**.

BATTERY

Since batteries used in marine applications endure far more rigorous treatment than those used in an automotive electrical system, they are constructed differently. Marine batteries have a thicker exterior case to cushion the plates inside during tight turns and rough water operation. Thicker plates are also used, with each one individually fastened within the case to prevent premature failure. Spill-proof caps on the battery cells prevent electrolyte from spilling into the bilge.

> *CAUTION*
> *Sealed or maintenance-free batteries are **not** recommended for use with the un-regulated charging systems used on some Yamaha outboards. Excessive charging during continued high-speed operation will cause the electrolyte to boil, resulting in the loss of electrolyte. Since water cannot be added to such batteries, such overcharging will ruin the battery.*

Separate batteries may be used to provide power for any accessories such as lighting, fish finders and depth finder. To determine the required capacity of such batteries, calculate the average discharge rate of the accessories and refer to **Table 2**.

Batteries may be wired in parallel to double the ampere hour capacity while maintaining a 12-volt system (**Figure 1**). For accessories which require 24 volts, batteries may be wired in series (**Figure 2**), but only accessories specifically requiring 24 volts should be connected into the system. Whether wired in parallel or in series, disconnect and charge the batteries individually.

Excessive Battery Drain (1994 V4 and V6 Models)

Yamaha has determined that on some of the 1994 V4 and V6 models there is a possible problem with the battery draining over a prolonged period of storage. The digital speedometer memory hold circuit can cause excessive current drain on the battery since the fuel sender circuit remains active even after the ignition key is turned off.

If you have encountered this problem, a relay kit can be installed in the fuel sender circuit of the speedometer. Prior to purchasing and installing the relay kit, check the color of the plastic tape around the wiring harness on the back of the speedometer. If the tape color is gray, the speedometer has been modified and the relay kit is not necessary. If the tape is of another color, the relay kit should be installed.

The Speedometer Relay Kit (part No. 90891-40220-00) contains the relay, 1 yellow extension lead, 1 black extension lead and 1 tie wrap. The kit is available from a Yamaha outboard dealer.

1. Locate the speedometer wiring harness containing 5 wires (1 yellow, 1 white, 1 red and 2 black).

2. If there is an empty female connector on the boat wiring harness, connect the yellow and black wires on the relay to the corresponding colored wires on the boat/speedometer harness.

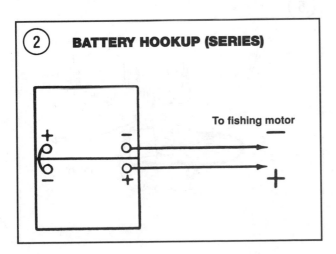

② **BATTERY HOOKUP (SERIES)**

To fishing motor

3. If there are no empty female connectors on the wiring harness, use the black and yellow jumper wires provided in the kit.

NOTE
There are 2 black wires on the speedometer sensor harness. Either black wire can be used for installation of the relay.

4. Locate and unplug the white wire from the speedometer harness (the wire leading from the speedometer is pink) (**Figure 3**).

5. Plug the male white connector on the relay into the white female wire connector on the speedometer harness. Plug the white female connector wire on the relay onto the pink male wire connector on the speedometer harness (**Figure 4**).

6. Use the tie wrap, furnished in the kit, tie the wiring and the relay neatly to the harness so it does not hang down from under the dashboard (**Figure 5**).

Battery Installation in Aluminum Boats

If a battery is not properly secured and grounded when installed in an aluminum boat, it may contact the hull and short to ground. This will burn out remote control cables, tiller handle cables or wiring harnesses.

The following preventive steps should be taken when installing a battery in a metal boat.

1. Choose a location as far as practical from the fuel tank while providing access for maintenance.

2. Install the battery in a plastic battery box with cover and tie-down strap (**Figure 6**).

3. If a covered container is not used, cover the positive battery terminal with a non-conductive shield or boot (**Figure 7**).

4. Make sure the battery is secured inside the battery box and also make sure the box is fastened in position with the tie-down strap.

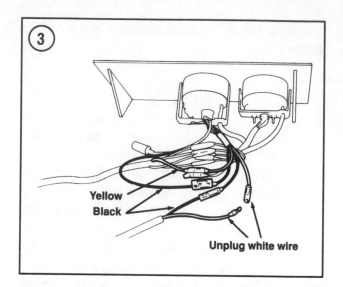

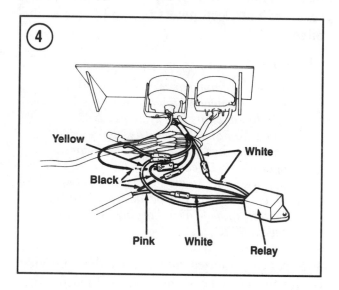

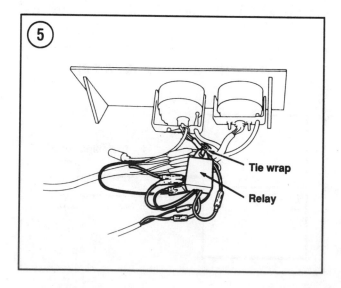

Care and Inspection

1. Remove the battery container cover (**Figure 6**) or hold-down (**Figure 7**).

2. Disconnect the negative (–) battery cable. Disconnect the positive (+) battery cable.

> *NOTE*
> *Some batteries have a built-in carry strap (**Figure 8**) for use in Step 3.*

3. Attach a battery carry strap to the terminal posts. Remove the battery from the battery tray or container.

4. Check the entire battery case for cracks or electrolyte leakage.

5. Inspect the battery tray or container for corrosion and clean if necessary with a solution of baking soda and water.

> *NOTE*
> *Keep cleaning solution out of the battery cells in Step 6 or the electrolyte will be seriously weakened.*

6. Clean the top of the battery with a stiff bristle brush using the baking soda and water solution (**Figure 9**). Rinse the battery case with clear water and wipe dry with a clean cloth or paper towel.

7. Position the battery in the battery tray or container.

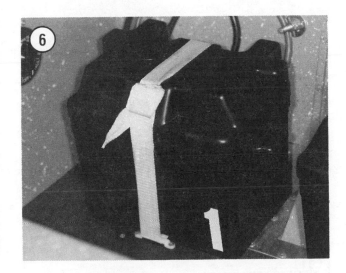

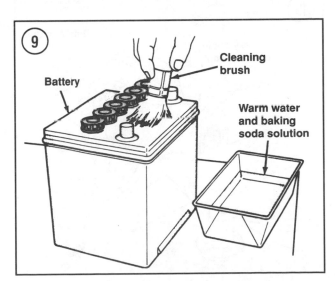

8. Clean the battery cable clamps with a stiff wire brush or one of the many tools made for this purpose (**Figure 10**). The same tool is used for cleaning the battery posts (**Figure 11**).

9. Reconnect the positive battery cable, then the negative cable.

> *CAUTION*
> *Be sure the battery cables are connected to their proper terminals. Connecting the battery backward will reverse the polarity and damage the rectifier and components of the electronic ignition system.*

10. Tighten the battery connections and coat with a petroleum jelly such as Vaseline or a light mineral grease.

> *NOTE*
> *Do not overfill the battery cells in Step 11. The electrolyte expands due to heat from charging and will overflow if the level is more than 4.8 mm (3/16 in.) above the battery plates.*

11. Remove the filler caps and check the electrolyte level. Add distilled water, if necessary, to bring the level up to 4.8 mm (3/16 in.) above the plates in the battery case (**Figure 12**).

> *NOTE*
> *If distilled water has been added, reinstall the filler caps, remove the battery and gently shake the battery for several minutes to mix the existing electrolyte with the new water. Properly secure the battery.*

Testing

Hydrometer testing is the best way to check battery condition. Use a hydrometer with numbered graduations from 1.100-1.300 rather than one with just color-coded bands. To use the hydrometer, squeeze the rubber ball, insert the tip in a cell and release the ball (**Figure 13**).

> *NOTE*
> *Do not attempt to test a battery with a hydrometer immediately after adding water to the cells. Charge the battery for 15-20 minutes at a rate high enough to cause vigorous gassing prior to testing the battery.*

Draw enough electrolyte to float the weighted float inside the hydrometer. When using a temperature-compensated hydrometer, release the electrolyte and repeat this process several times

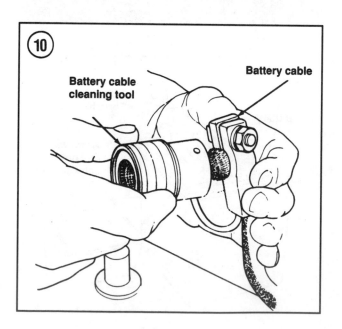

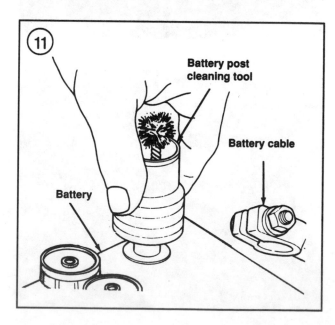

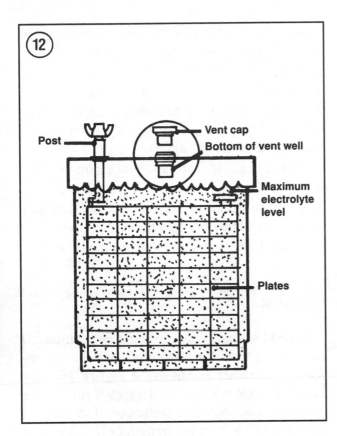

(12)

Post

Vent cap

Bottom of vent well

Maximum electrolyte level

Plates

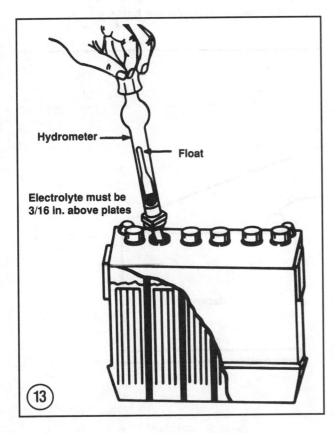

Hydrometer — Float

Electrolyte must be 3/16 in. above plates

(13)

to make sure the thermometer has adjusted to the electrolyte temperature before taking the reading.

Hold the hydrometer vertically and note the number in line with the surface of the electrolyte (**Figure 14**). This is the specific gravity for that cell. Return the electrolyte to the cell from which it came.

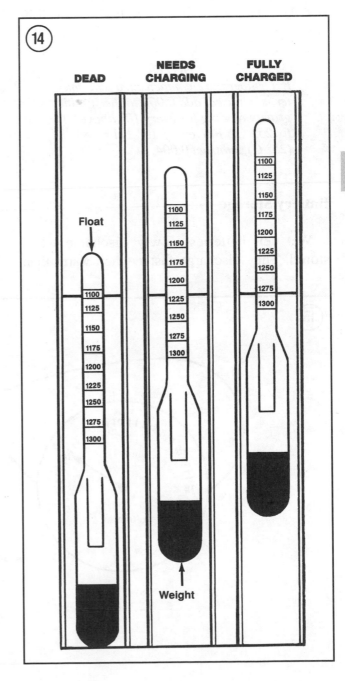

(14)

| DEAD | NEEDS CHARGING | FULLY CHARGED |

Float

Weight

7

The specific gravity of the electrolyte in each battery cell is an excellent indicator of that cell's condition. A fully charged cell will read 1.260 or more at 68° F (20° C). A cell that is 75 percent charged will read from 1.220-1.230 while one with a 50 percent charge reads from 1.170-1.180. If the cell tests below 1.120, the battery must be recharged and one that reads 1.100 or below is dead. Charging is also necessary if the specific gravity varies more than 50 points from cell to cell.

NOTE
If a temperature-compensated hydrometer is not used, add 0.004 to the specific gravity reading for every 10° above 80° F (25° C). For every 10° below 80° F (25° C), subtract 0.004.

Battery Storage

Wet cell batteries slowly discharge when stored. They discharge faster when warm than when cold. See **Table 3**. Before storing a battery for the season, perform the following.

1. Clean the case with a solution of baking soda and water. Rinse with clear water and wipe dry.
2. Charge the battery to a fully charged condition (no change in specific gravity when 3 readings are taken 1 hour apart).
3. Install the filler caps and make sure they are on tight.
4. Coat the battery posts with a petroleum jelly such as Vaseline or a light mineral grease.
5. Store the battery in a cool, dry location.

Charging

A good state of charge should be maintained in batteries used for starting. Check the battery with a voltmeter as shown in **Figure 15**. Any battery that cannot deliver at least 9.6 volts under a starting load should be recharged. If recharging does not bring it up to strength or if it does not hold the charge, replace the battery.

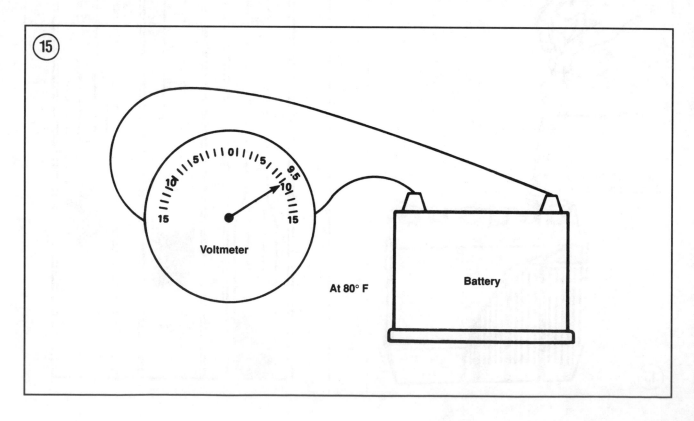

WARNING
During the charging process, highly ex-plosive hydrogen gas is released from the battery. The battery should be charged only in a well-ventilated area away from any open flames (including pilot lights on home gas appliances). Do not allow any smoking in the area. Never check the charge by arcing (connecting pliers or other metal objects) across the terminals; the resulting spark can ignite the hydrogen gas.

The battery does not have to be removed from the boat for charging, but it is a recommended safety procedure since a charging battery gives off highly explosive hydrogen gas. In many boats, the area around the battery is not well ventilated and the gas may remain in the area for hours after the charging process has been completed. Sparks or flames occurring near the battery can cause it to explode, spraying battery acid over a wide area. Also the corrosive mist that is emitted during the charging process will corrode all surrounding surfaces.

For this reason, it is important that you observe the following precautions:

a. Do not allow anyone to smoke around batteries that are charging or have been recently charged.

b. Do not break a live circuit at the battery terminals and cause an electrical arc that can ignite the hydrogen gas.

Connect the charger to the battery—negative to negative, positive to positive.

If the charger output is variable, select a 4 amp setting. Set the voltage regulator to 12 volts and plug the charger in. If the battery is severely discharged, allow it to charge for at least 8 hours.

Batteries that are not badly discharged require less charging time. **Table 3** gives approximate charge rates for batteries used primarily for cranking. Check the charging progress with the hydrometer.

Jump Starting

If the battery becomes severely discharged, it is possible to start and run an engine by jump starting it from another battery. If the proper procedure is not followed, however, jump starting can be dangerous. Check the electrolyte level before jump starting any battery. If it is not visible or if it appears to be frozen, *do not* attempt to jump start the battery.

WARNING
Use extreme caution when connecting a booster battery to the battery that is dis-charged to avoid personal injury or damage to the system.

1. Connect the jumper cables in the order and sequence shown in **Figure 16**.

WARNING
An electrical arc may occur when the final connection is made. This could cause an explosion if it occurs near either battery. For this reason, the final connection should be made to a good ground away from the battery and not to the battery itself.

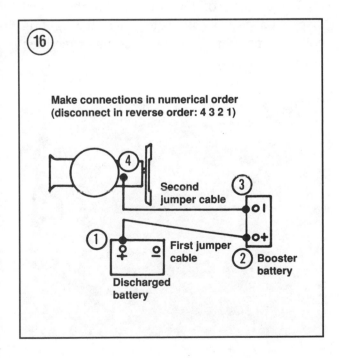

16

Make connections in numerical order (disconnect in reverse order: 4 3 2 1)

Second jumper cable

First jumper cable

Discharged battery

Booster battery

7

2. Check that all jumper cables are out of the way of moving engine parts.

> *CAUTION*
> *Running the engine at wide-open throttle may cause damage to the electrical system.*

3. Start the engine. Once it starts, run it at a moderate speed.

4. Remove the jumper cables in the exact reverse order shown in **Figure 16**. Remove the cables from point 4, then 3, 2 and 1.

New Battery Installation

When replacing the old battery with a new one, be sure to charge it completely (specific gravity, 1.260-1.280) before installing it in the boat. Failure to do so, or using the battery with a low electrolyte level will permanently damage the battery. When purchasing a new battery, be sure to purchase the correct battery capacity for your specific engine and boat.

> *NOTE*
> *Recycle your old battery. When you replace the old battery, be sure to turn in the old battery at that time. The lead plates and the plastic case can be recycled. Most outboard dealers will accept your old battery in trade when you purchase a new one, but if they will not, many automotive supply stores certainly will. **Never** place an old battery in your household trash since it is illegal, in most states, to place any acid or lead (heavy metal) contents in landfills. There is also the danger of the battery being crushed in the trash truck and spraying acid on the truck operator.*

BATTERY CHARGING SYSTEM

A battery charging system is standard on all electric start models. Manual start 6-30 hp models may be equipped with an AC lighting coil

system to operate lights and other AC electrical accessories.

The battery charging system consists of a charging coil (6-70 hp electric start models) or stator assembly (75-250 hp models), flywheel, rectifier (except electric start) or voltage regulator/rectifier (electric start) and related wiring. Rotation of the flywheel magnets creates alternating current (AC) in the charging coil(s) that is sent to the rectifier or voltage regulator/rectifier (A, **Figure 17**). The rectifier or regulator/rectifier converts (rectifies) the alternating current to direct current (DC) for storage in the battery (AC cannot be stored).

Figure 18 shows a typical battery charging system used on 9.9 and 15 hp models. Note that the components inside the dotted block are used on electric start models only.

System Inspection

A malfunction in the battery charging system generally results in an undercharged battery. Perform the following visual inspection to determine the cause of the problem. If the visual inspection proves satisfactory, test the lighting coil and rectifier, or voltage regulator/rectifier. See Chapter Three.

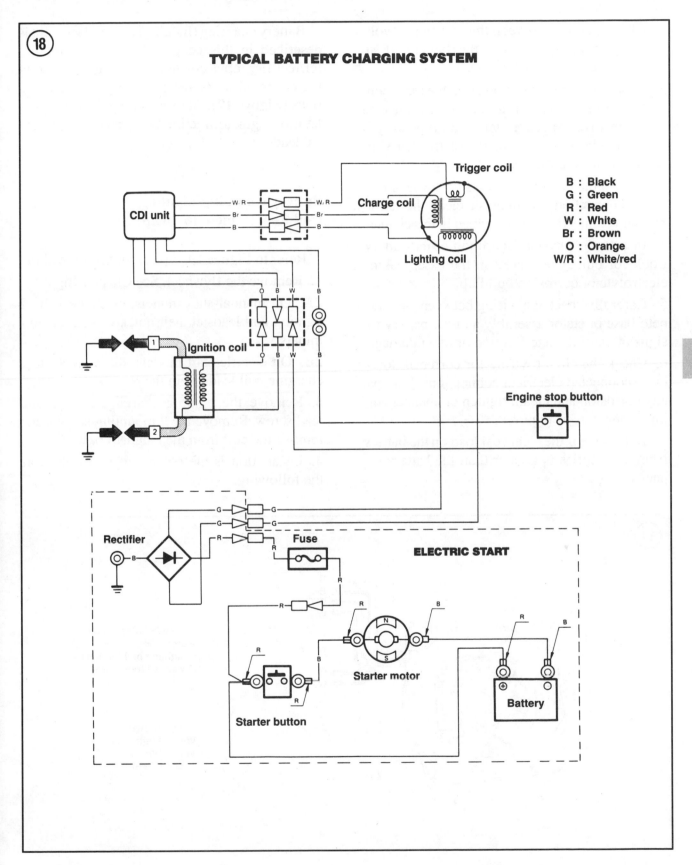

TYPICAL BATTERY CHARGING SYSTEM

B : Black
G : Green
R : Red
W : White
Br : Brown
O : Orange
W/R : White/red

7

1. Check the fuse between the rectifier, or voltage regulator/rectifier and the battery, if so equipped (B, **Figure 17**, typical).

2. Make sure that the battery cables are connected properly. The red cable must be connected to the positive (+) battery terminal. If polarity is reversed, check for a damaged rectifier or voltage regulator/rectifier.

3. Inspect the battery terminals for loose or corroded connections. Tighten or clean the terminals and connections as described in this chapter.

4. Inspect the physical condition of the battery. Look for bulges or cracks in the case, leaking electrolyte or corrosion build up.

5. Carefully check the wiring between the magneto base or stator assembly and the battery for signs of chafing, deterioration or other damage.

6. Check the circuit wiring for corroded, loose or disconnected electrical connections. Remove any corrosion and clean, tighten or connect wiring connectors as required.

7. Determine if the electrical load on the battery from accessories is greater than the battery capacity.

Battery charging (lighting) coil replacement is described in this chapter. Rectifier or regulator/rectifier replacement involves disconnecting the electrical leads and removing the attaching bolts (**Figure 17**). After installing the new regulator or regulator/rectifier, reconnect the electrical leads.

Battery Charging/Lighting Coil Replacement (6-70 hp)

Refer to **Figure 19**, typical for this procedure.

1. Remove the flywheel. See Chapter Eight.

2A. On manual start models, disconnect the 2 lighting coil leads at their quick-disconnect terminals.

2B. On electric start models, disconnect the 2 charging coil leads from the rectifier.

3. Remove the lighting charging coil ground lead screw. Remove the 2 mounting screws and remove the coil from the magneto base.

4. Installation is the reverse of removal. Note the following:

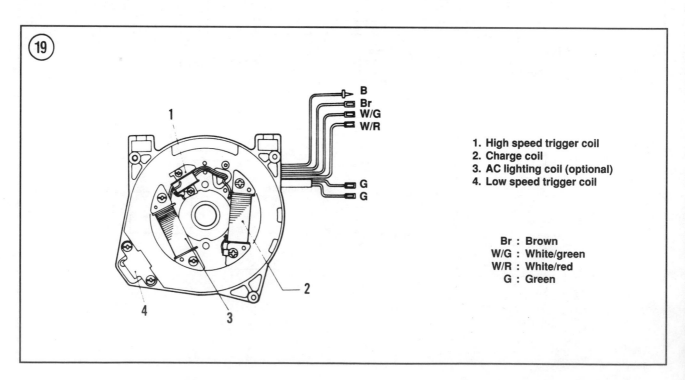

19

B
Br
W/G
W/R

G
G

1. High speed trigger coil
2. Charge coil
3. AC lighting coil (optional)
4. Low speed trigger coil

Br : Brown
W/G : White/green
W/R : White/red
G : Green

a. Be sure to reconnect the ground lead and route all wires so they do not contact or interfere with moving parts.

b. Make sure all electrical connectors are free of corrosion and are tight.

Charging Coil Replacement (75-90 hp)

1. Remove the flywheel. See Chapter Eight.
2. Remove the CDI unit cover and disconnect the 2 charging coil leads from the rectifier or regulator/rectifier.

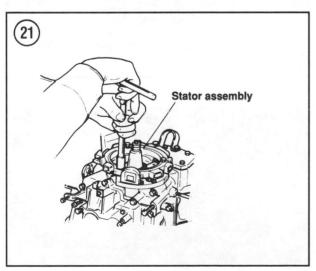

Stator assembly

3. Remove the charging coil ground lead screw. Remove the 2 mounting screws and remove the coil from the magneto base.
4. Installation is the reverse of removal. Note the following:
   a. Be sure to reconnect the ground lead and route all wires so they do not contact or interfere with moving parts.
   b. Make sure all electrical connectors are free of corrosion and are tight.

Battery Charging Coil and Ignition System Charging Coil Replacement (V4 and V6 Models)

The battery charging coils are combined with the ignition system charge coils in an alternator stator on V4 and V6 engines (**Figure 20**). The entire stator assembly must be replaced if either the battery charge or the ignition charging coils are defective.

1. Remove the flywheel. See Chapter Eight.
2. Remove the CDI unit cover and disconnect the stator leads from the rectifier or regulator/rectifier and the CDI unit.
3. Remove the bolts securing the stator assembly to the power head (**Figure 21**). Remove the stator assembly.
4. Installation is the reverse of removal. Note the following:
   a. Be sure to reconnect the ground lead and route all wires so they do not contact or interfere with any moving parts.
   b. Make sure all electrical connectors are free of corrosion and are tight.

ELECTRIC STARTING SYSTEM

Outboard motors covered in this manual either use a rope-operated manual rewind starting system or an electric (starter motor) starting system. Manual rewind starters are covered in Chapter Eleven.

7

The electric starting circuit consists of the battery, an ignition switch, neutral start switch, the starter motor, starter relay and connecting wiring.

The plunger-operated neutral start switch is located in the remote control box. A stop button (kill switch) connected to the ignition system can be used to shut the engine off in an emergency. Outboards equipped with a remote control box have this emergency switch located in the remote control box. On models using a tiller handle, the switch is generally located at the front of the lower cowling. **Figure 22** shows a typical switch installation as seen from the top of the engine.

Starting system operation and troubleshooting are described in Chapter Three.

Starter Motor

Marine starter motors used on Yamaha outboards are very similar in design and operation to those found on automotive engines. They use an inertia-type drive in which external spiral splines on the armature shaft mate with internal splines on the drive assembly.

The starter motor produces very high torque but only for a brief period of time, due to heat buildup. Never operate the starter motor continuously for more than 10 seconds. Let the motor cool for at least 2 minutes before operating it again.

If the starter motor does not turn operate, check the battery and all connecting wiring for loose or corroded connections. If this does not solve the problem, refer to Chapter Three. Except for brush replacement, service to the starter motor is limited to replacement with a new or rebuilt unit.

Yamaha outboard motors use a variety of starter motors, manufactured primarily by Hitachi. The starter motors are equipped with either 2, 3 or 4 brushes depending on the model.

Removal/Installation

1. Disconnect the negative battery cable.
2. Remove the engine cover.
3. Disconnect the electrical cables from the starter motor terminals (**Figure 23**).
4. Remove the mounting bolts. If equipped with a plastic pinion cover, remove the mounting bolt and the cover.
5. Remove the starter motor.
6. Installation is the reverse of removal. Tighten the mounting bolts to the torque specifications listed in **Table 5**.

Brush Replacement

Outboard motors use either a 2-, 3- or 4- brush starter design. Always replace the brushes in

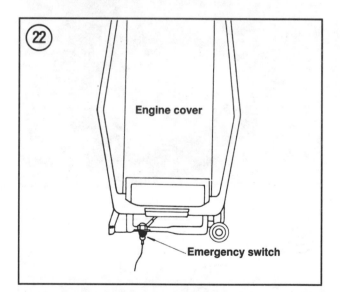

Engine cover

Emergency switch

complete sets. Refer to the following illustrations for the following procedure:

   a. **Figure 24**: 2-brush design, 9.9-15 hp, 25 hp models, typical.

   b. **Figure 25**: 2-brush design, 30-70 hp models, typical.

   c. **Figure 26**: 3-brush design, 115-250 hp models, typical.

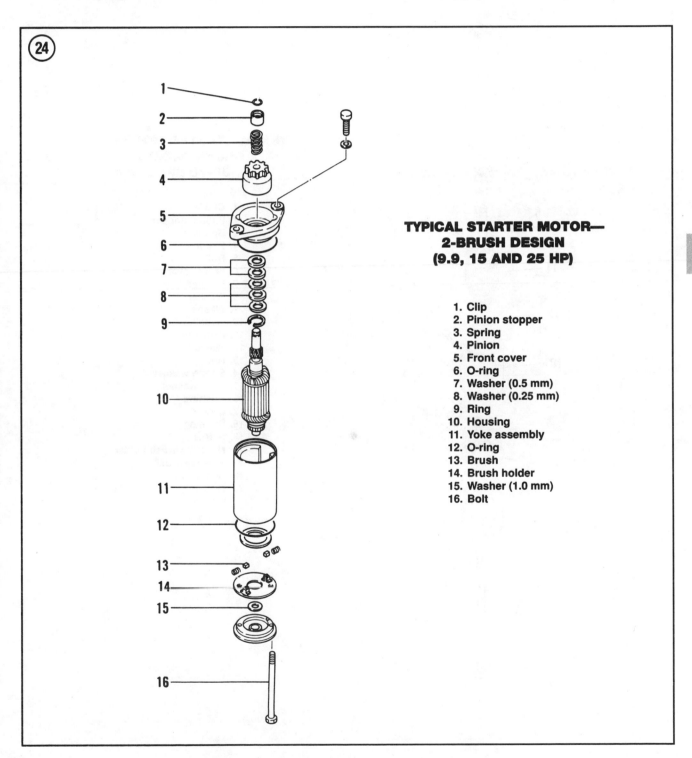

**TYPICAL STARTER MOTOR—
2-BRUSH DESIGN
(9.9, 15 AND 25 HP)**

1. Clip
2. Pinion stopper
3. Spring
4. Pinion
5. Front cover
6. O-ring
7. Washer (0.5 mm)
8. Washer (0.25 mm)
9. Ring
10. Housing
11. Yoke assembly
12. O-ring
13. Brush
14. Brush holder
15. Washer (1.0 mm)
16. Bolt

7

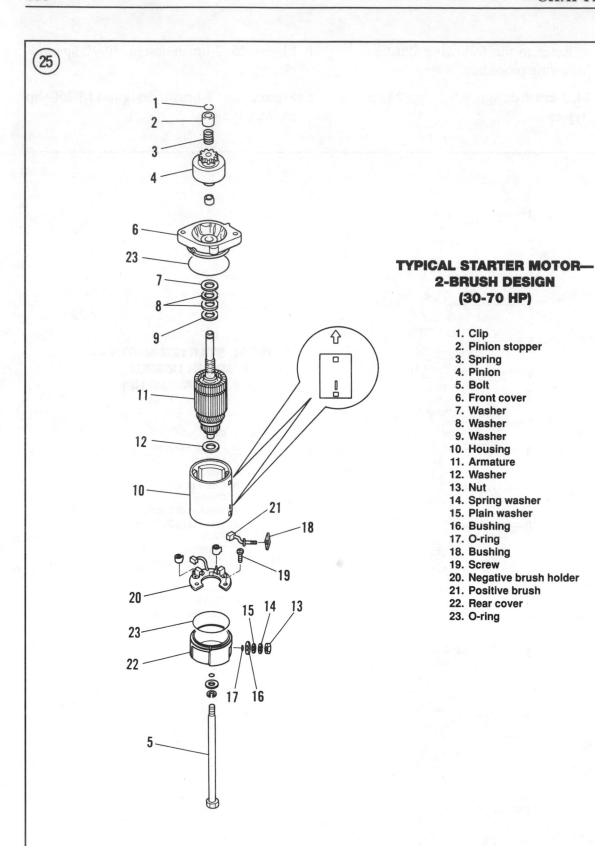

TYPICAL STARTER MOTOR— 2-BRUSH DESIGN (30-70 HP)

1. Clip
2. Pinion stopper
3. Spring
4. Pinion
5. Bolt
6. Front cover
7. Washer
8. Washer
9. Washer
10. Housing
11. Armature
12. Washer
13. Nut
14. Spring washer
15. Plain washer
16. Bushing
17. O-ring
18. Bushing
19. Screw
20. Negative brush holder
21. Positive brush
22. Rear cover
23. O-ring

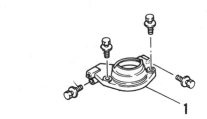

**TYPICAL STARTER MOTOR—
3-BRUSH DESIGN
(115-250 HP)**

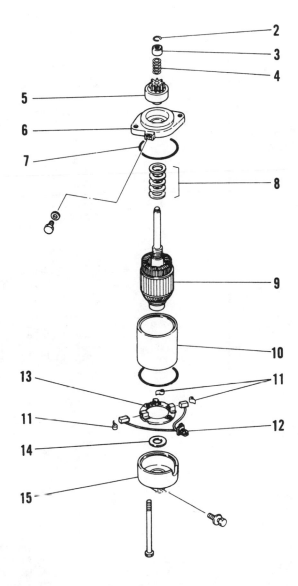

1. Pinion cover
2. Clip
3. Pinion stopper
4. Spring
5. Pinion (starter clutch)
6. Front cover
7. O-ring
8. Washer(s)
9. Armature
10. Housing
11. Brush springs
12. Brushes
13. Brush holder
14. Washer
15. Rear cover

7

d. **Figure 27**: 4-brush design, 85-90 hp models, typical.

1. Remove the starter as described in this chapter.

2. Remove the 2 through-bolts from the starter.

3. Remove the commutator end cap, circlip and thrust washer, if so equipped.

4. Lightly tap on starter drive with a rubber mallet until the lower end cap is free of the starter housing. Remove the end cap, taking care not to lose the brush springs.

NOTE
If corrosion causes the brushes to stick during Step 5, replace the brush holder plate.

5. Check the brush spring tension by pulling spring back and releasing it. Replace the spring if it does not snap the brush firmly into position.

6. Remove the brushes and springs from the brush holder plate. See **Figure 28** and **Figure 29**.

7. Inspect the brushes. Replace all brushes if any are pitted or oil-soaked. Measure each brush with a vernier caliper (**Figure 30**). Replace brushes if worn to the following dimension:

    a. 9.9-15 hp: 4.6 mm (0.18 in.)

    b. C25: 8.9 mm (0.35 in.)

    c. 25 hp: 7.6 mm (0.30 in.)

    d. 30-70 hp: 8.9 mm (0.35 in.)

    e. 75-250 hp: 12 mm (0.47 in.)

8A. If the brush holder is installed in the end cap, perform the following:

    a. Remove the positive terminal nut, insulators and O-ring (**Figure 31**, typical).

    b. Remove the screws holding the brush holder to the end cap (**Figure 32**, typical).

    c. Remove the brush holder plate from the end cap.

    d. Connect an ohmmeter between the insulated brush holder and ground (**Figure 33**). Replace the brush holder plate if the meter shows continuity.

    e. Determine whether or not brushes are fitted with leads and terminals. Make sure you

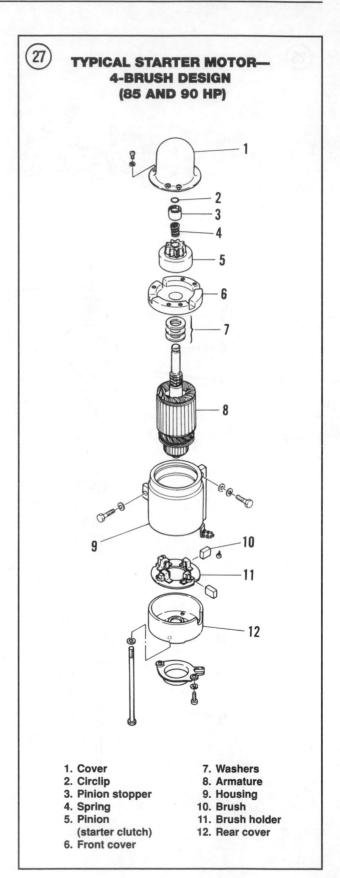

27 **TYPICAL STARTER MOTOR—**
4-BRUSH DESIGN
(85 AND 90 HP)

1. Cover	7. Washers
2. Circlip	8. Armature
3. Pinion stopper	9. Housing
4. Spring	10. Brush
5. Pinion	11. Brush holder
(starter clutch)	12. Rear cover
6. Front cover	

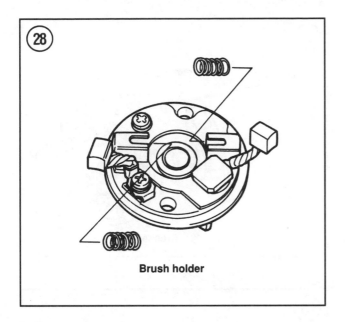

Brush holder

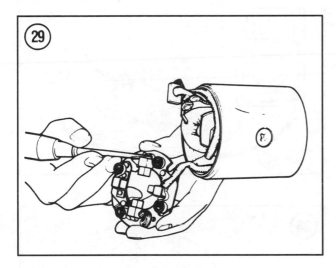

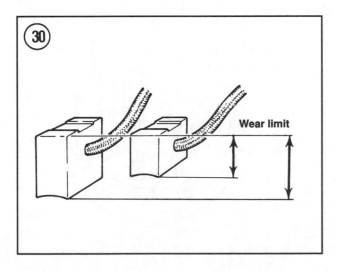

Wear limit

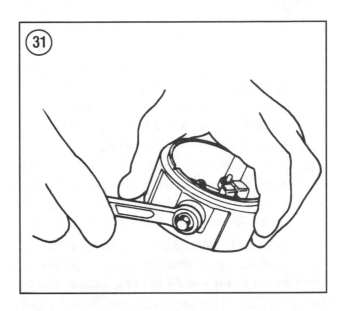

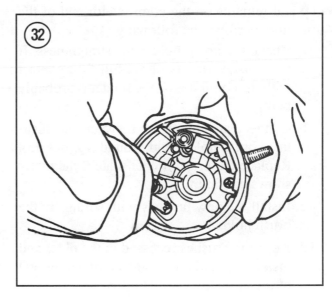

7

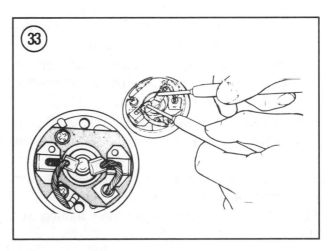

have the correct type of replacement brushes.

f. *Brushes with leads and terminals*: Remove the screw holding the old brush. Remove the brush from the end cap holder. Install the new brush in the end cap holder and attach to the cap with a screw.

g. *Brushes without leads*: Remove the old brush and spring from the brush holder. Insert the new brush with the spring in the holder. Reattach the holder to the end cap.

h. Press the brushes into the holders and use a narrow strip of flexible metal or plastic as shown in **Figure 34** to keep them in place.

8B. If the brush holder is separate from the end cap and remains on the commutator end of the armature, perform the following:

a. Check the brush holder for straightness. If the brushes do not show full-face contact with the commutator, the holder is probably bent.

b. Connect an ohmmeter between the insulated brush holder and ground (**Figure 35**). Replace the brush holder plate if the meter shows continuity.

c. Install the new brushes with springs in the brush holder.

d. Keep the brushes recessed in the older and install the holder onto the commutator end of the armature shaft (**Figure 36**).

e. Align the cutouts in the brush holder with the holes in the front cover to permit insertion of the through bolts (**Figure 37**). If the brush holder is part of the end cap, remove the temporary brush retainer as the brushes slide over the commutator.

9. On models so equipped, make sure the O-ring is in place on the front cover. Install the front cover.

10. Align the notch in the rear cover with the projection on the field coil case (**Figure 38**).

11. Install the through-bolts and tighten securely.

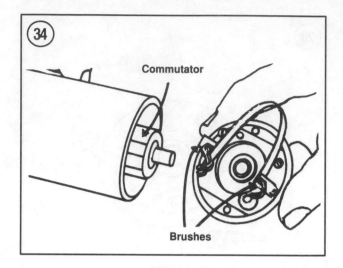

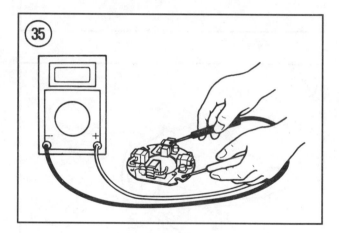

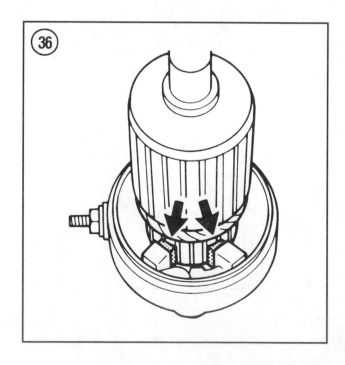

12. On models so equipped, install the thrust washer, circlip and end cap cover.

13. Install the starter cable and the terminal nut.

14. Install the starter as described in this chapter.

Starter Relay Replacement

1. Disconnect the negative battery cable.

2. Remove the engine cover.

3. Disconnect the electrical leads from the starter relay connectors.

4. Disconnect the battery and starter cables from the relay terminals.

5. Remove the bolts securing the relay to the cowling or relay bracket. On some models, a

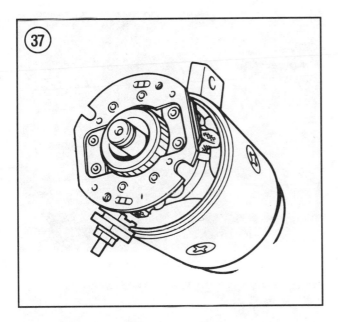

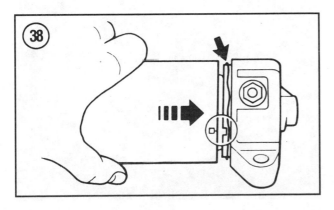

ground lead is installed under one of the mounting bolts.

6. Installation is the reverse of removal. Make sure all electrical connectors are free of corrosion and are tight.

IGNITION SYSTEMS

The outboards covered in this manual use one of the following ignition systems:
    a. Magneto breaker point.
    b. Simultaneous CDI (capacitor discharge ignition).
    c. Independent CDI (capacitor discharge ignition).
    d. Yamaha microcomputer ignition system (YMIS).

Refer to Chapter Three for troubleshooting and test procedures.

MAGNETO BREAKER POINT IGNITION (1990-1994 2 HP)

The 1990-1994 2hp models use a magneto ignition with a combined primary/secondary ignition coil, a condenser and one set of breaker points. The components are mounted on the stator base under the crankshaft driven flywheel. The system is self-energizing and does not require the use of a battery to provide electrical current.

Troubleshooting and test procedures are given in Chapter Three.

Operation

As the flywheel rotates, magnets around its outer diameter create a current that flows through the closed breaker points to the ignition coil primary windings. This flow of current through the coil primary winding builds a strong magnetic field. When the cam opens the point set, the magnetic field collapses, inducing a high voltage (approximately 18,000 volts) in the coil secondary windings. This voltage is sent to the spark plug where it jumps the plug gap and fires the cylinder. The condenser absorbs any residual current remaining in the primary windings. This eliminates arcing at the points and produces a stronger spark at the plug. This process is duplicated with each revolution of the flywheel.

Magneto Base
Removal/Installation

Magneto base removal is not required to replace a component on the base. Remove the base only if damaged or if the power head it being disassembled.

1. Remove the engine cover.
2. Remove the fuel tank. See Chapter Six.
3. Remove the rewind starter assembly. See Chapter Ten.
4. Remove the flywheel. See Chapter Eight.
5. Disconnect the spark plug lead from the spark plug.
6. Disconnect the stator lead wires at their bullet connectors. Disconnect the ground wire attached to the cylinder block (**Figure 39**).
7. Remove the 2 screws holding the magneto base to the power head (A, **Figure 40**). Remove the magneto base.
8. Installation is the reverse of removal. Make sure all electrical connectors are free of corrosion and are tight.

Breaker Point and
Condenser Replacement

See *Tune-up*, Chapter Four.

Ignition Coil
Removal/Installation

1. Remove the flywheel. See Chapter Eight.

2. Disconnect the coil lead wires from the breaker point set and ground.
3. Remove the spark plug lead. Remove the plug boot from the lead.
4. Remove the 2 screws holding the coil to the magneto base (B, **Figure 40**).
5. Pull the spark plug lead through the magneto base grommet and remove the coil.
6. Installation is the reverse of removal. Note the following:
   a. Insert the spark plug lead through the magneto base cutout before installing the coil mounting screws.
   b. Make sure all electrical connectors are free of corrosion and are tight.

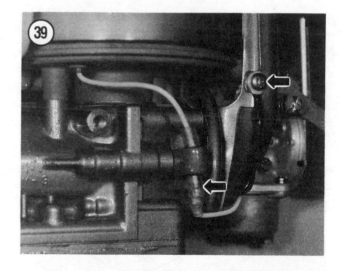

CAPACITOR DISCHARGE IGNITION (2-55 HP AND PRO 50 MODELS)

NOTE
The 1995 2 hp outboard is the first year for this model to have a capacitor discharge ignition (CDI) ignition system.

The 2-5 hp single cylinder models have a CDI ignition system using a single ignition coil, 1 charge coil and 1 pulser coil.

The 6-15 hp, C25 and C40 2-cylinder models have a simultaneous CDI ignition system using a single ignition coil, 1 charge coil and 1 pulser coil. The CDI unit fires the single ignition coil with 2 spark plug leads.

The 25 hp, C30 and C55 2-cylinder models have an independent CDI ignition system using 2 ignition coils, 1 charge coil and 2 pulser coils.

The CDI unit fires the 3 ignition coils to fire the spark plugs as required.

The 40 and 50 hp and Pro 50 3-cylinder models have an independent CDI ignition system using 3 ignition coils, 1 charge coil and 3 pulser coils. The CDI unit fires the 2 ignition coils to fire the spark plugs as required.

Operation

The major components of the CDI ignition system on all 2-55 hp models are the flywheel, charge coil, pulser coil, CDI unit, ignition coil(s), spark plug(s) and connecting wiring. **Figure 41** shows a typical 2-cylinder simultaneous CDI ignition system.

The charge coil is located under the flywheel on the magneto base plate. The flywheel is fitted with permanent magnets inside its outer rim

7

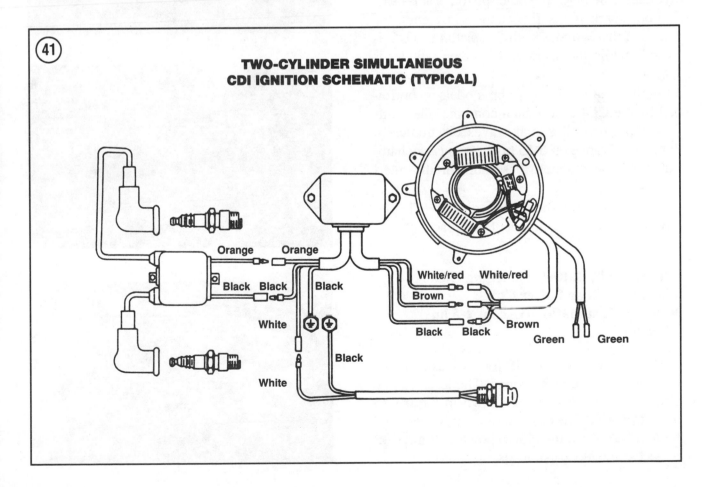

(41)

TWO-CYLINDER SIMULTANEOUS CDI IGNITION SCHEMATIC (TYPICAL)

Orange   Orange

Black   Black   Black

White/red   White/red

Brown

White

Brown

Black   Black

Black   Green   Green

Black

White

(**Figure 42**). As the crankshaft and flywheel rotate, the flywheel magnets pass the stationary charge coil, creating an AC voltage in the charge coil. The AC voltage is sent to the CDI unit (switch box) where it is rectified and stored in a capacitor for release.

A pulser coil assembly is also mounted under the flywheel (2-5 hp engines use a low- and high-speed coil). A second set of magnets located around the flywheel hub pass the stationary pulser coil assembly, triggering an AC voltage in the pulser coil(s). The AC voltage is routed to an electronic switch (SCR) in the CDI unit. The SCR discharges the capacitor in to the ignition coil at the correct time and in the correct firing order sequence for multicylinder engines.

The simultaneous ignition system on 6-15 hp, C25 and C40 2-cylinder models is also called a "waste spark" system. When the piston in one cylinder is at TDC, the other piston is at BTDC. If both spark plugs fire at the same time, the spark in the cylinder with the piston at TDC is "used" while the spark in the other cylinder is "wasted."

Ignition advance on 2-5 hp models is controlled by the CDI unit, which combines the 2 different pulser coil signal waves electronically. Ignition advance on 6-55 hp models is mechanical, with the magneto base and throttle interlocked.

Ignition timing should be adjusted (Chapter Five) whenever a component is replaced.

Charge Coil, Battery Charging Coil, Lighting Coil or Pulser Coil Removal/Installation (Except 2-5 hp Models)

Refer to **Figures 43-45** for various types of CDI unit connector housings. The leads can be pulled out of the housing shown in **Figure 43** and **Figure 44**. The cover screws and cover must be removed from the types shown in **Figure 45** to access the electrical leads.

1. Disconnect the negative battery cable; if so equipped.

2. Remove the engine cover.

3. Remove the screws securing the CDI cover (**Figure 45**) and remove the cover.

4. Remove the flywheel. See Chapter Eight.

5. Disconnect the defective coil's electrical connectors (**Figure 46**) from the CDI unit or from the rectifier if removing the battery charging coil.

6. Disconnect the magneto base link from the magneto control lever.

7. Remove the screws securing the magneto base to the retainer plate or power head. Remove the magneto base (**Figure 47**).

8. Loosen the clamp screw holding the defective coil's electrical lead to the magneto base.

9. Remove the 2 screws and washers securing the defective coil to the magneto base.

10. Remove the defective coil from the stator base, pulling its lead(s) through the base cutout or clamp and protective sleeve (if so equipped).

11. Installation is the reverse of removal. Note the following:

   a. Apply a light coat of Yamalube All-purpose Marine Grease to the retainer ring and all other points where the base will contact other components.

   b. Apply blue Loctite (No. 242) to the coil and magneto base mounting screws prior to installation. Tighten the screws securely.

   c. Make sure all electrical connectors are free of corrosion and are tight.

Charge Coil or Pulser Coil Removal/Installation (2-5 hp Models)

1. Remove the engine cover.

2. Remove the flywheel. See Chapter Eight.

3. Disconnect the defective coil's electrical connectors (**Figure 43**, typical) from the CDI unit.

4A. On 2 hp models, remove the 2 screws, lockwashers and washers securing the magneto base to the crankcase halves. Remove the base (**Figure 48**, typical).

4B. On 3-5 hp models, remove the 2 screws securing the magneto base to the crankcase halves. Remove the base (**Figure 48**).

5. On 3 hp models, the charge coil and the high-speed pulser coil are mounted on the top surface of the magneto base and the low-speed pulser coil is mounted on the bottom surface of the magneto base.

6. On 4 hp and 5 hp engines, **Figure 49** shows the location of the charge coil (A), low-speed pulser coil (B) and the high-speed pulser coil (C).

7. On 3-5 hp engines, remove the electrical wiring harness clamp and screw (A, **Figure 50**) from the magneto base.

8. Remove the 2 screws and washers securing the defective coil(s) to the magneto base.

9. Remove the defective coil(s) from the stator base, pulling its lead(s) through the base cutout rubber grommet.

10. Installation is the reverse of removal. Note the following:

   a. Check the O-ring and grease seal (models so equipped) on the magneto base (B, **Figure 50**) and replace if damaged.

   b. Lubricate the O-ring with Yamalube All-purpose Marine Grease. Apply a light coat of Yamalube All-purpose Marine Grease to the retainer ring and all other points where the base will contact other components.

   c. Apply blue Loctite (No. 242) to the coil and magneto base mounting screws prior to installation. Tighten the screws securely.

   d. Make sure all electrical connectors are free of corrosion and are tight.

CDI Unit Replacement

1. Disconnect the negative battery cable; if so equipped.

2. Remove the engine cover.

3. Remove the CDI housing cover (if so equipped) and disconnect the CDI unit electrical leads from their connectors.

4. Disconnect the black CDI unit ground lead.

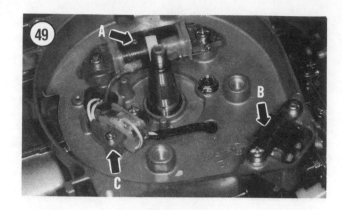

5. Remove the bolts securing the CDI unit to the mounting bracket or power head. See **Figure 51** or **Figure 52**, typical.

6. Remove the CDI unit.

7. Installation is the reverse of removal. Note the following:

   a. Tighten the bolts to 4.9-5.9 N·m (43-52 in.-lb.).

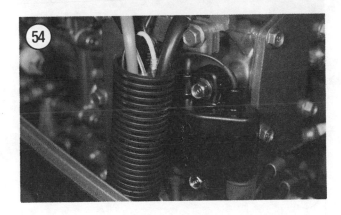

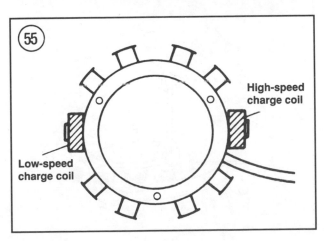

b. Make sure all electrical connectors are free of corrosion and are tight.

Secondary Ignition Coil Replacement

1. Disconnect the negative battery cable; if so equipped.

2. Remove the engine cover.

3. Disconnect the spark plug lead(s) from the spark plug(s).

4A. On models with simultaneous ignition, disconnect the magneto base lead from the secondary coil.

4B. On models with independent ignition, disconnect the coil primary leads from their bullet connectors.

5. Remove the bolts and washer securing the ignition coil(s). For typical installation, refer to **Figure 53** for single-cylinder models or **Figure 54** for 2-cylinder models. Remove the coil(s) from the mounting bracket.

6. Installation is the reverse of removal. Note the following:

   a. If the coil has a black ground lead attached, be sure to reinstall it under one of the mounting bolts.

   b. Tighten the bolts securely.

   c. Make sure all electrical connectors are free of corrosion and are tight.

CAPACITOR DISCHARGE IGNITION (75-200 HP [EXCEPT 1992-ON 90 HP])

The 75-200 hp models (except 1992-on 90 hp) use an alternator stator containing 2 charge coils and 8 battery charging coils (**Figure 55**, typical). A timer base underneath the stator contains 2 pulser coils (75-130 hp) or 3 pulser coils (150-200 hp) enclosed in iron to help build up the magnetic field and prevent interference from external sources.

Operation

The outer rim of the flywheel contains a series of magnets which create a magnetic field during rotation. This magnetic field cuts through the charge coil windings and produces an alternating current of positive and negative waveforms. The current is sent to the CDI unit where it is changed into direct current by an internal rectifier and stored in a capacitor.

The rotation of the timing magnet in the flywheel hub past the pulser coils on the timer base also creates a magnetic field (**Figure 56**). As the flywheel continues to rotate, this magnetic field collapses, inducing a small voltage in the pulser coil. This pulser voltage causes an electronic switch in the CDI unit to close, discharging the stored voltage into the appropriate ignition coil where it is stepped up to a higher voltage and sent to the spark plug.

Ignition advance is mechanical, with the timer base and throttle interlocked. Ignition timing should be adjusted (Chapter Five) whenever a component is replaced.

Alternator Stator
Removal/Installation

1. Disconnect the negative battery cable.

2. Remove the engine cover.

3. Remove the flywheel. See Chapter Eight.

4. Remove the CDI unit cover. Disconnect all stator leads from the CDI unit (**Figure 57**, typical).

5. Remove the screws securing the alternator stator to the timer base (**Figure 58**). Remove the alternator stator.

6. Installation is the reverse of removal. Make sure all electrical connectors are free of corrosion and are tight.

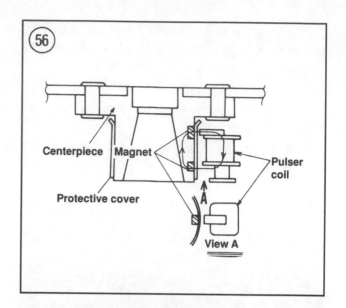

Timer Base
Removal/Installation

1. Remove the alternator stator as described in this chapter.
2. Disconnect the timer base link from the control lever.
3. Remove the CDI unit cover. Disconnect the pulser coil leads from the CDI unit (**Figure 57**, typical).
4. Remove the screws securing the timer base. Remove the timer base (**Figure 59**, typical).
5. Installation is the reverse of removal. Make sure all electrical connectors are free of corrosion and are tight.

Charge Coil or Battery
Charging Coil Replacement

The alternator stator is replaced as an assembly if any coil is defective.

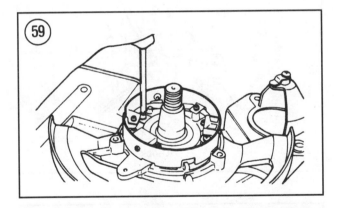

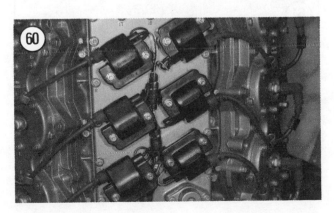

Pulser Coil Replacement

The alternator stator is replaced as an assembly if any coil is defective.

CDI Unit Replacement

1. Disconnect the negative battery cable.
2. Remove the engine cover.
3. Remove the CDI unit cover.

NOTE
The CDI unit electrical leads are grouped in sets of 3 or 4 and installed in grommets on some models to assist in proper reconnection. Do not remove the leads from the grommets unless replacing a component.

4. Disconnect the CDI unit electrical leads from the CDI unit terminals (**Figure 57**).
5. Remove the top and bottom bolts securing the CDI unit to the mounting bracket. Remove the CDI unit from its mounting bracket.
6. Installation is the reverse of removal. Note the following:
    a. Tighten the bolts securely.
    b. Make sure all electrical connectors are free of corrosion and are tight.

Secondary Ignition
Coil Replacement

1. Disconnect the negative battery cable; if so equipped.
2. Remove the engine cover.
3. Disconnect the coil primary leads from their bullet connectors.
4. Disconnect the spark plug leads from the spark plugs.
5. Remove the bolts and washers securing the ignition coil (**Figure 60**, typical). Remove the coil from the mounting bracket.
6. Installation is the reverse of removal. Note the following:

7

a. If the coil has a black ground lead attached, be sure to reinstall it under one of the mounting bolts.

b. Tighten the bolts securely.

c. Make sure all electrical connectors are free of corrosion and are tight.

YAMAHA MICROCOMPUTER IGNITION SYSTEM (YMIS) (1992-ON PRO 60, 70 HP, 90 HP 3-CYLINDER AND ALL 225-250 HP V6 MODELS)

The Yamaha microcomputer electronic ignition system is similar to the ignition system used on other 3-cylinder and V6 outboards, but it uses a microcomputer to control engine operation and ignition timing electronically, according to data received from a variety of sensors.

On 1992-on Pro 60, 70 hp and 90 hp engines, the microcomputer within the CDI unit receives voltage signals from the crank position sensor and a thermoswitch in the cylinder head. On V6 models, the microcomputer within the CDI unit receives voltage signals from the throttle position sensor (**Figure 61**), the crank position sensor (**Figure 62**), cylinder head knock sensor (**Figure 63**), a thermosensor (**Figure 64**) and a thermoswitch in each cylinder head (**Figure 65**). The microcomputer compares the data provided by the sensors to the operating strategies program in its memory and determines the correct

ignition timing for a specific operating condition. The microcomputer then signals the CDI unit to advance the timing as desired.

On V6 engines, the microcomputer also:

a. Provides a fixed amount of advance during engine cranking.

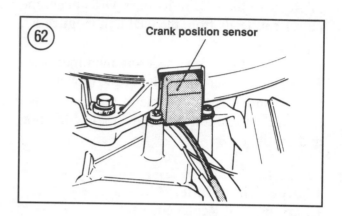

Crank position sensor

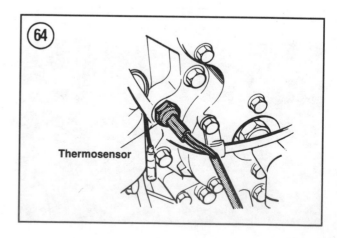

Knock sensor

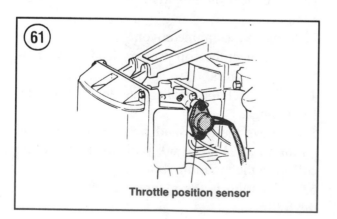

Throttle position sensor

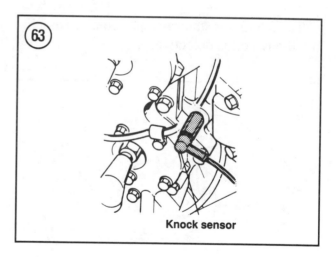

Thermosensor

b. Retards timing whenever engine detonation is detected by the knock sensor.

c. Alternately misfires the cylinders if engine speed exceeds 5,900-6,300 rpm until the engine speed returns to a safe level.

d. Misfires all cylinders to stop the engine if it is shifted into REVERSE while cruising. At low speeds, this system is disabled and allows REVERSE to be used as a brake when docking.

e. Misfires the cylinders in a specified order whenever engine temperature exceeds a predetermined level, until the temperature returns to a safe level.

Proper operation of an outboard equipped with YMIS depends upon the use of the correct fuel (see Chapter Four), correct linkage adjustment (see Chapter Five) and a fully charged battery. If battery voltage drops below 7 volts, the ignition timing will be fixed at 7° BTDC. In addition, engine speed may vary by 1,000-1,500 rpm, and maximum engine speed will not exceed 4,300-4,800 rpm should battery voltage become low. Yamaha recommends installation of a voltmeter to check battery condition before operating the outboard motor.

The YMIS system is quite complex, sophisticated and expensive. *Never* remove the cover

Thermoswitch

from the microcomputer unit and always handle it carefully whenever removal from the engine is necessary.

Component Replacement

The YMIS microcomputer is an integral part of the CDI unit and is attached to the mounting bracket on the starboard side of the engine on 3-cylinder engines or to the ignition coil bracket on the aft of the engine on V4 and V6 engines. Remove and disconnect the electrical connectors then the mounting bolts and remove the unit.

To remove and install all other related electrical components (alternator rotor, timer base, ignition coil) see *Yamaha 75-200 hp Engines CDI (Capacitor Discharge Ignition)* in this chapter.

On V4 and V6 engines, the throttle position sensor removal, installation and adjustment procedures are covered in Chapter Five. Replacement of all other sensors is covered in Chapter Eight.

**Ignition Stator Replacement
(1990-1991 250 hp V6 Engines Only)**

Yamaha has determined that some 1990 and 1991 250 hp V6 engines may have an internal failure in the stator assembly when subjected to hot climates. This condition could result in ignition misfire or complete ignition system failure.

If you have encountered this situation, Yamaha has developed an improved replacement stator assembly that will eliminate this problem. Prior to purchasing and installing the new stator assembly, check to see if there is a gray-color band around the wiring harness adjacent to one of the electrical connectors.

If there is a gray-colored band in place, the improved stator assembly has already been installed. If there is no gray band, install the new stator assembly.

The stator assembly (part No. 61A-84410-00) is available from a Yamaha outboard dealer.

7

Table 1 ELECTRICAL CONNECTOR ADAPTERS

Model	Part No.	Description
Pro 50, 70, 90 hp	6H0-ADPKT-93-94	Adapts 1993 engine to 1994 harness
Pro 50, 70, 90 hp	6H0-ADPKT-94-93	Adapts 1994 engine to 1993 harness
115-225 hp (V4 and V6)	6R3-ADPKT-93-94	Adapts 1993 engine to 1994 harness
115-225 hp (V4 and V6)	6R3-ADPKT-94-93	Adapts 1994 engine to 1993 harness

Table 2 BATTERY CAPACITY (HOURS)

Accessory draw	80 amp-hour battery provides continuous power for:	Approximate recharge time
5 amps	13.5 hours	16 hours
15 amps	3.5 hours	13 hours
25 amps	1.8 hours	12 hours

Accessory draw	105 amp-hour battery provides continuous power for:	Approximate recharge time
5 amps	15.8 hours	16 hours
15 amps	4.2 hours	13 hours
25 amps	2.4 hours	12 hours

Table 3 SELF-DISCHARGE RATE

Temperature	Approximate allowable self-discharge per day for first 10 days (specific gravity)
100° F (37.8° C)	0.0025 points
80° F (26.7° C)	0.0010 points
50° F (10.0° C)	0.0003 points

Table 4 STATE OF BATTERY CHARGE

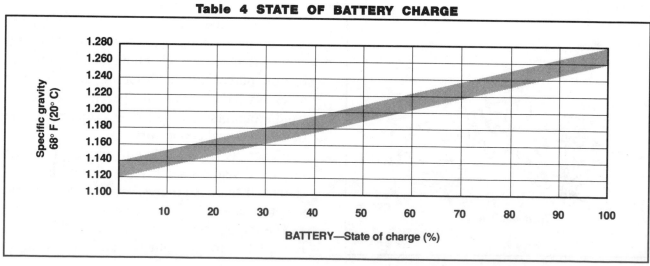

Table 5 TIGHTENING TORQUES

Fastener	ft.-lb.	N•m
M5 bolt or 8 mm nut	3.6	5
M6 bolt or 10 mm nut	5.8	8
M8 bolt or 12 mm nut	13	18
M10 bolt or 14 mm nut	25	36
M12 bolt or 17 mm nut	30	42

7

Chapter Eight

Power Head

This chapter covers the basic repair of Yamaha outboard power heads. The procedures involved are similar from model to model, with minor differences. Some procedures require the use of special tools, which can be purchased from a dealer or directly from Kent-Moore SPX Corporation, 29784 Little Mack, Roseville MI. 48066-2298. These special tools are specified in some procedures and are listed with a part No. prefix of YB-0000 or YU-0000. Certain tools may also be fabricated by a machinist, often at substantial savings. Power head stands are available from specialty shops such as Bob Kerr's Marine Tool Co., P.O. Box 1135, Winter Garden, FL 32787.

Work on the power head requires considerable mechanical ability. You should carefully consider your own capabilities before attempting any operation involving major disassembly of the engine.

Much of the labor charge for dealer repairs involves the removal and disassembly of other parts to reach the defective component. Even if you decide not to tackle the entire power head overhaul after studying the text and illustrations in this chapter, it can be cheaper to perform the preliminary operations yourself and then take the power head to your dealer. Since many marine dealers have lengthy waiting lists for service (especially during the spring and summer), this practice can reduce the time your unit is out of the boat and in the shop. If you have done much of the preliminary work, your repairs can be scheduled and performed much quicker.

Repairs go much faster and easier if the engine and related assemblies are clean before you begin work. There are special cleaners on the market, like Simple green or Bel-Ray degreaser, for washing the engine and related parts. Just spray or brush on the cleaning solution following the manufacturers' instructions, let it stand the specified length of time, then rinse it away with a garden hose. If compressed air is available, apply low air pressure and blow away water residue from the crevices of the engine. Clean all oily or greasy parts with fresh solvent as you remove them. Place the parts with their fasteners in trays or cupcake tins in their order of removal. This will speed assembly while helping to ensure that all parts are properly reinstalled

WARNING
Never use gasoline as a cleaning agent. It presents an extreme fire hazard. Be sure to work in a well-ventilated area when using cleaning solvents. Keep a fire extinguisher rated for gasoline and oil fires nearby in case of emergency.

Once you have decided to do the job yourself, read this chapter thoroughly until you have a good idea of what is involved in completing the overhaul satisfactorily. Make arrangements to buy or rent any special tools necessary and obtain replacement parts before you start. It is frustrating and time-consuming to start an overhaul and then be unable to complete it because the necessary tools or parts are not at hand.

Before beginning the job, read Chapter Two of this manual again. You will do a better job with this information fresh in your mind.

Remember that new engine break-in procedures should be followed after an engine has been overhauled. Refer to your owner's manual for specific instructions.

Since this chapter covers a large range of models over a lengthy time period, the procedures are sometimes generalized to accommodate all models. Where individual differences occur, they are specifically pointed out. The power heads shown in the accompanying pictures are current designs. While it is possible that the components shown in the pictures may not be identical with those being serviced, the step-by-step procedures may be used with all models covered in this manual. The serial and model numbers should be used when ordering any replacement parts for all engine components.

Tables 1-3 are at the end of the chapter.

NOTE
The "L" series outboard motors (counter rotation models) are included in all procedures. Unless there is a separate procedure designated for an "L" series model, refer to the procedure that relates to the same horsepower rating. If you are working on an L200, refer to the 200 hp procedure.

FASTENERS AND TORQUE

Always replace a worn or damaged fastener with one of the same size, type and torque requirement. Unless a thread-locking compound such as Loctite or ThreeBond is specified, bolt threads should be lubricated with Yamalube Two-Cycle Outboard oil before torque is applied.

Unless otherwise specified, power head fasteners should be tightened in 2 steps. Tighten to 50 percent of the torque value in the first step, then to 100 percent in the second step. Power head tightening torques are listed in **Table 1**.

Power head torque sequences are provided in this chapter. They are also embossed on the power head components. The embossed sequence should be followed if it differs from that given in this chapter, as it reflects a product change during the model run.

Retighten the power head fasteners after the engine has been run for 15 minutes and allowed to cool. It is a good idea to retorque them again after 10 hours of operation. To retighten the power head mounting fasteners properly, back them out 1 turn, then tighten to the correct torque specification.

When spark plug(s) are reinstalled after an overhaul, tighten to the specified torque. Warm the engine to normal operating temperature, let it cool down and retorque the plug(s).

8

ENGINE SERIAL NUMBER

Yamaha outboard motors are identified by engine serial number and model number. The engine serial number is stamped on a welch plug installed in the power head (**Figure 1**). Exact location of the welch plug varies according to model. The model and serial number are stamped on a plate riveted to the port side clamp bracket.

This information identifies the outboard motor and indicates if there are unique parts or if internal changes have been made during the model run. The serial and model numbers should be used when ordering any replacement parts for your outboard.

GASKETS AND SEALANTS

Yamaha Gasket Maker is applied in a thin, even coat covering the entire mating surface when sealing the crankcase cover and cylinder block. Both mating surfaces must be free of all sealant residue, dirt and oil. Lacquer thinner, acetone or similar solvents work well when used with a broad, flat scraper or a somewhat dull putty knife. Solvents with an oil, wax or petroleum base should not be used. Clean the aluminum surfaces carefully to avoid nicking them with the scraper or putty knife.

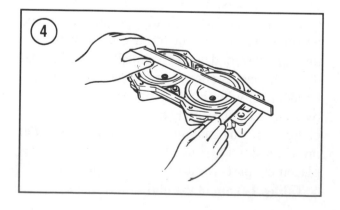

> *NOTE*
> *If a piece of glass is used for surface checking, it must be **plate glass**, not ordinary window glass. Plate glass has a very uniform surface flatness. Window glass is not uniform and cannot be used as it will give a false indication of warpage.*

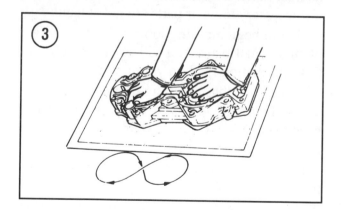

Once the gasket surfaces are clean, place the mating surface of each component on a surface plate or large pane of plate glass. Apply uniform downward pressure on the component and check for warpage (**Figure 2**). Replace any component that shows more than a 0.1 mm (0.004 in.) warpage. In cases where warpage is slight, it can often

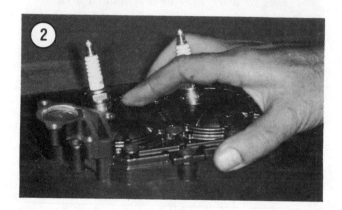

be eliminated by placing the mating surface of each component on a large sheet of 400-600 grit wet sandpaper that is placed on a surface plate or large piece of plate glass. Apply a slight amount of pressure and move the component in a figure-8 pattern (**Figure 3**). Remove the component from the sandpaper, then recheck the surface flatness on the surface plate or pane of plate glass. It may be necessary to repeat this procedure 2-3 times to remove a small piece of gasket material, eliminate warpage and produce a uniform mating surface. When finished, check for warpage with a straight edge and flat feeler gauge as shown in **Figure 4**.

Unless otherwise specified, gaskets used between components contain a heat-activated sealant and require no additional sealant. When newly installed, heat-activated gaskets may leak slightly until the engine has warmed up sufficiently to trigger the necessary chemical reaction in the gasket. For this reason, some service tech-

nicians feel that the application of Gasket Maker on a power head mounting gasket (**Figure 5**) provides additional protection against water leakage.

FLYWHEEL

Removal/Installation

1. Remove the engine cowling or cover.
2. Disconnect the spark plug lead(s) to prevent accidental starting of the engine.
3. If so equipped, remove the rewind starter as described under *Rope and Spring Replacement* in Chapter Eleven.
4. On models so equipped, remove the bolts and washers securing the rewind starter cup (A, **Figure 6**, typical). Remove the starter cup.
5. Remove the hole cover (B, **Figure 6**, typical).
6. On models so equipped, remove the screws and lockwashers securing the flywheel protector and remove the protector.
7. On electric start models, remove the starter motor. See Chapter Seven.
8. Install the flywheel holder (part No. YB-6139, or equivalent) onto the flywheel to lock it in place while loosening the flywheel nut.
9. Hold the flywheel stationary and using a suitable size socket, loosen the flywheel nut (**Figure 7**). Unscrew the nut until it is flush with the top

of the crankshaft end—do not remove the nut at this time.

CAUTION
Do not thread the puller bolts into the flywheel more than 12.7 mm (1/2 in.) in Step 8 or damage may result to the charge coil or trigger assemblies located beneath the flywheel.

10. Install the flywheel puller (part No. YB-6117, or equivalent) onto the flywheel and secure it with the special puller bolts.

CAUTION
Do not strike the puller center bolt with excessive force in Step 11 or crankshaft and/or bearing damage may result.

11. Hold the puller body with the puller handle and tighten the center bolt (**Figure 8**). If the flywheel does not pop from the crankshaft taper, lightly tap the puller center bolt with a soft-faced mallet or brass hammer (**Figure 9**).

12. Remove the puller from the flywheel. Remove the flywheel nut and washer. Remove the flywheel from the end of the crankshaft.

NOTE
*The Woodruff key may fall out of the crankshaft keyway as the flywheel is removed in Step 12. **Figure 10** shows the Woodruff key lodged between the crankshaft and the condenser on a 2 hp engine. Be sure to locate and retrieve the key.*

13. Remove the Woodruff key (**Figure 11**) from the crankshaft if it does not come off with the flywheel.

14. Thoroughly inspect the flywheel as described in this chapter.

15. Inspect the crankshaft and flywheel tapers. They must be perfectly dry and free of oil. Clean the tapered surfaces with a lint-free cloth and solvent, then blow dry with compressed air.

16. Installation is the reverse of removal. Note the following:

a. Install the Woodruff key (**Figure 11**) in the crankshaft slot with the outer edge of the key parallel to the crankshaft centerline.

b. Position the flywheel over the crankshaft so its keyway is aligned with the Woodruff key in the crankshaft. Install the flywheel.

c. Install the flywheel washer and nut.

d. Use the same tool set-up used for removal to keep the flywheel from turning while tightening the flywheel nut. Tighten the flywheel nut to the specification listed in **Table 1**.

Inspection

1. Check the flywheel carefully for cracks or fractures.

> *WARNING*
> *A cracked or chipped flywheel must be replaced. A damaged flywheel may fly apart at high rpm, throwing metal fragments over a large area. Do **not** attempt to repair a damaged flywheel.*

2. Check the tapered bore of the flywheel and crankshaft taper for signs of fretting or working.

3. On electric start models, check the flywheel teeth for excessive wear or damage.

4. Check the crankshaft and flywheel nut threads for wear or damage.

5. Replace the flywheel, the crankshaft and/or flywheel nut as required.

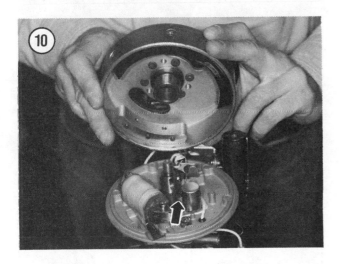

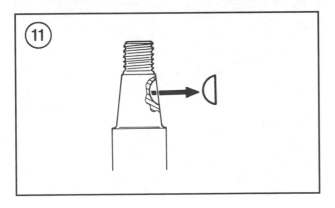

POWER HEAD REMOVAL/INSTALLATION

When removing any power head, it is a good idea to make a sketch or take an instant picture of the location, routing and positioning of electrical wiring, brackets and J-clamps for reassembly reference. This is especially important with 70-250 hp engines, as the wiring, vacuum and fuel hose arrangements become progressively more complex with each increase in engine size.

Take notes as you remove wires, hoses and washers so they can be reinstalled in their correct position. Unless specified otherwise, install lockwashers on the engine side of electrical leads to assure a good ground connection. Make sure the ground surface on the engine is clean and free of oil, grease or paint. The surface must be bare metal.

Professional mechanics find that the removal and installation of the power head is much faster and easier when they disconnect or remove only the components necessary to allow the power head to be removed. This is especially important with the larger displacement engines.

For example, there is no point in disconnecting all the lines to the fuel pumps on a V-block engine unless the pumps require service. Simply unbolt the pumps from the cylinder block and allow them to rest against the bottom cowling.

Components such as the CDI unit must be disconnected to remove the power head, but need not be taken off until it is out of the cowling and on a clean work bench.

Other components may not require removal at all, depending upon the purpose of power head removal. For example, if the power head is being removed to replace a base gasket, there is no need to remove the flywheel.

The following procedures assume that the power head is being removed for disassembly and overhaul. If you are removing it for some other reason, apply logic, common sense and good judgement—perform only those steps nec-

8

essary to remove the power head with the least amount of time and effort.

> *CAUTION*
> *After overhauling an oil-injected engine, it must be run with a 50:1 fuel/oil mixture in addition to the lubricant supplied by the injection pump. Refer to **Break-in Procedure** in Chapter Thirteen.*

Whenever grease is recommended in the following procedures, use Yamalube All-purpose Marine grease.

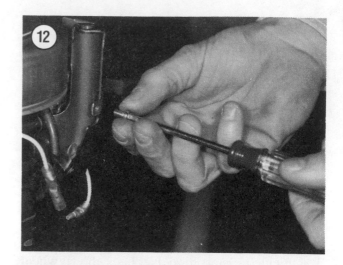

2 hp Models

1. Remove the screws securing the 2 halves of the engine cover. Remove the engine covers.
2. Remove the fuel tank. See Chapter Six.
3. Remove the rewind starter and flywheel as described in this chapter.
4. Remove the carburetor. See Chapter Six.
5. Disconnect the spark plug lead.
6. Disconnect the magneto leads as follows:
   a. On 1990-1994 models, disconnect the magneto white electrical lead at the bullet connector.
   b. On 1995 models, disconnect the magneto brown electrical lead at the bullet connector.
   c. On all models, remove the screw securing the magneto black ground lead to the rewind starter bracket (**Figure 12**).

7. Remove the screws securing the magneto base to the engine and remove the base (**Figure 13**).
8. Remove the 6 bolts and washers underneath the driveshaft housing that hold the power head and exhaust plate in place (**Figure 14**).
9. Carefully pry the power head and exhaust plate assembly from the drive shaft housing.
10. Separate the exhaust plate from the power head. Place the power head on a clean work surface and set the exhaust plate to one side and out of the way. Remove and discard the gaskets.

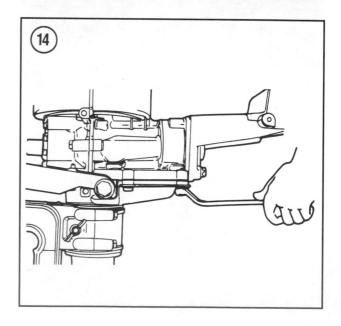

11. Clean the gasket residue from the drive shaft housing mating surfaces and make sure that the 2 locating pins are installed as shown in **Figure 15**.

12. Installation is the reverse of removal. Note the following:

    a. Coat the new gaskets with Yamabond No. 4 and install them between the power head, exhaust plate and the drive shaft housing.

    b. Lightly coat drive shaft splines with the recommended grease.

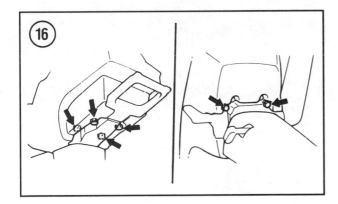

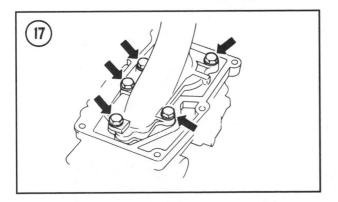

    c. Apply red Loctite (No. 271) to the power head mounting bolt threads prior to installation.

    d. Tighten all fasteners to the torque specifications listed in **Table 1**.

    e. Turn the fuel petcock to the ON position and check for fuel leakage.

    f. Perform engine timing, synchronization and linkage adjustment procedures. See Chapter Five.

3 hp Models

1. Remove the engine cover.

2. Remove the fuel tank. See Chapter Six.

3. Disconnect the spark plug leads to prevent accidental starting of the engine.

4. Remove the rewind starter and flywheel as described in this chapter.

5. Disconnect the 4 magneto base-to-CDI unit leads at the bullet connectors.

6. Remove the 2 magneto base fasteners and remove the magneto base.

7. Remove the air silencer cover, disconnect the throttle wire and choke linkage. If the power head is to be disassembled, remove the carburetor. See Chapter Six.

8. Remove the 6 bolts underneath the drive shaft housing holding the power head to the drive shaft housing (**Figure 16**).

NOTE
At this point, there should be no hoses, wires or linkage connecting the power head to the bottom cowling. Recheck to make sure that nothing will interfere with power head removal.

9. If necessary, tap the power head lightly with a soft-faced mallet to break the gasket seal. Lift the power head up and off the drive shaft housing.

10. Place the power head on a clean work bench. If the power head is to be disassembled, remove the exhaust manifold (**Figure 17**).

8

11. Remove and discard the power head mounting gasket.

12. Installation is the reverse of removal. Note the following:

a. Clean the power head mounting and drive shaft housing gasket surfaces of all gasket residue.

b. Install new seals in the top end of the exhaust manifold. The open side of the seals must face toward the bottom of the exhaust manifold. Lubricate the new seals with the recommended grease before installing the exhaust manifold on the power head.

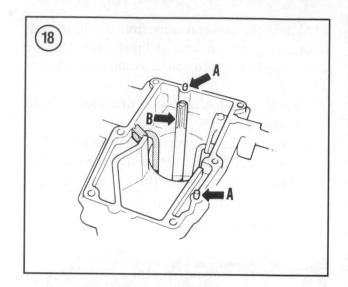

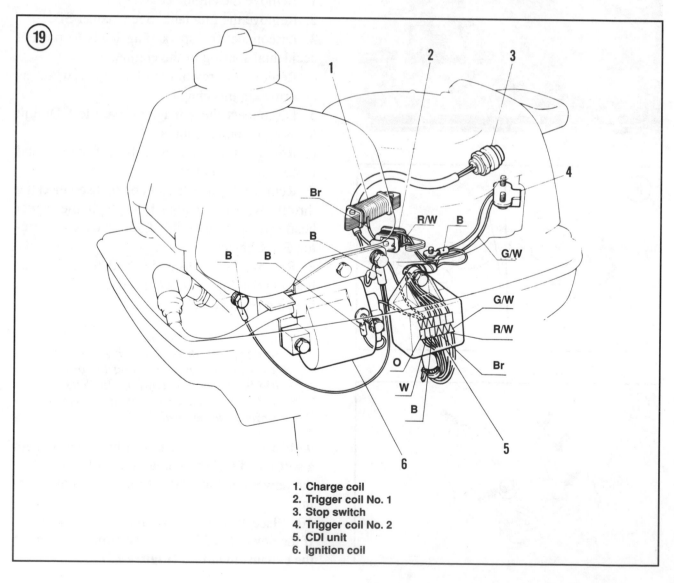

1. Charge coil
2. Trigger coil No. 1
3. Stop switch
4. Trigger coil No. 2
5. CDI unit
6. Ignition coil

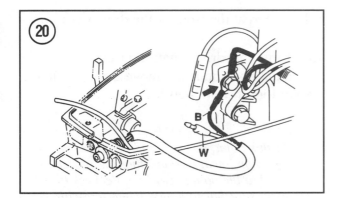

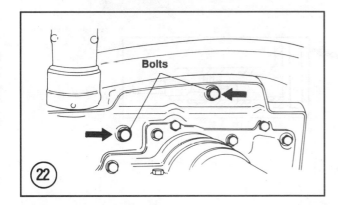

c. Make sure the locating pins (A, **Figure 18**) are correctly positioned in the drive shaft housing.

d. Install a new gasket on the drive shaft housing. Make sure the locating pins' holes are properly aligned.

e. Lightly coat the drive shaft splines (B, **Figure 18**) with the recommended grease.

f. Lower the power head into place. Rotate the propeller if necessary to mesh the drive shaft and crankshaft splines properly.

g. Connect the CDI-to-magneto base leads as shown in **Figure 19**.

h. Tighten all fasteners to the torque specifications listed in **Table 1**.

i. Turn the fuel petcock to the ON position and check for fuel leakage.

j. Perform engine timing, synchronization and linkage adjustment procedures. See Chapter Five.

4 and 5 hp Models

1. Remove the engine cover.

2. Remove the fuel tank. See Chapter Six.

3. Disconnect the spark plug leads to prevent accidental starting of the engine.

4. Disconnect the white stop switch lead at its bullet connector. Remove the screw securing the black magneto ground lead to the ignition coil bracket (**Figure 20**).

5. Disconnect the 4 magneto base-to-CDI unit electrical leads at their bullet connectors, then remove the leads from the bracket clamp on the magneto base side of the power head (**Figure 21**).

6. Remove the bolts (**Figure 22**) securing the CDI unit and coil mounting bracket. Move the bracket, CDI unit and coil assembly (**Figure 23**) out of the way. It is not necessary to remove this assembly completely.

7. Remove the rewind starter and flywheel as described in this chapter.

8. Remove the air silencer cover and disconnect the throttle wire and choke linkage. If the power head is to be disassembled, remove the carburetor. See Chapter Six.

9. Disconnect the magneto base linkage. Remove the 2 magneto base fasteners. Tap the underside of the magneto base with a soft-faced mallet to free it from the oil seal housing. Remove the magneto base.

10. Loosen the starter stop cable adjustment nut. Disconnect the cable from the stay, then remove the cable end from the linkage arm (**Figure 24**).

11. Disconnect the hairpin retaining clip from the starter lockout arm and disconnect the link from the arm (**Figure 24**).

12. Tilt the drive shaft housing up and remove the 3 bolts and washers as shown in **Figure 25**. Remove the 3 bolts and washers on the opposite side. Loosen but do not remove the remaining

bolt located at the front of the drive shaft housing.

13. Bring the drive shaft housing back to a horizontal position and remove the 7th bolt and washer loosened in Step 12.

NOTE
At this point, there should be no hoses, wires or linkage connecting the power head to the bottom cowling. Recheck to make sure that nothing will interfere with power head removal.

14. If necessary, tap the power head lightly with a soft-faced mallet to break the gasket seal. Lift the power head up and off the drive shaft housing.

15. Place the power head on a clean work bench. If the power head is to be disassembled, remove the bolt and washer, then remove the oil seal housing (**Figure 26**).

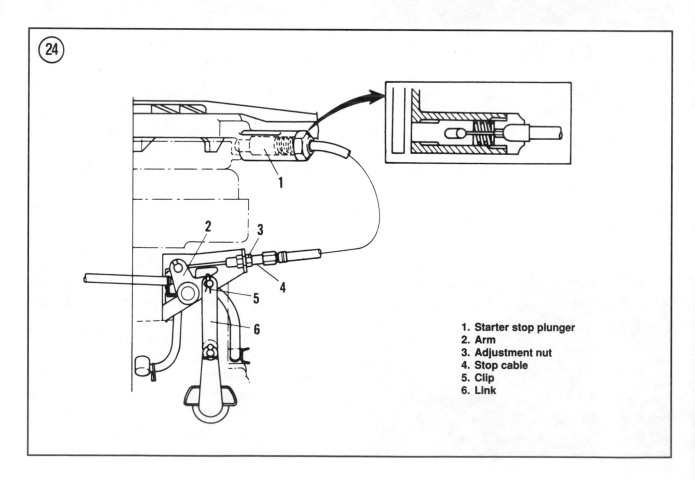

1. Starter stop plunger
2. Arm
3. Adjustment nut
4. Stop cable
5. Clip
6. Link

16. Remove and discard the power head mounting gasket.

17. Installation is the reverse of removal. Note the following:

    a. Clean the power head mounting and drive shaft housing gasket surfaces of all gasket residue.

    b. Install a new oil seal and O-ring seal in the lower oil seal housing. Lubricate the new seals with the recommended grease before installing the lower oil seal housing on the power head. Tighten the bolt securely.

    c. Install a new oil seal and O-ring seal in the magneto base. Lubricate the new seals with the recommended grease before installing the magneto base on the power head. Tighten the bolts securely.

    d. Lightly coat the drive shaft splines (A, **Figure 27**) with the recommended grease.

    e. Make sure the locating pins (B, **Figure 27**) are correctly positioned in the drive shaft housing.

    f. Install a new gasket on the drive shaft housing. Make sure the locating pins' holes are properly aligned.

    g. Lower the power head into place. Rotate the propeller, if necessary, to mesh the drive shaft and crankshaft splines properly.

    h. Connect the CDI-to-magneto base leads as shown in **Figure 28**.

    i. Tighten all fasteners to the torque specifications listed in **Table 1**.

8

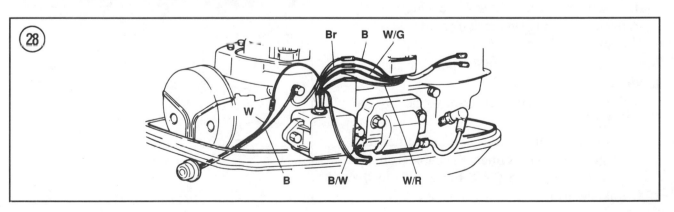

j. Turn the fuel petcock to the ON position and check for fuel leakage.

k. Perform engine timing, synchronization and linkage adjustment procedures. See Chapter Five.

6, 8, 9.9 and 15 hp Models

1. On models so equipped, disconnect the battery negative cable.

2. Remove the engine cover.

3. Disconnect the spark plug leads to prevent accidental starting of the engine.

4. Remove the rewind starter and flywheel as described in this chapter.

5A. On 6 and 8 hp engines, perform the following:

a. Remove the screws (A, **Figure 29**) and remove the magneto control lever (B, **Figure 29**).

b. Remove the mounting bolts (A, **Figure 30**).

c. Remove the throttle wire stay (B, **Figure 30**).

5B. On 9.9 and 15 hp engines, perform the following:

a. Disconnect the magneto control rod (A, **Figure 31**).

b. Remove the screws (B, **Figure 31**) then remove the magneto control lever (C, **Figure 31**).

c. Remove the bolt (A, **Figure 32**) and remove the magneto control lever (B, **Figure 32**).

d. Disconnect the water hose (**Figure 33**) from the fitting on the starboard side of the engine.

6A. On manual start models, perform the following:

a. On 6 and 8 hp engines, remove the arm rod (**Figure 34**).

b. Loosen the starter stop cable adjustment nut (**Figure 35**). Disconnect the cable from the stay, then remove the cable end from the linkage arm.

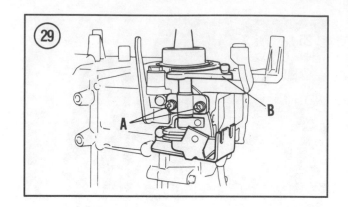

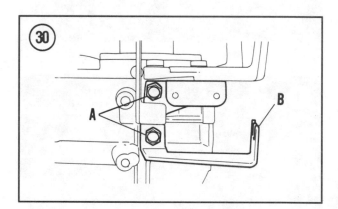

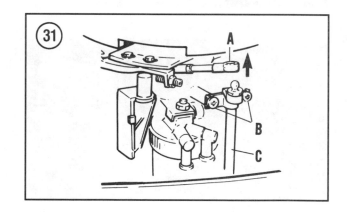

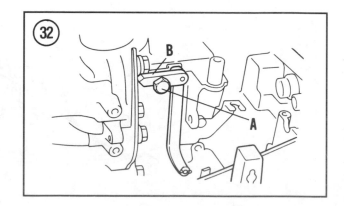

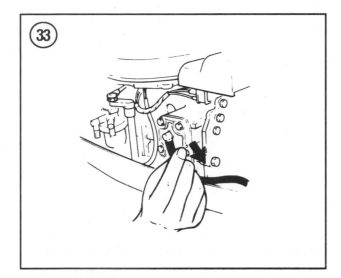

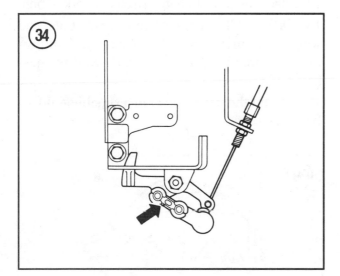

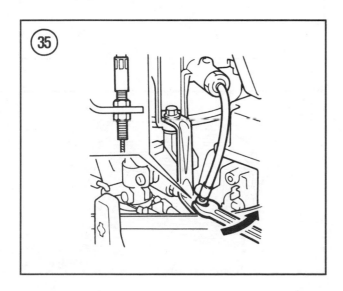

6B. On electric start models, remove the starter motor. See Chapter Seven.

7A. On 6 and 8 hp engines, perform the following:

   a. Remove the collar holding the CDI electrical leads (**Figure 36**).

   b. Disconnect the white stop switch lead.

   c. Remove the bolt securing the 2 black ground leads. Reinstall the bolt in the power head to prevent its loss.

7B. On 9.9 and 15 hp engines, perform the following:

   a. Remove the CDI cover.

   b. Disconnect and unclamp the white stop switch lead and the 2 black leads.

   c. Remove the bullet connectors from their holders on each side of the CDI unit (**Figure 37**). Disconnect all electrical leads.

   d. Remove the ignition coil from the CDI bracket.

8

e. Remove the CDI bracket.

8. Remove the bolts and washers securing the magneto base. Remove the magneto base with an upward rotating motion.

9. Remove the bolts and washers securing the magneto base retaining plate. Remove the retaining plate and gasket.

10A. On 6 and 8 hp engines, perform the following:

a. Disconnect the choke link from the carburetor.

b. Loosen the throttle wire adjustment bolts. Remove the adjustment bolts from the throttle wire stay. Disconnect the throttle wire ends from the throttle control lever.

10B. On 9.9 and 15 hp engines, perform the following:

a. Remove the neutral start arm and link, then disconnect the stop wire from the arm.

b. Loosen the stop wire adjustment bolt locknut and remove the wire from the bracket.

c. Disconnect the choke and throttle linkage from the carburetor (**Figure 38**).

d. Remove the inner and outer air silencer covers.

11. Tilt the drive shaft housing up and remove 3 bolts and washers (A, **Figure 39**) on one side. Remove only 2 bolts and washers on the opposite side. Loosen but do not remove the remaining bolt on that side of the drive shaft housing.

12. Bring the drive shaft housing back to a horizontal position and remove the remaining bolt and washer loosened in Step 11.

NOTE
At this point, there should be no hoses, wires or linkage connecting the power head to the bottom cowling. Recheck to make sure that nothing will interfere with power head removal.

13. If necessary, tap the power head lightly with a soft-faced mallet to break the gasket seal (B, **Figure 39**). Lift the power head up and off the drive shaft housing.

14. Place the power head on a clean work bench.

15. On 6 and 8 hp engines, remove the bolts and washers securing the exhaust manifold and remove the manifold and gasket. Discard the gasket.

16. Mount the power head in a suitable holding fixture.

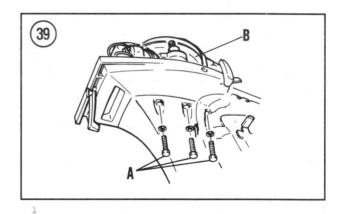

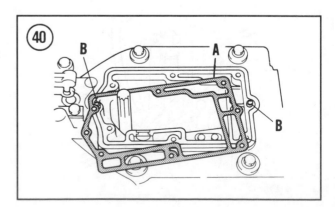

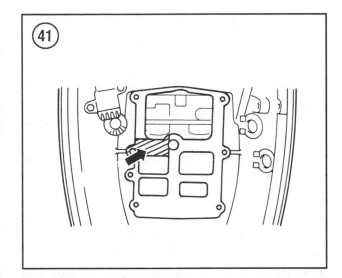

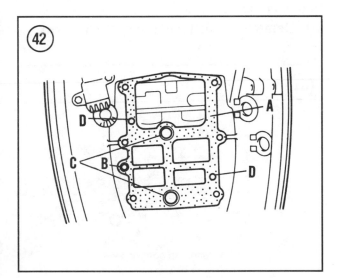

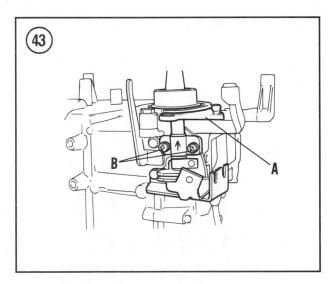

17. If the power head is going to be disassembled, remove the lower oil seal housing and all remaining fuel and electrical components.

18. Remove and discard the power head mounting gasket, and on 9.9 and 15 hp engines, the 2 small water seals.

19. Installation is the reverse of removal. Note the following:

   a. Clean the power head mounting and drive shaft housing gasket surfaces of all gasket residue.

   b. On 6 and 8 hp engines, install the exhaust manifold and a new gasket.

   c. Install a new oil seal and O-ring seal in the lower oil seal housing. Lubricate the new seals with Yamalube All-purpose Marine grease, or equivalent, before installing the lower oil seal housing on the power head. Tighten the bolt securely.

   d. On 6 and 8 hp engines, install a new power head gasket (A, **Figure 40**) on the driveshaft housing. Make sure the locating pins' (B, **Figure 40**) holes are properly aligned.

   e. On 9.9 and 15 hp engines, coat the cross-hatched area of the gasket as shown in (**Figure 41**) with Yamaha Gasket maker. Install the gasket (A, **Figure 42**) and install the 1 small (B, **Figure 42**) and 2 large water seals (C, **Figure 42**). Make sure the locating pins (D, **Figure 42**) are in place.

   f. Lightly coat the drive shaft splines with the recommended grease.

   g. Lower the power head into place. Rotate the propeller, if necessary, to mesh the drive shaft and crankshaft splines properly.

   h. Lubricate the magneto base retainer ring with the recommended grease.

   i. On 6 and 8 hp engines, apply the recommended grease to the inner and outer surfaces of the magneto base bushing.

   j. On 6 and 8 hp engines, install the magneto control lever (A, **Figure 43**). Position the

8

bracket with the arrow pointing UP and tighten the screws (B, **Figure 43**) securely.

k. Tighten all fasteners to the torque specifications listed in **Table 1**.

l. Turn the fuel petcock to the ON position and check for fuel leakage.

m. Perform engine timing, synchronization and linkage adjustment procedures. See Chapter Five.

25 and 30 hp Models

1. On models so equipped, disconnect the negative battery cable.

2. Remove the engine cover.

3. Disconnect the spark plug leads to prevent accidental starting of the engine.

4A. On manual start models, perform the following:

a. Disconnect the starter lockout cable from the rewind starter. Be careful not to lose the cable plunger or spring.

b. Remove the rewind starter as described under *Rope and Spring Replacement* in Chapter Eleven.

c. Disconnect the stop switch leads from the CDI unit bullet connectors.

4B. On electric start models, perform the following:

a. Disconnect the leads from the starter motor terminals. Remove the mounting bolts and remove the starter.

b. Disconnect the electrical leads from the starter relay.

c. Disconnect the neutral switch electrical leads.

d. Remove the starter mounting bracket screw holding the 2 ground leads. Reinstall the screw in the bracket to prevent its loss.

e. Disconnect the rectifier electrical leads.

f. Disconnect the CDI unit lead(s), from the wiring harness, that will interfere with the removal of the power head.

g. Remove the nut on the CDI unit ground lead bolt. Remove the lead from the bolt, then reinstall the nut.

5. Remove the flywheel as described in this chapter.

6. Remove the CDI magneto assembly. See Chapter Seven.

7. Disconnect all linkage at the magneto control lever (**Figure 44**, typical).

8. Remove the magneto base linkage. Remove the 4 bolts securing the magneto base assembly to the retainer plate. Remove the magneto base assembly.

9. Remove the fuel filter and plug the fuel line to prevent leakage.

10. Remove the fuel pump. See Chapter Six.

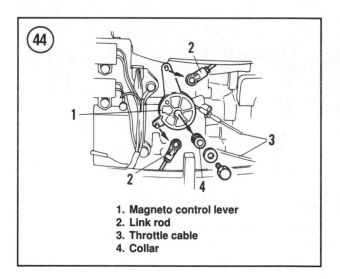

1. Magneto control lever
2. Link rod
3. Throttle cable
4. Collar

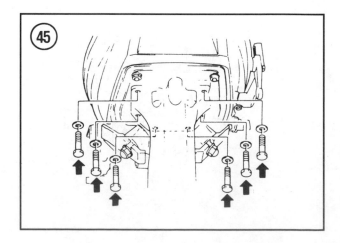

11. Disconnect the choke and throttle linkage from the carburetor.

12. On models so equipped, remove the fuel enrichment solenoid. See Chapter Six.

13. Remove the bolts and washer securing the flywheel retainer plate and ring and then remove the plate and ring.

14. Remove the intake silencer and carburetor assembly. See Chapter Six.

NOTE
At this point, there should be no hoses, wires or linkage connecting the power head to the bottom cowling. Recheck to make sure that nothing will interfere with power head removal.

15. Tilt the drive shaft housing up and remove 3 bolts and washers (**Figure 45**) on one side. Remove only 2 bolts and washers on the opposite side. Loosen but do not remove the 3rd bolt on that side of the drive shaft housing.

16. Bring the drive shaft housing back to a horizontal position and remove the 3rd bolt and washer loosened in Step 15.

17. If necessary, tap the power head lightly with a soft-faced mallet to break the gasket seal. Lift the power head up and off the drive shaft housing.

18. Place the power head on a clean work bench.

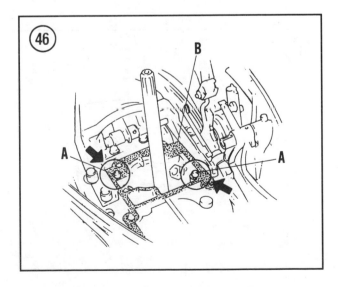

19. Mount the power head on an appropriate holding fixture.

20. If the power head if going to be disassembled, remove the lower oil seal housing and all remaining fuel and electrical components.

21. Remove and discard the power head mounting gasket.

22. Installation is the reverse of removal. Note the following:

   a. Clean the power head mounting and drive shaft housing gasket surfaces of all gasket residue.

   b. Install a new oil seal and O-ring seal in the lower oil seal housing. Lubricate the new seals with Yamalube All-purpose Marine grease, or equivalent, before installing the lower oil seal housing on the power head. Tighten the bolt securely.

   c. Make sure the locating pins are securely installed (A, **Figure 46**), then install a new power head gasket on the driveshaft housing (B, **Figure 46**).

   d. Lightly coat the drive shaft splines with the recommended grease.

   e. Lower the power head into place. Rotate the propeller, if necessary, to mesh the drive shaft and crankshaft splines properly.

   f. Lubricate the magneto base retainer ring with the recommended grease.

   g. Tighten all fasteners to the torque specifications listed in **Table 1**.

   h. Turn the fuel petcock to the ON position and check for fuel leakage.

   i. Perform engine timing, synchronization and linkage adjustment procedures. See Chapter Five.

40 hp, 50 hp and C55 Models

1. On models so equipped, disconnect the negative (–) battery cable.

2. Remove the engine cover.

3. Disconnect the spark plug leads to prevent accidental starting of the engine.

4A. On manual start models, perform the following:

  a. Disconnect the starter lockout cable from the rewind starter. Be careful not to lose the cable plunger or spring.

  b. Remove the rewind starter as described under *Rope and Spring Replacement* in Chapter Eleven.

  c. Disconnect the stop switch leads from the CDI unit bullet connectors.

  d. Remove the cotter pin, washer and wave washer connecting the shift lever arm to the linkage (**Figure 47**, typical). Separate the linkage.

4B. On electric start models, perform the following:

  a. Disconnect the electrical leads from the starter motor terminals. Remove the mounting bolts and remove the starter.

  b. Disconnect the electrical leads from the starter relay.

  c. Disconnect the neutral switch electrical leads.

  d. On models so equipped, remove the hairpin clips and disconnect the remote control cables.

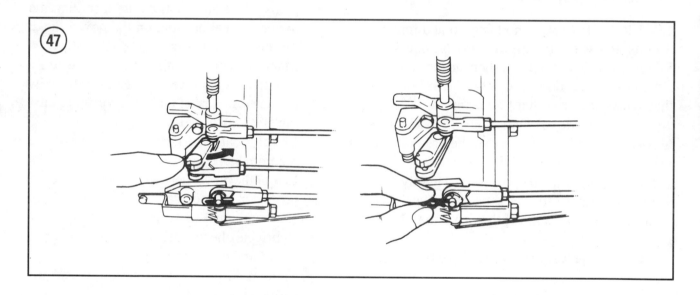

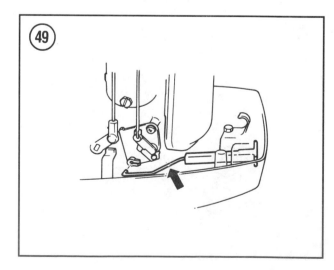

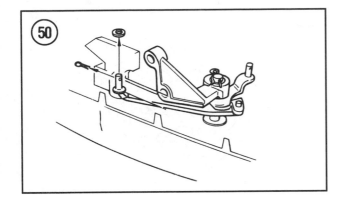

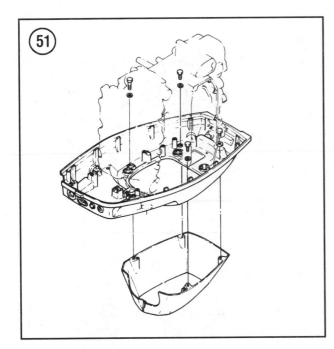

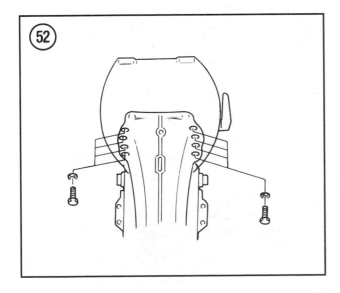

e. Disconnect the CDI unit lead(s), from the wiring harness, that will interfere with the removal of the power head.

5. Remove the oil tank. Disconnect the injection pump and remove the control unit. See Chapter Twelve.

6. Remove the air silencer cover (**Figure 48**).

7. Disconnect the choke (**Figure 49**, typical) and throttle linkage (**Figure 50**, typical) from the carburetors.

8. Disconnect the linkage from the magneto control arm.

9. Remove the flywheel as described in this chapter.

10. Remove the bolts securing the magneto base assembly to the power head. Remove the magneto base assembly and gasket.

11. On C40 models, remove the bolts securing the retainer plate. Remove the retainer plate and gasket.

12. Disconnect the fuel line from the inlet side of the fuel filter. Plug the fuel line to prevent leakage.

13. Remove the bolts securing the apron to the lower cowling (**Figure 51**, typical). Remove the apron.

NOTE
At this point, there should be no hoses, wires or linkage connecting the power head to the bottom cowling. Recheck to make sure that nothing will interfere with power head removal.

14. Tilt the drive shaft housing up and remove 4 bolts and washers (**Figure 52**) on one side. Remove only 3 bolts and washers on the opposite side. Loosen but do not remove the 4th bolt on that side of the drive shaft housing.

15. Bring the drive shaft housing back to a horizontal position and remove the 4th bolt and washer loosened in Step 14.

16. If necessary, tap the power head lightly with a soft-faced mallet to break the gasket seal. Lift the power head up and off the drive shaft housing.

8

17. Place the power head on a clean work bench.

18. Remove the oil seal housing from the bottom of the power head.

19. Mount the power head on an appropriate power head holding fixture.

20. If the power head if going to be disassembled, remove the lower oil seal housing and all remaining fuel and electrical components.

21. Remove and discard the power head mounting gasket.

22. Installation is the reverse of removal. Note the following:

   a. Clean the power head mounting and drive shaft housing gasket surfaces of all gasket residue.

   b. Install a new oil seal and O-ring seal in the lower oil seal housing. Lubricate the new seals with the recommended grease before installing the lower oil seal housing on the power head. Tighten the bolt securely.

   c. Make sure the locating pins are securely installed (**Figure 53**), then install a new power head gasket on the driveshaft housing.

   d. Lightly coat the drive shaft splines with the recommended grease.

   e. Lower the power head into place. Rotate the propeller, if necessary, to mesh the drive shaft and crankshaft splines properly.

   f. Lubricate the magneto base retainer ring with the recommended grease.

   g. Tighten all fasteners to the torque specifications listed in **Table 1**.

   h. Turn the fuel petcock to the ON position and check for fuel leakage.

   i. Perform engine timing, synchronization and linkage adjustment procedures. See Chapter Five.

Pro 60, 70 hp, C75, C85 and 90 hp Models

1. Disconnect the negative battery cable.

2. Remove the engine cover.

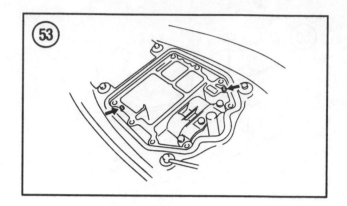

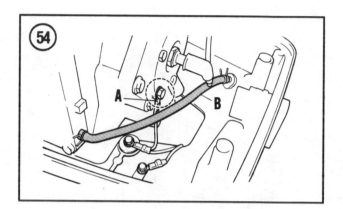

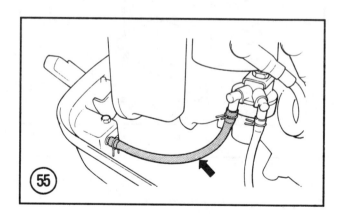

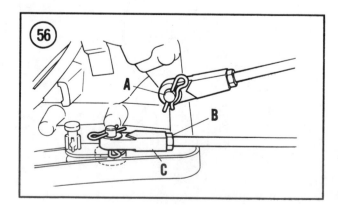

3. Disconnect the spark plug leads to prevent accidental starting of the engine.

4A. On manual start models, perform the following:

    a. Disconnect the starter lockout cable from the rewind starter. Be careful not to lose the cable plunger or spring.

    b. Remove the rewind starter as described under *Rope and Spring Replacement* in Chapter Eleven.

    c. Disconnect the stop switch leads from the CDI unit bullet connectors.

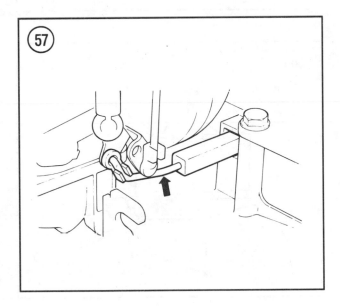

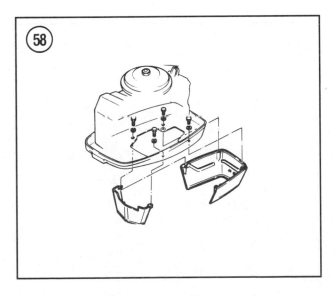

4B. On electric start models, perform the following:

    a. Disconnect the electrical leads from the starter motor terminals. Remove the mounting bolts and remove the starter.

    b. Disconnect the electrical leads from the starter relay.

    c. Disconnect the neutral switch electrical leads.

    d. On models so equipped, remove the hairpin clips and disconnect the remove control cables.

    e. Disconnect the CDI unit lead(s) that will interfere with the removal of the power head.

5. Disconnect the ground lead from the cylinder head cover (A, **Figure 54**).

6. Disconnect the cooling water pilot hose (B, **Figure 54**).

7. Disconnect the oil level sensor electrical lead.

8. Remove the oil tank. Disconnect the injection pump and remove the control unit. See Chapter Twelve.

9. On models so equipped, remove the power trim and tilt relays. See Chapter Twelve.

10. Remove the CDI cover and disconnect the electrical leads at the starter relay. Remove the starter relay.

11. Disconnect the fuel line from the inlet side of the fuel filter (**Figure 55**). Plug the fuel line to prevent leakage.

12. Remove the hairpin clip and disconnect the throttle cable (A, **Figure 56**).

13. Loosen the locknut (B, **Figure 56**), then remove the hairpin clip and disconnect the shift cable (C, **Figure 56**).

14. Disconnect the choke link (**Figure 57**) from the carburetors.

15. Remove the bolts and washers securing the front and rear apron to the lower cowling (**Figure 58**). Remove the aprons.

NOTE
At this point, there should be no hoses, wires or linkage connecting the power

8

head to the bottom cowling. Recheck to make sure that nothing will interfere power head removal.

16. Remove the bolts and washers (**Figure 59**) securing the power head to the bottom cowling. The 60 and 70 hp uses 8 bolts and the 75-90 hp uses 10 bolts.

17. If necessary, insert a wooden pry bar between the power head and bottom cowling as shown in **Figure 60** to break the gasket seal. Lift the power head up and off the bottom cowling.

18. Place the power head on a clean work bench.

19. Remove the oil seal housing from the bottom of the power head.

20. Mount the power head in an appropriate power head holding fixture.

21. If the power head if going to be disassembled, remove the flywheel and magneto base and/or the timer base, the oil injection pump and driven gear and all remaining fuel and electrical components.

22. Remove and discard the power head mounting gasket.

23. Installation is the reverse of removal. Note the following:

   a. Clean the power head mounting and bottom cowling gasket surfaces of all gasket residue.

   b. Make sure the locating pins are securely installed (**Figure 61**), then install a new power head gasket on the bottom cowling.

   c. Install a new oil seal and O-ring seal in the lower oil seal housing. Lubricate the new seals with the recommended grease, before installing the lower oil seal housing on the power head. Tighten the bolt securely.

   d. Lightly coat the drive shaft splines with the recommended grease.

   e. Lower the power head into place. Rotate the propeller, if necessary, to mesh the drive shaft and crankshaft splines properly.

   f. Lubricate the magneto base retainer ring with the recommended grease.

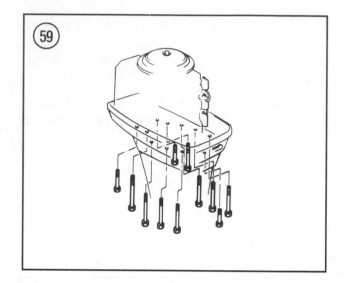

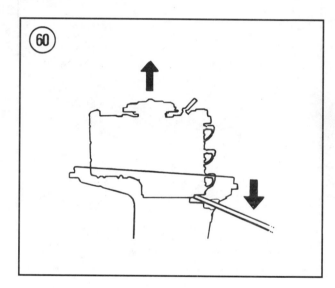

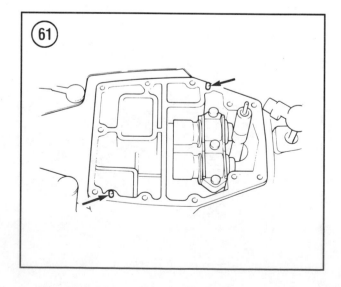

g. Tighten all fasteners to the torque specifications listed in **Table 1**.

h. Turn the fuel petcock to the ON position and check for fuel leakage.

i. Perform engine timing, synchronization and linkage adjustment procedures. See Chapter Five.

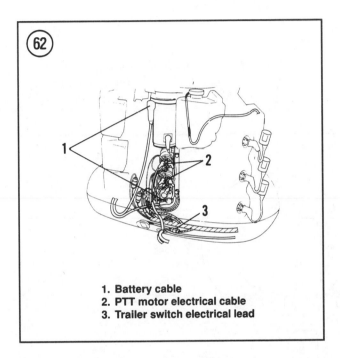

1. Battery cable
2. PTT motor electrical cable
3. Trailer switch electrical lead

115-130 hp V4 and
150-200 hp 90° V6 Models

1. Disconnect the battery negative cable.
2. Remove the engine cover.
3. Disconnect the spark plug leads to prevent accidental starting of the engine.
4. Remove the bolts securing the flywheel cover and remove the cover.
5. Remove the hairpin clip securing the shift cable. Remove the shift cable and bushing.
6. Remove the bolts securing the shift rod bracket to the crankcase. Remove the bracket.
7. Refer to **Figure 62** and disconnect the battery cables (1), the power trim and tilt electrical leads (2) and the trailer switch lead (3).
8. Refer to **Figure 63** and disconnect the power trim sensor electrical leads (1), the ground lead (2), the pilot water hose (3) and the cooling water outlet hose (4).
9. Refer to **Figure 64** and disconnect the remote control wiring harness (1), the power trim meter electrical lead (2), the oil level meter electrical lead (3) and the remote oil tank electrical lead (4).

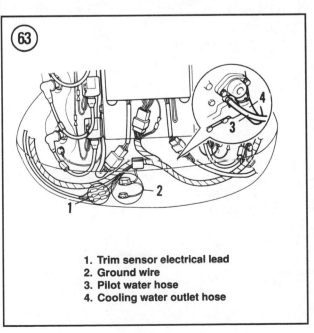

1. Trim sensor electrical lead
2. Ground wire
3. Pilot water hose
4. Cooling water outlet hose

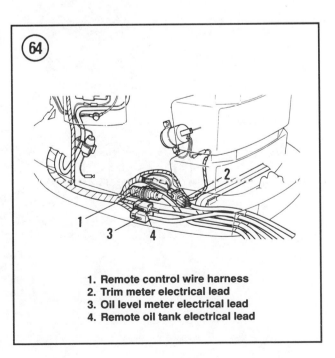

1. Remote control wire harness
2. Trim meter electrical lead
3. Oil level meter electrical lead
4. Remote oil tank electrical lead

8

10. Refer to **Figure 65** and perform the following:

a. Disconnect the fuel hose from the inlet side of the fuel filter (1). Plug the fuel line end with a golf tee to prevent leakage.

b. Disconnect the oil hose (2) from the oil tank.

c. Remove the shift bracket (3).

d. Remove the choke knob link (4).

11. Remove the nut securing the flywheel as described in this chapter.

12. Refer to **Figure 66** and remove the front bolts (1) securing the front apron. Remove the front apron (2). Remove the rear bolts (3) securing the front apron. Remove the rear apron (4).

NOTE
At this point, there should be no hoses, wires or linkage connecting the power head to the bottom cowling. Recheck to make sure that nothing will interfere with power head removal.

NOTE
The bolts and nuts had a locking agent applied to the threads during assembly and may be difficult to loosen in Step 13.

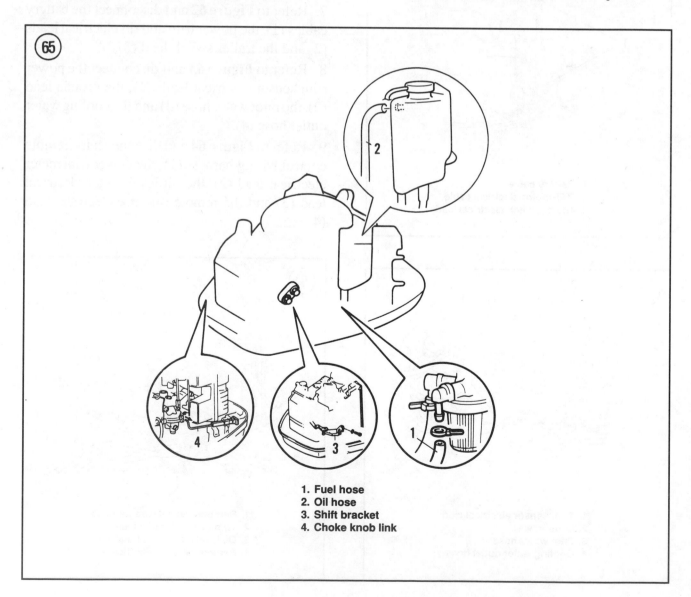

1. Fuel hose
2. Oil hose
3. Shift bracket
4. Choke knob link

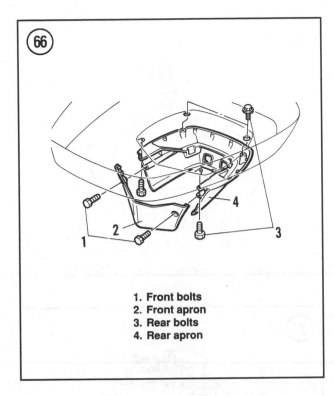

66

1. Front bolts
2. Front apron
3. Rear bolts
4. Rear apron

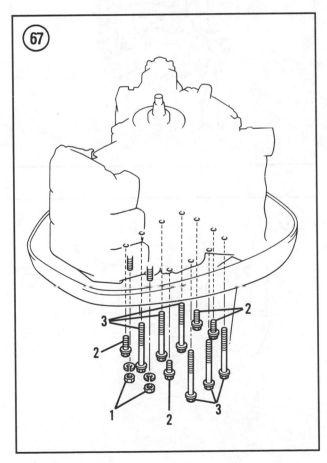

67

If necessary, use an impact driver and hammer to break them loose.

13. Refer to **Figure 67** and remove the 2 nuts and lockwashers (1), the 4 short bolts (2) and 6 long bolts (3) securing the power head to the bottom cowling.

14. Thread the lifting hook (part No. YB-6202) onto the end of the crankshaft (**Figure 68**). Make sure the lifting hook is screwed on tight.

WARNING
If a hoist is not available for use in Step 15, have at least 2 assistants help with power head removal to avoid possible serious personal injury.

CAUTION
The power head must be lifted straight up in Step 15. Since most of the weight is on the cylinder side, the power head will tend to lift at an angle unless a pry bar is used as specified in Step 15. Lifting up and removing the power head at an angle may damage the crankshaft and the drive shaft splines.

15. Attach a hoist to the lifting hook. Insert a wooden prybar between the power head and the

8

68

bottom cowling as shown in **Figure 69** to help break the gasket seal. Carefully pull the power head *straight up* and off the bottom cowling.

16. Lower the power head onto a clean work bench. Check the base of the power head and the bottom cowling for the 2 locating pins. If they stayed with the power head, remove them and install in the bottom cowling.

17. Mount the power head on an appropriate power head holding fixture (**Figure 70**).

18. Unhook the hoist and unscrew the lifting eye.

19. If the power head is going to be disassembled, perform the following:

    a. Remove the flywheel: See this chapter.

    b. Remove the oil pump and driven gear: See Chapter Twelve.

    c. Remove all remaining electrical components: See Chapter Seven.

    d. Remove all remaining fuel components: See Chapter Six.

20. Remove and discard the power head mounting gasket.

21. Installation is the reverse of removal. Note the following:

    a. Clean the power head mounting and bottom cowling gasket surfaces of all gasket residue.

    b. Make sure the locating pins (A, **Figure 71**) are securely installed then install a new power head gasket (B, **Figure 71**) on the bottom cowling.

    c. Install a new oil seal and O-ring seal in the lower oil seal housing. Lubricate the new seals with Yamalube All-purpose Marine grease, or equivalent, before installing the lower oil seal housing on the power head. Tighten the bolt securely.

    d. Lightly coat the drive shaft splines with the recommended grease.

    e. Lower the power head into place. Rotate the propeller, if necessary, to mesh the drive shaft and crankshaft splines properly.

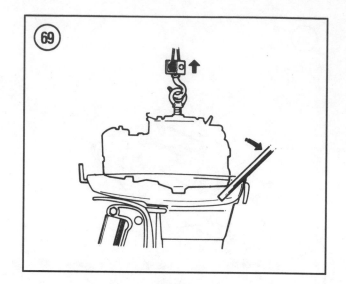

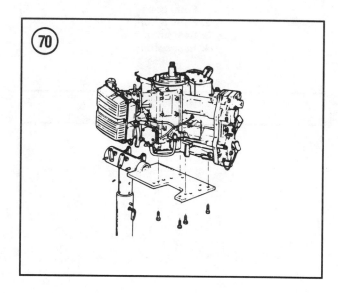

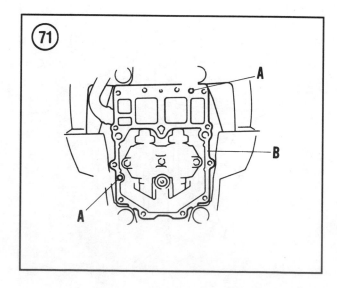

f. Apply red Loctite (No. 271) to the power head mounting bolts prior to installation.

g. Tighten all fasteners to the torque specifications listed in **Table 1**.

h. Turn the fuel petcock to the ON position and check for fuel leakage.

i. Perform engine timing, synchronization and linkage adjustment procedures. See Chapter Five.

225-250 hp 76° V6 Models

1. Disconnect the battery negative cable.
2. Remove the engine cover.
3. Disconnect the spark plug leads to prevent accidental starting of the engine.
4. Disconnect the fuel filter hose (1, **Figure 72**). Plug the end to prevent leakage.
5. Disconnect the fuel feed pump hoses (2, **Figure 72**). Plug the to prevent leakage.

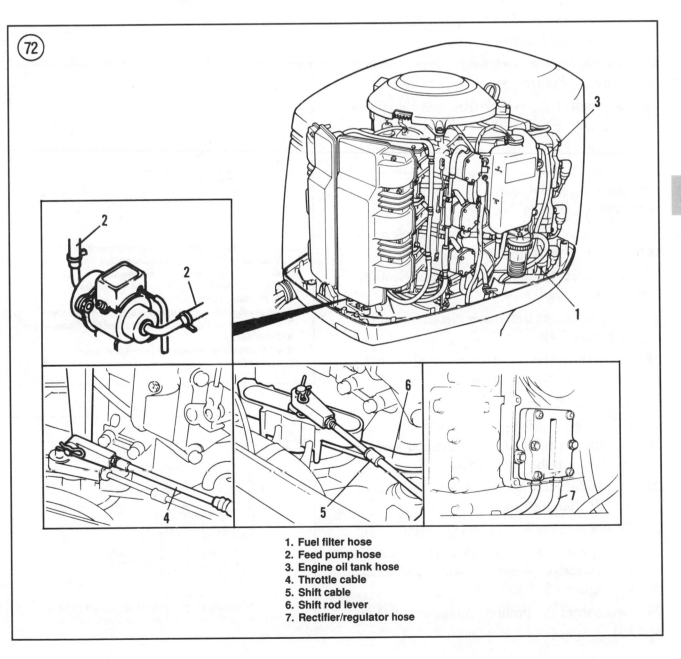

1. **Fuel filter hose**
2. **Feed pump hose**
3. **Engine oil tank hose**
4. **Throttle cable**
5. **Shift cable**
6. **Shift rod lever**
7. **Rectifier/regulator hose**

8

6. Disconnect the oil tank line from the power head (3, **Figure 72**). Plug the line to prevent leakage.

7. Remove the hairpin clip securing the throttle cable (4, **Figure 72**). Remove the throttle cable and bushing.

8. Remove the hairpin clip securing the shift cable (5, **Figure 72**). Remove the shift cable and bushing.

9. Remove the shift rod lever (6, **Figure 72**).

10. Disconnect the hose (7, **Figure 72**) from the pilot hole on the rectifier/regulator.

11. Disconnect the fuel feed pump electrical connector (1, **Figure 73**).

12. Disconnect the power trim and tilt switch electrical connector (2, **Figure 73**).

13. Disconnect the trim angle electrical connector (1, **Figure 74**).

14. Disconnect the shift cut switch electrical connector (2, **Figure 74**).

15. Disconnect the oil level gauge electrical connector (3, **Figure 74**).

16. Disconnect the remote control unit electrical connector (4, **Figure 74**).

17. Disconnect the trim meter electrical connector (5, **Figure 74**).

18. Disconnect the oil level warning indicator electrical connector (6, **Figure 74**).

19. Disconnect the electromagnetic priming pump electrical connector (7, **Figure 74**).

20. Disconnect the negative electrical lead (1, **Figure 75**) from the starter motor.

21. Disconnect the positive electrical lead (2, **Figure 75**) from the electrical box.

22. Disconnect the fuse holder (8, **Figure 74**).

23. Disconnect the power trim and tilt electrical harness connectors located inside the electrical box (9, **Figure 74**).

24. Disconnect the ground connector (10, **Figure 74**).

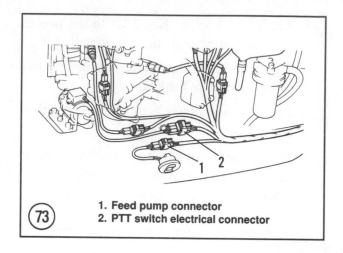

73
1. Feed pump connector
2. PTT switch electrical connector

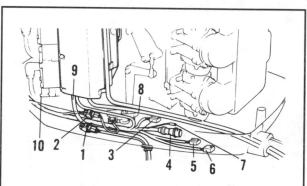

1. Trim angle sensor electrical connector
2. Shift cut switch electrical connector
3. Oil level gauge electrical connector
4. Remote control unit electrical connector
5. Trim meter electrical connector
6. Oil level warning indicator electrical connector
7. Electromagnetic priming pump electrical connector
8. Fuse holder
9. PTT electrical harness (in electrical box)
10. Ground wire

74

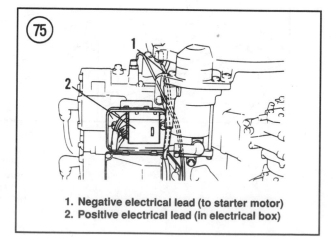

75

1. Negative electrical lead (to starter motor)
2. Positive electrical lead (in electrical box)

25. Remove the bolts securing the flywheel cover (A, **Figure 76**) and remove the cover.

26. Remove the 2 bolts and washers securing the front apron (B, **Figure 76**). Remove the 2 bolts and washers from the bottom and the 2 bolts from the inside of the bottom cowling securing the rear (C, **Figure 76**). Remove both aprons.

NOTE
At this point, there should be no hoses, wires or linkage connecting the power

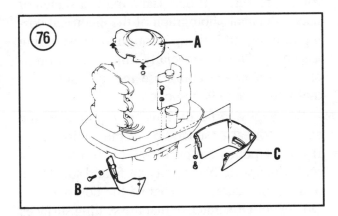

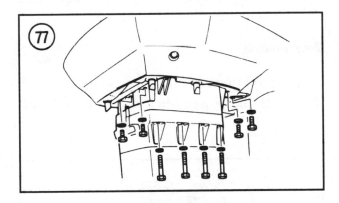

head to the bottom cowling. Recheck to make sure that nothing will interfere power head removal.

27. Remove the nut securing the flywheel as described in this chapter.

NOTE
The bolts and nuts are secured with tread locking compound during assembly and may be difficult to loosen in Step 28. If necessary, use an impact driver and hammer to break them loose.

28. Remove the bolts and lockwashers (**Figure 77**) securing the power head to the bottom cowling.

29. Thread the lifting hook (part No. YB-6442) onto the end of the crankshaft (**Figure 78**). Make sure the lifting hook is screwed on tight.

WARNING
If a hoist is not available for use in Step 30, have at least 2 assistants help with power head removal to avoid possible serious personal injury.

CAUTION
The power head must be lifted straight up in Step 30. Since most of the weight is on the cylinder side, the power head will tend to lift at an angle unless the power head is held in an upright position during removal. Lifting up and removing the power head at an angle may damage the crankshaft and the drive shaft splines.

30. Attach a hoist to the lifting hook and carefully lift the power head *straight up* and off the bottom cowling.

31. Lower the power head onto a clean work bench. Check the base of the power head and the bottom cowling for the 2 locating pins. If they stayed with the power head, remove them and install in the bottom cowling.

32. Mount the power head on a suitable holding fixture.

33. Unhook the hoist and unscrew the lifting eye.

8

34. If the power is going to be disassembled, perform the following:

35. Remove the flywheel. See this chapter.

36. Remove the oil pump and driven gear. See Chapter Twelve.

37. Remove all remaining electrical components. See Chapter Seven.

38. Remove all remaining fuel components. See Chapter Six.

39. Remove and discard the power head mounting gasket.

40. Installation is the reverse of removal. Note the following:

  a. Clean the power head mounting and bottom cowling gasket surfaces of all gasket residue.

  b. Make sure the locating pins (A, **Figure 79**) are securely installed and install a new power head gasket (B, **Figure 79**) on the bottom cowling.

  c. Install a new oil seal and O-ring seal in the lower oil seal housing. Lubricate the new seals with Yamalube All-purpose Marine grease, or equivalent, before installing the lower oil seal housing on the power head. Tighten the bolt securely.

  d. Lightly coat the drive shaft splines with the recommended grease.

  e. Lower the power head into place. Rotate the propeller, if necessary, to mesh the drive shaft and crankshaft splines properly.

  f. Tighten all fasteners to the torque specifications listed in **Table 1**.

  g. Turn the fuel petcock to the ON position and check for fuel leakage.

  h. Perform engine timing, synchronization and linkage adjustment procedures. See Chapter Five.

POWER HEAD DISASSEMBLY

A large number of bolts and screws of different lengths are used to secure the various covers and components. Tag all similar internal parts for location and mark all mating parts for position. Record the number and thickness of any shims as they are removed. Small parts can be identified by placing them in plastic sandwich bags. Seal and label them with masking tape. Place parts from a specific area of the power head into plastic boxes to keep them separated. This will make reassembly easier and faster.

Refer to the appropriate chapter and remove all electrical, fuel, oil and mechanical components attached to the power head, noting the locations of J-clamps or other electrical lead routing retainers. If necessary, make a sketch or take an instant photograph of the electrical wiring routing and J-clamp location to assist during assembly. This is especially important in properly reconnecting crankcase recirculation lines that will have to be removed.

Some power heads have pry points in the casting for easier separation of the components. If no pry points are provided, break the gasket seal with a wide-blade putty knife and soft-faced mallet, then carefully separate the components. Do not gouge, scratch or mar the sealing surfaces as this will result in a vacuum and/or fluid leak.

2 hp models

Refer to **Figure 80** for this procedure.

1. Secure the power head in a vise with soft jaws.

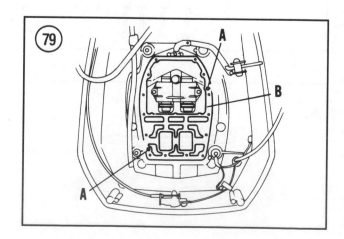

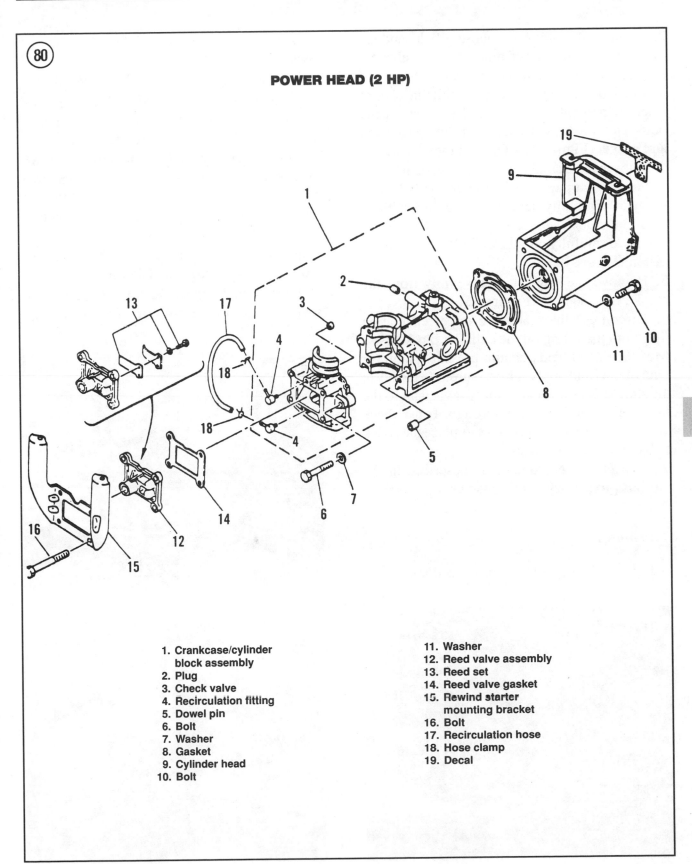

80

POWER HEAD (2 HP)

1. Crankcase/cylinder block assembly
2. Plug
3. Check valve
4. Recirculation fitting
5. Dowel pin
6. Bolt
7. Washer
8. Gasket
9. Cylinder head
10. Bolt
11. Washer
12. Reed valve assembly
13. Reed set
14. Reed valve gasket
15. Rewind starter mounting bracket
16. Bolt
17. Recirculation hose
18. Hose clamp
19. Decal

8

2. Remove the bracket mounting bolts and remove the rewind starter bracket, reed valve assembly and gasket. Discard the gasket.

3. Loosen the 4 cylinder head bolts in several stages to prevent head warpage, then remove the bolts and washers. Remove the cylinder head and gasket (**Figure 81**). Discard the gasket.

4. Loosen the 2 crankcase bolts in several stages to prevent warpage, then remove the bolts and washers. Carefully separate the cylinder block from the crankcase. Hold the crankshaft in one hand and carefully pull the cylinder block off the piston (**Figure 82**).

5. Remove the crankshaft assembly from the crankcase assembly (**Figure 83**).

6. Disconnect the crankcase upper circulation line from the fitting on the cylinder block. Use a Mity-Vac hand held vacuum/pressure pump (or equivalent) and apply air pressure into the hose; air should pass through. Apply a vacuum to the hose; air should not pass through. If the check valve fails either of these tests, replace the check valve in the cylinder block.

7. Inspect all components as described in the various procedures in this chapter.

3 hp models

Refer to **Figure 84** for this procedure.

1. Secure the power head in a vise with soft jaws.

2. Remove the carburetor. See Chapter Six.

3. Remove the bolts (**Figure 85**) securing the reed valve assembly, then remove the reed valve assembly and gasket. Discard the gasket.

4. Loosen the 5 cylinder head bolts (**Figure 86**) in several stages to prevent head warpage, then remove the bolts and washers. Remove the cylinder head cover and its gasket and the cylinder head and its gasket. Discard both gaskets.

5. Remove the thermostat cover bolts and remove the cover, gasket and thermostat.

6. Loosen the 6 crankcase bolts (**Figure 87**) in several stages to prevent warpage, then remove

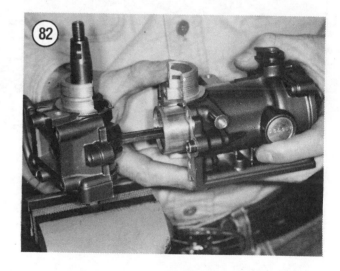

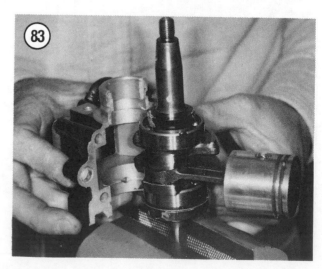

POWER HEAD (3 HP)

84

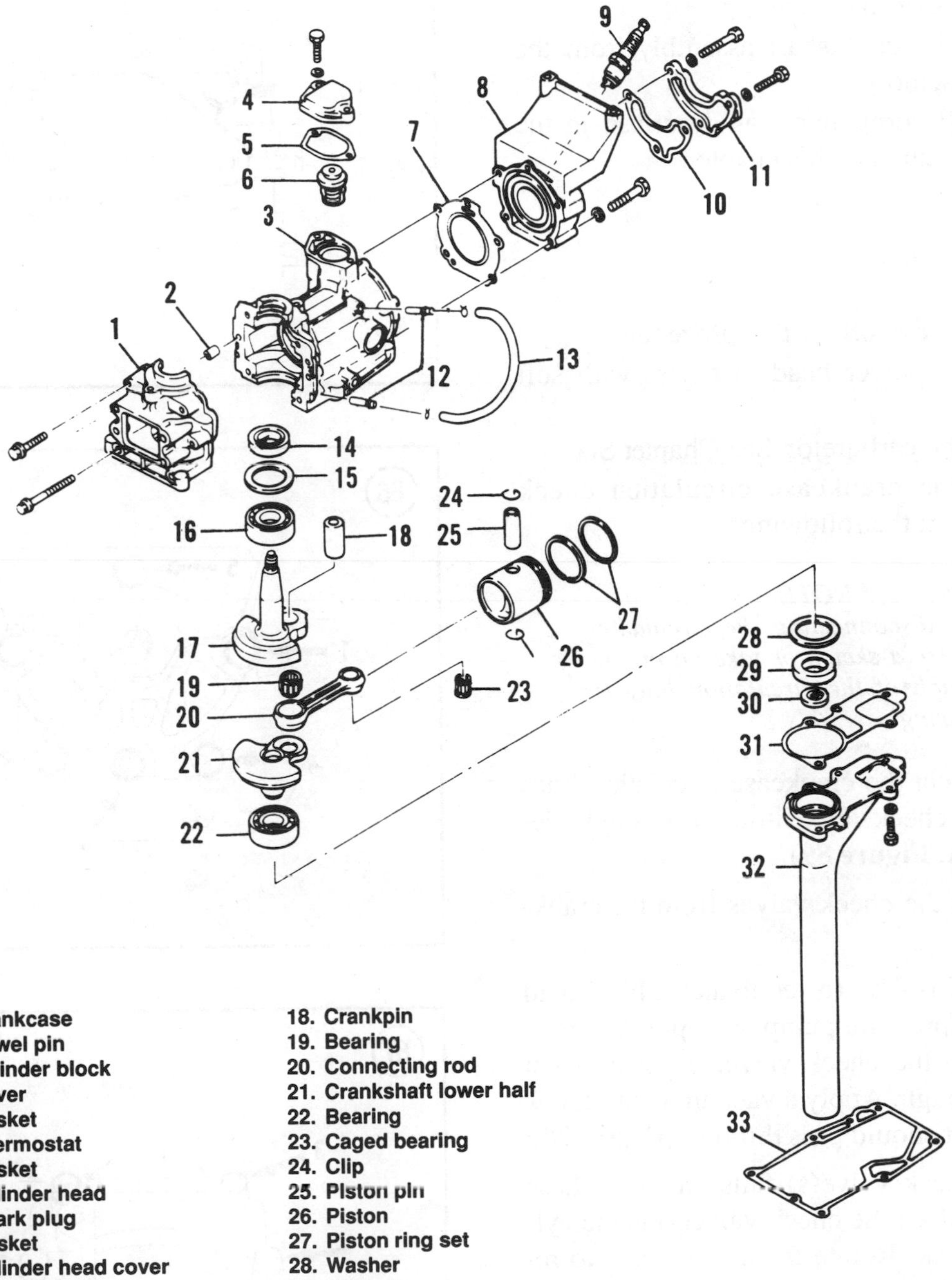

1. Crankcase
2. Dowel pin
3. Cylinder block
4. Cover
5. Gasket
6. Thermostat
7. Gasket
8. Cylinder head
9. Spark plug
10. Gasket
11. Cylinder head cover
12. Hose fitting
13. Recirculation hose
14. Oil seal
15. Washer
16. Bearing
17. Crankshaft upper half

18. Crankpin
19. Bearing
20. Connecting rod
21. Crankshaft lower half
22. Bearing
23. Caged bearing
24. Clip
25. Piston pin
26. Piston
27. Piston ring set
28. Washer
29. Oil seal
30. Oil seal
31. Gasket
32. Exhaust manifold
33. Gasket

8

the bolts and washers. Carefully separate the cylinder block from the crankcase. Hold the crankshaft in one hand and carefully pull the cylinder block off the piston.

7. Remove the crankshaft assembly from the crankcase assembly.

8. Inspect all components as described in the various procedures in this chapter.

4 and 5 hp models

Refer to **Figure 88** for this procedure.

1. Secure the power head in a vise with soft jaws.

2. Remove the carburetor. See Chapter Six.

3. To test the crankcase circulation check valves, perform the following:

> *NOTE*
> *Prior to disconnecting the circulation lines, make a sketch or take an instant photograph of the circulation lines to assist during assembly.*

a. Disconnect the crankcase circulation lines from the check valve fittings on the cylinder block (A, **Figure 89**).

b. Remove the check valves from the crankcase.

c. Use a Mity-Vac (or equivalent) hand-held vacuum/pressure pump and apply air pressure into the check valve; air should not pass through. Apply a vacuum to the check valve; air should pass through (**Figure 90**).

d. If the check valve(s) fails either of these tests, replace the check valve(s) in the cylinder block. Rotate the check valve to remove it. Do not pry it out.

e. Make sure the hose joint (B, **Figure 89**) is clear.

4. Remove the bolts securing the reed valve assembly, then remove the reed valve assembly and gasket. Discard the gasket.

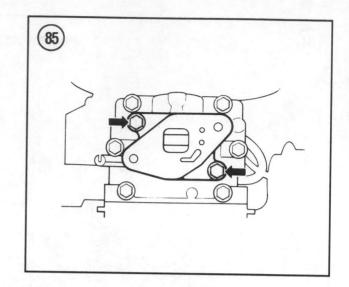

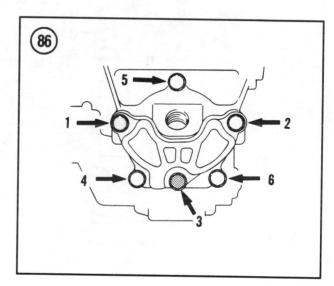

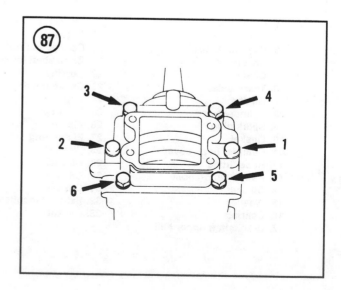

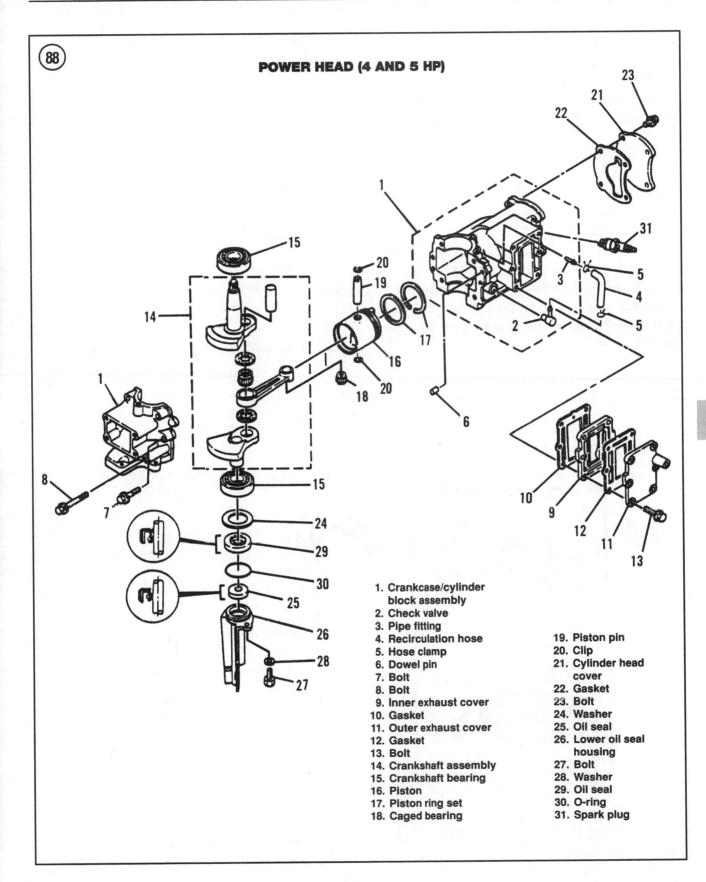

POWER HEAD (4 AND 5 HP)

1. Crankcase/cylinder block assembly
2. Check valve
3. Pipe fitting
4. Recirculation hose
5. Hose clamp
6. Dowel pin
7. Bolt
8. Bolt
9. Inner exhaust cover
10. Gasket
11. Outer exhaust cover
12. Gasket
13. Bolt
14. Crankshaft assembly
15. Crankshaft bearing
16. Piston
17. Piston ring set
18. Caged bearing
19. Piston pin
20. Clip
21. Cylinder head cover
22. Gasket
23. Bolt
24. Washer
25. Oil seal
26. Lower oil seal housing
27. Bolt
28. Washer
29. Oil seal
30. O-ring
31. Spark plug

8

5. If still in place, remove the bolt and washer securing the oil seal housing to the bottom of the power head and remove the housing.

6. Remove the bolts securing the exhaust cover assembly; remove the covers and gaskets (**Figure 91**).

7. Remove the thermostat from the inner exhaust cover (**Figure 92**).

8. Remove the bolts securing the cylinder head cover and remove the cover and gasket (**Figure 93**). Discard the gasket.

9. Loosen the 6 crankcase bolts (A, **Figure 94**) in several stages to prevent warpage, then remove the bolts. Carefully pry apart and separate the crankcase cover from the cylinder block (B, **Figure 94**). Remove the crankcase cover (**Figure 95**).

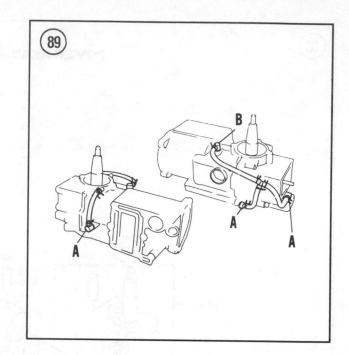

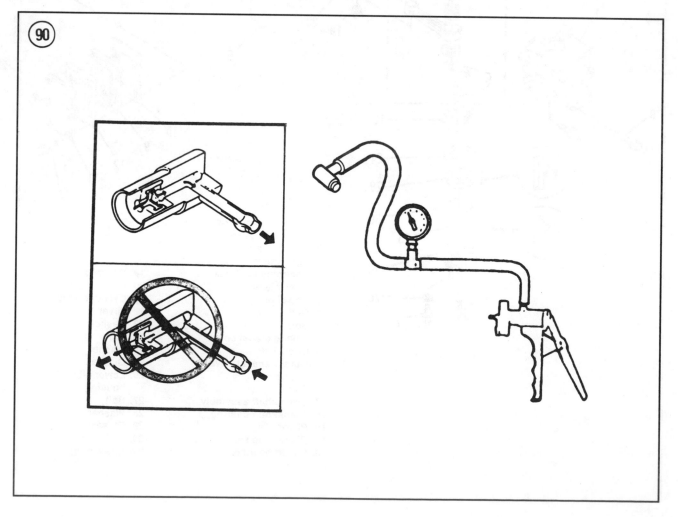

10. Using a soft-faced mallet, carefully tap on the underside of the crankshaft to loosen the piston and crankshaft bearings (**Figure 96**). Carefully pull the crankshaft and piston assembly from the cylinder block.

11. Inspect all components as described in the various procedures in this chapter.

6 and 8 hp
(2-cylinder)

Refer to **Figure 97** for this procedure.

1. Secure the power head in a vise with soft jaws.

2. If not removed previously, remove the flywheel as described in this chapter.

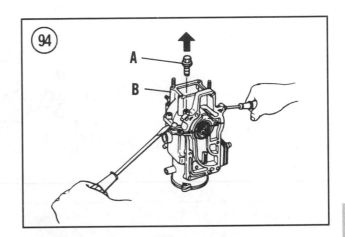

8

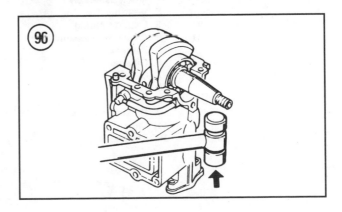

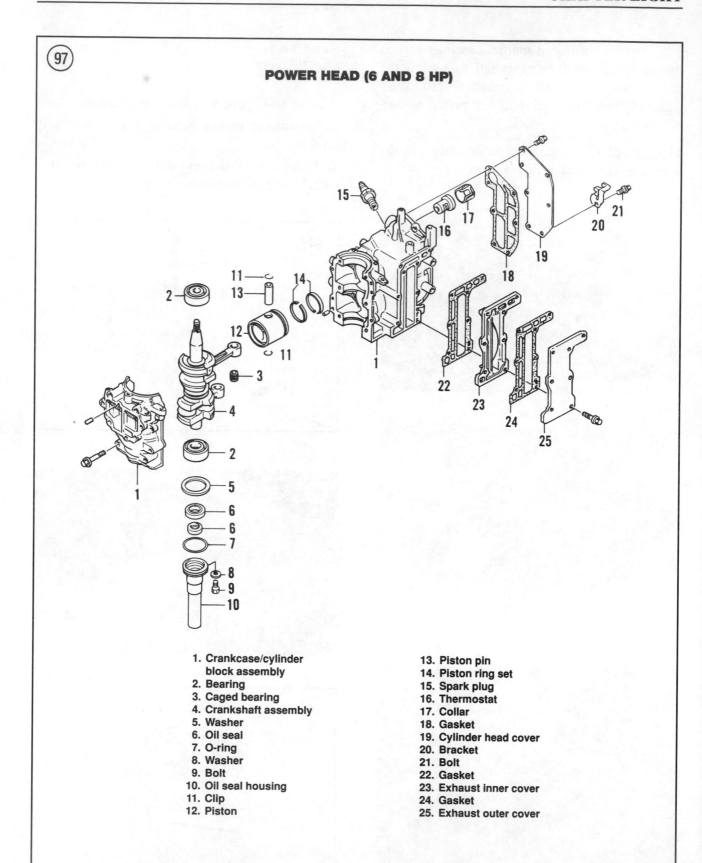

POWER HEAD (6 AND 8 HP)

1. Crankcase/cylinder block assembly
2. Bearing
3. Caged bearing
4. Crankshaft assembly
5. Washer
6. Oil seal
7. O-ring
8. Washer
9. Bolt
10. Oil seal housing
11. Clip
12. Piston
13. Piston pin
14. Piston ring set
15. Spark plug
16. Thermostat
17. Collar
18. Gasket
19. Cylinder head cover
20. Bracket
21. Bolt
22. Gasket
23. Exhaust inner cover
24. Gasket
25. Exhaust outer cover

3. Remove the carburetor. See Chapter Six.

4. To test the crankcase circulation check valves, perform the following:

NOTE
Prior to disconnecting the circulation lines, make a sketch or take an instant photograph of the circulation lines to assist during assembly.

a. Disconnect the crankcase circulation lines from the check valve fittings on the cylinder block.

b. Remove the check valves from the crankcase.

c. Use a Mity-Vac (or equivalent) hand-held vacuum/pressure pump and apply air pressure into the check valve; air should not pass through. Apply a vacuum to the check valve; air should pass through (**Figure 90**).

d. If the check valve(s) fails either of these tests, replace the check valve(s) in the cyl-inder block. Rotate the check valve for removal, do not pry it out.

e. Make sure the hose joint (**Figure 90**) is clear.

5. Remove the bolts securing the intake manifold (A, **Figure 98**) and the reed valve assembly. Remove the intake manifold (B, **Figure 98**), gasket, reed valve assembly and gasket. Discard both gaskets. Don't lose the locating pin.

6. Remove the bolts and washers (C, **Figure 98**) securing the exhaust manifold to the bottom of the power head and remove the manifold (D, **Figure 98**) and gasket. Discard the gasket.

7. Remove the bolts securing the exhaust cover assembly. Then remove the covers and gaskets and discard the gaskets.

8. Remove the bolts securing the cylinder head cover and remove the cover and gasket. Discard the gasket. Note the location of the clamp on one of the lower bolts.

9. Remove the thermostat from the cylinder head cover.

10. Loosen the 6 crankcase bolts in several stages to prevent warpage, then remove the bolts. Carefully pry apart and separate the crankcase cover from the cylinder block (**Figure 99**). Remove the crankcase cover.

11. Using a soft-faced mallet, carefully tap on the underside of the crankshaft to loosen the pistons and crankshaft bearings. Carefully pull the crankshaft and piston assembly from the cylinder block (**Figure 100**).

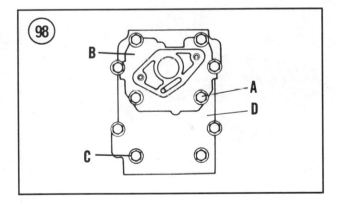

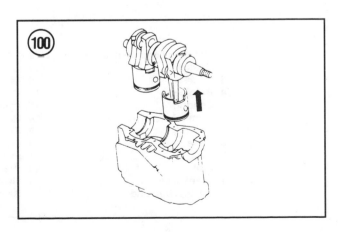

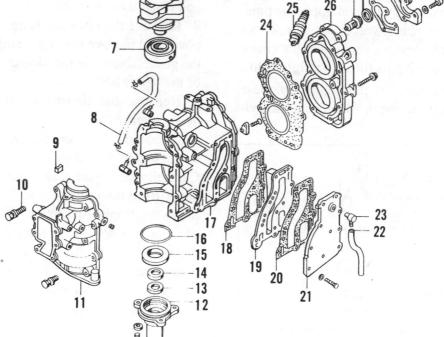

101

POWER HEAD (9.9 AND 15 HP)

1. Magneto base retainer
2. Gasket
3. Oil seal
4. Retainer
5. Bearing
6. Crankshaft assembly
7. Bearing
8. Hose
9. Pad
10. Bolt
11. Crankcase
12. Oil seal housing

13. Oil seal
14. Oil seal
15. Oil seal
16. O-ring
17. Cylinder block
18. Gasket
19. Exhaust inner cover
20. Gasket
21. Exhaust outer cover
22. Hose
23. Fitting
24. Gasket

25. Spark plug
26. Cylinder head
27. Thermostat
28. Washer
29. Gasket
30. Thermostat cover
31. Piston ring set
32. Piston
33. Clip
34. Piston pin
35. Washer
36. Loose needle bearings

12. Inspect all components as described in the various procedures in this chapter.

9.9 and 15 hp and C25 (2-Cylinder)

Refer to the following illustrations for this procedure:

a. **Figure 101**: 9.9 and 15 hp engines.

b. **Figure 102**: C25 engine.

1. Remove the carburetor. See Chapter Six.

2. To test the crankcase circulation check valves, perform the following:

NOTE
Prior to disconnecting the circulation lines, make a sketch or take an instant

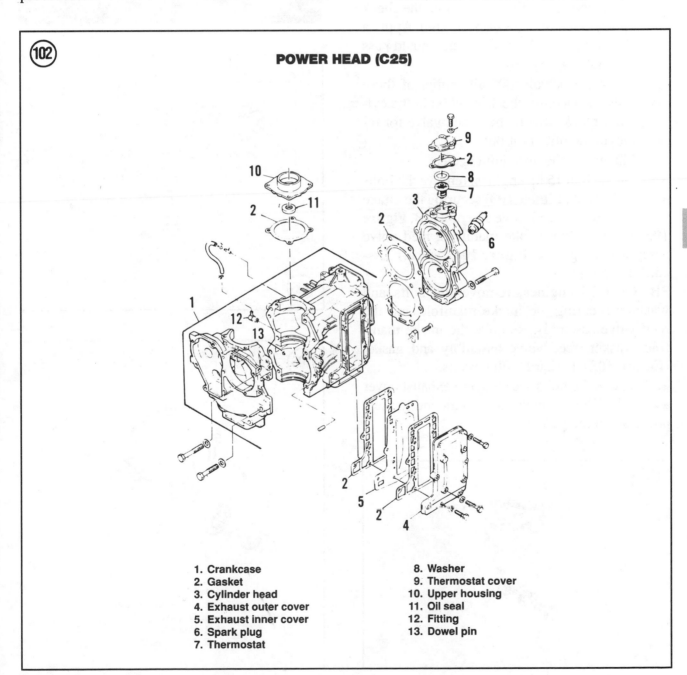

POWER HEAD (C25)

1. Crankcase
2. Gasket
3. Cylinder head
4. Exhaust outer cover
5. Exhaust inner cover
6. Spark plug
7. Thermostat
8. Washer
9. Thermostat cover
10. Upper housing
11. Oil seal
12. Fitting
13. Dowel pin

photograph of the circulation lines to assist during assembly.

a. Disconnect the crankcase circulation lines from the check valve fittings on the cylinder block.

b. Remove the check valves from the crank-case.

c. Use a Mity-Vac hand held vacuum/pressure pump and apply air pressure into the check valve; air should not pass through. Apply a vacuum to the check valve; air should pass through (**Figure 90**).

d. If the check valve(s) fails either of these tests, replace the check valve(s) in the cylinder block. Rotate the check valve for removal, do not pry it out.

e. Make sure the hose joint is clear.

3A. On 9.9 and 15 hp engines, remove the bolts and washers (A, **Figure 103**) securing the intake manifold and the reed valve assembly (B, **Figure 103**). Remove the intake manifold, reed valve assembly and gasket (**Figure 104**, typical). Discard the gasket.

3B. On C25 engines, remove the bolts and washers securing the intake manifold and the reed valve assembly. Remove the intake manifold, gasket, reed valve assembly and gasket (**Figure 105**). Discard both gaskets.

4. Remove the bolts securing the exhaust cover assembly. Then remove the covers and gaskets and discard the gaskets.

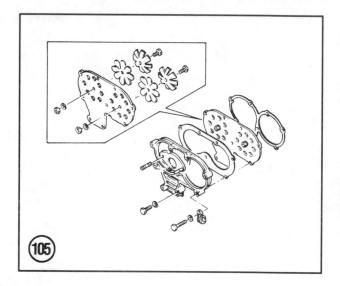

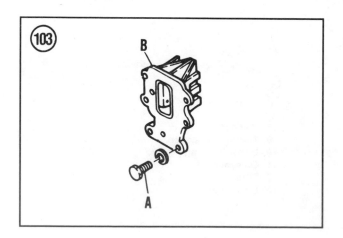

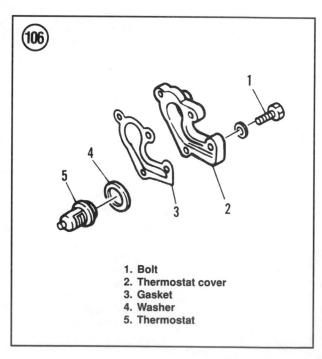

1. Bolt
2. Thermostat cover
3. Gasket
4. Washer
5. Thermostat

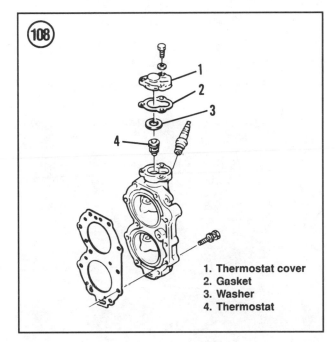

1. Thermostat cover
2. Gasket
3. Washer
4. Thermostat

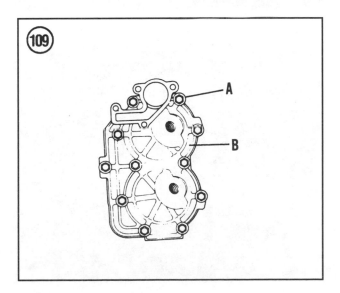

5A. On 9.9 and 15 hp engines, refer to **Figure 106** and remove the bolts and washers that secure the thermostat cover to the front of the cylinder head (**Figure 107**, typical). Remove the cover (2, **Figure 106**), gasket (3), washer (4) and thermostat (5).

5B. On C25 engines, remove the bolts and washers securing the thermostat cover to the top of the cylinder head. Remove the cover, gasket, washer and thermostat (**Figure 108**).

6. Loosen the cylinder head bolts in several stages to prevent warpage, then remove the bolts (A, **Figure 109**). Carefully separate the cylinder head (B, **Figure 109**) from the cylinder block. Remove the cylinder head and gasket (**Figure 110**). Discard the gasket.

7. Loosen the exhaust cover bolts in several stages to prevent warpage, then remove the bolts. Remove the outer cover, gasket, inner cover and gasket (**Figure 111**). Discard both gaskets.

8

8. Loosen the 10 crankcase bolts (A, **Figure 112**) in several stages to prevent warpage, then remove the bolts. Carefully separate the crankcase (B, **Figure 112**) from the cylinder block. Remove the crankcase (**Figure 113**).

9. Using a soft-faced mallet, carefully tap on the underside of the crankshaft to loosen the pistons and crankshaft bearings. Carefully pull the crankshaft and piston assembly out of the cylinder block (**Figure 114**).

10. Inspect all components as described in the various procedures in this chapter.

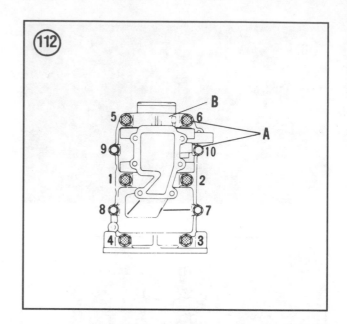

25 hp, C30, C40 and C55
(2-cylinder)

Refer to the following illustrations for this procedure:

a. **Figure 115**: 25 hp engine.

b. **Figure 116**: C30 engine.

c. **Figure 117**: C40 engine.

d. **Figure 118**: C55 engine.

1. Secure the power head in a suitable holding fixture.

2. Remove the carburetors. See Chapter Six.

3. To test the crankcase circulation check valves, perform the following:

NOTE
Prior to disconnecting the circulation lines, make a sketch or take an instant photograph of the circulation lines to assist during assembly.

a. Disconnect the crankcase circulation lines from the check valve fittings on the cylinder block.

b. Remove the check valves from the crankcase.

c. Use a Mity-Vac (or equivalent) hand-held vacuum/pressure pump and apply air pressure to the check valve; air should not pass through. Apply a vacuum to the check valve; air should pass through (**Figure 90**).

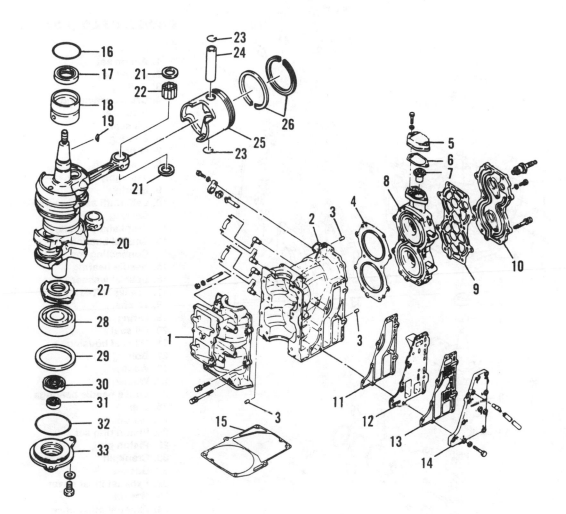

⑪⑤

POWER HEAD (25 HP)

8

1. Crankcase
2. Cylinder block
3. Dowel pin
4. Gasket
5. Cover
6. Gasket
7. Thermostat
8. Cylinder head
9. Gasket
10. Cylinder head cover
11. Gasket

12. Exhaust inner cover
13. Gasket
14. Exhaust outer cover
15. Gasket
16. O-ring
17. Oil seal
18. Bearing
19. Woodruff key
20. Crankshaft assembly
21. Washer
22. Loose needle bearings

23. Clip
24. Piston pin
25. Piston
26. Piston ring set
27. Oil pump drive gear
28. Bearing
29. Washer
30. Oil seal
31. Oil seal
32. O-ring
33. Oil seal housing

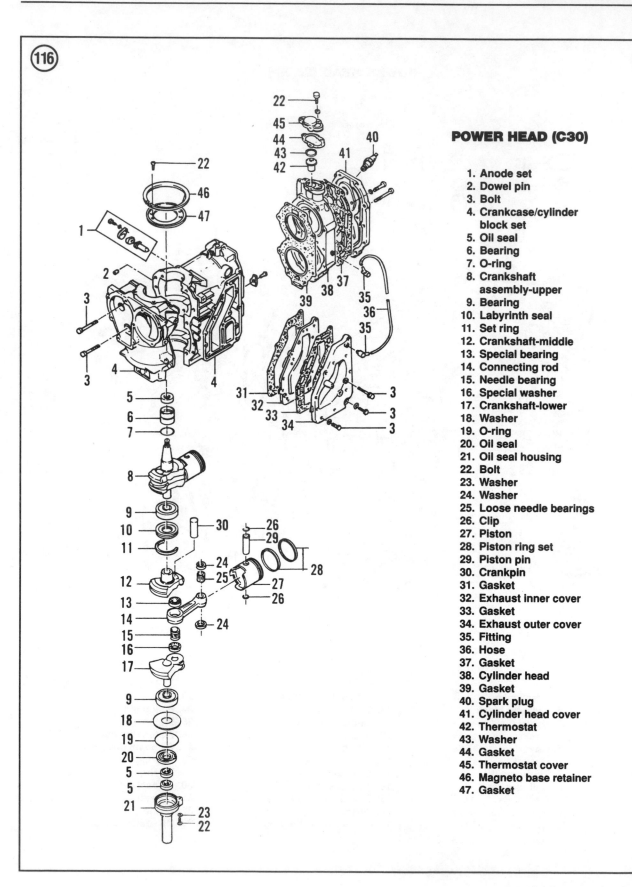

116

POWER HEAD (C30)

1. Anode set
2. Dowel pin
3. Bolt
4. Crankcase/cylinder block set
5. Oil seal
6. Bearing
7. O-ring
8. Crankshaft assembly-upper
9. Bearing
10. Labyrinth seal
11. Set ring
12. Crankshaft-middle
13. Special bearing
14. Connecting rod
15. Needle bearing
16. Special washer
17. Crankshaft-lower
18. Washer
19. O-ring
20. Oil seal
21. Oil seal housing
22. Bolt
23. Washer
24. Washer
25. Loose needle bearings
26. Clip
27. Piston
28. Piston ring set
29. Piston pin
30. Crankpin
31. Gasket
32. Exhaust inner cover
33. Gasket
34. Exhaust outer cover
35. Fitting
36. Hose
37. Gasket
38. Cylinder head
39. Gasket
40. Spark plug
41. Cylinder head cover
42. Thermostat
43. Washer
44. Gasket
45. Thermostat cover
46. Magneto base retainer
47. Gasket

117

POWER HEAD (C40)

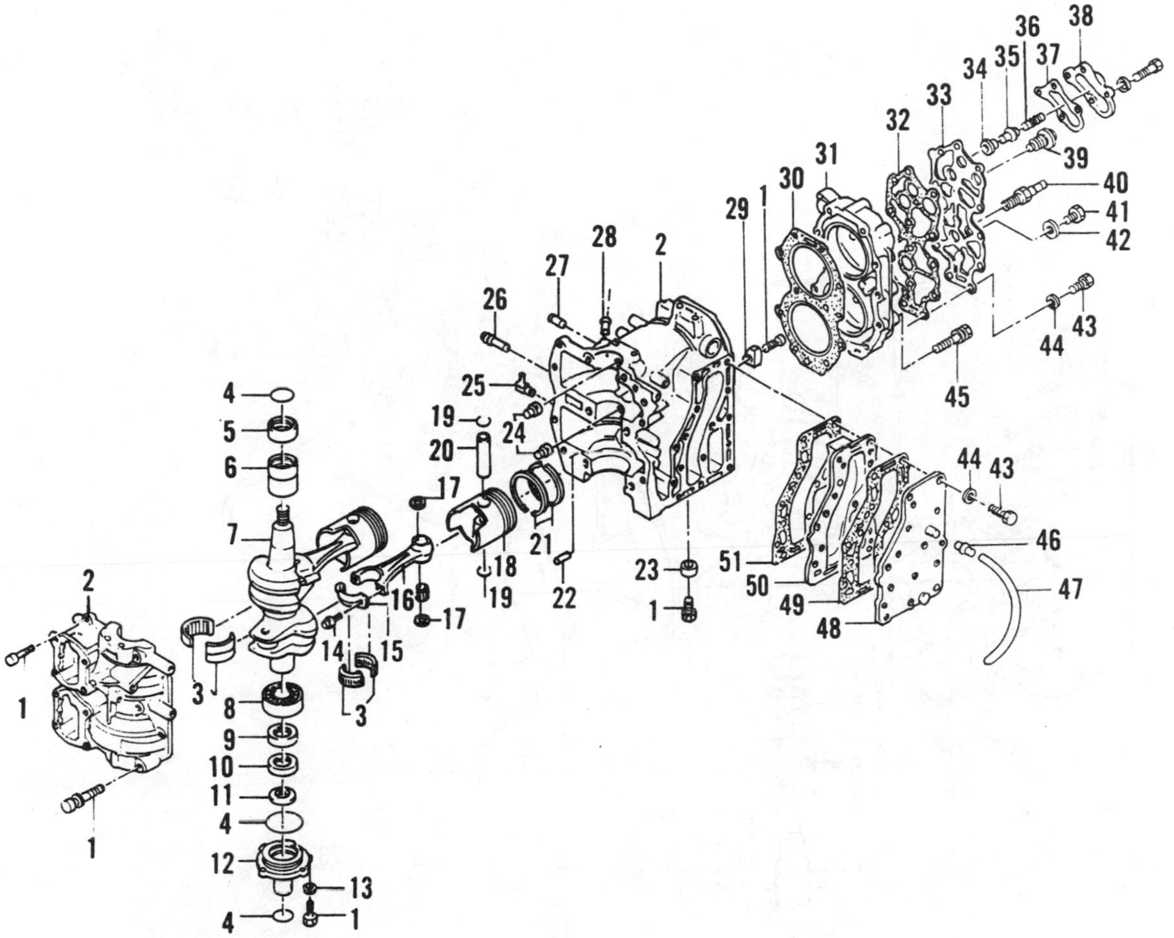

1. Bolt	18. Piston	35. Pressure control valve
2. Crankcase/cylinder block assembly	19. Clip	36. Spring
	20. Piston pin	37. Gasket
3. Roller bearing	21. Piston ring set	38. Thermostat cover
4. O-ring	22. Locating pin	39. Thermostat
5. Oil seal	23. Plug	40. Spark plug
6. Bearing	24. Screw	41. Bolt
7. Crankshaft	25. Fitting	42. Washer
8. Ball bearing	26. Pin	43. Bolt
9. Oil seal	27. Fitting	44. Washer
10. Oil seal	28. Fitting	45. Special bolt
11. Oil seal	29. Anode	46. Fitting
12. Oil seal housing	30. Gasket	47. Hose
13. Washer	31. Cylinder head	48. Exhaust outer cover
14. Bolt	32. Gasket	49. Gasket
15. Connecting rod end cap	33. Cylinder head cover	50. Exhaust inner cover
16. Connecting rod	34. Grommet	51. Gasket
17. Washer		

8

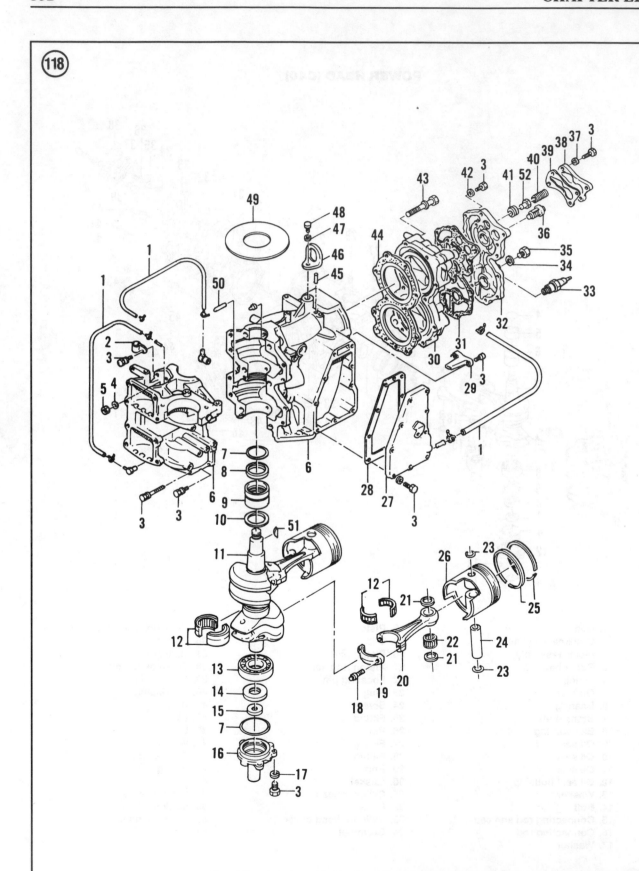

POWER HEAD (C55)

1. Recirculation hoses
2. Clamp
3. Bolt
4. Washer
5. Nut
6. Crankcase/cylinder block assembly
7. O-ring
8. Oil seal
9. Bearing
10. Washer
11. Crankshaft assembly
12. Roller bearing
13. Ball bearing
14. Oil seal
15. Oil seal
16. Oil seal housing
17. Washer
18. Bolt
19. Connecting rod end cap
20. Connecting rod
21. Washer
22. Loose needle bearings
23. Clip
24. Piston pin
25. Piston ring set
26. Piston
27. Exhaust cover
28. Gasket
29. Anode
30. Cylinder head
31. Gasket
32. Cylinder head cover
33. Spark plug
34. Washer
35. Bolt
36. Thermostat
37. Washer
38. Thermostat cover
39. Gasket
40. Spring
41. Grommet
42. Washer
43. Bolt
44. Gasket
45. Pin
46. Bracket
47. Washer
48. Bolt
49. Washer
50. Locating pin
51. Woodruff key
52. Pressure control valve

8

d. If the check valve(s) fails either of these tests, replace the check valve(s) in the cylinder block. Rotate the check valve to remove it. Do not pry it out.

e. Make sure the hose joint is clear.

NOTE
On C55 engines, the intake manifolds are held in place by the same nuts that secure the carburetors.

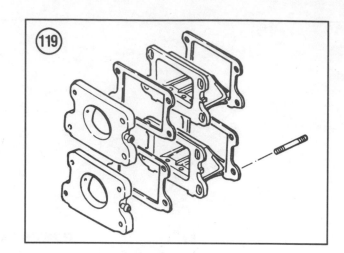

4A. On C55 engines, remove the intake manifolds, gaskets, reed valves and gaskets (**Figure 119**).

4B. On all other engines, remove the bolts and washers securing the intake manifold and the reed valve assembly (**Figure 120**, typical). Remove the intake manifold, reed valve assembly and gasket(s). Discard the gasket(s).

5. Remove the bolts securing the exhaust cover assembly; remove the cover(s) and gasket(s). Discard the gasket(s).

6A. On C40 and C55 engines, refer to **Figure 121** and remove the bolts and washers securing the thermostat cover to the front of the cylinder head. Remove the cover, gasket and thermostat.

6B. On 25 hp and C30 engines, remove the bolts and washers securing the thermostat cover to the top of the cylinder head. Remove the cover, gasket, washer and thermostat (**Figure 122**).

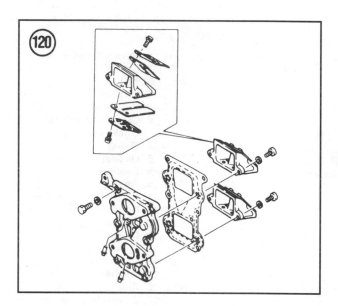

7A. On 25 hp and C30 engines, perform the following:

a. Loosen the cylinder head bolts in several stages to prevent warpage, then remove the bolts.

b. Tap the edge of the cylinder head with a soft-faced mallet to break the gasket seal. Carefully separate the cylinder head and cover assembly from the cylinder block and remove the assembly.

c. Place the cylinder head assembly on a flat, solid surface, use a suitable tool at the pry points (**Figure 123**) and carefully pry the cover free from the cylinder head. Separate

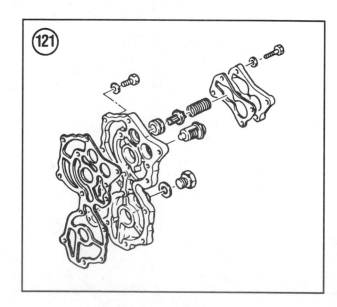

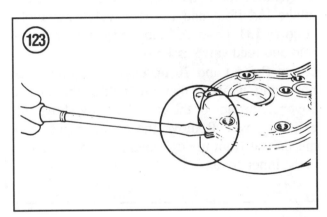

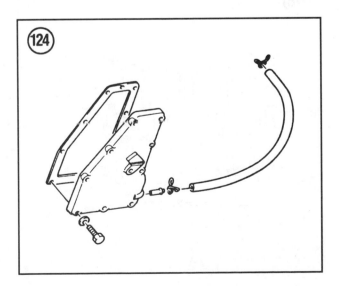

the cover from the cylinder head. Discard the gaskets.

7B. On C40 and C55 hp engines, perform the following:

a. Loosen the cylinder head cover bolts in several stages to prevent warpage, then remove the bolts.

b. Remove the cylinder head cover and gasket. Discard the gasket.

c. Loosen the cylinder head bolts in several stages to prevent warpage, then remove the bolts.

d. Tap the edge of the cylinder head with a soft-faced mallet to break the gasket seal. Carefully separate the cylinder head and gasket from the cylinder block and remove the assembly (**Figure 123**). Discard the gasket.

8. Disconnect the hose from the exhaust cover.

9A. On C55 engines, loosen the exhaust cover bolts in several stages to prevent warpage, then remove the bolts. Remove the cover and gasket (**Figure 124**). Discard the gasket.

9B. On all other engines, loosen the exhaust cover bolts in several stages to prevent warpage, then remove the bolts. Remove the outer cover, gasket, inner cover and gasket (**Figure 125**). Discard both gaskets.

8

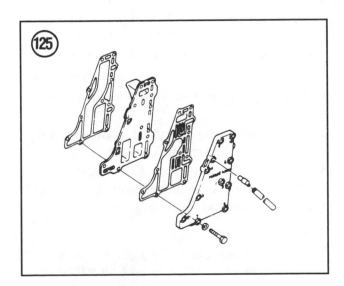

10. Loosen the crankcase bolts in several stages to prevent warpage, then remove the bolts. Carefully pry apart and separate the crankcase from the cylinder block. Remove the crankcase. Do not lose the locating pins (**Figure 126**).

11. On C55 engines, remove the lower half of the crankshaft main bearing from the crankcase.

> *NOTE*
> *On C40 and C55 engines, if the connecting rods are going to be disassembled from the crankshaft, you may want to loosen (do not remove) the connecting rod cap bolts at this time. The cylinder block makes a great holding fixture.*

12. Using a soft-faced mallet, carefully tap on the underside of the crankshaft to loosen the pistons, crankshaft bearings and oil seals. Carefully pull the crankshaft and piston assembly from the cylinder block (**Figure 100**).

13. On C55 engines, remove the upper half of the crankshaft main bearing from the cylinder block.

14. Inspect all components as described in the various procedures in this chapter.

All 3-cylinder Models

Refer to the following illustrations for this procedure:

    a. **Figure 127**: 30 hp engine.

    b. **Figure 128**: 40 and 50 hp engines.

    c. **Figure 129**: Pro 60 and 70 hp engines.

    d. **Figure 130**: C75, C85 and 90 hp engines.

1. Secure the power head in a suitable holding fixture.

2. If not previously removed, remove the flywheel as described in this chapter.

3. Remove the carburetors. See Chapter Six.

4. To test the crankcase circulation check valves, perform the following:

> *NOTE*
> *Prior to disconnecting the circulation lines, make a sketch or take an instant photograph of the circulation lines to assist during assembly.*

    a. Disconnect the crankcase circulation lines from the check valve fittings on the cylinder block.

    b. Remove the check valves from the crankcase.

    c. Use a Mity-Vac (or equivalent) hand-held vacuum/pressure pump and apply air pressure into the check valve; air should not pass through. Apply a vacuum to the check valve; air should pass through (**Figure 90**).

    d. If the check valve(s) fails either of these tests, replace the check valve(s). Rotate the check valve for removal, do not pry it out.

    e. Make sure the hose joint(s) is clear.

5. Remove the bolts and washers securing the intake manifold and the reed valve assembly (**Figure 131**, typical). Remove the intake manifold and reed valve assembly.

6. On Pro 60 and 70 hp engines, remove the bolts and washers that secure the thermostat cover to the side of the cylinder body above the exhaust cover. Remove the cover, gasket and thermostat from the cylinder block and the exhaust inner cover.

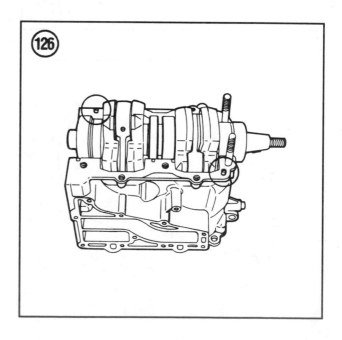

(126)

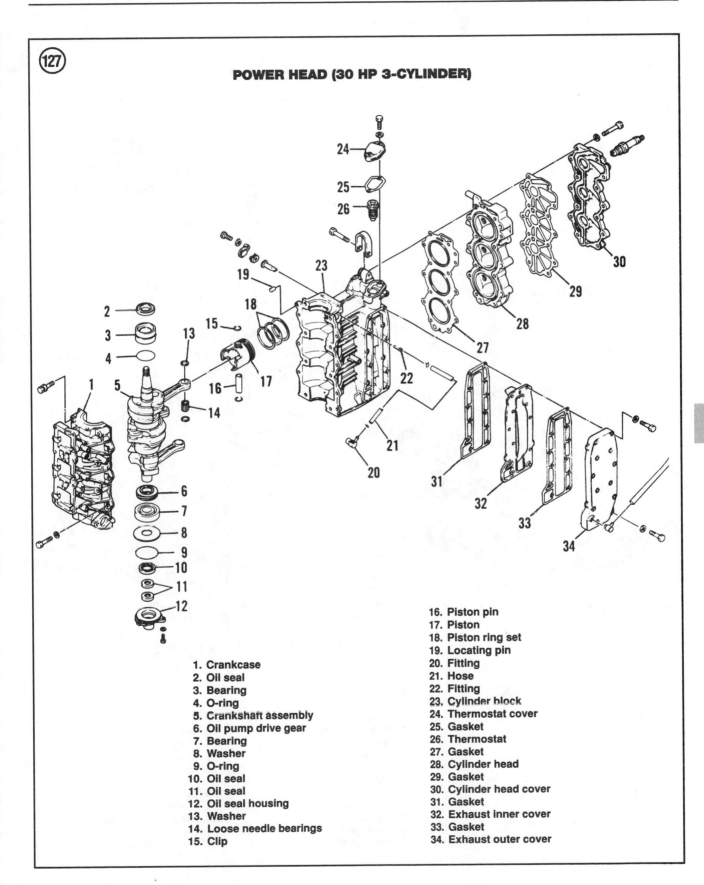

POWER HEAD (30 HP 3-CYLINDER)

1. Crankcase
2. Oil seal
3. Bearing
4. O-ring
5. Crankshaft assembly
6. Oil pump drive gear
7. Bearing
8. Washer
9. O-ring
10. Oil seal
11. Oil seal
12. Oil seal housing
13. Washer
14. Loose needle bearings
15. Clip

16. Piston pin
17. Piston
18. Piston ring set
19. Locating pin
20. Fitting
21. Hose
22. Fitting
23. Cylinder block
24. Thermostat cover
25. Gasket
26. Thermostat
27. Gasket
28. Cylinder head
29. Gasket
30. Cylinder head cover
31. Gasket
32. Exhaust inner cover
33. Gasket
34. Exhaust outer cover

8

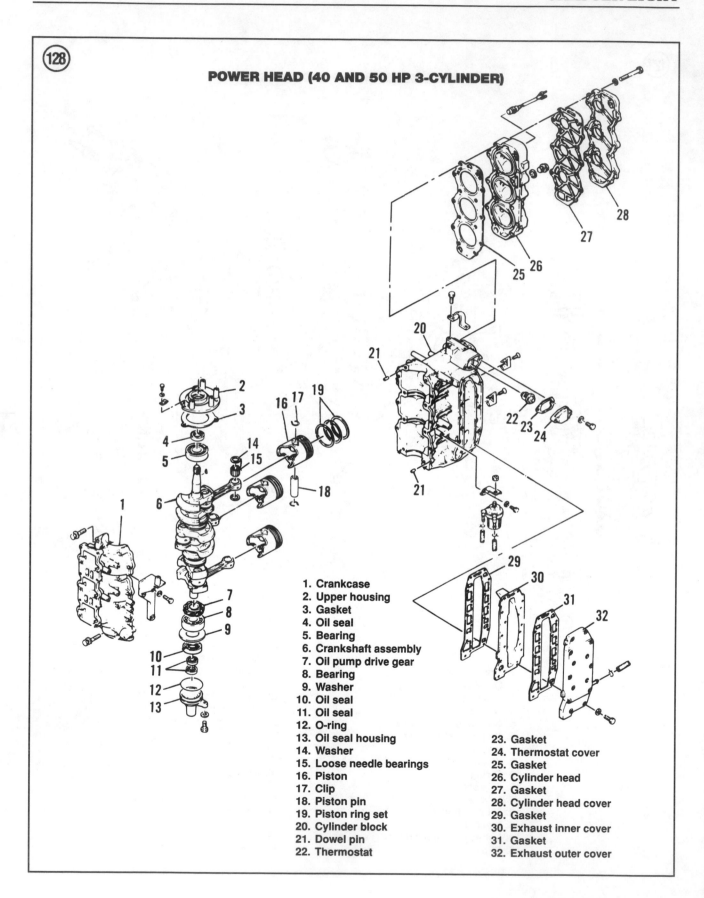

(128)

POWER HEAD (40 AND 50 HP 3-CYLINDER)

1. Crankcase
2. Upper housing
3. Gasket
4. Oil seal
5. Bearing
6. Crankshaft assembly
7. Oil pump drive gear
8. Bearing
9. Washer
10. Oil seal
11. Oil seal
12. O-ring
13. Oil seal housing
14. Washer
15. Loose needle bearings
16. Piston
17. Clip
18. Piston pin
19. Piston ring set
20. Cylinder block
21. Dowel pin
22. Thermostat
23. Gasket
24. Thermostat cover
25. Gasket
26. Cylinder head
27. Gasket
28. Cylinder head cover
29. Gasket
30. Exhaust inner cover
31. Gasket
32. Exhaust outer cover

POWER HEAD (PRO 60 AND 70 HP 3-CYLINDER)

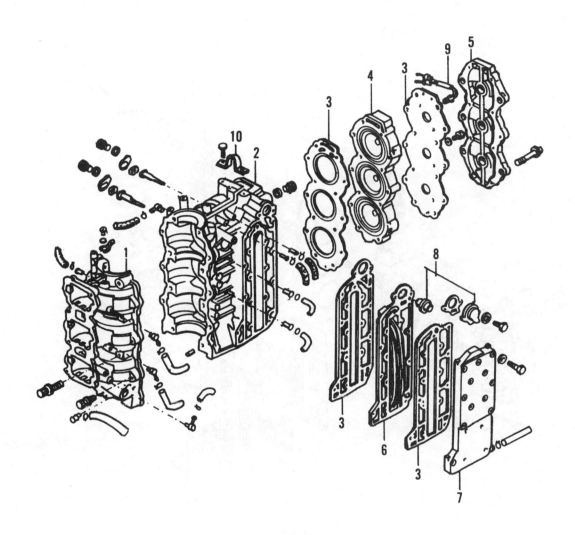

1. Crankcase
2. Cylinder block
3. Gasket
4. Cylinder head
5. Cylinder head cover
6. Exhaust inner cover
7. Exhaust outer cover
8. Thermostat and
   cover assembly
9. Thermoswitch
10. Lifting eye

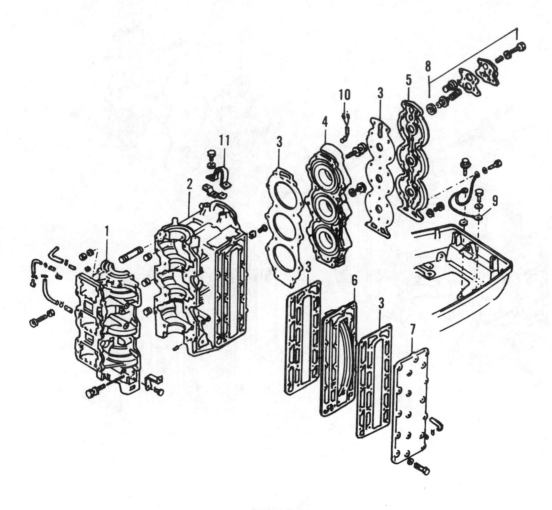

POWER HEAD (C75, C85 AND 90 HP 3-CYLINDER)

1. Crankcase
2. Cylinder block
3. Gasket
4. Cylinder head
5. Cylinder head cover
6. Exhaust inner cover
7. Exhaust outer cover
8. Thermostat and
   cover assembly
9. Ground lead
10. Thermoswitch
11. Lifting eye

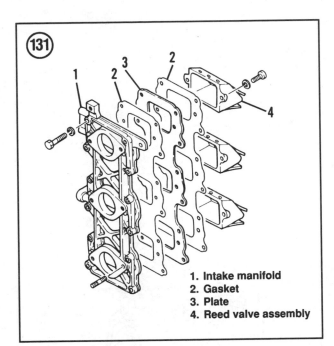

1. Intake manifold
2. Gasket
3. Plate
4. Reed valve assembly

7. Disconnect the hose from the exhaust cover.

8. Loosen the exhaust cover bolts in several stages to prevent warpage, then remove the bolts. Insert a flat-blade screwdriver between the cover lugs and the exhaust manifold and carefully pry the cover assembly from the cylinder block. Remove the outer cover, gasket, inner cover and gasket (**Figure 132**, typical). Discard both gaskets.

9A. On C75, C85 and 90 hp engines, refer to **Figure 133** and remove the bolts and washers securing the thermostat cover to the front of the cylinder head. Remove the cover, gasket and thermostat.

9B. On 30-50 hp engines, remove the bolts and washers securing the thermostat cover to the top

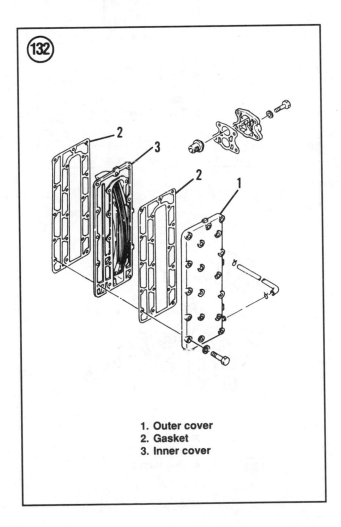

1. Outer cover
2. Gasket
3. Inner cover

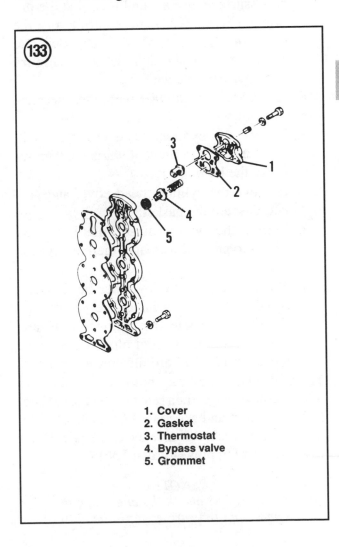

1. Cover
2. Gasket
3. Thermostat
4. Bypass valve
5. Grommet

8

of the cylinder block. Remove the cover, gasket, washer and thermostat (**Figure 134**).

10A.　On 30-70 hp and Pro 60 engines, perform the following:

    a. Loosen the cylinder head bolts in several stages to prevent warpage, then remove the bolts.

    b. Tap the edge of the cylinder head with a soft-faced mallet to break the gasket seal. Carefully separate the cylinder head and cover assembly from the cylinder block and remove the assembly.

    c. On 40 and 50 hp engines, remove the 4 bolts and washers securing the cylinder head cover and gasket to the cylinder head.

    d. Place the cylinder head assembly on a flat, solid surface, use a suitable tool at the pry points (**Figure 123**) and carefully pry the cover free from the cylinder head. Separate the cover from the cylinder head (**Figure 135**). Discard the gaskets.

10B.　On C75, C85 and 90 hp engines, perform the following:

    a. Loosen the cylinder head cover bolts in several stages to prevent warpage, then remove the bolts.

    b. Remove the cylinder head cover and gasket. Discard the gasket.

    c. Loosen the cylinder head bolts in several stages to prevent warpage, then remove the bolts.

    d. Tap the edge of the cylinder head with a soft-faced mallet to break the gasket seal. Carefully separate the cylinder head and gasket from the cylinder block and remove the assembly. Discard the gasket.

11.　Loosen the crankcase bolts in several stages to prevent warpage, then remove the bolts. Carefully pry apart and separate the crankcase from the cylinder block. Remove the crankcase. Don't lose the locating pins (**Figure 136**).

NOTE
On C75, C85 and 90 hp engines, if the connecting rods are going to be disas-

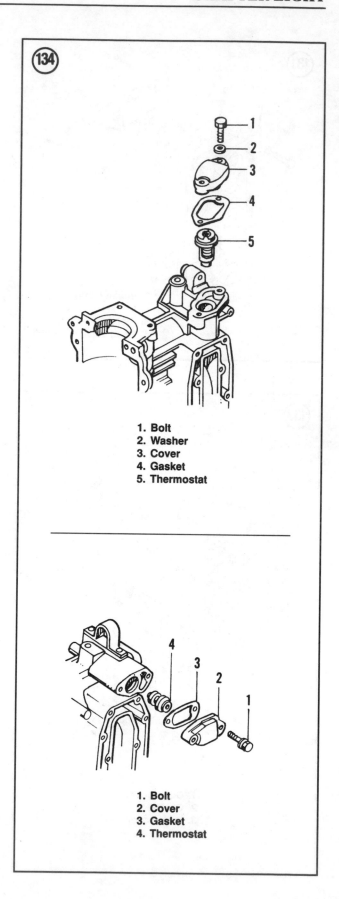

1. Bolt
2. Washer
3. Cover
4. Gasket
5. Thermostat

1. Bolt
2. Cover
3. Gasket
4. Thermostat

sembled from the crankshaft, you may want to loosen (do not remove) the connecting rod cap bolts at this time. The cylinder block makes a great holding fixture.

12. Using a soft-faced mallet, carefully tap on the underside of the crankshaft to loosen the crankshaft bearings and oil seals. Carefully pull the crankshaft and piston assembly from the cylinder block.

13. Inspect all components as described in the various procedures in this chapter.

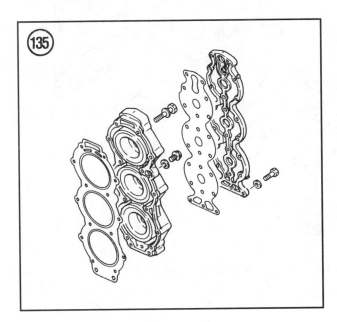

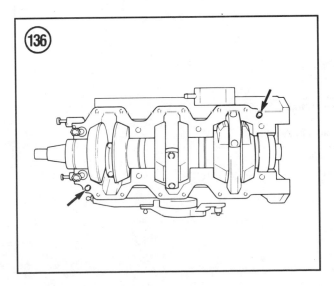

All V4 and All 90° V6 Engines

Refer to the following illustrations for this procedure:

a. **Figure 137**: Intake manifolds and reed valve assembly (Pro V 150, Pro V 175 and Pro V 200 models).

b. **Figure 138**: Power head components (all models) and intake manifolds and reed valve assembly (115-225 hp-except Pro V 150, Pro V 175 and Pro V 200 models)

NOTE
Cover the workbench surface with a flat sheet of heavy rubber or piece of clean masonite to protect all sealing surfaces of the engine. The work bench must also be level so the power head will be stable during the disassembly procedure.

CAUTION
The complete power head assembly is heavy and also very tall and top heavy during the initial part of the disassembly procedure. When breaking bolts loose or taping off a stubborn component, hold the power head so it will not fall over. If necessary, have an assistant hold the power head during the difficult removal of a component.

1. Remove the carburetors. See Chapter Six.

2. Remove the flywheel as described in this chapter.

3. To test the crankcase circulation check valves, perform the following:

NOTE
Prior to disconnecting the circulation lines, make a sketch or take an instant photograph of the circulation lines to assist during assembly.

a. Disconnect the crankcase circulation lines from the check valve fittings on the engine.

b. Remove the check valves from the crankcase.

c. Use a Mity-Vac (or equivalent) hand-held vacuum/pressure pump and apply air pres-

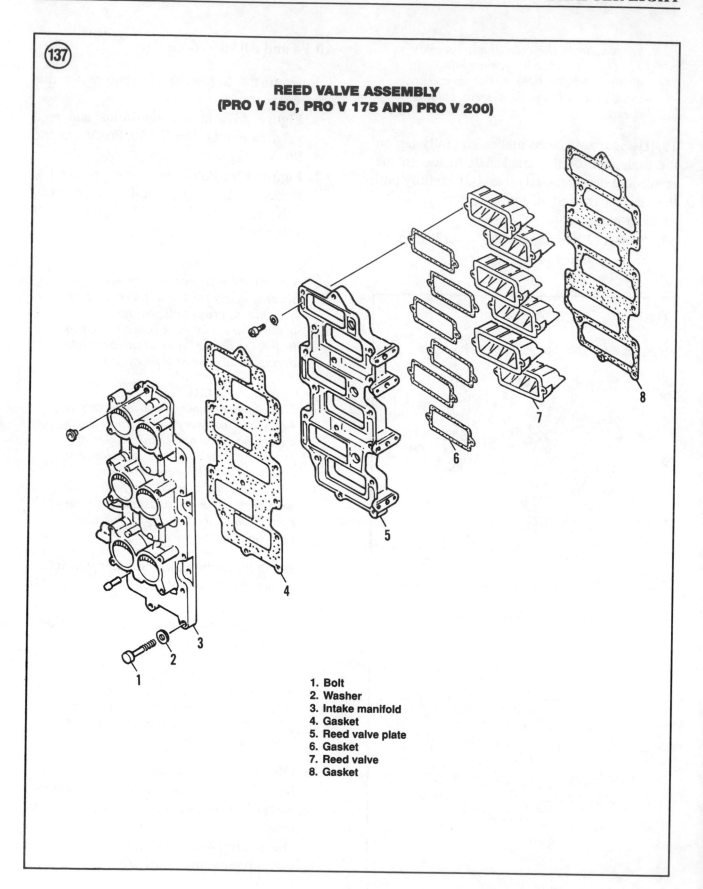

**REED VALVE ASSEMBLY
(PRO V 150, PRO V 175 AND PRO V 200)**

137

1. Bolt
2. Washer
3. Intake manifold
4. Gasket
5. Reed valve plate
6. Gasket
7. Reed valve
8. Gasket

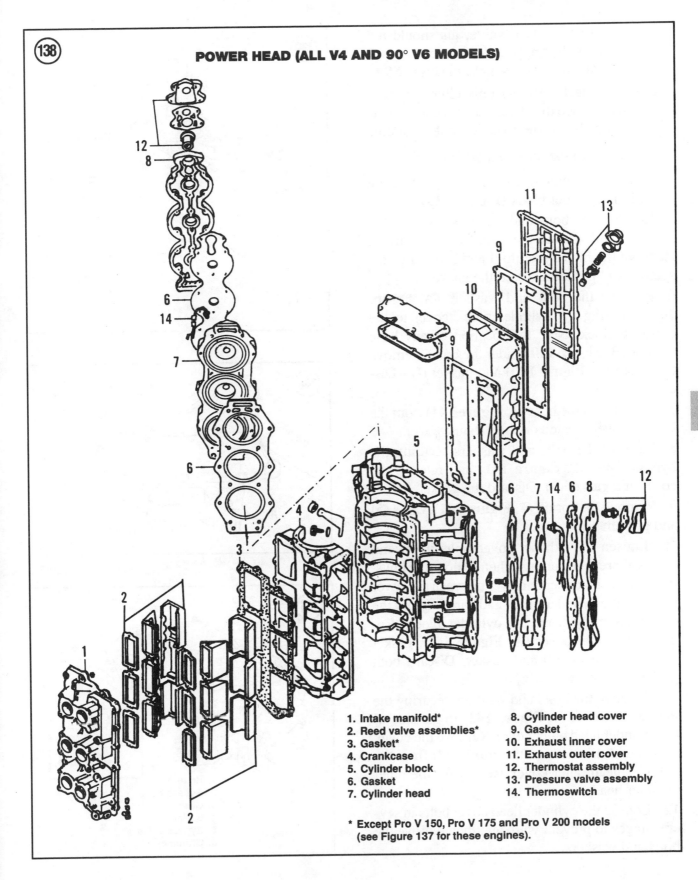

POWER HEAD (ALL V4 AND 90° V6 MODELS)

1. Intake manifold*
2. Reed valve assemblies*
3. Gasket*
4. Crankcase
5. Cylinder block
6. Gasket
7. Cylinder head
8. Cylinder head cover
9. Gasket
10. Exhaust inner cover
11. Exhaust outer cover
12. Thermostat assembly
13. Pressure valve assembly
14. Thermoswitch

* Except Pro V 150, Pro V 175 and Pro V 200 models
(see Figure 137 for these engines).

8

sure into the check valve; air should not pass through. Apply a vacuum to the check valve; air should pass through (**Figure 90**).

d. If the check valve(s) fails either of these tests, replace the check valve(s). Rotate the check valve for removal, do not pry it out.

e. Make sure the hose joint(s) is clear.

4. Unbolt and remove the engine stop on each side of the cylinder block (**Figure 139**).

5. Remove the bolts and washers securing the intake manifold and the reed valve assembly. Remove the intake manifold and reed valve assembly and gasket. Discard the gasket.

6. Remove the bolts and washers (A, **Figure 140**) securing the cylinder block cover to the cylinder block. Note the location of any hose clamps (B, **Figure 140**) under the bolts. Remove the cover (C, **Figure 140**) and gasket (D). Discard the gasket.

7. Disconnect the hose (1, **Figure 141**) from the bypass cover located on the exhaust cover.

8. Remove the bolts and washers securing the bypass cover (2, **Figure 141**) and remove the cover and gasket (3). Discard the gasket.

9. Remove the spring (4, **Figure 141**), valve (5) and grommet (6).

10. Loosen the exhaust cover bolts in several stages to prevent warpage, then remove the bolts. Insert a flat-blade screwdriver between the cover lugs and the cylinder block and carefully pry the cover assembly from the cylinder block. Remove the outer cover (A, **Figure 142**), gasket (B), inner cover (C) and gasket. Discard both gaskets.

11. Remove the bolts and washers securing the thermostat cover (1, **Figure 143**) to the side of the cylinder head outer cover. Remove the cover, gasket and thermostat (2, **Figure 143**) from the cylinder head outer cover. Repeat for the other cylinder head cover.

12. Loosen the cylinder head cover bolts in several stages to prevent warpage, then remove the bolts and washers.

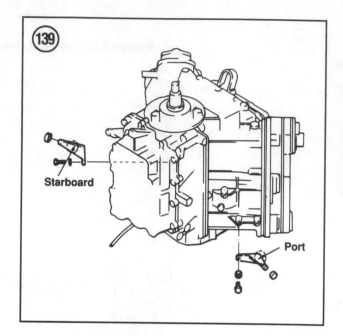

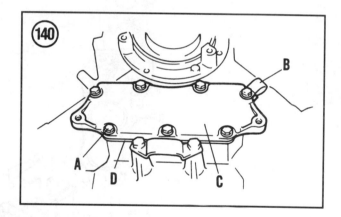

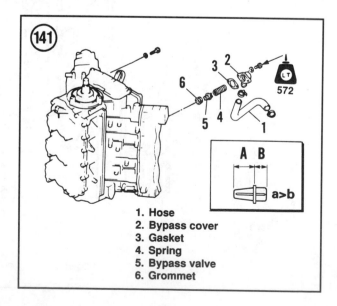

1. Hose
2. Bypass cover
3. Gasket
4. Spring
5. Bypass valve
6. Grommet

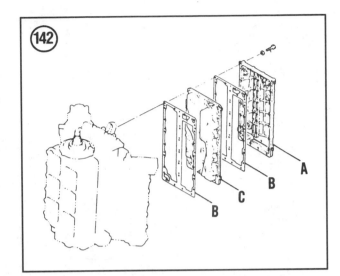

(142)

13. Tap the edge of the cylinder head cover with a soft-faced mallet to break the gasket seal. Carefully separate the cylinder head cover (3, **Figure 143**) and gasket from the cylinder head.

14. Unscrew the thermoswitch (4, **Figure 143**) from the cylinder head.

15. Loosen the cylinder head bolts in several stages to prevent warpage, then remove the bolts and washers.

16. Tap the edge of the cylinder head with a soft-faced mallet to break the gasket seal. Carefully separate the cylinder head (5, **Figure 143**) and gasket from the cylinder block and remove the assembly.

17. Repeat for the other cylinder head.

18. Remove the bolts and remove the 2 anodes located in the water jacket in the top of each side of the cylinder block (**Figure 144**). Remove all 4 anodes.

19. Remove the bolts and washers securing the lower bearing housing (A, **Figure 145**) and the

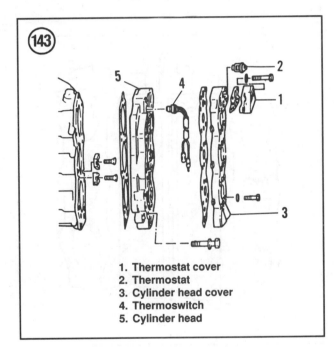

(143)

1. Thermostat cover
2. Thermostat
3. Cylinder head cover
4. Thermoswitch
5. Cylinder head

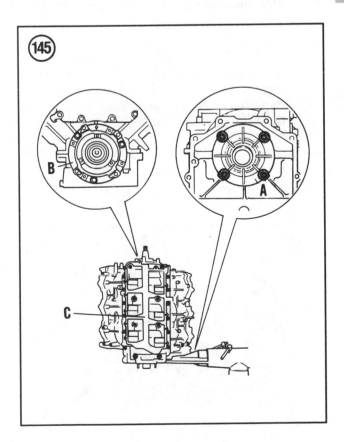

(145)

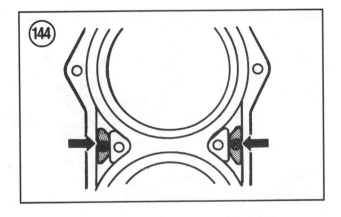

(144)

upper oil seal housing (B, **Figure 145**) to the crankcase and the cylinder block.

20. Loosen the crankcase bolts in several stages to prevent warpage, then remove the bolts. Carefully pry apart and separate the crankcase from the cylinder block. Remove the crankcase (C, **Figure 145**). Don't lose the locating pins (**Figure 146**, typical).

21. Remove the lower bearing housing and upper oil seal housing from the crankshaft and cylinder block.

NOTE
Figure 147 identifies the cylinder numbers for both the V4 and V6 engines. Refer to this illustration when marking pistons, connecting rods and connecting rod end caps. The port and starboard designation relates to the engine as it sits on the boat not as it sits on your workbench.

22. Refer to the preceding NOTE and correctly mark the connecting rods and caps with their respective cylinder numbers.

NOTE
*At this time do **not** remove the disc seal rings from the crankshaft. They will be inspected in a later procedure and replaced at that time if necessary.*

23. Loosen the connecting rod end cap bolts in several stages, then remove the bolts. Remove the end caps and the lower half of the big end

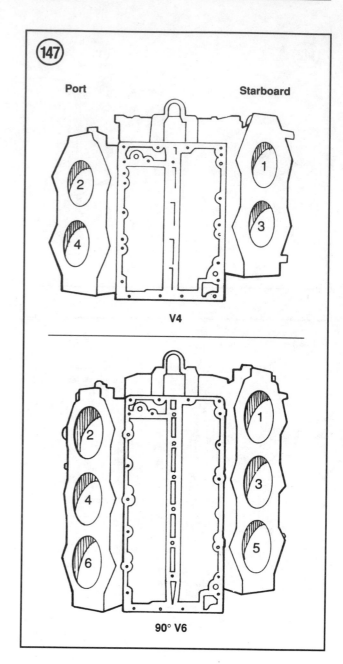

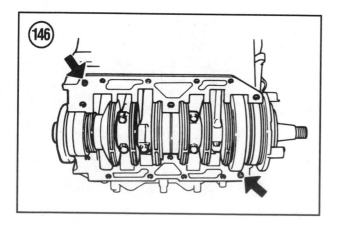

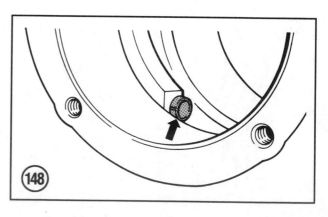

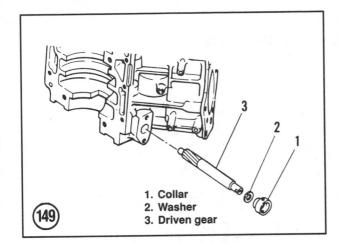

(149)

1. Collar
2. Washer
3. Driven gear

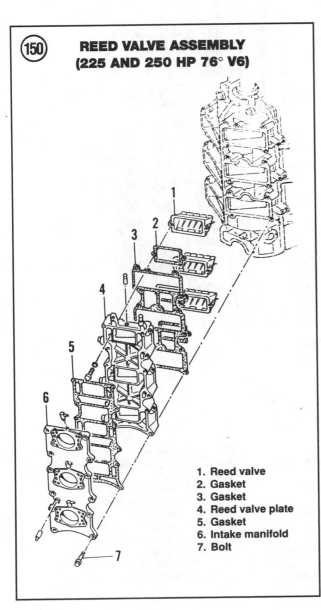

(150) **REED VALVE ASSEMBLY
(225 AND 250 HP 76° V6)**

1. Reed valve
2. Gasket
3. Gasket
4. Reed valve plate
5. Gasket
6. Intake manifold
7. Bolt

roller bearings. Place the bolts, end cap and roller bearing half in separate containers marked with the cylinder number.

24. Carefully pull up on the crankshaft, the lower bearing housing and upper oil seal housing assembly and remove from the cylinder block. If necessary, carefully tap on the each end of the crankshaft with a soft-faced mallet to break it loose. Place the crankshaft on the workbench and block it so it will not roll in any direction.

25. Remove the upper half of the big end roller bearings from the cylinder block and place them in the correct containers used in Step 21.

26. Refer to NOTE preceding Step 20 and correctly mark the piston crowns with their respective cylinder numbers.

CAUTION
Center the lower end of the connecting rod within the cylinder bore during piston and connecting rod removal. Do not allow the lower end of the connecting rod to contact and scratch the cylinder wall during removal.

27. Carefully push the piston and connecting rod assemblies out through the top of the cylinder block.

28. Remove the oil injection pump bushing (**Figure 148**) from the end of the pump drive shaft.

29. Refer to **Figure 149** and remove the collar (1), washer (2) and driven gear (3) from the cylinder block.

All 76° V6 Models

Refer to the following illustrations for this procedure:

   a. **Figure 150**: Intake manifold and reed valve assembly.

   b. **Figure 151**: Power head components.

NOTE
Cover the workbench surface with a flat sheet of heavy rubber or piece of clean

8

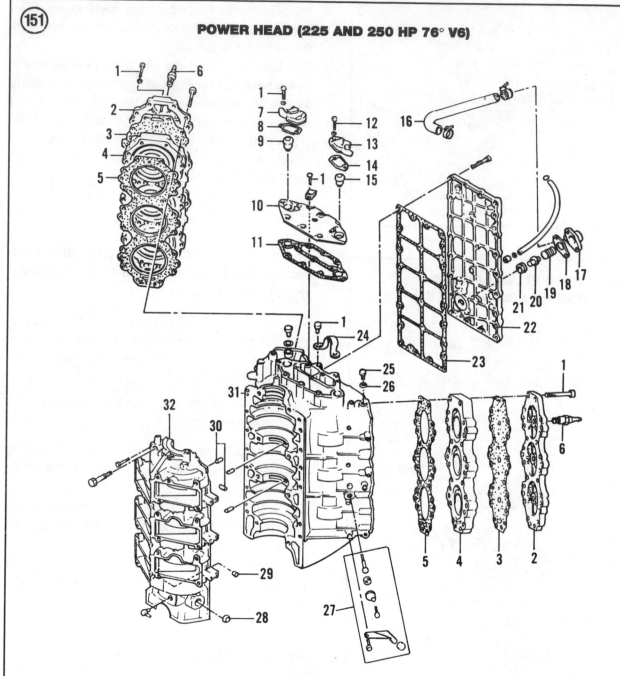

POWER HEAD (225 AND 250 HP 76° V6)

1. Bolt
2. Cylinder head cover
3. Gasket
4. Cylinder head
5. Gasket
6. Spark plug
7. Thermostat cover
8. Gasket
9. Thermostat
10. Cylinder block cover
11. Gasket

12. Screw
13. Thermostat cover
14. Gasket
15. Thermostat
16. Hose
17. Bypass cover
18. Gasket
19. Spring
20. Pressure valve
21. Grommet
22. Exhaust cover

23. Gasket
24. Engine hanger
25. Bolt
26. Washer
27. Engine stopper
    assembly
28. Formed bushing
29. Formed bushing
30. Locating pin
31. Cylinder block
32. Crankcase

masonite to protect all sealing surfaces of the engine. The work bench must also be level so the power head will be stable during the disassembly procedure.

CAUTION
The complete power head assembly is heavy and also very tall and top heavy during the initial part of the disassembly procedure. When breaking bolts loose or removing a stubborn component, securely hold the power head so it will not

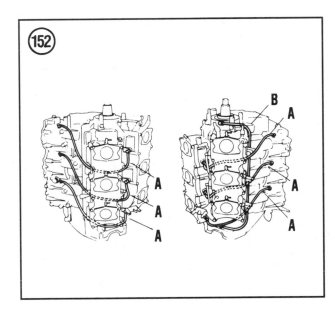

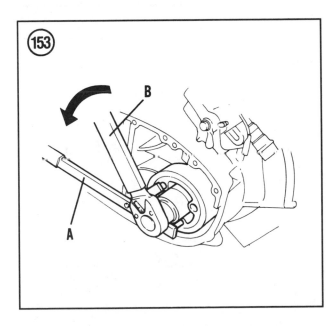

fall over. If necessary, have an assistant hold the power head during the removal of a difficult component.

1. Remove the carburetors See Chapter Six.
2. To test the crankcase circulation check valves, perform the following:

NOTE
Prior to disconnecting the circulation lines, make a sketch or take an instant photograph of the circulation lines to assist during assembly.

   a. Disconnect the crankcase circulation lines from the check valve fittings (A, **Figure 152**) on the engine.

   b. Remove the check valves from the crankcase.

   c. Use a Mity-Vac (or equivalant) hand held vacuum/pressure pump and apply air pressure into the check valve; air should not pass through. Apply a vacuum to the check valve; air should pass through.

   d. If the check valve(s) fails either of these tests, replace the check valve(s). Rotate the check valve for removal, do not pry it out.

   e. Make sure the hose joint(s) is clear.

3. Remove the torsional damper from the lower end of the crankshaft as follows:

   a. Install a flywheel holder (part No. YB-6139) to hold the torsional damper while loosening the nut (A, **Figure 153**).

   b. Loosen the torsional damper nut with an appropriate size socket wrench (B, **Figure 153**).

   c. Install a flywheel puller (part No. YB-6117) onto the torsional damper. Make sure it is installed straight.

CAUTION
Do not strike the puller screw with excessive force in sub-step d or the crankshaft may be damaged. Heat should not be used, as it will cause the torsional damper to seize to the crankshaft.

8

d. Hold the puller body straight and tighten the center bolt (**Figure 154**). If the torsional damper does not pop from the end of the crankshaft, lightly tap the puller center bolt with a soft-faced mallet to break the damper loose.

e. Remove the torsional damper from the crankshaft and remove the puller from the damper.

4. Remove the flywheel as described in this chapter.

5. Unbolt and remove the engine stop on each side of the cylinder block (**Figure 155**). Remove both engine stops.

6. Remove the bolts and covers and remove the 2 grommets and anodes located on both sides of the cylinder block and on the cylinder head covers (**Figure 156**). Remove all anodes.

7. Disconnect the hose (1, **Figure 157**) from the pressure valve cover located on the exhaust cover.

8. Remove the bolts and washers securing the bypass cover (2, **Figure 157**) and remove the cover and gasket (3). Discard the gasket.

9. Remove the spring (4, **Figure 157**) and valve (5) from the grommet (6) in the exhaust cover.

10. Remove the bolts securing the engine hanger (1, **Figure 158**) and remove the hanger.

11. Remove the bolts and washers securing each thermostat cover to the cylinder block cover. Remove the covers (2, **Figure 158**), gasket (3) and thermostats (4) from the cylinder head outer cover.

12. Remove the bolts and washers securing the cylinder block cover to the cylinder block. Note the location of any hose clamp(s) under the bolts. Remove the cover (5, **Figure 158**) and gasket (6). Discard the gasket.

13. Remove the oil injection pump as described in Chapter Thirteen.

14. Remove the distance collar (1, **Figure 159**) and O-ring (2), washer (3) and driven gear (4) from the cylinder block.

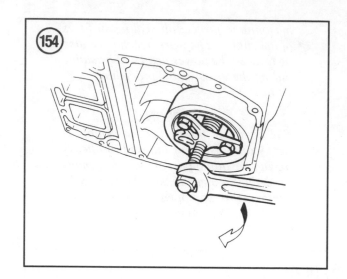

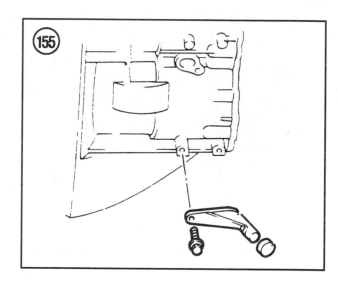

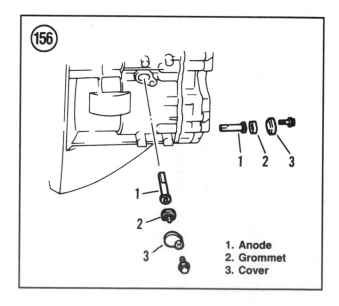

1. Anode
2. Grommet
3. Cover

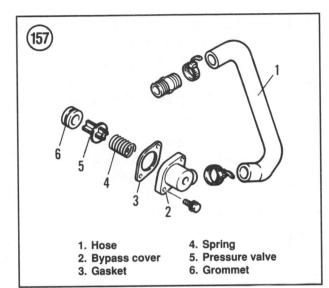

1. Hose
2. Bypass cover
3. Gasket
4. Spring
5. Pressure valve
6. Grommet

15. Remove the bolts and washers securing the intake manifold and the reed valve assembly. Remove the intake manifold and reed valve assembly and gasket. Discard the gasket.

16. Loosen the exhaust cover bolts in several stages to prevent warpage, then remove the bolts. Insert a flat-blade screwdriver between the cover lugs and the cylinder block and carefully pry the cover assembly from the cylinder block. Remove the cover (A, **Figure 160**) and gasket (B). Discard the gasket.

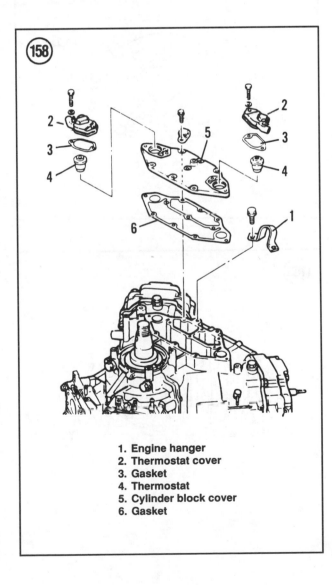

1. Engine hanger
2. Thermostat cover
3. Gasket
4. Thermostat
5. Cylinder block cover
6. Gasket

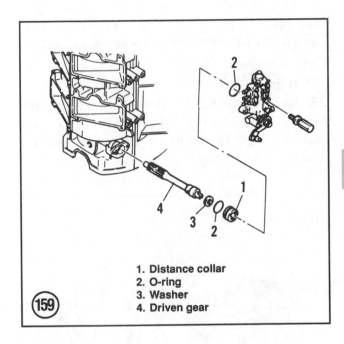

1. Distance collar
2. O-ring
3. Washer
4. Driven gear

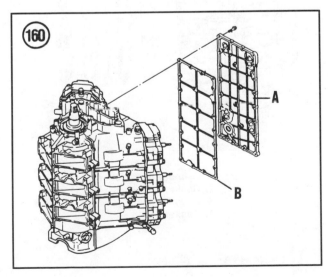

8

17. Loosen the cylinder head cover 6 bolts in several stages to prevent warpage, then remove the bolts and washers.

18. Tap the edge of the cylinder head cover with a soft-faced mallet to break the gasket seal. Carefully separate the cylinder head cover (1, **Figure 161**) and gasket (2) from the cylinder head.

19. Loosen the cylinder head bolts in several stages to prevent warpage, then remove the bolts and washers.

20. Tap the edge of the cylinder head with a soft-faced mallet to break the gasket seal. Carefully separate the cylinder head (3, **Figure 161**) and gasket (4) from the cylinder block and remove the assembly.

21. Repeat for the other cylinder head.

22. Remove the bolts and washers securing the lower oil seal housing (**Figure 162**) to the crankcase and the cylinder block. Slide the lower oil seal housing off the crankshaft.

23. Loosen the crankcase bolts in several stages to prevent warpage, then remove the bolts. Carefully pry apart and separate the crankcase from the cylinder block, then remove the crankcase. Don't lose the locating pins (**Figure 163**).

NOTE
Figure 164 identifies the cylinder numbers. Refer to this illustration when

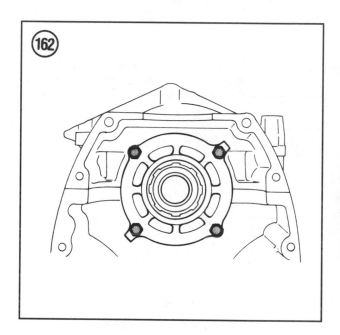

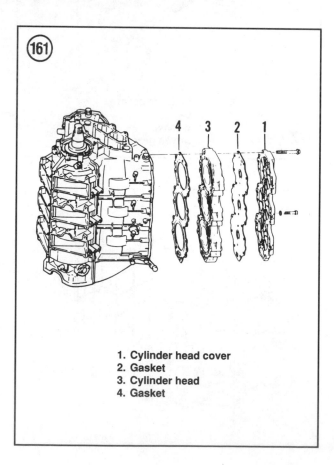

1. Cylinder head cover
2. Gasket
3. Cylinder head
4. Gasket

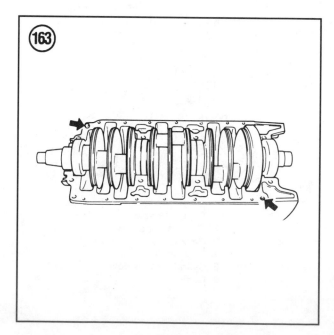

marking pistons, connecting rods and connecting rod end caps. The port and starboard designation relates to the outboard as mounted on the boat, not as it sits on your workbench.

24. Refer to the preceding NOTE and correctly mark the connecting rods and caps with their respective cylinder numbers.

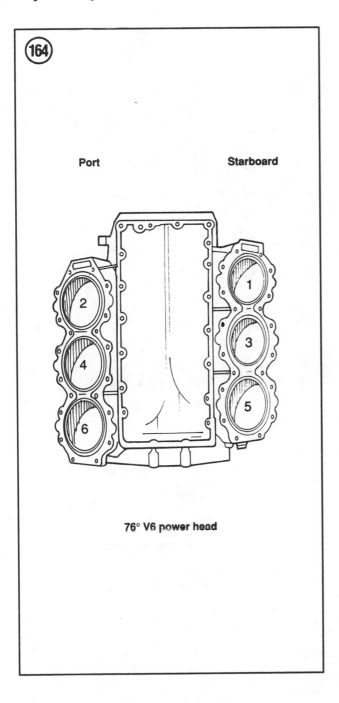

76° V6 power head

NOTE
*At this time do **not** remove the disc seal rings from the crankshaft. They will be inspected in a later procedure and replaced at that time if necessary.*

25. Loosen the connecting rod end cap bolts in several stages, then remove the bolts. Remove the end caps and the lower half of the big end roller bearings. Place the bolts, end cap and roller bearing half in separate containers marked with the cylinder number.

26. Carefully pull up on the crankshaft and remove the assembly from the cylinder block. If necessary, carefully tap on the each end of the crankshaft with a soft-faced mallet to break it loose. Place the crankshaft on the workbench and block it so it will not roll in any direction.

27. Remove the upper halves of the big end roller bearings from the cylinder block and place them in the correct containers used in Step 25.

28. Refer to NOTE preceding Step 24 and correctly mark the piston crowns with their respective cylinder numbers.

CAUTION
Center the lower end of the connecting rod within the cylinder bore during piston and connecting rod removal. Do not allow the lower end of the connecting rod to contact and scratch the cylinder wall during removal.

29. Carefully push the piston and connecting rod assemblies out through the top of the cylinder block.

CRANKSHAFT ASSEMBLY AND CYLINDER BLOCK

Piston/Crankshaft Disassembly (1-5 hp 1-Cylinder, 2-Cylinder [except C40, C55], 3-Cylinder [30-50 hp, Pro 50, Pro 60 and 70 hp])

The connecting rods *cannot* be disassembled from the crankshaft on these models. If either the rod(s) or the crankshaft is defective, replace the entire crankshaft assembly.

Refer to the following illustrations for this procedure:

a. **Figure 165**, typical: 1-cylinder engine.
b. **Figure 166**, typical: 2-cylinder engine.
c. **Figure 167**, typical: 3-cylinder engine.

NOTE
On 2- and 3-cylinder inline power heads, the No. 1 cylinder is the top cylinder.

1. Remove the crankshaft and piston assembly as described in this chapter.
2. On 2- and 3-cylinder engines, mark the pistons with a scribe or permanent marker so they will be reinstalled onto the correct connecting rod during assembly.
3. Before removing the piston(s), hold the rod tightly and rock the piston as shown in **Figure 168**. Any rocking motion (do not confuse with the normal sliding motion) indicates wear on the piston pin, piston pin bore or connecting rod small-end bearing, or more likely a combination of these.
4. If necessary, remove the piston rings as described in this chapter. Otherwise, leave the rings installed on the piston.

WARNING
Wear protective eyeglasses while performing Step 5.

5. Remove the clips from each side of the piston pin bore with a small screwdriver, scribe or needlenose pliers (**Figure 169**). Hold your thumb over one edge of the clip when removing it to prevent the clip from springing out.
6. Use a proper size wooden dowel or socket extension and push out the piston pin. Mark the piston and pin so that they will be reassembled into the same set.

CAUTION
Be careful when removing the pin to avoid damaging the connecting rod. If it is necessary to tap the pin gently to re-

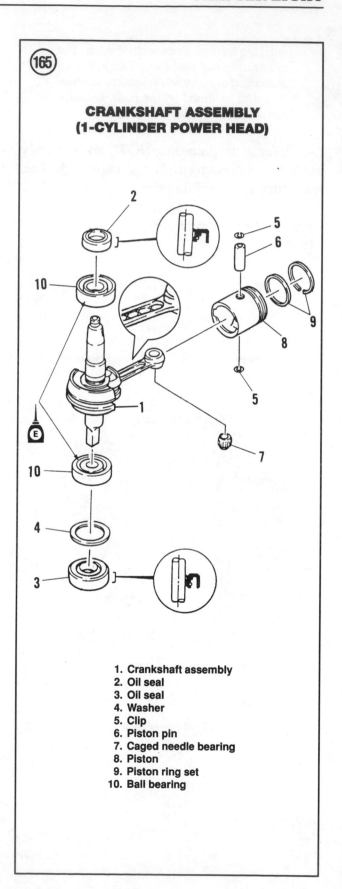

(165)

**CRANKSHAFT ASSEMBLY
(1-CYLINDER POWER HEAD)**

1. Crankshaft assembly
2. Oil seal
3. Oil seal
4. Washer
5. Clip
6. Piston pin
7. Caged needle bearing
8. Piston
9. Piston ring set
10. Ball bearing

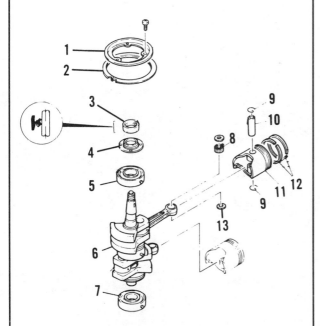

**CRANKSHAFT ASSEMBLY
(2-CYLINDER POWER HEAD
[EXCEPT C40, C55])**

1. **Magneto base retainer**
2. **Gasket**
3. **Oil seal**
4. **Retainer**
5. **Ball bearing**
6. **Crankshaft assembly**
7. **Ball bearing**
8. **Loose needle bearings**
9. **Clip**
10. **Piston pin**
11. **Piston**
12. **Piston ring set**
13. **Washer**

move it, be sure that the piston is properly supported so that lateral shock is not transmitted to the connecting rod lower bearing.

7. If the piston pin is difficult to remove, heat the piston and pin with a butane torch. Heat the piston to only about 140° F (60° C) (too warm to touch, but not excessively hot). If the pin is still difficult to push out, use a homemade tool as shown in **Figure 170**.

8A. On 2-8 hp engines, lift the piston off the connecting rod. Remove the caged needle bearing from the connecting rod (**Figure 171**).

NOTE
Be prepared to catch the loose needle bearings and washers in the next step. Do not drop or lose any of the loose rollers or retaining washers from the bearing if they are going to be reused.

8B. On 9.9-70 hp engines, lift the piston off the connecting rod. Catch the loose roller bearings and retaining washers (**Figure 172**).

9. Inspect the piston assembly as described in this chapter.

10. On 2- and 3-cylinder engines, repeat Steps 2-8 for the remaining piston(s).

NOTE
Yamaha suggests that the needle bearing(s) be replaced every time the piston is removed. If old bearings must be reused, store them in a clean container along with the piston and piston pin from the same cylinder.

11. Remove any oil seals and/or spacers from the crankshaft.

12. Inspect the upper and/or lower crankcase ball bearings and replace, if necessary, as described in this chapter.

8

**CRANKSHAFT ASSEMBLY
(3-CYLINDER POWER HEAD [30-50 HP, PRO 50, PRO 60 AND 70 HP])**

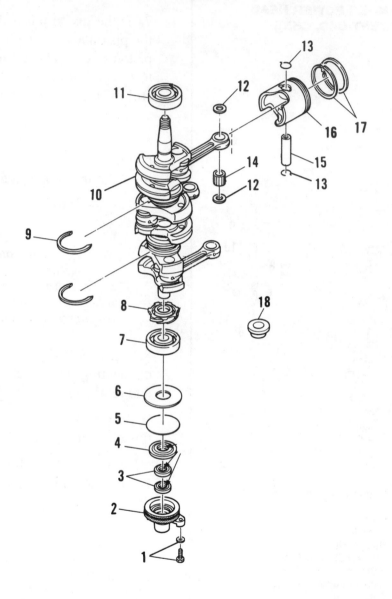

1. Bolt and washer
2. Oil seal housing
3. Oil seal
4. Oil seal
5. O-ring
6. Washer
7. Ball bearing

8. Oil pump drive gear
9. Set ring
10. Crankshaft assembly
11. Ball bearing
12. Washer
13. Clip

14. Loose needle bearings
15. Piston pin
16. Piston
17. Piston ring set
18. Spacer
(models so equipped)

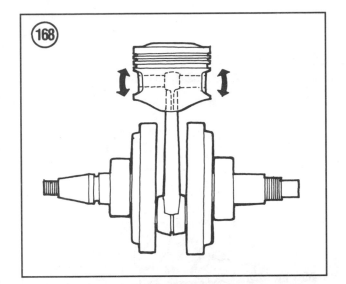

168

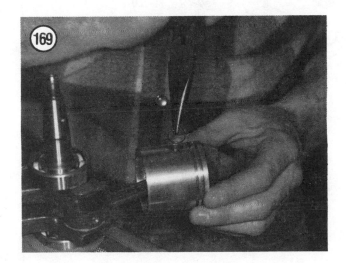

169

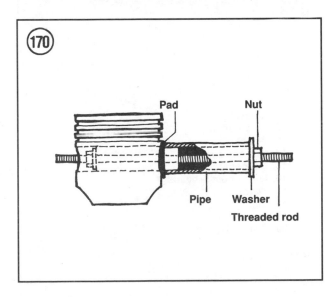

170

Pad

Nut

Pipe

Washer

Threaded rod

Piston/Crankshaft Disassembly (2-cylinder [C40, C55], 3-cylinder [C75, C85, 90 hp] and all V-Block Models)

The connecting rods can be removed from the crankshaft on these models. In addition, the connecting rods or crankshaft can be replaced separately, if necessary.

Refer to the following illustrations for this procedure:

a. **Figure 173**, typical: 2- and 3-cylinder engines.

b. **Figure 174**, typical: V-block engines.

1A. On 2- and 3-cylinder engines, perform the following:

a. Remove the crankshaft and piston assembly as described in this chapter.

b. Remove the needle bearing assembly from the top end of the crankshaft.

c. On 2-cylinder engines, remove the rotary bearing from the top end of the crankshaft.

171

172

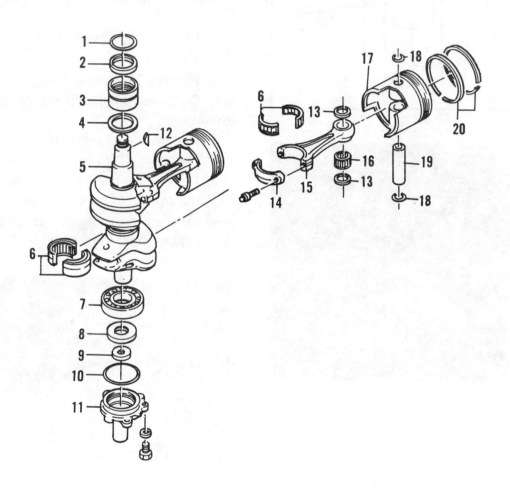

**CRANKSHAFT ASSEMBLY
(2-CYLINDER MODELS [C40, C55]; 3-CYLINDER [C75, C85, 90 HP])**

1. O-ring
2. Oil seal
3. Bearing
4. Washer
5. Crankshaft
6. Roller bearing
7. Ball bearing
8. Oil seal
9. Oil seal
10. O-ring
11. Oil seal housing
12. Woodruff key
13. Washer
14. Rod end cap
15. Connecting rod
16. Loose needle bearings
17. Piston
18. Clip
19. Piston pin
20. Piston ring set

1B. On V-block engines, perform the following:

  a. Remove the crankshaft as described in this chapter.

NOTE
*Note that the large circlip groove in the main bearing sleeve is located toward the **top end** of the crankshaft. Remember this during installation.*

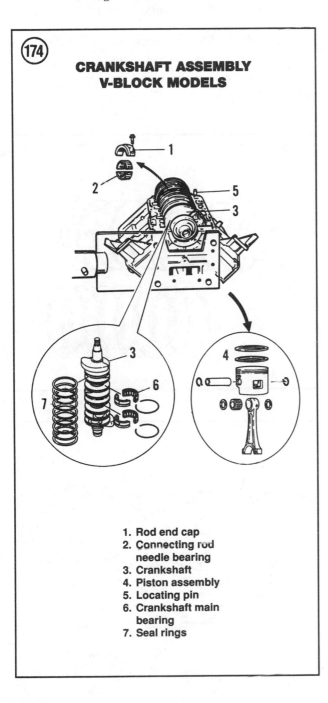

174

**CRANKSHAFT ASSEMBLY
V-BLOCK MODELS**

1. Rod end cap
2. Connecting rod needle bearing
3. Crankshaft
4. Piston assembly
5. Locating pin
6. Crankshaft main bearing
7. Seal rings

b. Remove the large circlip(s) and remove the crankshaft main bearing(s) from the crankshaft (**Figure 175**). There is one crankshaft main bearing on V4 engines and 2 crankshaft main bearings on V6 engines.

NOTE
On V-block engines, inspect the crankshaft sealing rings while still installed on the crankshaft. Do not remove the sealing rings from the crankshaft unless excessively worn or damaged.

2. On V-block engines, inspect the crankshaft sealing rings as follows:

  a. Insert a flat feeler gauge between the sealing ring and the ring groove in the crankshaft. The wear should not exceed 0.1 mm (0.004 in.), as shown in **Figure 176**.

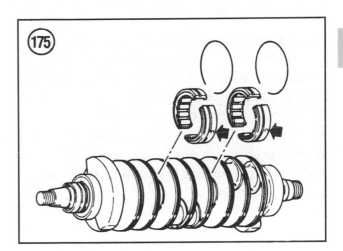

175

8

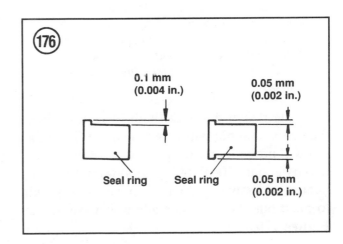

176

0.1 mm
(0.004 in.)

0.05 mm
(0.002 in.)

Seal ring   Seal ring

0.05 mm
(0.002 in.)

b. If the crankshaft seal rings (**Figure 177**) require replacement, remove and install them with a piston ring expander using the same method as described under piston ring removal/installation in this chapter.

3. Before removing the piston, hold the rod tightly and rock the piston as shown in **Figure 168**. Any rocking motion (do not confuse with the normal sliding motion) indicates wear on the piston pin, piston pin bore or connecting rod small-end bearing or, more likely, a combination of all three.

4. If necessary, remove the piston rings as described in this chapter. Otherwise leave the rings installed on the piston.

WARNING
Wear protective eyeglasses while performing Step 5.

5. Remove the clips from each side of the piston pin bore with a small screwdriver, scribe or needlenose pliers. Hold your thumb over one edge of the clip when removing it to prevent the clip from springing out.

6. Use a proper size wooden dowel or socket extension and push out the piston pin. Mark the piston and pin so that they will be reassembled into the same set.

CAUTION
Be careful when removing the pin to avoid damaging the connecting rod. If it is necessary to tap the pin gently to remove it, be sure that the piston is properly supported so that lateral shock is not transmitted to the connecting rod lower bearing.

7. If the piston pin is difficult to remove, heat the piston and pin with a butane torch. Then the pin will probably push right out. Heat the piston to only about 140° F (60° C) (too warm to touch, but not excessively hot). If the pin is still difficult to push out, use a homemade tool as shown in **Figure 170**.

8A. On 1993 and later V-block engines, lift the piston off the connecting rod. Remove the caged needle bearing from the connecting rod.

NOTE
Be prepared to catch the loose needle bearings and washers in the next step. Do not drop or lose any of the loose rollers or retaining washers from the bearing if they are going to be reused.

8B. On 1990-1992 V-block and all other engines, lift the piston off the connecting rod. Catch the loose roller bearings and retaining washers (**Figure 172**).

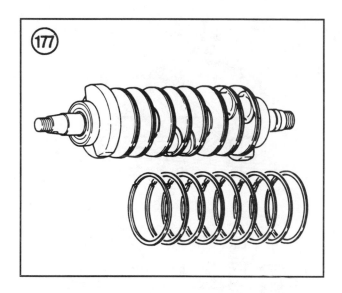

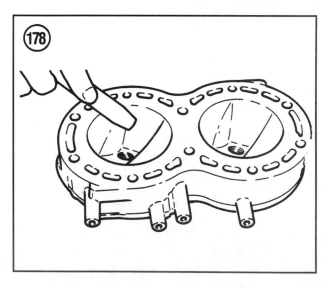

9. Inspect the piston assembly as described in this chapter.

10. Repeat Steps 3-8 for the remaining piston(s).

> *NOTE*
> *Yamaha suggests that the needle bearing(s) be replaced every time the piston is removed. If old bearings must be reused, store them in a clean container along with the piston and piston pin from the same cylinder.*

11. Inspect the upper and/or lower crankcase ball bearings and replace, if necessary, as described in this chapter.

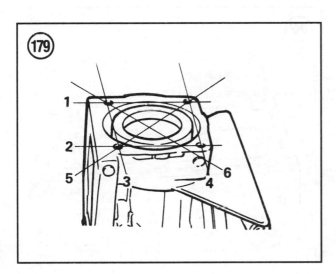

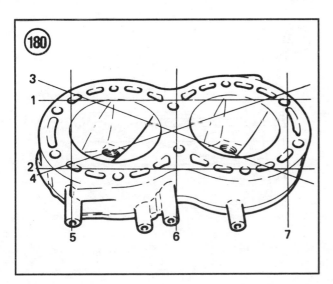

Cylinder Block and Crankcase Cleaning and Inspection (All Models)

This procedure represents all single cylinder, inline and V-type power head components. The procedures apply to all engine types unless otherwise specified

The cylinder block and crankcase are a matched and a line-bored assembly. For this reason, you should not attempt to assemble an engine with parts salvaged from other blocks. If inspection indicates that either the cylinder block or crankcase requires replacement, replace both as an assembly.

1. Carefully remove all gasket and sealant residue from the cylinder block and crankcase mating surfaces with lacquer thinner.

2. Clean the aluminum surfaces carefully to avoid nicking them. A dull putty knife can be used, but a piece of Lucite with one edge ground to a 45° angle is more efficient and will also eliminate the possibility of damage to the surfaces. When reassembling the crankcase and cylinder block, both mating surfaces must be free of all sealant residue, dirt and oil or leaks will develop.

3. Remove all carbon deposits from the combustion chambers, exhaust ports and cylinder head(s) (**Figure 178**). Use a hardwood or Lucite scraper and solvent. Be careful not to scratch or gouge the areas while cleaning.

4. Once all carbon is removed, clean the cylinder block and cylinder head thoroughly with solvent and a brush, then dry with compressed air.

5. On V-block engines, clean the lower oil seal housing in solvent and dry with compressed air.

6. Carefully remove all gasket and sealant residue from all mating surfaces.

7. Check the cylinder head gasket mating surface with a straightedge and flat feeler gauge. Check for warpage in the directions shown in **Figures 179-181** and correct as required. Refer

8

to *Gaskets and Sealants* at the beginning of this chapter.

8. Check the exhaust port surfaces for warpage as described in Step 7. Follow the directions shown in **Figure 182** or **Figure 183** and correct as required.

9. Check the block, cylinder head(s) and cover for cracks, fractures, stripped bolt or spark plug threads or other damage.

10. Check the gasket mating surfaces for nicks, grooves, cracks or excessive distortion. Any of these defects will cause compression leakage. Replace as required.

11. Check all oil and water passages in the cylinder block and crankcase for obstructions. Make sure any plugs installed are properly tightened.

NOTE
With older engines, it is a good idea to have the cylinder walls lightly honed with a medium stone even if they are in good condition. This will break up any glaze that might reduce compression.

12. Check each cylinder bore for aluminum transfer from the pistons to the cylinder wall. If scoring is present but not excessive, have the cylinders honed by a dealer or qualified machine shop.

13. Measure each cylinder bore front-to-rear with an inside micrometer or bore gauge (**Figure 184**) at top, center and bottom just above the exhaust port (**Figure 185**). Record the readings.

14. Turn the cylinder 90° and repeat the measurements. Subtract the smallest from the largest reading. If the difference between the 2 measurements exceeds the maximum allowable taper or out-of-round listed in **Table 2**, have all cylinders rebored by a dealer or qualified machine shop and install oversize pistons.

NOTE
Obtain the new pistons and measure them before having the cylinders bored. This allows for variations in piston size due to manufacturing tolerances. Re-

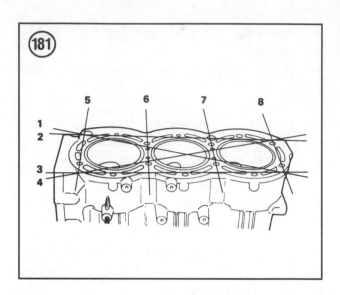

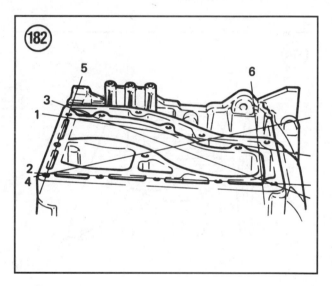

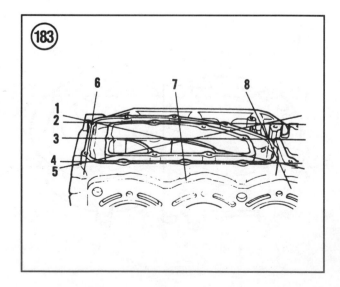

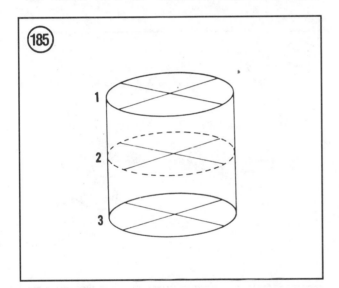

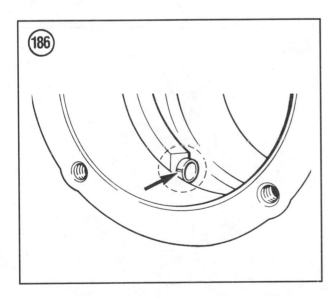

*member to allow for piston-to-cylinder wall clearance listed in **Table 2** when reboring.*

15. If check valve replacement is required, on models so equipped, remove the defective valve with pliers using a rotating motion. Clean all sealing compound from the mounting hole, coat the new check valve stem with Gasket Maker or equivalent and install with a suitable driver.

16. On models so equipped, if the oil pump driven gear shaft bushing requires replacement, be sure to install the new bushing with the slit (**Figure 186**) facing the lower oil seal housing.

Crankshaft and Connecting Rod Needle Bearings Cleaning and Inspection (All Models)

Bearings can be reused if they are in good condition. To be on the safe side, however, it is a good idea to discard all removable bearings and install new ones whenever the engine is disassembled. New bearings are inexpensive compared to the cost of a power head failure caused by the use of marginal bearings.

NOTE
Clean one set of needle bearings at a time to prevent any possible mixup.

1. Place needle bearings in a fine mesh wire basket and submerge in a suitable container of fresh solvent. The bottom of the basket should not touch the bottom of the container.

2. Carefully agitate basket to loosen all grease, sludge and other contamination.

3. Dry the caged needle bearings with dry filtered low-pressure compressed air. Be careful not to spin the bearings as they will be damaged.

4. Inspect for rust, wear, scuffed surfaces, heat discoloration or other defects. Check bearings for flat spots; if one needle is defective, replace the entire bearing. Always replace connecting rod big end needle bearings as a complete set—

8

never replace only half of the set as this will lead to premature bearing failure.

5. Lubricate the bearings with a light coat of Yamalube Two-Cycle Outboard Oil.

6. Repeat Steps 2-5, cleaning one bearing set at a time to prevent any possible mixup.

Crankshaft Main Bearings Removal, Cleaning, Inspection and Installation (All Models)

Bearings can be reused if they are in good condition. To be on the safe side, however, it is a good idea to discard all removable bearings and install new ones whenever the engine is disassembled. New bearings are inexpensive compared to the cost of a power head failure caused by the use of marginal bearings.

The main ball bearings, or bearing housings, must be pressed on and off the crankshaft with a bearing separator, a bearing installer and a hydraulic press. If you do not have access to a press and the additional special tools, have the bearings removed and installed by a dealer or machine shop.

Crankshaft Bearing Removal

1-, 2- and 3-cylinder power heads

1. On models so equipped, remove the circlip (A, **Figure 187**) securing the bearing (B).

2. Install a bearing separator under the ball bearing (**Figure 188**).

3. Place the crankshaft assembly in a hydraulic press.

4. Carefully press the bearing off the crankshaft. Be sure to hold the crankshaft securely during bearing removal—do not allow the crankshaft to drop to the floor.

5. Repeat this procedure to remove the remaining bearing.

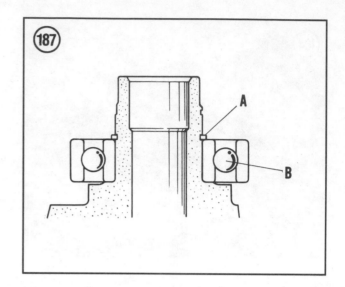

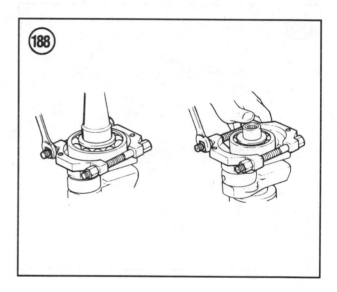

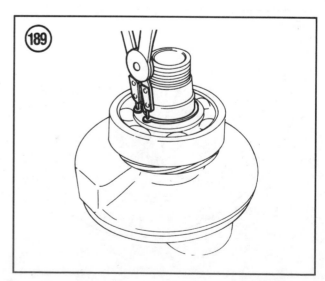

76° V6 power head

1. To remove the *upper* ball bearing from the crankshaft, first remove the circlip (**Figure 189**) from the crankshaft.

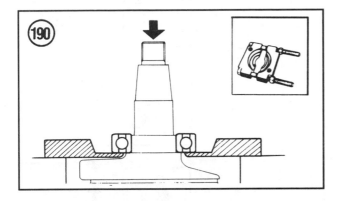

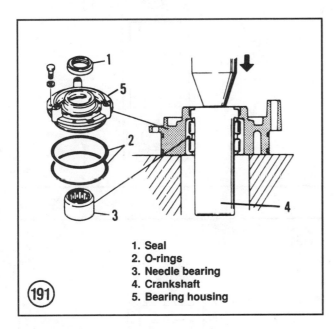

1. Seal
2. O-rings
3. Needle bearing
4. Crankshaft
5. Bearing housing

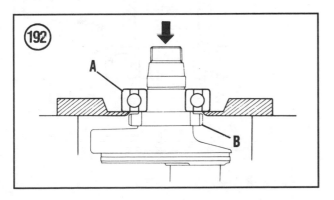

2. Install a bearing separator under the upper ball bearing (**Figure 190**).

3. Place the crankshaft assembly in a hydraulic press.

4. Carefully press the bearing off the crankshaft. Be sure to hold the crankshaft securely during bearing removal—do not allow the crankshaft to fall out of the press.

5. Repeat this procedure to remove the crankshaft lower bearing.

V4 and 90° V6 power heads

1. To remove the *upper* needle bearing from the upper bearing housing, first slide the bearing housing assembly off the crankshaft, if not previously removed.

2. Remove the oil seal (1, **Figure 191**) from the end of the housing.

3. Remove the O-ring seals (2, **Figure 191**) from the housing.

4. Place the bearing housing (5, **Figure 191**) on the hydraulic press. Position the bearing housing so the crankshaft side of the housing is facing down.

5. Install Yamaha bearing installer (part No. YB-6205) into the bearing housing and rest it on top of the bearing assembly.

6. Carefully press the bearing (3, **Figure 191**) out of the housing. Be sure to hold the bearing installer during removal—do not allow the installer to drop out of the housing.

7. Repeat this procedure to remove the crankshaft lower bearing.

Oil Pump Drive Gear Removal
(All V4 and V6 Power Heads)

1. Press the crankshaft lower bearing (A, **Figure 192**) off the crankshaft as previously outlined.

2. Install a bearing separator under the oil pump drive gear (B, **Figure 192**).

8

3. Place the crankshaft assembly in a hydraulic press. Carefully press the drive gear off the crankshaft. Hold the crankshaft securely during gear removal—do not allow the crankshaft to fall to the floor.

Bearing Cleaning and Inspection

1. Remove any sealer from outer edge of bearings with a scraper, then clean bearing surface with solvent.

2. Place the bearings in a wire basket and submerge in a suitable container of fresh solvent. The bottom of the basket should not touch the bottom of the container.

3. Carefully agitate the basket containing bearings to loosen all grease, sludge and other contamination within the bearings.

4. Dry ball bearings with dry filtered low-pressure compressed air. Be careful not to spin the bearings as they will be damaged.

5. Inspect for rust, wear, scuffed surfaces, heat discoloration or other defects. Check bearings for flat spots; if one needle is defective, replace the entire bearing. Replace as required. Always replace each connecting rod big end needle bearings as a complete set—never replace only half of the set as this will lead to premature bearing failure.

6. Turn each bearing by hand. Make sure the bearings turn smoothly. Replace the bearing(s) if they are noisy or have excessive axial and/or radial play (**Figure 193**).

Crankshaft Bearing Installation

1-, 2- and 3-cylinder power heads

1. Place the crankshaft in a hydraulic press. Make sure the crankshaft is positioned exactly vertical.

2. Lubricate the bearing inner diameter with Yamalube Two-Cycle Outboard oil. Position the bearing on the end of the crankshaft, with its

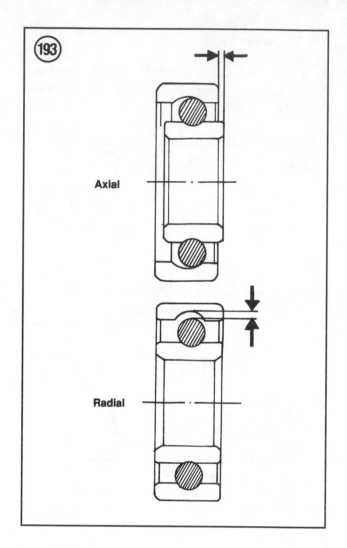

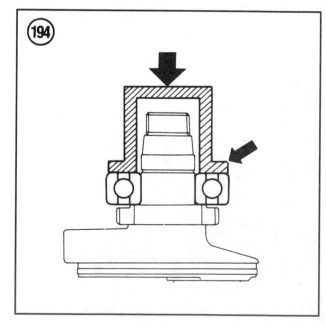

manufacturer's mark facing away from the crankshaft.

3. Place a suitable bearing installer on the bearing. Make certain the tool contacts the inner race of the bearing. See **Figure 194**.

4. Carefully press the bearing on the crankshaft until it bottoms out.

5. On models so equipped, install the circlip. Make sure the circlip is fully seated in its groove.

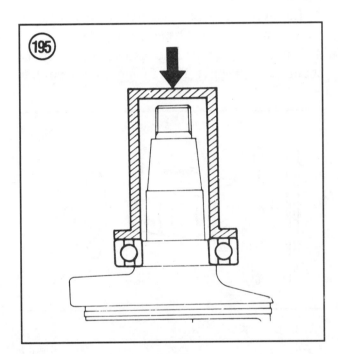

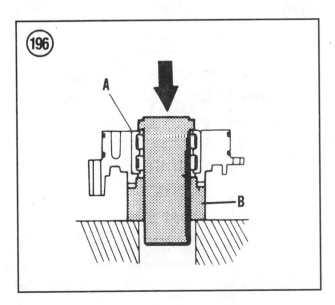

6. Repeat this procedure to install the remaining bearing.

76° V6 power head

1. To install the upper bearing, place the crankshaft assembly in the hydraulic press. Make sure the crankshaft is positioned exactly vertical.

2. Lubricate the inner diameter of the upper bearing with Yamalube Two-Cycle Outboard Oil. Place the bearing on the crankshaft, with its manufacturer's mark facing away from the crankshaft.

3. Install a suitable bearing installer (**Figure 195**) on the bearing. Make sure the installer contacts only the bearing inner race.

4. Carefully press the bearing on the crankshaft until fully seated.

5. Install the bearing circlip, on models so equipped. Make sure the circlip is fully seated in its groove.

CAUTION
If removed, be sure to install the oil pump drive gear before pressing the lower bearing on the crankshaft.

6. Install the oil pump drive gear (if removed) on the crankshaft as outlined in this chapter. Repeat this procedure to install the crankshaft lower bearing.

V4 and 90° V6 power heads

1. To install the crankshaft upper needle bearing and oil seal into the upper bearing housing, first place the bearing housing on the hydraulic press table. Position the housing so its crankshaft side is facing up.

2. Lubricate the needle bearing inner and outer diameters with Yamalube Two-Cycle Outboard oil.

3. Place the bearing (A, **Figure 196**) into position on the bearing housing.

8

4. Install Yamaha bearing installer (part No. YB-6205) under the bearing housing and into the inside race of the bearing as shown in B, **Figure 196**.

5. Carefully press the bearing into the housing until it bottoms. Remove the bearing installer.

6. Press a new oil seal (A, **Figure 197**) into the housing. Make sure the seal is fully bottomed out in the housing.

7. Install new O-rings (B, **Figure 197**) into the bearing housing.

CAUTION
If removed, be sure to install the oil pump drive gear prior to pressing the lower bearing on the crankshaft.

8. Install the oil pump drive gear on the crankshaft as outlined in this chapter.

9. Place the crankshaft in the hydraulic press. Make sure the crankshaft is positioned exactly vertical.

10. Lubricate the inner diameter of the lower bearing with Yamalube Two-Cycle Outboard Oil. Place the bearing on the crankshaft, with its manufacturer's mark facing away from the crankshaft.

11. Place a suitable bearing installer on the bearing. Make sure the bearing installer contacts only the bearing inner race.

12. Press the bearing on the crankshaft until fully seated.

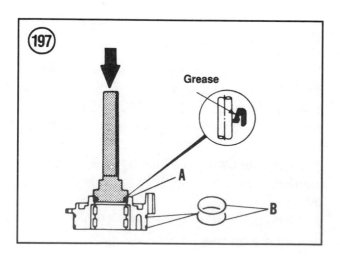

Oil Pump Drive Gear Installation (All V4 and V6 Power Heads)

NOTE
The crankshaft lower bearing must be installed on the crankshaft before installing the oil pump drive gear.

1. Place the crankshaft assembly in a hydraulic press. Make sure the crankshaft is positioned exactly vertical.

2. Lubricate the inner diameter of the drive gear with Yamalube Two-Cycle Outboard Oil.

3. Place the gear on the crankshaft, with its shoulder (A, **Figure 198**) facing away from the

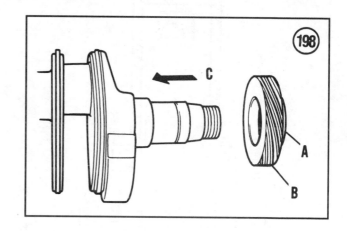

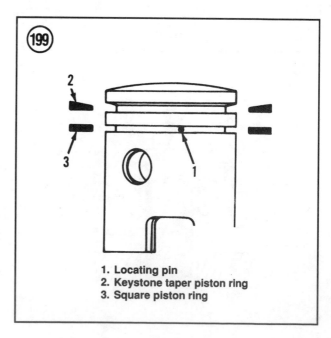

1. Locating pin
2. Keystone taper piston ring
3. Square piston ring

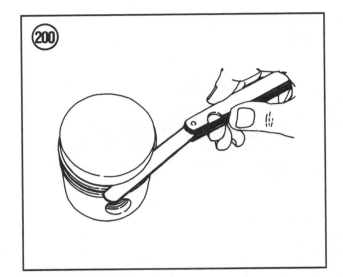

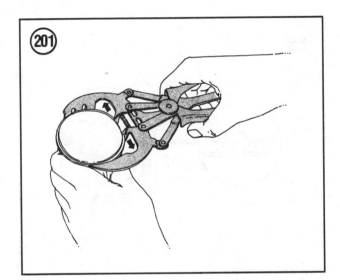

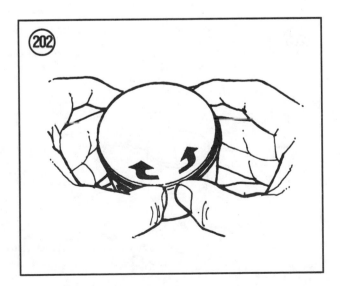

crankshaft. Press the gear (B, **Figure 198**) on the crankshaft (C).

Piston Ring Inspection and Replacement (All Power Heads)

Pistons use a keystone design top ring. The second ring is either a keystone design or a flat design as shown in **Figure 199**.

> *WARNING*
> *The edges of all piston rings are very sharp. Be careful when handling them to avoid cutting your fingers.*

1. Measure the side clearance of each ring in its groove with a flat feeler gauge (**Figure 200**) and compare to specifications given in **Table 2**. If the clearance is greater than specified, the rings must be replaced. If the clearance is still excessive with the new rings, the piston must also be replaced.

2. Remove the old rings with a ring expander tool (**Figure 201**) or by spreading the ends with your thumbs just enough to slide the ring up over the piston (**Figure 202**). Repeat for the remaining ring.

3. Clean and inspect the piston as described in this chapter.

4. Check the end gap of each ring. To check the ring, insert the ring into the cylinder, one at a time, just above the intake and exhaust ports. Square the ring in the cylinder by gently tapping it with the bottom of the piston. Measure the gap with a flat feeler gauge (**Figure 203**) and com-

pare to dimensions in **Table 2**. If the gap is greater than specified, the rings should be replaced. When installing new rings, measure their end gap as previously outlined. If the gap is less than specified, carefully file the ends with a fine-cut file until the gap is correct.

> *NOTE*
> *If the top ring has a manufacturer's mark on it, install that ring with the mark facing UP as shown in Figure 204.*

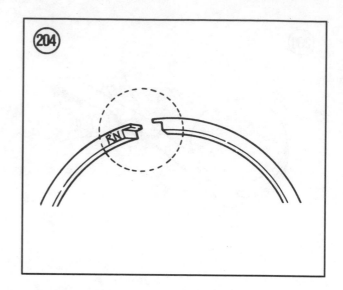

5. Once the ring clearance and end gap are correct, install the rings as follows:

  a. Install the lower ring first, then the top ring—by carefully spreading the ends with your thumbs and slipping the rings over the top of the piston.

  b. Rotate each ring so the locating pin in the ring groove fits into the ring gap (**Figure 205**). Proper ring positioning is necessary to minimize compression loss and to prevent the ring ends from catching on the cylinder ports.

  c. Make sure the rings are seated completely in their grooves all the way around the piston.

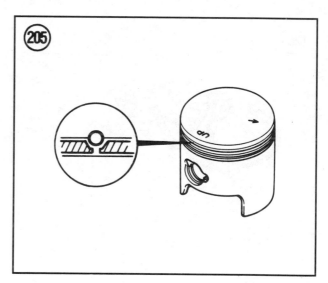

6. If new rings are installed, measure the side clearance of each ring in its groove with a flat feeler gauge (**Figure 200**) and compare to specifications given in **Table 2**.

7. After the rings are installed, apply clean Yamalube Two-Cycle Outboard Oil around the circumference of each ring. This will ensure proper oiling when the engine is first started.

Piston Cleaning and Inspection
(All Models)

1. Check the piston(s) for scoring, cracking, cracked or worn piston pin bosses or metal damage (**Figure 206**). Replace the piston and pin as an assembly if any of these defects are noted.

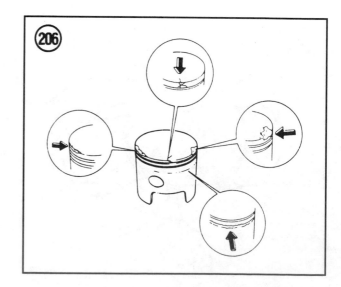

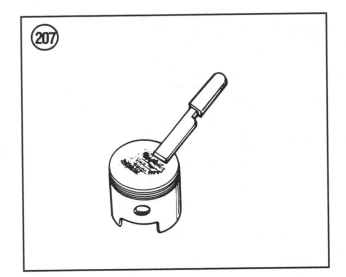

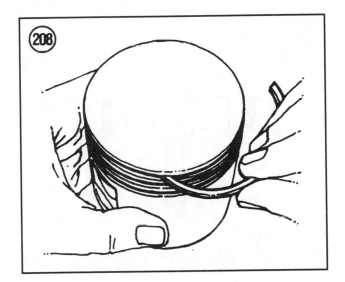

2. Remove carbon deposits from the piston crown with a hardwood or plastic scraper (**Figure 207**).

3. Carefully remove all carbon buildup from the ring grooves with a broken piston ring (**Figure 208**). Do not use an automotive ring groove cleaning tool as it can damage the piston groove locating pin.

4. Inspect the grooves carefully for burrs, nicks, broken or cracked lands, distortion, loose ring locating pins or excessive wear. If the flexing action of the rings has not kept the lower surface of the ring grooves free of carbon, clean with a bristle brush and solvent. Recondition or replace the piston if necessary.

5. Immerse the pistons in a carbon removal solution to remove any carbon deposits remaining from Step 4. If the solution does not remove all of the carbon, carefully use a fine wire brush and avoid burring or rounding of the machined edges. Clean the piston skirt with crocus cloth.

6. Measure the piston diameter at a right angle to the piston pin with a micrometer (**Figure 209**). Refer to **Table 2** for the exact measurement point on the piston skirt.

7. Measure the piston bore diameter in the cylinder block with a bore gauge (**Figure 210**) at the point indicated in **Table 2**.

8

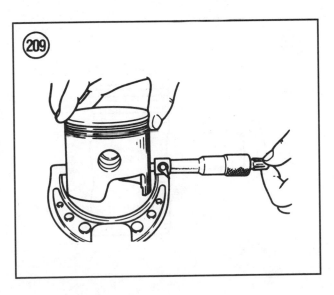

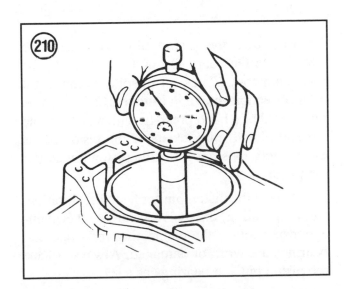

8. Subtract the measurement obtained in Step 6 from the Step 7 measurement to determine the cylinder-to-piston clearance (**Figure 211**). Compare clearance to specifications (**Table 2**). If the clearance exceeds specification, have the cylinder block rebored by a dealer or machine shop and install oversize pistons.

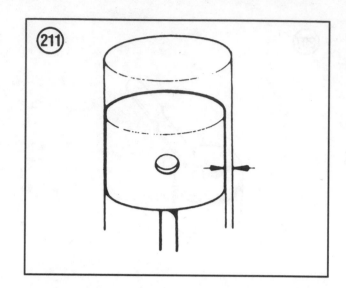

NOTE
Obtain the new pistons and measure them before having the cylinders bored. This allows for variations in piston size due to manufacturing tolerances.

9. Check the piston pin for wear as follows:

a. Lubricate the piston pin with Yamalube Two-Cycle Outboard Oil. Install either the loose roller bearings or the caged bearing in the connecting rod small end.

b. Insert the piston pin into the rod bearing. Slowly rotate the piston pin and check for radial and axial play (**Figure 212**). If any play exists, the piston pin should be replaced, providing the rod bearing is in good condition.

c. Remove the piston pin and small end bearings.

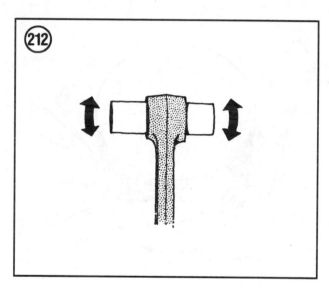

10. Lubricate the piston pin with Yamalube Two-Cycle Outboard Oil and insert it into the piston pin boss. Check for freeplay by moving it in the direction shown in **Figure 213**. The piston pin should be a hand press-fit with no noticeable vertical play. If play exists or the piston pin is excessively loose, replace the piston pin and/or the piston.

11. Inspect the piston pin for heat discoloration, fretting, galling, excessive wear or other damage, especially if the connecting rod small end bearings are worn or damaged. Always replace the piston pin and bearings as a set.

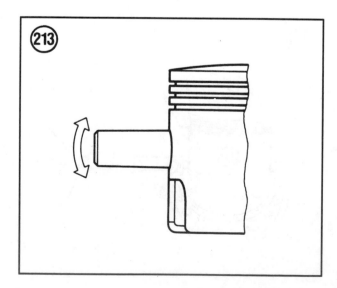

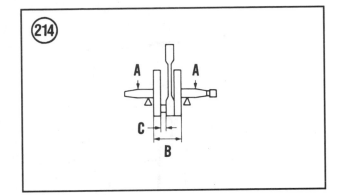

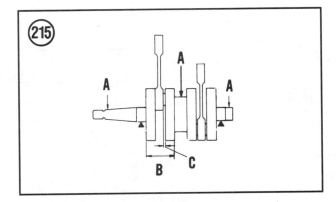

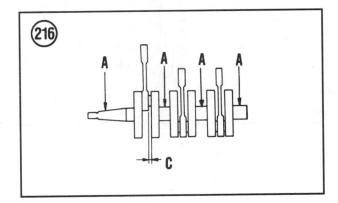

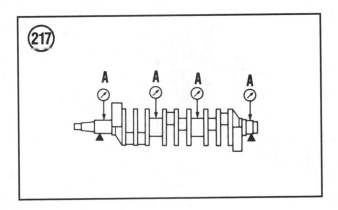

Crankshaft Cleaning and Inspection (All Models)

Only on the C40, C55 and 75-250 hp models, can the connecting rods be removed from the crankshaft. On all other engines, if either the rod(s) and/or the crankshaft is defective, replace the entire assembly.

1. Clean the crankshaft thoroughly with solvent and a brush. Blow dry with dry compressed air and lubricate with a light coat of Yamaha Outboard Motor oil.

2. Check the crankshaft journals and crankpins for scratches, heat discoloration or other damage.

3. Check the drive shaft splines, flywheel taper and threads, keyway and the oil injection pump drive gear (if so equipped) for wear or damage. Replace crankshaft as required.

4. Check the crankshaft oil seal surfaces for grooving, pitting or scratches.

5. Check the crankshaft bearing surfaces for rust, water marks, chatter marks and excessive or uneven wear. Minor cases of rust and water or chatter marks can be cleaned up with 320 grit carborundum cloth.

6. If 320 grit cloth is used, clean the crankshaft in solvent and recheck the surfaces. If they did not clean up properly, replace the crankshaft.

7. If crankshaft ball bearings have not been removed, grasp the outer race and try to work it back and forth. Replace bearing(s) if excessive axial play is noted.

8. Lubricate all ball bearings with Yamalube Two-Cycle Outboard Motor oil and rotate the outer race. Replace the bearing if it sounds or feels rough or if it does not rotate smoothly.

9. Support the crankshaft on a pair of V-blocks and check runout with a dial indicator at points marked "A" in the following:

    a. **Figure 214**: 1-cylinder engine.

    b. **Figure 215**: 2-cylinder engine.

    c. **Figure 216**: 3-cylinder engine.

    d. **Figure 217**: V4 and V6 engine.

8

Refer to **Table 2** for crankshaft runout tolerances and replace if necessary.

10. On 2-70 hp (except C40 and C55) engines, check the connecting rod deflection at the piston end of the connecting rod (**Figure 218**, typical). Maximum allowable deflection is listed in **Table 2**. If deflection exceeds the maximum, replace the crankshaft/connecting rod assembly.

11. On 1-cylinder and 2-cylinder engines only, check the crankshaft web width marked B, **Figure 214** for 1-cylinder models or **Figure 215** for 2-cylinder models. Web width is not within the specification listed in **Table 3**, replace the crankshaft assembly.

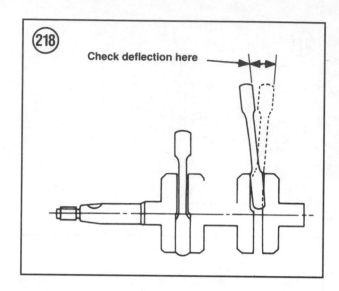

Check deflection here

NOTE
*Yamaha does not provide big end side clearance for all models. Refer to **Table 3** to make sure the engine you are working on is listed.*

12. Slide the connecting rod to one side of the crankshaft. Use a flat feeler gauge to measure the big end side clearance between the connecting rod and the crankshaft web (C, **Figures 214-216** for 1-3 cylinder engines or C, **Figure 219** for V4 and V6 engines). Refer to **Table 3** for specifications.

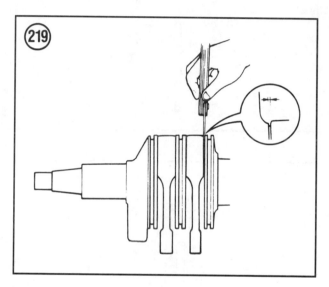

13. With all pistons removed and the crankshaft on V-blocks, check wear and condition of the big end of the connecting rod. Hold the crankshaft steady and move the connecting rod up and down with your hand (**Figure 220**). Make sure there is not a rattle in the big end.

14. On V4 and V6 engines, inspect the crankshaft sealing rings as described under *Piston/Crankshaft Disassembly (C40, C55 2-cylinder, All 3-cylinder and V-Block Engines)* in this chapter.

15. Replace the entire crankshaft and connecting rod assembly if any of the dimensions in Steps 9-13 are not within specifications. On V4 and V6 engines, replace the sealing rings as required.

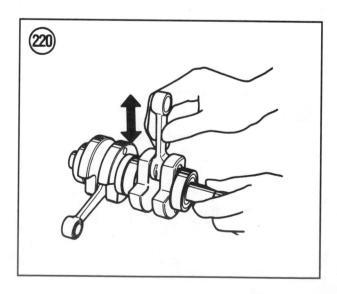

**Connecting Rod Cleaning and Inspection
(C40, C55, 75-250 hp)**

1. Check each connecting rod assembly for straightness. Place each rod and cap assembly on a smooth flat surface (plate glass) and press downward on the rod—it should not wobble under pressure. Try inserting a 0.05 mm (0.002 in.) flat feeler gauge between the machined surface portion of the rod and the flat surface. If you can insert the feeler gauge, replace the connecting rod assembly.

2. Inspect the big end bearings for rust, wear, scuffed surfaces, heat distortion or other damage. Replace as a set if faulty.

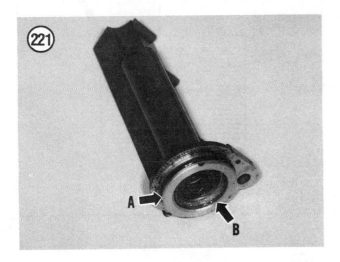

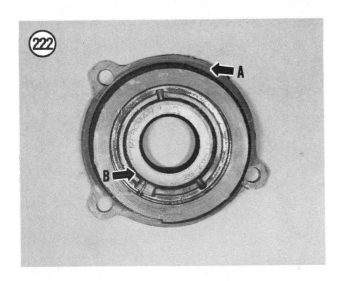

3. Check the connecting rod small and big end bearing surfaces for rust, water marks, chatter marks, heat discoloration and excessive or uneven wear.

4. Slight damage noted in Step 3 can be cleaned up as follows:

   a. Reassemble the rod cap to the connecting rod. Make sure the match marks made before disassembly are aligned. Tighten the cap bolts securely.

   b. Clean the bearing surfaces with crocus cloth.

   c. Clean the piston pin bearing surfaces with 320 carborundum cloth.

   d. Wash the connecting rod assembly in solvent to remove the abrasive grit, then recheck the bearing surface condition.

   e. Replace any connecting rod and cap assembly that does not clean up properly.

   f. Lightly oil all bearing surfaces on the connecting rod and cap assemblies with Yamalube Two-Cycle Outboard oil.

**Upper and Lower
Oil Seal Housing**

Figure 221 shows the lower housing used on the smaller displacement engines, and Figure 222 shows the lower housing equipped on the larger displacement engines. The upper housing used on some engines is similar and may contain a roller bearing.

1. Remove the O-ring(s) (A, Figure 221 and Figure 222) from the housing. Some models use one O-ring; others use two.

2. Note the position of the oil seal lips and remove the oil seal(s) (B, Figure 221 and B, Figure 222) from the housing. Depending on the model, the lower housing may contain 1-3 seals.

3. If the upper housing contains a roller bearing that must be replaced, remove the old bearing and install a new one using a hydraulic press.

4. Clean the housing with solvent and dry with compressed air.

8

5. Lubricate the outer diameter of the seal(s) with Gasket Maker or equivalent.

6. Position the seal with the seal lip(s) facing the same direction as noted in Step 2. Install the new seal(s) with a suitable size mandrel.

7. Remove any excess Gasket Maker and lubricate the seal lip(s) with Yamalube All-purpose Marine Grease.

8. Install new O-ring(s) and lubricate with the recommended grease.

Thermostat Inspection (All Engines so Equipped)

There are several different thermostats used among the different models. The temperature rating is stamped on the thermostat flange and if replacement is necessary, replace the old thermostat with one of the same temperature rating.

1. Clean all gasket residue from the thermostat and its cover.

2. Inspect the thermostat cover for cracks or corrosion damage. Replace if necessary.

3. Remove the rubber washer or collar (**Figure 223**) and wash the thermostat with clean water.

4. Suspend the thermostat and thermometer in a container of water that can be heated. Support the thermostat with wire so it does not touch the sides or bottom of the container (**Figure 224**).

5. Heat the container of water and note the temperature at which the thermostat starts to open. It should be approximately the same temperature as that stamped on the thermostat flange. If not, replace the thermostat.

6. Measure the maximum lift of the thermostat valve. To do this, mark a small screwdriver at a point 3 mm (0.12 in.) from the tip. Use the screwdriver tip to measure the valve lift when the valve is fully open. If the valve lift is less than 3 mm (0.12 in.) at the indicated temperature rating or more, replace the thermostat.

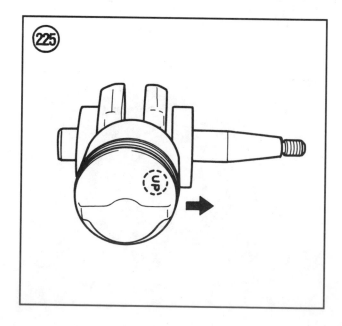

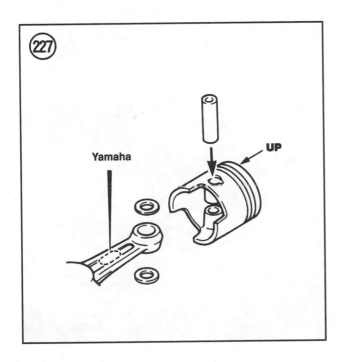

1. Caged needle
   bearing
2. Piston
3. Piston pin
4. Clip

Piston and Connecting Rod Assembly

If the piston(s) were removed from the connecting rod(s), they must be correctly oriented when reassembling. The UP mark on the piston crown must face toward the top of the power head (**Figure 225**).

Use Yamalube Two-Cycle Outboard Oil when the procedure specifies lubrication with oil. Use Yamalube Marine Grease if grease is specified.

Caged small end bearings

Refer to **Figure 226** for this procedure.

1. Coat the piston pin, piston pin bore and connecting rod small end bore and bearing assembly with oil.

2. On engines with the connecting rod separated from the crankshaft, position the connecting rod with the YAMAHA mark facing up, prior to installing the piston (**Figure 227**).

3. Position the piston with the UP mark facing toward the flywheel, or top of the power head. Install a new piston pin clip into the lower side of the piston using needlenose pliers. Use a screwdriver to make sure the clip is properly seated in its groove. This will prevent the piston pin from falling through the piston during piston pin installation.

4. Partially insert the piston pin into the piston.

5. Install the caged bearing in the small end of the connecting rod (**Figure 228**).

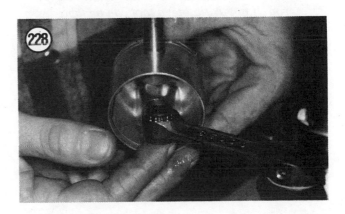

6. Position the piston with the UP mark facing toward the top of the power head and fit it over the connecting rod.

7. Align the piston pin with the caged bearing in the connecting rod.

8. Slowly push the piston pin through the caged bearing and into the other side of the piston. Push it in until it bottoms out against the previously installed piston pin clip.

9. Install the other new piston pin clip with needlenose pliers. Use a screwdriver to make sure the clip is properly seated in the piston bore groove (**Figure 229**).

10. Repeat Steps 1-9 and install all remaining pistons.

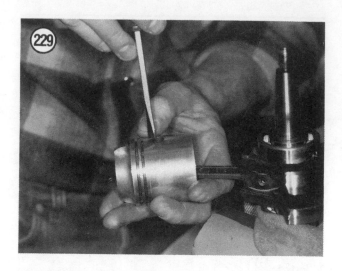

Loose small end bearings

Refer to **Figure 230** for this procedure.

1. Coat the piston pin and the piston pin bore with oil.

2. On engines with the connecting rod separated from the crankshaft, position the connecting rod with the YAMAHA mark facing up, prior to installing the piston (**Figure 230**).

3. Partially insert the piston pin into the piston.

4. Apply a light coat of cold grease to the inner surface of the connecting rod small end. This will help hold the loose needle bearing roller in place.

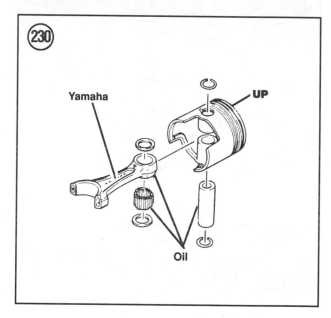

> *NOTE*
> *The manufacturer has a small end bearing installer tool available to ease bearing roller installation in the connecting rod. If not available, a tool can be fabricated from a short section of a discarded piston pin or other appropriately sized sleeve. Place the tool inside the connecting rod small end bore and install the bearing rollers around it.*

5. Install a suitable size bushing (to act as a spacer) into the connecting rod. Install the needle bearing rollers individually (**Figure 231**). Be sure to install the same number of rollers that were removed.

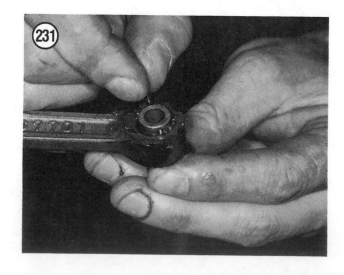

6. After all needle bearing rollers are in place, position the washers (**Figure 232**) with their convex side facing the piston (**Figure 233**).

NOTE
If possible, position the crankshaft, or individual connecting rod, so the connecting rod small end is in a horizontal position. This may help keep the bushing from falling out of the connecting rod small end after the needle bearings are installed.

7. Position the piston with the UP mark facing toward the top of the power head. Fit the piston over the connecting rod being careful not to disturb the bearings and washers.

CAUTION
*Prior to installing the piston pin, look into the piston to make sure that **both washers are still in place**. Both washers must be in place or premature piston wear will occur. Also, a loose washer*

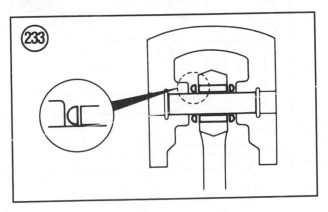

inside the engine can cause severe damage.

8. Align the piston pin with the washers and bearings in the connecting rod.
9. Slowly push the piston pin through the washers and bearings while pushing out the bushing used as a spacer. Push the piston pin in until it is centered in the piston.
10. Install the new lower piston pin clip with needlenose pliers. Use a screwdriver to make sure the clip is properly seated in the piston bore groove (**Figure 229**). Repeat for the upper piston pin clip.

NOTE
Refer to the CAUTION ahead of Step 8 and make sure that both washers are still properly in place.

11. Repeat Steps 1-10 and install all remaining pistons.

**Crankshaft Assembly
(All Models)**

Refer to the following illustrations for this procedure:
   a. **Figure 165**: 1-cylinder engine.
   b. **Figure 166**: 2-cylinder engine (crankshaft and connecting rods assembly).
   c. **Figure 167**: 3-cylinder engine (crankshaft and connecting rods assembly).
   d. **Figure 173**: 2 and 3 cylinder engines (removable connecting rods).
   e. **Figure 174**: V-block engines.

Use Yamalube Two-Cycle Outboard Oil if the procedure specifies lubrication with oil. Use Yamalube Marine Grease if grease is specified.
1. Install the crankshaft main bearings (if removed) as described in this chapter. Lubricate the bearings with oil, then slowly rotate them to make sure the oil is evenly distributed. Add additional oil if necessary.
2. If still removed, install the pistons on the connecting rods as described in this chapter.

8

3. Lubricate the lips of the new oil seals with grease and install new oil seals and spacers in their proper locations. Refer to the crankshaft illustrations in the *Crankshaft Assembly and Cylinder Block Disassembly* procedures at the beginning of this section in this chapter.

4. If the crankshaft is equipped with a split-sleeve center main bearing(s), install it as follows:

    a. Apply a light coat of grease to the crankshaft main bearing journals.

NOTE
*On V4 and V6 engines, the large circlip groove in the main bearing sleeve is located toward the **top end** of the crankshaft.*

NOTE
On most engines, the locating pin is located toward the lower end of the engine, away from the flywheel end of the crankshaft. Check the location of the pins of the engine you are working on to make sure the bearing hole and pin align correctly.

    b. Correctly position the bearing on the crankshaft journal so the locating hole in the bearing correctly aligned with the locating pin in the cylinder block upon installation.

CAUTION
Do not expand the circlip any more than necessary to install it on the bearing. The circlip must fit snug against the bearings to hold them in place.

    c. Install both bearing halves, then install the large circlip that secures them to the crankshaft (**Figure 234**). Make sure the circlip is correctly seated in the groove in each bearing half.

5. On V4 and V6 engines, if the crankshaft seal rings were removed, make sure they are installed correctly as described in this chapter.

6. On V4 and 90° V6 engines, make sure the oil seal and O-ring(s) are installed in the crankshaft upper bearing housing. Lubricate the bearings with oil and slowly rotate them to make sure the oil is evenly distributed. Add additional oil if necessary. Also check the oil seals in the lower oil seal housing. Apply a light coat of grease to the oil seal lips.

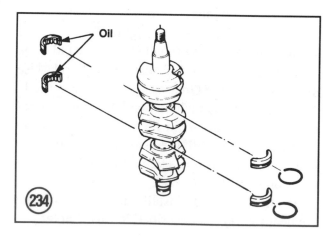

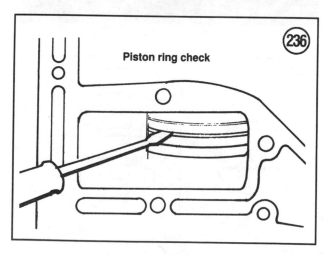

Piston ring check

Crankshaft Installation
(2-70 hp Models [Except C40 and C55])

Use Yamalube Two-Cycle Outboard Oil whenever the procedure specifies lubrication with oil.

1. Coat the crankshaft, piston(s), rings and cylinder bore(s) with oil.

2. Place the cylinder block on a clean, level work bench.

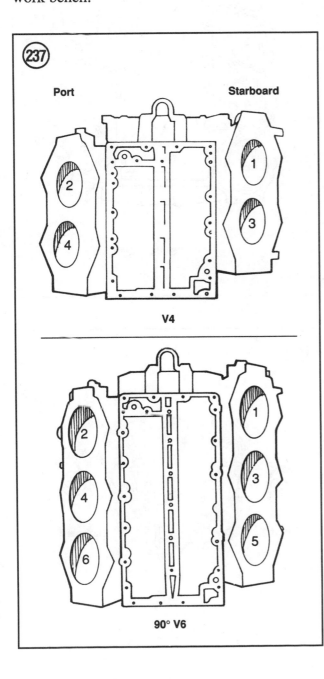

Port   Starboard

V4

90° V6

3. On engines so equipped, install the lower bearing.

> *CAUTION*
> *Be sure that the piston ring end gaps remain aligned with the ring groove locating pins as the piston enters the cylinder bore in the following steps.*

4. Carefully lower the crankshaft assembly until the No. 1 piston starts to enter the cylinder bore. Compress the rings on the piston with your fingers and slowly work the piston/ring assembly into the cylinder. On multi-cylinder engines, rotate the crankshaft and repeat this step to fit each remaining piston into its bore.

5. When all piston/ring assemblies have entered the cylinder bores, apply sufficient downward pressure to seat the pistons in their bores and the crankshaft within the crankcase.

6. Rotate the crankshaft ball bearing races to align their locating pin with the pin recess in the cylinder block (A, **Figure 235**). On some engines it is necessary to align the lower bearing washer and the labyrinth seal and center bearing circlips in their respective crankcase cutouts (B, **Figure 235**).

7. Reach through the exhaust ports and lightly depress each ring with a small screwdriver blade (**Figure 236**). The ring should snap back when pressure is released. If it does not, the ring was broken during piston installation and must be replaced. Remove the crankshaft assembly from the cylinder block and replace the broken ring(s).

Piston and Connecting Rod
Installation (C40, C55, 75-250 hp Models)

Refer to the following illustrations for this procedure:

    a. **Figure 237**: V4 and 90° V6 engines.

    b. **Figure 238**: 76° V6 engines.

Use Yamalube Two-Cycle Outboard Oil whenever the procedure specifies lubrication with oil.

8

1. Coat the pistons, rings and cylinder bores with oil.

2. Place the cylinder block on a clean, level work bench.

3. Check the piston number made during disassembly and match the piston with its correct cylinder bore.

CAUTION
On V4 and V6 engines, the piston crown is marked with a P (port) or S (starboard) (Figure 239). Be sure to install the pistons in their proper locations or the engine will not run. Remember that port and starboard relates to the outboard motor as it sits on the boat, not as it sits on your workbench.

4. Insert the piston into its cylinder bore with the UP mark facing the top of the power head (**Figure 240**).

5. Make sure the rings are properly positioned in their grooves and that the ring gaps are correctly positioned in relation to the ring groove locating pins.

6. Install a suitable ring compressor over the piston dome and rings. With the ring compressor resting on cylinder head, tighten it until the rings are compressed sufficiently to enter the bore.

7. Hold the connecting rod end with one hand to prevent it from scraping or scratching the cylinder bore and slowly push the piston into the cylinder (**Figure 241**).

8. Remove the ring compressor tool and repeat the procedure to install the remaining pistons.

9. Reach through the exhaust ports and lightly depress each ring with a small screwdriver blade (**Figure 236**). The ring should snap back when pressure is released. If it does not, the ring was broken during piston installation and must be replaced. Remove the piston and connecting rod assembly from the cylinder block and replace the broken ring(s).

10. Temporarily install the cylinder head(s) to prevent the piston assemblies from falling out.

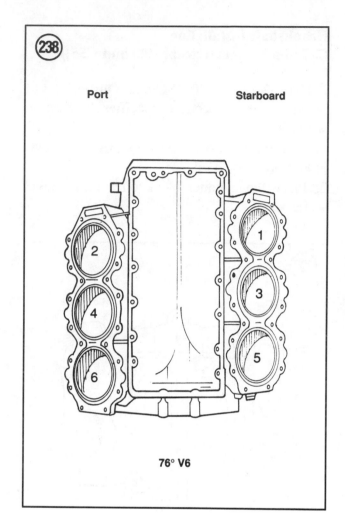

Port   Starboard

76° V6

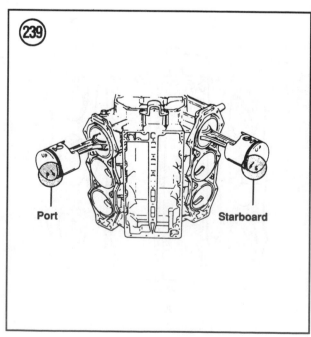

Port   Starboard

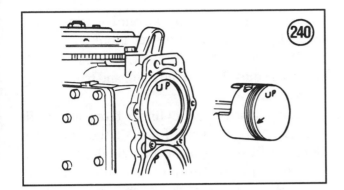

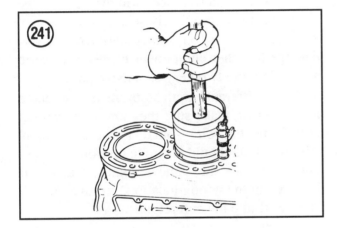

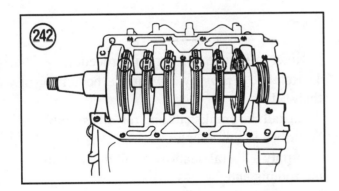

Crankshaft Installation
(C40, C55, 75-250 hp Models)

Use Yamalube Two-Cycle Outboard Oil whenever the procedure specifies lubrication with oil.

1. Install the piston and connecting rods as described in this chapter.

2. Remove the connecting rod caps. Coat connecting rod bearing surfaces and bearing cages with oil. Install a bearing cage in the rods.

3. Lubricate the crankshaft with oil and partially install it in the cylinder block. Rotate the crankshaft bearing(s) to align the locating hole(s) with the pin(s) in the cylinder block. After alignment is correct, lower the crankshaft and make sure it seats correctly. The crankshaft must completely bottom out in the cylinder block, otherwise you will be unable to install the crankcase cover.

4. On V4 and V6 engines, rotate the seal rings so their end gaps face out (**Figure 242**) directly away from the cylinder block.

CAUTION
*Do not allow the connecting rod to contact and nick the rod journals on the crankshaft. Pull the connecting rod **straight** onto the crankshaft journal.*

5. Pull up and guide the connecting rod onto the crankshaft so the crankshaft bearing surface will not be damaged by the connecting rod during installation. Make sure the top half of the bearing is still in place in the rod. Repeat for all connecting rods.

6. Lightly coat the exposed part of each crankpin with oil. Install the remaining bearing cages on the crankpins.

7. Correctly install the rod caps on the connecting rods. Be sure to install the correct cap on its respective connecting rod. Refer to marks made during the removal procedure. Also correctly align the factory match marks on both parts (**Figure 243**).

8. Install the connecting rod cap bolts and tighten as follows:

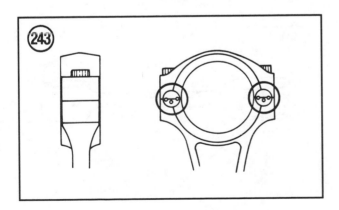

8

a. Apply oil to the bolt threads.

b. Install the bolts and tighten to the 1st torque step listed in **Table 1**.

c. Check to see that the cap and rod are aligned properly. If not, remove the bolt and caps and reposition.

d. Tighten the bolts to the 2nd torque step in **Table 1**.

e. Loosen the bolts 1/2 turn, then retighten to the 2nd torque step in **Table 1**.

> *CAUTION*
> *The procedure detailed in Step 9 is very important to proper engine operation as it affects bearing action. If not done properly, major engine damage will result. It can also be a time-consuming and frustrating process. Work slowly and with patience. If alignment cannot be achieved, replace the connecting rod and cap assembly.*

9. Run a dental pick or pencil point along the cap match marks to check cap offset (**Figure 244**). The rod and cap must be aligned so that the dental pick or pencil point will pass smoothly across the fracture line at each of the 3 faces indicated by the arrows in **Figure 244**. If alignment is not correct, return to Step 8.

10. Rotate the crankshaft to check for binding. If the connecting rod does not float freely over the full length of the crankpin, loosen the rod cap and repeat Step 8.

POWER HEAD ASSEMBLY

Assembly Tips

1. Use Yamalube Two-Cycle Outboard Oil whenever the procedure specifies lubrication with oil. Use Yamalube All-purpose Marine grease whenever grease is specified.

2. Make sure the mating surfaces of the cylinder block and crankcase are thoroughly clean. Prior to coating the mating surface with Gasket Maker, clean the mating surfaces with aerosol electrical contact cleaner, isopropyl alcohol or acetone and wipe dry with a clean lint-free cloth.

3. Use Gasket Maker sealant, or equivalent. If using an equivalent, avoid thick and hard-setting materials.

4. The crankcase and cylinder block should fit together without using force. If the crankcase does not fit snug against the cylinder block, do not attempt to pull it down with the crankcase bolts. Remove the crankcase and investigate the cause of the interference. Maybe one of the bearings is not completely seated or an oil seal may be hung up on something. Do not risk damage to either component by using force to assemble these two very expensive parts.

5. When different length bolts are used to secure a component, make sure they are in the correct hole. Install the bolts—but do not screw them in. All bolt heads should protrude up from the component surface the same amount. If a bolt is installed in the wrong location, remove the bolt and insert into the correct hole.

2 hp

Refer to **Figure 245** for this procedure.

1. Refer to *Assembly Tips* at the beginning of this section.

2. Install the crankshaft and piston assembly as described in this chapter.

3. Apply a liberal quantity of oil to the connecting rod big end.

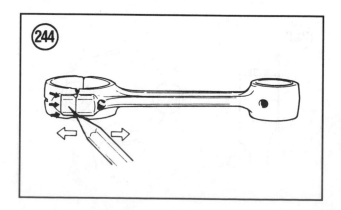
(244)

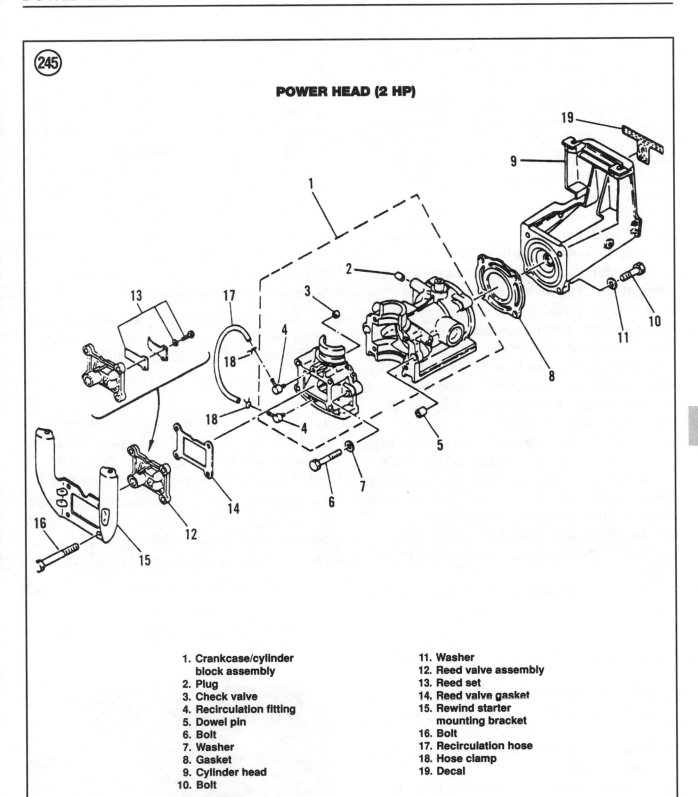

POWER HEAD (2 HP)

1. Crankcase/cylinder
   block assembly
2. Plug
3. Check valve
4. Recirculation fitting
5. Dowel pin
6. Bolt
7. Washer
8. Gasket
9. Cylinder head
10. Bolt
11. Washer
12. Reed valve assembly
13. Reed set
14. Reed valve gasket
15. Rewind starter
    mounting bracket
16. Bolt
17. Recirculation hose
18. Hose clamp
19. Decal

4. Apply a thin coat of Gasket Maker, or equivalent, to the mating surfaces of the cylinder block and the crankcase (**Figure 246**).

5. Make sure the dowel pins are in place.

6. Install the crankcase onto the cylinder block and install the bolts. Be sure to install the J-clamp under the bolt on the starboard side of the engine. Tighten the bolts in 2 stages to the specifications listed in **Table 1**.

7. Rotate the crankshaft several turns to check for binding. If the crankshaft does not turn easily, disassemble and correct the interference.

8. Connect the crankcase upper circulation hose fitting to the cylinder block.

9. Install the cylinder head with a new gasket. Make sure the water passages in the cylinder head, gasket and cylinder block align.

10. Apply blue Loctite (No. 242) to the cylinder head bolt threads prior to installation. Install the 4 bolts and tighten to the specifications listed in **Table 1** in a diagonal pattern.

11. Install the reed valve assembly with a new gasket. Position the rewind starter bracket against the reed valve assembly and install the bolts. Tighten the bolts to the specifications listed in **Table 1** in a diagonal pattern.

12. Install the carburetor. See Chapter Six.

13. Install the flywheel as described in this chapter.

14. Install the power head as described in this chapter.

3 hp engines

Refer to **Figure 247** for this procedure.

1. Refer to *Assembly Tips* at the beginning of this section.

2. Install the crankshaft and piston assembly as described in this chapter.

3. Apply a liberal quantity of oil to the connecting rod big end.

4. Apply a thin coat of Gasket Maker, or equivalent, to the mating surfaces of the cylinder block and the crankcase (**Figure 246**).

5. Make sure the dowel pins are in place (**Figure 248**).

6. Install the crankcase onto the cylinder block and install the 6 bolts. Tighten the bolts in 2 stages to the specifications listed in **Table 1** in the sequence shown in **Figure 249**.

7. Rotate the crankshaft several turns to check for binding. If the crankshaft does not turn easily, disassemble and correct the interference.

8. Connect the crankcase upper circulation hose fitting to the cylinder block.

9. Install the thermostat, cover and new gasket. Tighten the bolts securely.

10. Install the cylinder head with a new gasket. Make sure that the water passages in the cylinder head, gasket and cylinder block align.

11. Install the cylinder head cover and new gasket.

12. Apply blue Loctite (No. 242) to the cylinder head bolt threads prior to installation. Install the 5 bolts and tighten to the specifications listed in **Table 1** in the sequence shown in **Figure 250**.

13. Install the reed valve assembly with a new gasket. Tighten the bolts to the specifications listed in **Table 1** in a diagonal pattern.

14. Install the carburetor. See Chapter Six.

15. Install the flywheel as described in this chapter.

16. Install the power head as described in this chapter.

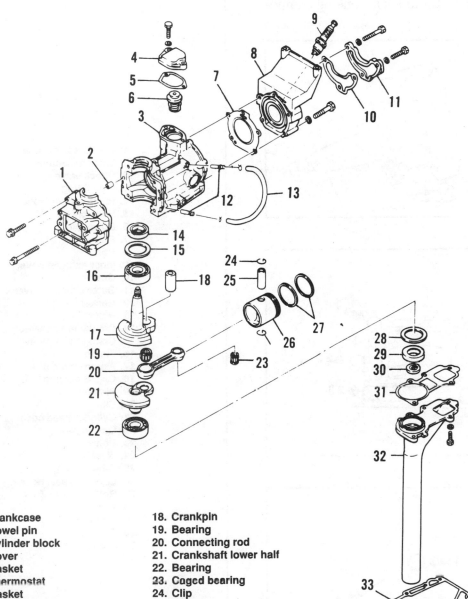

POWER HEAD (3 HP)

8

1. Crankcase
2. Dowel pin
3. Cylinder block
4. Cover
5. Gasket
6. Thermostat
7. Gasket
8. Cylinder head
9. Spark plug
10. Gasket
11. Cylinder head cover
12. Hose fitting
13. Recirculation hose
14. Oil seal
15. Washer
16. Bearing
17. Crankshaft upper half

18. Crankpin
19. Bearing
20. Connecting rod
21. Crankshaft lower half
22. Bearing
23. Caged bearing
24. Clip
25. Piston pin
26. Piston
27. Piston ring set
28. Washer
29. Oil seal
30. Oil seal
31. Gasket
32. Exhaust manifold
33. Gasket

4 and 5 hp

Refer to **Figure 251** for this procedure.

The 4 and 5 hp engines have the correct bolt torque sequence cast into each housing compo-

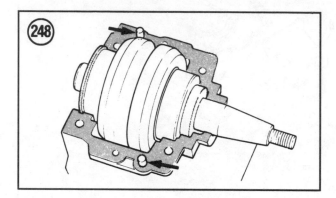

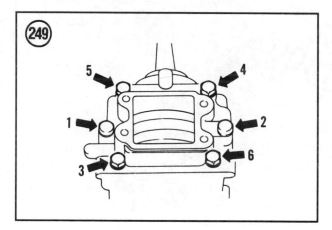

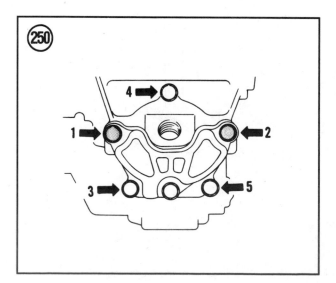

**POWER HEAD
(4 AND 5 HP)**

1. Crankcase/cylinder
   block assembly
2. Check valve
3. Pipe fitting
4. Recirculation hose
5. Hose clamp
6. Dowel pin
7. Bolt
8. Bolt
9. Inner exhaust cover
10. Gasket
11. Outer exhaust cover
12. Gasket
13. Bolt
14. Crankshaft assembly
15. Crankshaft bearing
16. Piston
17. Piston ring set
18. Caged bearing
19. Piston pin
20. Clip
21. Cylinder head cover
22. Gasket
23. Bolt
24. Washer
25. Oil seal
26. Lower oil seal housing
27. Bolt
28. Washer
29. Oil seal
30. O-ring
31. Spark plug

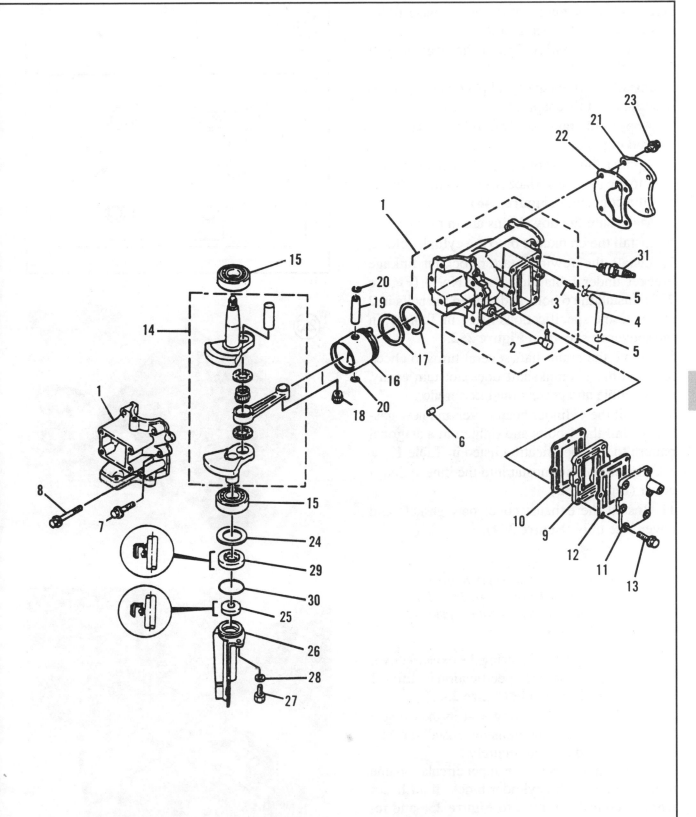

nent. Follow the numbered sequence when tightening the bolts to specification.

1. Refer to *Assembly Tips* at the beginning of this section.

2. Install the crankshaft and piston assembly as described in this chapter.

3. Apply a liberal quantity of oil to the connecting rod big end.

4. Apply a thin coat of Gasket Maker, or equivalent, to the mating surfaces of the cylinder block and the crankcase (**Figure 246**).

5. Make sure the dowel pins are in place.

6. Install the crankcase onto the cylinder block.

7. Install the rewind starter lockout linkage bracket under bolts No. 2 and No. 3 (**Figure 252**). Install the 6 bolts and tighten the bolts in 2 stages to the specifications listed in **Table 1**, in the sequence shown in **Figure 252**.

8. Rotate the crankshaft several turns to check for binding. If crankshaft does not turn easily, disassemble and correct the interference.

9. Install the cylinder head cover and new gasket. Install the 4 bolts and tighten in a diagonal pattern to the specification listed in **Table 1**.

10. Install the thermostat into the inner exhaust cover (**Figure 253**).

11. Install the exhaust cover new gaskets and cover assembly (**Figure 254**).

> *NOTE*
> *There are 3 different length 6 mm bolts securing the exhaust cover. Install the bolts in the correct location prior to tightening them.*

12. Install the 9 bolts securing the exhaust cover assembly and tighten to specification in **Table 1** in the sequence shown in **Figure 255**.

13. Apply oil to the O-ring seal in the oil seal housing and install the housing. Install the bolt and washer and tighten securely.

14. Connect the crankcase upper circulation line to the fitting on the cylinder block. If all hoses were disconnected, refer to **Figure 256** and reconnect the hoses.

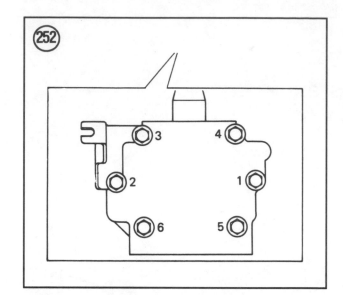

15. Install the reed valve assembly (A, **Figure 257**) with a new gasket (B, **Figure 257**). Tighten the bolts (C, **Figure 257**) to the specification listed in **Table 1** in a diagonal pattern.

16. Install the carburetor. See Chapter Six.

17. Install the flywheel as described in this chapter.

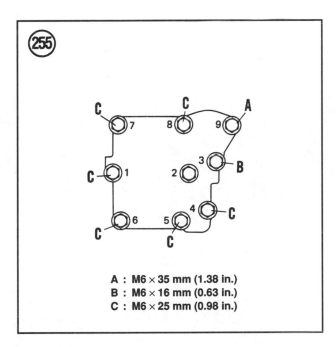

A : M6 × 35 mm (1.38 in.)
B : M6 × 16 mm (0.63 in.)
C : M6 × 25 mm (0.98 in.)

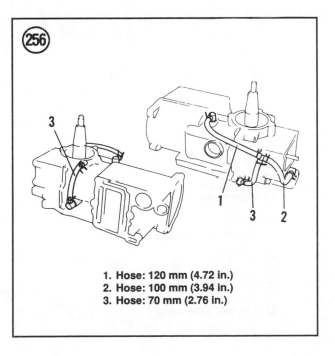

1. Hose: 120 mm (4.72 in.)
2. Hose: 100 mm (3.94 in.)
3. Hose: 70 mm (2.76 in.)

18. Install the power head as described in this chapter.

6 and 8 hp (2-cylinder)

Refer to **Figure 258** for this procedure.

1. Refer to *Assembly Tips* at the beginning of this section.

2. Install the crankshaft and piston assembly as described in this chapter.

3. Apply a liberal quantity of oil to the big end of the connecting rods.

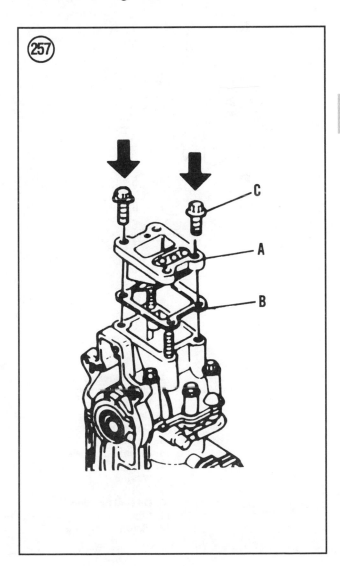

8

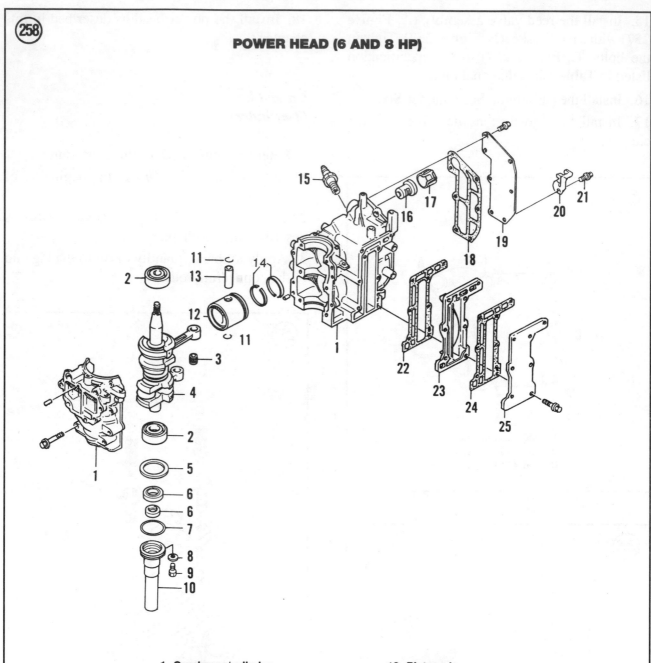

POWER HEAD (6 AND 8 HP)

1. Crankcase/cylinder block assembly
2. Bearing
3. Caged bearing
4. Crankshaft assembly
5. Washer
6. Oil seal
7. O-ring
8. Washer
9. Bolt
10. Oil seal housing
11. Clip
12. Piston
13. Piston pin
14. Piston ring set
15. Spark plug
16. Thermostat
17. Collar
18. Gasket
19. Cylinder head cover
20. Bracket
21. Bolt
22. Gasket
23. Exhaust inner cover
24. Gasket
25. Exhaust outer cover

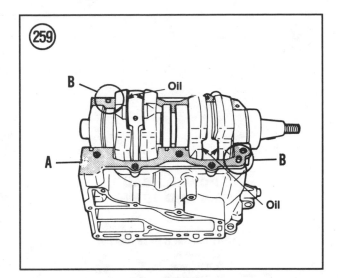

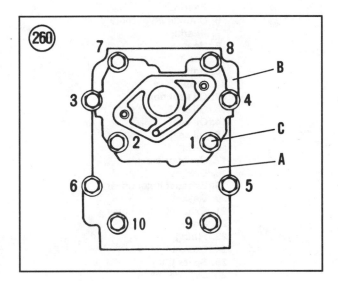

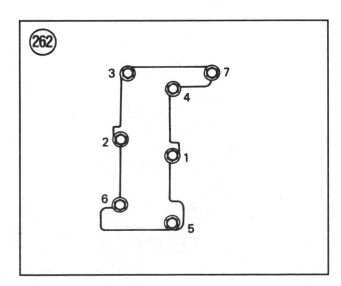

1. Gasket
2. Exhaust inner cover
3. Exhaust outer cover
4. Bolt

4. Apply a thin coat of Gasket Maker, or equivalent, to the mating surfaces of the cylinder block and the crankcase (A, **Figure 259**).

5. Make sure the dowel pins are in place (B, **Figure 259**).

6. Install the crankcase onto the cylinder block (A, **Figure 260**).

7. Install the 6 bolts securing the crankcase, but do not tighten the bolts at this time.

8. Install the reed valve assembly with a new gasket and the intake manifold with a new gasket (B, **Figure 260**).

9. Install the remaining bolts and tighten all 10 bolts to the specifications listed in **Table 1** in the sequence shown in C, **Figure 260**.

10. Rotate the crankshaft several turns to check for binding. If the crankshaft does not turn easily, disassemble and correct the interference.

11. Apply oil to the O-ring seal in the oil seal housing and grease to the mounting surface of the housing. Install the housing, the bolt and washer and tighten securely.

12. Refer to **Figure 261** and install the exhaust inner cover gasket (1), inner cover (2), outer cover gasket (1) and outer cover assembly (4).

13. Apply red Loctite (No. 271) to the cover bolt threads prior to installation. Install the bolts and tighten to the specifications listed in **Table 1** in the sequence shown in **Figure 262**.

14. Install the exhaust manifold and new gasket. Install the bolts and tighten securely.

15. Install the thermostat and collar into the cylinder head.

16. Install the cylinder head cover and new gasket.

17. Apply oil to the cylinder head cover bolt threads prior to installation. Install the bolts and tighten to the specifications listed in **Table 1** in the sequence shown in **Figure 263**.

18. Install the carburetor. See Chapter Six.

19. Install the flywheel as described in this chapter.

20. Install the power head as described in this chapter.

9.9 and 15 hp and C25 (2-cylinder)

Refer to the following illustrations for this procedure:

    a. **Figure 264**: 9.9 and 15 hp engines.

    b. **Figure 265**: C25 engine.

1. Refer to *Assembly Tips* at the beginning of this section.

2. Install the crankshaft and piston assembly as described in this chapter.

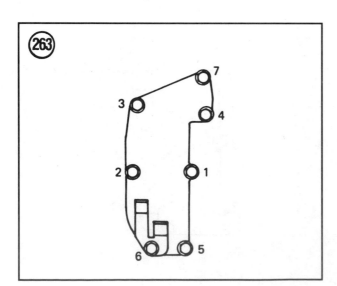

POWER HEAD (9.9 AND 15 HP)

1. Magneto base retainer
2. Gasket
3. Oil seal
4. Retainer
5. Bearing
6. Crankshaft assembly
7. Bearing
8. Hose
9. Pad
10. Bolt
11. Crankcase
12. Oil seal housing
13. Oil seal
14. Oil seal
15. Oil seal
16. O-ring
17. Cylinder block
18. Gasket
19. Exhaust inner cover
20. Gasket
21. Exhaust outer cover
22. Hose
23. Fitting
24. Gasket
25. Spark plug
26. Cylinder head
27. Thermostat
28. Washer
29. Gasket
30. Thermostat cover
31. Piston ring set
32. Piston
33. Clip
34. Piston pin
35. Washer
36. Loose needle bearings

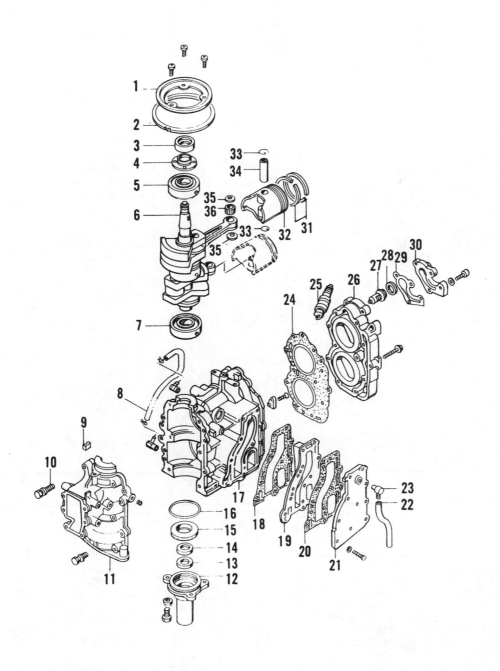

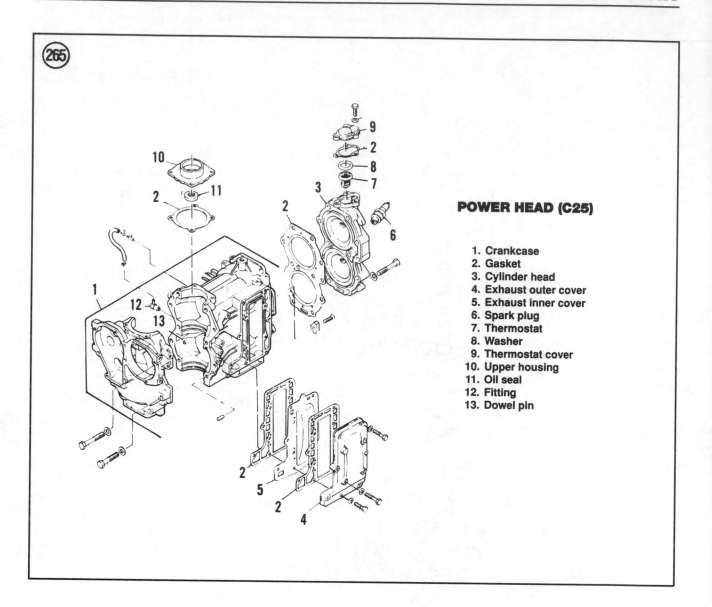

POWER HEAD (C25)

1. Crankcase
2. Gasket
3. Cylinder head
4. Exhaust outer cover
5. Exhaust inner cover
6. Spark plug
7. Thermostat
8. Washer
9. Thermostat cover
10. Upper housing
11. Oil seal
12. Fitting
13. Dowel pin

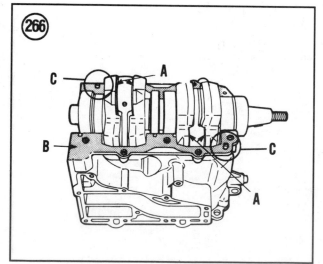

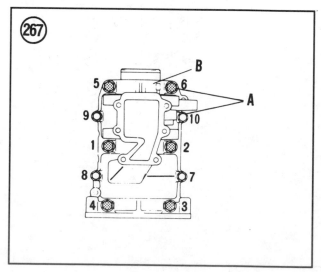

3. Apply a liberal quantity of oil to the connecting rod big end bearings (A, **Figure 266**).

4. Apply a thin coat of Gasket Maker, or equivalent, to the mating surfaces of the cylinder block and the crankcase (B, **Figure 266**).

5. Make sure the dowel pins are in place (C, **Figure 266**).

6. Install the crankcase onto the cylinder block.

7. Apply blue Loctite (No. 242) to the crankcase bolt threads prior to installation.

8. Install the four 6 mm bolts and the six 8 mm bolts securing the crankcase. Tighten all 10 bolts to the specifications listed in **Table 1** in the sequence shown in (**Figure 267**).

9. Rotate the crankshaft several turns to check for binding. If the crankshaft does not turn easily, disassemble and correct the interference.

10. Apply oil to the O-ring seal in the oil seal housing, and apply grease to the mounting surface of the housing. Install the housing, the bolt and washer and tighten securely.

NOTE
*If removed, install the spacer (A, **Figure 268**), nut (B), bolt and lockwasher (C) to the reed valve. Tighten the bolt securely.*

11. Apply a light coat of Gasket Maker to both sides of the reed valve gasket as shown in **Figure 269**.

12. Install the reed valve assembly with a new gasket. Install the bolts and lockwasher and tighten to the specification listed in **Table 1**.

13. Refer to **Figure 270** and install the exhaust inner cover gasket (1), inner cover (2), outer cover gasket (1) and outer cover assembly (4).

14. Apply red Loctite (No. 271) to the exhaust cover bolt threads prior to installation. Install the exhaust cover bolts and tighten to the specifica-

8

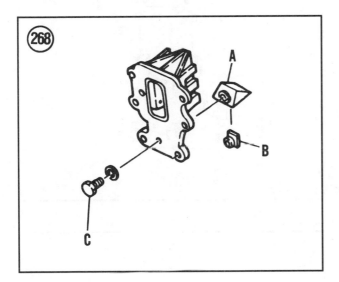

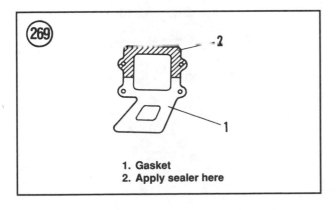

1. Gasket
2. Apply sealer here

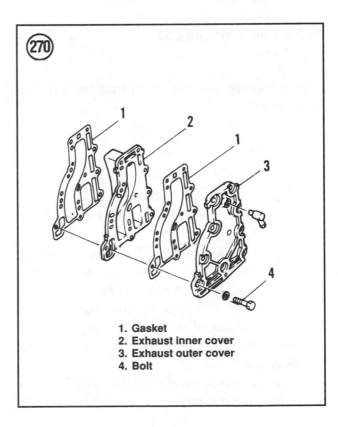

1. Gasket
2. Exhaust inner cover
3. Exhaust outer cover
4. Bolt

tion listed in **Table 1** in the sequence shown in **Figure 271**.

15. Install the cylinder head cover and new gasket.

16. Apply oil to the cylinder head cover bolt threads prior to installation. Install the bolts and tighten to the specifications listed in **Table 1** in the sequence shown in **Figure 272**.

17A. On 9.9 and 15 hp engines, install the thermostat, washer, gasket and cover to the front of the cylinder head. Install the bolts and tighten securely.

17B. On C25 engines, install the thermostat, washer, gasket and cover to the top of the cylinder head. Install the bolts and tighten securely.

18. Connect the crankcase upper circulation line to the fitting on the cylinder block.

19. Install the carburetor. See Chapter Six.

20. Install the flywheel as described in this chapter.

21. Install the power head as described in this chapter.

25 hp, C30, C40 and C55 (2-cylinder)

Refer to the following illustrations for this procedure:

    a. **Figure 273**: 25 hp engine.

    b. **Figure 274**: C30 engine.

    c. **Figure 275**: C40 engine.

    d. **Figure 276**: C55 engine.

1. Refer to *Assembly Tips* at the beginning of this section.

2. On C55 models, apply a light coat of grease to the oil seal housing O-rings and oil seal lips. Align the mounting bolt holes (**Figure 277**) and install the oil seal housing into the cylinder block. Do not install the mounting bolts yet.

3. Install the crankshaft assembly as described in this chapter.

4. Apply a liberal quantity of oil to the big end of the connecting rods.

5. Apply a thin coat of Gasket Maker, or equivalent, to the mating surfaces of the cylinder block and the crankcase (A, **Figure 278**).

6. Make sure the dowel pins are in place (B, **Figure 278**).

7. Install the crankcase onto the cylinder block.

8. Apply blue Loctite (No. 242) to the crankcase bolt threads prior to installation.

9. Install the 10 bolts (25 hp and C30) or 14 bolts (C40, C55) securing the crankcase. Tighten all 10 or 14 bolts to the specifications listed in **Table 1** in the sequence shown in the following illustrations:

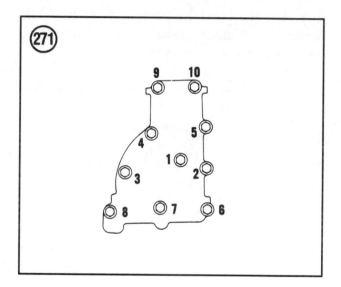

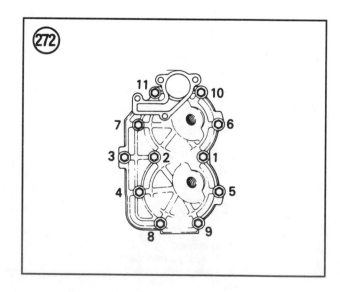

POWER HEAD (25 HP)

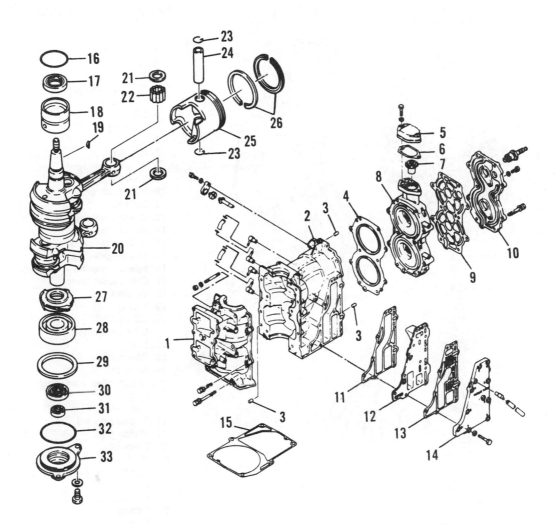

8

1. Crankcase
2. Cylinder block
3. Dowel pin
4. Gasket
5. Cover
6. Gasket
7. Thermostat
8. Cylinder head
9. Gasket
10. Cylinder head cover
11. Gasket

12. Exhaust inner cover
13. Gasket
14. Exhaust outer cover
15. Gasket
16. O-ring
17. Oil seal
18. Bearing
19. Woodruff key
20. Crankshaft assembly
21. Washer
22. Loose needle bearings

23. Clip
24. Piston pin
25. Piston
26. Piston ring set
27. Oil pump drive gear
28. Bearing
29. Washer
30. Oil seal
31. Oil seal
32. O-ring
33. Oil seal housing

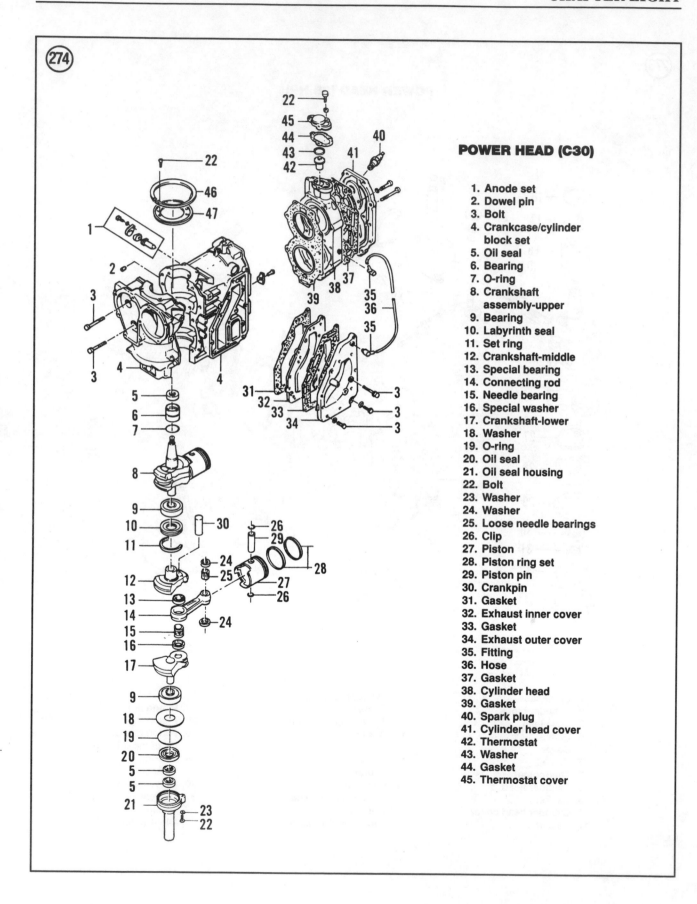

POWER HEAD (C30)

1. Anode set
2. Dowel pin
3. Bolt
4. Crankcase/cylinder block set
5. Oil seal
6. Bearing
7. O-ring
8. Crankshaft assembly-upper
9. Bearing
10. Labyrinth seal
11. Set ring
12. Crankshaft-middle
13. Special bearing
14. Connecting rod
15. Needle bearing
16. Special washer
17. Crankshaft-lower
18. Washer
19. O-ring
20. Oil seal
21. Oil seal housing
22. Bolt
23. Washer
24. Washer
25. Loose needle bearings
26. Clip
27. Piston
28. Piston ring set
29. Piston pin
30. Crankpin
31. Gasket
32. Exhaust inner cover
33. Gasket
34. Exhaust outer cover
35. Fitting
36. Hose
37. Gasket
38. Cylinder head
39. Gasket
40. Spark plug
41. Cylinder head cover
42. Thermostat
43. Washer
44. Gasket
45. Thermostat cover

POWER HEAD (C40)

275

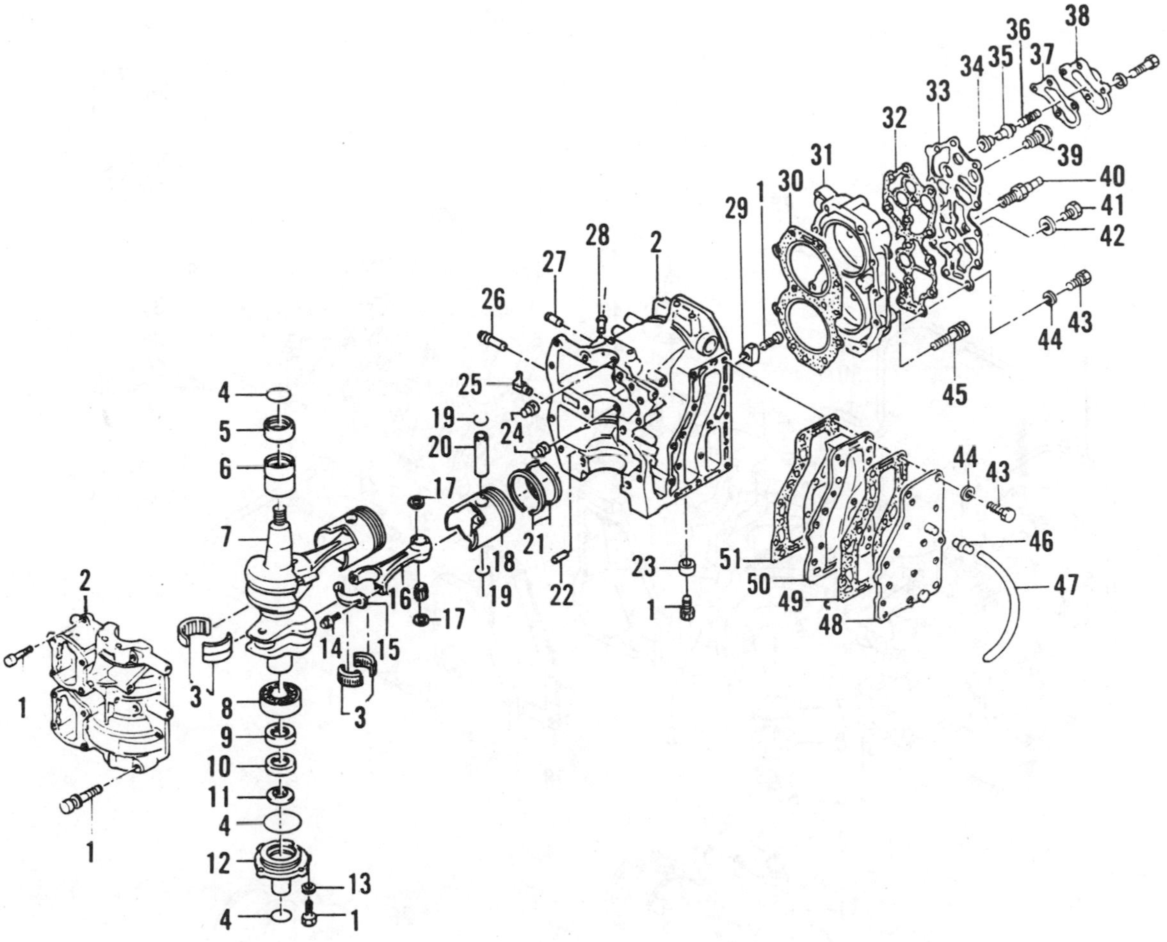

1. Bolt
2. Crankcase/cylinder
   block assembly
3. Bearing
4. O-ring
5. Oil seal
6. Bearing
7. Crankshaft
8. Bearing
9. Oil seal
10. Oil seal
11. Oil seal
12. Oil seal housing
13. Washer
14. Bolt
15. Connecting rod end cap
16. Connecting rod
17. Washer

18. Piston
19. Clip
20. Piston pin
21. Piston ring set
22. Locating pin
23. Plug
24. Screw
25. Fitting
26. Pin
27. Fitting
28. Fitting
29. Anode
30. Gasket
31. Cylinder head
32. Gasket
33. Cylinder head cover
34. Grommet

35. Pressure control valve
36. Spring
37. Gasket
38. Thermostat cover
39. Thermostat
40. Spark plug
41. Bolt
42. Washer
43. Bolt
44. Washer
45. Special bolt
46. Fitting
47. Hose
48. Exhaust outer cover
49. Gasket
50. Exhaust inner cover
51. Gasket

8

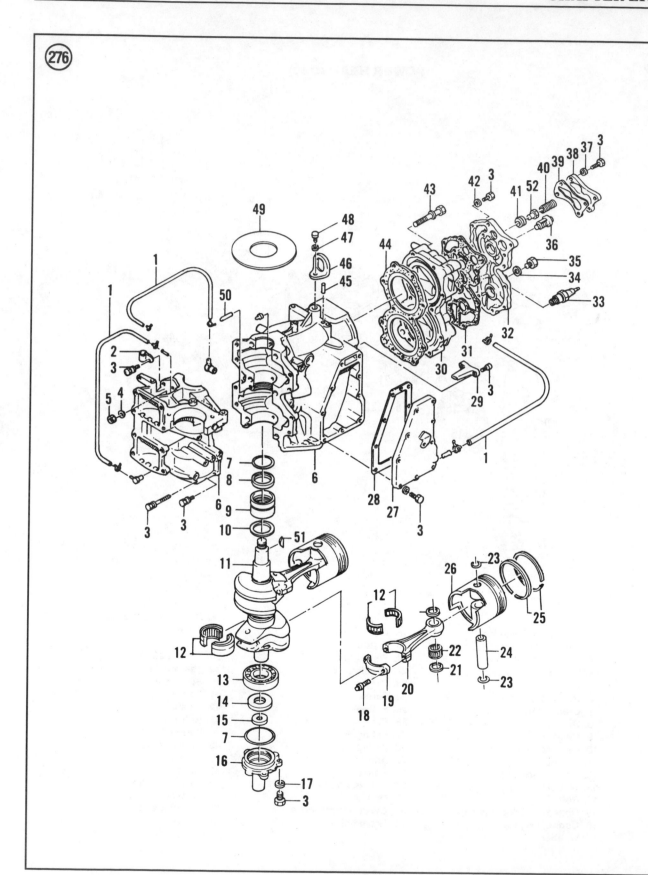

8

POWER HEAD (C55)

1. Recirculation hoses
2. Clamp
3. Bolt
4. Washer
5. Nut
6. Crankcase/cylinder block assembly
7. O-ring
8. Oil seal
9. Bearing
10. Washer
11. Crankshaft assembly
12. Roller bearing
13. Ball bearing
14. Oil seal
15. Oil seal
16. Oil seal housing
17. Washer
18. Bolt
19. Connecting rod end cap
20. Connecting rod
21. Washer
22. Loose needle bearings
23. Clip
24. Piston pin
25. Piston ring set
26. Piston

27. Exhaust cover
28. Gasket
29. Anode
30. Cylinder head
31. Gasket
32. Cylinder head cover
33. Spark plug
34. Washer
35. Bolt
36. Thermostat
37. Washer
38. Thermostat cover
39. Gasket
40. Spring
41. Grommet
42. Washer
43. Bolt
44. Gasket
45. Pin
46. Bracket
47. Washer
48. Bolt
49. Washer
50. Locating pin
51. Woodruff key
52. Pressure control valve

a. **Figure 279**: 25 hp.

b. **Figure 280**: C30.

c. **Figure 281**: C40.

d. **Figure 282**: C55.

10. Rotate the crankshaft several turns to check for binding. If the crankshaft does not turn easily, disassemble and correct the interference.

11A. On C55 engines, install the bolts and washers securing the oil seal housing installed in Step 2. Tighten the bolts securely.

11B. On all other engines, apply oil to the O-ring seal in the oil seal housing and apply grease to the mounting surface of the housing. Install the housing, the bolt(s) and washer(s) and tighten securely.

12A. On 25 hp and C30 engines, perform the following:

a. Assemble the cylinder head gasket, the cylinder head, the cylinder head cover gasket and the cylinder head on a workbench. Make sure all bolt holes are aligned.

b. Apply red Loctite (No. 271) to the cylinder head bolt threads prior to installation.

c. Install the cylinder head assembly onto the cylinder block.

d. Install the 10 bolts (25 hp) or 11 bolts (C30) securing the cylinder head. Tighten all 10 or 11 bolts to the specification listed in

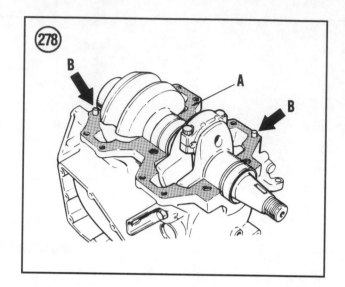

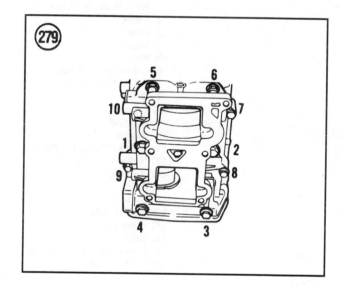

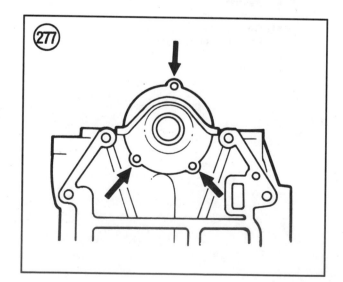

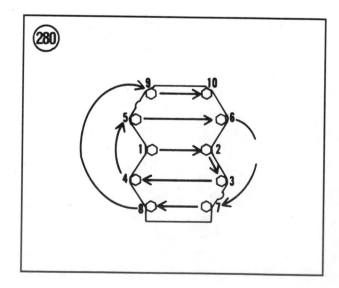

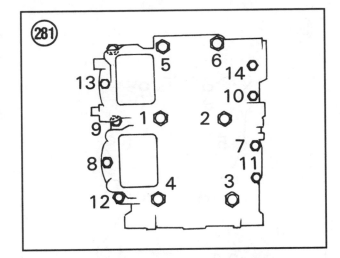

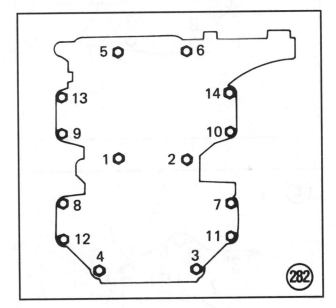

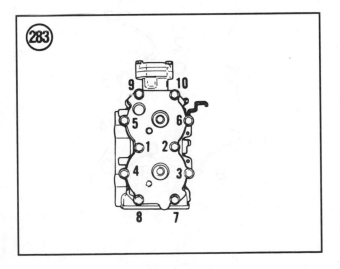

Table 1 in the sequence shown in **Figure 283** (25 hp) or **Figure 284** (C30).

12B. On C40 hp engines, perform the following:

a. Apply red Loctite (No. 271) to the cylinder head and cylinder head cover bolt threads prior to installation.

b. Install the cylinder head gasket and the cylinder head onto the cylinder head. Make sure all bolt holes align.

c. Install the bolts securing the cylinder head—do not tighten at this time.

d. Install the cylinder head cover gasket and the cylinder head cover onto the cylinder head. Make sure all bolt holes align.

e. Install the bolts securing the cylinder head cover.

f. Tighten the 11 bolts securing the cylinder head cover and cylinder head to specifica-

8

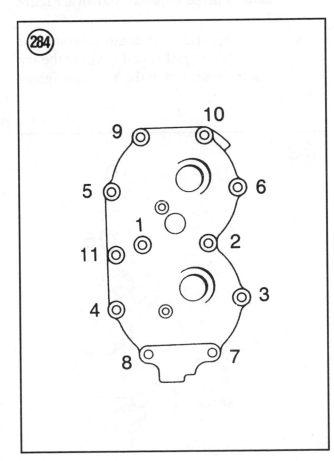

tion in **Table 1** in the sequence shown in **Figure 285**.

12C. On C55 hp engines, perform the following:

a. Apply red Loctite (No. 271) to the cylinder head and cylinder head cover bolt threads prior to installation.

b. Install the cylinder head gasket and the cylinder head onto the cylinder head. Make sure all bolt holes align.

c. Install the 10 bolts securing the cylinder head and tighten to the specification listed in **Table 1** in the sequence shown in **Figure 286**.

d. Install the cylinder head cover gasket and the cylinder head cover onto the cylinder head. Make sure all bolt holes align.

e. Install the bolts securing the cylinder head cover and tighten to the specification listed in **Table 1** in the sequence shown in **Figure 287**.

13A. On 25 hp and C30 engines, install the thermostat, washer, gasket and cover to the top of the cylinder head. Install the bolts and tighten securely.

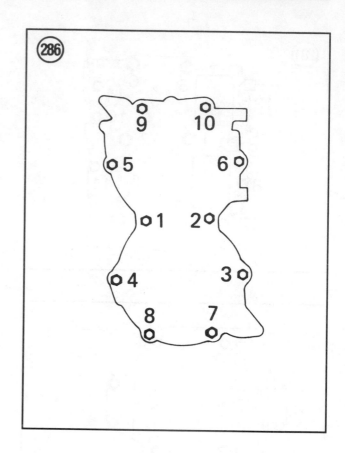

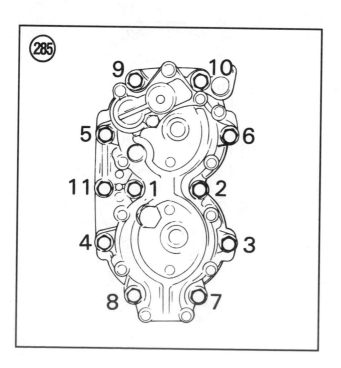

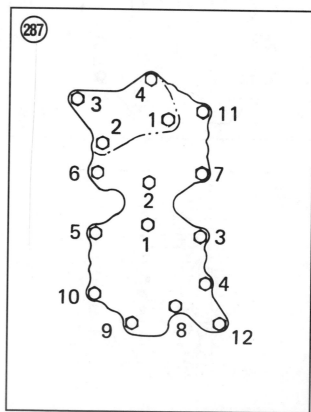

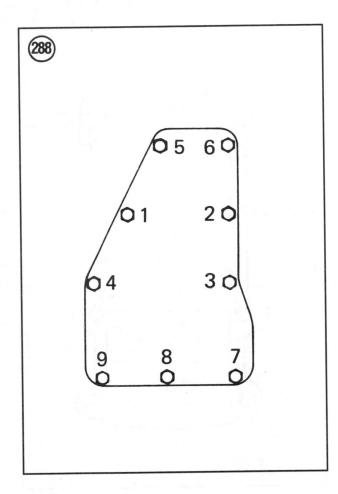

13B. On C40 and C55 engines, install the thermostat, washer, gasket and cover to the front of the cylinder head. Install the bolts and on C40 engines, tighten securely. On C55 engines, tighten to the specification listed in **Table 1**.

14A. On C55 engines, perform the following:

    a. Apply red Loctite (No. 271) to the exhaust cover bolt threads prior to installation.

    b. Install the exhaust cover gasket and exhaust cover.

    c. Install the 9 exhaust cover bolts and tighten to the specification listed in **Table 1** in the sequence shown in **Figure 288**.

14B. On all other models, perform the following:

    a. Apply red Loctite (No. 271) to the exhaust cover bolt threads prior to installation.

    b. Install the gasket, inner cover, gasket and outer cover. Make sure all bolt holes align.

    c. Install the bolts and washers securing the exhaust cover and tighten to the specification listed in **Table 1** in the sequence shown in the following illustrations:

    1. **Figure 289**: 25 hp engine.

    2. **Figure 290**: C30 engine.

8

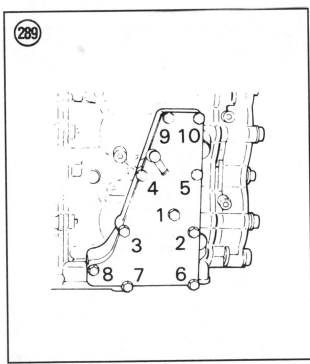

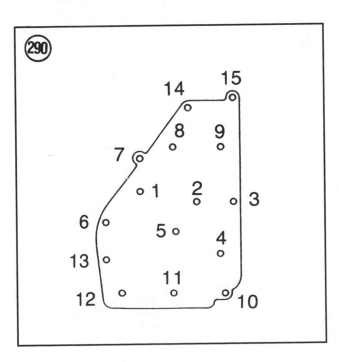

3. **Figure 291**: C40 engine.

15. Connect the hose to the exhaust cover fitting.

16A. On C55 engines, perform the following:

   a. Install the gasket, reed valves, gasket and the 2 intake manifolds onto the crankcase studs gaskets.

   b. Install the carburetors. See Chapter Six.

   c. Install the carburetor/reed valve assembly mounting nuts and lockwashers. Tighten the nuts to the specification listed in **Table 1** following the sequence shown in **Figure 292**.

16B. On all other models, perform the following:

   a. Install the gasket(s), reed valve assembly and intake manifold.

   b. Install the intake manifold/reed valve mounting bolts and washers. Tighten the bolts to the specification listed in **Table 1** following the sequence shown in **Figure 293** (25 hp), **Figure 294** (C30) or **Figure 295** (C40).

17. Connect the crankcase upper circulation line to the fitting on the cylinder block.

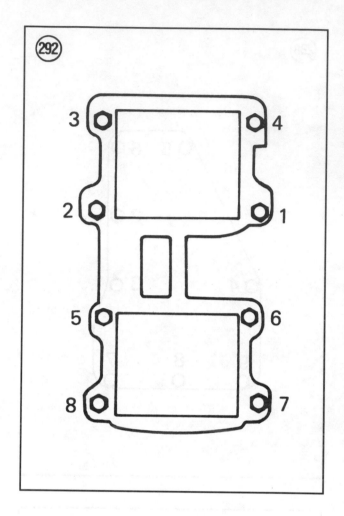

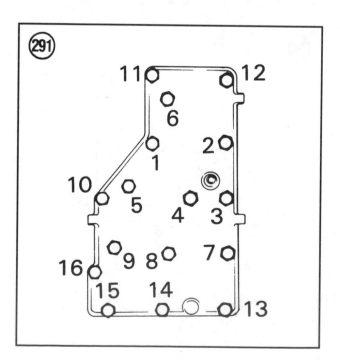

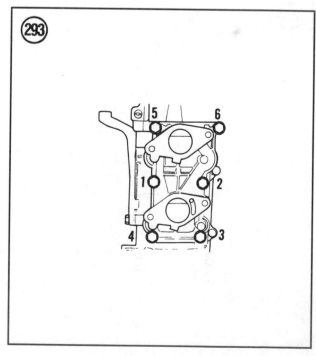

18. On all models except C55, install the carburetors. See Chapter Six.

19. Install the flywheel as described in this chapter.

20. Install the power head as described in this chapter.

All 3-cylinder Engines

Refer to the following illustrations for this procedure:

    a. **Figure 296**: 30 hp.

    b. **Figure 297**: 40 hp and Pro 50.

    c. **Figure 298**: Pro 60 and 70 hp.

    d. **Figure 299**: C75, C85 and 90 hp.

1. Refer to *Assembly Tips* at the beginning of this section.

2. Install the oil seal housing as follows:

    a. Apply a light coat of grease to the oil seal housing O-rings and oil seal lips. Pack the

oil seal lip and outer surface of the O-ring with grease.

    b. Install the oil seal housing into the cylinder block and align the mounting bolt holes (**Figure 300**).

3. Install the crankshaft and piston assembly as described in this chapter.

4. Apply a liberal quantity of oil to the connecting rods big end.

5. Apply a thin coat of Gasket Maker, or equivalent, to the mating surfaces of the cylinder block and the crankcase (A, **Figure 301**).

6. Make sure the dowel pins are in place (B, **Figure 301**).

7. Install the crankcase onto the cylinder block.

8. Apply blue Loctite (No. 242) to the crankcase bolt threads prior to installation.

9. Install the 14 bolts (30 hp, 40 hp, 50 hp, Pro 60, 70 hp) or 20 bolts (75 hp, 85 hp, 90 hp) securing the crankcase. Tighten all bolts to the specification listed in **Table 1** in the sequence shown in the following illustrations:

    a. **Figure 302**: 30 hp, Pro 60, 70 hp engine.

    b. **Figure 303**: 40 hp, Pro 50 engine.

    c. **Figure 304**: C75, 85 hp, 90 hp engine.

8

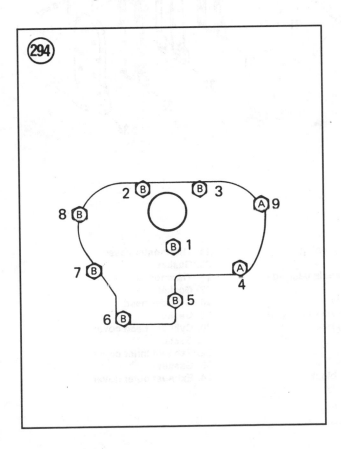

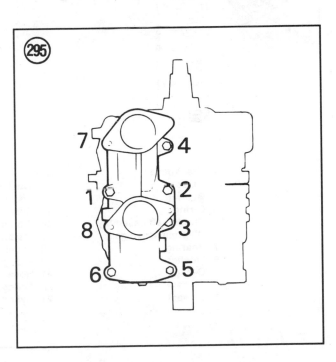

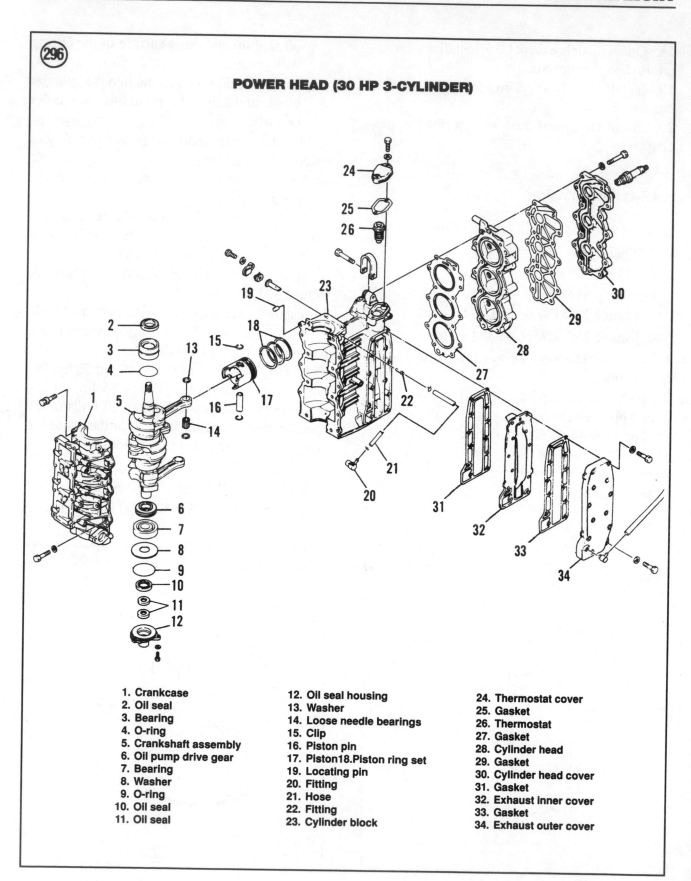

POWER HEAD (30 HP 3-CYLINDER)

1. Crankcase
2. Oil seal
3. Bearing
4. O-ring
5. Crankshaft assembly
6. Oil pump drive gear
7. Bearing
8. Washer
9. O-ring
10. Oil seal
11. Oil seal

12. Oil seal housing
13. Washer
14. Loose needle bearings
15. Clip
16. Piston pin
17. Piston
18. Piston ring set
19. Locating pin
20. Fitting
21. Hose
22. Fitting
23. Cylinder block

24. Thermostat cover
25. Gasket
26. Thermostat
27. Gasket
28. Cylinder head
29. Gasket
30. Cylinder head cover
31. Gasket
32. Exhaust inner cover
33. Gasket
34. Exhaust outer cover

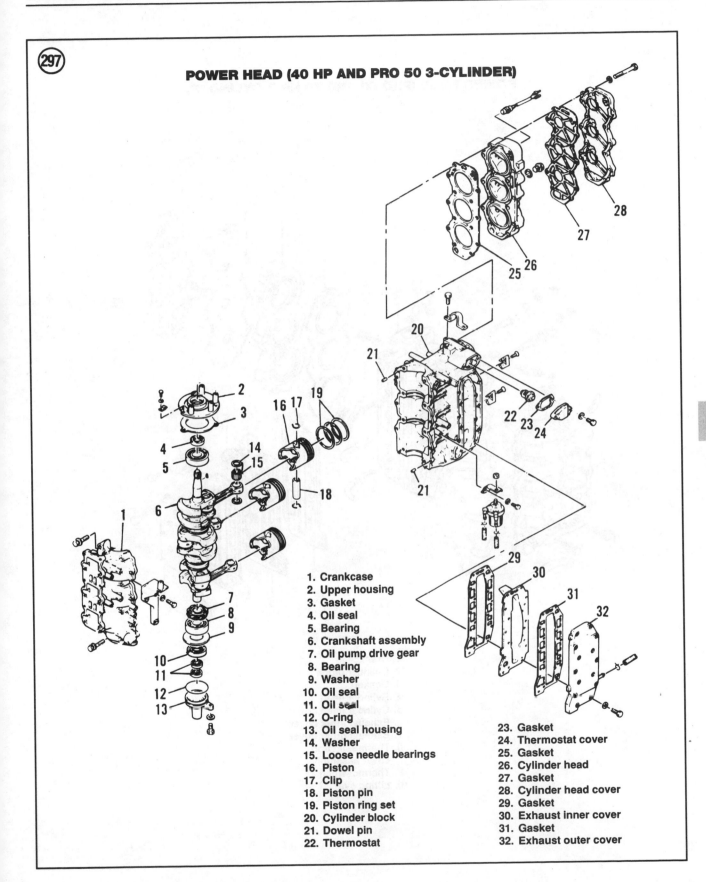

POWER HEAD (40 HP AND PRO 50 3-CYLINDER)

1. Crankcase
2. Upper housing
3. Gasket
4. Oil seal
5. Bearing
6. Crankshaft assembly
7. Oil pump drive gear
8. Bearing
9. Washer
10. Oil seal
11. Oil seal
12. O-ring
13. Oil seal housing
14. Washer
15. Loose needle bearings
16. Piston
17. Clip
18. Piston pin
19. Piston ring set
20. Cylinder block
21. Dowel pin
22. Thermostat
23. Gasket
24. Thermostat cover
25. Gasket
26. Cylinder head
27. Gasket
28. Cylinder head cover
29. Gasket
30. Exhaust inner cover
31. Gasket
32. Exhaust outer cover

8

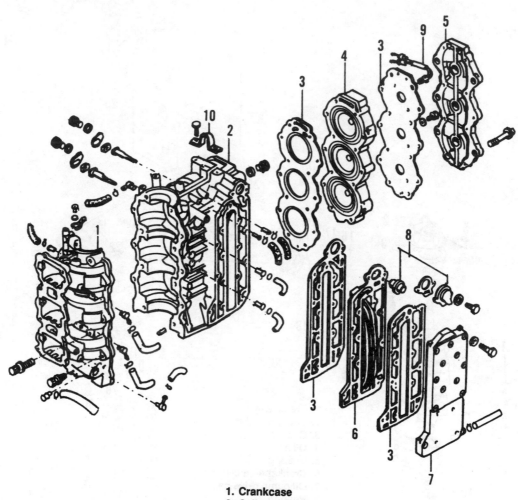

POWER HEAD (PRO 60 AND 70 HP 3-CYLINDER)

1. Crankcase
2. Cylinder block
3. Gasket
4. Cylinder head
5. Cylinder head cover
6. Exhaust inner cover
7. Exhaust outer cover
8. Thermostat and
   cover assembly
9. Thermoswitch
10. Lifting eye

POWER HEAD (C75, C85 AND 90 HP 3-CYLINDER)

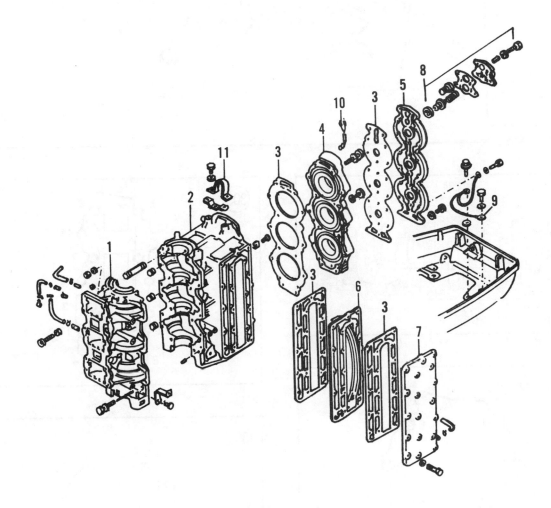

8

1. Crankcase
2. Cylinder block
3. Gasket
4. Cylinder head
5. Cylinder head cover
6. Exhaust inner cover
7. Exhaust outer cover
8. Thermostat and
   cover assembly
9. Ground lead
10. Thermoswitch
11. Lifting eye

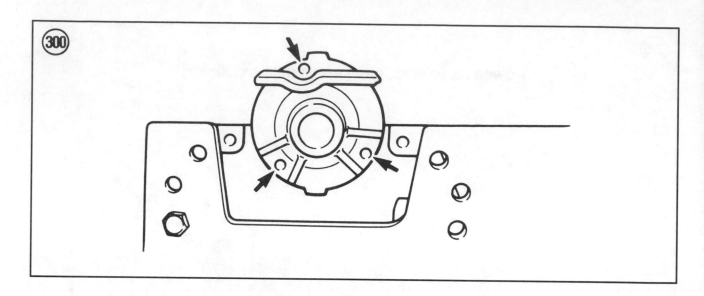

(300)

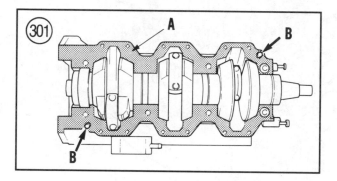

(301)

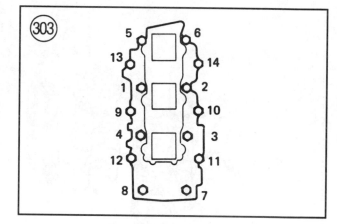

(303)

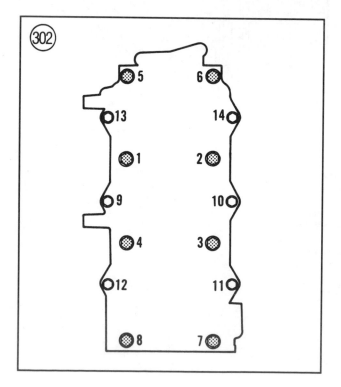

(302)

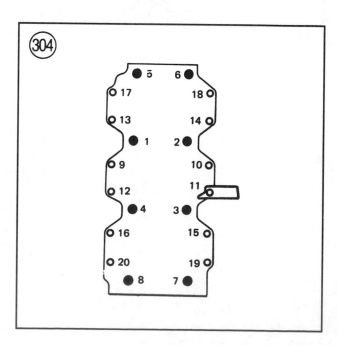

(304)

10. Rotate the crankshaft several turns to check for binding. If the crankshaft does not turn easily, disassemble and correct the interference.

11. Install the bolts and washers that secure the oil seal housing installed in Step 2. Tighten the bolts securely.

12A. On 30-70 hp and Pro 60 engines, perform the following:

    a. Assemble the cylinder head gasket, the cylinder head, the cylinder head cover gasket and the cylinder head on a workbench. Make sure all bolt holes are aligned.

    b. On 40 hp and Pro 50 engines, install the 4 bolts and washers securing the cylinder head cover and gasket to the cylinder block. Tighten the bolts securely.

    c. Apply red Loctite (No. 271) to the cylinder head bolt threads prior to installation.

    d. Install the cylinder head assembly onto the cylinder block.

    e. Install the 14 bolts that secure the cylinder head. Tighten the bolts to the specifications listed in **Table 1** in the sequence shown in the following illustrations: **Figure 305** (30 hp, 40 hp, Pro 50) or **Figure 306** (Pro 60, 70 hp, C75, C85 and 90 hp).

12B. On C75, C85 and 90 hp, perform the following:

    a. Apply red Loctite (No. 271) to the cylinder head and cylinder head cover bolt threads prior to installation.

    b. Install the cylinder head gasket and cylinder head on the cylinder block.

    c. Install the 14 bolts that secure the cylinder head. Tighten the bolts to the specifications listed in **Table 1** in the sequence shown in **Figure 305**.

    d. Install the cylinder head cover gasket and cylinder head cover on the cylinder head.

    e. Install the 22 bolts that secure the cylinder head cover. Tighten the bolts to the specifi-

8

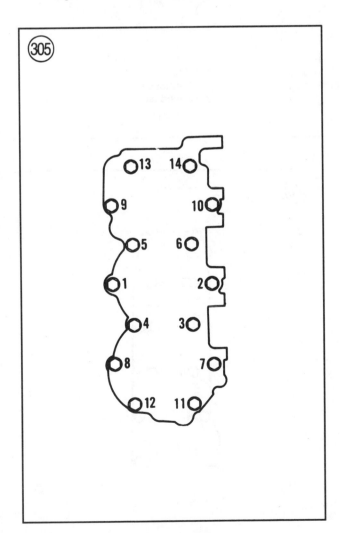

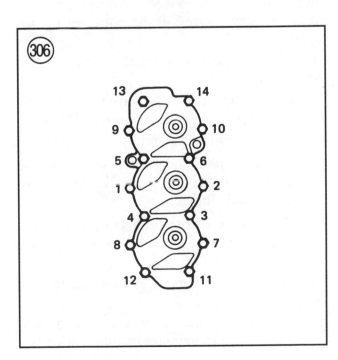

cation listed in **Table 1** in the sequence shown in **Figure 307**.

13A. On 30-50 hp engines, install the thermostat, washer, gasket and cover top of the cylinder block. Install the bolts and tighten securely.

13B. On C75, C85 and 90 hp engines, install the thermostat, washer, gasket and cover to the front of the cylinder head. Install the bolts and tighten securely.

14. To install the exhaust cover, perform the following:

a. Apply red Loctite (No. 271) to the exhaust cover bolt threads prior to installation.

b. Install the gasket, inner cover, gasket and outer cover. Make sure all bolt holes align.

c. Install the bolts and washers that secure the exhaust cover and tighten to the specification listed in **Table 1** in the sequence shown in the following illustrations:

1. **Figure 308**: 30 hp.
2. **Figure 309**: 40 hp and Pro 50.
3. **Figure 310**: Pro 60 and 70 hp.
4. **Figure 311**: C75, C85 and 90 hp.

15. On Pro 60 and 70 hp engines, install the thermostat, washer, gasket and cover to the exhaust inner cover. Install the bolts and tighten securely.

16. Connect the hose onto the exhaust cover fitting.

17A. On 30 hp engines, perform the following:

a. Install the reed valve assembly, gasket and intake manifold assembly.

b. Install the bolts and washers that secure the intake manifold and reed valve assembly to the cylinder block.

c. Tighten the bolt to the specification listed in **Table 1** in the sequence shown in **Figure 312**.

17B. On all other engines, perform the following:

a. Install the reed valve assembly, gasket, plate, gasket and intake manifold assembly.

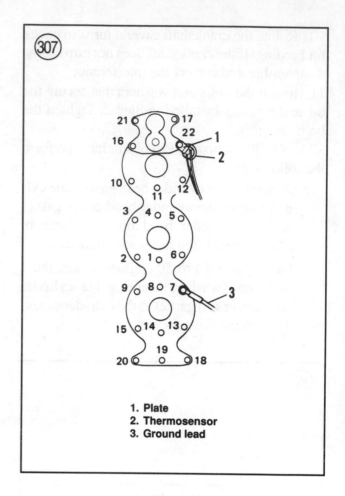

1. Plate
2. Thermosensor
3. Ground lead

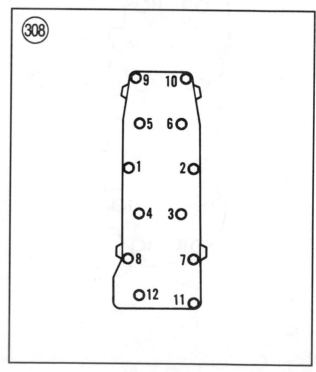

b. Install the bolts and washer securing the intake manifold and reed valve assembly to the cylinder block.

c. Tighten the bolt to specifications in **Table 1** in the crisscross pattern.

18. Connect the crankcase upper circulation lines to the fittings on the cylinder block.

19. Install the carburetors. See Chapter Six.

20. Install the flywheel as described in this chapter.

21. Install the power head as described in this chapter.

V4 and 90° V6 Models

Refer to the following illustrations for this procedure:

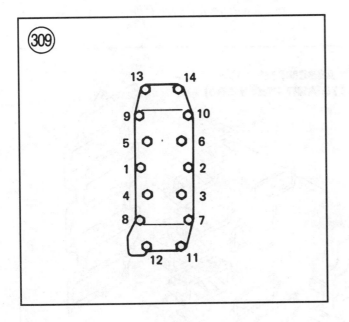

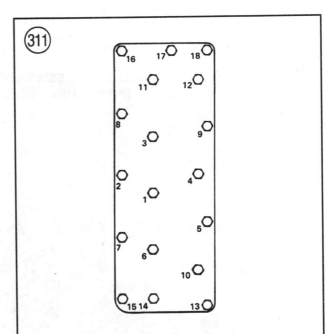

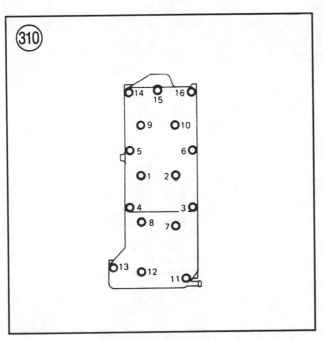

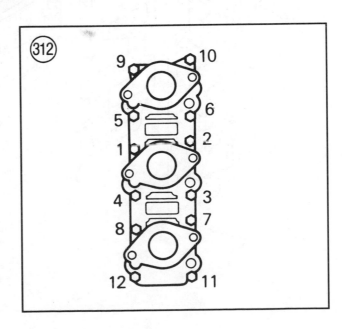

a. **Figure 313**: Intake manifold and reed valve assembly (Pro V 150, Pro V 175 and Pro V 200).

b. **Figure 314**: Engine components (all models) and intake manifolds and reed valve assembly (115-225 hp except Pro V 150, Pro V 175 and Pro V 200).

NOTE
Cover the workbench surface with a flat sheet of heavy rubber or piece of clean

masonite to protect all sealing surfaces of the engine. The work bench must also be level so that the power head will be stable during the assembly procedure.

CAUTION
When the power head is completely assembled, it will be very heavy and also very tall and top heavy during the final part of the assembly procedure. When tightening bolts, hold the power head so that it will not fall over. If necessary, have

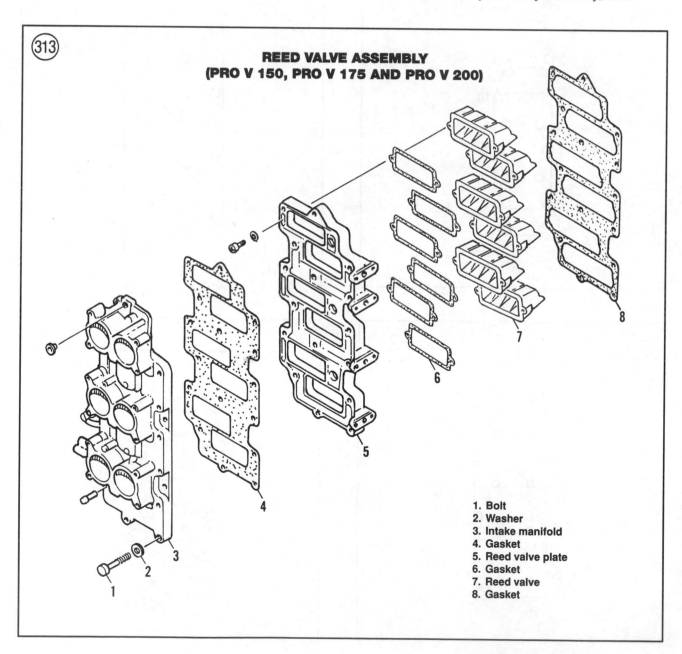

REED VALVE ASSEMBLY
(PRO V 150, PRO V 175 AND PRO V 200)

1. Bolt
2. Washer
3. Intake manifold
4. Gasket
5. Reed valve plate
6. Gasket
7. Reed valve
8. Gasket

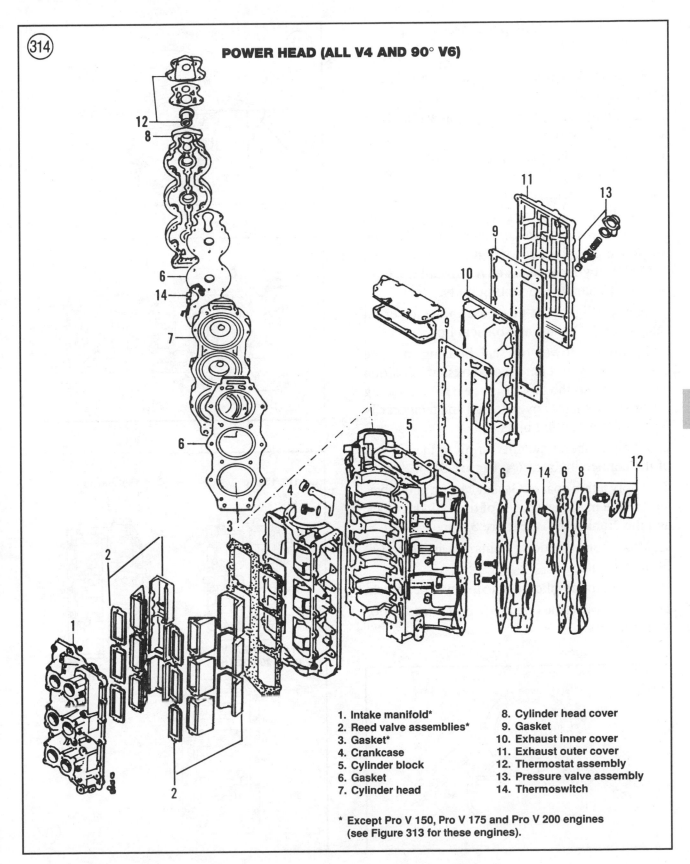

POWER HEAD (ALL V4 AND 90° V6)

8

1. Intake manifold*
2. Reed valve assemblies*
3. Gasket*
4. Crankcase
5. Cylinder block
6. Gasket
7. Cylinder head
8. Cylinder head cover
9. Gasket
10. Exhaust inner cover
11. Exhaust outer cover
12. Thermostat assembly
13. Pressure valve assembly
14. Thermoswitch

* Except Pro V 150, Pro V 175 and Pro V 200 engines
(see Figure 313 for these engines).

an assistant hold the power head to help steady the assembly.

1. Refer to *Assembly Tips* at the beginning of this section.

2. Install the crankshaft and piston assembly as described in this chapter.

3. Apply a light coat of grease to the upper bearing housing O-rings and oil seal lips. Pack the oil seal lip with grease.

4. Install the upper bearing housing into the cylinder block and onto the crankshaft. Position the housing so the arrow (**Figure 315**) is facing toward the cylinder block cover. Install and temporarily tighten the mounting bolts.

5. Apply a light coat of grease to the lower oil seal housing O-rings and oil seal lips.

6. Install the lower oil seal housing into the cylinder block and onto the crankshaft. Position the housing so the tabs (**Figure 316**) are facing toward the exhaust cover. Install and temporarily tighten the mounting bolts.

7. Apply a liberal quantity of oil to the big end of the connecting rods (A, **Figure 317**).

8. Apply a thin coat of Gasket Maker, or equivalent, to the mating surfaces of the cylinder block and the crankcase (B, **Figure 317**).

9. Make sure the dowel pins are in place (C, **Figure 317**).

10. Install the crankcase onto the cylinder block.

11. Apply oil to the crankcase bolt threads prior to installation.

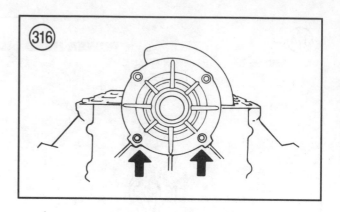

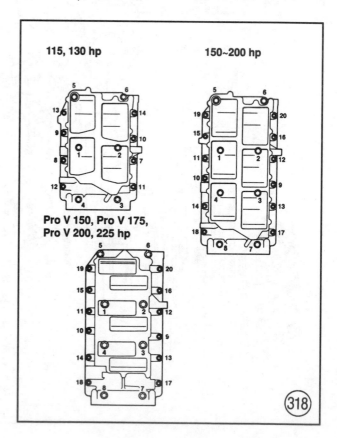

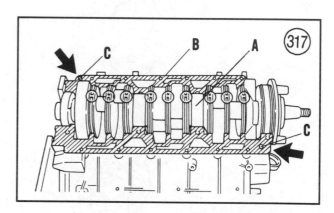

115, 130 hp   150~200 hp

Pro V 150, Pro V 175, Pro V 200, 225 hp

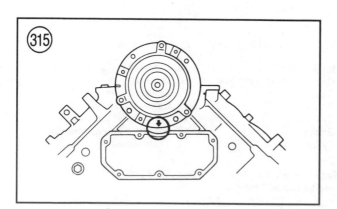

12. Install the 15 bolts (V4 engines), or 20 bolts (V6 engines) that secure the crankcase. Tighten the bolts to the specifications listed in **Table 1** in the sequence shown in **Figure 318**.

13. Rotate the crankshaft several turns to check for binding. If the crankshaft does not turn easily, disassemble and correct the interference.

14. Tighten the bolts that secure the upper bearing housing and lower oil seal housing to the

specifications listed in **Table 1** in a crisscross pattern.

15. To install the oil pump driven gear, refer to **Figure 319** and perform the following:

   a. Apply oil to the driven gear, install the driven gear (1, **Figure 319**) into the cylinder block and rotate it slowly to engage it with the drive gear on the crankshaft. Push it in all the way.

   b. Install the washer (2, **Figure 319**), O-ring (3) and collar (4) into the cylinder block.

16. Install the 2 new anodes and bolts in the top of the water jackets located on each side of the cylinder block.

17. Refer to **Figure 320**, perform the following:

   a. Apply red Loctite (No. 271) to the cylinder head and cylinder head cover bolt threads prior to installation.

   b. Install the cylinder head gasket (1, **Figure 320**) and cylinder head (2) on the cylinder block.

   c. Install the 10 bolts (V4 engines) or 14 bolts (V6 engines) securing the cylinder head. Tighten all bolts to the specifications listed in **Table 1** in the sequence shown in **Figure 321** for 115 and 130 hp or **Figure 322** for 150-225 hp engines.

   d. Screw the thermoswitch (3, **Figure 320**) into the cylinder head.

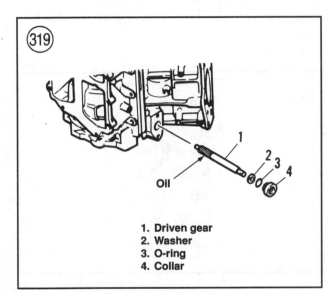

(319)

Oil

1. Driven gear
2. Washer
3. O-ring
4. Collar

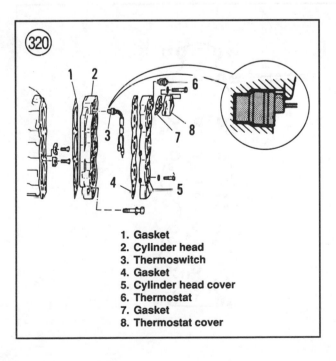

(320)

1. Gasket
2. Cylinder head
3. Thermoswitch
4. Gasket
5. Cylinder head cover
6. Thermostat
7. Gasket
8. Thermostat cover

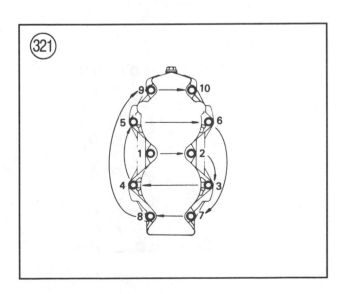

(321)

e. Install the cylinder head cover gasket (4, **Figure 320**) and cylinder head cover (5) on the cylinder head.

f. Install the 16 bolts (V4 engines) or 22 bolts (V6 engines) that secure the cylinder head. Tighten all bolts to the specifications listed in **Table 1** in the sequence shown in **Figure 323**.

g. Repeat for the other cylinder head assembly.

18. Install the thermostat (6, **Figure 320**), gasket (7) and the thermostat cover (8) to the side of the cylinder head outer cover. Install the bolts and tighten securely. Repeat for the other cylinder head cover.

19. Install the exhaust cover inner gasket, the inner cover, gasket and outer cover onto the cylinder block. Install the bolts and tighten to the specifications listed in **Table 1** in the sequence shown in **Figure 324**.

20. Install the water bypass valve as follows:

a. Install the grommet into the exhaust outer cover.

b. Position the valve with the longest portion going into the cover and install the valve.

c. Install the spring, new gasket and cover.

d. Install the cover bolts and washers and tighten securely.

e. Connect the hose to the bypass cover.

21. Install a new gasket and the cylinder block cover onto the top of the cylinder block. Install the bolts and any hose clamps noted during removal. Tighten the bolts securely.

22A. On 115-130 hp engines, perform the following:

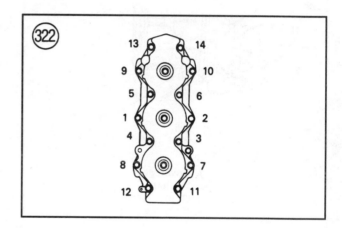

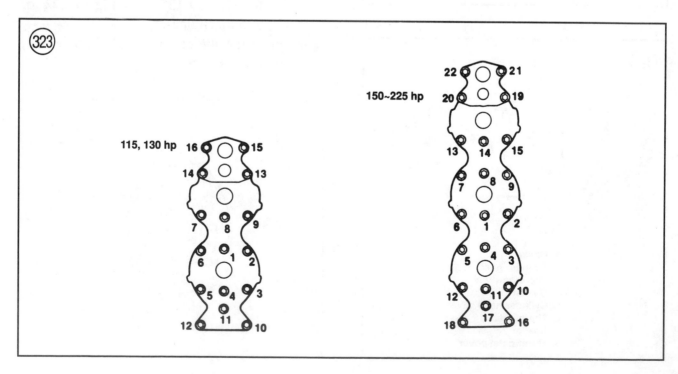

a. Install the reed valve assembly, gasket and intake manifold assembly.

b. Install the bolts and washer that secure the intake manifold and reed valve assembly to the cylinder block.

c. Tighten the bolts to specifications listed in **Table 1** in the sequence shown in **Figure 325**.

22B. On 150-225 hp engines, perform the following:

a. Install the reed valve assembly, gasket, plate, gasket and intake manifold assembly.

b. Install the bolts and washer securing the intake manifold and reed valve assembly to the cylinder block.

c. Tighten the bolt to specifications in **Table 1** in the sequence shown in **Figure 326**.

23. Connect the crankcase upper circulation lines to the fittings on the cylinder block as

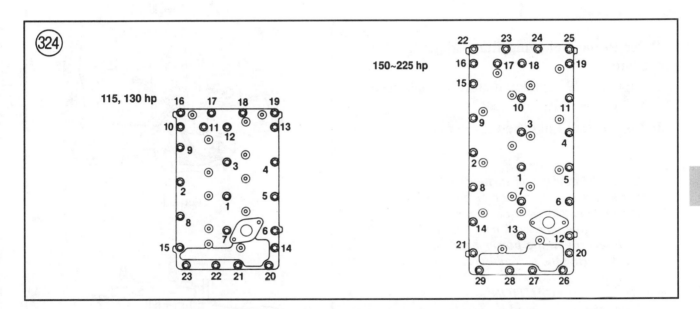

8

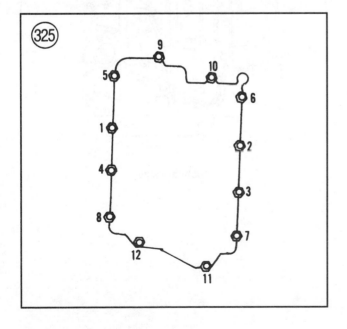

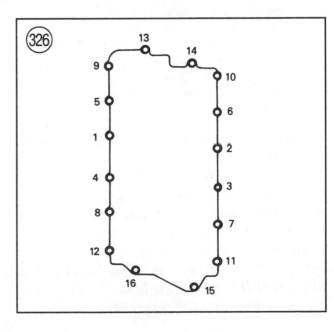

shown in **Figure 327** for 115-130 hp engines or **Figure 328** for 150-225 hp engines.

24. Install the engine stop on each side of the cylinder block and tighten the bolts securely.

25. Install the carburetors. See Chapter Six.

26. Install the flywheel as described in this chapter.

27. Install the power head as described in this chapter.

All 76° V6 Engines

Refer to the following illustrations for this procedure:

a. **Figure 329**: Intake manifolds and reed valve assembly.

b. **Figure 330**: Engine components.

NOTE
Cover the workbench surface with a flat sheet of heavy rubber or piece of clean masonite to protect all sealing surfaces of the engine. The work bench must also be level so that the power head will be stable during the assembly procedure.

CAUTION
When the power head is completely assembled, it will be very heavy and also very tall and top heavy during the final part of the assembly procedure. When tightening the bolts, hold the power head so that it will not fall over. If necessary, have an assistant hold the power head to help steady the assembly.

1. Refer to *Assembly Tips* at the beginning of this section.

2. Install the crankshaft and piston assembly as described in this chapter.

3. Apply a light coat of grease to the lower oil seal housing O-rings and oil seal lips.

4. Install the lower bearing housing into the cylinder block and onto the crankshaft. Install 2 of the bolts (**Figure 331**) to hold the assembly in place. Do not tighten at this time.

115-130 HP

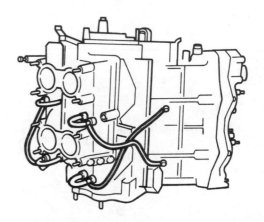

Port side

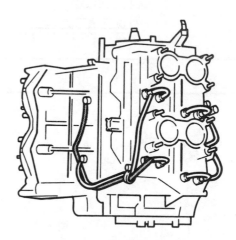

Starboard side

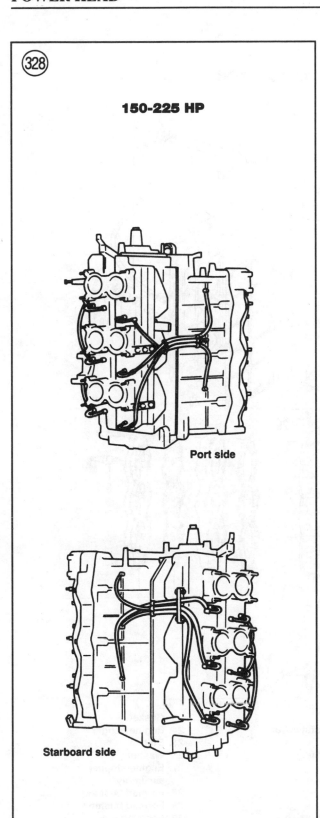

328

150-225 HP

Port side

Starboard side

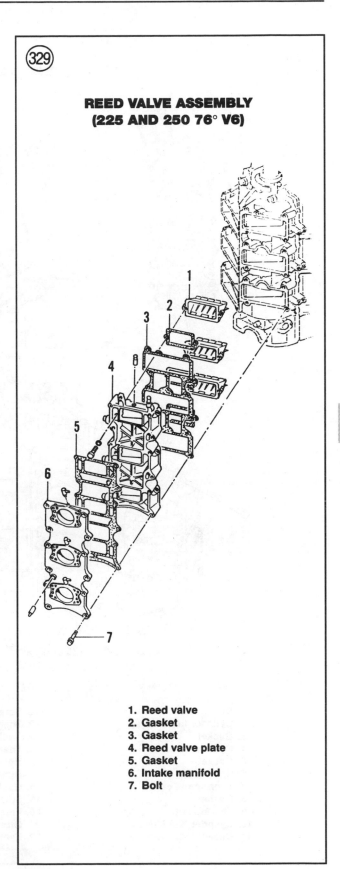

329

**REED VALVE ASSEMBLY
(225 AND 250 76° V6)**

1. Reed valve
2. Gasket
3. Gasket
4. Reed valve plate
5. Gasket
6. Intake manifold
7. Bolt

8

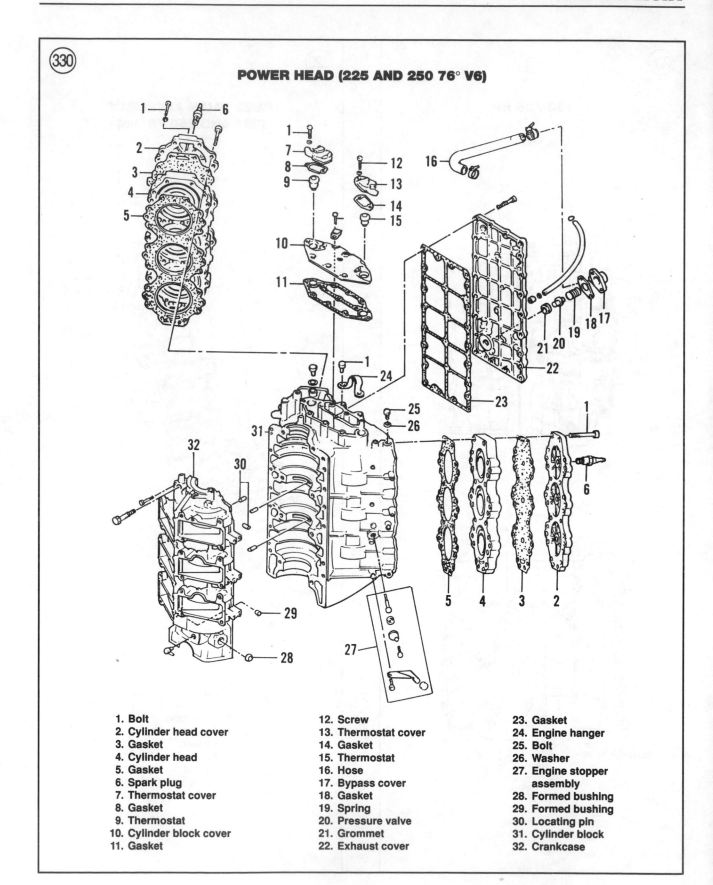

POWER HEAD (225 AND 250 76° V6)

1. Bolt	12. Screw	23. Gasket
2. Cylinder head cover	13. Thermostat cover	24. Engine hanger
3. Gasket	14. Gasket	25. Bolt
4. Cylinder head	15. Thermostat	26. Washer
5. Gasket	16. Hose	27. Engine stopper
6. Spark plug	17. Bypass cover	assembly
7. Thermostat cover	18. Gasket	28. Formed bushing
8. Gasket	19. Spring	29. Formed bushing
9. Thermostat	20. Pressure valve	30. Locating pin
10. Cylinder block cover	21. Grommet	31. Cylinder block
11. Gasket	22. Exhaust cover	32. Crankcase

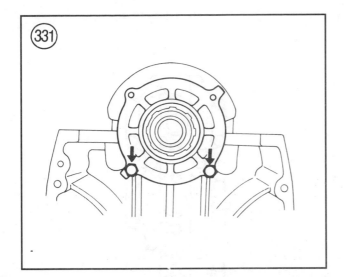

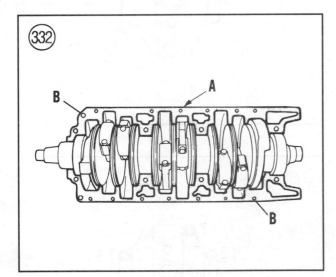

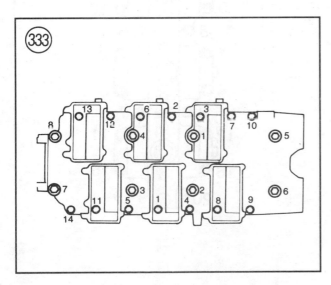

5. Apply a liberal quantity of oil to the big end of the sealing rings.

6. Apply a thin coat of Gasket Maker, or equivalent, to the mating surfaces of the cylinder block and the crankcase (A, **Figure 332**).

7. Make sure the dowel pins are in place (B, **Figure 332**).

8. Install the crankcase onto the cylinder block.

9. Apply oil to the crankcase bolt threads prior to installation.

10. Install the 14 bolts that secure the crankcase. Tighten the bolts to the specification listed in **Table 1** in the sequence shown in **Figure 333**.

11. Rotate the crankshaft several turns to check for binding. If the crankshaft does not turn easily, disassemble and correct the interference.

12. Install the remaining bolts. Tighten the 4 bolts that secure the lower oil seal housing securely in a crisscross pattern (**Figure 334**).

13. On the work bench, assemble the cylinder head assembly as follows:

   a. Place the cylinder head cover gasket on the cylinder head.

   b. Apply red Loctite (No. 271) to the cylinder head cover bolt threads prior to installation.

   c. Install the cylinder head cover on this assembly and install the 6 bolts. Tighten the

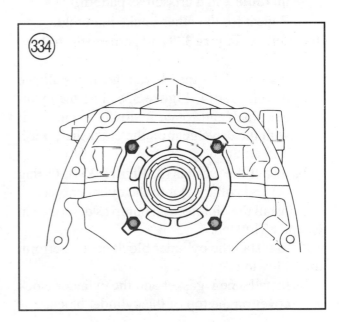

bolts to the specifications listed in **Table 1** in the sequence shown in **Figure 335**.

d. Apply oil to the cylinder head bolt threads and lower bolt head face prior to installation.

e. Install the cylinder head gasket on the cylinder block and install the cylinder head and cylinder head cover assembly onto the gasket.

f. Install the 20 bolts that secure the cylinder head. Tighten the bolts to the specification listed in **Table 1** in the sequence shown in **Figure 336**.

g. Repeat for the other cylinder head assembly.

14. Install the exhaust cover gasket and cover onto the cylinder block. Install the bolts and tighten to the specification listed in **Table 1** in the sequence shown in **Figure 337**.

15. To install the reed valve assembly, perform the following:

a. Install the reed valve assembly, gasket, plate, gasket and intake manifold assembly.

b. Install the bolts and washer that secure the intake manifold and reed valve assembly to the cylinder block.

c. Tighten the bolts to the specification listed in **Table 1** in a crisscross pattern.

d. Repeat for the other intake manifold.

16. Refer to **Figure 338** and perform the following:

a. Apply oil to the driven gear, install the driven gear (4, **Figure 338**) into the cylinder block and rotate it slowly to engage it with the drive gear on the crankshaft. Push it in all the way.

b. Install the washer (3, **Figure 338**), O-ring (2) and collar (1) into the cylinder block.

17. Install the oil injection pump as described in Chapter Thirteen.

18. To install the cylinder block cover, perform the following:

a. Install a new gasket and the cylinder block cover on the top of the cylinder block.

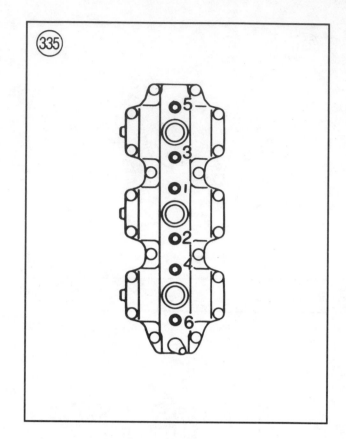

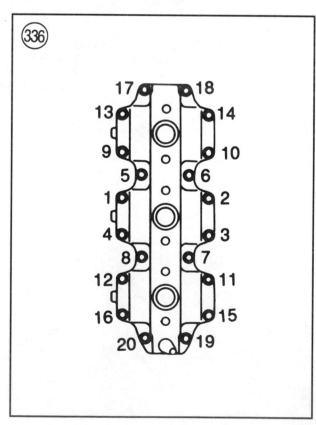

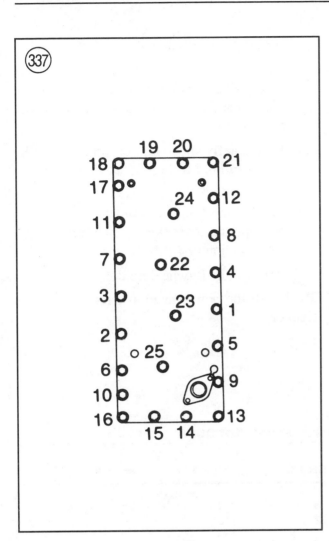

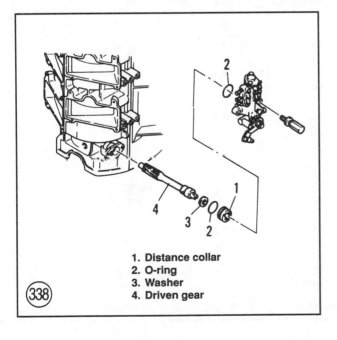

1. **Distance collar**
2. **O-ring**
3. **Washer**
4. **Driven gear**

b. Apply red Loctite (No. 271) to the cylinder block cover and thermostat cover bolt threads prior to installation.

c. Install the cover bolts and hose clamps under the bolts as noted during removal. Tighten the bolts securely in a crisscross pattern.

d. Install both thermostats, new gaskets and thermostat covers. Install the bolts and tighten securely.

e. Install the engine hanger and bolts and tighten securely.

19. Install the water bypass valve as follows:

a. Install the grommet into the exhaust outer cover.

b. Install the valve, the spring, new gasket and cover.

c. Apply red Loctite (No. 271) to the valve cover bolt threads prior to installation.

d. Install the cover bolts and washers and tighten securely.

e. Connect the hose to the bypass cover. Make sure the hose clamp is secure.

20. Install the anode, grommet, cover and bolt on both sides of the cylinder block and on the cylinder head covers. Tighten the bolts securely.

21. Install the engine stop on each side of the cylinder block and tighten the bolts securely.

22. Connect the crankcase circulation lines to the fittings on the scavenger ports and intake manifold (A, **Figure 339**) and from the upper bearing to the lower bearing (B, **Figure 339**).

8

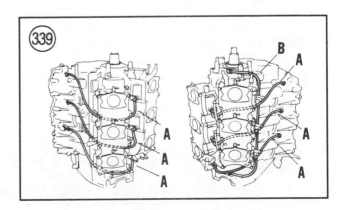

23. Install the carburetors. See Chapter Six.

24. Install the flywheel as described in this chapter.

25. To install the torsional damper onto the lower end of the crankshaft, proceed as follows:

a. Remove all foreign material from the crankshaft taper and the taper within the torsional damper.

CAUTION
Make sure there is no grease residue on the crankshaft taper. If necessary, clean it off with a non-petroleum based solvent. This surface must be grease-free to ensure a good lock of the torsional damper taper to the crankshaft taper.

b. Install the torsional damper onto the crankshaft.

c. Apply oil to the torsional damper mounting nut threads and seat, then install the nut finger-tight.

d. Install a flywheel holder (part No. YB-6139) to hold the torsional damper while tightening the nut.

e. Tighten the torsional damper nut with an appropriate size socket wrench to the torque specification in **Table 1**.

f. Remove the flywheel holder.

26. Install the power head as described in this chapter.

Table 1 POWER HEAD TIGHTENING TORQUES

Fastener	N•m Step 1	Step 2	ft.-lb. Step 1	Step 2
Connecting rod bolts				
C40, C55, C75, C85, C115	17	35	12	25
115-130 hp V4, 150-225 hp 90° V6 225-250 hp	17	37	12	27
76° V6	28	45	20	32
Crankcase-to-cylinder block bolts				
2 hp	5	10	3.6	7.2
3 hp	5	11	3.6	8.0
4, 5 hp	6	12	4.3	8.8
6, 8 hp	6	11	4.3	8.0
9.9, 15 hp				
6 mm bolts	6	12	4.3	8.8
8 mm bolts	15	30	11	22
C25	15	28	11	20
25, 30 hp				
6 mm bolts	5	11	3.6	8.0
8 mm bolts	15	28	11	20
C30	15	27	11	19
C40, C55				
6 mm bolts	6	12	4.3	8.8
10 mm bolts	20	40	15	29
40, 50 hp, Pro 50				
6 mm bolts	5	11	3.6	8.0
8 mm bolts	15	28	11	20

(continued)

Table 1 POWER HEAD TIGHTENING TORQUES (continued)

	N•m		ft.-lb.	
Fastener	Step 1	Step 2	Step 1	Step 2
Pro 60, 70 hp, 90 hp				
6 mm bolts	4	12	2.9	8.7
8 mm bolts	10	20	7.2	14
10 mm bolts	20	40	15	29
C75, C85				
6 mm bolts	6	12	4.3	8.7
10 mm bolts	20	40	15	29
C115				
8 mm bolts	10	18	7.2	13
10 mm bolts	20	40	15	29
115-130 hp V4, 150-225 hp 90° V6				
8 mm bolts	10	18	7.2	13
10 mm bolts	20	40	15	29
225-250 hp 76° V6				
6 mm bolts	4	8	2.9	5.8
10 mm bolts	20	40	15	29
Cylinder head bolts				
2 hp	5	10	3.6	7.2
3 hp	5	11	3.6	8.0
4, 5, 6, 8 hp	N/A			
9.9, 15 hp	8	17	5.8	12
C25, 25 hp, 30 hp	15	28	11	20
C30	15	27	11	19
C40, 55 hp	15	30	11	22
40, 50, Pro 50	15	28	11	20
Pro 60, 70 hp, 90 hp	15	32	11	23
C75, C85, C115	15	30	11	22
115-130 hp V4,				
150-225 hp 90° V6	15	30	11	22
225-250 hp 76° V6	15	28	11	20
Cylinder head cover bolts				
4, 5 hp	3	9	2.2	6.5
6, 8 hp	4	8	2.9	5.8
C30	15	27	11	19
115-250 V4 and V6	4	8	2.9	5.8
Exhaust cover (or manifold)				
2 hp	N/A			
3 hp	3	8	2.2	5.8
4, 5 hp	3	9	2.2	6.5
6, 8 hp	4	8	2.2	6.5
9.9, 15 hp	6	12	4.3	8.8
C25, 25 hp, 30 hp, C30	4	8	2.9	6.5
C40	3	7	2.2	5.1
40, 50, Pro 50, C55	4	8	2.9	6.5
Pro 60, 70 hp, 90 hp				
6 mm bolt	3	8	2.2	5.8
8 mm bolt	9	18	6.5	13
C75, C85	4	8	2.9	6.5
115-250 hp V4 and V6	4	8	2.9	5.8

(continued)

8

Table 1 POWER HEAD TIGHTENING TORQUES (continued)

Fastener	N•m Step 1	N•m Step 2	ft.-lb. Step 1	ft.-lb. Step 2
Intake manifold				
2, 3 hp	5	10	3.6	7.2
4, 5 hp	3	9	2.2	6.5
6, 8 hp	6	11	4.3	8.0
9.9, 15 hp	4	8	2.9	6.5
C25, 25 hp, 30 hp, C30	4	8	2.9	6.5
C40	10	21	7	15
40 hp, 50 hp, Pro 50, C55	4	8	2.9	6.5
Pro 60, 70 hp	4	8	2.9	6.5
90 hp, C75, C85	4	12	2.9	8.8
115-225 hp V4 and 90° V6	4	8	2.9	5.8
225-250 hp 76° V6	—	10	—	7.2
Lower oil seal housing				
All models	—	6-8	—	4.3-5.8
Flywheel nut				
2, 3, 4, 5, 6, 8 hp	—	45	—	32
9.9, 15 hp	—	115	—	85
C25, 25 hp	—	100	—	73
30, 40, 50 hp, Pro 50	—	110	—	81
C30	—	140	—	103
C40, C55, Pro 60, 70 hp, 90 hp, C75, C85, C115	—	160	—	118
115-250 V4 and V6	—	190	—	140
Power head mounting fasteners				
2 hp	*			
3, 4, 5 hp	3	8	2.2	5.8
9.9, 15 hp	*			
C25, 25 hp, C40	—	21	—	15
30 hp	—			
C30	15	28	10.8	20.3
40, 50 hp, Pro 50	*			
All other engines	—	21	—	15
Spark plug				
2 hp (1990-1994), 30 hp	—	20	—	14
C25, C30	—	28	—	20.3
All other engines	—	25	—	18
Starter motor				
9.9, 15 hp	*			
C25, 25, 30 hp	—	18	—	13
C30, C40, C55	—	21	—	15
40, 50 hp, Pro 50	*			
C30, C40, C55	—	20	—	14
C75, C85	—	18	—	13
C115, 115-130 V4, 150-225 hp 90° V6	—	30	—	22
225-250 hp 76° V6	*			
Thermostat cover				
All engines	—	8	—	5.8
Upper bearing housing				
All models so equipped	*			

N/A—Not applicable. Power head not equipped with this component.
* Specifications not available for these fasteners, tighten securely.

Table 2 POWER HEAD SPECIFICATIONS

Item	Specification mm (In.)
Connecting rod	
Big end side clearance	
2, 3 hp	0.30-0.60 (0.012-0.024)
4, 5, 6, 8 hp	0.20-0.70 (0.008-0.028)
9.9, 15 hp	*
C25	1.90-2.10 (0.075-0.082)
25, 30 hp, C30	0.20-0.70 (0.008-0.028)
C40, C55, C75, C85	*
40, 50 hp, Pro 50, Pro 60, 70 hp	0.20-0.70 (0.008-0.028)
90 hp	0.12-0.26 (0.005-0.010)
C115	0.20-0.32 (0.008-0.0126)
V4 and V6	0.12-0.26 (0.005-0.010)
Small end free play limit	
76° V6	0.5 (0.0020)
All other engines	2.0 (0.08)
Cylinder head warp limit	0.1 (0.004)
Cylinder bore	
Diameter	
2 hp	39.00-39.02 (1.535-1.536)
3 hp	46.00-46.02 (1.811-1.812)
4 hp	50.00-50.02 (1.9685-1.9697)
5 hp	54.00-54.02 (2.1260-2.1268)
6, 8 hp	50.00-50.02 (1.9685-1.9697)
9.9, 15 hp	56.00-56.02 (2.2047-2.2055)
C25, 25 hp	67.00-67.02 (2.638-2.639)
30 hp	59.50-59.52 (2.3425-2.3444)
C30	72.00-72.02 (2.8346-2.8354)
C40	75.00-75.02 (2.953-2.954)
40, 50 hp, Pro 50	67.00-67.02 (2.638-2.639)
C55, C75, C85, 90 hp	82.00-82.02 (3.228-3.229)
50, 60 hp	72.00-72.02 (2.8346-2.8354)
V4 and V6	90.00-90.02 (3.543-3.544)
Taper limit	0.08 (0.003)
Out-of-round limit	0.05 (0.002)
Piston	
Diameter	
2 hp	38.967-38.969 (1.5341-1.5349)
3 hp	45.965-45.990 (1.8096-1.8106)
4 hp	49.97-50.00 (1.9673-1.9685)
5 hp	53.97-54.00 (2.1248-2.1260)
6, 8 hp	49.955-49.980 (1.9667-1.9677)
9.9, 15 hp	55.940-55.985 (2.2024-2.2041)
C25	66.980-67.000 (2.637-2.638)
25 hp	66.960-66.980 (2.636-2.637)
30 hp	59.46-59.48 (2.341-2.342)
C30	71.94-71.96 (2.8323-2.8331)
C40	74.945-74.970 (2.9506-2.9516)
40, 50 hp, Pro 50	66.940-67.000 (2.6354-2.6378)
C55, C75, C85, 90 hp	81.935-81.962 (3.2258-3.2268)

(continued)

8

Table 2 POWER HEAD SPECIFICATIONS (continued)

Item	Specification mm (in.)
Piston	
Diameter (continued)	
Pro 60, 70 hp	71.945-71.970 (2.8325-2.8335)
C115, 115 hp, P115,	
130 hp, L130, 150 hp,	
L150, 175 hp, 200 hp,	
L200, Pro V 200, 225 hp	89.92-89.94 (3.540-3.541)
Pro V 150, Pro V 175	89.91-89.93 (3.539-3.540)
225, L225, 250 hp, L250	
76° V6	89.850-89.870 (3.5374-3.5382)
Measuring point	10 (0.40) up from bottom of skirt
Clearance in bore	
2, 3, 4, 5 hp	0.030-0.035 (0.0012-0.0014)
6, 8 hp	0.040-0.045 (0.0016-0.0018)
9.9, 15 hp	0.035-0.040 (0.0014-0.0016)
C25, C30	0.060-0.065 (0.0024-0.0025)
25, 30 hp	0.040-0.045 (0.0016-0.0018)
C40, Pro 60, 70 hp	0.050-0.055 (0.0020-0.0022)
40, 50 hp, Pro 50,	
C55, C75, C85, 90 hp	0.060-0.065 (0.0024-0.0025)
C115, 115 hp, Pro 115,	
130 hp, L130, 150 hp,	
L150, 175 hp, 200 hp,	
L200, Pro V 200, 225 hp	0.080-0.085 (0.0031-0.0033)
Pro V 150, Pro V 175	0.090-0.095 (0.0035-0.0037)
225, L225 76° V6	0.145-0.150 (0.0057-0.0059)
250 hp, L250 76° V6	0.135-0.140 (0.0053-0.0055)
Oversize diameter	
2 hp	
1st	39.25 (1.545)
2nd	39.50 (1.555)
3 hp 1st	46.50 (1.831)
4, 5 hp	*
6, 8 hp	
1st	50.25 (1.978)
2nd	50.50 (1.988)
9.9, 15 hp	
1st	56.25 (2.215)
2nd	56.50 (2.224)
C25	*
25 hp	67.50 (2.657)
30 hp	
1st	59.75 (2.352)
2nd	60.00 (2.362)
C30, Pro 60, 70 hp	
1st	72.25 (2.844)
2nd	72.50 (2.854)
C40	75.50 (2.972)
40, 50 hp, Pro 50	
1st	67.25 (2.648)
2nd	67.50 (2.657)

(continued)

Table 2 POWER HEAD SPECIFICATIONS (continued)

Item	Specification mm (in.)
Piston	
Oversize diameter (continued)	
C55, C75, C85, 90 hp	
1st	82.25 (3.238)
2nd	82.50 (3.248)
C115	*
115 hp, Pro 115, 130 hp, L130	
150 hp, L150, Pro V 150, 175 hp,	
Pro V 175, 200 hp, L200, Pro V 200, 225	
1st	90.25 (3.553)
2nd	90.50 (3.563)
225 hp, L225, 250 hp, L250	
76° V6	90.36 (3.557)
Off set	
2, 3 hp	N/A
4, 5, 6, 8 hp	0.5 (0.02)
9.9, 15 hp	1.0 (0.04)
C25, 25, 30 hp, C30	N/A
C40, C55, C75, C85	1.5 (0.059)
40, 50 hp, Pro 50	N/A
Pro 60, 70 hp	0.5 (0.02)
90 hp	1.0 (0.04)
V4 and V6	N/A
Piston rings	
End gap	
2, 3 hp	0.10-0.30 (0.004-0.012)
4, 5, 6, 8 hp, 9.9, 15 hp	0.15-0.35 (0.006-0.014)
C25, 25 hp	0.40-0.60 (0.016-0.023)
30 hp	0.15-0.30 (0.006-0.012)
C30	0.20-0.35 (0.008-0.014)
C40, Pro 60, 70 hp	0.30-0.50 (0.012-0.020)
40, 40 hp, Pro 50,	
C55, C75, C85, 90 hp	0.40-0.60 (0.016-0.023)
V4 and V6	0.30-0.40 (0.012-0.016)
Side clearance	
2 hp	0.03-0.07 (0.001-0.003)
3, 6, 8 hp	
Top	0.02-0.06 (0.0008-0.0024)
2nd	0.03-0.07 (0.001-0.003)
4, 5, hp	0.02-0.06 (0.0008-0.0024)
9.9, 15 hp	
Top	0.02-0.06 (0.0008-0.0024)
2nd	0.04-0.08 (0.0016-0.0031)
C25	
Top	0.03-0.05 (0.0012-0.0020)
2nd	0.03-0.07 (0.001-0.003)
25 hp, C40	
Top	0.02-0.06 (0.0008-0.0024)
2nd	0.03-0.07 (0.0012-0.0028)
30 hp	0.05-0.09 (0.002-0.004)

(continued)

8

Table 2 POWER HEAD SPECIFICATIONS (continued)

Item	Specification mm (in.)
Piston rings	
Side clearance (continued)	
C30	*
40, 50 hp, Pro 50	
Top	0.04-0.08 (0.0016-0.0031)
2nd	0.03-0.07 (0.0012-0.0028)
C55, C75, C85	
Top	0.03-0.065 (0.0012-0.0026)
2nd	0.03-0.07 (0.001-0.003)
Pro 60, 70 hp	0.03-0.07 (0.001-0.003)
90 hp	0.03-0.06 (0.001-0.0024)
V4 and V6	0.02-0.06 (0.0008-0.0024)
Seal ring clearance	
wear limit (V4 and V6)	0.10 (0.004)

N/A—Not applicable.
* Specification not available.

Table 3 CRANKSHAFT SPECIFICATIONS

Model	Maximum runout mm (in.)	Dimension B mm (in.)	Dimension C mm (in.)
2 hp	0.02 (0.001)	27.90-27.95 (1.098-1.100)	0.30-0.60 (0.012-0.024)
3 hp	0.03 (0.001)	35.00-36.00 (1.098-1.100)	0.30-0.60 (0.012-0.024)
4, 5, 6, 8 hp	0.03 (0.001)	39.90-39.95 (1.571-1.573)	0.20-0.70 (0.008-0.028)
9.9, 15 hp	0.03 (0.001)	46.90-46.95 (1.846-1.848)	*
C25	0.03 (0.001)	53.90-53.95 (2.122-2.124)	1.90-2.10 (0.075-0.082)
25, 30 hp	0.03 (0.001)	49.90-49.95 (1.965-1.967)	0.20-0.70 (0.008-0.028)
C30	0.03 (0.001)	56.90-56.95 (2.240-2.242)	0.20-0.70 (0.008-0.028)
C40	0.03 (0.001)	60.25-60.50 (2.372-2.382)	*
40, 50, Pro 50	0.03 (0.001)	53.90-53.95 (2.122-2.124)	0.20-0.70 (0.008-0.028)
C55	0.02 (0.0008)	*	*
Pro 60, 70 hp	0.03 (0.001)	57.90-57.95 (2.280-2.281)	0.20-0.70 (0.008-0.028)
C75, C85	0.02 (0.0008)	284.2-284.8 (11.189-11.213)	*
90 hp	0.05 (0.002)	57.90-57.95 (2.280-2.281)	0.12-0.26 (0.005-0.010)

(continued)

Table 3 CRANKSHAFT SPECIFICATIONS (continued)

Model	Runout mm (in.)	Dimension B mm (in.)	Dimension C mm (in.)
V4 and 90° V6	0.02 (0.0008)	N/A	*
76° V6	0.05 (0.0020)	N/A	0.12-0.26 (0.005-0.010)

* Specification not available.
** Total dimension across all three cylinder crankshaft webs.
N/A—Not applicable.

Chapter Nine

Gearcase and Drive Shaft Housing

Torque is transferred from the power head's crankshaft to the gearcase by a drive shaft. A pinion gear on the drive shaft meshes with a drive gear in the gearcase to change the vertical power flow into a horizontal flow through the propeller shaft. The power head drive shaft rotates clockwise continuously when the engine is running, but propeller rotation is controlled by the gear train shifting mechanism.

On Yamaha outboards with a reverse gear, a sliding clutch engages the appropriate gear in the gearcase when the shift mechanism is placed in FORWARD or REVERSE. This creates a direct coupling that transfers the power flow from the pinion to the propeller shaft. **Figure 1**, typical shows the operation of the gear train for regular rotation engines.

Some models are *counter rotational* and are so designated with a "L" in front of the horsepower model designation (e.g. L200T). On these models, the propeller rotates in the opposite direction than on regular models and is used when dual engines are mounted in the boat to equalize the propellers directional churning force on the water. This allows the operator to maintain a true course instead of being pulled off toward one side while underway.

NOTE
The "L" series outboards (counter rotation models) are included in all procedures. Unless there is a separate procedure designated for the "L" series model, refer to the procedure that relates to the same horsepower rating. If you are working on an L200, refer to the 200 hp procedure.

The gearcase can be removed without removing the entire outboard from the boat. This chapter contains removal, overhaul and installation procedures for the gearcase, water pump and propeller.

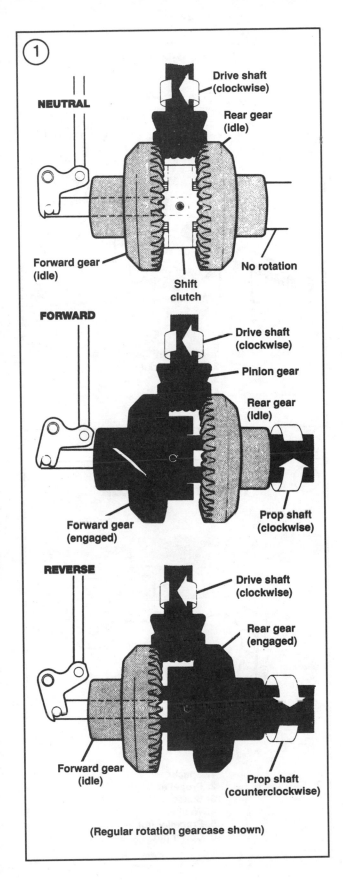

NEUTRAL

Drive shaft
(clockwise)

Rear gear
(idle)

Forward gear
(idle)

No rotation

Shift
clutch

FORWARD

Drive shaft
(clockwise)

Pinion gear

Rear gear
(idle)

Forward gear
(engaged)

Prop shaft
(clockwise)

REVERSE

Drive shaft
(clockwise)

Rear gear
(engaged)

Forward gear
(idle)

Prop shaft
(counterclockwise)

(Regular rotation gearcase shown)

The gearcases covered in this chapter differ somewhat in design and construction over the years covered and require slightly different service procedures. The chapter is arranged in a normal disassembly/assembly sequence. When only a partial repair is required, follow the procedure(s) for your gearcase to the point where the faulty parts can be replaced, then reassemble the unit.

Since this chapter covers a wide range of models, the gearcases shown in the accompanying illustrations are the most common ones. While it is possible that the components shown in the pictures may not be identical to those being serviced, the step-by-step procedures may be used with all models covered in this manual.

Tables 1-3 are located at the end of the chapter.

SERVICE PRECAUTIONS AND NOTES

Whenever you work on a Yamaha outboard, there are several good procedures to keep in mind that will make your work easier, faster and more accurate.

1. Never use elastic stopnuts more than twice. It is a good idea to replace such nuts each time they are removed. Never use non-locking nuts or worn-out stop nuts.

2. Use special tools where noted. In some cases, it may be possible to perform the procedure with makeshift tools, but this is not recommended. The use of makeshift tools can damage the components and may cause serious personal injury.

3. Use a vise with protective jaws to hold housings or parts. If protective jaws are not available, insert wooden blocks on each side of the part(s) before clamping them in the vise.

4. Remove and install pressed-on parts with an appropriate special tool or mandrel, a support and a hydraulic press. Do not try to pry, hammer or otherwise force them on or off. If you do not have access to a press, have the components removed and installed by a Yamaha dealer or qualified machine shop.

5. Refer to **Table 1** at the end of the chapter for torque values. Proper torque is essential to ensure long life and satisfactory service from outboard components.

6. Apply Yamalube All-purpose Marine grease to the outer surfaces of all bearing carrier and retainer mating surfaces during reassembly.

7. Discard all O-rings and oil seals during disassembly. Apply Yamalube All-purpose Marine grease to the new O-rings and seal lips to prevent damage when the engine is first started.

8. Keep a record of all shims and where they came from. As soon as the shims are removed, inspect them for damage and write down their thickness and location. Wire the shims together for correct reassembly and store them in a safe place. Follow shimming instructions closely. If gear backlash is not properly set, the unit will be noisy and suffer premature gear failure. Incorrect bearing preload will result in premature bearing failure.

9. Work in an area where there is good lighting and sufficient space for component storage. Keep an ample number of clean containers available for storing small parts. Cover parts with clean shop cloths when you are not working on them.

10. Use Yamaha Gearcase Lube whenever the procedure specifies lubrication with oil. Use Yamalube All-purpose Marine grease where grease is specified.

PROPELLER

The outboards covered in this manual use variations of 2 propeller attachment designs. All 2-5 hp models use a shear pin design (**Figure 2**). In this design a metal pin installed in the propeller shaft engages a slot in the propeller hub. As the shaft rotates, the pin rotates the propeller. The shear pin is designed to break if the propeller hits an obstruction in the water. This design has 2 advantages. The pin absorbs the impact to prevent possible propeller and gearcase damage. It

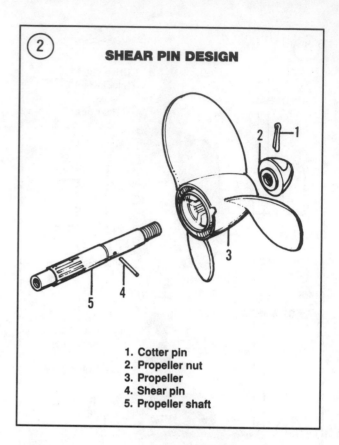

SHEAR PIN DESIGN

1. Cotter pin
2. Propeller nut
3. Propeller
4. Shear pin
5. Propeller shaft

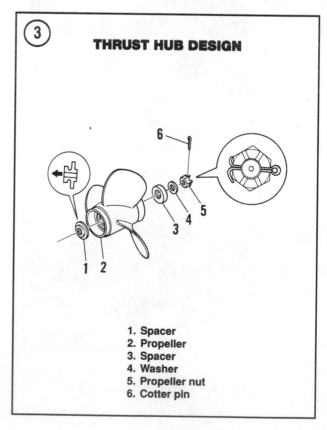

THRUST HUB DESIGN

1. Spacer
2. Propeller
3. Spacer
4. Washer
5. Propeller nut
6. Cotter pin

also alerts the user that something is wrong, since the engine speed will increase immediately if the pin breaks. Most Yamaha outboards are equipped with spare shear pins and cotter pins installed in the bottom cowl near the power head.

Propellers on Yamaha 6-250 hp outboards use some variation of the thrust hub design (**Figure 3**). The propeller drives on a ratchet-type rubber bushing or a spline drive rubber hub and is retained by a castellated nut and cotter pin. Any underwater impact is absorbed by the propeller bushing/hub.

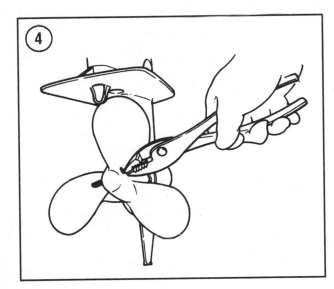

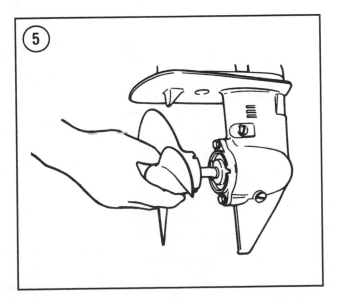

WARNING
To prevent accidental engine starting when working on or around the propeller, disconnect the spark plug lead(s) from the plug(s) on manual and electric start models. In addition, electric start models should be shifted into NEUTRAL and the ignition key removed (if so equipped).

Propeller Removal/Installation (Shear Pin Design)

1. Disconnect the spark plug lead(s) to prevent accidental starting of the engine.

2A. On 2 hp models, remove the cotter pin (**Figure 4**), then remove the propeller (**Figure 5**). Discard the cotter pin as it must not be reused.

2B. On 3-5 hp models, refer to **Figure 6** and perform the following:

    a. Remove the cotter pin (1, **Figure 6**). Discard the cotter pin as it must not be reused.

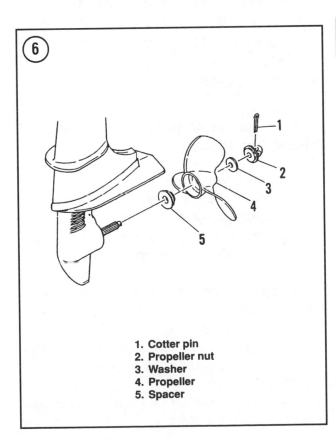

1. Cotter pin
2. Propeller nut
3. Washer
4. Propeller
5. Spacer

9

b. Unscrew the propeller nut (2, **Figure 6**).

c. Remove the washer (3, **Figure 6**), propeller (4) and spacer (5) from the shaft.

3. If the bearing housing or housing cap is going to be removed, remove the shear pin from the propeller shaft with an appropriate size punch or drift (**Figure 7**).

4. Clean the propeller shaft thoroughly.

5. Inspect the propeller as follows:

a. Inspect the blades for wear, damage and cavitation erosion (A, **Figure 8**).

b. Check the inner splines for wear or damage (B, **Figure 8**). If the inner splines are worn or damaged, inspect the outer splines on the propeller shaft as they may be damaged also.

c. Inspect the pin engagement slot in the propeller hub and hole in the propeller shaft for wear or damage. Replace if necessary.

6. Installation is the reverse of removal. Note the following:

a. If removed, install a new shear pin.

b. Lubricate the propeller shaft with grease.

c. Tighten the nut securely.

d. Install a new cotter pin and bend the ends over completely.

Propeller Removal/Installation
(Thrust Hub Design)

Refer to **Figure 9** for this procedure.

1. Disconnect the spark plug leads to prevent accidental starting of the engine.

2. Remove the cotter pin (1, **Figure 9**) from the propeller nut. Discard the cotter pin as it must not be reused.

3. Place a piece of wood between the propeller blades and the antiventilation plate to prevent the propeller from rotating.

4. Remove the propeller castellated nut (2, **Figure 9**), washer (3) and splined spacer (4) from the shaft.

5. Remove the propeller (5, **Figure 9**) and inner spacer (6) from the shaft.

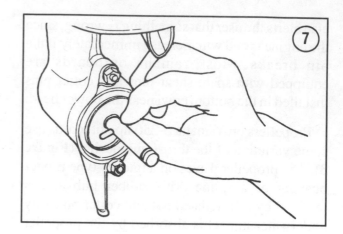

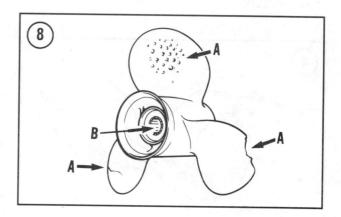

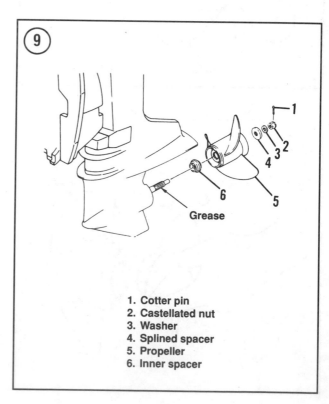

1. Cotter pin
2. Castellated nut
3. Washer
4. Splined spacer
5. Propeller
6. Inner spacer

6. Clean the propeller shaft splines thoroughly.

7. Inspect the propeller as follows:

   a. Inspect the blades for wear, damage or cavitation erosion (A, **Figure 8**).

   b. Check the inner splines for wear or damage (B, **Figure 8**). If the inner splines are worn or damaged, inspect the outer splines on the propeller shaft as they may also be damaged.

8. Installation is the reverse of removal. Note the following:

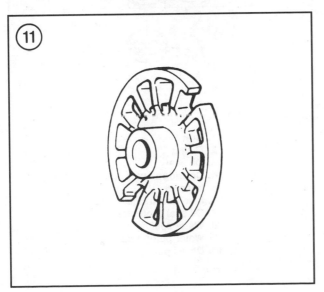

   a. Lubricate the propeller shaft with grease.

   b. Use the same tool set-up used during removal to hold the propeller in place and tighten the nut to the specification in **Table 1**.

   c. Align the recess in the propeller nut with the hole in the propeller shaft and install a new cotter pin (**Figure 10**). Bend the ends over completely.

   d. Recheck the propeller nut torque after the first time the outboard is operated. Tighten if necessary and install a new cotter pin.

Test Propeller Installation

Some test procedures in other chapters in this book specify the installation of a test propeller to perform an "engine running" test or adjustment procedure safely.

The test propeller (**Figure 11**) (part No. YB-1629) is available from a Yamaha marine dealer. Purchase one for the specific outboard to be worked on and follow the manufacturer's instructions for installation.

9

WATER PUMP

The water pump is mounted on top of the gearcase housing on all outboards covered in this manual. On 2-5 hp models, the pump impeller is fastened to the drive shaft by a key that fits into the drive shaft and into a similar cutout in the pump impeller hub. On 6-250 hp models, the impeller is secured by a key that engages a flat area or a slot in the drive shaft and a cutout in the impeller hub. As the drive shaft rotates, the impeller rotates with it. Water between the impeller blades and pump housing is pumped up to the power head through the water tube.

The offset center of the pump housing causes the impeller vanes to flex during rotation. At low speeds, the pump operates as a displacement type pump. At high speeds, water resistance forces the vanes to flex inward and the pump becomes a centrifugal type pump (**Figure 12**).

All seals and gaskets should be replaced whenever the water pump is removed. Since proper water pump operation is critical to outboard operation, it is also a good idea to install a new impeller at the same time.

Never turn a used impeller over and reuse it. The impeller rotates in a clockwise direction with the drive shaft and the vanes gradually take a set in one direction. Turning the impeller over will cause the vanes to move in a direction opposite to that which caused the set. This will result in premature impeller failure and can cause extensive power head damage.

**Removal and Disassembly
(2 hp)**

Refer to **Figure 13** for this procedure.

1. Remove the gearcase as described in this chapter.
2. Secure the gearcase in a suitable holding fixture or a vise with protective jaws. If protective jaws are not available, position the gearcase upright in the vise with the skeg between wooden blocks.
3. Remove the water tube from the pump housing.
4. Remove the bolts and washers securing the water pump housing to the gear housing.
5. If necessary, insert flat-bladed screwdrivers at the fore and aft end of the pump housing and carefully pry the housing up. Remove the housing from the drive shaft.
6. Remove the cartridge outer plate.

NOTE
If the impeller is corroded and adhered onto the shaft, the impeller may have to be carefully split with a hammer and chisel for removal in Step 7.

7. Remove the impeller, then the dowel pin from the drive shaft.

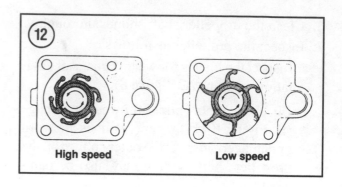
High speed Low speed

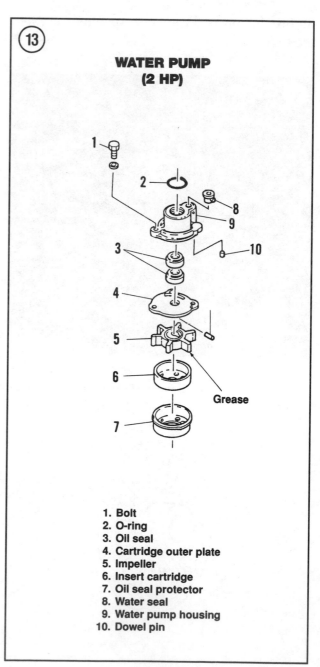

**WATER PUMP
(2 HP)**

Grease

1. Bolt
2. O-ring
3. Oil seal
4. Cartridge outer plate
5. Impeller
6. Insert cartridge
7. Oil seal protector
8. Water seal
9. Water pump housing
10. Dowel pin

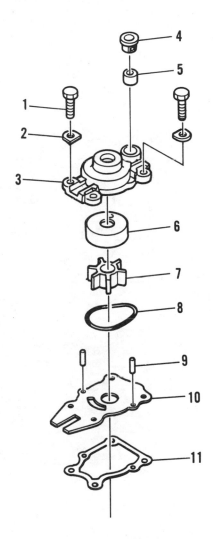

**WATER PUMP
(3-52 HP, C25, 40-50 HP, PRO 50)**

1. Bolt
2. Special washer
3. Water pump housing
4. Water seal cover
5. Water seal
6. Insert cartridge
7. Impeller
8. O-ring
9. Dowel pin
10. Cartridge plate
11. Gasket

8. Remove the insert cartridge and the oil seal protector from the gear housing.

9. Clean and inspect all parts as described in this chapter.

**Removal and Disassembly
(3-5 hp, C25, 40 hp, 50 hp
and Pro 50, Models)**

Refer to **Figure 14**, typical for this procedure.

1. Remove the gearcase as described in this chapter.

2. Secure the gearcase in a suitable holding fixture or a vise with protective jaws. If protective jaws are not available, position the gearcase upright in the vise with the skeg between wooden blocks.

3. Remove the water tube from the pump housing.

4. Remove the bolts and washers securing the water pump housing to the gear housing. On 3-5 hp engines, remove the support plates under the bolts. Do not bend, distort or damage the plates during removal.

> *NOTE*
> *Don't lose the dowel pin(s) that may either come off with the pump housing or stay with the gear housing.*

5. If necessary, insert flat-bladed screwdrivers at the fore and aft end of the pump housing and carefully pry the housing up. Remove the pump housing and gasket, or O-ring, from the drive shaft. Discard the gasket or O-ring.

> *NOTE*
> *The insert cartridge may stay within the pump housing or may stay with the impeller.*

6. If it is still in place, remove the insert cartridge from the impeller.

> *NOTE*
> *If the impeller is corroded and stuck to the shaft, the impeller may have to be*

9

carefully split with a hammer and chisel for removal in Step 7.

7. Remove the impeller, then the dowel pin, or Woodruff key, from the drive shaft.

8A. On 3-5 hp models, remove the outer plate from the top of the base plate.

8B. On C25 models, remove the outer plate, gasket, inner plate and gasket from the top of the gear housing. Separate the inner and outer plates from the gaskets and discard the gaskets.

9. On 3-5 hp models, perform the following:

   a. Remove the shift rod from the base plate.

   b. On 4-5 hp models, remove the bolt and washer securing the base plate and gasket to the gear housing.

   c. If necessary, insert flat-bladed screwdrivers at the fore and aft end of the base plate and carefully pry the base plate up. Remove the base plate and gasket from the drive shaft and the gear housing. Discard the gasket.

10. Clean and inspect all parts as described in this chapter.

Removal and Disassembly (All Other Models)

Refer to **Figure 15**, typical for this procedure.

1. Remove the gearcase as described in this chapter.

2. Secure the gearcase in a suitable holding fixture or a vise with protective jaws. If protective jaws are not available, position the gearcase upright in the vise with the skeg between wooden blocks.

3. Remove the water tube from the pump housing.

4. Remove the bolts and washers securing the water pump housing to the gear housing (**Figure 16**). On 6-15 hp and C30 models, remove the support plate(s) under the bolts. Do not bend, distort or damage the plate(s) during removal.

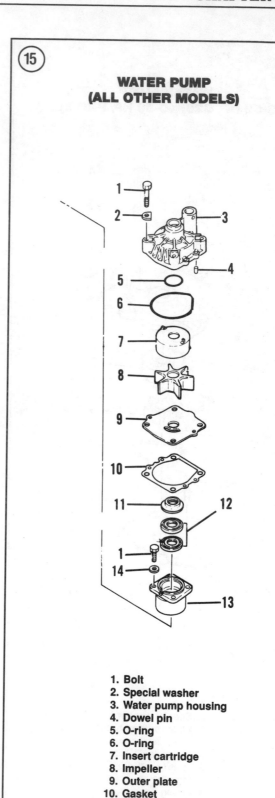

(15)

WATER PUMP (ALL OTHER MODELS)

1. Bolt
2. Special washer
3. Water pump housing
4. Dowel pin
5. O-ring
6. O-ring
7. Insert cartridge
8. Impeller
9. Outer plate
10. Gasket
11. Oil seal
12. Oil seal
13. Oil seal housing
14. Washer

NOTE
Don't lose the dowel pins that may either come off with the pump housing or stay with the gear housing.

5. If necessary, insert flat-bladed screwdrivers at the fore and aft end of the pump housing and carefully pry the pump housing up. Remove the pump housing and gasket, or O-ring(s), from the drive shaft. Discard the gasket or O-ring(s).

NOTE
The insert cartridge may stay within the pump housing or may stay with the impeller.

6. If it is still in place, remove the insert cartridge from the impeller.
7. On 115-250 hp models (except C115), slide the cap, collar, spring washer and plain washer, located above the impeller, up and off the drive shaft.

NOTE
If the impeller is corroded and stuck to the shaft, the impeller may have to be carefully split with a hammer and chisel for removal in Step 8.

8. Remove the impeller, then the Woodruff key from the drive shaft (**Figure 17**).
9. Remove the outer plate and gasket from the top of the oil seal housing. Separate the outer plate from the gasket and discard the gasket.

NOTE
The water pump base is also the oil seal housing. It is not necessary to remove this assembly unless it is to be serviced.

10. If oil seal housing removal is necessary, perform the following:

NOTE
On some models, the oil seal housing is bolted in place and on other models the housing is held in place by the bolts that secure the water pump housing.

a. On models so equipped, remove the bolts and washers securing the oil seal housing to the gear housing.

b. If necessary, insert flat-bladed screwdrivers at the fore and aft end of the oil seal housing and carefully pry the housing up.

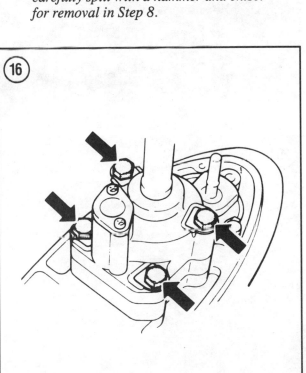

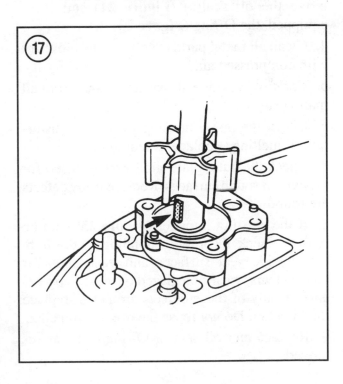

c. Remove the oil seal housing and gasket, or O-ring, from the drive shaft (**Figure 18**). Discard the gasket or O-ring(s).

11. Clean and inspect all parts as described in this chapter.

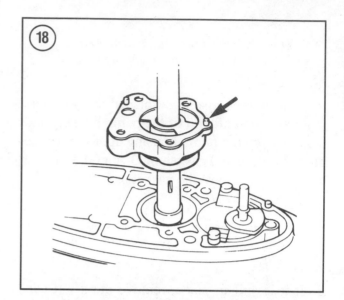

Cleaning and Inspection (All Models)

When removing seals from the water pump housing, note and record the direction in which each seal lip faces for proper reinstallation.

1. If the insert cartridge stayed with the water pump housing, insert a drift through the drive shaft opening and carefully drive the cartridge from the housing (**Figure 19**).

2. On models so equipped, remove the drive shaft rubber grommet and water tube seal (**Figure 20**) from the pump housing. Inspect these rubber parts for wear, hardness or deterioration and replace if necessary.

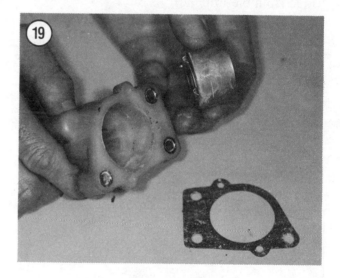

3. If the water pump base plate or oil seal housing were removed from the gear housing, remove the oil seal(s) (**Figure 21**) and if so equipped, the O-ring (**Figure 22**).

4. Clean all metal parts in solvent and blow dry with compressed air.

5. Carefully remove all gasket residue from all mating surfaces.

6. Check the pump housing for cracks, distortion or melting. Replace as required.

7. Check the outer plate and cartridge insert for grooves or rough surfaces. Replace if any defects are found.

8. If the existing impeller (**Figure 23**) is to be reused, check the rubber bonding to the hub. Check side seal surfaces and vane ends for cracks, tears, wear or a glazed or melted appearance. If any of these defects are noted, replace the impeller. Do *not* reuse the original impeller.

9. Replace any oil seal or O-ring that was removed.

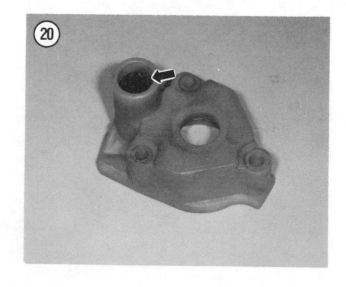

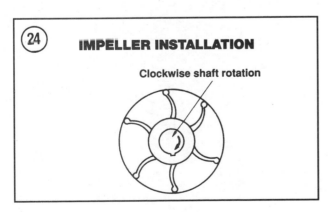

IMPELLER INSTALLATION

Clockwise shaft rotation

Assembly and Installation
(2 hp Models)

Refer to **Figure 13** for this procedure.

1. Secure the gearcase in a suitable holding fixture or a vise with protective jaws. If protective jaws are not available, position the gearcase upright in the vise with the skeg between wooden blocks.

2. Install the oil seal protector and insert the cartridge onto the gear housing.

3. Install the dowel pin into the drive shaft.

> *CAUTION*
> *If the original impeller is to be reused, install it in the same rotational direction as removed to avoid premature failure. The curl of the blades should be positioned in a counterclockwise direction as shown in* **Figure 24**.

4. Apply grease to the impeller hub. Slide the impeller onto the shaft and align the slot in the impeller hub with the dowel pin and push it all the way down.

5. Check impeller rotation by rotating the drive shaft clockwise. The impeller should rotate smoothly with the shaft. If not, remove and reposition the impeller to engage the dowel pin properly.

6. Install the cartridge outer plate and align the mounting bolt holes in the gearing housing.

7. Apply a light coat of grease to the lips of the oil seals in the housing cover.

8. Slide the housing cover over the drive shaft and align the mounting bolt holes in the gear housing and cartridge outer plate. Push down on the housing cover while slowly rotating the drive shaft clockwise to assist the impeller in entering the cover without damage. If necessary, guide the impeller into the housing with your fingers.

9. Apply Loctite (No. 242) to the housing cover bolt threads prior to installation.

10. Install the bolts and washers securing the water pump housing to the gear housing. Tighten the bolts securely.

9

11. Install the water tube onto the pump housing.

12. Install the gearcase as described in this chapter.

Assembly and Installation (3-5 hp, C25, 40 hp, 50 hp and Pro 50, Models)

Refer to **Figure 14**, typical for this procedure.

1. Secure the gearcase in a suitable holding fixture or a vise with protective jaws. If protective jaws are not available, position the gearcase upright in the vise with the skeg between wooden blocks.

2. Make sure the dowel pin(s) are in place on the gear housing.

3. On 3-5 hp models, perform the following:

   a. Apply Gasket Maker to both surfaces of the gasket.

   b. Install the base plate and new gasket over the drive shaft and onto the gear housing. Align the bolt holes.

   c. On 4-5 hp models, install the bolt and washer securing the base plate and gasket to the gear housing. Tighten the bolt securely.

   d. Install the shift rod through the base plate.

4A. On 3-5 hp models, install the outer plate onto the top of the base plate.

4B. On C25 models, install the new gasket, inner plate, new gasket, outer plate and new gasket onto the gear housing (**Figure 25**). Align the bolt holes.

5. Install the dowel pin, or Woodruff key, into the drive shaft.

> *CAUTION*
> *If the original impeller is to be reused, install it in the same rotational direction as removed to avoid premature failure. The curl of the blades should be positioned in a counterclockwise direction as shown in Figure 24.*

6. Apply grease to the impeller hub. Slide the impeller onto the shaft and align the slot in the impeller hub with the dowel pin, or Woodruff key, and push it all the way down.

7. Check impeller rotation by rotating the drive shaft clockwise. The impeller should rotate smoothly with the shaft. If not, remove and reposition the impeller to engage the dowel pin or Woodruff key properly.

8. If a new insert cartridge is being installed, coat the insert mating area in the water pump housing with Loctite PST seal and 657. Align the locating pin(s) or tab(s) with the receptacle(s) in the top of the water pump housing and install the cartridge into the housing.

9. Apply a light coat of grease to the lips of the oil seals in the housing cover.

10. Install a new housing gasket, or O-ring.

11. Slide the pump housing over the drive shaft and onto the impeller. If necessary, guide the impeller into the cartridge with your fingers. Align the mounting bolt holes with those in the

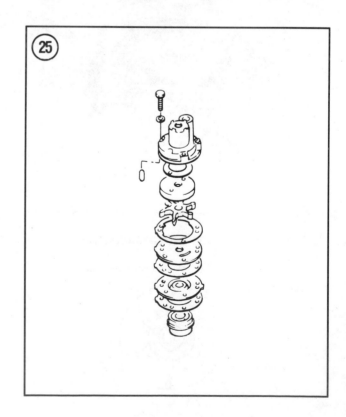

gear housing and plates and gaskets. Push down on the pump housing until it bottoms out.

12. Apply Loctite (No. 242) to the pump housing bolt threads prior to installation.

13. Install the bolts and washers securing the water pump housing to the gear housing. On 3-5 hp models, install the support plates under the bolts. Tighten the bolts securely.

14. Install the water tube onto the pump housing.

15. Install the gearcase as described in this chapter.

Assembly and Installation (All Other Models)

Refer to **Figure 15**, typical for this procedure.

1. Secure the gearcase in a suitable holding fixture or a vise with protective jaws. If protective jaws are not available, position the gearcase upright in the vise with the skeg between wooden blocks.

2. If the oil seal housing was removed, perform the following:

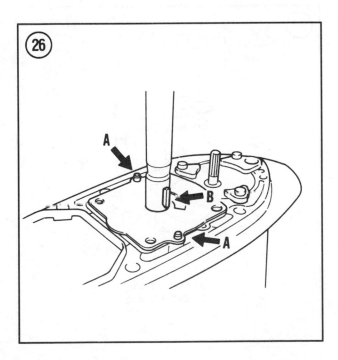

a. Apply grease to the lips of the oil seals in the housing.

b. Install a new gasket or O-ring(s).

c. Install the oil seal housing down the drive shaft and into position in the gear housing. Push it down until it bottoms out in the gear housing. Align the bolt holes (if so equipped).

d. On models equipped with mounting bolts, apply Loctite (No. 242) to the oil seal housing bolt threads prior to installation.

e. On models equipped with mounting bolts, install the bolts and washers securing the oil seal housing to the gear housing. Tighten the bolts securely.

3. Install the outer plate and new gasket over the drive shaft and onto the oil seal housing. Align the bolt holes.

4. Install the dowel pins (A, **Figure 26**) outer plate.

5. Install the Woodruff key (B, **Figure 26**) into the drive shaft.

CAUTION
*If the original impeller is to be reused, install it in the same rotational direction as removed to avoid premature failure. The curl of the blades should be positioned in a counterclockwise direction as shown in **Figure 24**.*

6. Apply grease to the impeller hub. Pull up on the drive shaft and slide the impeller onto the shaft and align the slot in the impeller hub with the Woodruff key, and push it all the way down.

7. Check impeller rotation by rotating the drive shaft clockwise. The impeller should rotate smoothly with the shaft. If not, remove and reposition the impeller to engage the Woodruff key properly. Apply a light coat of grease to the impeller blades.

NOTE
The C115 outboard motor is not equipped with items installed in Step 8.

8. On 115-250 hp models (except C115), refer to **Figure 27** and perform the following:

 a. Apply a light coat of grease to the impeller blades (1, **Figure 27**).

 b. Slide the plain washer (2, **Figure 27**) wave washer (3) and plain washer (4) onto the drive shaft.

 c. Install the spacer (5, **Figure 27**) on the drive shaft. Push it down against the contour of the drive shaft.

 d. Install the collar (6, **Figure 27**) and slide it down over the spacer (5). Push it all the way down until it seats completely.

9. If a new insert cartridge is being installed, coat the insert mating area in the water pump housing with Loctite PST sealant 657. Align the locating pin(s) or tab(s) with the receptacle(s) in the top of the water pump housing and install the cartridge into the housing.

10. Apply a light coat of grease to the lips of the oil seals in the housing cover.

11. Install a new housing gasket, or O-ring.

12. Slide the pump housing over the drive shaft and onto the impeller. If necessary, guide the impeller into the cartridge with your fingers. Align the mounting bolt holes with those in the gear housing and outer plate and gasket. Push down on the pump housing until it bottoms out.

13. Apply Loctite (No. 242) to the pump housing bolt threads prior to installation.

14. Install the bolts and washers securing the water pump housing to the gear housing. On 6-15 hp and C30 models, install the support plate(s) under the bolts. Tighten the bolts securely.

15. Install the water tube onto the pump housing.

16. Install the gearcase as described in this chapter.

GEARCASE

When removing the gearcase mounting fasteners, it is not uncommon to find that they are

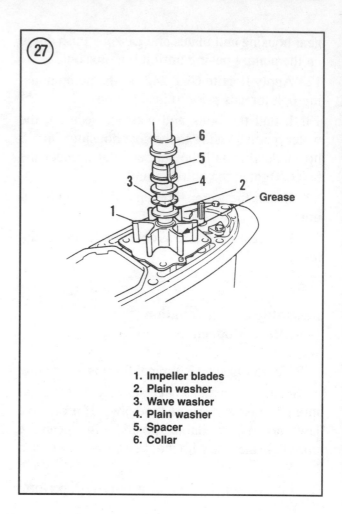

1. Impeller blades
2. Plain washer
3. Wave washer
4. Plain washer
5. Spacer
6. Collar

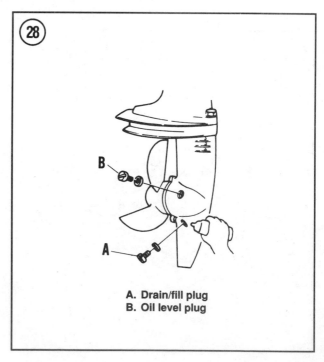

A. Drain/fill plug
B. Oil level plug

corroded. Such fasteners should be discarded and replaced during installation and assembly.

If water has entered the gearcase area, it may have also corroded the water tubes and the driveshaft/crankshaft connection, making it impossible to remove the unit with hand pressure. In this situation, it will be necessary to pry the gearcase free from the drive shaft housing. Some extreme cases may require the use of heat to free the corroded components. Remember that excessive use of heat and/or prying force can result in damage to the drive shaft, crankshaft and/or the gearcase housing.

CAUTION
If heat is necessary to free components, protect any surrounding components (plastic parts) that may be damaged by the heat. Also make sure there are no traces of spilled gasoline or gasoline fumes remaining in the gearcase area.

Removal (All Models)

Preliminary removal steps

1. Remove the engine cover and disconnect the spark plug lead(s) to prevent any accidental starting of the engine during lower unit removal.
2. Place the shift lever into NEUTRAL.

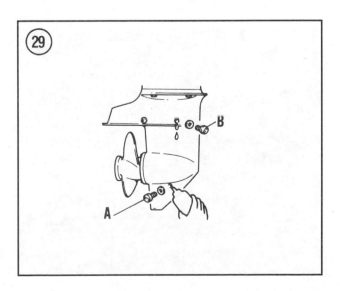

3. Tilt the outboard to the full out position and engage the tilt lock lever.
4. Place a suitable container under the gearcase drain/fill plug and remove the plug. Refer to A, **Figure 28** for 2 hp models or to A, **Figure 29** for all other models. Remove the oil level plug. Refer to B, **Figure 28** for 2 hp models or to B, **Figure 29** for all other models. Drain the lubricant from the unit.

NOTE
If the lubricant is white or creamy in color or metallic particles are found in Step 5, the gearcase must be completely disassembled to determine and correct the cause of the problem.

5. Wipe a small amount of lubricant on a finger and rub the finger and thumb together. Check for the presence of metallic particles in the lubricant. Note the color of the lubricant. A white or creamy color indicates water in the lubricant. Check the drain container for signs of water separation from the lubricant.
6. Remove the propeller as described in this chapter. On 2-5 hp models, if the gearcase is going to be disassembled, also remove the shear pin from the shaft.

2 hp models

1. Perform the *Preliminary Removal Steps* as previously described.
2. Remove the bolt and washer from the top surface of the upper case and the bolt and washer on the lower surface of the gear housing.
3. Carefully separate the gear housing from the upper case.
4. Remove the pipe from the drive shaft.
5. Remove the antiventilation plate from the gear housing. Don't lose the dowel pin in the gear housing.
6. If the gearcase is going to be disassembled, mount the gearcase in a suitable holding fixture. If the gearcase is not going to be serviced, place

it on a clean work surface and cover with clean shop cloths.

3-8 hp models

1. Perform the *Preliminary Removal Steps* as previously described.

2A. On 3-5 hp models, place the shift lever (1, **Figure 30**) into REVERSE. Remove the rubber grommet (2, **Figure 30**) from the port side of the gear housing. Then, loosen the bolt (3, **Figure 30** or **Figure 31**) approximately 3 turns on the shift rod connector.

2B. On 6-8 hp models, remove the bolt and nut (A, **Figure 32**) securing the shift rod connector (B, **Figure 32**) and remove the connector from the rods.

3. Remove the 2 or 4 bolts and washers securing the gear housing to the drive shaft housing (**Figure 33**).

4. Partially separate the gear housing from the drive shaft housing and disconnect the shift rods at the connector.

5. If the gear housing is going to be disassembled, mount the gear housing in a suitable holding fixture. If the gear housing is not going to be serviced, place on a clean work surface and cover with clean shop cloths.

9-50 hp including "C" series models

1. Perform the *Preliminary Removal Steps* as previously described.

2. On C25, 30 hp, C30, C40 models, perform the following:
   a. Scribe a mark on the trim tab for reassembly reference.
   b. Remove the bolt and washer securing the trim tab and remove the trim tab.

3. Place the shift lever into REVERSE.

4. On 25 hp models, disconnect the reverse interlock hook (**Figure 34**) from the shift rod.

5. On all models except 40-50 hp, and Pro 50, perform the following:

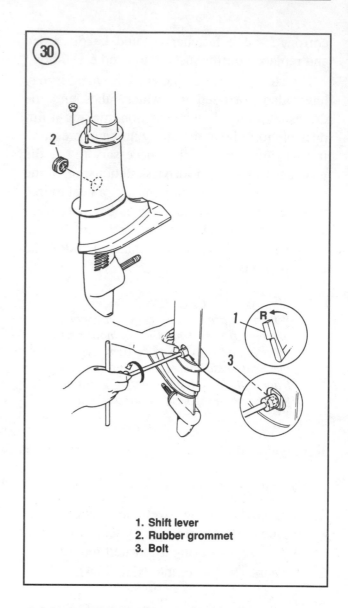

1. Shift lever
2. Rubber grommet
3. Bolt

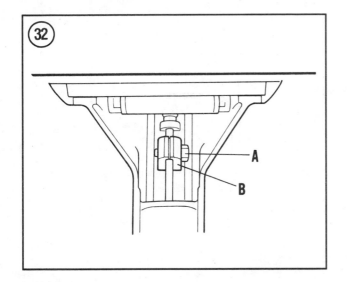

a. Hold onto the nut with a suitable size wrench, then loosen the locknut (A, **Figure 35**).

b. Unscrew the nut (B, **Figure 35**) and disconnect the upper shift shaft from the lower shift shaft.

NOTE
Some models are equipped with lockwashers as well as plain washers on some mounting bolts. Note their location.

6. Remove the 4 or 6 bolts and washers securing the gear housing to the drive shaft housing (**Figure 36**, typical).

7. Separate the gear housing from the drive shaft housing.

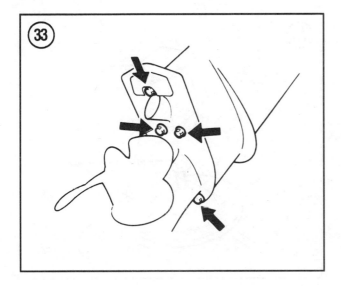

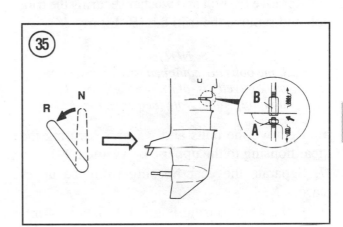

9

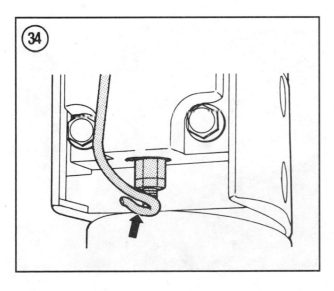

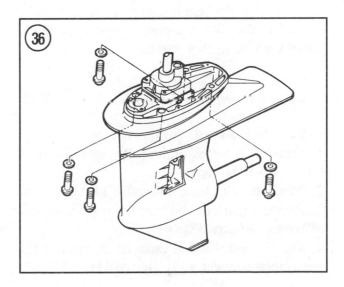

8. If the gear housing is going to be disassembled, mount the gear housing in a suitable holding fixture. If the gear housing is not going to be serviced, place it on a clean work surface and cover with clean shop cloths.

55-90 hp including C series models

1. Perform the *Preliminary Removal Steps* as previously described.
2. Place the shift lever into NEUTRAL.
3. Scribe a mark on the trim tab for reassembly reference (**Figure 37**).
4. Pry the plastic plug (A, **Figure 38**) from the rear of the drive shaft housing to expose the trim tab bolt (**Figure 39**).
5. Remove the bolt and washer securing the trim tab and remove the trim tab (B, **Figure 38**).

> *NOTE*
> *Some bolts are equipped with lockwashers as well as plain washers on the mounting bolts. Note their location.*

6. Remove the bolts and washers securing the gear housing to the upper case (**Figure 40**).
7. Separate the gear housing from the upper case.
8. If the gear housing is going to be disassembled, mount the gear housing in a suitable holding fixture. If the gear housing is not going to be serviced, place it on a clean work surface and cover with clean shop cloths.

115-250 hp including C115 models

Refer to **Figure 41** for this procedure.
1. Perform the *Preliminary Removal Steps* as previously described.
2. Place the shift lever into NEUTRAL.
3. Scribe a mark on the trim tab for reassembly reference (**Figure 37**).
4. On V4 and 90° V6 models, disconnect the speed tube connector (1, **Figure 41**).

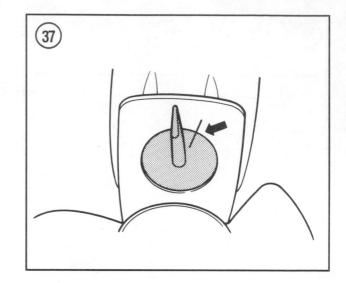

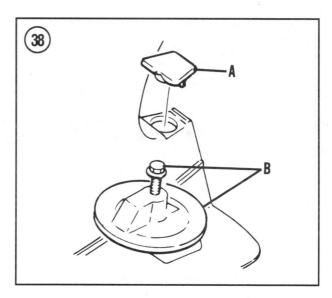

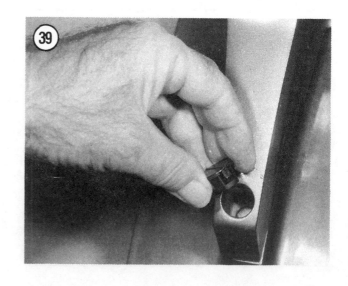

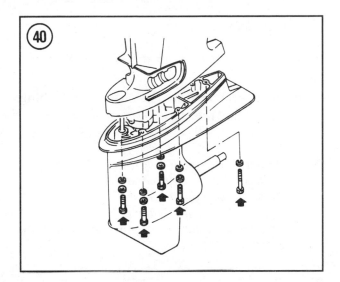

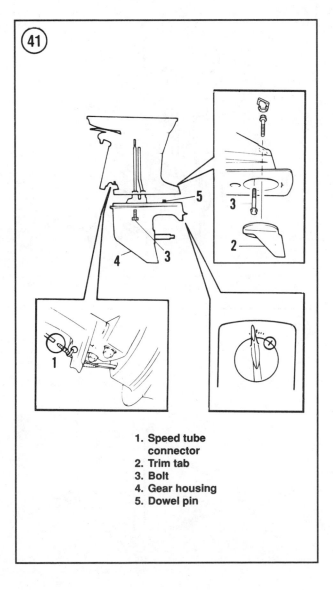

1. Speed tube
   connector
2. Trim tab
3. Bolt
4. Gear housing
5. Dowel pin

9

5. Pry the plastic plug from the rear of the drive shaft housing to expose the trim tab bolt.

6. Remove the bolt and washer securing the trim tab and remove the trim tab (2, **Figure 41**).

7. Remove the bolts and washers (3, **Figure 41**) securing the gear housing to the upper case.

8. Separate the gear housing (4, **Figure 41**) from the upper case. Don't lose the locating dowel (5, **Figure 41**).

9. If the gear housing is going to be disassembled, mount the gearcase in a suitable holding fixture. If the gear housing is not going to be serviced, place on a clean work surface and cover with clean shop cloths.

Installation

2 hp models

1. Lubricate the inside of the drive shaft sleeve and water tube seals with grease.

2. If removed, install the drive shaft sleeve down over the drive shaft and position it in the water pump housing.

3. Make sure the locating pins are in place in the gear housing.

4. Install the antiventilation plate onto the gear housing and onto the dowel pins.

5. Apply red Loctite (No. 271) to the gear housing bolt threads prior to installation.

> *CAUTION*
> *Do **not** rotate the propeller shaft counterclockwise in Step 6 as this can damage the water pump impeller.*

6. Position and correctly seat the gear housing against the upper case. Align the drive shaft splines with the crankshaft and guide the water tube into the upper case properly. If necessary, rotate the propeller shaft clockwise to align the crankshaft and drive shaft splines.

7. Install the gear housing bolts and washers and tighten to the specification listed in **Table 1**.

8. Install the propeller as described in this chapter.

9. Reconnect the spark plug lead and refill the gearcase with the proper type and quantity of lubricant. See Chapter Four.

3 hp models

1. Lubricate the inside of the drive shaft sleeve and water tube seals with grease (A, **Figure 42**).

2. Make sure the locating pins are in place in the gear housing.

3. Apply red Loctite (No. 271) to the gear housing bolt threads prior to installation.

CAUTION
*Do **not** rotate the propeller shaft counterclockwise in Step 4 as this can damage the water pump impeller.*

4. Position and correctly seat the gear housing against the upper case. Align the drive shaft splines with the crankshaft and the guide water tube into the upper case properly. If necessary, rotate the propeller shaft clockwise to align the crankshaft and drive shaft splines.

5. Install the gearcase bolts and washers (B, **Figure 42**) and tighten to the specification listed in **Table 1**.

6. Properly connect the lower shift rod to the upper shift rod connector and tighten the bolt securely (**Figure 43**).

7. Check shift operation in FORWARD and NEUTRAL. If the unit does not shift properly, the problem may either be in the connector (**Figure 31**) or in the gearcase.

8. If the unit shifts properly, install the rubber grommets into the port side of the gear housing. If it does not shift properly, remove the gear housing and locate the problem.

9. Install the propeller as described in this chapter.

10. Reconnect the spark plug lead and refill the gear housing with the proper type and quantity of lubricant. See Chapter Four.

4-8 hp models

1. Place the shift lever in the REVERSE position.

2. Shift the gearcase into REVERSE by pushing the shift rod downward.

CAUTION
Do not grease the top of the drive shaft in Step 2. This may excessively preload the drive shaft and crankshaft when the mounting bolts are tightened and cause a premature failure of the power head or gearcase.

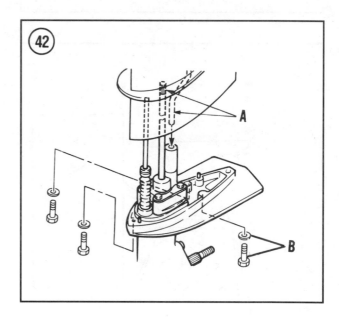

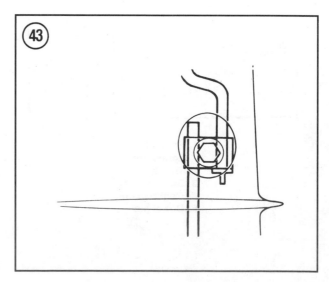

3. Lightly lubricate the drive shaft and splines with grease. Wipe any excessive grease off the top of the drive shaft.

4. Apply red Loctite (No. 271) to the gear housing bolt threads prior to installation.

NOTE
The lower shift rod must pass through a connector and grommet located in the reverse lock plate in the drive shaft housing when installing the gearcase (Figure

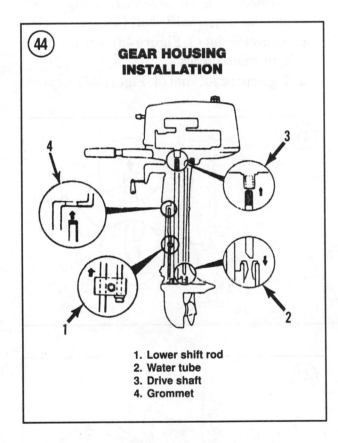

GEAR HOUSING INSTALLATION

1. Lower shift rod
2. Water tube
3. Drive shaft
4. Grommet

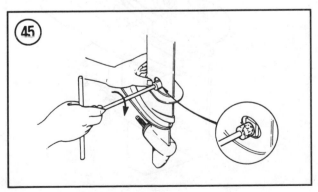

44). If the grommet came off during removal, reinstall it after completing Step 4.

5A. On 4-5 hp models, slide the drive shaft into the drive shaft housing, aligning the lower shift rod with the upper shift rod connector and the water pump with the water tube. Keep the upper case and the gear housing mating surfaces parallel during assembly.

5B. On 6-8 hp models, perform the following:

a. Fit the drive shaft into the drive shaft housing and align the water pump with the water tube. Keep the upper case and the gear housing mating surfaces parallel during assembly.

b. Align the lower and upper shift rods and install the connector (B, **Figure 32**) and the bolt and the nut (A, **Figure 32**). Tighten the bolt and nut securely.

CAUTION
*Do **not** rotate the propeller shaft counterclockwise in Step 6 as this can damage the water pump impeller.*

6. Position and correctly seat the gear housing against the upper case. Align the drive shaft splines with the crankshaft and guide the water tube into the upper case properly. If necessary, rotate the propeller shaft clockwise to align the crankshaft and drive shaft splines.

7. Install the gearcase bolts and washers and tighten to the specification listed in **Table 1** (B, **Figure 42**).

8A. On 3-5 hp models, with the lower and upper shift rods properly aligned in the connector, tighten the bolt securely (**Figure 45**).

8B. On 6-8 hp models, align the lower and upper shift rods and install the connector (B, **Figure 32**) onto both rods. Install the bolt and nut (A, **Figure 32**) and tighten securely.

9. Check shift operation in FORWARD, NEUTRAL and REVERSE. If the unit does not shift properly, the problem may either be in the connector (**Figure 31**) or in the gearcase.

9

10. If the unit shifts properly, install the rubber grommet into the port side of the gear housing. If it does not shift properly, remove the gear housing and locate the problem.

11. Install the propeller as described in this chapter.

12. Reconnect the spark plug leads and refill the gear housing with the proper type and quantity of lubricant. See Chapter Four.

9-50 hp including C series models

1. Place the shift lever in the REVERSE.

> *CAUTION*
> *Do not grease the top of the drive shaft in Step 2. This may excessively preload the drive shaft and crankshaft when the mounting bolts are tightened and cause a premature failure of the power head or gearcase.*

2. Lightly lubricate the drive shaft and splines with grease. Wipe any excess grease off the top of the drive shaft.

3. Apply red Loctite (No. 271) to the gear housing bolt threads prior to installation.

> *CAUTION*
> *Do **not** rotate the propeller shaft counterclockwise in Step 4 as this can damage the water pump impeller.*

> *NOTE*
> *In Step 4, on 40-50 hp and Pro 50 models, also align the shift shaft with the upper case during assembly.*

4. Position and correctly seat the gear housing against the upper case. Align the drive shaft splines with the crankshaft and guide the water tube into the upper case properly (**Figure 46**). If necessary, rotate the propeller shaft clockwise to align the crankshaft and drive shaft splines.

> *NOTE*
> *Some models are equipped with lock-washers as well as plain washers on*

some mounting bolts. Install the lock-washers on the correct bolts as noted during disassembly.

5. Install the gearcase bolts and washers and tighten to specification listed in **Table 1** (**Figure 47**).

6. On all models except 40-50 hp and Pro 50, perform the following:

   a. If not already in this position, shift the upper and lower shift shafts into REVERSE.

   b. Connect the lower shift shaft (1, **Figure 48**) onto the upper shift shaft (2).

   c. Screw the nut (3, **Figure 48**) onto the upper shift shaft 5 turns.

   d. Tighten the locknut (4, **Figure 48**) securely.

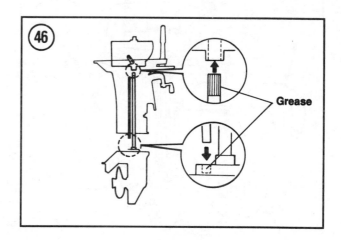

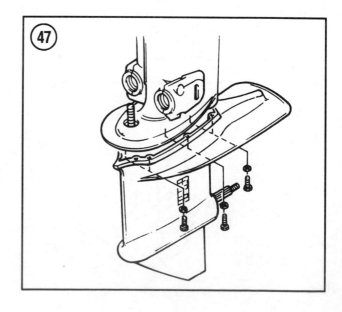

7. On 25 hp models, connect the reverse interlock hook (**Figure 34**) onto the shift rod.

8. On C25, 30 hp, C30, C40 models, install the trim tab and align the marks made during disassembly. Install the bolt and washer and tighten securely.

9. Check shift operation in FORWARD, NEUTRAL and REVERSE. If the unit does not shift properly, the problem may either be in the shift rod connector or in the gearcase.

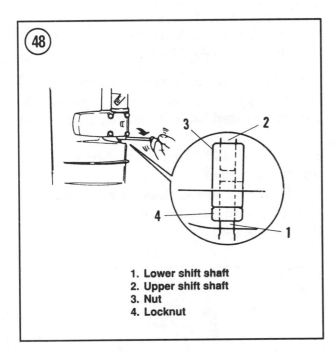

1. Lower shift shaft
2. Upper shift shaft
3. Nut
4. Locknut

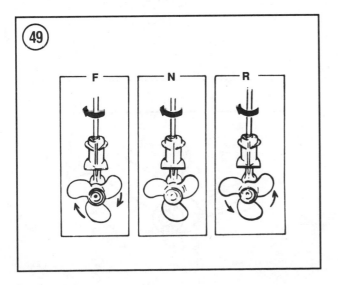

10. If the unit does not shift properly, remove the gear housing and locate the problem.

11. Install the propeller as described in this chapter.

12. Reconnect the spark plug leads and refill the gear housing with the proper type and quantity of lubricant. See Chapter Four.

55-90 hp including C series models

> *CAUTION*
> *Do not grease the top of the drive shaft in Step 1. This may excessively preload the drive shaft and crankshaft when the mounting bolts are tightened and cause a premature failure of the power head or gearcase.*

1. Lightly lubricate the drive shaft and splines with grease. Wipe any excess grease off the top of the drive shaft.

> *CAUTION*
> *In Step 2, work carefully and slowly to avoid damaging the crankshaft lower oil seal with the drive shaft.*

2. If removed, fit the drive shaft into the gear case housing. Make sure that the drive shaft is properly meshed with its mating gear in the gearcase.

3. Install the shift handle (part No. YB-6052) onto the shift shaft.

4. Slowly rotate the drive shaft clockwise and check the shift operation as follows (**Figure 49**):

    a. FORWARD—propeller shaft will rotate only clockwise.

    b. NEUTRAL—propeller shaft will rotate freely in both directions.

    c. REVERSE—propeller shaft will rotate only counterclockwise.

5. Remove the special shift handle tool.

6. If the unit does not shift properly, locate the problem.

7. After checking the action, return the lever to the NEUTRAL position and align the shift lever

mark with the arrow on the bottom cowling. Refer to **Figure 50** for C55 or **Figure 51** for all other models.

8. On C55 models, if removed, install the reverse rod guide in the upper case (**Figure 52**).

9. If removed, install the water tube and shift shaft into the gear housing and make sure they are properly aligned.

10. Apply red Loctite (No. 271) to the gear housing bolt threads prior to installation.

> *CAUTION*
> *Do **not** rotate the propeller shaft counterclockwise in Step 11 as this can damage the water pump impeller.*

11. Position and correctly seat the gear housing against the upper case. Align the drive shaft splines with the crankshaft and guide the water tube into the upper case properly (**Figure 53**). If necessary, rotate the propeller shaft clockwise to align the crankshaft and drive shaft splines.

> *NOTE*
> *Some bolts are equipped with lockwashers as well as plain washers. Install the lockwashers on the correct bolts as noted during disassembly.*

12. Install the gearcase bolts and washers (**Figure 40**) and tighten to specification listed in **Table 1**.

13. Install the trim tab and align the marks made during disassembly. Install the bolt and washer and tighten securely.

14. Install the plastic plug into the rear of the drive shaft housing (**Figure 39**).

15. Install the propeller as described in this chapter.

16. Reconnect the spark plug leads and refill the gear housing with the proper type and quantity of lubricant. See Chapter Four.

115-250 hp including C115 models

Refer to **Figure 41** for this procedure.

> *CAUTION*
> *Do not grease the top of the drive shaft in Step 1. This may excessively preload the drive shaft and crankshaft when the mounting bolts are tightened and cause a premature failure of the power head or gearcase.*

1. Lightly lubricate the drive shaft and splines with grease. Wipe any excessive grease off the top of the drive shaft.

> *CAUTION*
> *In Step 2, work carefully and slowly to avoid damaging the crankshaft lower oil seal with the drive shaft.*

2. If removed, fit the drive shaft into the gearcase housing. Make sure that the drive shaft is properly meshed with its mating gear in the gearcase.

3. Install the shift handle (part No. YB-6052) onto the shift shaft.

4A. On regular rotation models, rotate the drive shaft clockwise and check the shift operation as follows (**Figure 54**):

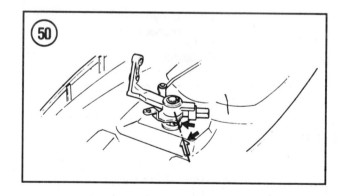

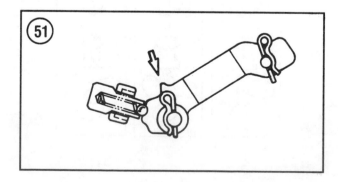

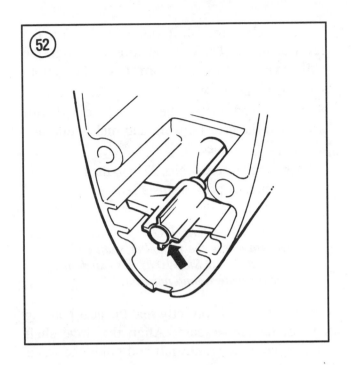

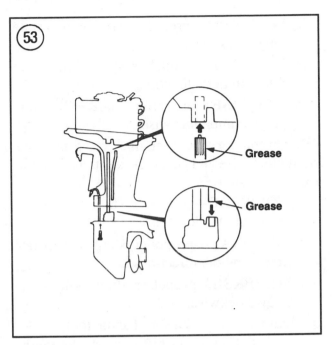

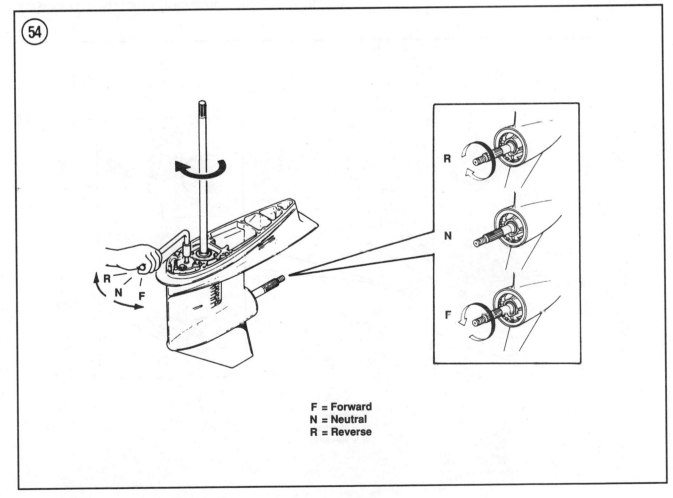

F = Forward
N = Neutral
R = Reverse

a. FORWARD—propeller shaft will rotate only clockwise.

b. NEUTRAL—propeller shaft will rotate freely in both directions.

c. REVERSE—propeller shaft will rotate only counterclockwise.

4B. On counter rotation engines, rotate the drive shaft clockwise and check the shift operation as follows (**Figure 55**):

a. FORWARD—propeller shaft will rotate only counterclockwise.

b. NEUTRAL—propeller shaft will rotate freely in both directions.

c. REVERSE—propeller shaft will rotate only clockwise.

5. Remove the special shift handle tool.

6. If the unit does not shift properly, locate the problem.

7. After checking shift operation, return the lever to the NEUTRAL position and align the shift lever mark with the arrow on the bottom cowling (**Figure 56**).

8. If removed, install the water tube and shift shaft into the gear housing and make sure they are properly aligned.

9. Apply red Loctite (No. 271) to the gear housing bolt threads prior to installation.

CAUTION
*Do **not** rotate the propeller shaft counterclockwise in Step 10 as this can damage the water pump impeller.*

10. Position and correctly seat the gear housing against the upper case. Align the drive shaft splines with the crankshaft and guide the water tube into the upper case properly. If necessary,

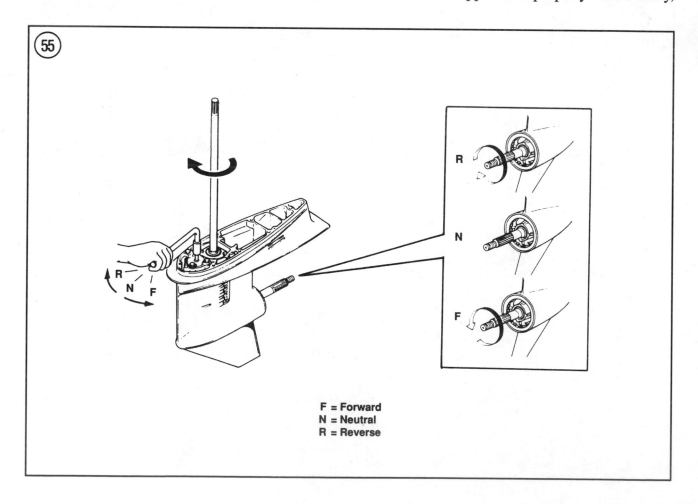

F = Forward
N = Neutral
R = Reverse

rotate the propeller shaft clockwise to align the crankshaft and drive shaft splines.

11. Install the gearcase bolts and washers and tighten to the specification listed in **Table 1** (**Figure 40**, typical).

12. Install the trim tab and align the marks made during disassembly (**Figure 57**). Install the bolt and washer and tighten securely.

13. Install the plastic plug into the rear of the drive shaft housing.

14. On V4 and 90° V6 models, connect the speed tube connector.

15. Install the propeller as described in this chapter.

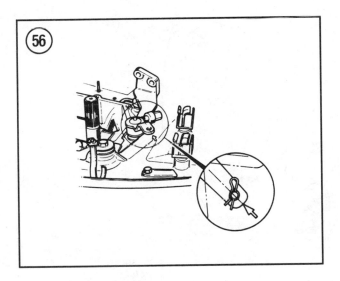

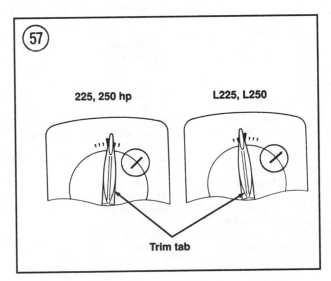

16. Reconnect the spark plug leads and refill the gear housing with the proper type and quantity of lubricant. See Chapter Four.

GEARCASE DISASSEMBLY/INSPECTION/ REASSEMBLY

The following exploded view drawings are of the gearcases covered in this chapter. Refer to the appropriate drawing for the specific model being worked on for all service procedures:

  a. **Figure 58**: 2 hp gearcase.
  b. **Figure 59**: 3 hp gearcase.
  c. **Figure 60**: 4 and 5 hp gearcase.
  d. **Figure 61**: 6 and 8 hp gearcase.
  e. **Figure 62**: 9.9 and 15 hp gearcase.
  f. **Figure 63**: C25 gearcase.
  g. **Figure 64**: 25 hp gearcase.
  h. **Figure 65**: C30 hp gearcase.
  i. **Figure 66**: 30 hp gearcase.
  j. **Figure 67**: C40 and C55 gearcase.
  k. **Figure 68**: 40 and 50 hp and Pro 50 gearcase.
  l. **Figure 69**: Pro 60, 70 hp, C75, C85 and 90 hp gearcase.
  m. **Figure 70**: C115 V4 gearcase.
  n. **Figure 71**: 115-130 hp V4 and 150-225 90° V6 Regular Rotation gearcase.
  o. **Figure 72**: L130 V4 Counter Rotation gearcase.
  p. **Figure 73**: L150 and L200 90° V6 Counter Rotation gearcase.
  q. **Figure 74**: 225 and 250 hp 76° V6 Regular Rotation gearcase.
  r. **Figure 75**: L225 and L250 hp 76° V6 Counter Rotation gearcase.

Bearing Carrier and Propeller Shaft Removal (2-15 hp, 25 hp, C30, 40-50 hp, Pro 50 models)

1. Remove the propeller as described in this chapter.

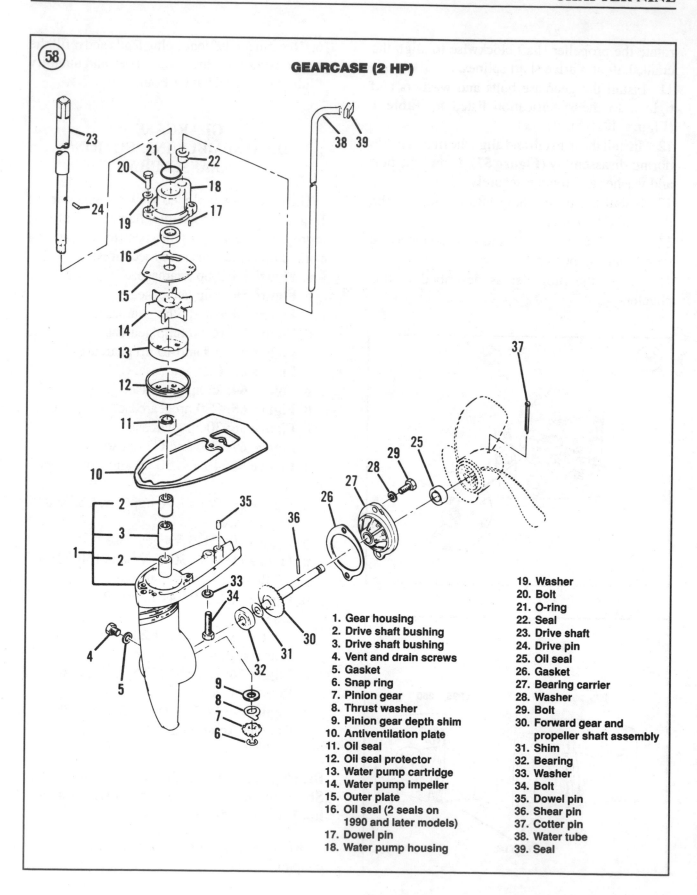

GEARCASE (2 HP)

1. Gear housing
2. Drive shaft bushing
3. Drive shaft bushing
4. Vent and drain screws
5. Gasket
6. Snap ring
7. Pinion gear
8. Thrust washer
9. Pinion gear depth shim
10. Antiventilation plate
11. Oil seal
12. Oil seal protector
13. Water pump cartridge
14. Water pump impeller
15. Outer plate
16. Oil seal (2 seals on 1990 and later models)
17. Dowel pin
18. Water pump housing
19. Washer
20. Bolt
21. O-ring
22. Seal
23. Drive shaft
24. Drive pin
25. Oil seal
26. Gasket
27. Bearing carrier
28. Washer
29. Bolt
30. Forward gear and propeller shaft assembly
31. Shim
32. Bearing
33. Washer
34. Bolt
35. Dowel pin
36. Shear pin
37. Cotter pin
38. Water tube
39. Seal

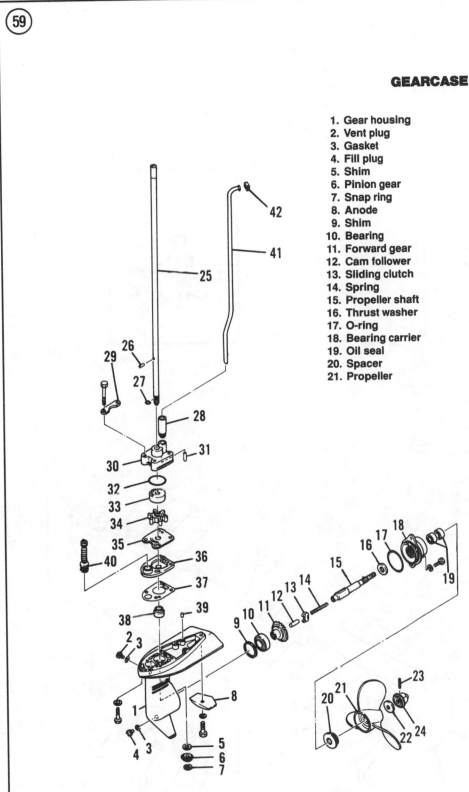

GEARCASE (3 HP)

1. Gear housing
2. Vent plug
3. Gasket
4. Fill plug
5. Shim
6. Pinion gear
7. Snap ring
8. Anode
9. Shim
10. Bearing
11. Forward gear
12. Cam follower
13. Sliding clutch
14. Spring
15. Propeller shaft
16. Thrust washer
17. O-ring
18. Bearing carrier
19. Oil seal
20. Spacer
21. Propeller
22. Washer
23. Shear pin
24. Propeller nut
25. Drive shaft
26. Pin
27. Clip
28. Seal
29. Plate
30. Water pump housing
31. Dowel pin
32. O-ring
33. Insert
34. Impeller
35. Plate
36. Water pump base
37. Gasket
38. Oil seal
39. Dowel pin
40. Boot
41. Water tube
42. Seal

9

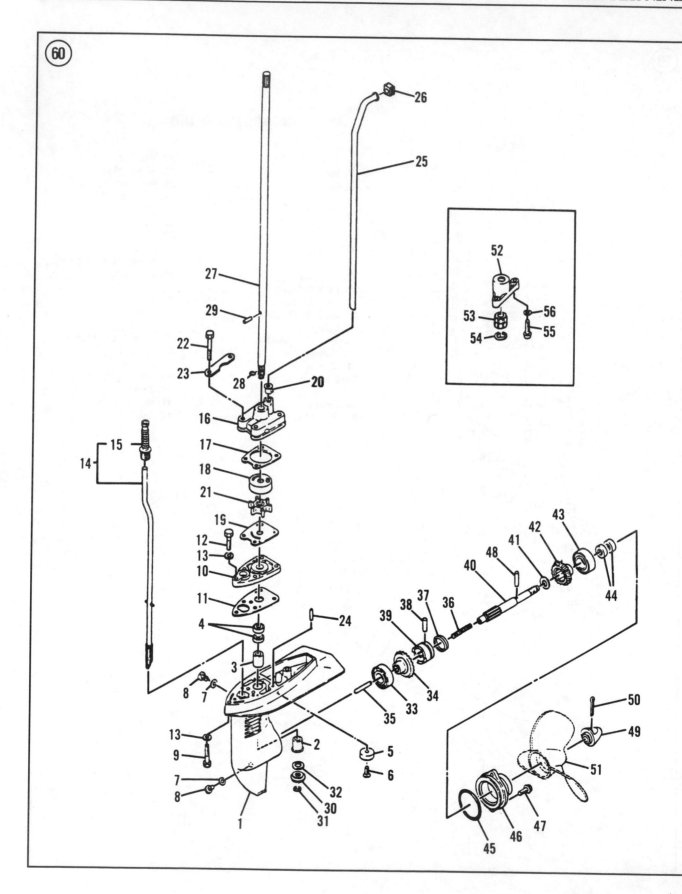

GEARCASE (4 AND 5 HP)

1. Gear housing
2. Bushing
3. Bushing
4. Oil seal
5. Anode
6. Screw
7. Gasket
8. Plug
9. Bolt
10. Water pump base
11. Gasket
12. Bolt
13. Washer
14. Lower shift rod
15. Boot
16. Water pump housing
17. Gasket
18. Insert
19. Outer plate
20. Seal
21. Impeller
22. Bolt
23. Support plate
24. Dowel pin
25. Water tube
26. Seal
27. Drive shaft
28. Clip
29. Dowel pin
30. Pinion gear
31. Snap ring
32. Thrust washer
33. Ball bearing
34. Forward gear
35. Cam follower
36. Compression spring
37. Cross pin retaining ring
38. Cross pin
39. Sliding clutch
40. Propeller shaft
41. Thrust washer
42. Reverse gear
43. Ball bearing
44. Oil seal
45. O-ring
46. Gear housing cap
    (bearing carrier)
47. Bolt
48. Shear pin
49. Propeller nut
50. Cotter pin
51. Propeller
52. Bushing housing*
53. Bushing*
54. Snap ring*
55. Bolt*
56. Washer*

* Long drive shaft models only.

9

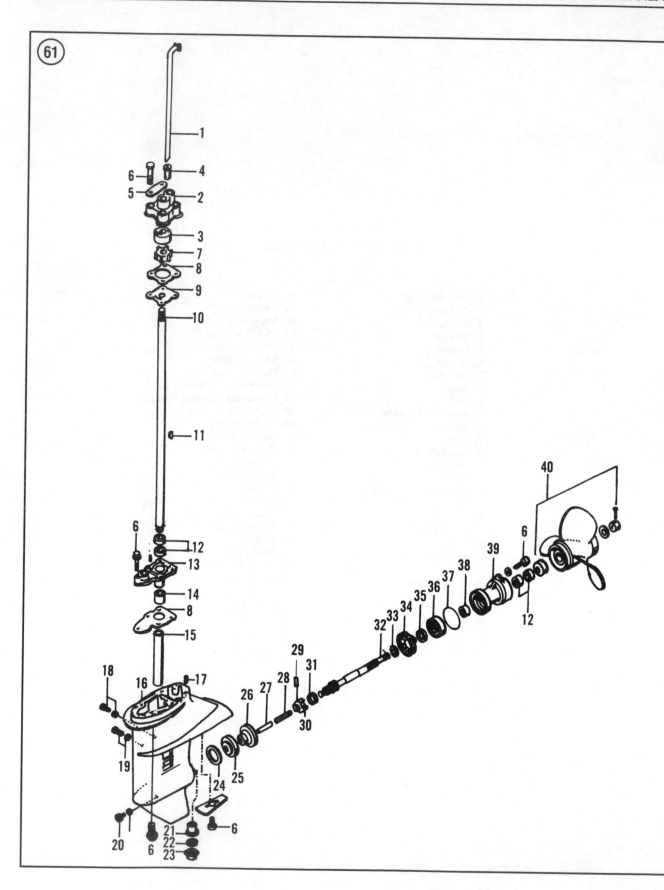

GEARCASE
(6 AND 8 HP)

1. Water tube
2. Water pump cover
3. Cover insert
4. Seal
5. Support plate
6. Bolt
7. Impeller
8. Gasket
9. Face plate
10. Drive shaft
11. Drive key
12. Oil seal
13. Oil seal housing
14. Upper bushing
15. Sleeve
16. Gearcase housing
17. Dowel pin
18. Vent plug/washer
19. Plug/washer
20. Drain/fill plug
21. Bushing
22. Thrust washer
23. Pinion gear
24. Shim
25. Bearing
26. Forward gear
27. Shift plunger
28. Spring
29. Cross pin
30. Clutch dog
31. Retaining spring
32. Propeller shaft
33. Thrust bearing
34. Reverse gear
35. Shim
36. Bearing
37. O-ring
38. Needle bearing
39. Bearing housing
40. Propeller assembly

9

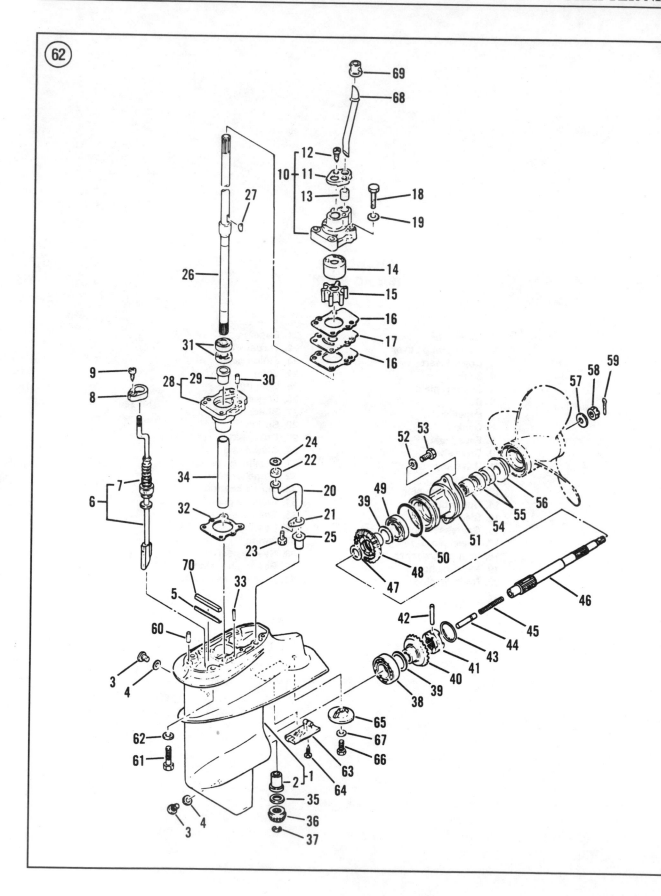

GEARCASE
(9.9 AND 15 HP)

1. Gear housing
2. Bushing
3. Plug
4. Gasket
5. Seal guide
6. Shift cam assembly
7. Shift rod boot
8. Bracket
9. Screw
10. Water pump housing
11. Water pump cover
12. Screw
13. Seal
14. Water pump insert
15. Impeller
16. Gasket
17. Outer plate
18. Bolt
19. Washer
20. Water pickup tube
21. Retainer plate
22. Seal
23. Screw
24. Washer
25. Seal
26. Drive shaft
27. Woodruff key
28. Bearing housing
    (water pump base)
29. Bushing
30. Dowel pin
31. Oil seal
32. Gasket
33. Dowel pin
34. Drive shaft tube
35. Thrust washer
    (adjusting shim)
36. Pinion gear
37. Snap ring
38. Ball bearing
39. Shim
40. Forward gear
41. Sliding clutch
42. Cross pin
43. Cross pin
    retaining ring
44. Cam follower
45. Spring
46. Propeller shaft
47. Thrust washer
48. Reverse gear
49. Ball bearing
50. O-ring
51. Bearing carrier
52. Bolt
53. Washer
54. Needle bearing
55. Oil seal
56. Thrust washer
57. Washer
58. Propeller nut
59. Cotter pin
60. Dowel pin
61. Bolt
62. Washer
63. Inlet cover
64. Screw
65. Anode
66. Bolt
67. Washer
68. Water tube
69. Seal
70. Seal

9

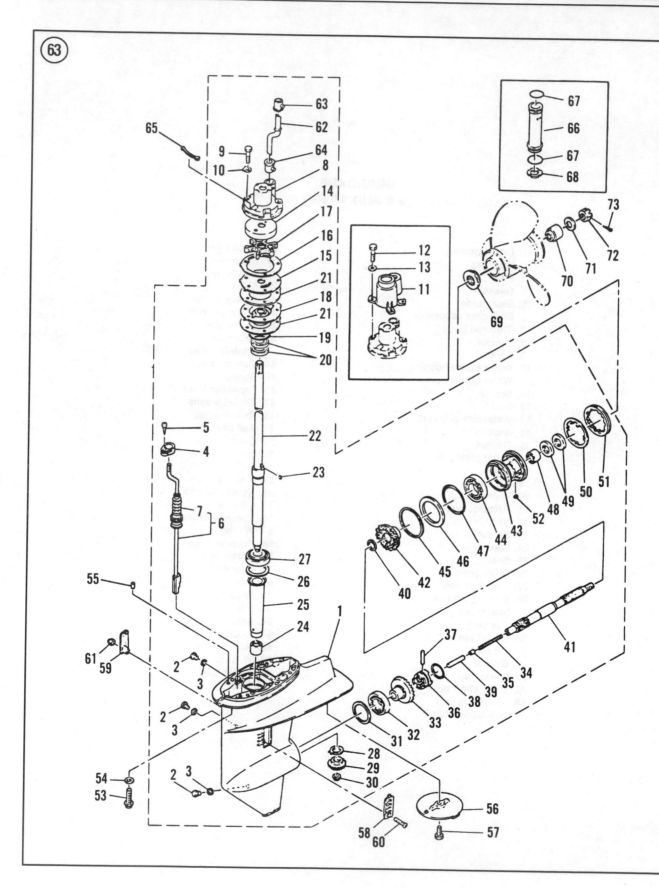

GEARCASE
(C25)

1. Gear housing
2. Plug
3. Gasket
4. Bracket
5. Screw
6. Lower shift shaft assembly
7. Boot
8. Water pump housing
9. Bolt
10. Washer*
11. Housing extension
12. Housing and extension bolt**
13. Washer**
14. Cartridge insert
15. Outer plate
16. Gasket
17. Impeller
18. Water pump base
19. O-ring
20. Oil seal
21. Gasket
22. Drive shaft
23. Woodruff key
24. Needle bearing
25. Drive shaft sleeve
26. Shim
27. Tapered roller bearing
28. Thrust washer
29. Pinion gear
30. Nut
31. Shim
32. Tapered roller bearing
33. Forward gear
34. Compression spring
35. Shift slide
36. Sliding clutch
37. Cross pin

38. Cross pin retaining ring
39. Shift plunger
40. Thrust washer
41. Propeller shaft
42. Reverse gear
43. Bearing carrier
44. Ball bearing
45. Shim
46. Thrust washer
47. O-ring
48. Needle bearing
49. Oil seal
50. Tab washer
51. Cover nut
52. Key
53. Bolt
54. Washer
55. Dowel pin
56. Trim tab
57. Bolt
58. Port water inlet cover
59. Starboard water inlet cover
60. Cover screw
61. Nut
62. Water tube
63. Seal
64. Seal
65. Spacer
66. Water tube extension***
67. O-ring
68. Plate
69. Forward thrust hub
70. Reverse thrust hub
71. Washer
72. Propeller nut
73. Cotter pin

  * Short shaft only
 ** Long shaft only
*** Long and Super Ultra Long shaft only.

9

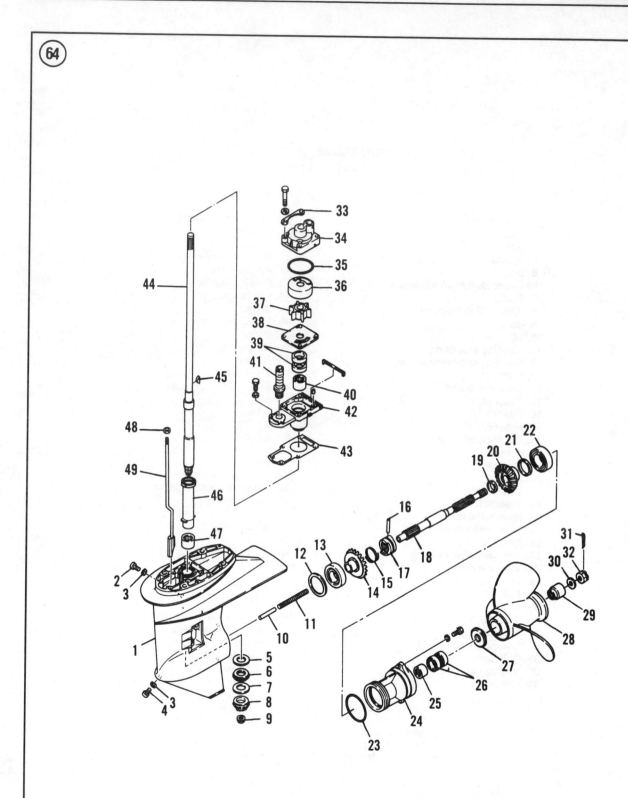

GEARCASE
(25 HP)

1. Gear housing
2. Vent plug
3. Gasket
4. Fill plug
5. Thrust washer
6. Bearing
7. Shim
8. Pinion gear
9. Nut
10. Cam follower
11. Spring
12. Shim
13. Bearing
14. Forward gear
15. Cross pin retainer ring
16. Cross pin
17. Sliding clutch
18. Propeller shaft
19. Plate washer
20. Reverse gear
21. Shim
22. Bearing
23. O-ring
24. Bearing carrier
25. Bearing

26. Oil seal
27. Spacer
28. Propeller
29. Spacer
30. Washer
31. Cotter pin
32. Nut
33. Plate
34. Water pump housing
35. O-ring
36. Insert
37. Impeller
38. Plate
39. Oil seals
40. Bearing
41. Boot
42. Oil seal housing
43. Gasket
44. Drive shaft
45. Woodruff key
46. Drive shaft sleeve
47. Bearing
48. Nut
49. Shift rod assembly

9

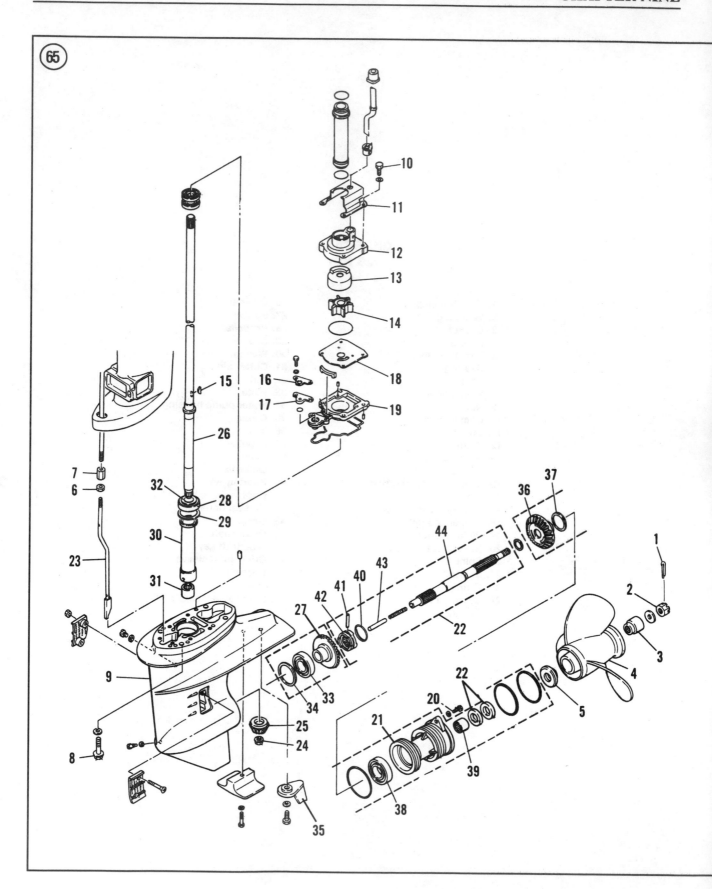

**GEARCASE
(C30)**

1. Cotter pin
2. Nut
3. Spacer
4. Propeller
5. Spacer
6. Locknut
7. Joint nut
8. Bolt
9. Gear housing
10. Bolt
11. Plate
12. Water pump housing
13. Insert cartridge
14. Impeller
15. Woodruff key
16. Bracket
17. Plate
18. Outer plate
19. Oil seal housing
20. Bolt
21. Bearing carrier
22. Oil seals
23. Shift cam
24. Nut
25. Pinion gear
26. Drive shaft
27. Forward gear assembly
28. Bearing outer race
29. Shim
30. Drive shaft sleeve
31. Needle bearing
32. Bearing inner race
33. Ball bearing
34. Shim
35. Trim tab
36. Reverse gear
37. Shim
38. Ball bearing
39. Needle bearing
40. Cross pin ring
41. Cross pin
42. Dog clutch
43. Shift plunger
44. Propeller shaft

9

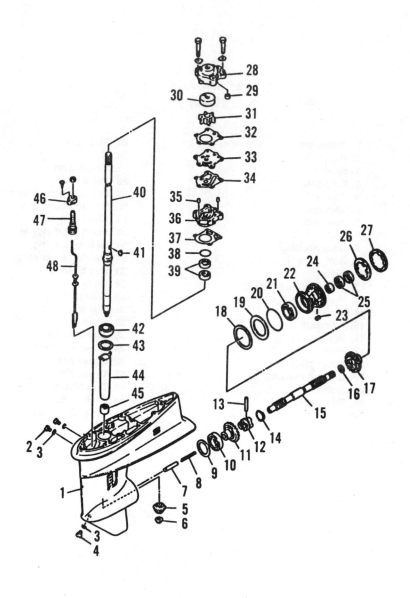

GEARCASE
(30 HP)

1. Gear housing
2. Vent plug
3. Gasket
4. Fill plug
5. Pinion gear
6. Nut
7. Cam follower
8. Spring
9. Shim
10. Bearing
11. Forward gear
12. Sliding clutch
13. Cross pin
14. Cross pin retainer ring
15. Propeller shaft
16. Washer
17. Reverse gear
18. Shim
19. Thrust washer
20. O-ring
21. Bearing
22. Bearing carrier
23. Key
24. Bearing

25. Seals
26. Washer
27. Nut
28. Water pump housing
29. Damper
30. Insert
31. Impeller
32. Gasket
33. Plate
34. Gasket
35. Dowel pin
36. Water pump base
37. Gasket
38. O-ring
39. Oil seals
40. Drive shaft
41. Woodruff key
42. Bearing
43. Shim
44. Drive shaft sleeve
45. Bearing
46. Bracket
47. Boot
48. Shift rod assembly

9

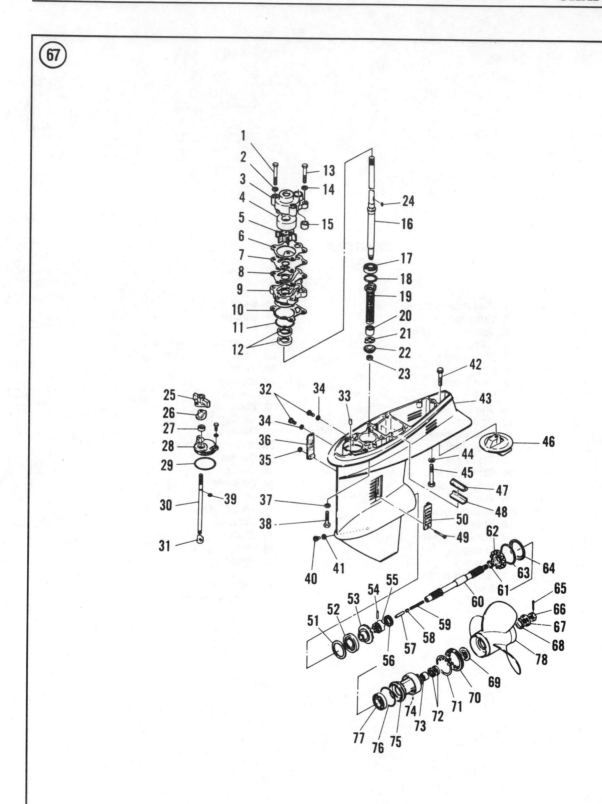

GEARCASE
(C40 AND C55 HP)

1. Bolt
2. Washer
3. Water pump housing
4. Cartridge insert
5. Impeller
6. Gasket
7. Outer plate
8. Gasket
9. Water pump base
10. Gasket
11. O-ring
12. Oil seal
13. Bolt
14. Washer
15. Water seal
16. Drive shaft
17. Taper roller bearing
18. Shim
19. Drive shaft sleeve
20. Needle bearing
21. Bearing*
22. Pinion gear*
23. Nut*
24. Woodruff key
25. Reverse rod guide
26. Reverse rod cam
27. Oil seal
28. Plate
29. O-ring
30. Shift rod
31. Shift cam
32. Plug
33. Dowel pin
34. Gasket
35. Nut
36. Water inlet cover
37. Washer
38. Bolt
39. Circlip
40. Plug
41. Gasket
42. Bolt
43. Gear housing
44. Spring washer
45. Bolt
46. Trim tab
47. Seal rubber
48. Seal rubber guide
49. Screw
50. Water inlet cover
51. Shim
52. Taper roller bearing
53. Forward gear
54. Cross pin
55. Sliding clutch
56. Cross pin retainer ring
57. Shift plunger
58. Shift slide
59. Compression spring
60. Propeller shaft
61. Washer
62. Reverse gear
63. Shim
64. Thrust washer
65. Cotter pin
66. Castellated nut
67. Spacer
68. Thrust plate cap
69. Spacer
70. Cover nut
71. Tab washer
72. Oil seal
73. Needle bearing
74. Bearing carrier key
75. Bearing carrier
76. O-ring
77. Ball bearing
78. Propeller

* Models so equipped.

9

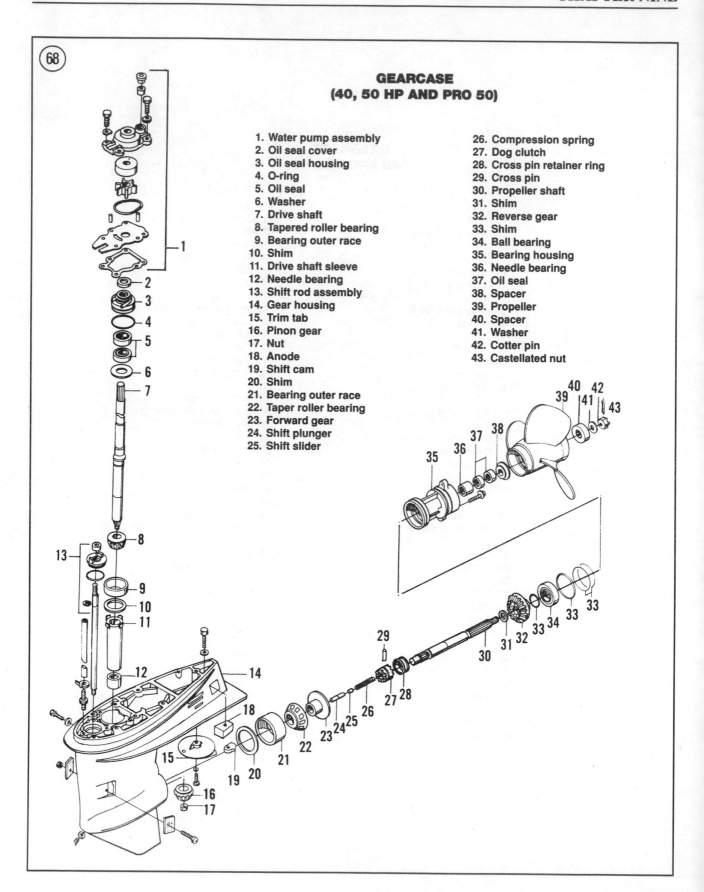

**GEARCASE
(40, 50 HP AND PRO 50)**

1. Water pump assembly
2. Oil seal cover
3. Oil seal housing
4. O-ring
5. Oil seal
6. Washer
7. Drive shaft
8. Tapered roller bearing
9. Bearing outer race
10. Shim
11. Drive shaft sleeve
12. Needle bearing
13. Shift rod assembly
14. Gear housing
15. Trim tab
16. Pinon gear
17. Nut
18. Anode
19. Shift cam
20. Shim
21. Bearing outer race
22. Taper roller bearing
23. Forward gear
24. Shift plunger
25. Shift slider
26. Compression spring
27. Dog clutch
28. Cross pin retainer ring
29. Cross pin
30. Propeller shaft
31. Shim
32. Reverse gear
33. Shim
34. Ball bearing
35. Bearing housing
36. Needle bearing
37. Oil seal
38. Spacer
39. Propeller
40. Spacer
41. Washer
42. Cotter pin
43. Castellated nut

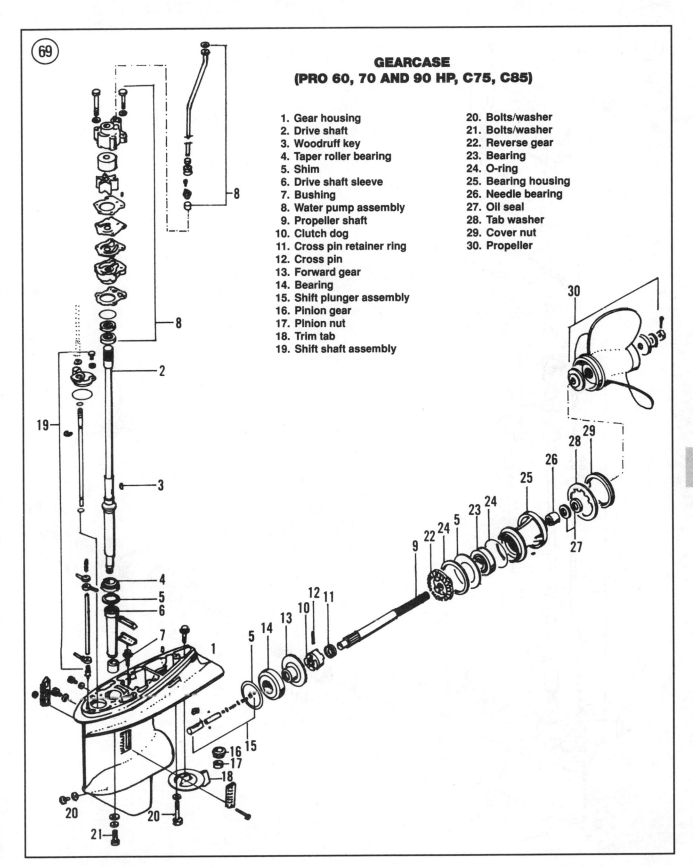

**GEARCASE
(PRO 60, 70 AND 90 HP, C75, C85)**

1. Gear housing
2. Drive shaft
3. Woodruff key
4. Taper roller bearing
5. Shim
6. Drive shaft sleeve
7. Bushing
8. Water pump assembly
9. Propeller shaft
10. Clutch dog
11. Cross pin retainer ring
12. Cross pin
13. Forward gear
14. Bearing
15. Shift plunger assembly
16. Pinion gear
17. Pinion nut
18. Trim tab
19. Shift shaft assembly
20. Bolts/washer
21. Bolts/washer
22. Reverse gear
23. Bearing
24. O-ring
25. Bearing housing
26. Needle bearing
27. Oil seal
28. Tab washer
29. Cover nut
30. Propeller

9

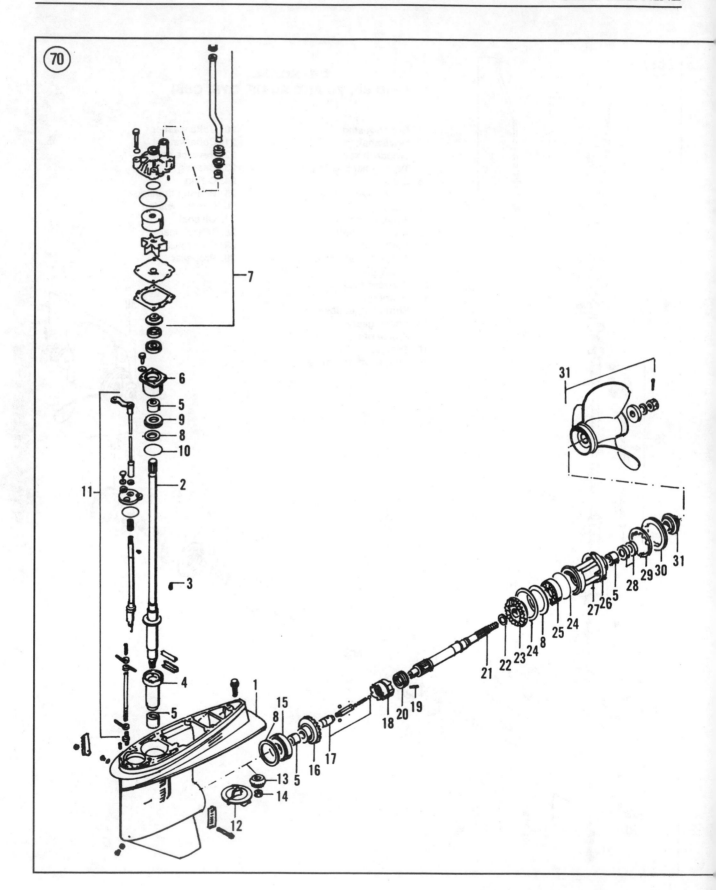

GEARCASE
(C115 V4)

1. Gearcase housing
2. Drive shaft
3. Woodruff key
4. Drive shaft sleeve
5. Needle bearing
6. Thrust bearing housing
7. Water pump assembly
8. Shim
9. Taper roller bearing
10. O-ring
11. Shift shaft assembly
12. Trim tab
13. Pinion gear
14. Nut
15. Bearing
16. Forward gear
17. Shift plunger assembly
18. Clutch dog
19. Cross pin
20. Cross pin retainer ring
21. Propeller shaft
22. Thrust washer
23. Reverse gear
24. O-ring
25. Bearing
26. Bearing housing
27. Housing key
28. Oil seal
29. tab washer
30. Cover nut
31. Propeller assembly

9

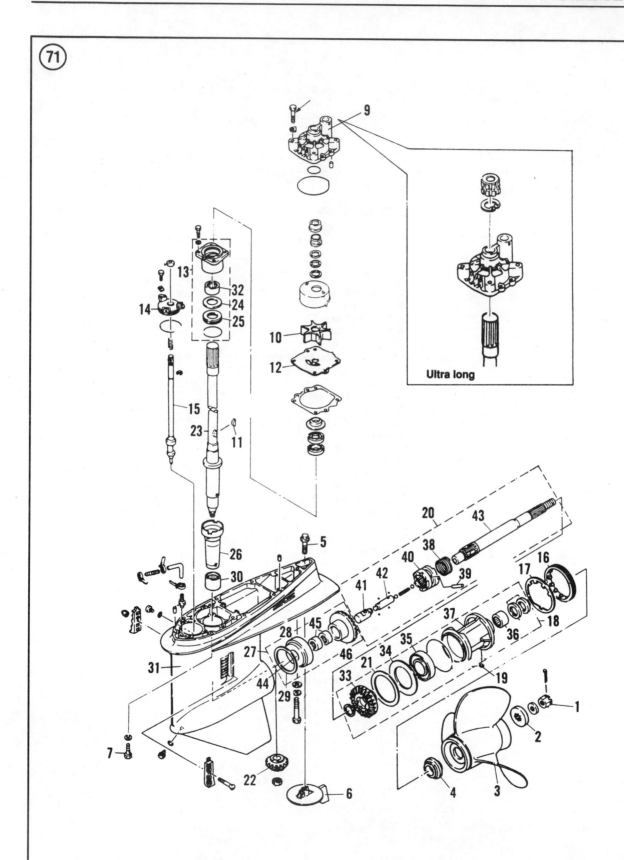

Ultra long

GEARCASE
(115-225 HP V4 AND 90° V6 [REGULAR ROTATION])

1. Nut
2. Spacer (rear)
3. Propeller
4. Spacer (front)
5. Bolt
6. Trim tab
7. Bolt
8. Lower unit assembly
9. Water pump housing
10. Impeller
11. Woodruff key
12. Impeller plate
13. Bearing housing
14. Bracket
15. Shift rod
16. Ring nut
17. Tab washer
18. Bearing housing
19. Straight key
20. Propeller shaft assembly
21. Shim
22. Pinion gear
23. Drive shaft

24. Shim
25. Thrust bearing
26. Drive shaft sleeve
27. Forward gear assembly
28. Bearing outer race
29. Shim
30. Needle bearing
31. Lower casing
32. Needle bearing
33. Reverse gear
34. Thrust washer
35. Ball bearing
36. Needle bearing
37. Bearing housing
38. Cross pin retainer ring
39. Cross pin
40. Dog clutch
41. Shifter
42. Shift slider
43. Propeller shaft
44. Bearing inner race
45. Needle bearing
46. Forward gear

9

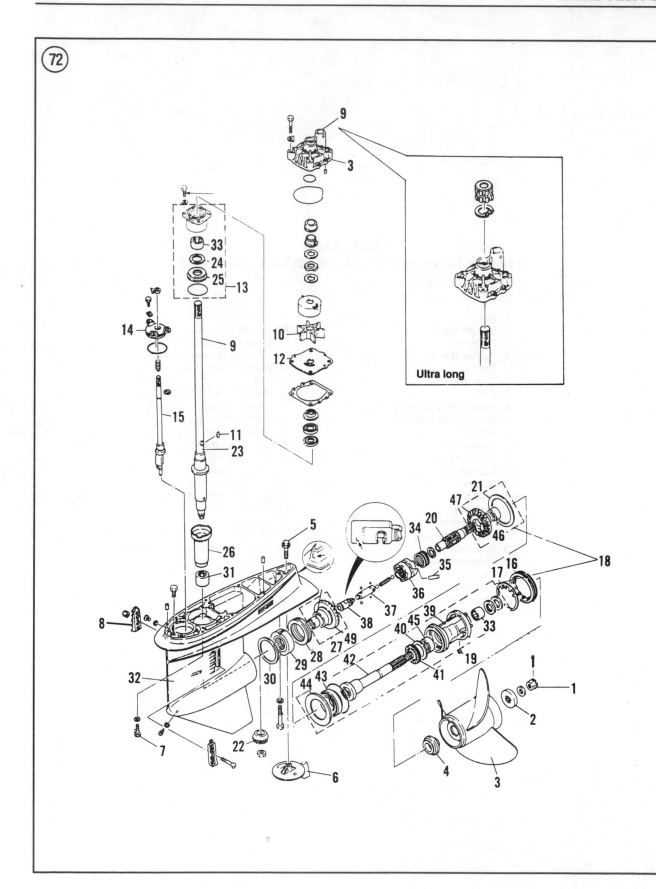

Ultra long

GEARCASE
(L130 V4 [COUNTER ROTATION])

1. Nut
2. Spacer (rear)
3. Propeller
4. Spacer (front)
5. Bolt
6. Trim tab
7. Bolt
8. Lower unit assembly
9. Water pump housing
10. Impeller
11. Woodruff key
12. Impeller plate
13. Bearing housing
14. Bracket
15. Shift rod
16. Ring nut
17. Claw washer
18. Bearing housing
19. Straight key
20. Front propeller
    shaft assembly
21. Shim
22. Pinion gear
23. Drive shaft
24. Shim

25. Thrust bearing
26. Drive shaft sleeve
27. Reverse gear assembly
28. Thrust bearing
29. Roller bearing
30. Shim
31. Needle bearing
32. Lower casing
33. Needle bearing
34. Cross pin retainer ring
35. Cross pin
36. Dog clutch
37. Shifter
38. Shift slider
39. Bearing housing
40. Shim
41. Thrust bearing
42. Rear propeller shaft
43. Taper roller bearing
44. Thrust washer
45. Needle bearing
46. Needle bearing
47. Forward gear
48. Needle bearing
49. Reverse gear

9

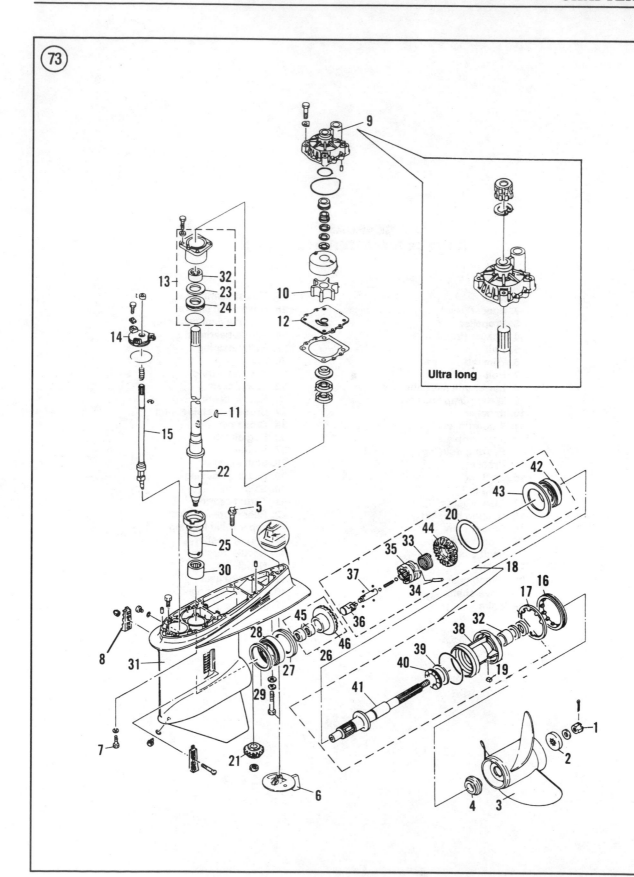

Ultra long

GEARCASE
(L150 AND L200 90° V6 [COUNTER ROTATION])

1. Nut
2. Spacer (rear)
3. Propeller
4. Spacer (front)
5. Bolt
6. Trim tab
7. Bolt
8. Lower unit assembly
9. Water pump housing
10. Impeller
11. Woodruff key
12. Impeller plate
13. Bearing housing
14. Bracket
15. Shift rod
16. Ring nut
17. Claw washer
18. Bearing housing
19. Straight key
20. Shim
21. Pinion gear
22. Drive shaft
23. Shim
24. Thrust bearing
25. Drive shaft sleeve
26. Reverse gear assembly
27. Thrust bearing
28. Roller bearing
29. Shim
30. Needle bearing
31. Lower casing
32. Needle bearing
33. Cross pin retainer ring
34. Cross pin
35. Dog clutch
36. Shifter
37. Shift slider
38. Bearing housing
39. Shim
40. Thrust bearing
41. Propeller shaft
42. Taper roller bearing
43. Thrust washer
44. Forward gear
45. Needle bearing
46. Reverse gear

9

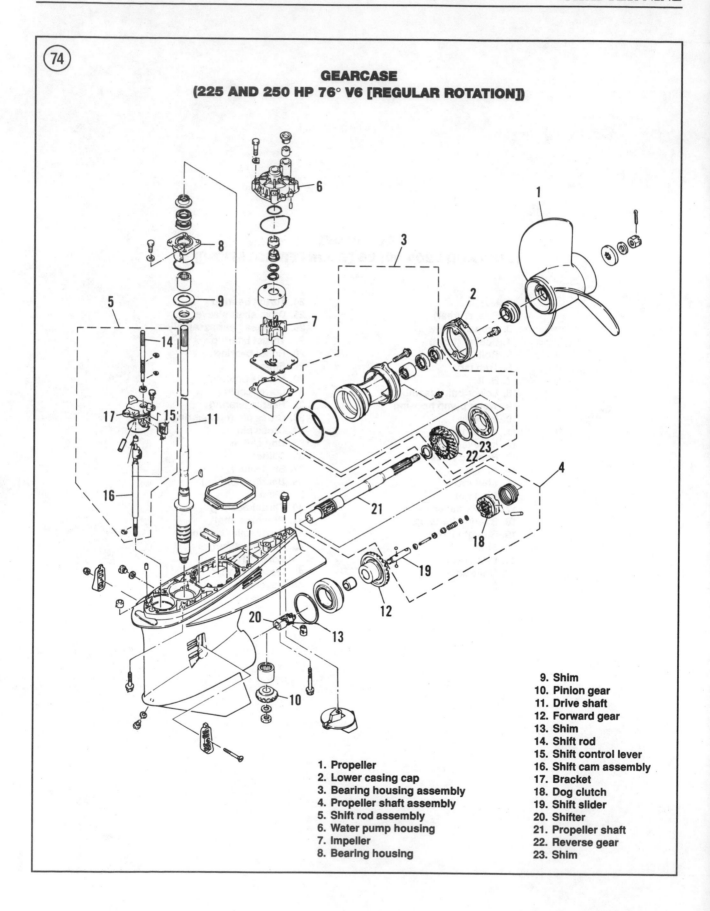

**GEARCASE
(225 AND 250 HP 76° V6 [REGULAR ROTATION])**

74

1. Propeller
2. Lower casing cap
3. Bearing housing assembly
4. Propeller shaft assembly
5. Shift rod assembly
6. Water pump housing
7. Impeller
8. Bearing housing
9. Shim
10. Pinion gear
11. Drive shaft
12. Forward gear
13. Shim
14. Shift rod
15. Shift control lever
16. Shift cam assembly
17. Bracket
18. Dog clutch
19. Shift slider
20. Shifter
21. Propeller shaft
22. Reverse gear
23. Shim

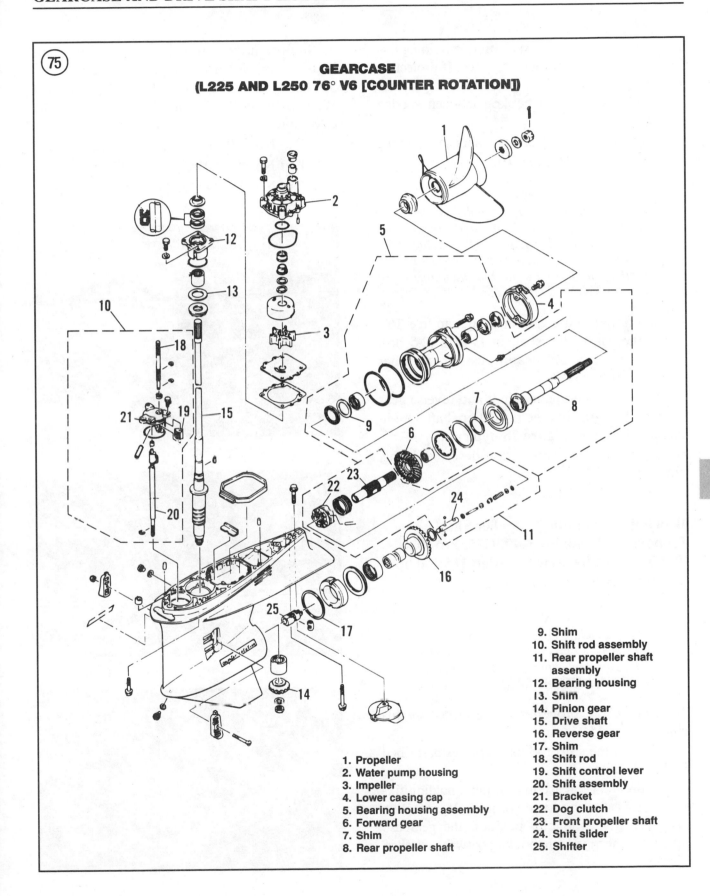

**GEARCASE
(L225 AND L250 76° V6 [COUNTER ROTATION])**

9

1. Propeller
2. Water pump housing
3. Impeller
4. Lower casing cap
5. Bearing housing assembly
6. Forward gear
7. Shim
8. Rear propeller shaft

9. Shim
10. Shift rod assembly
11. Rear propeller shaft assembly
12. Bearing housing
13. Shim
14. Pinion gear
15. Drive shaft
16. Reverse gear
17. Shim
18. Shift rod
19. Shift control lever
20. Shift assembly
21. Bracket
22. Dog clutch
23. Front propeller shaft
24. Shift slider
25. Shifter

2. Secure the gearcase in a suitable holding fixture or a vise with protective jaws. If protective jaws are not available, position the gearcase upright in the vise with the skeg between wooden blocks.

3. Remove the 2 bolts and washers securing the gear housing cap (**Figure 76**).

> *NOTE*
> *If the gear housing cap assembly is corroded in the prop shaft bore and cannot be removed easily by hand in Step 4, tap on the side of the cap with a soft-faced mallet and/or rotate the bolt mounting ears and carefully pry it out.*

4. Carefully pry the gear housing cap free. Remove the cap and gasket, or O-ring (2-5 hp). Remove the cap and bearing carrier (all other engines) (**Figure 77**).

5. Remove the propeller shaft and reverse gear (except 2-3 hp) from the propeller shaft bore in the gear housing (**Figure 78**, typical).

6. Clean and inspect all parts as described in this chapter.

Bearing Carrier and Propeller Shaft Removal (C25, 30 hp, C40, C55, Pro 60, 70-90 hp and Regular Rotation 115-130 hp V4, 150-225 hp 90° V6 Models)

> *NOTE*
> *This procedure covers the **regular rotation** 115-225 hp outboards. Refer to the following procedure for counter rotation L130 V4, L150 and L200 V6 outboards.*

1. Remove the propeller as described in this chapter.

2. Remove the shift rod assembly as described in this chapter.

3. Secure the gearcase in a suitable holding fixture or a vise with protective jaws. If protective jaws are not available, position the gearcase upright in the vise with the skeg between wooden blocks.

4. Straighten the bent tab(s) on the prop shaft housing tab washer with a punch and hammer.

5. The following special tool (Ring Nut Wrench) is required to loosen and remove the cover nut:

    a. Part No. YB-6075: C25 and 30 hp.

    b. Part No. YB-6048: C40 and C55.

    c. Part No. YB-34447: All other models.

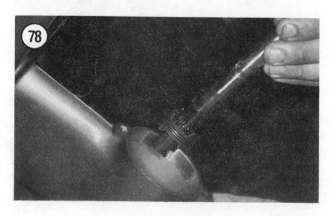

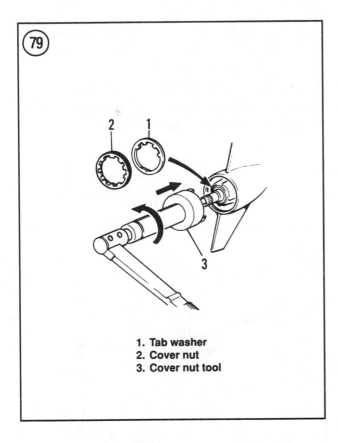

1. Tab washer
2. Cover nut
3. Cover nut tool

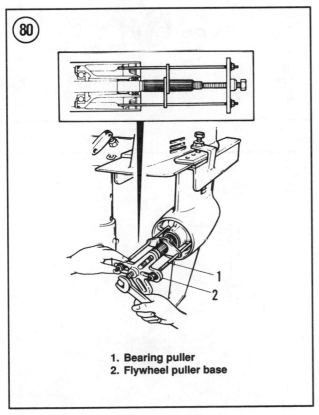

1. Bearing puller
2. Flywheel puller base

NOTE
If the cover nut is corroded and frozen in place and cannot be removed in Step 6, even with the assistance of heat and tapping on the removal tool, carefully drill out one side of the nut, then remove the cover nut. This will permit removal of the cover nut without damage to the gear housing.

6. Install the special tool onto the cover nut (**Figure 79**) and turn the tool counterclockwise to loosen, then remove the cover nut and the special tool. Remove the tab washer.

7. The following special tools (claws) and (puller) are required to remove the bearing housing:

    a. Part No. YB-6117: Universal puller (all models).

    b. Part No. YB-6234: Bearing puller claws (C25, C30, C40 and C55).

    c. Part No. YB-6207: Bearing puller claws (all other models).

8. Attach the bearing puller claws onto the universal puller assembly.

9. Attach the puller claws onto the backside of the horizontal legs on the bearing housing, then place the center bolt of the universal puller on the end of the propeller shaft (**Figure 80**, typical).

10. Slowly tighten the center bolt of the puller to break the bearing assembly loose from the propeller shaft bore. If necessary, tap on the end of the puller with a hammer to break the bearing assembly loose.

NOTE
A locating key is used to locate the bearing assembly within the gear housing. This key may come out with the bearing assembly or fall into the housing after the bearing assembly is removed. Locate and save the key as it must be used during installation.

11. Remove the bearing housing, propeller shaft and the puller assembly from the gear housing.

9

Separate the special tools from the bearing housing.

12. Clean and inspect all parts as described in this chapter.

Bearing Carrier and Propeller Shaft Removal (L130 V4, L150 and L200 V6 Counter Rotation Models)

NOTE
The L130 gearcase is equipped with front and rear propeller shafts and both must be removed in this procedure.

1. Remove the propeller as described in this chapter.

2. Remove the shift rod assembly as described in this chapter.

3. Secure the gearcase in a suitable holding fixture or a vise with protective jaws. If protective jaws are not available, position the gearcase upright in the vise with the skeg between wooden blocks.

4. Straighten the bent tab(s) on the prop shaft housing tab washer with a punch and hammer.

5. The special ring nut wrench (part No. YB-34447) is required to loosen and remove the cover nut.

NOTE
If the cover nut is corroded and frozen in place and cannot be removed in Step 6 even with the assistance of heat and tapping on the removal tool, carefully drill out one side of the nut, then remove the cover nut. This will permit removal of the cover nut without damage to the gear housing.

6. Install the ring nut wrench onto the cover nut (**Figure 79**) and turn the tool counterclockwise to loosen, then remove the cover nut (A, **Figure 81**). Remove the tab washer (B, **Figure 81**).

7. The following special tools are required to remove the bearing housing:

  a. Part No. YB-6335: Propeller shaft puller.

  b. Part No. YB-6096: Slide hammer puller.

8. Screw the propeller shaft puller onto the end of the propeller shaft. Attach the slide hammer to the end of the puller.

9. Using quick in and out strokes on the slide hammer, withdraw the bearing housing from the propeller shaft bore (**Figure 82**).

NOTE
A locating key is used to locate the bearing assembly within the gear housing.

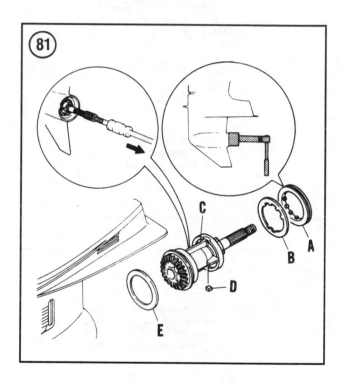

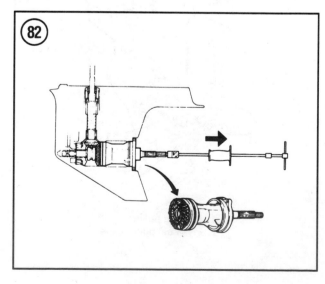

This key may come out with the bearing assembly or fall into the housing after the bearing assembly is removed. Locate and save the key as it must be used during installation.

10A. On L130 models, remove the bearing housing and *rear* propeller shaft assembly (C,

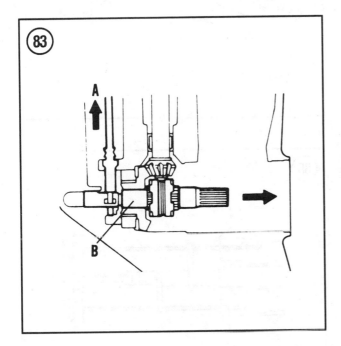

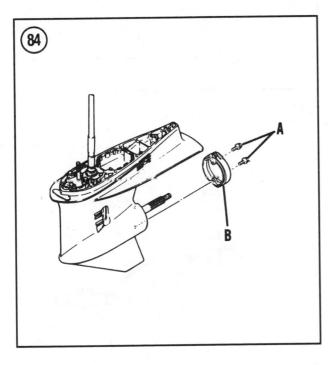

Figure 81), locating key (D, **Figure 81**), forward thrust shim (E, **Figure 81**) and the puller assembly from the gear housing. Separate the special tools from the front propeller shaft.

10B. On L150 and L200 models, remove the bearing housing and propeller shaft assembly (C, **Figure 81**), locating key (D, **Figure 81**), forward thrust shim (E, **Figure 81**) and the puller assembly from the gear housing. Separate the special tools from the propeller shaft.

11. On L130 models, make sure the shift rod (A, **Figure 83**) is removed, then remove the *front* propeller shaft assembly (B, **Figure 83**).

12. Clean and inspect all parts as described in this chapter.

Bearing Carrier and Propeller Shaft Removal (225-250 hp 76° V6 Regular Rotation Models)

NOTE
*This procedure covers the **regular rotation** 225-250 hp models. Refer to the following procedure for counter rotation L225 and L250 V6 models.*

1. Remove the propeller as described in this chapter.

2. Remove the shift rod assembly as described in this chapter.

3. Secure the gearcase in a suitable holding fixture or a vise with protective jaws. If protective jaws are not available, position the gearcase upright in the vise with the skeg between wooden blocks.

CAUTION
The bolts securing the lower casing cap had a thread locking compound applied during installation. It may be necessary to use an impact driver and appropriate size socket to loosen these bolts.

4. Remove the 2 bolts (A, **Figure 84**) securing the lower casing cap (B, **Figure 84**). Remove the cap from the gear housing.

5. Remove the 2 bolts (A, **Figure 85**) securing the bearing housing.

6. The following special tools are required to remove the bearing housing:

    a. Part No. YB-6117: Universal puller.

    b. Part No. YB-6207: Bearing puller claws.

7. Attach the bearing puller claws to the universal puller assembly.

8. Attach the puller claws onto the backside of the horizontal legs on the bearing housing, then place the center bolt of the universal puller on the end of the propeller shaft (**Figure 86**).

9. Slowly tighten the center bolt of the puller to break the bearing assembly loose from the propeller shaft bore. If necessary, tap on the end of the puller with a hammer to break the bearing assembly loose.

10. Remove the bearing housing (B, **Figure 85**), propeller shaft and the puller assembly from the gear housing. Separate the special tools from the bearing housing.

11. Clean and inspect all parts as described in this chapter.

Bearing Carrier and Propeller Shafts Removal (L225 and L250 76° V6 Counter Rotation Models)

> *NOTE*
> *The L225 and L250 models are equipped with front and rear propeller shafts and both must be removed in this procedure.*

1. Remove the propeller as described in this chapter.

2. Remove the shift rod assembly as described in this chapter.

3. Secure the gearcase in a suitable holding fixture or a vise with protective jaws. If protective jaws are not available, position the gearcase upright in the vise with the skeg between wooden blocks.

4. Remove the 2 bolts (A, **Figure 84**) securing the lower casing cap (B, **Figure 84**). Remove the cap from the gear housing.

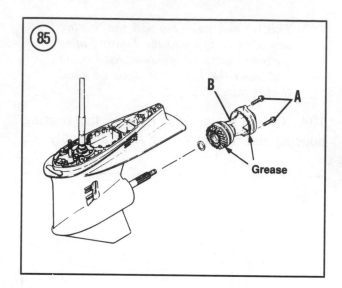

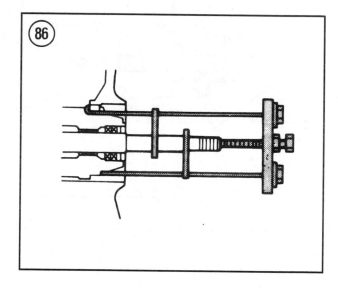

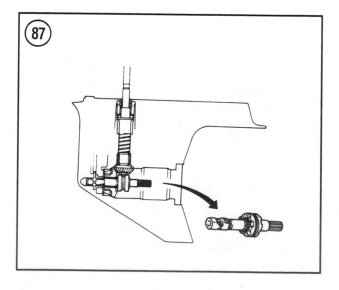

5. Remove the 2 bolts (A, **Figure 85**) securing the bearing housing.

6. The following special tools are required to remove the bearing housing:

   a. Part No. YB-6335: Propeller shaft puller.

   b. Part No. YB-6096: Slide hammer puller.

7. Screw the propeller shaft puller onto the end of the propeller shaft. Attach the slide hammer to the end of the puller.

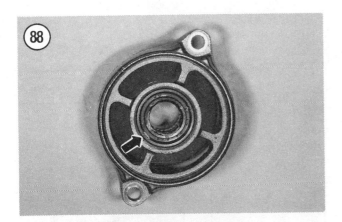

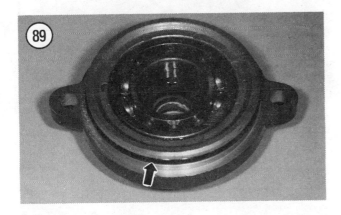

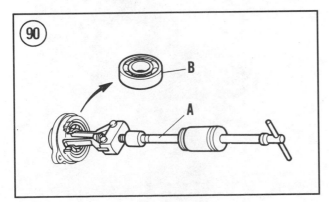

8. Using quick in and out strokes on the slide hammer, withdraw the bearing housing from the propeller shaft bore (**Figure 82**).

9. Remove the bearing housing and *rear* propeller shaft assembly from the gear housing. Separate the special tools from the front propeller shaft.

10. Make sure the shift rod is removed, then remove the *front* propeller shaft assembly (**Figure 87**).

11. Clean and inspect all parts as described in this chapter.

Bearing Carrier Disassembly/Assembly (2-5 hp)

NOTE
Do not remove the bearing or oil seals for inspection purposes. Only remove the bearing and/or oil seals if replacement is necessary.

1. Remove the propeller shaft from the bearing carrier as described in this chapter.

2. Remove all traces of old gasket residue from the propeller shaft housing cap.

3. Remove and discard the propeller shaft oil seals from the housing (**Figure 88**).

4. Remove and discard the O-ring seal (**Figure 89**).

5. On 4-5 hp models, use slide hammer part No. YB-6096 (A, **Figure 90**) and remove the reverse gear ball bearing (B, **Figure 90**) from the housing cap.

6. Clean the cap with solvent and blow dry with compressed air.

   If the ball bearing is still in place, do not allow the bearing to spin while using compressed air.

7. Install new oil seals as follows:

   a. Apply grease to the outer diameter of the oil seals to aid in installation.

   b. Position both new oil seals with their open end going in first.

   c. Carefully tap both oil seals in with an oil seal installer (part No. YB-6023), or a suitable size socket or piece of pipe that matches the *outer surface* of the seal (**Figure 91**). Do not drive the oil seals in using the inner surface as the oil seals will be damaged. Tap both oil seals in until they bottom out.

8. If removed, install the new bearing as follows:

   a. Apply oil to the bearing outer race and to the balls within the bearing.

   b. Position the ball bearing with its manufacturer's marks facing up (A, **Figure 92**).

   c. Carefully tap the ball bearing in with a bearing installer (part No. YB-6016), or a suitable size socket or piece of pipe that matches the *outer race* (B, **Figure 92**). Do not drive the bearing in using the inner race as the bearing will be damaged. Tap the bearing in until it bottoms out.

9. Apply grease to the lips of both oil seals.

10. Install a new O-ring (**Figure 89**) into the groove in the shaft housing cap. Make sure it is seated correctly in the groove, then apply a light coat of grease to the O-ring.

Bearing Housing Disassembly/Assembly (6-90 hp and C115 V4 Models)

> *CAUTION*
> *The oil seals and needle bearing (not the large reverse gear ball bearing) must be reinstalled in the **exact same location** within the bearing housing in order for them to function correctly. Prior to removing the oil seals and needle bearing, measure their location inside the housing. If you feel unqualified to perform this procedure, have the oil seals and needle bearing removed and installed by a Yamaha dealer.*

> *NOTE*
> *Do not remove the ball or needle bearings or oil seals for inspection purposes. Only remove the bearing(s) and/or oil seals if they must be replaced.*

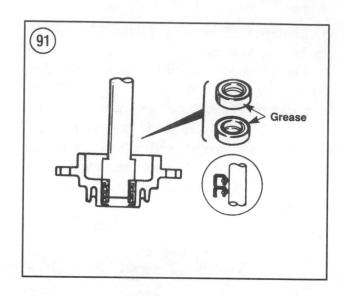

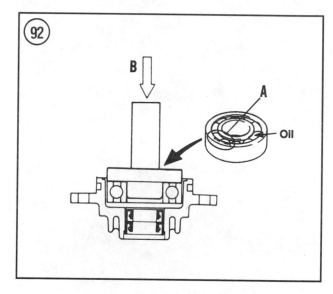

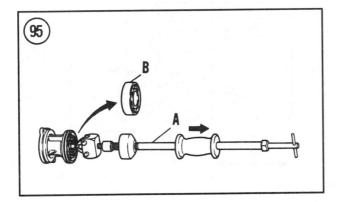

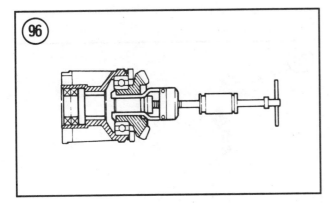

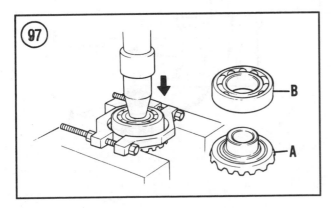

1. Remove the propeller shaft from the bearing housing as described in this chapter.

2. Remove and discard the O-ring seal(s) (**Figure 93**).

3A. To remove the reverse gear and ball bearing on 6-15 hp models, perform the following:

    a. Carefully pry the reverse gear from the bearing housing with 2 flat-bladed screwdrivers as shown in **Figure 94**.

    b. Remove the gear and any shims located behind the gear. Keep these shim(s) with the gear so they will be reinstalled correctly.

    c. Insert a slide hammer special tool (part No. YB-6096) into the backside of the reverse gear ball bearing.

    d. Using quick in and out strokes on the slide hammer, withdraw the ball bearing from the bearing housing (A, **Figure 95**).

    e. Remove the ball bearing (B, **Figure 95**).

3B. On all other models, to remove the reverse gear and ball bearing, perform the following:

    a. Insert slide hammer (part No. YB-6096), or equivalent into the backside of the reverse gear and the ball bearing.

    b. Using quick in and out strokes on the slide hammer, withdraw the reverse gear, any shim(s), thrust washer (models so equipped) and ball bearing from the bearing housing (**Figure 96**).

    c. Install bearing separator (part No. YB-6219 or equivalent) under the bearing outer race and between the gear.

    d. Place the bearing separator on the hydraulic press plate and using a suitable size socket or piece of pipe, press the reverse gear (A, **Figure 97**) out of the ball bearing (B, **Figure 97**).

CAUTION
*Prior to removing the oil seals and/or needle bearing from the bearing housing, measure their location within the housing as described in Step 4. This must be an **accurate measurement** made with either metric or decimal measurements (fractional measurements cannot be*

9

used) due to close tolerances of all components within the bearing housing.

4. Prior to the removing the oil seals and needle bearing, perform the following:

   a. Refer to **Figure 98** for a typical bearing housing with the oil seals and needle bearing still in place.

   b. Place a metal straight edge on the outer surface of the bearing housing, then use a depth gauge or steel ruler with fine metric or decimal increments.

   c. Measure the distance from the outer surface of the bearing housing to the face of the outer oil seal (A, **Figure 98**) and to the needle bearing (B, **Figure 98**). Note both of these measurements as they will be used during installation.

5A. On 6-15 hp, 40-50 hp and Pro 50 models, perform the following:

   a. Place the bearing housing on a piece of soft wood with the mounting flange end of the housing facing down.

   b. Place bearing driver (part No. YB-6071) or suitable size socket on top of the needle bearing.

   c. Carefully drive both oil seals (A, **Figure 99**) and the needle bearing (B, **Figure 99**) out of the bearing housing as an assembly.

   d. Discard the needle bearing and oil seals. After removal, they cannot be reused.

5B. On all other models, perform the following:

   a. Insert slide hammer (part No. YB-6096 or equivalent) into the backside of both oil seals (A, **Figure 100**).

   b. Using quick in and out strokes on the slide hammer, withdraw both oil seals from the bearing housing.

   c. Place a suitable size socket, or piece of pipe on top of the needle bearing.

   d. Carefully drive the needle bearing (B, **Figure 100**) out of the bearing housing.

   e. Discard the needle bearing and oil seals. After removal, they cannot be reused.

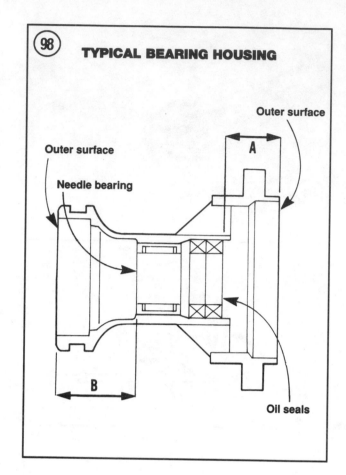

98 **TYPICAL BEARING HOUSING**

Outer surface

Outer surface

Needle bearing

A

B

Oil seals

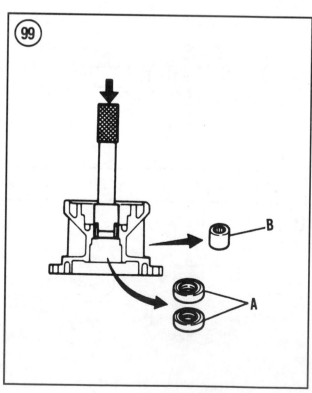

99

B

A

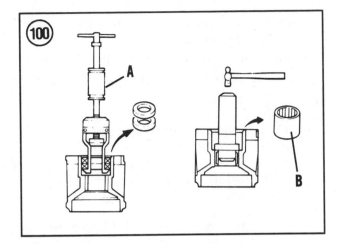

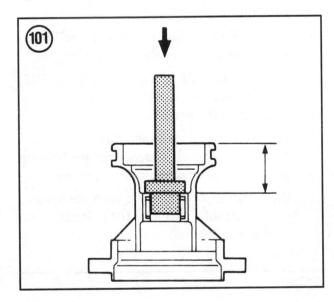

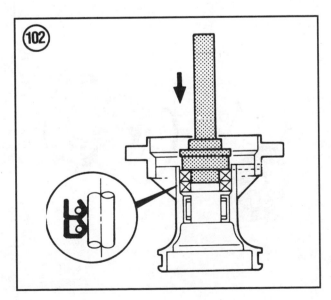

6. Clean the bearing housing with solvent and blow dry with compressed air. If the ball bearing is still in place, do not allow the bearing to spin while using compressed air.

CAUTION
Refer to the CAUTION at the beginning of this procedure. The following components must be installed in the specified location within the bearing housing.

7. If removed, install the new needle bearing as follows:

a. Apply oil to the outer surface of the outer race and to the needles within the bearing.

b. Position the needle bearing with its manufacturer's marks facing up.

c. Carefully tap the needle bearing in with a bearing installer, or a suitable size socket or piece of pipe that matches the outer edge of the bearing (**Figure 101**). Tap the bearing in the same distance (A, **Figure 98**) as noted during removal Step 5B.

8. Install new oil seals as follows:

a. Apply grease to the outer diameter of the oil seals to aid in installation.

b. Position both new oil seals with their open end going in last.

c. Carefully tap both oil seals in with an oil seal installer, or a suitable size socket or piece of pipe that matches the *outer surface* of the seal (**Figure 102**). Do not drive the oil seals in using the inner surface as the oil seals will be damaged. Tap both oil seals in the same distance (B, **Figure 98**) as noted during removal Step 5A.

9A. To install the reverse gear and ball bearing into the bearing housing on 6-15 hp engines, perform the following:

a. Apply oil to the outer surface of the outer race and to the balls within the bearing. Also lubricate the bearing receptacle within the bearing housing.

b. Position the ball bearing with its manufacturer's marks facing up.

c. Carefully tap the ball bearing in with a bearing installer (part No. YB-6015) and drive shaft holder (part No. YB-6071) or a suitable size socket or piece of pipe that matches the *outer race* (**Figure 103**). Do not drive the bearing in using the inner race as the bearing will be damaged. Tap the ball bearing in until it bottoms out.

d. Install the shim(s) (A, **Figure 104**) (same number and thickness as removed) onto the reverse gear.

e. Apply oil to the outer surface of the reverse gear and to the inner surface of the inner race of the ball bearing.

f. Carefully tap the reverse gear, and shim(s) into the ball bearing. Tap the gear (B, **Figure 104**) in until it bottoms out in the bearing.

e. Install a new O-ring (C, **Figure 104**) into the groove in the bearing housing. Make sure it is seated correctly in the grove, then apply a light coat of grease to the O-ring.

9B. To install the reverse gear and ball bearing on all other models, perform the following:

a. Place the reverse gear on a piece of soft wood. Then set the wooden block and gear on the hydraulic press plate with the gear portion facing down.

b. Install the shim(s) (same number and thickness as removed) onto the gear shoulder.

NOTE
On some models, the thrust washer has a chamfer on the inner diameter (A, Figure 105). On these models position the thrust washer with the chamfered side going on first.

c. Install the thrust washer (B, **Figure 105**) on top of the shim(s) already installed on the gear shoulder.

d. Apply oil to the inner race of the ball bearing and to the outer shoulder of the gear.

e. Position the ball bearing (C, **Figure 105**) with its manufacturer's marks facing up, away from the gear.

f. Using a suitable size mandrel or socket that fits the inner bearing race, press the bearing onto the gear shoulder until it bottoms out.

g. Press the bearing housing onto the reverse gear assembly (**Figure 106**). Press it on until it bottoms out.

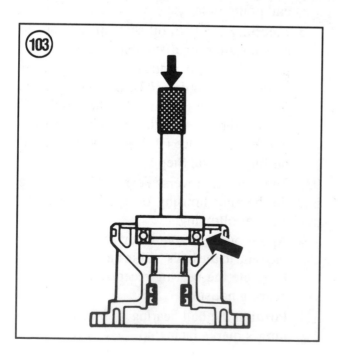

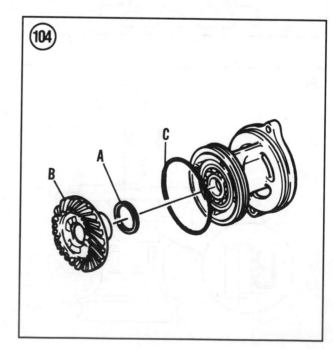

10. Install the propeller shaft into the bearing housing as described in this chapter.

Bearing Housing Disassembly/Assembly (115-225 hp V4 and All V6 Normal Rotation Models)

CAUTION
The oil seals and needle bearing (not the large reverse gear ball bearing) must be

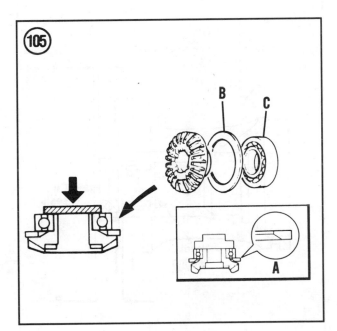

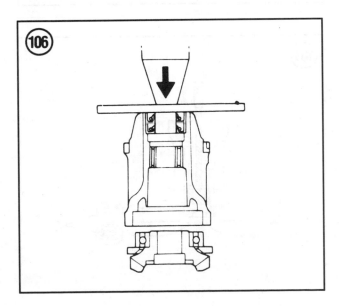

*reinstalled in the **exact same location** within the bearing housing to function correctly. Prior to removing the oil seals and needle bearing, measure their location inside the housing. If you feel unqualified to perform this procedure, have the oil seals and needle bearing removed and installed by a Yamaha dealer.*

NOTE
Do not remove the ball or needle bearings or oil seals for inspection purposes. Only remove the bearing(s) and/or oil seals if they must be replaced.

1. Remove the propeller shaft from the bearing housing as described in this chapter.

2. To remove the reverse gear and ball bearing, perform the following:

a. Insert slide hammer (part No. YB-6096 or equivalent) into the backside of the reverse gear and the ball bearing.

b. Using the slide hammer, withdraw the reverse gear, any shim(s), thrust washer and ball bearing from the bearing housing (**Figure 96**).

c. Install a bearing separator (part No. YB-6219 or equivalent) under the bearing outer race and between the gear.

d. Place the bearing separator on a press plate and using a suitable size socket or piece of pipe, press the reverse gear out of the ball bearing.

CAUTION
*Prior to removing the oil seals and/or needle bearing from the bearing housing measure their location within the housing as described in Step 4. This must be an **accurate measurement** made with either metric or decimal measurements (fractional measurements cannot be used) due to close tolerances of all components within the bearing housing.*

3. Prior to removing the oil seals and needle bearing, perform the following:

a. Refer to **Figure 107** for a bearing housing with the oil seals and needle bearing still in place.

b. Place a metal straight edge on the outer surface of the bearing housing, then use a depth gauge or steel ruler with fine metric or decimal increments.

c. Measure the distance from the outer surface of the bearing housing to the face of the outer oil seal (A, **Figure 107**) and to the needle bearing (B, **Figure 107**). Note both of these measurements as they will be used during installation.

4. To remove the oil seals and needle bearing, perform the following:

a. Place the bearing housing on 2 pieces of soft wood with the mounting flange end of the housing facing down. There must be room for the oil seals and needle bearing to exit the housing.

b. Place bearing drivers (part No. YB-6071 and YB-6196 or equivalent) on top of the needle bearing.

c. Carefully drive both oil seals (A, **Figure 108**) and the needle bearing (B, **Figure 108**) out of the bearing housing as an assembly.

d. Discard the needle bearing and oil seals. After removal, they cannot be reused.

5. Clean the bearing housing with solvent and blow dry with compressed air. If the ball bearing is still in place, do not allow the bearing to spin while using compressed air.

CAUTION
Refer to the CAUTION at the beginning of this procedure. The following components must be installed in the specified location within the bearing housing.

6. If removed, install the new needle bearing as follows:

a. Apply oil to the outer surface of the outer race and to the bearing rollers within the bearing.

b. Position the needle bearing with its manufacturer's marks facing up.

NOTE
There is no built-in stop, or shoulder, within the bearing housing that will limit the travel of the needle bearing. Tap the bearing in slowly and check the dimension several times to ensure the bearing is positioned correctly.

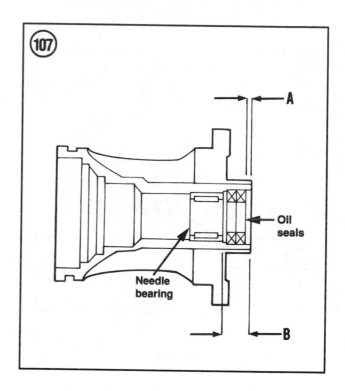

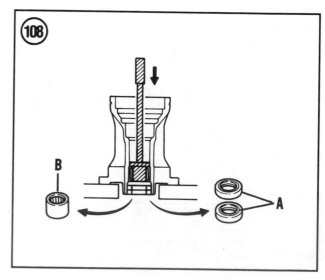

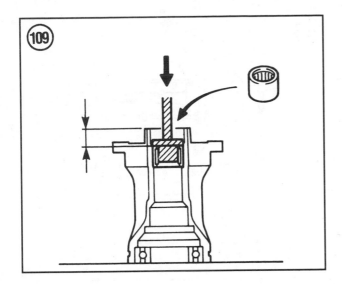

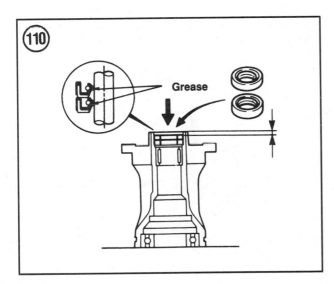

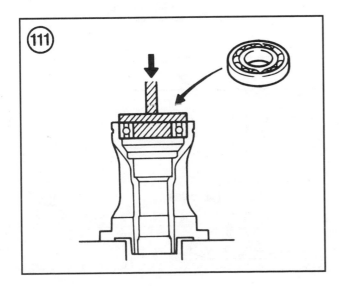

c. Use the same set of special tools used for removal and carefully tap the needle bearing into place (**Figure 109**). Tap the bearing in the same distance (B, **Figure 107**) as noted during removal Step 3B.

7. Install new oil seals as follows:

a. Apply grease to the outer diameter of the oil seals to aid in installation.

b. Position both new oil seals with their open end going in last.

c. Carefully tap both oil seals in with an oil seal installer, or a suitable size socket or piece of pipe that matches the *outer surface* of the seal (**Figure 110**). Do not drive the oil seals in using the inner surface as the oil seals will be damaged. Tap both oil seals in the same distance (A, **Figure 107**) as noted during removal Step 3A.

8. To install the reverse gear and ball bearing into the bearing housing, perform the following:

a. Apply oil to the outer surface of the outer race and to the balls within the bearing. Also lubricate the bearing receptacle within the bearing housing.

b. Position the ball bearing with its manufacturer's marks facing down into the bearing housing.

c. Carefully tap the ball bearing in with bearing installer (part No. YB-6430 or equivalent) and drive shaft holder (part No. YB-6071 or equivalent) or a suitable size socket or piece of pipe that matches the *outer race* (**Figure 111**). Do not drive the bearing in using the inner race as the bearing will be damaged. Tap the ball bearing in until it bottoms out.

d. Install the shim(s) (same number and thickness as removed) and thrust washer onto the reverse gear.

e. Apply oil to the outer surface of the reverse gear and to the inner surface of the inner race of the ball bearing.

9

f. Carefully tap the reverse gear, thrust washer and shim(s) into the ball bearing. Tap the gear in until it bottoms out in the bearing.

g. Install a new O-ring into the groove in the bearing housing. Make sure it is seated correctly in the grove, then apply a light coat of grease to the O-ring.

Bearing Housing Disassembly/Assembly and Propeller Shaft Removal/Installation (L130 V4, L150 and L200 90° V6 Counter Rotation Models)

> *NOTE*
> *The L130 is equipped with 2 propeller shafts. The rear propeller shaft must be pressed out of the bearing housing. This operation is covered in this procedure. However, the front propeller shaft is installed in the gearcase housing; this operation is covered in a separate procedure.*

> *CAUTION*
> *The oil seals and needle bearing (not the large forward gear taper roller bearing) must be reinstalled in the **exact same location** within the bearing housing for them to function correctly. Prior to removing the oil seals and needle bearing, measure their location inside the housing. If you feel unqualified to perform this procedure, have the oil seals and needle bearing removed and installed by a dealer.*

> *NOTE*
> *Do not remove the taper roller or needle bearings or the oil seals for inspection purposes. Only remove the bearing(s) and/or oil seals if they are faulty and must be replaced.*

1. The following special tools are required to remove the propeller shaft and the forward drive gear from the bearing housing:

   a. Part No. YB-6117: Universal puller.

   b. Part No. YB-6207: Bearing puller claws.

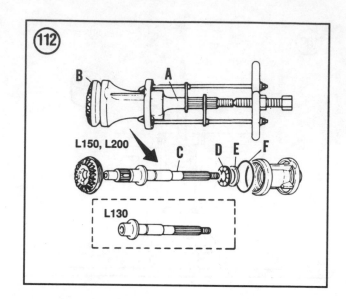

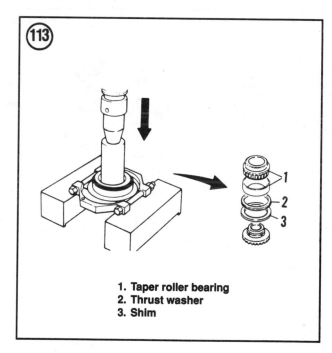

1. Taper roller bearing
2. Thrust washer
3. Shim

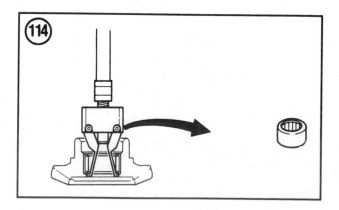

2. Attach the bearing puller claws to the universal puller assembly.

3. Attach the puller claws onto the backside of the horizontal legs on the bearing housing, then place the center bolt of the universal puller on the end of the propeller shaft.

4. Slowly tighten the center bolt of the puller to break the rear propeller shaft (A, **Figure 112**) and forward gear (B, **Figure 112**) loose from the bearing housing bore. If necessary, tap on the end of the puller with a hammer to break the assembly loose.

5. Refer to **Figure 112** and remove the forward gear/roller bearing assembly (B), propeller shaft (C), thrust bearing (D) and shim (E) from the bearing housing. Remove the O-ring seal (F, **Figure 112**) and discard it.

6. Separate the special tools from the bearing housing.

7. To remove the tapered roller bearing from the forward gear, perform the following:

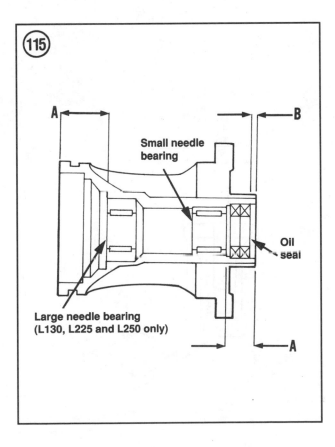

a. Install bearing separator (part No. YB-6219 or equivalent) between the bearing and gear.

b. Place the bearing separator on the hydraulic press plate and using a suitable size socket or piece of pipe, press the forward gear out of the tapered roller bearing (**Figure 113**).

c. Remove the taper roller bearing assembly (1, **Figure 113**), thrust washer (2) and shim (3) from the forward gear.

8. To remove the needle bearing from the forward gear on L130 models, perform the following:

a. Place the forward gear in a vise with soft jaws and tighten securely. Do not overtighten to avoid damage to the gear teeth.

b. Insert slide hammer (part No. YB-6096 or equivalent) and bearing puller (part No. 90890-06535 or equivalent) into the forward gear and onto the needle bearing.

c. Using the slide hammer, withdraw the needle bearing from the forward gear (**Figure 114**).

> *CAUTION*
> *Prior to removing the oil seals and/or needle bearing from the bearing housing measure their location within the housing as described in Step 9. This must be an **accurate measurement** made with either metric or decimal measurements (fractional measurements cannot be used) due to close tolerances of all components within the bearing housing.*

9. Prior to the removing the oil seals and needle bearing, perform the following:

a. Refer to **Figure 115** for a bearing housing with the oil seals and needle bearing still in place.

b. Place a metal straight edge on the outer surface of the bearing housing, then use a depth gauge or steel ruler with fine metric or decimal increments.

c. Measure the distance from the outer surface of the bearing housing to the face of the outer oil seal (B, **Figure 115**) and to the needle bearing(s) (A, **Figure 115**). Note both of these measurements as they will be used during installation.

> *NOTE*
> *The bearing housing on the L130 engines, has an additional needle bearing located at the end where the forward gear is located.*

10. On L130 engines, to remove the large needle bearing from the gear housing, perform the following:

    a. Insert slide hammer (part No. YB-6096 or equivalent) and bearing puller (part No. 90890-06535) into the bearing housing and onto the needle bearing.

    b. Using the slide hammer, withdraw the large needle bearing from the gear housing (**Figure 116**).

11. On all models, to remove the oil seals and small needle bearing, perform the following:

    a. Place the bearing housing on 2 pieces of soft wood with the mounting flange end of the housing facing down. There must be room between the wooden blocks for the oil seals and needle bearing to exit the housing.

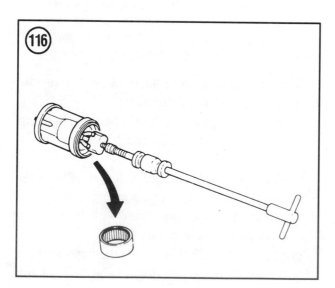

    b. Place special tools (part No. YB-6071 and YB-6196) or suitable size socket on top of the needle bearing.

    c. Carefully drive both oil seals (A, **Figure 117**) and the small needle bearing (B, **Figure 117**) out of the bearing housing as an assembly.

    d. Discard the needle bearing and oil seals, after removal, they cannot be reused.

12. Clean the bearing housing with solvent and blow dry with compressed air. If the taper roller bearing is still in place, do not allow the bearing to spin while using the compressed air.

> *CAUTION*
> *Refer to the CAUTION at the beginning of this procedure. The following components must be installed in the specified location within the bearing housing.*

13. On all models, install a new small needle bearing into the bearing housing as follows:

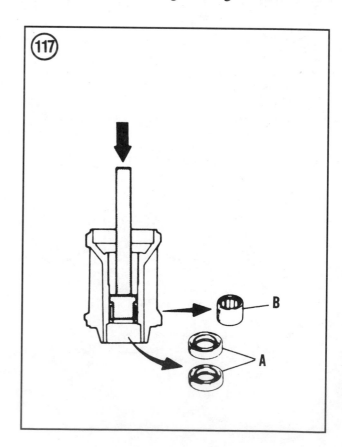

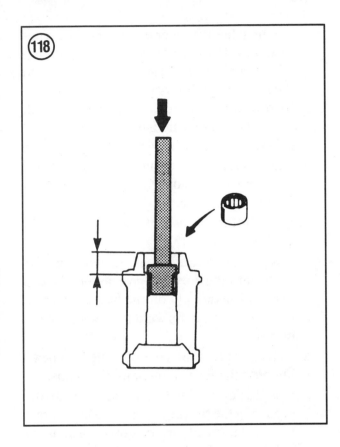

a. Apply oil to the outer surface of the outer race and to the needles within the bearing.

b. Position the small needle bearing with its manufacturer's marks facing up.

> *NOTE*
> *There is no built-in stop, or shoulder, within the bearing housing that will limit the travel of the needle bearing. Tap the bearing in slowly and check the dimension several times to ensure the bearing is positioned correctly.*

c. Use the same set of special tools used for removal and carefully tap the small needle bearing into place (**Figure 118**). Tap the bearing in the same distance (A, **Figure 115**) as noted during removal Step 9.

14. On all models, install new oil seals as follows:

a. Apply grease to the outer diameter of the oil seals to aid in installation.

b. Position both new oil seals with their open end going in last.

c. Carefully tap both oil seals in with an oil seal installer, or a suitable size socket or piece of pipe that matches the *outer surface* of the seal (**Figure 119**). Do not drive the oil seals in using the inner surface as the oil seals will be damaged. Tap both oil seals in the same distance (B, **Figure 115**) as noted during removal Step 3A.

15. On L130 models, install the large needle bearing into the gear housing, as follows:

a. Apply oil to the outer surface of the outer race and to the needles within the bearing.

b. Position the large needle bearing with its manufacturer's marks facing up.

> *NOTE*
> *There is no built-in stop, or shoulder, within the bearing housing that will limit the travel of the needle bearing. Tap the bearing in slowly and check the dimension several times to ensure the bearing is positioned correctly.*

9

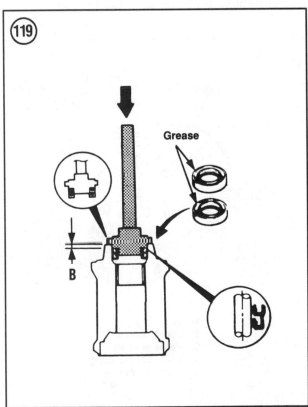

c. Use the same set of special tools used for removal and carefully tap the large needle bearing into place (**Figure 120**). Tap the bearing in the same distance (A, **Figure 115**) as noted during removal Step 10.

16. On L130 models, install the needle bearing into the forward gear, as follows:

a. Apply oil to the outer surface of the outer race and to the needles within the bearing.

b. Position the needle bearing with the manufacturer's marks facing up.

c. Use a socket that matches the bearing outer race and carefully tap the needle bearing into place.

17. To assemble and install the propeller shaft and the taper roller bearing into the bearing housing refer to **Figure 121** and perform the following:

a. Apply oil to the outer surface of the outer race and to the rollers within the bearing. Also lubricate the bearing surfaces of the front propeller shaft.

b. Install the shim (1, **Figure 121**), thrust bearing (2) and propeller shaft (3) into the bearing housing.

c. Install the taper roller bearing (4, **Figure 121**) and the outer race (5).

d. Place the bearing housing on the hydraulic press plate and using a suitable size socket

that matches the outer diameter of the outer race, or a flat piece of heavy metal on top of the outer race. Press the outer race into the housing until it bottoms out.

18. To install the forward drive gear into the ball bearing in the bearing housing refer to **Figure 122** and perform the following:

a. Apply oil to the outer surface of the forward gear and to the inner surface of the ball bearing inner race.

b. Place the thrust washer (2, **Figure 122**) onto the forward gear (3).

c. Position the bearing housing and propeller shaft onto the forward gear assembly and place this assembly on the hydraulic press plate. Protect the forward gear with a stand or base.

d. Carefully press the gear housing ball bearing onto the forward gear until it stops.

e. Install a new O-ring (1, **Figure 122**) into the groove in the bearing housing. Make sure it is seated correctly in the grove, then apply a light coat of grease to the O-ring.

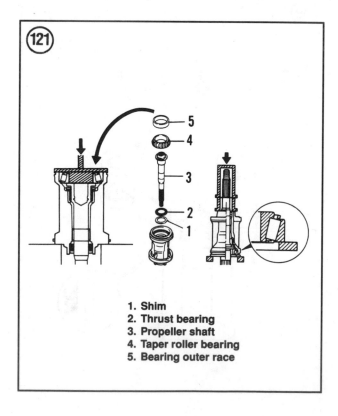

121

1. Shim
2. Thrust bearing
3. Propeller shaft
4. Taper roller bearing
5. Bearing outer race

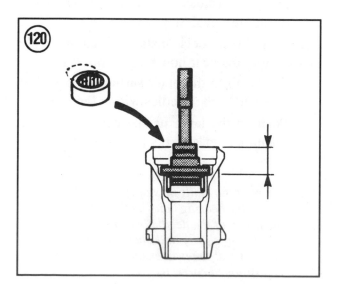

120

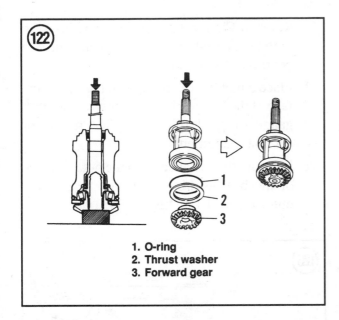

1. O-ring
2. Thrust washer
3. Forward gear

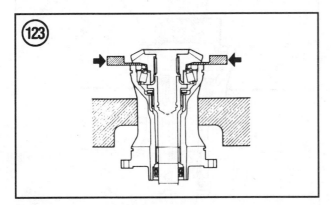

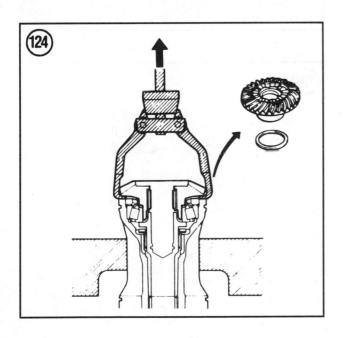

Bearing Housing Disassembly/Assembly and Rear Propeller Shaft Removal/Installation (L225 and L250 76° V6 Counter Rotation Models)

NOTE
The rear propeller shaft must be pressed out of the bearing housing. These models are equipped with 2 propeller shafts with the rear propeller shaft installed in the bearing housing. This operation is covered in this procedure. The front propeller shaft is installed in the gear housing. Front propeller shaft removal/installation is covered in a separate procedure earlier in this chapter.

CAUTION
*The oil seals and needle bearing (not the large forward gear taper roller bearing) must be reinstalled in the **exact same location** within the bearing housing in order for them to function correctly. Prior to removing the oil seals and needle bearing, measure their location inside the housing. If you feel unqualified to perform this procedure, have the oil seals and needle bearing removed and installed by a dealer.*

NOTE
Do not remove the tapered roller, needle bearings or the oil seals for inspection purposes. Remove the bearing(s) and/or oil seals only if they must be replaced.

1. Install bearing separator (part No. YB-6219 or equivalent) between the forward gear and bearing housing. Carefully tighten the nuts on the bearing separator until the forward gear moves away from the bearing housing enough to install the bearing puller legs under the bearing. See **Figure 123**. Then, remove the bearing separator.

2. Insert slide hammer (part No. YB-6096 or equivalent) onto the bearing puller legs (part No. YB-6334), then position the puller legs under the forward gear (**Figure 124**).

9

3. Using the slide hammer, withdraw the forward gear. Remove the forward gear and shim(s) from the gear housing.

4. Use ring nut wrench (part No. YB-6048 or equivalent) and unscrew the ring nut (**Figure 125**). Remove the ring nut and washer from the gear housing.

5. The following special tools are required to remove the rear propeller shaft and the forward drive gear tapered roller bearing from the bearing housing:

    a. Part No. YB-6117: Universal puller.

    b. Part No. YB-6207: Bearing puller claws.

6. Attach the bearing puller claws onto the universal puller assembly.

7. Attach the puller claws onto the backside of the horizontal legs on the bearing housing, then place the center bolt of the universal puller on the end of the rear propeller shaft. See **Figure 126**.

8. Slowly tighten the center bolt of the puller to break the forward drive gear taper roller bearing and rear propeller shaft loose from the bearing housing bore. If necessary, tap on the end of the puller with a hammer to break the assembly loose.

9. Remove the forward gear/roller bearing assembly (A, **Figure 126**), rear propeller shaft (B), thrust bearing (C) and shim (D) from the bearing housing.

10. Separate the special tools from the bearing housing.

CAUTION
*Prior to removing the oil seals and/or needle bearing from the bearing housing measure their location within the housing as described in Step 11. This must be an **accurate measurement** made with either metric or decimal measurements (fractional measurements cannot be used) due to close tolerances of all components within the bearing housing.*

11. Prior to removing the oil seals and needle bearing, perform the following:

    a. Refer to **Figure 115** for a bearing housing with the oil seals and small and large needle bearings still in place.

    b. Place a metal straightedge on the outer surface of the bearing housing, then use a depth gauge or steel ruler with fine metric or decimal increments.

    c. Measure the distance from the outer surface of the bearing housing to the face of the outer oil seal (B, **Figure 115**) and to the

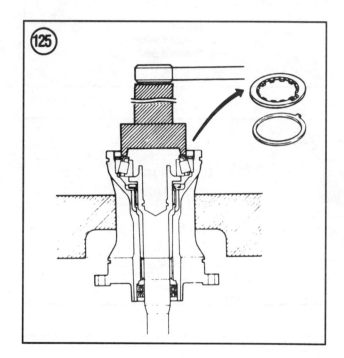

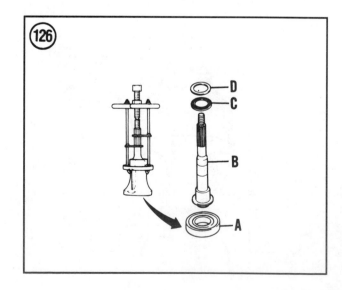

needle bearing(s) (A, B, **Figure 115**). Note both of these measurements as they will be used during installation.

12. Insert slide hammer (part No. YB-6096 or equivalent) onto the bearing puller and position the puller legs under the large needle bearing (**Figure 127**).

13. Using the slide hammer, withdraw the large needle bearing from the gear housing.

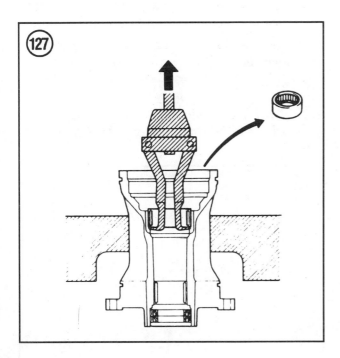

14. To remove the oil seals and small needle bearing from the bearing housing, perform the following:

a. Place the bearing housing on 2 pieces of soft wood with the mounting flange end of the housing facing down. There must be enough room between the wooden blocks for the oil seals and needle bearing to exit the housing.

b. Place special tools (part No. YB-6071 and YB-6196) or a suitable size socket on top of the needle bearing.

c. Carefully drive both oil seals (A, **Figure 128**) and the needle bearing (B, **Figure 128**) from the bearing housing as an assembly.

d. Discard the needle bearing and oil seals. After removal, they cannot be reused.

15. To remove the needle bearing from the forward gear, perform the following:

a. Place the forward gear in a vise with soft jaws and tighten securely but do not over-tighten to avoid damage to the gear teeth.

b. Insert slide hammer (part No. YB-6096 or equivalent) and bearing puller into the forward gear and onto the needle bearing.

c. Using quick in and out strokes on the slide hammer, withdraw the needle bearing from the forward gear (**Figure 129**).

9

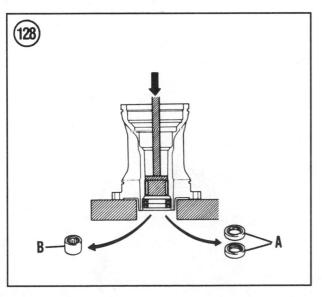

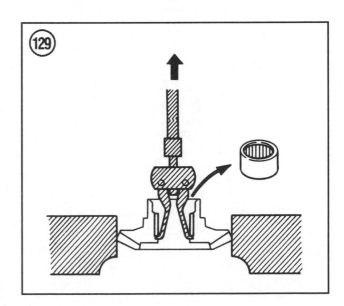

16. Clean the bearing housing with solvent and blow dry with compressed air. If the ball bearing is still in place, do not allow the bearing to spin while using the compressed air.

CAUTION
Refer to the CAUTION at the beginning of this procedure. The following components must be installed in the specified location within the bearing housing.

17. To install the large needle bearing into the gear housing, perform the following:

  a. Apply oil to the outer surface of the outer race and to the needles within the bearing.

  b. Position the large needle bearing with the manufacturer's marks facing up.

NOTE
There is no built-in stop, or shoulder, within the bearing housing that will limit the travel of the needle bearing. Tap the bearing in slowly and check the dimen-

sion several times to ensure the bearing is positioned correctly.

  c. Use the same set of special tools used for removal and carefully tap the needle bearing into place (**Figure 130**). Tap the bearing in the same distance (A, **Figure 115**) as noted during removal Step 12.

18. Install the new small needle bearing as follows:

  a. Apply oil to the outer surface of the outer race and to the needles within the bearing.

  b. Position the small needle bearing with its manufacturer's marks facing up.

NOTE
There is no built-in stop, or shoulder, within the bearing housing that will limit

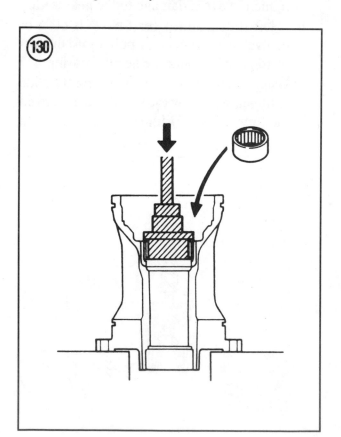

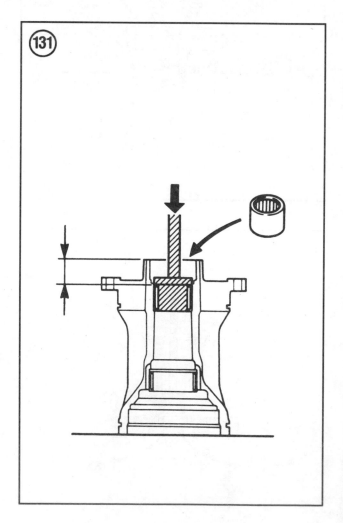

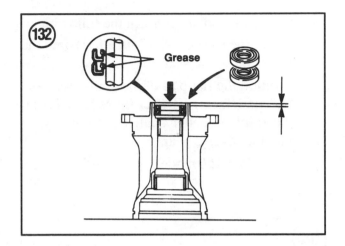

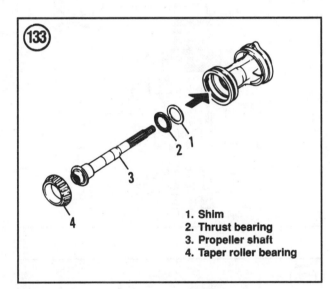

1. Shim
2. Thrust bearing
3. Propeller shaft
4. Taper roller bearing

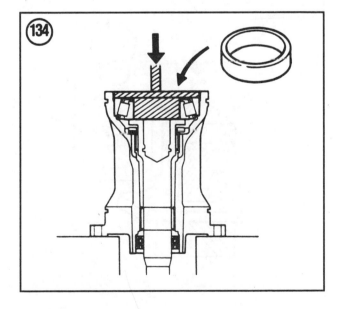

the travel of the needle bearing. Tap the bearing in slowly and check the dimension several times to ensure the bearing is positioned correctly.

c. Use the same set of special tools used for removal and carefully tap the needle bearing into place (**Figure 131**). Tap the bearing in the same distance (C, **Figure 115**) as noted during removal Step 14.

19. Install new oil seals as follows:

a. Apply grease to the outer diameter of the oil seals to aid in installation.

b. Position both new oil seals with their open end going in last.

c. Carefully tap both oil seals in with an oil seal installer, or a suitable size socket or piece of pipe that matches the *outer surface* of the seal (**Figure 132**). Do not drive the oil seals in using the inner surface as the oil seals will be damaged. Tap both oil seals in the same distance (B, **Figure 115**) as noted during removal Step 11.

20. To assemble and install the rear propeller shaft and the tapered roller bearing into the bearing housing, refer to **Figure 133** and perform the following:

a. Apply oil to the outer surface of the outer race and to the rollers within the bearing. Also, apply oil to the bearing surfaces of the rear propeller shaft.

b. Install the shim (1, **Figure 133**), thrust bearing (2) and rear propeller shaft (3) into the bearing housing.

c. Install the tapered roller bearing (4, **Figure 133**) and the outer race.

d. Place the bearing housing on the hydraulic press plate. Using a suitable size socket that matches the outer diameter of the outer race, or a flat piece of heavy metal on top of the outer race, press the outer race into the housing until it bottoms out (**Figure 134**).

21. Install the washer and ring nut into the gear housing. Use a ring nut wrench (part No. YB-

9

6048 or equivalent) and tighten the ring nut (**Figure 135**) to the torque specification in **Table 1**.

22. To install the needle bearing into the forward gear, perform the following:

   a. Apply oil to the outer surface of the outer race and to the bearing. Also, apply oil to the bearing surfaces of the gear.

   b. Place the forward gear on a stand with the gear portion facing down.

   c. Position the bearing with its manufacturer's marks facing up and set it on the gear shoulder (A, **Figure 136**).

   d. Place the gear and stand on the hydraulic press plate. Using a suitable size socket that matches the outer diameter of the outer race, press the bearing into the gear until it bottoms out (**Figure 136**).

23. To assemble and install the forward gear and shim(s) into the gear housing and onto the propeller shaft perform the following:

   a. Apply oil to the outer race of the bearing in the gear housing. Also apply to the bearing surfaces of the front propeller shaft.

   b. Install the shim(s) onto the forward gear and place the forward gear on a test stand with the gear portion facing down.

   c. Place the gear and stand on the hydraulic press plate.

   d. Position the gear housing and propeller shaft assembly onto the gear on the press plate.

   e. Press the gear housing and propeller shaft assembly onto the forward gear until it bottoms out.

Front Propeller Shaft Removal/Installation (L130 V4 and L225, L250 76° V6 Counter Rotation Models)

1. Remove the rear propeller shaft and bearing housing, as described in this chapter.

2. Withdraw the front propeller shaft straight out of the gear housing.

3A. On L130 models, perform the following:

   a. Install the washer (A, **Figure 137**) onto the front end of the shaft.

   b. Position the flat part of the shifter with the "L" mark facing UP (B, **Figure 137**). Install the front propeller shaft (C, **Figure 137**) into the reverse gear.

3B. On L225, L250 models, perform the following:

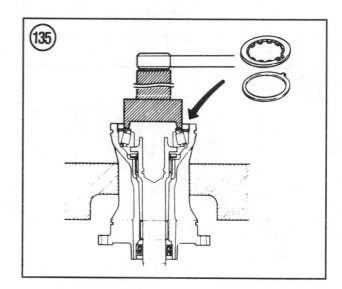

a. Position the flat part of the shifter with the "L" mark facing UP (A, **Figure 138**).

b. Apply a light coat of cold grease to the shift cam to hold it in place in the next step.

c. Position the shift cam with the "O" mark (B, **Figure 138**) facing down and to the front, then place it on the shifter.

d. Make sure the dog clutch is in the NEU-TRAL position (C, **Figure 138**).

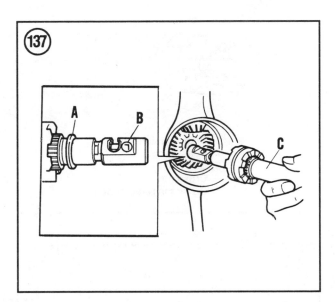

4. Install the front propeller shaft into the reverse gear.

Propeller Shaft Disassembly/Assembly (2 hp Models)

The propeller shaft is removed during the *Bearing Carrier and Propeller Shaft Removal (2-25 hp)* in this chapter. The propeller shaft on these models cannot be disassembled.

Propeller Shaft Disassembly/Assembly (3 hp Models)

Refer to **Figure 139** for this procedure.

1. Remove the propeller shaft as described in this chapter.

2. Withdraw the cam follower from the end of the propeller shaft.

3. Push the sliding clutch toward the propeller end of the propeller shaft and compress the spring.

4. Withdraw the sliding clutch from the propeller shaft.

9

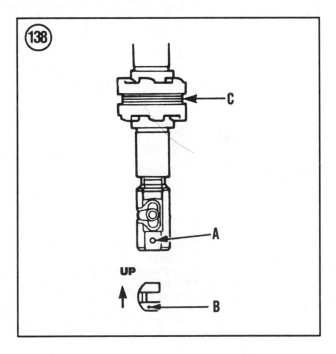

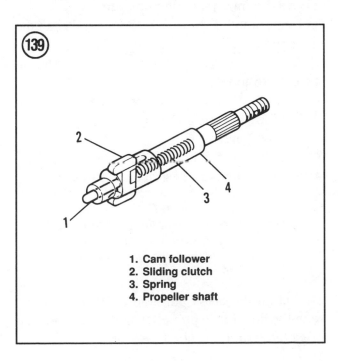

1. Cam follower
2. Sliding clutch
3. Spring
4. Propeller shaft

5. Rotate the propeller shaft on end and remove the spring.

6. Assembly by reversing these disassembly steps.

7. Make sure the eared end of the sliding clutch faces toward the forward gear.

Propeller Shaft Disassembly/Assembly (4-50 hp, Pro 50, C55, C75, C85 Models)

Refer to the following illustrations for this procedure:

    a. **Figure 140**: 4-30 hp engines.

    b. **Figure 141**: 40-50 hp, Pro 50, C55, C75, C85 models.

1. Remove the propeller shaft as described in this chapter.

2. Insert the end of an awl, seal pick, or thin-blade screwdriver under one end of the cross pin retaining ring (**Figure 142**).

3. Lift up the end of the retaining ring and unwind it from the dog clutch. Remove the ring.

4. Hold onto the propeller shaft and place the cam follower against a solid object, then push on the other end of the propeller shaft. This will relieve the internal spring pressure.

5. Use a small drift or screwdriver and push the cross pin out of the dog clutch (**Figure 143**).

6. Remove the tool and release the pressure on the cam follower.

7. Remove the shift plunger or cam follower, shift slide (models so equipped) and the compression spring.

8. Slide the dog clutch off the propeller shaft.

9. Clean all parts as described in this chapter.

NOTE
On models so identified, position the "F" (forward) mark stamped on the dog, facing toward the front end of the propeller shaft.

10. Align the cross pin hole in the dog clutch with the hole in the propeller shaft, then slide the dog clutch onto the shaft.

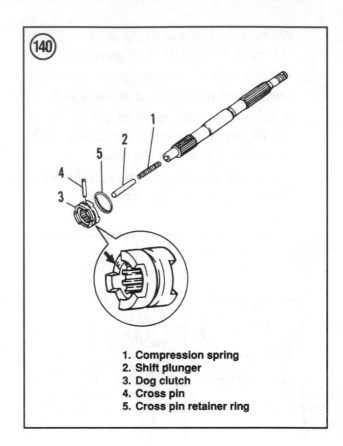

1. Compression spring
2. Shift plunger
3. Dog clutch
4. Cross pin
5. Cross pin retainer ring

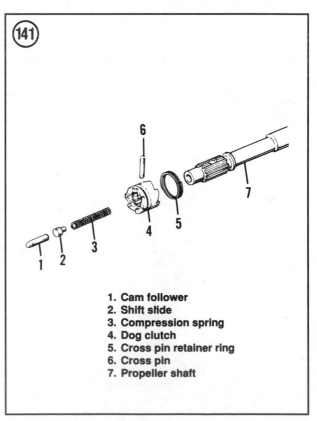

1. Cam follower
2. Shift slide
3. Compression spring
4. Dog clutch
5. Cross pin retainer ring
6. Cross pin
7. Propeller shaft

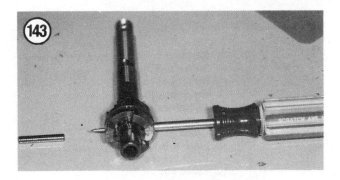

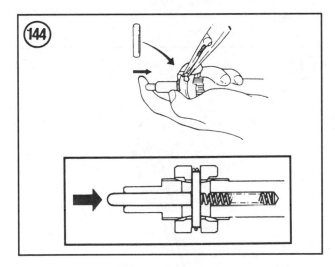

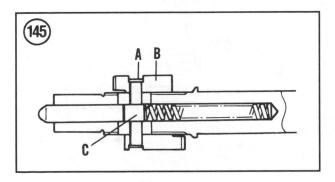

NOTE
On models so equipped, align the cross pin hole in the shift slide with the hole in the dog clutch. In Step 11B, the cross pin must pass through the dog clutch, the propeller shaft and the shift slide.

11A. On 4-30 hp models, install the compression spring and shift plunger into the end of the propeller shaft.

11B. On all other models, install the compression spring, shift slide and cam follower into the end of the propeller shaft.

12. Apply pressure on the end of the shift plunger or cam follower to compress the spring.

13. To align the holes in all of the parts, insert a small drift or punch through the holes in the dog clutch, the shift slide (models so equipped) and the propeller shaft.

14A. On 4-30 hp models, with the spring compressed, from the end opposite the drift installed in Step 13, install the cross pin through the propeller shaft and dog clutch and in front of the spring (**Figure 144**). Pull the drift out as the cross pin is being inserted.

14B. On all other models, with the spring compressed, from the end opposite the drift installed in Step 13, install the cross pin (A, **Figure 145**) through the dog clutch (B, **Figure 145**), propeller shaft and shift slide (C, **Figure 145**). Pull the drift out as the cross pin is being inserted.

15. Release pressure on the shift plunger or cam follower and remove it from the end of the propeller shaft.

CAUTION
Do not over stretch the retaining ring during installation in Step 16. If stretched, or distorted, it will lose its ability to secure the cross pin in place properly.

16. Carefully start one end of the retaining ring around the dog clutch groove and wrap the entire length of the ring around the dog clutch. Make sure the ring is seated correctly in the dog clutch groove so it will secure the cross pin in place.

17. Apply a small amount of cold grease to the inner end of the shift plunger or cam follower and reinstall it in the end of the propeller shaft. The cold grease will help hold it in place during propeller shaft installation.

Propeller Shaft Disassembly/Assembly (Pro 60, 90-130 hp V4, 150-225 hp 90° V6 Models, including L130, L150, L200)

> *NOTE*
> *On the L130 counter rotation outboard, this procedure relates to the short front propeller shaft. This model is equipped with 2 propeller shafts, and the rear propeller shaft does not include any of the small shift mechanism parts that are part of the front shaft.*

Refer to **Figure 146** for this procedure.
1. Remove the propeller shaft(s) as described in this chapter.
2. Insert the end of an awl, seal pick or thin-blade screwdriver under one end of the cross pin retaining ring (**Figure 142**).
3. Lift up the end of the retaining ring and unwind it from the dog clutch. Remove the ring.
4. Use a small drift or screwdriver and push the cross pin out of the dog clutch (**Figure 143**).
5. Remove the tool—but do not allow the shifter assembly to come out of the propeller shaft.
6. Slide the dog clutch off the propeller shaft. On L130 models, also slide the washer off propeller shaft.

> *NOTE*
> *Perform the next step over an open pan or box to catch the small steel balls that will come out with the shift slider.*

7. Working over an open pan or box, insert a small screwdriver, between the slider shoulder and end of the propeller shaft (**Figure 147**) and carefully pry the slider and shift slider loose from the propeller shaft.

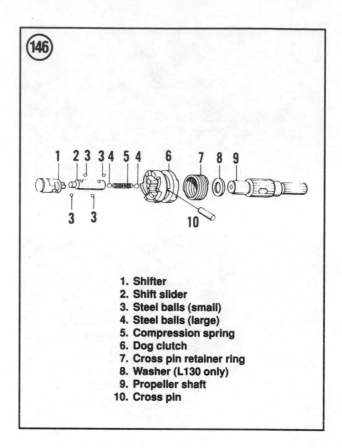

1. Shifter
2. Shift slider
3. Steel balls (small)
4. Steel balls (large)
5. Compression spring
6. Dog clutch
7. Cross pin retainer ring
8. Washer (L130 only)
9. Propeller shaft
10. Cross pin

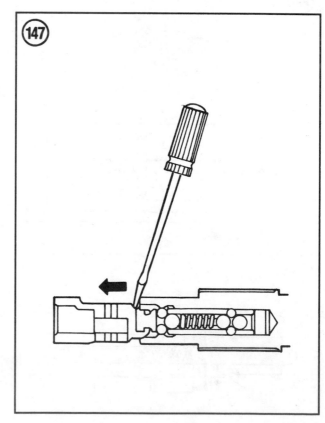

8. Slowly remove the shifter and the shift slider along with the 4 small steel balls from the shift slider. Do not lose any of the 4 balls as they all must be reinstalled.

9. Disconnect the shifter from the shift slider.

NOTE
In the next step, the 2 large steel balls and spring may come out with the shift slider or stay inside the propeller shaft.

10. Remove the 2 large steel balls and spring from the shift slider or from the propeller shaft.

11. Clean all parts as described in this chapter.

12. Apply a coat of cold grease to the large steel balls to hold them in place.

13. Install 1 large steel ball, the spring and the other large steel ball into the shift slider.

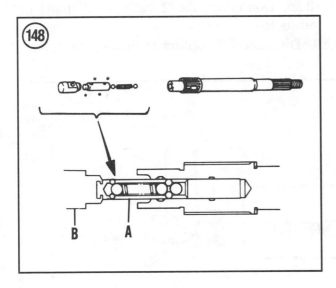

14. Apply a coat of cold grease to the 4 small steel balls to hold them in place, then install the 4 small steel balls into the holes in the shift slider.

15. Position the shift slider with the open end (containing the steel balls and spring) going in first. Install this assembly (A, **Figure 148**) partially into the end of the propeller shaft.

16. Connect the shifter onto the shift slider, then push the assembly in until it clicks into the neutral position in the propeller shaft (B, **Figure 148**). Don't push in any farther.

17. Rotate the shifter to the NEUTRAL position.

NOTE
On models so identified, position the "F" (forward) mark stamped on the dog clutch, facing toward the front end of the propeller shaft.

18. On L130 models, install the washer onto the propeller shaft.

19. Align the cross pin hole in the dog clutch with the hole in the propeller shaft (A, **Figure 149**), then slide the dog clutch (B, **Figure 149**) onto the shaft.

20. To align the holes in all of the parts, insert a small drift or punch through the holes in the dog clutch and the propeller shaft.

21. From the end opposite the drift installed in Step 20, install the cross pin (C, **Figure 149**) through the propeller shaft and dog clutch. Pull the drift out as the cross pin is being inserted.

CAUTION
Do not over stretch the retaining ring during installation in Step 22. If stretched, or distorted, it will lose its ability to secure the cross pin in place properly.

22. Carefully start one end of the retaining ring (D, **Figure 149**) around the dog clutch groove. Wrap the entire length of the ring around the dog clutch. Make sure the ring is seated correctly in the dog clutch groove so it will secure the cross pin in place.

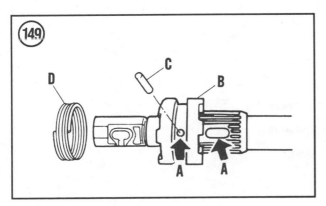

Propeller Shaft Disassembly/Assembly (225-250 hp 76° V6 Models, including L225 and L250)

NOTE
On L225 and L250 counter rotation outboards, this procedure relates to the short front propeller shaft. These models are equipped with 2 propeller shafts and the rear propeller shaft does not include any of the small shift mechanism parts that are part of the front shaft.

Refer to **Figure 150** for this procedure.

1. Remove the propeller shaft as described in this chapter.

2. Insert the end of an awl, seal pick or thin-blade screwdriver under one end of the cross pin retaining ring (**Figure 142**).

3. Lift up the end of the retaining ring and unwind it from the dog clutch. Remove the ring.

4. Use a small drift or screwdriver and push the cross pin out of the receptacle in the dog clutch (**Figure 143**).

5. Remove the tool—but do not allow the shifter assembly to come out of the propeller shaft.

6. Slide the dog clutch off the propeller shaft.

NOTE
Perform the next step over an open pan or box to catch the small steel balls that will come out with the shift slider.

7. Working over an open pan or box, insert a small screwdriver, between the slider shoulder and end of the propeller shaft (**Figure 147**) and carefully pry the shifter and shift slider loose from the propeller shaft.

8. Slowly remove the shifter and the shift slider along with the 2 large steel balls from the shift slider. Don't lose the 2 balls as all must be reinstalled.

9. Disconnect the shifter from the shift slider.

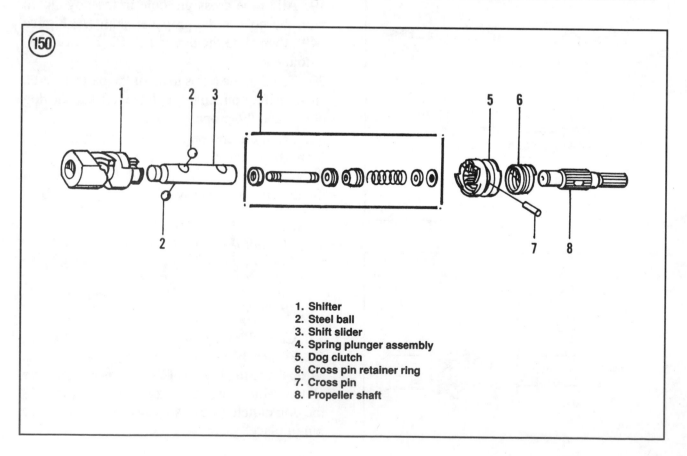

1. Shifter
2. Steel ball
3. Shift slider
4. Spring plunger assembly
5. Dog clutch
6. Cross pin retainer ring
7. Cross pin
8. Propeller shaft

10. Turn the shifter upside down and tap the closed end to loosen the spring assembly inside. Remove the spring assembly and note the orientation of the spring assembly. The spring assembly must be reinstalled in the same direction.

11. Clean all parts as described in this chapter.

12. Position the spring assembly in the same direction noted during removal, with the spring end going in last.

13. Push the spring assembly (A, **Figure 151**) into the shift slider until the end of it aligns with the steel ball holes (B, **Figure 151**) in the shift slider.

14. Apply a coat of cold grease to the 2 large steel balls to hold them in place, then install the 2 large steel balls (C, **Figure 151**) into the holes (B, **Figure 151**) in the shift slider.

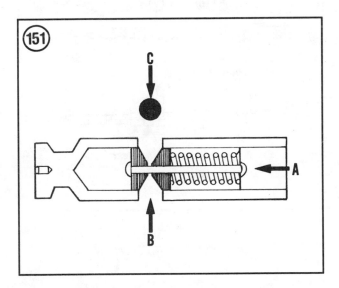

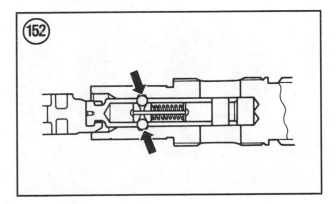

15. Position the shift slider with the open end (containing the spring assembly) going in first and partially install this assembly into the end of the propeller shaft.

16. Connect the shifter onto the shift slider, then push the assembly in until the steel balls (**Figure 152**) click into the neutral position in the propeller shaft. Don't push in any farther.

17. Rotate the shifter to the NEUTRAL position.

NOTE
On models so identified, position the "F" (forward) mark stamped on the dog clutch, facing toward the front end of the propeller shaft.

18. Align the cross pin hole in the dog clutch with hole in the propeller shaft (A, **Figure 149**), then slide the dog clutch (B, **Figure 149**) onto the shaft.

19. To align the holes in all of the parts, insert a small drift or punch through the holes in the dog clutch, the shift slider and the propeller shaft.

20. From the end opposite the drift installed in Step 19, install the cross pin (C, **Figure 149**) through the dog clutch, the shift slider and the propeller shaft. Pull the drift out as the cross pin is being inserted.

CAUTION
Do not over stretch the retaining ring during installation in Step 21. If stretched, or distorted, it will lose its ability to secure the cross pin in place properly.

21. Carefully start one end of the retaining ring (D, **Figure 149**) around the dog clutch groove. Wrap the entire length of the ring around the dog clutch. Make sure the ring is seated correctly in the dog clutch groove so it will secure the cross pin in place.

9

Gearcase Housing and Propeller Shaft Cleaning and Inspection (All Models)

1. Clean all parts in solvent and dry with compressed air.

2. On all counter rotation models, the rear propeller shaft must be pulled out of the bearing housing with special tools to inspect the propeller shaft. Refer to the procedure described in this chapter for shaft removal.

3. Check the bearing carrier and bearing contact points on the propeller shaft (A, **Figure 153**). Replace the shaft and bearing carrier bearing(s) if the shaft shows pitting, grooving, scoring, heat discoloration or embedded metallic particles.

4. Inspect the propeller shaft surfaces where the oil seal lips contact. If grooved, replace the propeller shaft and oil seals.

5. Install the propeller shaft(s) on V-blocks at the bearing locations. Refer to **Figure 154** for both types of propeller shafts. Position the dial indicator at the center of the shaft and zero the dial gauge. Slowly rotate the shaft several complete revolutions and note the readings. Replace the shaft if runout exceeds 0.02 mm (0.0008 in.).

6. Check the propeller shaft splines and threads for wear, rust or corrosion damage (B, **Figure 153**). Replace the shaft if necessary.

7. Apply a light coat of oil to the reverse gear ball bearing and rotate the bearing to check for rough spots. Push and pull on the reverse gear to check for side wear. If movement is excessive, replace the bearing with special tools and a hydraulic press.

8. Inspect the reverse gear teeth (A, **Figure 155**). If teeth are pitted, chipped, broken or excessively worn, replace the gear.

9. Inspect the dogs on the gear and the dog clutch (B, **Figure 155**). If the clutch dogs are chipped or rounded off, replace the gear and the dog clutch as an assembly. Such damage can be caused by improper shift adjustment, excessive idle speed or shifting too slowly.

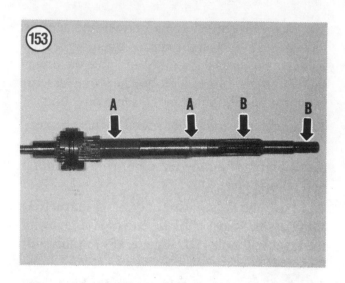

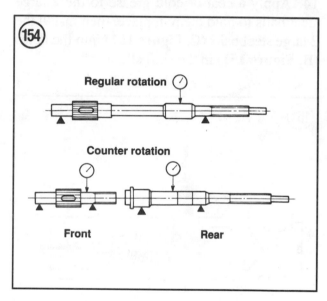

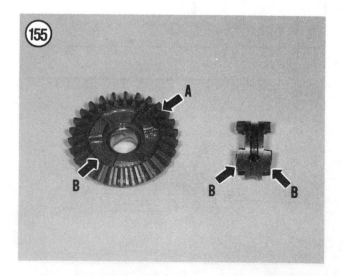

10. Inspect the propeller shaft compression spring for weakness or sagging. Replace as required.

11. Inspect the retainer ring for weakness. Replace as required.

12. On models so equipped, inspect the cover nut for cracks, and broken or corroded threads. Replace as required.

13. On models so equipped, inspect the tab washer. There must be sufficient locking tabs in good condition for reinstallation. If not, replace the washer. It's good practice to replace the tab

washer every other time the bearing carrier is removed.

Bearing Carrier and Propeller Shaft Installation (2-15 hp, 25 hp, C30, 40-15 hp, Pro 50 Models)

1. Secure the gearcase in a suitable holding fixture or a vise with protective jaws. If protective jaws are not available, position the gearcase upright in the vise with the skeg between wooden blocks.

2. On models so equipped, install the reverse gear thrust washer over the threaded end of the propeller shaft.

3. Install the propeller shaft and reverse gear (except 2-3 hp) into the propeller shaft bore in the gear housing (**Figure 156**, typical).

4. Apply a light coat of grease to the gear housing and O-ring.

5A. On 2-5 hp, install a new gasket under the cap, then install the cap.

5B. On all other models, install the bearing carrier and cap (**Figure 157**).

6. Apply blue Loctite (No. 242) to the bolt threads prior to installation.

7. Install the 2 bolts and washers securing the gear housing cap (**Figure 158**) and tighten to the specification in **Table 1**.

8. On 6-25 hp models, check the forward and reverse gear backlash as described in this chapter.

9. Install the propeller as described in this chapter.

Bearing Housing and Propeller Shaft Installation (C25, 30 hp, C40, C55, Pro 60, 70-90 hp and Regular Rotation 115-130 V4, 150-225 hp 90° V6 Models)

NOTE
*This procedure covers the **regular rotation** 115-225 hp outboards. Refer to the*

9

*following procedure for counter rotation
L130 V4, L150 and L200 V6 models.*

1. Secure the gearcase in a suitable holding fixture or a vise with protective jaws. If protective jaws are not available, position the gearcase upright in the vise with the skeg between wooden blocks.

2. On models so equipped, install the propeller thrust washer over the threaded end of the propeller shaft.

3. Apply a light coat of grease to the outer diameter of the bearing housing at all points where the housing contacts the gearcase bore.

4. On models so equipped, install the reverse gear shimming between the gear and the thrust washers.

5A. On Pro 60 and 70-90 hp models, place the shift cam on the shifter with the "F" mark on the shift cam facing forward, then install the propeller shaft into the bore in the bearing housing (**Figure 159**).

5B. On C115, 115-130 hp V4, 150-225 hp 90° V6 models, position the flat part of the shifter up and install the propeller shaft in the bore in the bearing housing.

5C. On all other models, install the propeller shaft into the bore in the bearing housing.

6. Install the propeller shaft and bearing housing into the gearcase bore.

7. Align the key slots in the bearing housing and the gearcase, then rotate the driveshaft clockwise to mesh with the pinion and reverse gears.

8. When the housing is fully seated, install the locating key in the slots (**Figure 160**). Make sure it is properly seated in both parts.

9. Install a *new* tab washer. If a new washer is not available, the old one may be reused providing different tabs are bent up in Step 13.

10. Apply a light coat of grease to the cover nut threads prior to installation. Install the cover nut and tighten finger-tight to make sure it is not cross-threaded (**Figure 161**).

11. Use the same special tools used during Removal Step 6, (**Figure 162**) and tighten as much

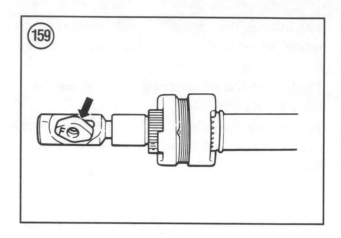

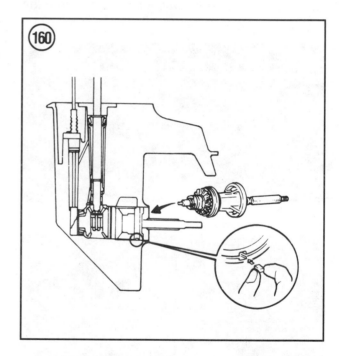

as possible by hand, then tighten to the specification in **Table 1**.

12. Check the forward and reverse gear backlash as described in this chapter.

13. Bend one of the lock tabs on the lockwasher into the cover nut slot. Bend the remaining tabs 90° in the opposite direction.

14. Install the shift rod assembly as described in this chapter.

15. Install the propeller as described in this chapter.

Bearing Housing and Propeller Shaft Installation (L130 V4, L150 and L200 V6 Counter Rotation Models)

1. Secure the gearcase in a suitable holding fixture or a vise with protective jaws. If protective jaws are not available, position the gearcase

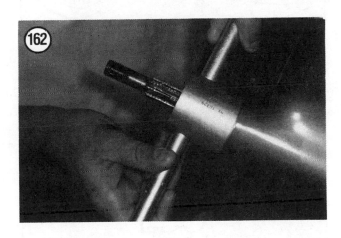

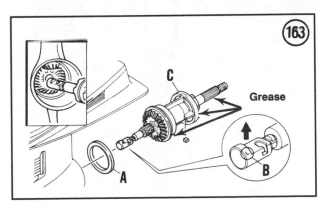

upright in the vise with the skeg between wooden blocks.

2. Apply a light coat of grease to the outer diameter of the bearing housing at all points where the housing contacts the gearcase bore.

3. Install the forward gear shim (A, **Figure 163**) onto the front of the bearing housing.

4. On L150 and L200 models, position the flat part (marked "L") of the shifter facing up (B, **Figure 163**).

5A. On L130 V4 models, perform the following:

   a. Install the front propeller shaft assembly as described in this chapter.

   b. Install the rear propeller shaft and bearing housing into the gearcase bore and onto the front propeller shaft assembly.

5B. On L150 and L200 V6 models, install the rear propeller shaft and bearing housing (C, **Figure 163**) in the gearcase bore and into the front propeller shaft.

6. Align the key slots in the bearing housing and the gear case, then rotate the driveshaft clockwise to mesh with the pinion and reverse gears.

7. When the bearing housing is fully seated, install the locating key into the slots (**Figure 164**). Make sure it is properly seated in both parts.

9

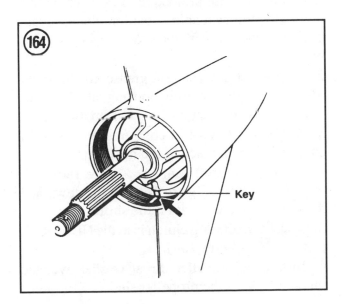

8. Install a *new* tab washer (A, **Figure 165**). If a new washer is not available, the old one may be reused providing different tabs be bent up in Step 12.

9. Apply a light coat of grease to the cover nut threads prior to installation. Install the cover nut (B, **Figure 165**) and tighten finger-tight to make sure it is not cross-threaded.

10. Use the same special tools used during Removal Step 5, and tighten as much as possible by hand, then tighten to the specification in **Table 1**.

11. Check the forward and reverse gear backlash as described in this chapter.

12. Bend one of the lock tabs on the lockwasher into the cover nut slot. Bend the remaining tabs 90° in the opposite direction.

13. Install the shift rod assembly as described in this chapter.

14. Install the propeller as described in this chapter.

Bearing Housing and Propeller Shaft Installation (225-250 hp 76° V6 Regular Rotation Models)

1. Secure the gearcase in a suitable holding fixture or a vise with protective jaws. If protective jaws are not available, position the gearcase upright in the vise with the skeg between wooden blocks.

2. Apply a light coat of grease to the outer diameter of the bearing housing at all points where the housing contacts the gearcase bore.

3. Apply a light coat of cold grease to the shift cam to hold it in place in the next step.

4. Position the shift cam (A, **Figure 166**) with the "O" mark (B, **Figure 166**) facing down and to the front and place it on the shifter.

5. Make sure the dog clutch is in the NEUTRAL position (C, **Figure 166**).

6. Install the propeller thrust washer over the threaded end of the propeller shaft.

7. Install the propeller shaft and bearing housing into the gearcase bore.

8. Align the key slots in the bearing housing and the gearcase, then rotate the driveshaft clockwise to mesh with the pinion and reverse gears.

9. When the housing is fully seated, install the locating key in the slots (A, **Figure 167**). Make sure it is properly seated in both parts.

10. Attach a grease gun to the grease fitting (B, **Figure 167**) and fill the propeller shaft bearing housing with grease until it begins to come out of the bearing housing.

11. Apply red Loctite (No. 271) to the lower casing cap bolt threads prior to installation.

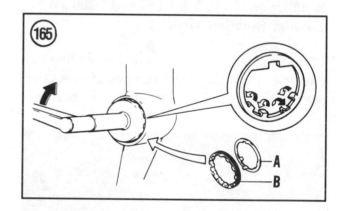

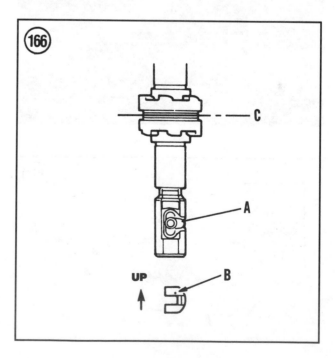

12. Install the lower casing cap and bolts and tighten securely.

13. Check the forward and reverse gear backlash as described in this chapter.

14. Install the shift rod assembly as described in this chapter.

15. Install the propeller as described in this chapter.

Bearing Housing and Propeller Shaft Installation (L225 and L250 76° V6 Counter Rotation Models)

1. Secure the gearcase in a suitable holding fixture or a vise with protective jaws. If protective jaws are not available, position the gearcase upright in the vise with the skeg between wooden blocks.

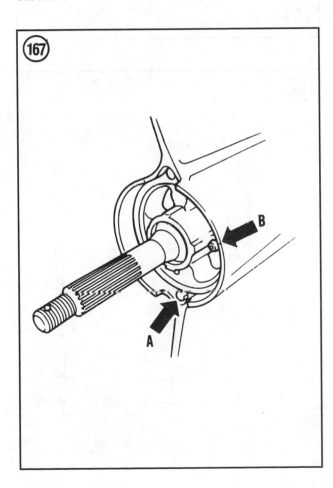

2. Apply a light coat of grease to the outer diameter of the bearing housing at all points where the housing contacts the gear case bore.

3. Install the front propeller shaft assembly as described in this chapter.

4. Install the rear propeller shaft and bearing housing into the gearcase bore and onto the front propeller shaft assembly.

5. Align the key slots in the bearing housing and the gear case, then rotate the driveshaft clockwise to mesh with the pinion and reverse gears.

6. When the bearing housing is fully seated, install the locating key in the slots. Make sure it is properly seated in both parts.

7. Attach a grease gun to the grease fitting and fill the propeller shaft bearing housing with grease until it begins to come out of the bearing housing.

8. Apply red Loctite (No. 271) to the lower casing cap bolt threads prior to installation.

9. Install the lower casing cap and bolts and tighten securely.

10. Check the forward and reverse gear backlash as described in this chapter.

11. Install the shift rod assembly as described in this chapter.

12. Install the propeller as described in this chapter.

PINION GEAR AND DRIVESHAFT

Removal (2-8 hp Models)

The pinion gear is secured to the drive shaft by a circlip.

1. Remove the water pump assembly as described in this chapter.

2. Remove the bearing carrier and propeller shaft assembly as described in this chapter.

3. Secure the gearcase in a suitable holding fixture or a vise with protective jaws. If protective jaws are not available, position the gearcase upright in the vise with the skeg between wooden blocks.

9

4. Use a hooked awl, needlenose pliers (**Figure 168**), or similar tool and remove the circlip securing the pinion gear to the driveshaft (A, **Figure 169**).

5A. On 2 hp models, remove the pinion gear, washer and shim from the end of the driveshaft.

5B. On all other models, remove the pinion gear (B, **Figure 169**) and shim (C, **Figure 169**).

6. Carefully withdraw the drive shaft (D, **Figure 169**) up through the top of the gearcase.

7. Clean and inspect all components as described in this chapter.

Removal (9-250 hp Models)

The pinion gear is secured to the drive shaft by a nut.

1. Remove the water pump assembly as described in this chapter.

2. Remove the bearing carrier and propeller shaft assembly as described in this chapter.

3. On all models except, C25, 25 hp, C40, 40-50 hp and Pro 50 models, remove the shift rod assembly as described in this chapter.

4. Secure the gearcase in a suitable holding fixture or a vise with protective jaws. If protective jaws are not available, position the gearcase upright in the vise with the skeg between wooden blocks.

5. Install a drive shaft holder onto the splines on top of the drive shaft to keep it from turning in the following step (A, **Figure 170**). Use the following special tool:

   a. 9.9-15 hp models: part No. YB-6228.

   b. 25 hp model: part No. YB-6368.

   c. C25, C30, C40, 30-50 hp, Pro 50 models: part No. YB-6079.

   d. C55, Pro 60, 70 hp models: part No. YB-6049.

   e. C75, C85, 90 hp models: part No. YB-6151.

   f. C115, 115-250 hp models: part No. YB-6201.

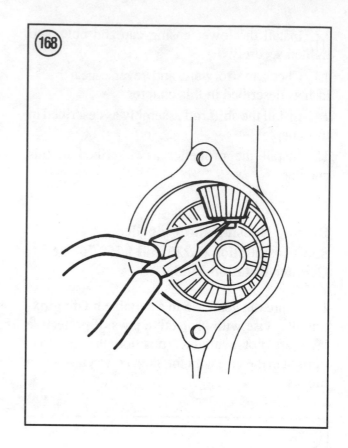

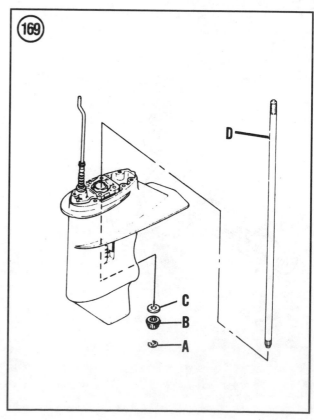

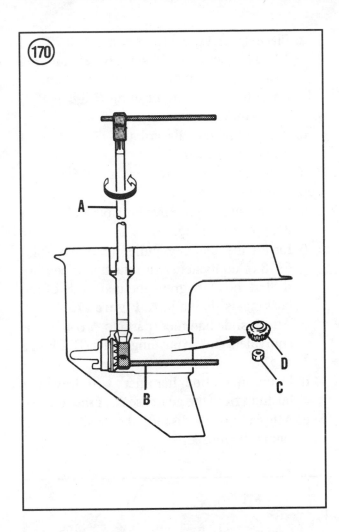

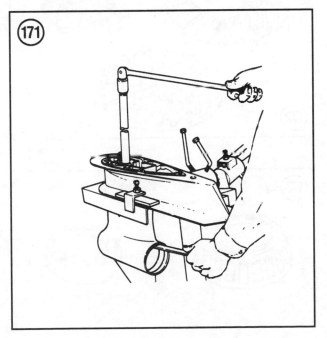

CAUTION
Pad the sides of the propeller shaft bore in the gearcase to prevent damage or distortion from contact with the wrench.

6. Hold the pinion gear nut using a box-end wrench or, if available, the following special tool (B, **Figure 170**):

   a. 9.9-30 hp, C25, C30, C40 models: part No. YB-6078.

   b. 40-50 hp, Pro 50 models: part No. 90890-06506.

   c. All other models: part No. 90890-06505.

7. Hold the pinion gear nut stationary and turn the driveshaft to loosen the nut (**Figure 171**).

8. Remove the special tools.

9A. On 9.9-15 hp models, remove the nut, pinion gear, shim, thrust bearing and washer from the lower end of the drive shaft.

9B. On 25 hp models, remove the nut, pinion gear, shim, thrust bearing and washer from the lower end of the drive shaft.

9C. On all other models, remove the nut (C, **Figure 170**) and the pinion gear (D, **Figure 170**) from the lower end of the drive shaft.

10. Carefully withdraw the drive shaft up through the top of the gearcase.

NOTE
On all other models, the drive shaft upper bearing must be removed prior to removal of the drive shaft sleeve as described in this chapter. The 225-250 76° V6 models are not equipped with a sleeve.

11. On 9.9-15, 25 hp models, remove the drive shaft sleeve up through the top of the gearcase. It may be necessary to tap the sleeve loose from the lower side of the gearcase.

12. Clean and inspect all components as described in this chapter.

9

Cleaning and Inspection
(All Models)

1. Clean the drive shaft and pinion gear with solvent. Blow dry with compressed air, if available.

2. Inspect the pinion gear for pitting, grooving, scoring, uneven or excessive wear and heat discoloration (**Figure 172**).

CAUTION
Do not remove any bushing or bearing from the gearcase unless replacement is required. The bushing or bearing will be damaged during removal and must not be reinstalled.

3. Inspect the drive shaft bushing, needle bearing and/or tapered bearings and tapered bearing contact surfaces for defects as described in Step 2 (**Figure 173**). Replace the bushing(s) and/or bearing(s) if any defects are found, as described in this chapter.

4. Inspect the drive shaft splines for wear or damage. If the splines are damaged, also inspect the splines on the associated gear for damage.

5. Inspect the drive shaft where the bushing, bearings and oil seals ride. Replace the drive shaft if grooves or other damage are found.

6. Inspect the water pump oil seal contact surface on the drive shaft.

Drive Shaft Bushing,
Bearing and Oil Seal(s)
Removal/Installation

NOTE
Do not remove the tapered roller bearing races, or needle bearings or the oil seals for inspection purposes. Only remove the bearing(s) and/or oil seals if replacement is necessary.

1. Remove the driveshaft as described in this chapter.

2. On 2-8 hp models, remove the drive shaft lower bushings as follows:

a. Place special tools (part No. YB-6027 and YB-6229) or suitable size socket and long socket extension on top of the bushing.

b. Carefully drive the bushing (**Figure 174**) out of the gearcase.

c. After removal, discard the bushing as it cannot be reused.

3. On 2-8 hp models, remove the drive shaft upper bushing as follows:

a. Use an awl and remove both oil seals above the upper bushing.

b. Install the bushing puller (part No. YB-6178 or equivalent) into the upper bearing so that the claw grabs the underside of the bushing as shown in A, **Figure 175**.

c. Attach slide hammer (part No. YB-6096 or equivalent) to the bushing puller (B, **Figure 175**).

d. Using the slide hammer, withdraw the bushing from the gearcase (C, **Figure 175**).

e. After removal, discard the bushing as it cannot be reused.

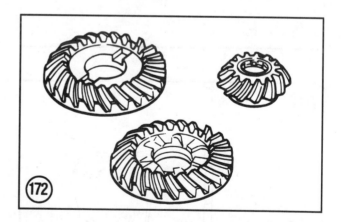

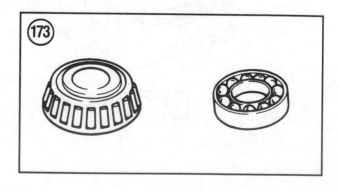

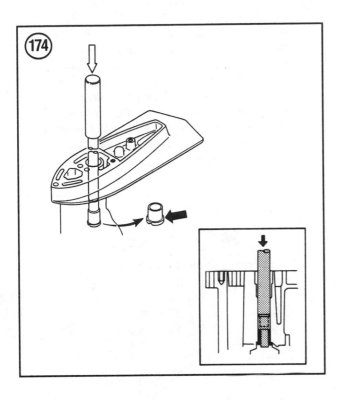

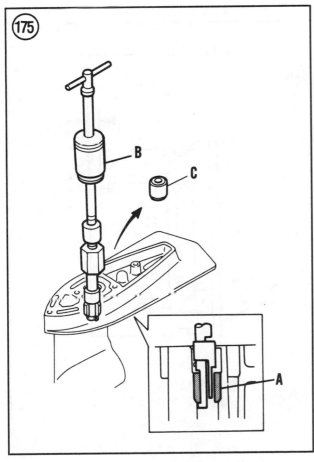

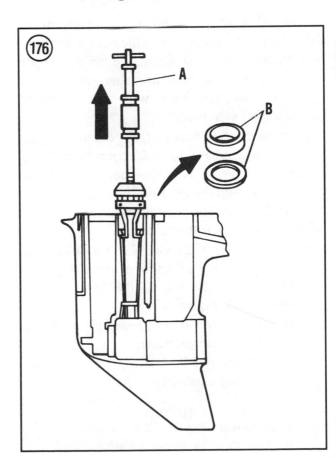

NOTE
On 9.9-15, 25 hp models, the oil seals and upper bearing are contained in the oil seal housing portion of the water pump assembly and their replacement is covered in the water pump section of this chapter. On V4 and all V6 models, the upper bearings and oil seal(s) are contained in the drive shaft bearing housing assembly and are covered in this procedure.

4. On all other models except V4 and all V6 models, perform the following:

   a. Remove the upper tapered roller bearing from the outer race.

   b. Attach slide hammer (part No. YB-6096 or equivalent) to the bearing puller (part No. 90890-06535).

   c. Insert the special tools into the bearing inner race and place the puller under the outer race (A, **Figure 176**).

d. Using the slide hammer, withdraw the outer race from the gearcase (B, **Figure 176**).

e. After removal, discard the outer race and the rest of the bearing set.

f. On models so equipped, remove the shim below the outer race.

5. On models so equipped, if still installed, remove the drive shaft sleeve (A, **Figure 177**) up through the top of the gearcase. It may be necessary to tap the sleeve loose from the lower side of the gear case.

CAUTION
*On C25, C30 and 30 hp models, measure the location of the lower needle bearing within the gearcase as described in Step 6 before removing it. This must be an **accurate measurement** made with either metric or decimal measurements (fractional measurements cannot be used) due to close tolerances of all components within the gear case.*

6. On C25, C30 and 30 hp engines, perform the following prior to removing the needle bearing:

a. Place a metal straightedge on the upper surface of the gearcase, then use a depth gauge or steel ruler with fine metric or decimal increments.

b. Measure the distance from the top surface of the gearcase to the upper face of the needle bearing. Note this measurement as it will be used during installation.

7. On C25, 30-90 hp models, remove the lower needle bearing as follows:

a. Insert driver rod (part No. YB-6071) and needle bearing attachment (part No. YB-6063) onto the top of the lower needle bearing (B, **Figure 177**).

b. Drive the lower needle bearing (C, **Figure 177**) out of the gearcase.

c. Discard the needle bearing after removal. The bearing cannot be reused.

CAUTION
Prior to removing the oil seals and needle bearing from the drive shaft bearing

*housing, measure their location within the drive shaft bearing housing as described in Step 8. This must be an **accurate measurement** made with either metric or decimal measurements (fractional measurements cannot be used) due to close tolerances of all components inside the gearcase and drive shaft bearing housing.*

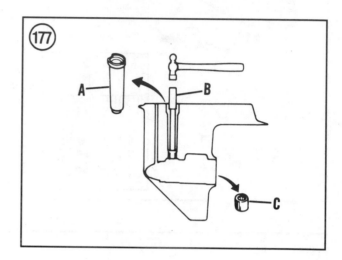

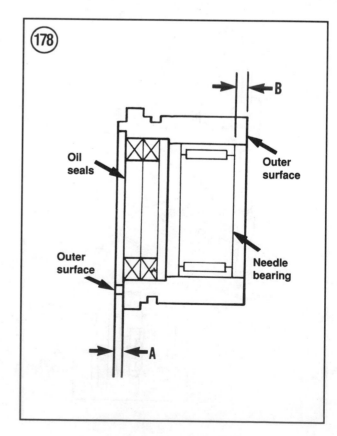

8. On V4 and all V6 models, perform the following prior to the removing the oil seals and needle bearing from the drive shaft bearing housing:

   a. Refer to **Figure 178** for a typical drive shaft bearing housing with the oil seals and needle bearing still in place.

   b. Place a metal straightedge on the outer surface of the bearing housing, then use a depth gauge or steel ruler with fine metric or decimal increments.

   c. Measure the distance from the outer surface of the bearing housing to the face of the outer oil seal (A, **Figure 178**) and to the needle bearing (B, **Figure 178**). Note both of these measurements as they will be used during installation.

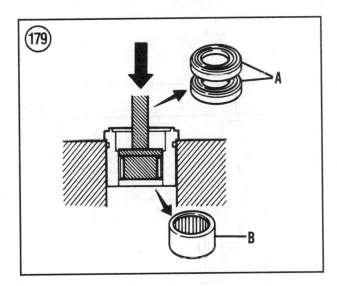

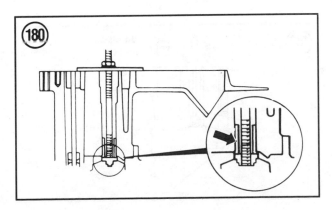

9. On V4 and all V6 models, remove the oil seals and upper bearing from the drive shaft bearing housing as follows:

   a. Use an awl and remove both oil seals (A, **Figure 179**) from the housing. Discard both oil seals.

   b. Place bearing driver (part No. YB-6071 and YB-6169), or suitable size socket and long socket extension on top of the bearing.

   c. Carefully drive the bearing (B, **Figure 179**) out of the gearcase.

   d. Discard the bushing.

NOTE
On 2-8 hp models, install the lower bushing first, then install the upper bushing. If the upper bushing is installed first, it will interfere with the special tools required to install the lower bushing.

NOTE
The lower bushing is pulled into the gearcase from the underside of the drive shaft bore. Special tools must be used to install the bushing.

10. On 2-8 hp models, install the drive shaft lower bushing as follows:

   a. Apply oil to the outer surface of the bushing outer surface and to the inner surface of the gearcase.

   b. Install bushing installer set (part No. YB-6169, YB-6029 and YB-6028) and the bushing into the gearcase.

   c. Carefully pull the bushing (**Figure 180**) into the gearcase by tightening the center bolt until the tool bottoms out on the gearcase.

   d. Remove the special tools.

11. On 2-8 hp models, install the drive shaft upper bushing as follows:

   a. Apply oil to the outer surface of the bushing outer surface and to the inner surface of the gear case.

   b. Correctly position the bushing in its bore in the gearcase.

9

c. Install the bushing installer set (part No. YB-6025 and YB-6229) onto the bushing and carefully drive the bushing into the gearcase until it bottoms out on the gearcase shoulder (**Figure 181**).

d. Apply grease to the outer diameter of the oil seals to aid in installation.

e. Position both new oil seals with their open end going in last (A, **Figure 182**).

f. Carefully tap both oil seals in with an oil seal installer, or a suitable size socket or piece of pipe that matches the *outer surface* of the seal. Do not drive the oil seals in using the inner surface as the oil seals will be damaged. Tap both oil seals in until the top seal is below the top surface of the gearcase by 1.0-1.5 mm (0.04-0.06 in.) (B, **Figure 182**).

NOTE
On 9.9-15, 25 hp models, the oil seals and upper bearing are contained in the oil seal housing portion of the water pump assembly and their replacement is covered in the water pump section of this chapter.

12. On C25 and 30-90 hp models, install the lower needle bearing as follows:

a. Apply oil to the outer surface of the needle bearing and to the inner surface of the gear case.

b. Position the needle bearing with its manufacturer's marks facing up.

c. Insert driver rod (part No. YB-6071) (A, **Figure 183**) and needle bearing attachment (part No. YB-6081[C25] or YB-6082[C30 and 30-90 hp]) (B, **Figure 183**) onto the top of the lower needle bearing.

NOTE
There is no built-in stop, or shoulder, within the gearcase that will limit the travel of the needle bearing. Tap the bearing in slowly and check the dimension several times to ensure the bearing is positioned correctly.

d. Carefully tap the needle bearing into place. Tap the bearing in the same distance (C, **Figure 183**) as noted during removal Step 7.

13. On V4 and all V6 models, install the upper bearing and oil seals into the drive shaft bearing housing as follows:

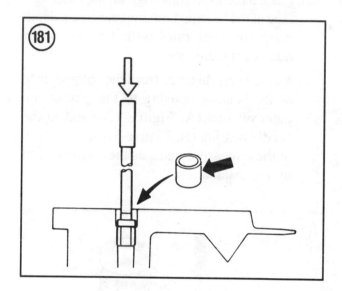

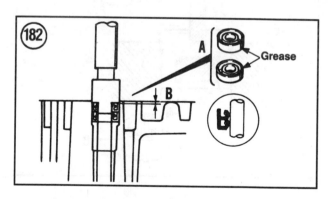

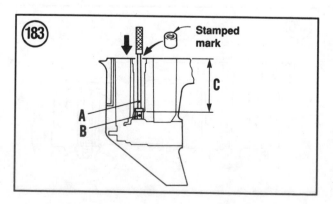

a. Apply oil to the outer surface of the needle bearing and to the inner surface of the drive shaft bearing housing.

b. Position the needle bearing with its manufacturer's marks facing up.

NOTE
There is no built-in stop, or shoulder, within the bearing housing that will limit the travel of the needle bearing. Tap the bearing in slowly and check the dimen-

sion several times to ensure the bearing is positioned correctly.

c. Use the same set of special tools used for removal and carefully tap the needle bearing into place (**Figure 184**). Tap the bearing in the same distance (B, **Figure 178**) as noted during removal Step 9.

d. Apply grease to the outer diameter of the oil seals to aid in installation.

e. Position both new oil seals with their open end going in last.

f. Carefully tap both oil seals in with an oil seal installer, or a suitable size socket or piece of pipe that matches the *outer surface* of the seal (**Figure 185**). Do not drive the oil seals in using the inner surface as the oil seals will be damaged. Tap both oil seals in the same distance (A, **Figure 178**) as noted during removal Step 9.

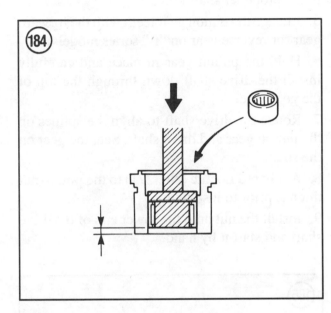

14. On models so equipped, install the drive shaft sleeve into the top of the gear case. Align the locating rib(s) on the sleeve with the recess in the top of the gearcase, then push the sleeve down making sure it is properly aligned and seated.

15. On models equipped with a tapered roller upper bearing, perform the following:

a. On models so equipped, install the pinion gear shim onto the sleeve below the outer race.

b. Apply oil to the outer surface of the bearing outer race and to the inner surface of the gearcase.

c. Correctly position the bearing outer race in its bore in the gear case.

d. Install a suitable size socket or piece of pipe onto the top of the outer race and carefully drive the race into the gearcase until it bottoms out.

16. Install the drive shaft as described in this chapter.

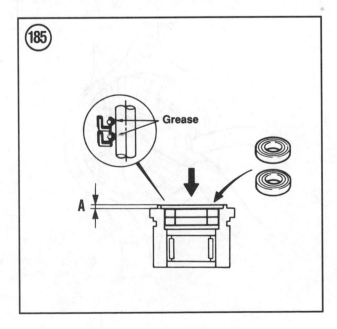

Grease

A

Driveshaft/Pinion Gear Installation (2-8 hp Models)

1. Secure the gearcase in a suitable holding fixture or a vise with protective jaws. If protective jaws are not available, position the gearcase upright in the vise with the skeg between wooden blocks.

2. Apply a light coat of grease to the exterior of the drive shaft and to the pinion gear teeth.

3A. On 2 hp models, install the shim, washer and pinion gear in the propeller shaft bore.

3B. On all other models, install the shim and the pinion gear in the propeller shaft bore.

4. Engage the pinion gear teeth with the forward gear.

5. Hold the pinion gear in place and carefully install the drive shaft down through the top of the gearcase.

6. Rotate the drive shaft to align the splines on the pinion gear and drive shaft, then seat the gear on the shaft.

7. Inside the propeller shaft bore, hold the pinion gear in place. Using needle nose pliers, install the circlip securing the gear in place (**Figure 186**). Make sure the circlip is properly engaged in the drive shaft groove.

8. Install the bearing carrier and propeller shaft assembly as described in this chapter.

9. Install the water pump assembly as described in this chapter.

Drive Shaft/Pinion Gear Installation (9-250 hp Models)

1. Secure the gearcase in a suitable holding fixture or a vise with protective jaws. If protective jaws are not available, position the gearcase upright in the vise with the skeg between wooden blocks.

2. On 9.9-15, 25 hp models, install the drive shaft sleeve down through the top of the gear case. Align the lower locating tab with the notch

in the gear case, then carefully tap on top of the sleeve to seat it into the gearcase completely.

3. Apply a light coat of grease to the exterior of the drive shaft and to the pinion gear teeth.

4A. On 9.9-25 hp models, install the washer, thrust washer, shim and pinion gear in the propeller shaft bore. Make sure the locating tab on the thrust washer is properly positioned in the housing slot.

4B. On all other models, install the pinion gear in the propeller shaft bore.

5. Engage the pinion gear teeth with the forward gear (or reverse gear on "L" series models).

6. Hold the pinion gear in place and carefully install the drive shaft down through the top of the gear case.

7. Rotate the drive shaft to align the splines on the pinion gear and drive shaft. Seat the gear on the shaft.

8. Apply red Loctite (No. 271) to the pinion nut threads prior to installation.

9. Install the nut onto the lower end of the drive shaft and start it by hand.

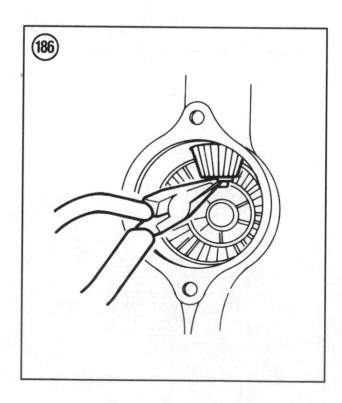

10. Install a drive shaft holder onto the splines on top of the drive shaft. Use the same special tool used during removal.

CAUTION
Pad the sides of the propeller shaft bore in the gearcase to prevent damage or distortion from contact with the wrench.

11. Place a box-end wrench on the pinion nut. While holding the pinion nut from turning, turn

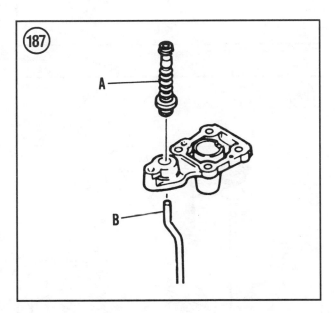

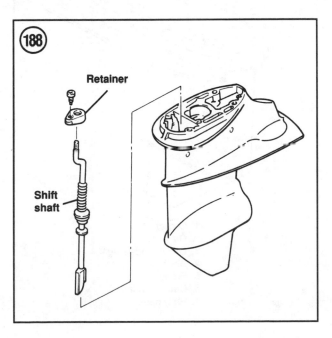

the drive shaft to tighten the nut (**Figure 171**) to the specification listed in **Table 1**.

12. On all models except C25, 25 hp, C40, 40-50 hp and Pro 50 models, install the shift rod assembly as described in this chapter.

13. Install the bearing carrier and propeller shaft assembly as described in this chapter.

14. Install the water pump assembly as described in this chapter.

SHIFT SHAFT

Removal, Inspection and Installation (All Models)

NOTE
The 2 hp outboard motor is not equipped with a shift shaft.

1A. On 3-5 hp models, perform the following:
   a. Remove the bolt and washer securing the plate to the gearcase.
   b. Remove the plate, gasket and shift shaft from the gearcase. Don't lose the locating pin(s).
   c. Slide the rubber boot up and off the upper end of the shift shaft. Discard the rubber boot.
   d. Withdraw the shift shaft out through the bottom of the plate.
1B. On 6-8 hp models, perform the following:
   a. Remove the bolt and washer securing the oil seal housing to the gear case.
   b. Remove the oil seal housing, gasket and shift shaft from the gear case. Don't lose the locating pin.
   c. Slide the rubber boot (A, **Figure 187**) up and off the upper end of the shift shaft. Discard the rubber boot.
   d. Withdraw the shift rod (B, **Figure 187**) through the bottom of the oil seal housing.
1C. On 9.9-15 hp, C25, 30 hp and C40 engines, remove the screw securing the shift shaft retainer to the gearcase withdraw the shift shaft assembly and retainer from the gearcase (**Figure 188**).

1D. On 25 hp and C30 models, perform the following:

  a. Remove the water pump as described in this chapter.

  b. On 25 hp models, remove the remaining bolt and washer securing the oil seal housing to the gearcase housing.

  c. On C30 engines, remove the bolts, washers, bracket and plate securing the oil seal housing to the gearcase housing.

  d. If necessary, insert flat-bladed screwdrivers at the fore and aft end of the oil seal housing and carefully pry the housing up (**Figure 189**). On C30 models, do not lose the locating pins.

  e. Lift the oil seal housing and gasket (or O-ring) up and over the drive shaft. Discard the gasket or O-ring(s).

  f. Withdraw the shift shaft assembly from the gearcase.

1E. On 40 hp, 50 hp, Pro 50, C55, C75, C85 models, refer to **Figure 190** and perform the following:

> *NOTE*
> *The forward gear and bearing must be removed to reach the shift cam attached to the lower end of the shift shaft.*

  a. Remove the forward gear and bearing as described in this chapter.

  b. Remove the water pump as described in this chapter.

  c. On C55, C75, C85 models, remove the bolts and washers securing the shift shaft oil seal housing to the gearcase (**Figure 191**).

  d. Carefully loosen the shift shaft oil seal housing from the gearcase.

  e. Withdraw the shift shaft and oil seal housing assembly from the gearcase (**Figure 192**).

  f. Remove the O-ring seal from the oil seal housing and discard it.

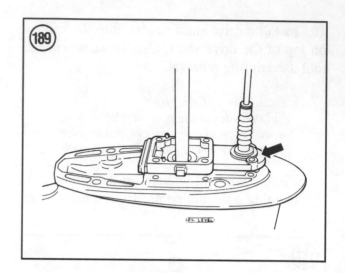

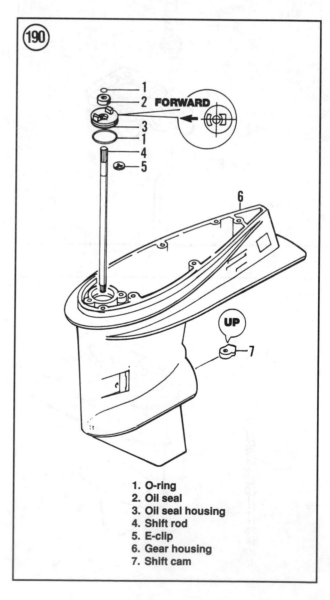

1. O-ring
2. Oil seal
3. Oil seal housing
4. Shift rod
5. E-clip
6. Gear housing
7. Shift cam

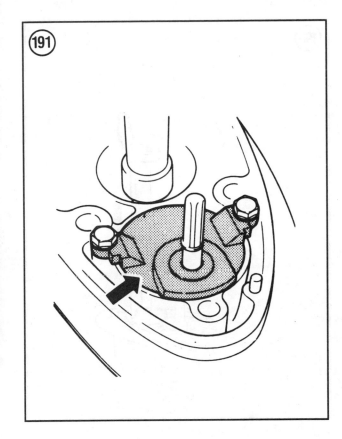

g. Remove the shift cam from the recess in the gearcase.

1F. On Pro 60, 70-250 hp models (except C75, C85), perform the following:

a. Install the shift shaft handle (part No. YB-6052) onto the shift shaft and make sure the gearcase is in the NEUTRAL position. Shift the gearcase if necessary.

b. Remove the water pump as described in this chapter.

c. Remove the bolts and washers securing the shift shaft retainer plate (**Figure 191**).

d. Withdraw the shift shaft and retainer plate assembly from the gearcase.

e. Remove the O-ring seal from the retainer plate and discard it.

2. Clean and inspect all components as described in this chapter.

3. Apply a light coat of grease to the lower half portion of the shift shaft.

4A. On 3-5 hp models, perform the following:

a. Install the shift shaft up through the bottom of the plate.

b. Install a new gasket onto the plate.

c. Make sure the locating pin(s) is in place on the gearcase.

d. Install the shift shaft, plate and gasket onto the gearcase.

e. Install the bolt and washer securing the plate and tighten securely.

f. Apply grease to the inner surface of the end openings of the new rubber boot.

g. Slide the new rubber boot down onto the shift shaft until it bottoms out on the plate.

4B. On 6-8 hp models, perform the following:

a. Install the shift shaft (B, **Figure 187**) up through the bottom of the oil seal housing.

b. Install a new gasket onto the oil seal housing.

c. Make sure the locating pin(s) is in place on the gear case.

d. Install the shift shaft, oil seal housing and gasket onto the gearcase.

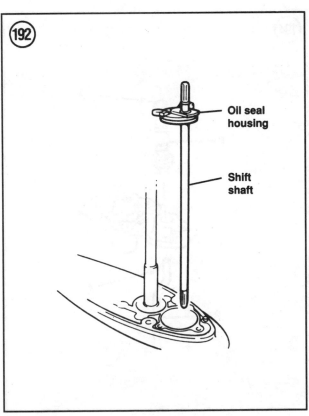

Oil seal housing

Shift shaft

9

e. Install the bolt and washer securing the oil seal housing and tighten securely.

f. Apply grease to the inner surface of the end openings of the new rubber boot.

g. Slide the new rubber boot (A, **Figure 187**) down onto the shift shaft until it bottoms out on the oil seal housing.

4C. On 9.9-15 hp, C25, 30 hp and C40 models, perform the following:

a. Insert the shift shaft assembly with the ramped face of the cam facing toward the drive shaft (**Figure 193**).

b. Install the shift shaft assembly into the gearcase.

c. Move the shift shaft retainer into position. Install the screw and tighten securely.

4D. On 25 hp and C30 models, perform the following:

a. Apply grease to the inner surface of the end openings of the new rubber boot, to the oil seal lips in the oil seal housing and to the end of the shift shaft assembly (A, **Figure 194**).

b. Insert the shift shaft assembly (B, **Figure 194**) up through the oil seal housing and install a new rubber boot (C, **Figure 194**) onto the shaft.

c. On C30 models, make sure the locating pins are in place in the gear housing.

d. Install a new gasket or O-ring onto the oil seal housing.

e. Position the shift shaft assembly with the ramped face of the cam facing toward the drive shaft.

f. Install the shift shaft assembly and oil seal housing over the drive shaft and into position on the gearcase.

g. On 25 hp models, apply red Loctite (No. 271) to the bolt threads prior to installation. Install the single bolt and washer, next to the rubber boot, securing the oil seal housing to the gear housing. Tighten the bolt securely.

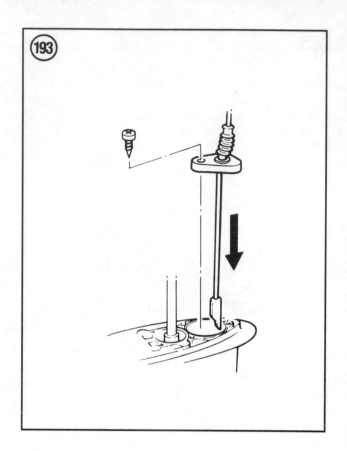

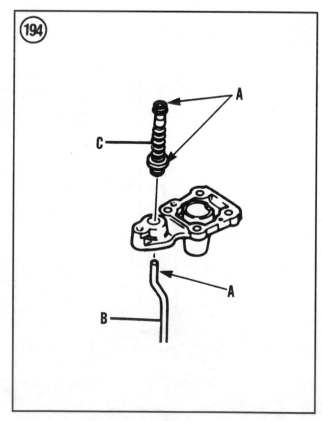

h. On C30 models, install the plate, bracket, bolts and washers securing the oil seal housing to the gear housing. Tighten the bolts securely.

i. Install the water pump as described in this chapter.

4E. On 40 hp, 50 hp, Pro 50, C55, C75 and C85 models, refer to **Figure 190** and perform the following:

a. Apply a light coat of grease to the shift cam to help hold it in place.

b. Position the shift cam with the UP mark (A, **Figure 195**) facing up and install it in the gearcase.

c. Install a new O-ring seal onto the oil seal housing.

d. Apply a light coat of grease to the new O-ring and to the lips on the oil seal in the top of the housing.

e. Make sure the circlip is still in place on the upper end of the shift shaft.

f. Insert the shift shaft up into the oil seal housing until it stops.

g. Install the shift shaft assembly (B, **Figure 195**) into the gearcase.

NOTE
Slightly rotate the shift shaft during the last part of its downward travel to align

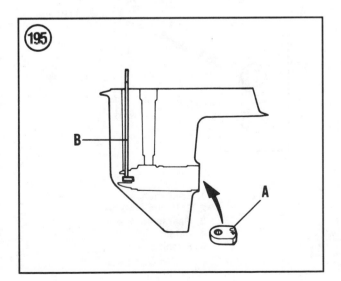

the splines on the shift shaft and shift cam in the gearcase.

h. On C55, C75 and C85 models, install the bolts and washers securing the oil seal housing and tighten securely.

i. On 40 hp, 50 hp and Pro 50 models, position the oil seal housing with the shift shaft hole facing forward as shown in **Figure 190**. This part is not symmetrical and must be installed correctly.

j. Carefully push the shift shaft oil seal housing down into the gearcase until it bottoms out. Make sure the shift shaft and cam splines are aligned. If not, the shift shaft will not travel to its limit into the gearcase.

CAUTION
*On 40 hp, 50 hp and Pro 50 models, if the oil seal housing is not positioned as indicated in **Figure 190**, the shift shaft will not be properly aligned and will bind.*

k. On 40 hp, 50 hp and Pro 50 models, make sure the oil seal housing is still correctly positioned with the shift shaft hole facing forward as shown in **Figure 190**.

l. Install the water pump as described in this chapter.

4F. On Pro 60, 70-130 hp (except C75, C85), 150-225 hp 90° V6 models, perform the following:

a. Install a new O-ring seal onto the shift shaft retainer plate.

b. Apply a light coat of grease to the new O-ring and to the lips of the oil seal in the top of the shift shaft retainer plate.

c. Make sure the circlip is still in place on the upper end of the shift shaft.

d. Insert the shift shaft up into shift shaft retainer plate until it stops.

e. On Pro 60 and 70-90 hp models, look through the hole in the gearcase. Slightly rotate the propeller shaft and align the shift shaft hole in the gearcase with the splined

9

hole in the shift cam, then install the shift shaft (**Figure 196**) into the gearcase.

f. On all other models, the shift dog must be in the NEUTRAL position and the flat part of the shifter must face upward for the shift shaft to engage properly. When these conditions are met, install the shift shaft into the gearcase.

g. Carefully push the shift shaft retainer plate down into the gearcase until it bottoms out.

h. Install the bolts and washers securing the shift shaft retainer plate and tighten securely.

i. Install the water pump as described in this chapter.

4G. On 225-250 hp 76° V6 models, perform the following:

a. If removed, insert the shift cam assembly (1, **Figure 197**) into the shift shaft retainer (2) while aligning the index marks on both gear teeth (3). Fit the detent (4, **Figure 197**) into the cutout part of the shift control bushing (5). This alignment is necessary for proper gear shifting.

b. Install a new O-ring seal onto the shift shaft retainer plate.

c. Apply a light coat of grease to the new O-ring and to the lips on the oil seal in the top of the shift shaft retainer plate.

d. The shift dog must be in the NEUTRAL position and the flat part of the shifter must face upward for the shift shaft to engage properly. When these conditions are met, install the shift shaft into the gearcase.

e. Carefully push the shift shaft retainer plate down into the gearcase until it bottoms out.

f. Install the bolts and washers securing the shift shaft retainer plate and tighten securely.

g. Install the water pump as described in this chapter.

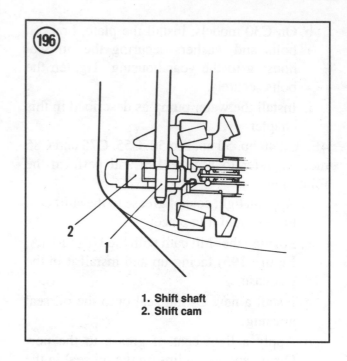

1. Shift shaft
2. Shift cam

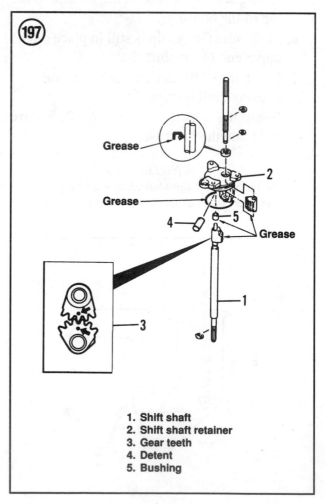

1. Shift shaft
2. Shift shaft retainer
3. Gear teeth
4. Detent
5. Bushing

Cleaning and Inspection (All Models)

1. Clean the shift shaft with solvent. Blow dry with compressed air, if available.

2. Inspect the shift cam ramps for wear or damage. Replace if necessary.

3. On models so equipped, discard the shift shaft boot as it cannot be reused.

4. On models so equipped, inspect the shift shaft retainer plate assembly for cracks or damage. Replace if necessary.

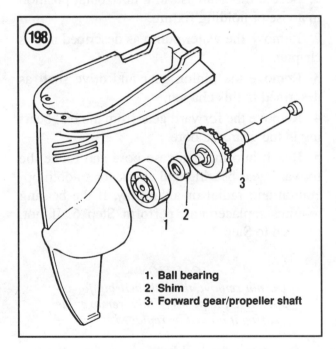

1. Ball bearing
2. Shim
3. Forward gear/propeller shaft

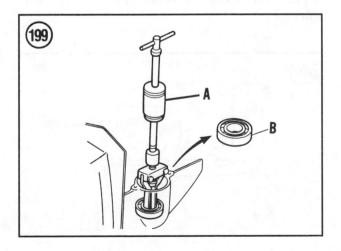

5. On models so equipped, install a new O-ring seal.

FORWARD GEAR OR REVERSE GEAR ("L" MODELS) AND BEARING ASSEMBLY

Removal/Inspection/Installation (2 hp Models)

Refer to **Figure 198** for this procedure.

1. Secure the gearcase in a horizontal position in a vise or holding fixture.

2. Remove the water pump as described in this chapter.

3. Remove the pinion gear and drive shaft as described in this chapter.

4. Withdraw the forward gear and propeller shaft assembly from the ball bearing in the gearcase bore. The shim(s) may come out with the forward gear or stick to the face of the ball bearing.

5. If the shim(s) did not come out in Step 3, reach into the gearcase bore and remove the shim(s) from the forward gear ball bearing.

6. Reach into the gearcase bore and rotate the forward gear bearing and check for smooth operation and radial or axial play. If the bearing requires replacement, perform Step 7. If not, proceed to Step 8.

CAUTION
Do not remove the ball bearing for inspection purposes. Only remove the bearing if it must be replaced.

7. To remove the ball bearing, perform the following:

    a. Attach slide hammer (part No. YB-6096 or equivalent) to the bearing puller (part No. 90890-06535).

    b. Insert the special tools into the bearing inner race and place the puller (A, **Figure 199**) under the inner race.

9

c. Using the slide hammer, withdraw the ball bearing (B, **Figure 199**) from the gearcase.

d. Discard the ball bearing.

8. Clean the gearcase bore in solvent and dry with compressed air. If the bearing was removed, make sure the bearing bore is free of burrs and any metal particles.

9. Clean the forward gear/propeller shaft in solvent and dry with compressed air.

NOTE
The forward gear is pressed onto the propeller shaft, and if either is defective, they must be replaced as an assembly.

10. Place the propeller shaft on V-blocks and measure the shaft runout with a dial indicator. Replace the propeller shaft assembly if the runout exceeds 0.02 mm (0.0008 in.).

11. Inspect the pinion gear and forward gear teeth for pitting, grooving scoring or uneven wear and heat discoloration. If either gear is defective, replace the pinion gear and forward gear/propeller shaft assembly as a set.

12. If the bearing was removed, perform the following:

a. Apply grease to the bearing bore in the gearcase and to the outer diameter of the new ball bearing.

b. Position the new bearing with its manufacturer's marks facing out.

c. Install the bearing installer (part No. YB-6014) onto the ball bearing and carefully tap the ball bearing straight into its bore in the gearcase. Tap the bearing in until it bottoms out.

13. Apply a liberal coat of oil to the balls within the ball bearing.

14. Apply a light coat of cold grease to the shim(s) to hold the shim(s) in place in Step 14.

15. Install the same number of shim(s) removed in Step 4 or Step 5 onto the forward gear end the propeller shaft.

16. Install the forward gear/propeller shaft assembly into the propeller shaft bore until it engages the ball bearing. Carefully push the assembly into the inner race until it stops.

17. Install the drive shaft and pinion gear as described in this chapter.

18. Check gear backlash as described in this chapter.

19. Install the water pump as described in this chapter.

Removal/Installation (3-5 hp Models)

1. Secure the gearcase in a horizontal position in a vise or holding fixture.

2. Remove the water pump as described in this chapter.

3. Remove the pinion gear and drive shaft as described in this chapter.

4. Remove the forward gear from the ball bearing in the gearcase bore.

5. Reach into the gearcase bore and rotate the forward gear bearing and check for smooth operation and radial or axial play. If the bearing requires replacement, perform Step 6. If not, proceed to Step 7.

CAUTION
Do not remove the ball bearing for inspection purposes. Only remove the bearing if it must be replaced.

6. To remove the ball bearing, perform the following:

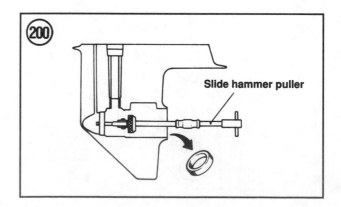
Slide hammer puller

a. Attach slide hammer special tool (part No. YB-6096 or equivalent) to the bearing puller (part No. 90890-06535).

b. Insert the special tools into the bearing inner race and place the puller under the inner race.

c. Using the slide hammer, withdraw the ball bearing from the gearcase (**Figure 200**).

d. Discard the ball bearing after removal. It cannot be reused as removal damages the bearing.

e. On 3 hp models, the shim(s) may come out with the ball bearing or stick to the face of the gearcase. Remove the shim from either part.

7. Inspect all components as described in this chapter.

8. If the bearing was removed, perform the following:

a. Apply grease to the bearing bore in the gearcase and to the outer diameter of the new ball bearing.

b. On 3 hp models, apply a light coat of cold grease to the shim(s) to hold the shim(s) in place.

c. On 3 hp models, install the shims (same thickness as removed) into the forward gear ball bearing bore.

d. Position the new bearing with its manufacturer's marks facing out.

e. Install the bearing installer (part No. YB-6270 and YB-6071) onto the ball bearing

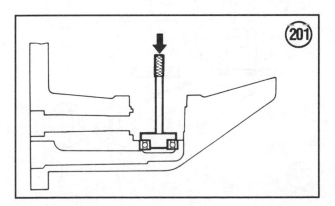

and carefully tap the ball bearing straight into its bore in the gearcase. Tap the bearing in until it bottoms out (**Figure 201**).

9. Apply a liberal coat of oil to the balls within the ball bearing.

10. Install the forward gear into the ball bearing.

11. Install the drive shaft and pinion gear as described in this chapter.

12. Check gear backlash as described in this chapter.

13. Install the water pump as described in this chapter.

Removal/Installation
(6-250 hp, Normal Rotation Models)

1. Secure the gearcase in a horizontal position in a vise or holding fixture.

2. Remove the propeller shaft assembly as described in this chapter.

3. Remove the pinion gear and drive shaft as described in this chapter.

NOTE
The tapered bearing outer race will remain in the gearcase and will be removed later in this procedure.

4. Remove the forward gear and the tapered bearing assembly from the bearing outer race in the gearcase bore.

CAUTION
Do not remove the tapered ball bearing outer race for inspection purposes. Remove the race only if the taper bearing assembly must be replaced.

5. To remove the tapered bearing outer race, perform the following:

a. Attach slide hammer (part No. YB-6096 or equivalent) to the bearing puller (part No. 90890-06535).

b. Insert the special tools into the bearing outer race and place the puller under the lips of the bearing outer race.

c. Using the slide hammer, withdraw the taper bearing outer race (A, **Figure 202**) from the gearcase.

d. Discard the bearing race after removal. It cannot be reused as removal damages the race.

e. Remove the shim(s) (B, **Figure 202**) that may come out with the bearing race or may stick to the face of the gearcase.

6. Inspect all components as described in this chapter.

CAUTION
The following special tools are required to install the tapered bearing outer race correctly. If substitute tools are used, the race may be damaged during installation.

7. If the tapered bearing outer race was removed, the following special tools are required to install the outer race in Step 8:

a. 6-8 hp models: part No. YB-6071 and YB-6167.

b. 9.9-30 hp, C25 and C30 models: part No. YB-6071 and YB-6085.

c. C40, 50 hp, Pro 50 and C55 models: part No. YB-6071 and YB-6109.

d. 40 hp models: part No. YB-6071 and YB-41446.

e. Pro 60, 70-90 hp, C75 and C85 models: part No. YB-6071 and YB-6276.

f. 115-130 hp, C115, Pro 115 V4 models: part No. YB-6071 and YB-6199.

g. 150-225 hp, Pro 150, Pro 175, Pro 200 90° V6 models: part No. YB-6071 and YB-6258.

h. 225-250 hp 76° V6 models: part No. YB-6071 and YB-6431.

8. If the bearing outer race was removed, perform the following:

a. Apply grease to the bearing outer race bore in the gearcase and to the outer diameter of the new bearing outer race.

b. Install the same number of shim(s) (A, **Figure 203**) removed in Step 4 into the bearing bore in the gearcase.

c. Position the new bearing outer race with its tapered side facing out.

d. Install the correct bearing installer, listed in Step 7, onto the bearing race and carefully tap the bearing race (B, **Figure 203**) straight into its bore in the gearcase. Tap the bearing race in until it bottoms out.

9. Apply a liberal coat of oil to the rollers within the tapered bearing and on the forward gear assembly.

10. Install the forward gear and tapered bearing assembly into the bearing outer race in the gearcase bore.

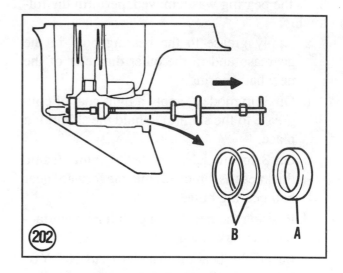

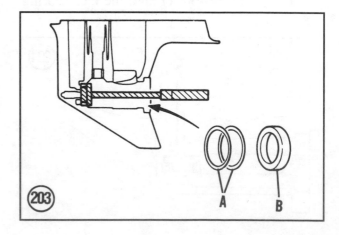

11. Install the drive shaft and pinion gear as described in this chapter.

12. Check pinion gear depth and forward gear backlash as described in this chapter.

13. Install the propeller shaft as described in this chapter.

Removal/Installation (L130, L150, L200, L225, L250 Counter Rotation Models)

1. Secure the gearcase in a horizontal position in a vise or holding fixture.

2. Remove the rear propeller shaft and forward gear assembly as described in this chapter.

3. Remove the front propeller shaft assembly as described in this chapter.

4. Remove the pinion gear and drive shaft as described in this chapter.

5. Remove the reverse gear and thrust bearing from the gearcase bore.

6. Reach into the gearcase bore and rotate the reverse gear needle bearing and check for smooth operation. If the bearing requires replacement, perform Step 7. If not proceed to Step 8.

CAUTION
Do not remove the needle bearing for inspection purposes. Remove the bearing only if it must be replaced.

7A. On L130, L225, L250 models, perform the following:

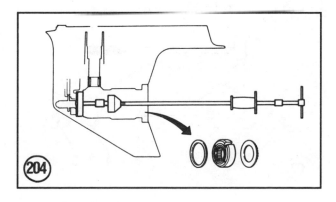

a. Attach slide hammer (part No. YB-6096 or equivalent) to the bearing puller.

b. Insert the special tools into the needle bearing, spacer and shim(s) and place the puller under the backside of the spacer and shim(s).

c. Using the slide hammer, withdraw the needle bearing, spacer and shim(s) from the gearcase (**Figure 204**).

d. Discard the needle bearing and spacer after removal. The bearing cannot be reused as removal will damage it.

e. Remove the shim(s).

7B. On L150, L200 models, perform the following:

a. Attach slide hammer (part No. YB-6096 or equivalent) to the bearing puller.

b. Insert the special tools into the needle bearing and shim(s) and place the puller under the backside of the needle bearing and shim(s).

c. Using the slide hammer, withdraw the needle bearing and shim(s) from the gear case.

d. Discard the needle bearing after removal. The bearing is damaged during removal and cannot be reused.

e. Remove the shim(s).

8. Inspect all components as described in this chapter.

CAUTION
The following special tools are required to install the needle bearing and spacer on models so equipped. If substitute tools are used, the bearing may be damaged during installation.

9. The following special tools are necessary to install the needle bearing (and spacer if so equipped).

a. L130 models: part No. YB-6071 and YB-6377.

b. L150 and L200 models: part No. YB-6071 and YB-6336.

c. L225 and L250 models: part No. YB-6071 and YB-6430.

10A. On L130 models, install the needle bearing and spacer as follows:

a. Lubricate the needle bearing bore in the gearcase with grease.

b. Install the shims (A, **Figure 205**).

c. Position the new spacer (B, **Figure 205**) with its oil grooves positioned at 6 and 12 o'clock (C) and its raised shoulder (D) facing toward the installation tool.

d. Install the correct bearing installer, listed in Step 9, on the bearing and spacer. Then, carefully tap the bearing and spacer straight into their bore in the gearcase. Continue tapping until the bearing and spacer are fully seated in the gearcase.

10B. On L150 and L200 models, install the needle bearing as follows:

a. Lubricate the needle bearing bore in the gearcase with grease.

b. Install the shims (A, **Figure 206**).

c. Position the new needle bearing (B, **Figure 206**) in its bore with its manufacturer's marks (C, **Figure 207**) facing toward the gearcase.

d. Using the correct bearing installer, tap the bearing straight into the gearcase until fully seated.

10C. On L225 and L250 models, install the needle bearing and spacer into the gearcase as follows:

a. Lubricate the needle bearing bore in the gearcase with grease.

b. Install the shims (A, **Figure 207**).

c. Position the new spacer (B, **Figure 207**) with its oil grooves positioned at 6 and 12 o'clock.

d. Using the correct bearing installer (listed in Step 9), tap the bearing and spacer straight into the gearcase until fully seated.

11. Thoroughly lubricate the needle bearing with oil.

12. Install the thrust bearing and reverse gear into the needle bearing inner race.

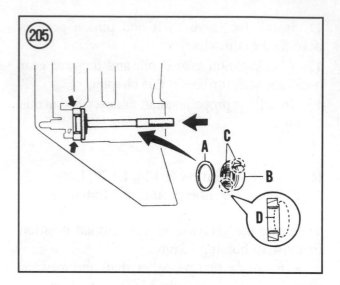

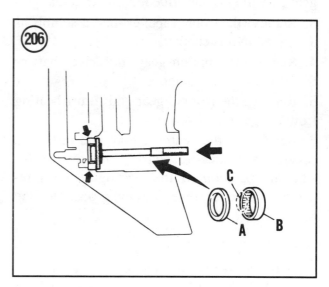

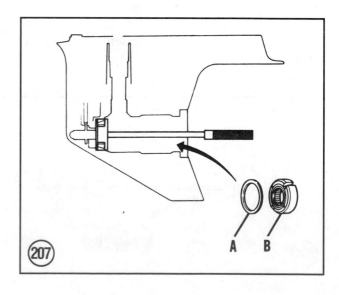

13. Install the drive shaft and pinion gear as described in this chapter.

14. Check pinion gear depth and forward gear backlash as described in this chapter.

15. Install the front propeller shaft assembly as described in this chapter.

16. Install the rear propeller shaft and forward gear assembly as described in this chapter.

Cleaning and Inspection
(Except 2 hp Models)

1. Clean the gearcase bore in solvent and dry with compressed air. If the bearing was removed, make sure the bearing bore is free of burrs and any metal particles.

2. Clean the gears and bearings in solvent and dry with compressed air. Do *not* allow the bearing to spin with the compressed air.

3. Inspect the pinion gear, forward gear and reverse gear teeth (A, **Figure 208**) for pitting, grooving, scoring, uneven wear and heat discoloration. If either gear is damaged, replace the pinion gear and forward, or reverse gear as a set.

4. If the clutch dogs (B, **Figure 208**) are chipped or rounded off, replace the gear. If the gear shows signs of heat discoloration, replace the gear.

5. On all models except counter rotating models, apply a light coat of oil to the forward gear bearing (**Figure 209**) and rotate the bearing to check for rough spots. Push and pull on the forward gear to check for side wear. If movement is excessive, replace the bearing as described in Step 6.

6. To remove the bearing from the forward gear, perform the following:
   a. Install a bearing separator between the bearing outer race and the gear (A, **Figure 210**).
   b. Place the bearing separator on a press plate and using a suitable size socket or piece of pipe (B, **Figure 210**), press the forward gear out of the bearing.
   c. Remove the bearing assembly from the forward gear.

7. To install the forward drive gear into the bearing perform, the following:
   a. Apply oil to the outer surface of the forward gear and to the inner surface of the bearing race.
   b. Place this assembly on the hydraulic press plate. Protect the forward gear with a stand or base (A, **Figure 211**).

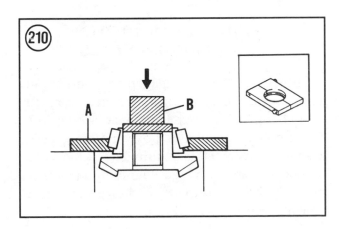

c. Use special tool (part No. YB-6276) or a suitable size socket that fits the inner race of the bearing and press the bearing (B, **Figure 211**) onto the forward gear until it stops.

GEARCASE HOUSING

Cleaning and Inspection
(All Models)

1. Clean the gearcase housing with solvent and dry with compressed air.

2. Inspect the water inlet cover, screw hole threads and cover nut or bearing cap screw threads for corrosion damage or stripped threads. Clean up any thread damage with the appropriate size thread tap if possible. Replace the gearcase if necessary.

3. Check the gearcase housing for cracks or other impact damage. Replace the gearcase if necessary.

4. Check the water inlet cover and all water passages for clogging or corrosion. Clean out as necessary.

5. Inspect the painted surfaces for flaking or corrosion. If found, touch up with Yamaha Zinc primer (part No. LUB-84PNT-PR-MR), or equivalent, and finish with the color of paint that matches the gearcase.

6. Inspect the anode(s) and trim tab as described in this chapter. Replace if necessary.

PINION GEAR DEPTH
AND GEAR BACKLASH

Proper pinion gear engagement and forward and reverse gear backlash are necessary for smooth operation and long gear service life. When components are remove and/or replaced, a shim adjustment is required to achieve the proper tolerances. Three shimming operations must be performed to set up the gearcase components properly as follows:

a. If the gearcase, drive shaft(s), bushing, pinion gear or thrust bearing is replaced, the pinion gear must be shimmed to the correct depth.

b. If the gearcase, forward or reverse gear bearing is replaced, the forward gear must be shimmed to the pinion gear for proper backlash.

c. If the gearcase, reverse gear, reverse gear bearing or bearing housing/cap is replaced, the reverse gear must be shimmed to the pinion gear for proper backlash.

Not all models require all three shimming procedures.

CAUTION
The backlash adjustment must be done correctly, or it will result in a noisy gear-

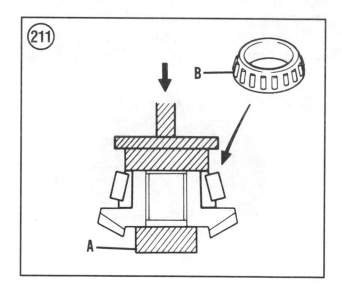

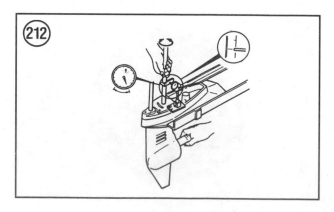

case as well as rapid wear of the affected gears. Do not risk damage to a newly installed set of gears with an incorrect adjustment. If you feel unqualified to complete this procedure correctly, have it performed by a Yamaha dealer or qualified machine shop familiar with outboard motors.

The gearcase on larger displacement outboard motors requires the use of expensive precision measuring equipment. It is recommended that measuring equipment also be used with smaller displacement models, but if it is not available, they may be checked by touch or sight. However, this method requires some degree of expertise to tell if the amount of backlash is within specifications.

Forward Gear Backlash
(2 hp Models)

NOTE
The water pump components must be removed during this procedure or they will restrict drive shaft movement.

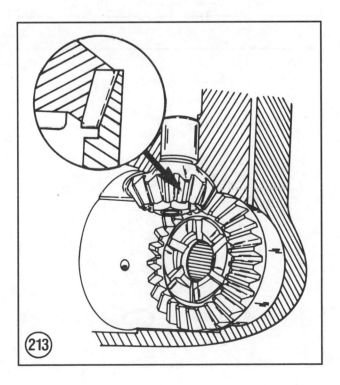

1. Install the gearcase in a holding fixture in the upright position.

2. Install the backlash indicator rod (part No. YB-6265) on the drive shaft.

3. Securely attach a dial indicator to the gearcase (**Figure 212**). The dial indicator plunger must contact the mark on the backlash indicator rod.

4. Set the dial indicator gauge to zero.

5. Pull up on the drive shaft while pushing inward on the propeller shaft. Slowly rock the drive shaft clockwise and counterclockwise.

6. Note the dial indicator reading when the needle reverses direction. This is the amount of backlash.

7. The correct amount of backlash is listed in **Table 2**.

8. If the backlash is incorrect, remove the shim located between the gearcase and the forward gear on the propeller shaft. Increase or decrease the shim thickness as required.

9. Available shim thicknesses are listed in **Table 3**.

Pinion Gear Depth
(All Models Except 2 hp)

NOTE
The water pump components must be removed during this procedure or they will restrict drive shaft movement.

1. Install the gearcase in a holding fixture.

2. Depress and hold the drive shaft down.

3. Reach into the propeller shaft bore and lightly push the pinion gear upward, away from the forward gear (or reverse gear on counter rotating models).

4. Check the engagement between the pinion gear and the forward gear by feel. The entire length of the gear teeth must be in contact as shown in **Figure 213**. There should be a *minimum* of up and down play in the drive shaft.

5. If necessary, adjust the position of the pinion gear by adding or subtracting shims located behind the pinion gear.

6. Available shim thickness are listed in **Table 3**.

Forward Gear Backlash
(3 hp Models)

> *NOTE*
> *The water pump components must **not** be installed during this procedure as it will restrict drive shaft movement.*

1. Perform *Pinion Gear Depth* as previously described.

2. Install the gearcase in a holding fixture in the upside down position.

3. Install the backlash indicator rod (part No. YB-6265) on the drive shaft.

4. Securely attach a dial indicator to the gearcase.

5. The dial indicator plunger must contact the mark on the backlash indicator rod (**Figure 212**).

6. Set the dial indicator gauge to zero.

7. Shift the unit into FORWARD.

8. Pull on the drive shaft while pushing on the propeller shaft, slowly rock the drive shaft back and forth.

9. Note the dial indicator reading when the needle reverses direction. This is the amount of backlash present.

10. The correct amount of backlash is listed in **Table 2**.

11. If the backlash is incorrect, remove the pinion gear shim located between the gearcase and the pinion gear on the drive shaft. Increase or decrease the shim thickness as required.

12. Available shim thicknesses are listed in **Table 3**.

13. If by adding or subtracting the pinion gear shim, the backlash is still not within specification, then add to or remove from the forward gear shim located between the gearcase and the forward gear bearing.

14. The forward gear shim is available in only one thickness.

15. If the forward gear shim was replaced in Step 13, repeat Steps 7-10 and recheck the pinion gear backlash and readjust if necessary.

16. Remove the measuring equipment.

Forward and Reverse Gear Backlash
(6-8 hp Models)

> *NOTE*
> *The water pump components must be removed during this procedure or they will restrict drive shaft movement.*

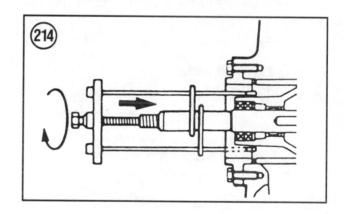

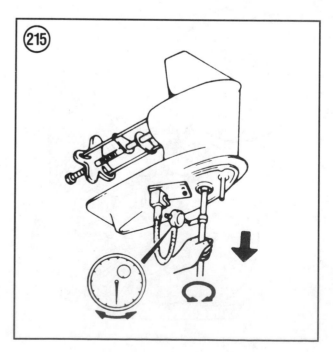

1. Perform *Pinion Gear Depth* as previously outlined (this chapter).

2. Install the gearcase in a holding fixture in the upside down position.

3. Temporarily install the propeller shaft and bearing housing (without the O-ring) into the gearcase.

4. Install the bearing housing puller (part No. YB-6234) and universal puller (part No. YB-6117) as shown in **Figure 214**. Lightly tighten the puller center bolt until the pressure of the propeller shaft on the forward gear restricts movement sufficiently to allow forward backlash measurement.

5. Install the backlash indicator rod (part No. YB-6265) onto the drive shaft.

6. Securely attach a dial indicator to the gearcase. The dial indicator plunger must contact the mark on the backlash indicator rod.

7. Set the dial indicator gauge to zero.

8. To check *forward* gear backlash, perform the following:

   a. Shift the unit into NEUTRAL.

   b. Pull down and slowly rock the drive shaft back and forth (**Figure 215**).

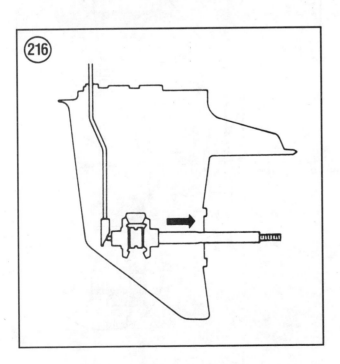

   c. Note the dial indicator reading when the needle reverses direction. This is the amount of backlash present.

   d. The correct amount of backlash is listed in **Table 2**.

   e. If the backlash is incorrect, remove the forward gear shim located between the gearcase and the forward gear bearing. Increase or decrease the shim thickness as required.

NOTE
The thinnest shim available is 0.10 mm. Therefore, if the measurement is between 0.25 mm and 0.75 mm do not change the shim.

   f. Available shim thicknesses are listed in **Table 3**.

9. To check *reverse* gear backlash, perform the following:

   a. Remove the bearing housing puller (part No. YB-6234) and universal puller (part No. YB-6117) installed in Step 3b.

   b. Make sure the unit is still in NEUTRAL.

   c. Pull out on the propeller shaft so the reverse gear restricts movement sufficiently to allow reverse backlash measurement (**Figure 216**).

   d. Pull down on the drive shaft and slowly rock the drive shaft back and forth.

   e. Note the dial indicator reading when the needle reverses direction. This is the amount of backlash.

   f. The correct amount of backlash is listed in **Table 2**.

   g. If the backlash is incorrect, remove the reverse gear shim located between the reverse gear and the reverse gear bearing. Increase or decrease the shim thickness as required.

   h. Available shim thicknesses are listed in **Table 3**.

10. Remove the measuring equipment.

Pinion Gear Clearance and Forward and Reverse Gear Backlash (9.9-15 hp Models)

NOTE
The water pump components must be removed during this procedure or they will restrict drive shaft movement.

1. Install the gearcase in a holding fixture in the upside down position.

2. To check *pinion gear clearance*, perform the following:

   a. Remove the propeller shaft assembly as described in this chapter.

   b. Install the Pinion Height Gauge (part No. YB-34232) onto the forward gear as shown in **Figure 217**.

   c. Insert a flat feeler gauge between the special tool and the end of the pinion gear (**Figure 218**).

   d. The specified clearance is listed in **Table 2**.

   e. If the clearance is incorrect, remove the pinion gear shim located between the pinion gear and the pinion gear thrust bearing. Increase or decrease the shim thickness as required.

   f. Available shim thicknesses are listed in **Table 3**.

   g. Remove the special tool.

3. To check *forward* gear backlash, perform the following:

   a. Shift the unit into NEUTRAL.

   b. Temporarily install the propeller shaft and bearing housing into the gearcase.

   c. Install the bearing housing puller (part No. YB-6234) and universal puller (part No. YB-6117) (**Figure 214**). Lightly tighten the puller center bolt until the pressure of the propeller shaft on the forward gear restricts movement sufficiently to allow forward backlash measurement.

   d. Install the backlash indicator rod (part No. YB-6265) on the drive shaft.

   e. Securely attach a dial indicator to the gearcase.

   f. The dial indicator plunger must contact the mark on the backlash indicator rod.

   g. Set the dial indicator gauge to zero.

   h. Pull down and slowly rock the drive shaft back and forth (**Figure 215**).

   i. Note the dial indicator reading when the needle reverses direction. This is the amount of backlash.

   j. The correct amount of backlash is listed in **Table 2**.

   k. If the backlash is incorrect, remove the forward gear shim located between the gearcase and the forward gear bearing. Increase or decrease the shim thickness as required.

NOTE
The thinnest shim available is 0.10 mm. Therefore, do not change the shim if the

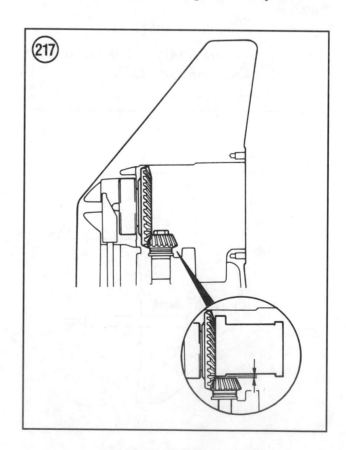

measurement is between 0.23 mm and 0.50 mm.

l. Available shim thicknesses are listed in **Table 3**.

4. To check *reverse* gear backlash, perform the following:

   a. Make sure the unit is still in NEUTRAL.

   b. Install the propeller without the front spacer and tighten the nut securely (**Figure 219**).

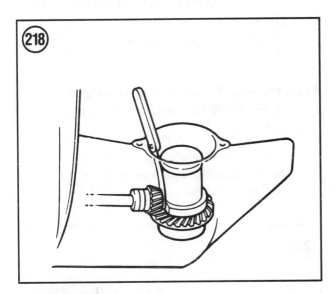

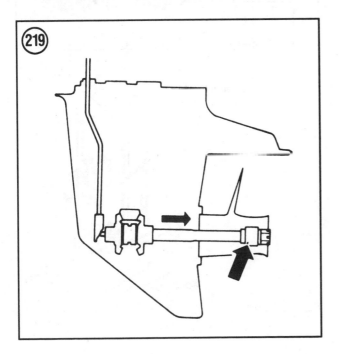

This will pull out on the propeller shaft so the reverse gear restricts movement sufficiently to allow reverse backlash measurement.

   c. Pull down on the drive shaft and slowly rock the drive shaft back and forth (**Figure 215**).

   d. Note the dial indicator reading when the needle reverses direction. This is the amount of backlash present.

   e. The correct amount of backlash is listed in **Table 2**.

   f. If the backlash is incorrect, remove the reverse gear shim located between the reverse gear and the reverse gear bearing. Increase or decrease the shim thickness as required.

> *NOTE*
> *The thinnest shim available is 0.10 mm. Therefore, do not change the shim if the measurement is between 0.82 mm and 1.17 mm.*

   g. Available shim thicknesses are listed in **Table 3**.

5. Remove the propeller assembly and the measuring equipment.

Pinion Gear Depth and Forward and Reverse Gear Backlash (25 hp Models)

> *NOTE*
> *The water pump components must be removed during this procedure or they will restrict drive shaft movement.*

1. Perform *Pinion Gear Depth* at the beginning of this procedure.

2. Install the gearcase in a holding fixture in the upright position.

3. After pinion gear depth is correct, perform the following:

   a. Temporarily install the propeller shaft and bearing housing into the gearcase as described in this chapter.

9

b. Install the bearing housing puller (part No. YB-6234) and universal puller (part No. YB-6117) as shown in **Figure 214**. Lightly tighten the puller center bolt until the pressure of the propeller shaft on the forward gear restricts movement sufficiently to allow forward backlash measurement.

c. Install the backlash indicator rod (part No. YB-6265) on the drive shaft.

d. Securely attach a dial indicator to the gearcase.

e. The dial indicator plunger must contact the mark on the backlash indicator rod (**Figure 220**).

f. Set the dial indicator gauge to zero.

4. To check *forward* gear backlash, perform the following:

a. Shift the unit into NEUTRAL.

b. Pull up and slowly rock the drive shaft back and forth (**Figure 220**).

c. Note the dial indicator reading when the needle reverses direction. This is the amount of forward gear backlash.

d. The correct amount of backlash is listed in **Table 2**.

e. If the backlash is incorrect, remove the forward gear shim located between the gearcase and the forward gear bearing. Increase or decrease the shim thickness as required.

f. Available shim thicknesses are listed in **Table 3**.

5. To check *reverse* gear backlash, perform the following:

a. Remove the bearing housing puller (part No. YB-6234) and universal puller (part No. YB-6117) installed in Step 3b.

b. Make sure the unit is still in NEUTRAL.

c. Install the reverse gear holding tool with the front side facing aft, then install the propeller nut and tighten securely (**Figure 221**).

d. Slowly rock the drive shaft back and forth (**Figure 220**).

e. Note the dial indicator reading when the needle reverses direction. This is the amount of reverse gear backlash.

f. The correct amount of backlash is listed in **Table 2**.

g. If the backlash is incorrect, remove the reverse gear shim located between the reverse gear and the reverse gear bearing. Increase or decrease the shim thickness as required.

h. Available shim thicknesses are listed in **Table 3**.

i. Remove the measuring equipment.

Forward and Reverse Gear Backlash (C25-C85, 30-90 hp and Pro 50 Models)

NOTE
The water pump components must be removed during this procedure or they will restrict drive shaft movement.

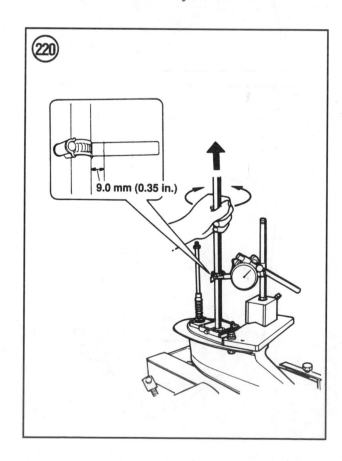

220

9.0 mm (0.35 in.)

1. Perform *Pinion Gear Depth* as described in this chapter.

2. Install the gearcase in a holding fixture in the upright position.

3. After pinion gear depth is correct, perform the following:

    a. Temporarily install the propeller shaft and bearing housing into the gearcase as described in this chapter.

    b. Install the bearing housing puller (part No. YB-6234) and universal puller (part No. YB-6117) as shown in **Figure 214**. Lightly tighten the puller center bolt until the pressure of the propeller shaft on the forward gear restricts movement sufficiently to allow forward backlash measurement.

    c. Install the backlash indicator rod (part No. YB-6265) on the drive shaft.

    d. Securely attach a dial indicator to the gearcase.

    e. The dial indicator plunger must contact the mark on the backlash indicator rod.

    f. Set the dial indicator gauge to zero.

4. To check *forward* gear backlash, perform the following:

    a. Shift the unit into NEUTRAL.

> *NOTE*
> *On 40-50 hp and Pro 50 models, push down on the drive shaft in sub-step 4b. On all other models, just rotate the drive shaft—do not apply any downward pressure.*

    b. Slowly rock the drive shaft back and forth (**Figure 222**).

    c. Note the dial indicator reading when the needle reverses direction. This is the amount of backlash forward gear.

    d. The correct amount of backlash is listed in **Table 2**.

    e. If the backlash is incorrect, remove the forward gear shim located between the gearcase and the forward gear bearing. Increase or decrease the shim thickness as required.

    f. Available shim thicknesses are listed in **Table 3**.

5. To check *reverse* gear backlash, perform the following:

    a. Make sure the unit is still in NEUTRAL.

9

b. Install the propeller backward onto the shaft and tighten the nut securely (**Figure 223**). This will pull out on the propeller shaft so the reverse gear restricts movement sufficiently to allow reverse backlash measurement.

NOTE
On 40-50 hp and Pro 50 models, push down on the drive shaft in sub-step 5c. On all other models, just rotate the drive shaft—do not apply any downward pressure.

c. Slowly rock the drive shaft back and forth (**Figure 222**).

d. Note the dial indicator reading when the needle reverses direction. This is the amount of reverse gear backlash.

e. The correct amount of backlash is listed in **Table 2**.

f. If the backlash is incorrect, remove the reverse gear shim located between the reverse gear and the reverse gear bearing. Increase or decrease the shim thickness as required.

g. Available shim thicknesses are listed in **Table 3**.

6. Remove the propeller assembly and the measuring equipment.

**Forward and Reverse Gear Backlash
(115-250 hp Regular Rotation Models)**

NOTE
The water pump components must be removed during this procedure or they will restrict drive shaft movement.

1. Perform *Pinion Gear Depth* as described in this chapter.

2. Install the gearcase in a holding fixture in the upright position.

3. After pinion gear depth is correct, perform the following:

a. Temporarily install the propeller shaft and bearing housing into the gearcase as described in this chapter.

b. Install the bearing housing puller (part No. YB-6207) and universal puller (part No. YB-6117) as shown in **Figure 224**. Lightly tighten the puller center bolt until the pressure of the propeller shaft on the forward gear restricts movement sufficiently to allow forward backlash measurement.

c. Install the backlash indicator rod (part No. YB-6265) on the drive shaft.

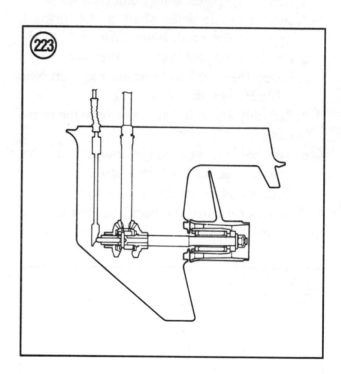

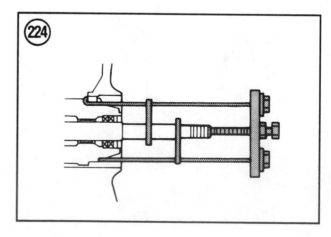

d. Securely attach a dial indicator to the gearcase.

e. The dial indicator plunger must contact the mark on the backlash indicator rod.

f. Set the dial indicator gauge to zero.

4. To check *forward* gear backlash, perform the following:

a. Shift the unit into NEUTRAL.

b. Pull up and slowly rock the drive shaft back and forth (**Figure 222**).

c. Note the dial indicator reading when the needle reverses direction. This is the amount of forward gear backlash.

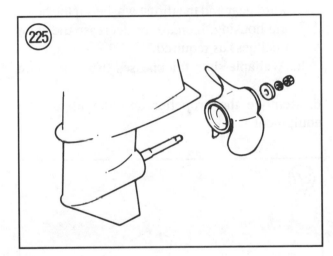

d. The correct amount of backlash is listed in **Table 2**.

e. If the backlash is incorrect, remove the forward gear shim located between the gearcase and the forward gear bearing. Increase or decrease the shim thickness as required.

f. Available shim thickness are listed in **Table 3**.

5. To check *reverse* gear backlash, perform the following:

a. Remove the bearing housing puller (part No. YB-6234) and universal puller (part No. YB-6117) installed in Step 3b.

b. Make sure the unit is still in NEUTRAL.

c. Install the propeller backward, install the nut and tighten securely (**Figure 225**).

d. Push up and slowly rock the drive shaft back and forth (**Figure 226**).

e. Note the dial indicator reading when the needle reverses direction. This is the amount of backlash.

f. The correct amount of backlash is listed in **Table 2**.

g. If the backlash is incorrect, remove the reverse gear shim located between the reverse gear and the reverse gear bearing. Increase or decrease the shim thickness as required.

h. Available shim thicknesses are listed in **Table 3**.

i. Remove the propeller and the measuring equipment.

Forward and Reverse Gear Backlash (L130, L150, L200 Counter Rotation Models)

NOTE
The water pump components must be removed during this procedure or they will restrict drive shaft movement.

1. Perform *Pinion Gear Depth* as described in this chapter.

9

2. Install the gearcase in a holding fixture in the upside down position.

3. After pinion gear depth is correct, perform the following:

> *NOTE*
> *On L130 models, install both the front and rear propeller shafts.*

a. Temporarily install the propeller shaft(s) and bearing housing into the gearcase as described in this chapter.

b. Install the bearing housing puller (part No. YB-6207) and universal puller (part No. YB-6117) as shown in **Figure 224**. Lightly tighten the puller center bolt until the pressure of the propeller shaft on the forward gear restricts movement sufficiently to allow reverse backlash measurement.

c. Install the backlash indicator rod (part No. YB-6265) on the drive shaft.

d. Securely attach a dial indicator to the gearcase.

e. The dial indicator plunger must contact the mark on the backlash indicator rod.

f. Set the dial indicator gauge to zero.

4. To check *reverse* gear backlash, perform the following:

a. Shift the unit into NEUTRAL.

b. Pull down and slowly rock the drive shaft back and forth (**Figure 227**).

c. Note the dial indicator reading when the needle reverses direction. This is the amount of reverse gear backlash.

d. The correct amount of backlash is listed in **Table 2**.

e. If the backlash is incorrect, remove the reverse gear shim located between the gearcase and the reverse gear bearing. Increase or decrease the shim thickness as required.

f. Available shim thickness are listed in **Table 3**.

5. To check *forward* gear backlash, perform the following:

a. Remove the bearing housing puller and universal puller installed in Step 3b.

b. Make sure the unit is still in NEUTRAL.

c. Install the propeller backward, install the nut and tighten securely (**Figure 225**).

d. Pull down and slowly rock the drive shaft back and forth (**Figure 227**).

e. Note the dial indicator reading when the needle reverses direction. This is the amount of forward gear backlash.

f. The correct amount of backlash is listed in **Table 2**.

g. If the backlash is incorrect, remove the forward gear shim located between the forward gear and the thrust washer in the bearing housing. Increase or decrease the shim thickness as required.

h. Available shim thicknesses listed in **Table 3**.

6. Remove the propeller and the measuring equipment.

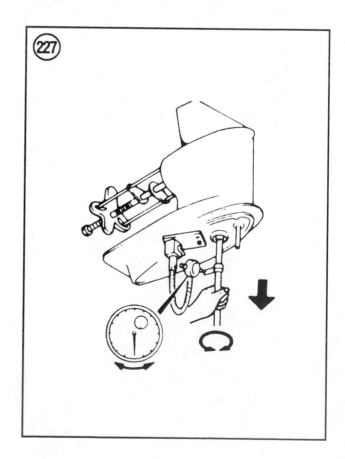

Forward and Reverse Gear Backlash (L225, L250 Counter Rotation Models)

NOTE
The water pump components must be removed during this procedure or they will restrict drive shaft movement.

1. Perform *Pinion Gear Depth* as described in this chapter.

2. Install the gearcase in a holding fixture in the right side up position.

3. After pinion gear depth is correct, perform the following:

   a. Temporarily install both propeller shafts and the bearing housing into the gearcase as described in this chapter.

   b. Install the bearing housing puller (part No. YB-6207) and universal puller (part No. YB-6117) as shown in **Figure 228**. Lightly tighten the puller center bolt until the pressure of both propeller shafts on the forward gear restricts movement sufficiently to allow forward gear backlash measurement.

   c. Install the backlash indicator rod (part No. YB-6265) on the drive shaft.

   d. Securely attach a dial indicator to the gearcase.

   e. The dial indicator plunger must contact the mark on the backlash indicator rod.

   f. Set the dial indicator gauge to zero.

4. To check *forward* gear backlash, perform the following:

   a. Shift the unit into NEUTRAL.

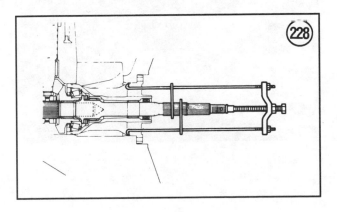

   b. Pull down and slowly rock the drive shaft back and forth (**Figure 226**).

   c. Note the dial indicator reading when the needle reverses direction. This is the amount of forward gear backlash.

   d. The correct amount of backlash is listed in **Table 2**.

   e. If the backlash is incorrect, remove the forward gear shim located between the forward gear shoulder and the end of the rear propeller shaft. Increase or decrease the shim thickness as required.

   f. Available shim thickness are listed in **Table 3**.

5. To check *reverse* gear backlash, perform the following:

   a. Remove the bearing housing puller and universal puller installed in sub-step 3b.

   b. Remove the forward gear and the forward gear bearing from the bearing housing as described in this chapter.

   c. Make sure the front propeller shaft is still installed in the gearcase.

   d. Reinstall the bearing housing and rear propeller shaft (without the forward gear and bearing) and housing assembly into the gearcase. Install the cap and tighten the bolts.

   e. Reinstall the bearing housing puller (part No. YB-6207) and universal puller (part No. YB-6117) as shown in **Figure 228**. Lightly tighten the puller center bolt until the pressure of the propeller shafts on the reverse gear restricts movement sufficiently to allow reverse gear backlash measurement.

   f. Make sure the unit is still in NEUTRAL.

   g. Pull up and slowly rock the drive shaft back and forth (**Figure 226**).

   h. Note the dial indicator reading when the needle reverses direction. This is the amount of reverse gear backlash.

   i. The correct amount of backlash is listed in **Table 2**.

9

j. If the backlash is incorrect, remove the reverse gear shim located between the reverse gear and the spacer in the gearcase. Increase or decrease the shim thickness as required.

k. Available shim thicknesses are listed in **Table 3**.

l. Remove the bearing housing puller and universal puller.

m. Remove the bearing housing and rear propeller shaft and reinstall the forward gear and bearing onto the rear propeller shaft and housing as described in this chapter.

6. Remove the measuring equipment.

TRIM TAB AND ANODE

All Yamaha outboard motors use a sacrificial zinc anode to protect against galvanic corrosion. On models equipped with a trim tab, the tab is the zinc anode. Smaller displacement models without a trim tab have a zinc anode attached under or near the antiventilation plate. The 70-250 hp models also have an anode on the transom bracket for protection when the gearcase is lifted out of the water. The anode is attached with a single bolt and can be easily removed for inspection (**Figure 229**). Trim tabs and zinc anodes should be replaced if they have been reduced to approximately 60 percent of their original size.

PRESSURE AND VACUUM TEST

Whenever a gearcase is disassembled and reassembled, it should be pressure and vacuum tested to check for leakage before refilling with gear lubricant. If the gearcase fails either the pressure or vacuum test, it must be disassembled and repaired before returning the unit to service. Failure to perform a pressure and vacuum test after gearcase service will result in either lubri-

cation being pushed out of the gearcase by pressure, or water being pulled into the gearcase by vacuum.

1. Install a pressure test gauge into the drain/fill plug hole.

2. Pump the pressure tester to 21-41 kPa (3-6 psi). If the pressure holds steady, increase the pressure to 110-124 kPa (16-18 psi). Rotate, push, pull and wiggle all shafts while observing the pressure gauge.

3. If the pressure drops, submerge the gearcase in water and check for air bubbles to indicate the source of the air leak.

4. If the pressure holds steady at 110-124 kPa (16-18 psi), release the air pressure and remove the pressure tester.

5. Install a vacuum tester gauge into the drain/fill plug hole.

6. Draw a 3-5 in.-Hg vacuum and note the vacuum gauge. If the vacuum holds steady, increase to 15 in.-Hg. If the vacuum does not hold at this level, apply oil around the suspected area to determine if the leak stops.

7. If the vacuum holds steady at 15 in.-Hg, release the vacuum and remove the tester.

8. If the source of the leak cannot be determined visually, disassemble the gearcase and locate the leak.

9. If no leakage is noted, fill the crankcase with the recommended lubricant, See Chapter Four.

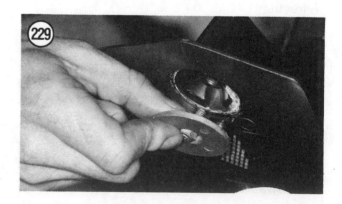

Table 1 GEARCASE TIGHTENING TORQUES

Fastener	N•m		ft.-lb.	
	Step 1	Step 2	Step 1	Step 2
Bearing housing/gearcase cap				
4, 5 hp	3	8	2.2	5.8
C30	—	11	—	8
40 hp, 50 hp, Pro 50	—	16	—	11
225, 250 hp 76° V6	—	24	—	17
Bearing housing ring nut				
C25, 30 hp	—	90	—	66
C40, C55, Pro 60, 70 hp	—	130	—	95
C75, C85, 90 hp,				
115-130 hp V4	—	145	—	106
150-225 90° V6	—	190	—	140
L225-L250 90° V6	—	110	—	81
Gearcase mounting fasteners				
C25	—	38	—	27
25 hp, 30 hp, 40 hp, 50 hp, Pro 50	—	40	—	29
C30	20	37	14.5	26.8
C40	—	21	—	15
C55	—	37	—	26.8
Pro 60, 70 hp, C75, C85, 90 hp,				
115-130 hp V4,				
150-225 hp 90° V6	—	40	—	29
76° V6	—	48	—	35
Grease nipple				
76° V6	—	6	—	4.3
Pinion nut				
9.9, 15 hp	—	25	—	18
C25	—	36	—	25
25 hp, 30 hp, C30	—	50	—	36
C40, 40 hp, Pro 50, C55	—	75	—	55
Pro 60, 70 hp, 90 hp	75	95	54	70
C75, C85, 115-130 hp V4,				
150-225 hp 90° V6	—	95	—	69
76° V6	—	145	—	106
Propeller nut				
6, 8, 9.9, 15 hp	—	17	—	12
C25, 40 hp, 50 hp, Pro 50	—	30	—	22
25 hp, 30 hp, C30, C40, C55,				
Pro 60, 70 hp, C75, C85, 90 hp	—	35	—	25
115-130 hp V4,				
150-250 hp V6	—	55	—	40
Shift rod lever				
4, 5 hp	—	6	—	4.3
Shift rod connector				
4, 5, 6, 8 hp	—	10	—	7.2
Water inlet bolt				
40 hp, 50 hp, Pro 50	—	5	—	3.6
Water pump cover and base				
6, 8 hp	—	1	—	8

(continued)

9

Table 1 GEARCASE TIGHTENING TORQUES (continued)

Standard torque values	N•m	ft.lb.
M5 bolt or 8 mm nut	5	3.6
M6 bolt or 10 mm nut	8	5.8
M8 bolt or 12 mm nut	18	13
M10 bolt or 14 mm nut	36	25
M12 bolt or 17 mm nut	30	42

Table 2 GEAR BACKLASH SPECIFICATIONS

Engine	Forward gear mm (in.)	Reverse gear mm (in.)
2 hp	0.27-0.99 (0.011-0.039)	N/A
3 hp	0.15-1.22 (0.006-0.048)	N/A
4, 5 hp	0.28-0.71 (0.011-0.028)	0.28-0.71 (0.011-0.028)
6, 8 hp	0.25-0.75 (0.009-0.029)	0.25-0.75 (0.009-0.029)
9.9, 51 hp	0.23-0.70 (0.009-0.027)	0.82-1.17 (0.032-0.046)
C25	0.10-0.25 (0.004-0.009)	0.35-0.50 (0.014-0.019)
25 hp	0.32-0.53 (0.013-0.021)	0.85-1.17 (0.034-0.046)
30 hp	0.20-0.50 (0.008-0.020)	0.70-1.00 (0.028-0.039)
C30	0.31-0.72 (0.012-0.028)	0.93-1.65 (0.037-0.065)
C40	0.10-0.25 (0.004-0.009)	0.40-0.55 (0.016-0.022)
40 hp, 50 hp, Pro 50	0.18-0.45 (0.007-0.018)	0.71-0.98 (0.028-0.039)
C55	0.05-0.15 (0.002-0.006)	0.40-0.50 (0.016-0.020)
Pro 60, 70 hp	0.09-0.28 (0.003-0.011)	0.75-1.13 (0.029-0.044)
90 hp	0.08-0.25 (0.003-0.009)	0.67-1.00 (0.026-0.039)
C75, C85	0.05-0.15 (0.002-0.006)	0.40-0.60 (0.016-0.024)
C115, L130	0.32-0.45 (0.013-0.018)	0.80-1.12 (0.031-0.044)
115 hp, Pro 115, 130 hp	0.32-0.50 (0.013-0.020)	0.80-1.17 (0.031-0.046)
150 hp	0.25-0.46 (0.009-0.018)	0.74-1.32 (0.029-0.052)
L150, L200	0.21-0.43 (0.008-0.017)	0.97-1.29 (0.038-0.051)
175, Pro V 175, 200 hp, Pro V 200	0.24-0.44 (0.009-0.017)	0.70-1.24 (0.028-0.049)
225 hp 90° V6	0.23-0.42 (0.009-0.016)	0.68-1.20 (0.027-0.047)
225-250 hp 76° V6	0.19-0.40 (0.007-0.015)	0.64-0.93 (0.025-0.036)

Table 3 GEAR BACKLASH SHIM THICKNESS

mm	In.
0.12	0.005
0.15	0.006
0.18	0.007
0.30	0.0118
0.40	0.0157
0.50	0.0196
1.13	0.044
1.20	0.047
2.0	0.079
2.1	0.083
2.2	0.087
2.3	0.091

Chapter Ten

Jet Drives

Yamaha first introduced the jet drives as an option in 1987. Five models have been offered. They are: 40, 50, 90, 115 and 200 hp. The jet drive model numbers reflect the equivalent prop-driven model's horsepower. However, because the jet drive is less efficient than a propeller, actual jet drive horsepower is lower. A Model 40 jet drive actual provides 28 horsepower from the jet pump. A Model 50 jet drive actual provides

35 horsepower from the jet pump. A Model 90 jet drive actual provides 65 horsepower from the jet pump. A Model 115 jet drive actual provides 80 horsepower from the jet pump. And a Model 200 jet drive actual provides 140 horsepower from the jet pump.

Service to the power head and its related components and the power tilt and trim assembly is the same as on prop-driven models. Refer to the appropriate chapter and service section for the model or component number you are servicing. Only service on the jet drive assembly is covered in this chapter

The jet drive serial number is stamped on the starboard side of the pump housing above the thrust gate pivot, and the jet drive model number is stamped into the port side of the pump housing above the thrust gate pivot (**Figure 1**).

NOTE
The "L" series models (counter rotation models) are included in all procedures. Unless there is a separate procedure designated for the "L" series refer to the procedure that relates to the same horse-

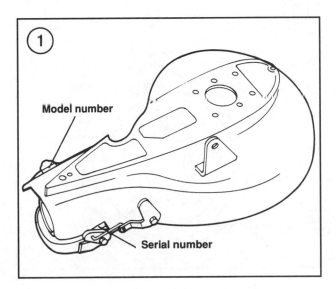

power rating. If you are working on an L200, refer to the 200 hp procedure.

MAINTENANCE

Outboard Mounting Height

A jet drive outboard motor must be mounted higher on the transom plate than an equivalent propeller driven outboard. If the jet drive is mounted too high, air will be allowed to enter the jet drive resulting in cavitation and power loss. If the jet drive is mounted too low, excessive drag, water spray and loss in speed will result.

To set the initial height of the outboard engine, proceed as follows:

1. Place a straightedge against the boat bottom *not* keel and abut the end of the straightedge with the jet drive intake.
2. The fore edge of the water intake housing should align with the top edge of the straightedge (**Figure 2**).
3. Secure the outboard motor at this setting, then test run the boat.
4. If cavitation occurs (over-revving; loss of thrust), the outboard must be lowered 6.35 mm (1/4 in.) at a time until uniform operation is noted.
5. If uniform operation is noted with the initial setting, raise the outboard at 6.35 mm (1/4 in.) increments until cavitation is noted. Then lower the outboard to the last uniform setting.

> *NOTE*
> *The outboard motor should be in a vertical position when the boat is on plane. Adjust trim setting as needed. If the outboard trim setting is altered, the outboard motor height must be checked and adjusted, if needed, as previously outlined.*

Steering Torque

A minor adjustment to the trailing edge of the drive outlet nozzle may be made if the boat tends

to pull in one direction when the boat and outboard motor are pointed in a straight-ahead direction. Should the boat tend to pull to the starboard side, bend the top and bottom trailing edge of the jet drive outlet nozzle 1.6 mm (1/16 in.) toward the starboard side of the jet drive (**Figure 3**).

Bearing Lubrication

The jet drive bearing(s) should be lubricated after *each* operating period, after every 10 hours

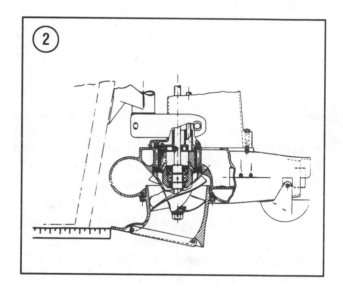

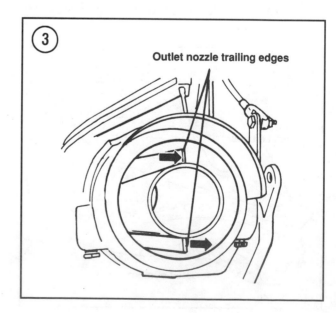

Outlet nozzle trailing edges

of operation and prior to storage. Also, additional grease should be pumped into the bearing(s) after every 50 hours of operation to purge any moisture. The bearing(s) is lubricated by first removing the cap on the end of the excess grease hose from the grease fitting on the side of the jet drive pump housing (**Figure 4**). Use a grease gun and inject grease into the fitting until grease exits from the capped end of the excess grease hose. Use only Yamalube All-purpose Marine grease or a NLGI No. 1 rated grease to lubricate the bearing(s).

Note the color of the grease being expelled from the excess grease hose. During the break-in period, some discoloration of the grease is normal. If the grease starts to turn a dark or dirty grey after the break-in period, the jet drive as-

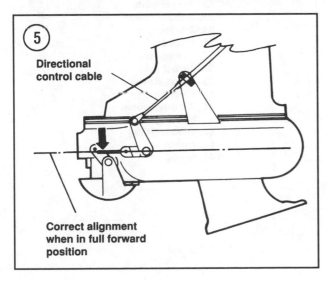

sembly should be disassembled as outlined under *JET DRIVE* and the seals and bearing(s) inspected and replaced as needed. If moisture is noted being expelled from the excess grease hose, the jet drive should be disassembled and the seals replaced and the bearing(s) inspected and replaced as needed.

Directional Control

The boat's operational direction is controlled by a thrust gate via a cable and lever. When the directional control lever is placed in the full forward position, the thrust gate should completely uncover the jet drive outlet nozzle opening and seat securely against the rubber pad on the jet drive pump housing. When the directional control lever is placed in full reverse position, the thrust gate should completely close off the pump outlet nozzle opening. Neutral position is located midway between the complete forward and complete reverse position.

NOTE
On remote control models, the control box shift cable must be approximately 30.5 cm (12 in.) longer for a jet drive model than a propeller driven model as the control cable connects directly to the jet drive thrust gate linkage.

The directional control cable is properly adjusted if after placing the directional control lever in the full forward position, the link between the thrust gate and the lower arm of the control cable pivot bracket are in alignment (**Figure 5**). The thrust gate should seat securely against the rubber pad on the jet drive pump housing.

WARNING
Always use the lower hole of the thrust gate lever to attach the control linkage. See arrow, Figure 5.

On manual models, a neutral stop adjustment is provided. To adjust, first find true neutral with the engine at idle position and retain this setting. Then loosen the nut (**Figure 6**) securing the stop position and move the stop to contact the directional control lever. Securely tighten the nut to retain this adjustment.

Impeller Clearance

1. Disconnect the spark leads to prevent accidental starting of the engine.
2. Insert a selection of feeler gauge thicknesses through the clearance between the impeller blades and the intake housing (**Figure 7**).
3. The impeller-to-intake housing clearance should be approximately 0.8 mm (1/32 in.).
4. If the clearance is incorrect, remove the six intake housing mounting bolts (**Figure 8** or **Figure 9**). Remove the intake housing.

**JET DRIVE
(MODELS 40 [28 HP] AND
50 [35 HP])**

1. Drive shaft
2. Woodruff key
3. Thrust ring
4. Nylon sleeve
5. Drive key
6. Impeller
7. Shim
8. Tab washer
9. Nut
10. Intake housing
11. Intake grille
12. Snap ring
13. Grease seal
14. Retaining ring
15. Upper seal carrier
16. Spacer washer
17. Collar
18. Thrust washer
19. Bearing
20. Bearing housing
21. Retaining ring
22. Grease seal
23. Bolts (short)
24. Bolts (long)
25. Washers
26. Water pump housing
27. Cartridge insert
28. Impeller
29. Gasket
30. Plate
31. Gasket
32. Dowel pin
33. Spacer plate
34. Rubber sleeve
35. Adapter plate
36. Pivot bracket
37. Linkage rod
38. Thrust gate
39. Nylon sleeve
40. Pivot pin
41. Jet drive pump
    housing
42. Grease fitting
43. Hose
44. O-ring

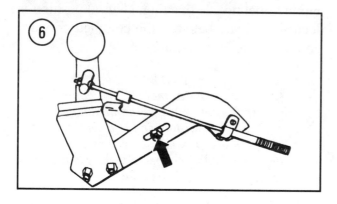

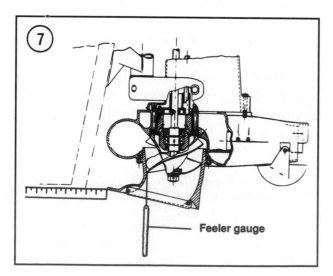

Feeler gauge

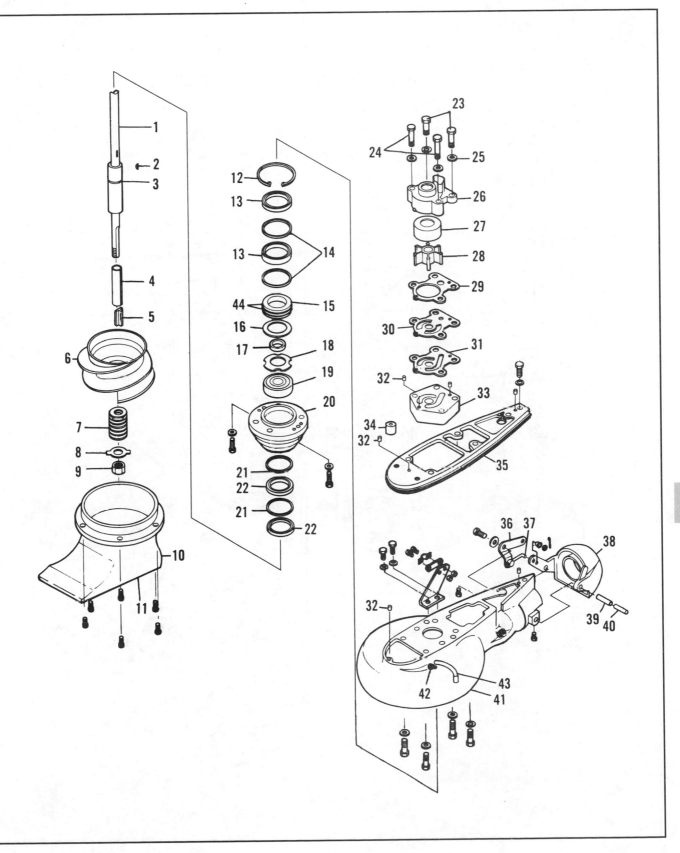

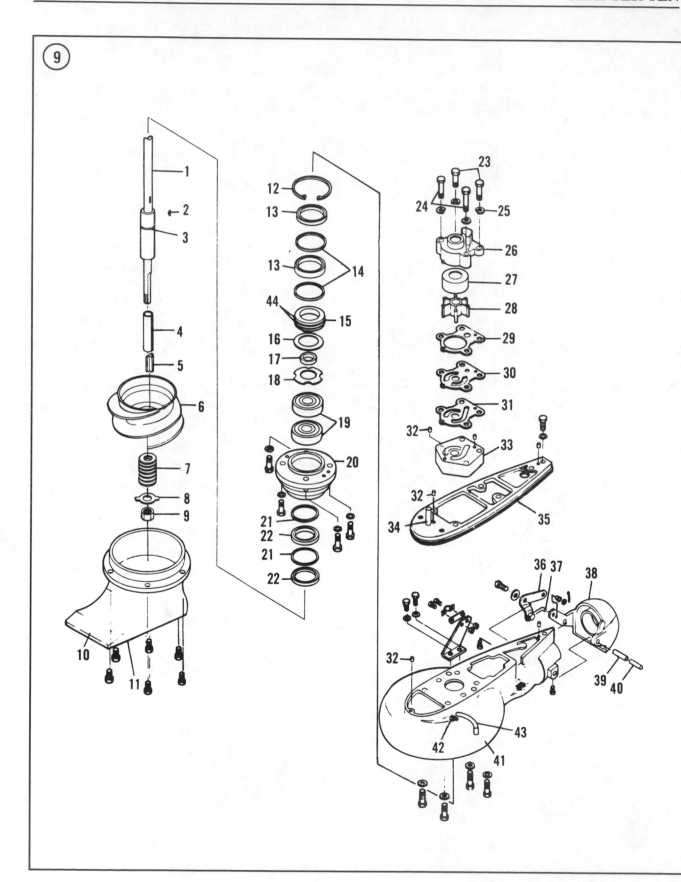

JET DRIVE
(MODELS 90 [65 HP] 115 [80 HP] AND 200 [140 HP])

1. Drive shaft
2. Woodruff key
3. Thrust ring
4. Nylon sleeve
5. Drive key
6. Impeller
7. Shim
8. Tab washer
9. Nut
10. Intake housing
11. Intake grille
12. Snap ring
13. Grease seal
14. Retaining ring
15. Upper seal carrier
16. Cupped washer
17. Collar
18. Thrust washer
19. Bearing
20. Bearing housing
21. Retaining ring
22. Grease seal
23. Bolts (short)
24. Bolts (long)
25. D-washers
26. Water pump housing
27. Cartridge insert
28. Impeller
29. Gasket
30. Plate
31. Gasket
32. Dowel pin
33. Spacer plate
34. Dowel pin
35. Adapter plate
36. Pivot bracket
37. Linkage rod
38. Thrust gate
39. Nylon sleeve
40. Pivot pin
41. Jet drive pump housing
42. Grease fitting
43. Hose
44. O-ring

10

5. Bend the ears on the washer retaining the jet drive impeller nut to allow a suitable tool to be installed on the impeller nut. Remove the nut, eared washer, lower shims, impeller and upper shims. Note the number of lower and upper shims.

> *NOTE*
> *Eight 0.8 mm (1/32 in.) shims are used to adjust the impeller-to-intake housing clearance on 40 and 50 hp models. Nine 0.8 mm (1/32 in.) shims are used to adjust the impeller-to-intake housing clearance on 90, 115 and 200 hp models.*

6. If clearance is excessive, remove the shims as needed from below the impeller (lower shims) and position above the impeller.

7. Install the impeller with the selected number of shims below the impeller.

8. Install the eared washer and impeller retaining nut onto the drive shaft. Tighten the nut with hand pressure while ensuring that the eared washer does not lodge in the drive shaft thread and jam the nut. Tighten the nut to the torque specification shown in **Table 1**.

9. Grease the threads of the six intake housing mounting bolts with Yamalube All-purpose Marine grease or an NLGI No. 1-rated grease.

10. Install the intake housing on the jet drive pump housing with the lowest part of the intake grill facing aft. Tighten the six intake housing bolts to the specification shown in **Table 1**.

11. Repeat Steps 2 and 3 to recheck impeller-to-intake housing clearance and Steps 4 through 10 if further adjustment is necessary.

12. After the correct clearance is measured, remove the six intake housing bolts and remove the intake housing.

13. Make sure the jet drive impeller retaining nut is correctly tightened to the specification shown in **Table 1**.

> *NOTE*
> *If the ears on the washer located behind the jet drive impeller retaining nut do not align with the flats on the nut, remove the*

> *nut and turn over the washer, reinstall the nut and then retighten to the specification shown in **Table 1**. **Make sure** the selected number of lower shims do not fall free.*

14. Bend the ears on the washer located behind the jet drive impeller retaining nut against the nut flats to retain the torque setting on the nut.

15. Grease the threads of the six intake housing bolts with Yamalube All-purpose Marine grease or an NLGI No.1-rated grease.

16. Install the intake housing on the jet drive pump housing with the lowest part of the intake grill facing aft. Tighten the six intake housing bolts to the specification shown in **Table 1**.

17. Install the directional control cable into the jet drive support bracket and reconnect the cable end to the lower arm of the control cable pivot bracket.

18. Refer to *Directional Control* in this chapter and adjust the cable to provide correct operation of the thrust gate.

19. Complete reassembly in the reverse of disassembly.

Cooling System Cleaning

The cooling system can become blocked by sand and salt deposits if it is not flushed occasionally. Clean the cooling system after each use in saltwater.

All factory equipped jet drives are equipped with a plug installed on the port side of the jet drive (**Figure 10**).

1. Remove the plug and gasket from the port side of the jet drive pump housing to gain access to flush passage (**Figure 10**).

2. Install adaptor (part No. 6E0-28193-00-94) into flush passage.

3. Connect a suitable freshwater supply to the adapter and turn on to full pressure (maximum output).

CAUTION
When the outboard motor is running, make sure a stream of water is discharged from the engine's tell-tale outlet. If not, stop the engine immediately and diagnose the problem.

CAUTION
Do not operate the outboard motor at high speed when connected to the flush adapter.

4. Start the engine and allow the freshwater to circulate for approximately 15 minutes.

5. Stop the engine, turn off the auxiliary water supply and disconnect the water supply from the adapter.

6. Remove the adapter.

7. Replace the gasket if damaged, then install the gasket on the plug.

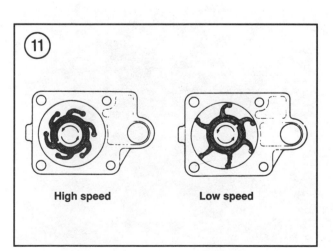

High speed   **Low speed**

8. Install the plug and gasket into the jet drive pump housing flush passage and tighten securely.

NOTE
To flush the jet drive impeller and intake housing, direct a freshwater supply into the intake passage housing area.

WATER PUMP

Refer to **Figure 8** or **Figure 9** for this procedure.

The water pump is mounted on top of the aluminum spacer on all models. The impeller is driven by a key which engages a groove in the drive shaft and a cutout in the impeller hub. As the drive shaft rotates, the impeller rotates with it. Water between the impeller blades and pump housing is pumped up to the power head through the water tube.

The offset center of the pump housing causes the impeller vanes to flex during rotation. At low speeds, the pump acts as a positive displacement type. At high speeds, water resistance forces the vanes to flex inward and the pump becomes a centrifugal type (**Figure 11**).

All gaskets should be replaced whenever the water pump is removed. Since proper water pump operation is critical to outboard operation, it is also a good idea to install a new impeller at the same time. Note that the impeller will only slide over the Woodruff key in one direction.

Removal and Disassembly

Refer to **Figure 8** or **Figure 9** for this procedure.

1. Remove the jet drive assembly as described in this chapter.

2. Remove the four bolts and washers (D washers on 90, 115 and 200 models) retaining the pump housing.

10

3. Withdraw the pump cover off of the impeller. Rotate the pump cover *counterclockwise* if needed to assist in cover removal.

> *CAUTION*
> *When removing the pump cover, do not rotate it **clockwise** or you will damage the impeller and have to replace it.*

> *NOTE*
> *In some cases, the impeller may come off with the pump cover. In extreme cases, the impeller hub may have to be split with a hammer and chisel to remove it in Step 4.*

4. If the impeller does not come off with the pump cover, slide it upward on the drive shaft. Remove the impeller.

5. Remove the impeller drive key (Woodruff key).

6. Remove the water pump face plate with top and bottom gaskets. Separate the face plate from the gaskets. Discard the gaskets.

Cleaning and Inspection

Refer to **Figure 8** or **Figure 9** for this procedure.

1. Remove the water pump cartridge insert from the pump cover.

2. Remove the water tube seal from the pump cover.

3. Clean all metal parts in solvent and blow dry with compressed air, if available.

4. Clean all gasket residue from all mating surfaces.

5. Check the pump cover for damage or distortion from overheating.

6. Check the face plate and cartridge insert for grooves or rough surfaces. Replace if any damage is found.

7. If the original impeller is to be reused, check the rubber bonding to the hub. Check the side seal surfaces and blade ends for cracks, tears, wear or a glazed or melted appearance (**Figure**

12, typical). If any of these conditions are noted, replace the impeller.

Assembly and Installation

Refer to **Figure 8** or **Figure 9** for this procedure.

1. If the pump cover cartridge insert was removed, reinstall the cartridge with tab on top engaging the slot in pump cover.

2. If removed, install a new water tube seal into the pump cover. The original water tube seal water tube seal can be reinstalled if it is not damaged.

3. Install the lower gasket, pump face and upper gasket.

4. Install the impeller drive key (Woodruff key).

5. Lightly lubricate the inner surfaces of the impeller with Yamalube All-purpose Marine grease or an NLGI No.1-rated grease. Slide the impeller onto the drive shaft. Align the slot in the impeller hub with the drive key and seat the impeller onto the water pump face plate.

6. Check the impeller installation by rotating the drive shaft *clockwise*. The impeller should rotate with the drive shaft. If not, remove and reposition the impeller to engage the drive key properly.

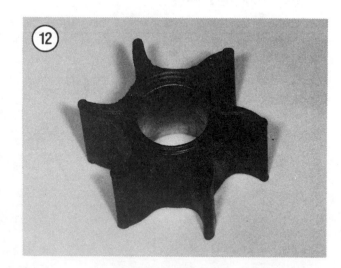

7. Slide the pump cover over the drive shaft. Push downward on the cover while rotating the drive shaft *clockwise* to assist the impeller in entering the cover without damage.

8. Grease the threads of the four bolts retaining the pump housing to the jet drive pump housing with Yamalube All-purpose Marine grease or an NLGI No.1-rated grease. Install the bolts and washers (D washers on 90, 115 and 200 models) and tighten the bolts in small increments following a crisscross pattern until the torque specified in **Table 1** is obtained.

9. Install the jet drive assembly as described in this chapter.

JET DRIVE

When removing the jet drive mounting fasteners, it is not uncommon to find that they are corroded. Such fasteners must be replace when the jet drive is installed. The threads on all mounting bolts should be greased with Yamalube All-purpose Marine grease or an NLGI No.1-rated grease.

Removal

1. Disconnect the spark plug leads to prevent accidental starting of the engine during jet drive removal.

2. Tilt the outboard to the full out position and engage the tilt lock lever.

3. Remove the directional control cable from the lower arm of the control cable pivot bracket. Remove the cable from the jet drive support bracket.

4. Remove the intake housing mounting bolts. Remove the intake housing. Refer to **Figure 8** or **Figure 9**.

5. Bend the ears on the washer retaining the jet drive impeller nut to allow a suitable tool to be installed on the impeller nut. Remove the nut and the eared washer.

NOTE
Eight 0.8 mm (1/32 in.) shims are used to adjust the impeller-to-intake housing clearance on 40 and 50 hp models. Nine 0.8 mm (1/32 in.) shims are used to adjust the impeller-to-intake housing clearance on 90, 115 and 200 hp models.

6. Remove the shims located below the impeller and note the number. Remove the impeller and the shims located above the impeller and note the number.

7. Slide the impeller sleeve and drive key off the drive shaft.

8. Remove the four bolts located on the inside of the jet drive pump housing and adjacent to the bearing housing and the one bolt at the external bottom aft end of the intermediate housing which secure the jet drive pump housing to the adapter plate, then withdraw the jet drive assembly.

Installation

Refer to **Figure 8** or **Figure 9** for this procedure.

1. Install the fore and aft dowel pin in the jet drive housing.

2. Lubricate the drive shaft splines and the water sub seal with Yamalube All-purpose Marine grease or an NLGI No.1-rated grease. Wipe excess grease off of the top of the shaft.

3. Grease all the mounting bolts with Yamalube All-purpose Marine grease or an NLGI No.1-rated grease.

4. Install the jet drive assembly and tighten the mounting bolts to the specification shown in **Table 1**.

5. Grease the drive shaft threads, drive key and jet drive impeller bore with Yamalube All-purpose Marine grease or an NLGI No.1-rated grease.

6. If the original bearing(s), bearing housing, jet drive pump housing, impeller and intake housing are reinstalled, install the shims located above and below the impeller in the same number and

10

location as removed. If any of the previously listed components were replaced, then install all of the adjustment shims below the impeller (next to the retaining nut) and proceed to *Impeller Clearance* in this chapter after completion of installation.

> *NOTE*
> *Eight 0.8 mm (1/32 in.) shims are used to adjust the impeller-to-intake housing clearance on 40 and 50 hp models. Nine 0.8 mm (1/32 in.) shims are used to adjust the impeller-to-intake housing clearance on 90, 115 and 200 hp models.*

7. Install the impeller sleeve into the jet drive impeller bore.

8. Install the shims above the impeller as noted in Step 6.

9. Slide the drive key and impeller onto the drive shaft.

10. Install the shims below the impeller as noted in Step 6.

11. Install the eared washer and impeller retaining nut on the drive shaft. Tighten the nut by hand while ensuring that the eared washer does not lodge in the drive shaft threads and jam the nut. Tighten the nut to the specification listed in **Table 1**.

12. Grease the threads of the six intake housing mounting bolts with Yamalube All-purpose Marine grease or an NLGI No.1-rated grease.

13. Install the intake housing on the jet drive pump housing with the lowest part of the intake grill facing aft. Tighten the intake housing bolts to the specification shown in **Table 1**.

14. Refer to *Impeller Clearance* in this chapter.

15. Remove the intake housing bolts and remove the intake housing.

16. Make sure the jet drive impeller retaining nut is correctly tightened to the specification shown in **Table 1**.

> *NOTE*
> *If the ears on the washer located behind the jet drive impeller retaining nut do not align with flats on the nut, remove the nut and turn over the washer. Then reinstall the nut and then retighten to the specification shown in **Table 1**. **Make sure** the lower shims do not fall free when the nut is removed.*

17. Bend the ears on the washer located behind the jet drive impeller retaining nut against the flats to retain the torque setting of the nut.

18. Reinstall the intake housing as previously outlined in Step 12 and Step 13.

19. Install the directional control cable in the jet drive support bracket and reconnect the cable end to the lower arm of the control cable pivot bracket.

20. Refer to *Directional Control* in this chapter and adjust the cable to provide correct operation of the thrust gate.

21. Complete reassembly in the reverse order of disassembly.

BEARING HOUSING

It is recommended that service to the bearing housing assembly be performed by an authorized Yamaha Outboard motor dealer. You can save some labor rate cost by removing and installing the jet drive assembly as outlined in this chapter, then taking the assembly to a dealer for

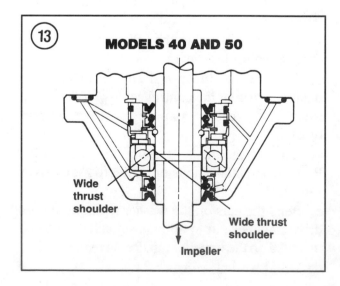

(13) **MODELS 40 AND 50**

Wide thrust shoulder

Wide thrust shoulder

Impeller

service. Should you elect to service the bearing housing yourself, read the following procedure completely before proceeding.

Refer to **Figure 8** or **Figure 9** for this procedure.

1. Remove the jet drive assembly as outlined under *Removal* in the *JET DRIVE* section in this chapter.

2. Remove the water pump assembly and impeller drive key (Woodruff key) as outlined under *WATER PUMP* in this chapter.

3. Withdraw the aluminum spacer.

4. Remove the bolts and washers securing the bearing housing to the jet drive housing. Withdraw the bearing housing assembly and drive shaft from the jet drive housing and place it on a clean work bench.

5. Remove the snap ring from the bore in the top of the bearing housing.

CAUTION
Do not apply excessive heat to the bearing housing as the grease seals may be damaged.

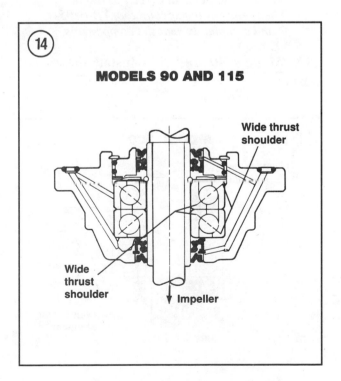

MODELS 90 AND 115

Wide thrust shoulder

Wide thrust shoulder

Impeller

WARNING
*Components will be **hot**. Take the necessary safety precautions to prevent personal injury.*

6. Apply heat to the bearing housing in increments. After each application of heat, strike the impeller end of the drive shaft against a wooden block. If the bearing housing has been heated to a sufficient temperature, the housing will slide down off the bearing(s). If not, apply additional heat to the bearing housing and reattempt removal of the bearing housing.

7. Withdraw the upper seal carrier and space washer (Models 40 and 50) or cupped washer (Models 90, 115 and 200) from the drive shaft.

8. Press the bearing(s) off of the drive shaft.

9. Slide the thrust washer off the drive shaft.

10. Remove the collar and the thrust ring from the drive shaft, if needed.

11. Remove the grease seals and retaining rings from the bearing housing.

12. Remove the grease seals and retaining rings from the upper seal carrier.

13. Clean and inspect the bearing housing, upper seal carrier and the drive shaft.

NOTE
If bearing(s) are pressed from the drive shaft, it is recommended to replace the bearings.

14A. *Models 40 and 50*—Install the thrust washer onto the drive shaft with the gray teflon coated side facing toward the jet drive impeller end. Press the new bearing onto the drive shaft. Press *only* against the inner race and position the bearing so that the bearing's thrust shoulders are positioned as shown in **Figure 13**.

14B. *Models 90, 115 and 200*—Install the thrust washer onto the drive shaft. Use Yamaha tool YB-06075 and press the new bearing onto the drive shaft. Press *only* against the inner races and position the bearings so that the bearing's thrust shoulders are positioned as shown in **Figure 14**

10

for Models 90 and 115 and **Figure 15** for Model 200.

15. Install new grease seals and retaining rings into the bearing housing and the upper carrier while noting the following:

a. Wipe a light film of Yamalube All-purpose Marine grease or an NLGI No.1-rated grease onto the surfaces of each retaining ring and grease seal prior to installation.

b. The grease seal open end or side with the lip faces outward. See **Figure 13** for Models 40 and 50, **Figure 14** for Models 90 and 115 and **Figure 15** for Model 200.

c. Position the outer retaining ring so its notched ends align with the small vent hole in the ring groove.

d. Fill the open end of each grease seal with Yamalube All-purpose Marine grease or an NLGI No.1-rated grease after installation.

e. Wipe a light film of Yamalube All-purpose Marine grease or an NLGI No.1-rated grease onto the inner surface of the bearing housing to ease the installation of the bearing(s) and upper seal carrier.

16. Slide the bearing housing on the drive shaft.

CAUTION
Do not apply excessive heat to the bearing housing as the grease seals may be damaged.

WARNING
*Components will be **hot**. Take the necessary safety precautions to prevent personal injury.*

17A. *Models 40 and 50*—Apply heat to the bearing housing in increments. If the bearing housing has been heated to a sufficient temperature, the housing will begin to slide onto the bearing(s). If not, apply additional heat to the bearing housing and reattempt the installation procedure. Make sure the bearing housing slides squarely onto the bearing. Use an arbor press to seat the bearings in the bearing housing. Press only against the inner race of the bearing. If the

bearing and bearing housing are properly aligned, only slight pressure is required to seat the components. *Do not* use a hammer to seat the components.

17B. *Models 90, 115 and 200*—Support the bearings and drive shaft with Yamaha tool YB-6205-2. Apply heat to the bearing housing in increments. If the bearing housing has been heated to a sufficient temperature, the housing should begin to slide onto the bearings. If not, apply additional heat to the bearing housing and reattempt the installation procedure. Make sure the bearing housing slides squarely onto the bearing. Use a hand press to seat the bearings in the bearing housing. Press only against the inner race of the bearing. If the bearing and bearing housing are properly aligned, only slight pressure should be required to seat the components. *Do not* use a hammer to seat the components.

NOTE
Yamaha tool YB-6205-2 will prevent the bearing housing and bearings from completely seating. After initial pressing, remove the special tool YB-6205-2 and install the upper seal carrier as a spacer. Then reinstall the special tool YB-6205-2 and completely seat the components.

18A. *Models 40 and 50*—Install the spacer washer.

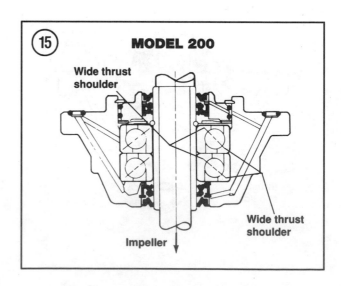

(15) **MODEL 200**

Wide thrust shoulder

Wide thrust shoulder

Impeller ↓

18B. *Models 90, 115 and 200*—Install the cupped washer and dished side facing upward.

19. Install two O-rings on the outside of the upper seal carrier.

20. Lightly seal the O-rings with Yamalube All-purpose Marine grease or an NLGI No.1-rated grease

21. Install the upper seal carrier. Only light hand pressure should be required.

22. Install the snap ring with the beveled side facing upward.

23. Install the bearing housing assembly and the drive shaft into the jet drive pump housing.

24. Apply Yamalube All-purpose Marine grease or an NLGI No.1-rated grease on the bearing housing retaining bolts.

25. Install the bearing retaining bolts and washers and tighten to the specification shown in **Table 1**.

26. Install the aluminum spacer on top of the jet drive housing.

27. Install the water pump assembly as outlined under *WATER PUMP* in this chapter.

28. Install the jet drive assembly as outlined under *Installation* in the *JET DRIVE* section in this chapter.

29. Grease the bearings as outlined under *Bearing Lubrication* in the *MAINTENANCE* section in this chapter

INTAKE HOUSING LINER

Replacement

1. Remove the six intake housing mounting bolts. Remove the intake housing. Refer to **Figure 8** or **Figure 9** for this procedure.
2. Identify the liner bolts for reassembly in the same location, then remove the bolts.
3. Tap the liner loose by inserting a long drift punch through the intake housing grille. Place the punch on the edge of the liner and tap with a hammer.
4. Withdraw the liner from the intake housing.
5. Install the new liner into the intake housing.
6. Align the liner bolt holes with their respective intake housing holes. Tap the liner into place with a soft face hammer if necessary.
7. Apply Yamalube All-purpose Marine grease or an NLGI No.1-rated grease on liner retaining bolts prior to installation.
8. Install the liner retaining bolts and tighten to the specification shown in **Table 1**.
9. Remove any burrs from the liner retaining bolt area.
10. Grease the threads of the six intake housing mounting bolts with Yamalube All-purpose Marine grease or an NLGI No.1-rated grease.
11. Install the intake housing on the jet drive pump housing with the lowest part of the intake grill facing aft. Tighten the six intake housing bolts to the specification listed in **Table 1**.
12. Refer to *Impeller Clearance* in this chapter.

10

Chapter Eleven

Automatic Rewind Starters

All manual start (and some electric start) models are equipped with a rope-operated rewind starter. Electric start models not equipped with a rewind starter have a flywheel drive cup and starter rope for emergency starts should the electric starting system fail.

The starter assembly is mounted above the flywheel on all models (**Figure 1**, typical). Pulling the rope handle causes the starter sheave shaft to rotate against spring tension, moving the drive pawl or pinion gear to engage the flywheel and crank the engine. When the rope handle is released, the spring inside the assembly reverses direction of the sheave shaft and rewinds the rope around the sheave.

All 4 hp and larger outboards are equipped with a starter lockout cable (**Figure 2**). When properly adjusted, this assembly prevents operation of the rewind starter unless the shift lever is in the NEUTRAL position.

Automatic rewind starters are relatively trouble-free; a broken or frayed rope is the most common malfunction. This chapter covers removal and installation of the rewind starter assembly, rope and spring replacement and starter lockout cable adjustment. **Figure 3** shows the

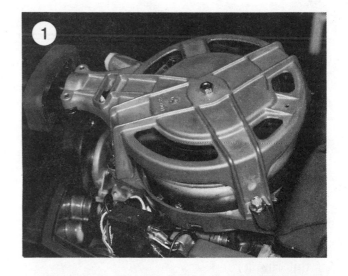

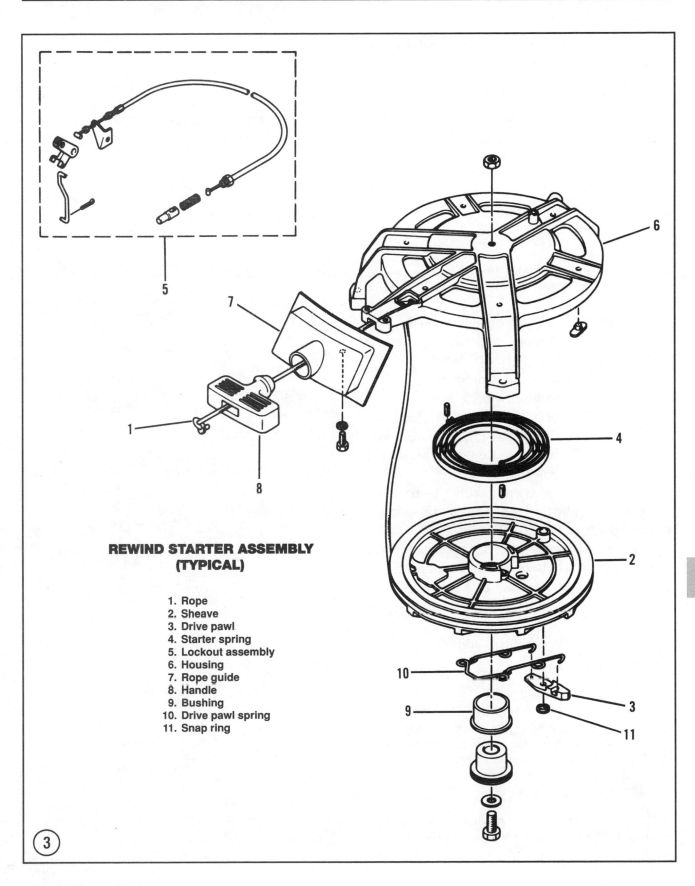

REWIND STARTER ASSEMBLY (TYPICAL)

1. Rope
2. Sheave
3. Drive pawl
4. Starter spring
5. Lockout assembly
6. Housing
7. Rope guide
8. Handle
9. Bushing
10. Drive pawl spring
11. Snap ring

3

11

components of a typical Yamaha rewind starter assembly for 5 hp and larger engines.

> *NOTE*
> *The "L" series outboards (counter rotation models) are included in all procedures. Unless there is a separate procedure designated for an "L" series model, refer to the procedure that relates to the same horsepower rating. If you are working on an L200, refer to the 200 hp procedure.*

Rope and Spring Replacement (2 and 3 hp Models)

The spring should only be removed if broken. If only replacing the rope, omit the steps dealing with spring removal and installation.

Refer to **Figure 4** for this procedure.

1. Remove the engine cowling.
2. Remove the 3 bolts and any related hardware holding the rewind starter assembly to the power head mounting brackets. Remove the rewind starter assembly (**Figure 5**).
3. Invert the rewind starter assembly on a clean work bench. Untie the knot in the starter rope and remove the rope from the handle.
4. Fit the rope in the sheave groove and let the sheave turn slowly to relax the starter spring.
5. Remove the starter shaft bolt and shaft.
6. Remove the drive pawl spring from the starter shaft.
7. Remove the drive pawl and return spring from the sheave.

> *WARNING*
> *Removing the starter sheave without holding the spring in place with a screwdriver will allow the spring to unwind violently and may result in serious personal injury. Wear safety glasses while removing and installing the spring.*

8. Insert a screwdriver in the sheave hole as shown in **Figure 6** and hold the starter spring in place.

**REWIND STARTER ASSEMBLY
(2 AND 3 HP ENGINES)**

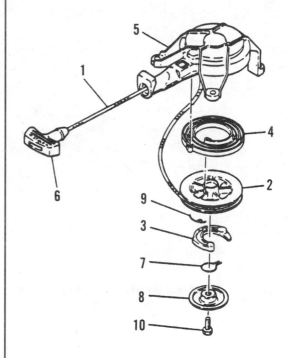

1. Rope
2. Sheave
3. Drive pawl
4. Starter spring
5. Housing
6. Handle
7. Drive pawl spring
8. Plate
9. Pawl return spring
10. Bolt

9. Remove the sheave and rope.

10. Untie the rope knot and remove the rope from the sheave.

11. If the spring requires replacement, place the rewind assembly housing on the floor right side up. Tap lightly on top of the housing while holding it tightly against the floor. The spring will fall out of the housing and unwind inside the housing mounting flanges. When the spring has unwound, pick the housing up off the floor and discard the spring.

12. Secure one housing leg in a vise with protective jaws and wipe the inside surface with Yamalube All-purpose Marine grease.

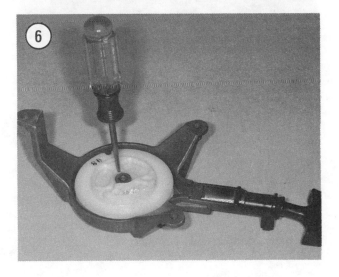

NOTE
Replacement springs are properly coiled at the factory. Do not uncoil the spring before installation.

13. Install the new spring coil in the starter housing. Fit the outer looped end over the housing catch. With the spring fully seated and connected in the housing, carefully remove the retaining tie straps. The spring will uncoil slightly and fill the housing cavity.

14. Tie a knot in one end of the starter rope and insert the rope through the sheave hole.

15. With the sheave facing flywheel end up, wind the rope 3 1/2 turns *counterclockwise* around it, then route the rope through the sheave groove.

16. Wipe the sheave with a light coat of Yamalube All-purpose Marine grease and install it in the starter housing. Make sure the inner spring hook is positioned over the sheave catch.

17. Install the drive pawl and return spring in the sheave.

18. Make sure the drive pawl and return spring is installed on the starter shaft (**Figure 7**).

19. Install the starter shaft on the sheave with open end of pawl spring engaging the round tab on the pawl.

20. Install the starter shaft bolt and tighten securely.

21. Depress the sheave and rotate it 3 turns *counterclockwise*. Maintain pressure on the

11

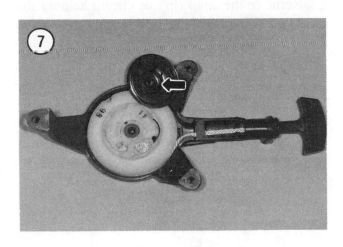

sheave and route the rope through the rope guide in the starter housing and handle. Tie a knot in the end of the rope as shown in **Figure 8**. Release the sheave slowly and allow it to take up any slack remaining in the rope.

22. Install the rewind starter assembly and any related hardware to the engine mounting brackets. Tighten the bolts securely.

23. Install the engine cowling.

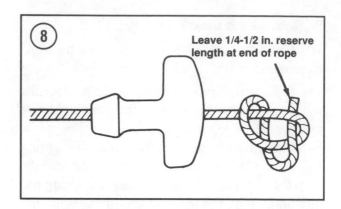

Rope and Spring Replacement (All Other Models)

The spring should be removed only if it is broken. When replacing only the rope, omit the steps dealing with the spring removal and installation. Refer to **Figure 3**, typical for this procedure.

1. Remove the engine cover.

2. Unscrew and disconnect the starter lockout cable from the starter housing (**Figure 9**, typical).

3. Remove the locknut plunger and spring from the cable end and place in a small container for reinstallation.

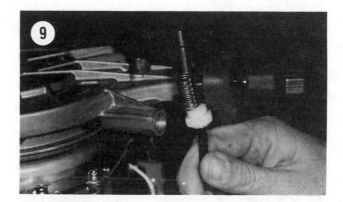

4. Remove attaching bolts and any related hardware holding the rewind starter assembly to the engine mounting brackets. Remove the rewind starter assembly and place it flywheel side up on a clean work bench (**Figure 10**).

5. Remove the snap ring or circlip holding the drive pawl in place. Carefully remove the drive pawl and spring assembly (**Figure 11**).

> *WARNING*
> *Apply sufficient pressure on the starter sheave in Step 6 to prevent it from unwinding rapidly. Wear safety glasses while removing and installing the spring.*

6. Hook the starter rope in the sheave groove. Depress the sheave and let it rotate slowly until all spring tension is removed.

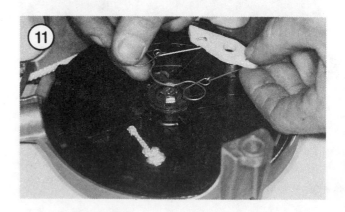

7. Untie the knot in the starter rope and remove the rope from the handle.

8. Remove the starter shaft bolt and nut. Remove the shaft (**Figure 12**).

> *WARNING*
> *Perform Step 9 slowly and carefully to prevent the spring from snapping out of the housing and unwinding. This can cause personal injury. Wear safety glasses while removing and installing the spring.*

9. Carefully lift one end of the starter sheave and insert a screwdriver under it to prevent the spring from flying up as the sheave is fully removed (**Figure 13**).

10. Untie the starter rope knot. Remove the rope and bushing from the sheave. Inspect the bushing for wear or damage and replace as required.

11. If the spring requires replacement, place the rewind assembly housing on the floor right side up. Tap lightly on top of the housing while

holding it tightly against the floor. The spring will fall out of the housing and unwind inside the housing mounting flanges. When the spring has unwound, pick the housing up off the floor and discard the spring.

12. Secure one housing leg in a vise with protective jaws and wipe the inside surface with Yamalube All-purpose Marine grease.

> *NOTE*
> *Replacement springs are properly coiled at the factory. Do not uncoil the spring before installation.*

13. Install the new spring coil in the starter housing. Fit the outer loop over the housing pin. With the spring fully seated and connected in the housing, carefully remove the retaining tie straps. The spring will uncoil slightly and fill the housing cavity (**Figure 14**).

> *NOTE*
> *Make sure the new rope is the same length as the old rope.*

14. Tie a knot in one end of the starter rope and insert the rope through the sheave hole.

15. With the sheave facing flywheel end up, wind the rope 2 1/2 turns *counterclockwise* around it, then route the rope through the sheave groove.

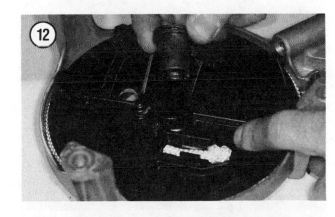

11

16. Lightly coat the sheave with Yamalube All-purpose Marine grease at the contact points and install it in the starter housing. Make sure the inner spring hook engages the sheave pin.

17. Wipe the starter shaft bushing and shaft with a light coat of Yamalube All-purpose Marine grease. Install the bushing and shaft in the housing.

> *NOTE*
> *Be sure to tighten the nut securely on the starter shaft bolt in Step 18. If the nut works loose and comes off, the spring will unwind inside the housing and the starter will not function.*

18. Apply Loctite 242 to the shaft bolt threads prior to installation. Install the washer and nut and tighten securely.

19. Depress the starter sheave and rotate it *counterclockwise* 5 full turns to tension the spring. Maintain the pressure to keep the sheave from unwinding and route the rope through the hole in the housing and handle.

20. Tie a knot in the end of the rope as shown in **Figure 8**. Release the sheave slowly and allow it to take up any slack remaining in the rope.

21. Install the drive pawl and spring assembly. Install the snap ring or circlip to hold the assembly in place, then bend the spring ends (if necessary) to make sure they will not slip out of the drive pawl.

22. Install the rewind starter assembly and any related hardware to the engine mounting brackets. Tighten the bolts securely.

23. Fit the lockout cable spring and plunger on the cable. Install the lockout cable assembly to the starter housing and tighten the attaching nut securely.

24. Adjust the lockout cable as described in this chapter.

25. Install the engine cover.

Starter Interlock Adjustment

1. Loosen the lockout cable adjusting locknuts (**Figure 15**, typical).

2. Adjust the nuts as required to permit the starter rope to be pulled out with the shift lever in NEUTRAL but not in FORWARD or REVERSE.

3. Tighten the adjusting locknuts securely.

Chapter Twelve

Power Trim and
Tilt Systems

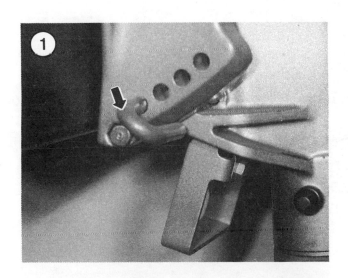

The usual method of raising and lowering small outboard motors is a mechanical one, consisting of a series of holes in the transom mounting bracket. To trim the outboard, an adjustment stud or trim pin (**Figure 1**) is removed from the bracket, the outboard motor is repositioned and the stud or pin is reinserted in the proper set of holes to retain the unit in place.

A power tilt system is standard on the 40TR, 50er, 50TH and Pro 50TR models as shown in **Figure 2**. A power trim and tilt system is standard on all 60-250 hp models and is shown in **Figure 3**.

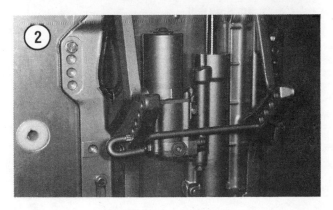

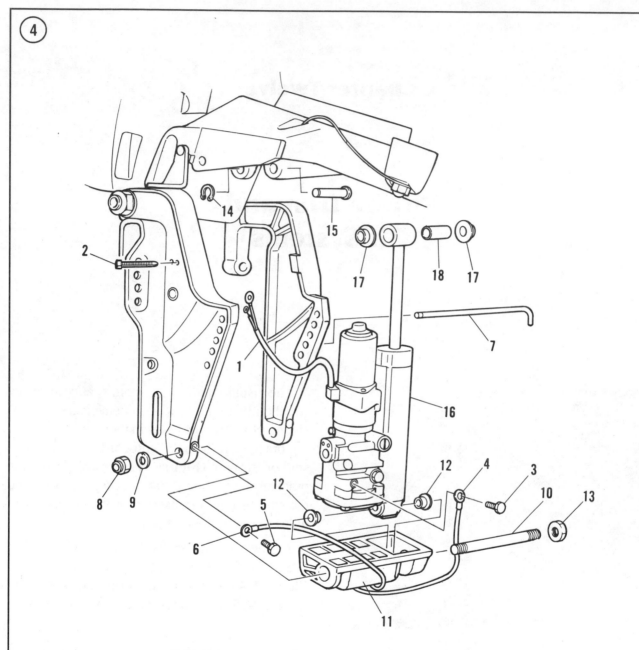

④

1. PTT motor
   electrical lead
2. Tie strap
3. Bolt/washer
4. Electrical lead
5. Bolt/washer
6. Electrical lead
7. Tilt rod assembly
8. Nut
9. Washer
10. Stud bolt
11. Clamp bracket
    spacer assembly
12. Bushing
13. Nut
14. Circlip
15. Shaft pin
16. Tilt unit
17. Bushing
18. Collar

This chapter includes maintenance, troubleshooting procedures and removal and installation of the power tilt and power trim/tilt systems.

NOTE
The "L" series models (counter rotation models), are included in all procedures. Unless there is a separate procedure designated for an "L" series model, refer to the procedure that relates to the same horsepower rating. If you are working on an L200, refer to the 200 hp procedure.

POWER TILT SYSTEM

Components

This system consists of a hydraulic pump (containing an electric motor, oil reservoir, oil pump and valve body) and a hydraulic tilt cylinder (**Figure 4**). A tilt switch located in the remote control box handle, sends current to the up/down relays mounted on the bottom cowling at the rear of the starter relay. The relays connect to a terminal assembly or junction box on the power head, sending current to the power tilt motor.

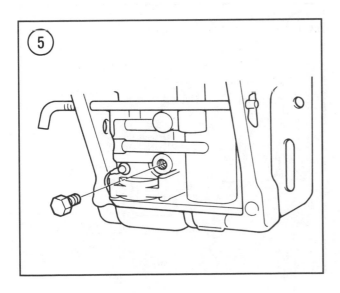

Operation

Moving the tilt switch to the UP position closes the pump motor circuit. The motor drives the oil pump, forcing oil into the up side of the tilt cylinder. The engine will move upward until it reaches its maximum position.

Moving the tilt switch to the DOWN position also closes the pump motor circuit. The reversible motor runs in the opposite direction, driving the oil pump to force oil into the down side of the tilt cylinder and bringing the engine back down to the desired position.

A shock absorbing system is used to prevent damage from striking an underwater object. If an impact occurs, the tilt piston moves up and hydraulic fluid flows through a valve in the piston. As the piston moves upward, a partial vacuum forms under it and allows the piston to move downward, absorbing the shock.

A manual release valve is provided on the hydraulic pump. Turning the valve screw opens the upper and lower tilt cylinder chambers to the reservoir. This permits manual raising and lowering of the outboard if the electrical system fails.

Hydraulic Pump Fluid Check

1. Tilt the outboard to its fully UP position.
2. Clean area around pump fill plug. Remove the plug (**Figure 5**) and visually check the fluid level in the pump reservoir. It should be at the bottom of the fill hole threads.
3. Top up if necessary with DEXRON Type II automatic transmission fluid (ATF).
4. Install the fill plug and tighten securely.

Hydraulic Pump Fluid Bleed and Refill

Follow this procedure if a large amount of fluid has been lost due to service or leakage.

12

If any of the internal parts of the trim or tilt cylinders or the interconnecting hydraulic lines have been removed or replaced the system must be bled with the use of special tools. Refer this operation to a Yamaha dealer.

1. Tilt the outboard to the fully UP position. Remove the fill plug and top off the reservoir with DEXRON Type II automatic transmission fluid (ATF). Install the fill plug.

2. Turn the manual valve screw clockwise until it stops.

3. Slowly pull upward on the tilt rod to allow the fluid to enter the lower tilt cylinder chamber.

4. Repeat Step 1. Turn the manual valve screw *counterclockwise* until it stops.

5. Slowly push down on the tilt rod to allow the fluid to enter the upper tilt cylinder chamber.

6. Repeat Steps 1-5 as required to purge the air completely and fill the tilt cylinder with ATF fluid.

Troubleshooting

If a problem develops in the power tilt system, the initial step is to determine whether the problem is in the electrical or hydraulic system. Electrical and hydraulic tests are given in this chapter. If the problem appears to be in the hydraulic system, refer it to a dealer or qualified specialist for necessary service.

1. Make sure the plug-in connectors are properly engaged and that all terminals and wires are free of corrosion. Tighten and clean as required.

2. Make sure the battery is fully charged. Charge or replace as required.

3. Check the hydraulic fluid level as described in this chapter. Top off if necessary.

4. Make sure the manual release valve is fully closed.

Tilt Relay Test

1. Disconnect the negative (–) battery lead, then disconnect the positive (+) battery lead.

2. Disconnect the three tilt relay leads (**Figure 6**).

3. Connect an ohmmeter or self-powered test lamp between the disconnected sky blue and black relay leads. The meter should indicate continuity (low resistance) or the test lamp should light.

4. Connect an ohmmeter or test lamp between the disconnected light green and black relay leads. The meter should indicate continuity (low resistance) or the test lamp should light.

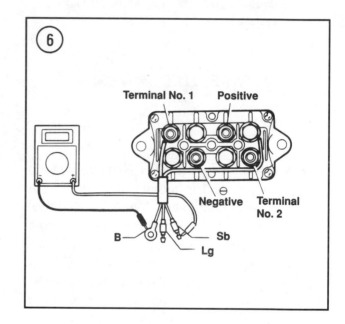

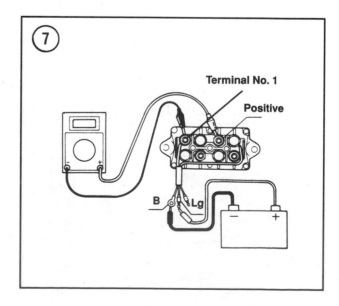

5. Connect an ohmmeter or test lamp between the relay No. 1 terminal and the negative (–) terminal. The meter should indicate continuity (low resistance) or the test lamp should light.

6. Connect an ohmmeter or test lamp between the relay No. 2 terminal and the negative (–) terminal. The meter should indicate continuity (low resistance) or the test lamp should light.

7. Connect an ohmmeter or test lamp between the relay No. 1 terminal and the positive (+) terminal. The meter should indicate no continuity (infinity) or the test lamp should not light.

8. Connect an ohmmeter or test lamp between the relay No. 2 terminal and the positive (+) terminal. The meter should indicate no continuity (infinity) or the test lamp should not light.

9. Use jumper leads and connect the positive (+) battery lead to the light green relay lead (**Figure 7**). Connect the negative (–) battery lead to the black relay lead. Connect an ohmmeter between the No. 1 terminal and the positive (+) terminal.

The meter should indicate continuity (low resistance) or the test lamp should light.

10. Use jumper leads and connect the positive (+) battery lead to the sky blue relay lead (**Figure 8**). Connect the negative (–) battery lead to the black relay lead. Connect an ohmmeter between the No. 2 terminal and the positive (+) terminal. The meter should indicate continuity (low resistance) or the test lamp should light.

11. If the relay fails any of these tests (Step 3-10), the relay is faulty and must be replaced.

Tilt Switch Test

The rocker-type switch is mounted in the remote control box handle.

1. Disconnect the negative (–) battery cable, then disconnect the positive (+) battery cable.

2. Remove the remote control box from its mounting bracket.

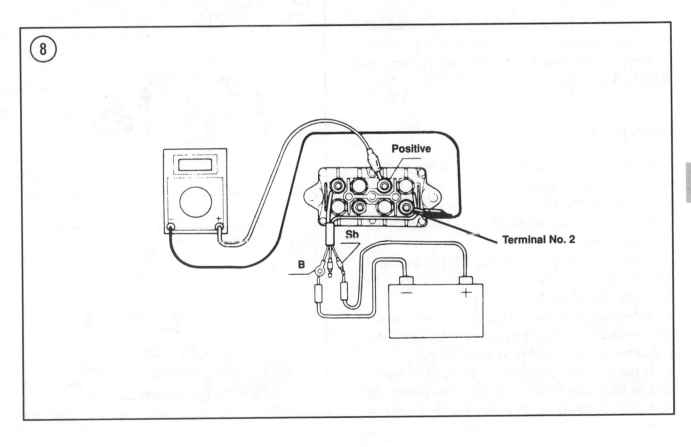

3. Remove the wire cover (**Figure 9**) and the back panel (**Figure 10**).

4. Disconnect the tilt relay electrical connector (**Figure 11**).

5. Connect an ohmmeter or test lamp between the sky blue and red terminals in the switch electrical connector. The meter should indicate continuity (low resistance) or the test lamp should light when the switch is depressed in the UP position.

6. Connect an ohmmeter or test lamp between the light green and red terminals in the switch electrical connector. The meter should indicate continuity (low resistance) or the test lamp should light when the switch is pushed to the DOWN position.

7. Connect an ohmmeter or test lamp between the terminals in the switch electrical connector without depressing the switch:

    a. Red and sky blue.

    b. Red and light green.

    c. Sky blue and light green.

There should be no continuity between any of the terminals with the switch in the OFF position.

8. Replace the switch if it does not perform as specified in Steps 5-7.

Hydraulic Test

1. Remove the tilt cylinder drain bolts and install the pressure gauge (part No. YB-6181) as shown in **Figure 12**.

2. Check the pump hydraulic level as described in this chapter.

3. Move the tilt switch to the UP position and run the outboard up as far as it will go. The pressure should read 500-570 psi.

4. Move the tilt switch to the down position and run the outboard down as far as it will go. The pressure gauge should read 430-500 psi.

5. If the pressure gauge does not read as specified in Step 3 and Step 4, remove the power tilt unit as described in this chapter and have it serviced by a Yamaha dealer or qualified specialist.

Removal/Installation

Refer to **Figure 4** for this procedure.

1. Disconnect the negative battery cable.

2. Remove the engine cover.

3. Disconnect the power tilt motor electrical leads at the terminal assembly or junction box.

4. Remove the tie wrap securing the tilt motor electrical leads to the clamp bracket.

5. Unbolt and remove the outboard from the boat. Secure it to a repair stand.

6. Remove the bolts and washers securing the lower electrical connectors to both clamp brackets.

7. Remove the tilt rod assembly.

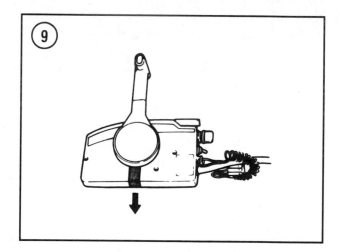

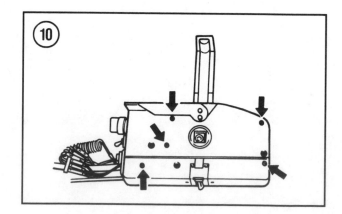

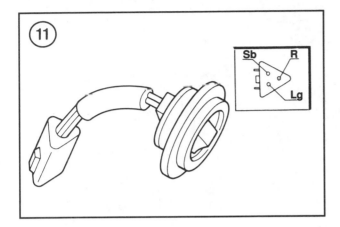

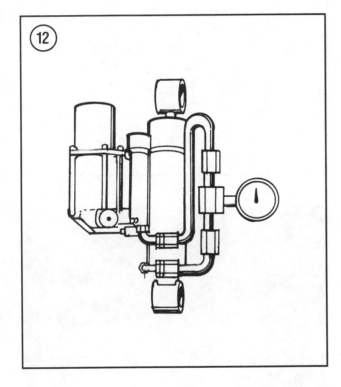

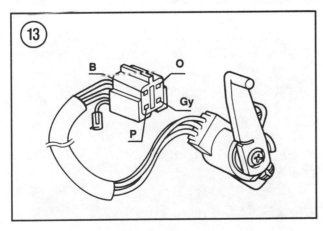

8. On the starboard clamp bracket, remove the nut and washer from the stud bolt.

9. Withdraw the stud bolt from the port side and lower the clamp bracket spacer assembly.

10. Remove the bushing from each side of the power tilt assembly unit where the stud bolt passes through.

11. Remove the circlip from the shaft pin.

12. Hold onto the power tilt assembly and drive the shaft pin out from the port side. Lower the power tilt assembly and remove it. Don't lose the collar in the power tilt assembly upper mount.

13. Remove the bushing from each side of the motor mount where the shaft pin passes through.

14. Installation is the reverse of removal. Note the following:

   a. Coat the shaft pin and stud bolt with Yamalube All-purpose Marine grease.

   b. If necessary, refill the hydraulic pump as described in this chapter.

Trim Sensor Test

1. Disconnect the trim sensor electrical connector.

2. Connect an ohmmeter between the pink and black terminals in the connector (**Figure 13**). The specified resistance is 360-540 ohms.

3. Connect an ohmmeter between the black and orange terminals, slowly turn the lever and observe the ohmmeter. The specified resistance is 800-1,200 ohms.

4. Replace the sensor if it fails either of these tests.

POWER TRIM/TILT SYSTEM

Components

This system consists of a manifold or trim/tilt housing containing a hydraulic pump (consisting of an electric motor, oil reservoir oil pump and valve body) and 2 hydraulic trim pistons. A separate hydraulic tilt cylinder is attached to the

12

housing by a shaft and bushings (**Figure 14**). A trim/tilt switch located in the remote control box handle sends current to the up/down relay mounted on the bottom of the cowling to the rear of the starter relay on 70-90 hp model or the power head relay bracket on 115-250 hp models. The relays connect to a terminal assembly or junction box on the power head, sending current to the power trim/tilt motor.

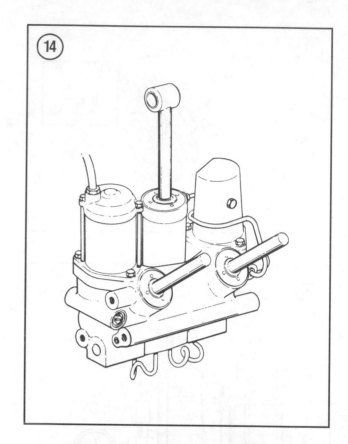

Operation

Moving the trim switch to the UP position closes the pump motor circuit. The motor drives the oil pump, forcing oil into the up side of the trim cylinders. The trim cylinder pistons push on the swivel bracket thrust pads to trim the outboard upward. Once the trim cylinders are fully extended, the hydraulic fluid is diverted into the tilt cylinder, which now moves the outboard throughout the remaining range of travel.

Moving the trim switch to the DOWN position also closes the pump motor circuit. The reversible motor runs in the opposite direction, forcing oil into the tilt cylinder and bringing the outboard back to a position where the swivel brackets rest on the trim cylinder pistons. The pistons then lower the outboard the remainder of the way.

The power trim/tilt system will temporarily maintain the outboard at any angle within its range to allow shallow water operation at slow speed, launching, beaching or trailering.

To prevent damage if the outboard strikes an underwater object, a relief valve in the hydraulic pump opens to allow the outboard to pivot upward quickly and return slowly, absorbing the shock.

A trim gauge sending unit is located on the inside of the port clamp bracket (**Figure 15**). Access to the sending unit requires the outboard motor to be fully tilted.

A manual release valve (A, **Figure 16**) is provided on the hydraulic pump. Opening this valve by turning its screw head permits manual

raising and lowering of the outboard motor if the electrical system fails.

Hydraulic Pump Fluid Check

1. Tilt the outboard to its fully UP position.
2. Clean the area around the pump fill plug. Remove the plug (B, **Figure 16**) and visually check the fluid level in the pump reservoir. It should be at the bottom of the fill hole threads.
3. Top up if necessary with DEXRON Type II automatic transmission fluid (ATF).
4. Install the fill plug and tighten securely.

Hydraulic Pump Fluid Bleed and Refill

Follow this procedure if a large amount of fluid has been lost due to service or leakage.
1. Tilt the outboard to its fully UP position.
2. Clean the area around the pump fill plug. Remove the plug (B, **Figure 16**) and visually check the fluid level in the pump reservoir. It should be at the bottom of the fill hole threads.
3. Top up if necessary with DEXRON Type II automatic transmission fluid (ATF).
4. Install the fill plug and tighten securely.

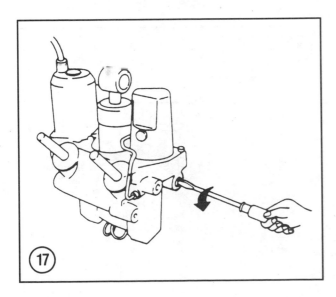

5. Turn the manual release valve to the closed position (**Figure 17**).
6. Operate the trim/tilt switch to completely lower, then raise the outboard to its full tilt position, adding more ATF fluid as required to keep the fluid level at the bottom of the fill plug hole.
7. Operate the outboard up and down several times.
8. Tilt the outboard to its fully UP position. Remove the fill plug and add ATF fluid to the reservoir as required to keep the fluid level at the bottom of the fill plug hole.
9. Repeat Step 7 and Step 8 until the fluid level stabilizes at the bottom of the fill plug hole. Install and tighten the fill plug securely.
10. Recharge the battery. See Chapter Seven.

Troubleshooting

If a problem develops in the power trim/tilt system, the initial step is to determine whether the problem is in the electrical or hydraulic system. Electrical and hydraulic tests are given in this chapter. If the problem appears to be in the hydraulic system, refer it to a dealer or qualified specialist for necessary service.

One of the most common problems causing leak-down of the power trim/tilt hydraulic cylinders is internal contamination of the oil or a defective valve, usually with the up side main valve.
1. Make sure the plug-in connectors are properly engaged and that all terminals and wires are free of corrosion. Tighten and clean as required.
2. Make sure the battery is fully charged. Charge or replace as required.
3. Check the hydraulic fluid level as described in this chapter. Top off if necessary.
4. Make sure the manual release valve is turned to the closed position (**Figure 17**).

12

Trim/Tilt Relay Test

60-90 hp models

1. Disconnect the negative (–) battery lead, then disconnect the positive (+) battery lead.

2. Disconnect the tilt relay electrical connector.

3. Connect an ohmmeter or test lamp between the relay No. 1 terminal and the positive (+) terminal (**Figure 18**). The meter should indicate no continuity (infinity) or the test lamp should not light.

4. Connect an ohmmeter or test lamp between the relay No. 2 terminal and the positive (+) terminal. The meter should indicate no continuity (infinity) or the test lamp should not light.

5. Connect an ohmmeter or test lamp between the relay No. 1 terminal and the negative (–) terminal. The meter should indicate continuity (low resistance) or the test lamp should light.

6. Connect an ohmmeter or test lamp between the relay No. 2 terminal and the negative (–) terminal. The meter should indicate continuity (low resistance) or the test lamp should light.

7. Use jumper leads and connect the positive (+) battery lead to the light green relay lead (**Figure 19**). Connect the negative (–) battery lead to the black relay lead. Connect an ohmmeter between the No. 1 terminal and the positive (+) terminal. The meter should indicate continuity (low resistance) or the test lamp should light.

8. Use jumper leads and connect the positive (+) battery lead to the sky blue relay lead (**Figure 20**). Connect the negative (–) battery lead to the black relay lead. Connect an ohmmeter between the No. 2 terminal and the positive (+) terminal. The meter should indicate continuity (low resistance) or the test lamp should light.

9. If the relay failed any of these tests in Step 3-8, the relay is faulty and must be replaced.

C115 models

1. Disconnect the negative (–) battery lead, then disconnect the positive (+) battery lead.

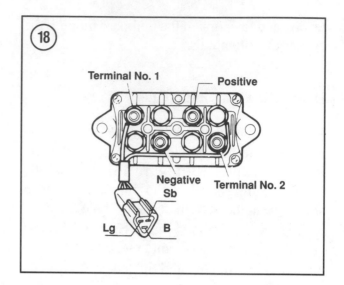

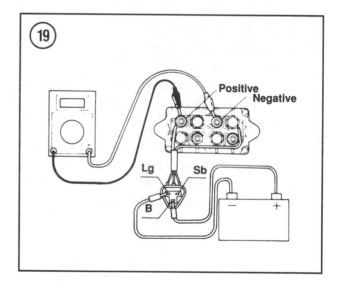

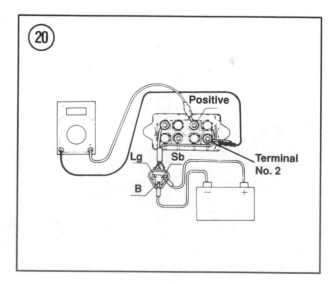

2. Disconnect the tilt relay electrical connectors.

3. Connect an ohmmeter or test lamp between the disconnected sky blue and black relay leads (**Figure 21**). The meter should indicate continuity (low resistance) or the test lamp should light.

4. Connect an ohmmeter or test lamp between the disconnected light green and black relay leads (**Figure 21**). The meter should indicate continuity (low resistance) or the test lamp should light.

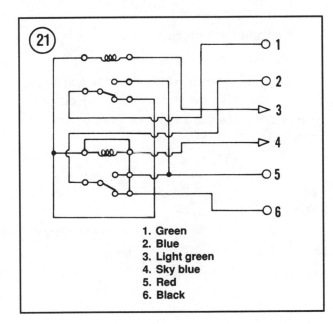

21

1. Green
2. Blue
3. Light green
4. Sky blue
5. Red
6. Black

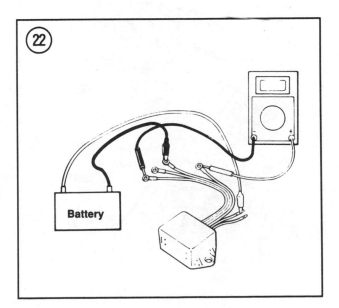

22

5. Use jumper leads and connect the positive (+) battery lead to the light green relay lead (**Figure 22**). Connect the negative (–) battery lead to the black relay lead. Connect an ohmmeter between the disconnected green and red relay leads. The meter should indicate continuity (low resistance) or the test lamp should light.

6. Use jumper leads and connect the positive (+) battery lead to the sky blue relay lead (**Figure 23**). Connect the negative (–) battery lead to the black relay lead. Connect an ohmmeter between the disconnected blue and red relay leads. The meter should indicate continuity (low resistance) or the test lamp should light.

7. If the relay failed any of these tests in Step 3-6, the relay is faulty and must be replaced.

115-250 hp models

1. Disconnect the negative battery lead, then disconnect the positive battery lead.

2. Disconnect the tilt relay electrical connectors.

3. Connect an ohmmeter or test lamp between the disconnected light blue and black leads (A,

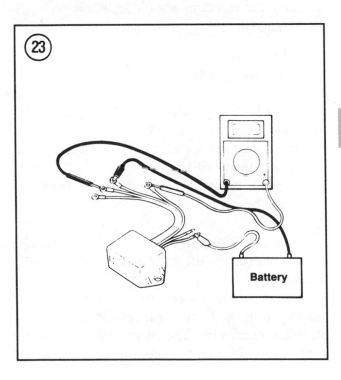

23

12

Figure 24). The meter should indicate no continuity (infinity) or the test lamp should not light.

4. Connect an ohmmeter or test lamp between the disconnected light green and black relay leads (B, **Figure 24**). The meter should indicate continuity (low resistance) or the test lamp should light.

5. Connect an ohmmeter or test lamp between the disconnected sky blue and black relay leads (C, **Figure 24**). The meter should indicate continuity (low resistance) or the test lamp should light.

6. Use jumper leads and connect the positive (+) battery lead to the sky blue relay lead (C, **Figure 24**). Connect the negative (–) battery lead to the black relay lead. Connect an ohmmeter between the disconnected light green and black relay leads. The meter should indicate no continuity (infinity) or the test lamp should not light.

7. Use jumper leads and connect the positive (+) battery lead to the sky blue relay lead (C, **Figure 24**). Connect the negative (–) battery lead to the black relay lead. Connect an ohmmeter between the disconnected light green and red relay leads. The meter should indicate continuity (low resistance) or the test lamp should light.

8. Replace the relay if it fails any of these tests.

Trim/Tilt Switch Test

The rocker-type trim/tilt switch is mounted in the remote control box handle.

1. Disconnect the negative (–) battery lead, then disconnect the positive (+) battery lead.

2. Remove the remote control box from its mounting bracket.

3. Remove the wire cover (**Figure 9**) and the back panel (**Figure 10**).

4. Disconnect the tilt relay electrical connector (**Figure 11**).

5. Connect an ohmmeter or test lamp between the sky blue and red terminals in the switch electrical connector. The meter should indicate continuity (low resistance) or the test lamp

should light when the switch is depressed in the UP position.

6. Connect an ohmmeter or test lamp between the light green and red terminals in the switch electrical connector. The meter should indicate continuity (low resistance) or the test lamp should light when the switch is depressed in the DOWN position.

7. Connect an ohmmeter or test lamp between the terminals in the switch electrical connector without depressing the switch:

    a. Red and sky blue.

    b. Red and light green.

    c. Sky blue and light green.

There should be on continuity between any of the terminals with the switch in the OFF position.

8. Replace the switch if it does not perform as specified in Steps 5-7.

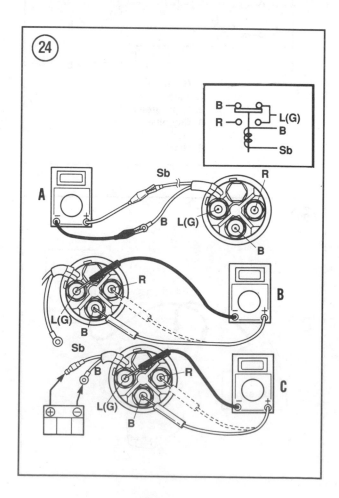

Trim/Tilt Motor Test

1. Disconnect the pump motor electrical connector from the wiring harness.

2. Connect the voltmeter red test lead to the blue wiring harness lead. Connect the black test lead to the black wiring harness lead.

3. Move the trim/tilt switch to the UP position. If the voltmeter does not indicated battery voltage, replace the UP relay.

4. Move the red test lead to the green wiring harness lead.

5. Move the trim/tilt switch to the DOWN position. If the voltmeter does not read battery voltage, replace the DOWN relay.

6. If the voltmeter readings are as specified in Step 3 and Step 5, but the motor still does not run, replace the motor.

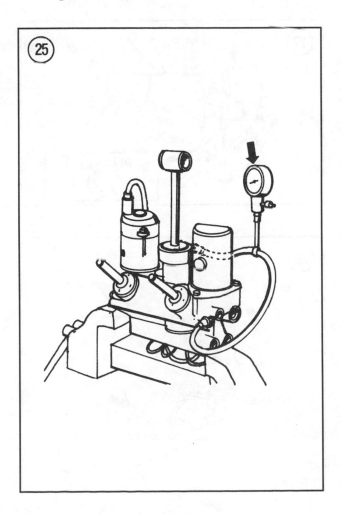

Hydraulic Test

115-200 hp and 90° 225 hp V6 models)

NOTE
Pressure gauge part No. YB-6181 is required for this test.

1. Turn the manual release valve toward the manual tilt position until it stops.

2. Place a suitable container under the fittings to be removed in the following steps to catch any hydraulic fluid that may leak out.

3. Disconnect the hydraulic line from the bottom of the reservoir and upper chamber of the tilt cylinder. Install the pressure gauge part No. YB-6181 to the reservoir and the reservoir and tilt cylinder fittings (**Figure 25**).

4. Turn the manual valve to the power tilt position and immediately operate the trim/tilt switch to tilt the outboard motor up and then down.

5. Turn the manual valve toward the manual tilt position until it stops (to bleed any air from the system), then return it to the power tilt position.

6. Check the hydraulic fluid level as described in this chapter. Top off if necessary.

7. Operate the trim/tilt switch to tilt the outboard motor up, noting the pressure gauge reading. The gauge should read 0-71 psi (0-489 kPa) during the upward movement and 1,351-1,636 psi (9.3-11.3 mPa) once the outboard motor has reached the full up position.

8. Return the outboard engine to the full down position, noting the pressure gauge readings. The gauge should read 85-156 psi (586-1,075 kPa) once the outboard engine has reached the full down position.

9. Remove the pressure gauge and reconnect the hydraulic line to the reservoir and tilt cylinder upper chamber. Tighten the fittings securely.

10. Turn the manual release valve toward the manual tilt position until it stops.

11. Place a suitable container under the fittings to be removed in the following steps to catch any hydraulic fluid that may leak out.

12

12. Disconnect the hydraulic line at the lower chambers of the trim cylinder and the tilt cylinder. Install pressure gauge part No. YB-6181 to the trim and tilt cylinder fittings (**Figure 26**).

13. Repeat Steps 4-6.

14. Operate the trim/tilt switch to drive the outboard motor up, noting the pressure gauge readings. The gauge should read 0-71 psi (0-489 kPa) during the upward movement and 0 psi once the outboard motor has reached the full up position.

15. Return the outboard motor to the full down position, noting the pressure gauge readings. The gauge should read 583-782 psi (4,019-5,391 kPa) once the outboard motor has reached the full down position.

16. Remove the pressure gauge and reconnect the hydraulic line to the trim and tilt cylinder chambers. Tighten the fittings securely.

17. Bleed and refill the reservoir with Dexron II automatic transmission fluid (ATF) as described in this chapter.

76° 225 and 250 hp V6 models

> *NOTE*
> *Two special gauges (part No. YB-6181) are required for this test, so the trim and tilt pressure can be measured at the same time.*

1. Turn the manual valve to the power tilt position and immediately operate the trim/tilt switch to drive the outboard motor up and then down.

2. Operate the trim/tilt switch to tilt the outboard motor up and then down.

3. Check the hydraulic fluid level as described in this chapter. Top off if necessary.

4. Turn the manual release valve toward the manual tilt position until it stops (**Figure 27**).

5. Place a suitable container under the fittings to be removed in the following steps to catch any hydraulic fluid that leaks out.

6. Disconnect both hydraulic lines from the reservoir and chamber of the tilt cylinder. Install

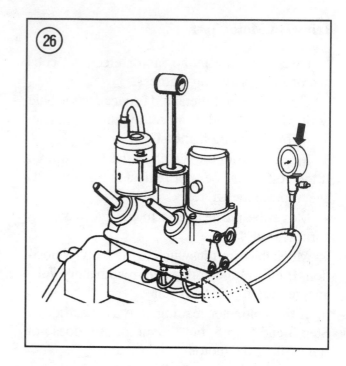

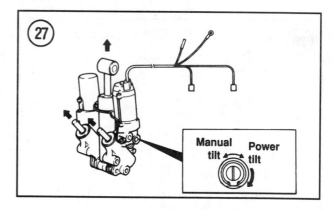

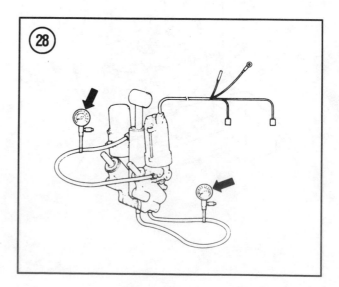

both sets of pressure gauges, part No. YB-6181, as shown in **Figure 28**.

7. Operate the trim/tilt switch to drive the outboard motor to the full down position, noting the pressure gauge readings. The "A" gauge should read 683-697 psi (4.7-4.8 mPa) and the "B" gauge should read 0 psi once the outboard motor has reached the full down position (**Figure 29**).

8. Operate the trim/tilt switch to drive the outboard motor to the full up position, noting the pressure gauge readings. The "A" gauge should read 0 psi and the "B" gauge should read 1,636-1,920 psi (11.3-13.2 mPa) once the outboard motor has reached the full up position (**Figure 30**).

9. Remove both sets of pressure gauges and reconnect the hydraulic lines to the trim and tilt cylinder chambers. Tighten the fittings securely.

10. Bleed and refill the reservoir with Dexron II automatic transmission fluid (ATF) as described in this chapter.

Trim/Tilt Housing
Removal/Installation

1. Disconnect the negative (–) battery cable.

2. Remove the engine cover.

3. Disconnect the ground lead connected to the grease nipple on the starboard swivel bracket.

4. Disconnect the power trim/tilt motor leads from the terminal assembly or junction box. Disconnect the trim sender leads.

5. Unbolt and remove the outboard motor from the boat. Secure it to a repair stand.

6. Turn the manual valve screw to the manual tilt position, tilt the swivel bracket up and lock it in place with the tilt lock lever.

7. Remove the adjustment stud or trim pin from the clamp brackets.

8. Remove the nut from the starboard side clamp bracket.

9. Remove the bolts holding the trim/tilt housing to each clamp bracket. Separate the clamp brackets slightly.

10. Pull the trim sender and motor leads through the hole in the port clamp bracket.

11. Support the trim/tilt housing and remove the snap ring at the end of the tilt cylinder upper pin

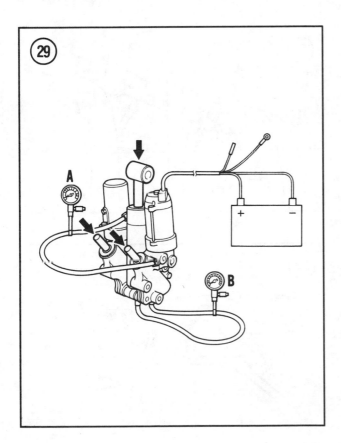

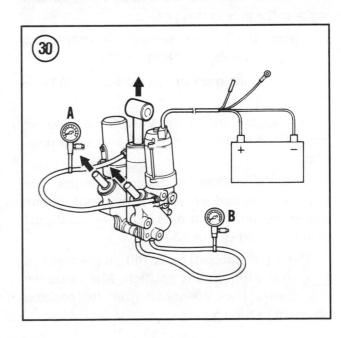

12

(**Figure 31**, typical). Carefully drive the upper pin out.

12. Remove the power tilt assembly.

13. Installation is the reverse of removal. Check, bleed and refill the unit (as required) with Dexron II automatic transmission fluid (ATF) as described in this chapter.

Trim Sender Removal/Installation

1. Raise the outboard to the full tilt position and support the unit in this position.

2. Disconnect the trim sender leads.

3. Remove the 2 screws holding the trim sender to the inside of the port clamp bracket (**Figure 32**).

4. Pull the trim sender leads through the hole in the port clamp bracket.

5. Installation is the reverse of removal. Adjust the trim sender as described in this chapter.

Trim Sender Adjustment

60-90 hp and 76° 225-250 hp V6 models

1. Raise the outboard to the full tilt position and support the unit in this position.

2. Loosen the 2 screws securing the trim sensor so it can move slightly (**Figure 33**).

3. Fully tilt the outboard to the full down position.

4. If disconnected, connect the outboard to the battery and set the main switch to the On position.

5. With the outboard in the down position, use a screwdriver and adjust the trim sensor so only one segment on the trim indicator on the digital meter goes on (**Figure 34**).

6. Raise the outboard to the full tilt position and support the unit in this position. Make sure the trim sensor does not move from the position obtained in Step 5.

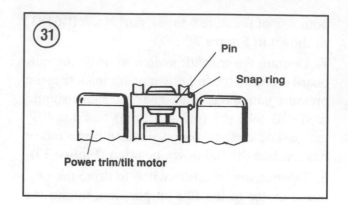

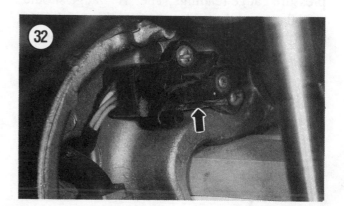

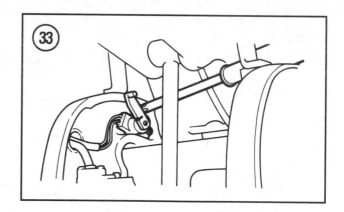

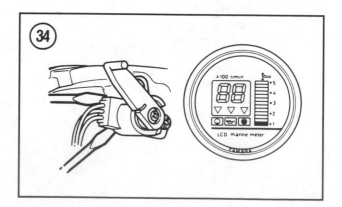

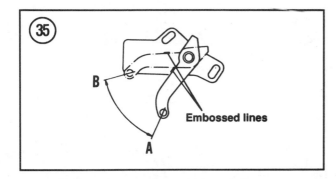

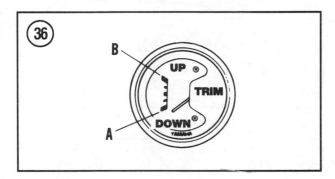

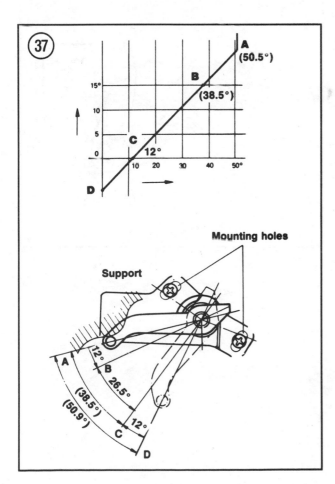

7. Tighten the 2 bolts securing the trim sensor securely (**Figure 33**).

All other models

1. Raise the outboard to the full tilt position and support the unit in this position.

2. Manually move the trim sender lever to position A, **Figure 35**. The trim sender gauge should read full DOWN (A, **Figure 36**).

3. Manually move the trim sender lever to position B, **Figure 35**. The trim sender gauge should read full UP (B, **Figure 36**).

4. If the sender gauge is not in agreement with the lever position in Step 2 or Step 3, loosen the trim sender attaching screws.

5. Repeat Step 2 while positioning the sender unit to achieve the correct gauge alignment. When adjustment is correct, the outboard will trim upward a maximum 50.5° (**Figure 37**).

Trim Sensor Test

60-90 hp models

1. Disconnect the trim sensor electrical connector.

2. Connect an ohmmeter between the pink and black terminals in the connector (**Figure 38**). The specified resistance is 360-540 ohms.

3. Connect an ohmmeter between the black and orange terminals, slowly turn the lever and ob-

12

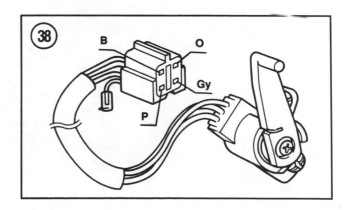

serve the ohmmeter. The specified resistance is 800-1,200 ohms.

4. Replace the trim sensor if it fails either one of these tests.

225-250 hp 76° V6 models

1. Disconnect the trim sensor electrical connector.

2. Connect an ohmmeter between the pink and orange terminals in the connector (**Figure 39**). The specified resistance is 494.4-741.6 ohms.

3. Connect an ohmmeter between the black and orange terminals, slowly turn the lever and observe the ohmmeter. The specified resistance is 800-1,200 ohms.

4. Replace the trim sensor if it fails either one these tests.

115-220 hp and 90° 225 hp V6 models

1. Disconnect the trim sensor electrical connector.

2. Connect an ohmmeter between the pink and black terminals in the connector (**Figure 40**). The specified resistance is 489-735 ohms.

3. Connect an ohmmeter between the black and orange terminals, slowly turn the lever and observe the ohmmeter. The specified resistance is 800-1,200 ohms.

4. Replace the trim sensor if it fails either one these tests.

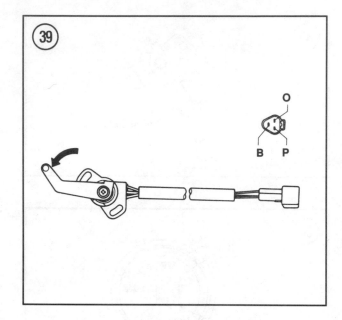

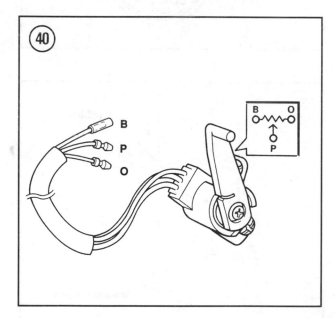

Chapter Thirteen

Oil Injection System

The fuel/oil ratio required by outboard motors depends upon engine demand. Without oil injection, oil must be hand-mixed with gasoline at a predetermined ratio to ensure that sufficient lubrication is provided at all operating speeds and engine load conditions. This ratio is adequate for high-speed operation, but contains more oil than required to lubricate the engine properly during idle and low-speed operation. The correct fuel-oil ratio for all models is listed in **Table 1**.

With oil injection, fuel/oil ration can be varied instantly and accurately to provide the optimum ratio for proper lubrication at any operating speed or engine load condition.

The 25-250 hp models, except "C" series (C25, C30, C40, C55, C75, C85 and C115) covered in this book are equipped with the Precision Blend oil injection system. This is mechanical oil injection system using a crankshaft-driven injection pump and integral oil tank. V-block engines also have a remote reserve oil tank which automatically supplies the integral tank on the engine as required. The pump draws oil from the oil tank and supplies it under pressure to intake manifold nozzles where it is sprayed into the air-fuel mixture. **Figure 1** shows a typical oil injection system. There are, however, minor differences among the various models covered in this book. A linkage rod connects the pump to the throttle and varies the pump stroke according to the throttle opening. The fuel-oil ratio ranges between 200:1 at idle to 100:1 at wide-open throttle on 25-50 hp models and 50:1 at wide-open throttle on 70-250 hp models.

Yamaha recommends the use of Yamalube Two-Cycle Outboard Oil that is certified TC-W3 by the National Marine Manufacturers Association (NMMA). If the Yamaha lubricant is not available, any high-quality 2-stroke oil intended for outboard motors may be substituted providing it meets the NMMA TC-W3 rating and specifies so on the container (**Figure 2**).

On models not equipped with an oil control unit, when the oil level in the oil tank is reduced to 10 percent of its capacity, the oil level sensor circuit closes to activate the engine rpm reduction system to lower the engine speed while activating the light on the motor pan and the buzzer on electric start models. On models equipped with an oil control unit, a 3-stage control unit monitors the oil level. The control unit informs the user of its status and automatically reduces engine speed while sounding a warning buzzer if the oil level is low or the injection system is not functioning properly.

This chapter covers the operation, troubleshooting and component replacement of the oil injection system.

Table 1 is at the end of the chapter.

NOTE
The "L" series models (counter rotation models), are included in all procedures. Unless there is a separate procedure designated for an "L" series model, refer to the procedure that relates to the same horsepower rating. If you are

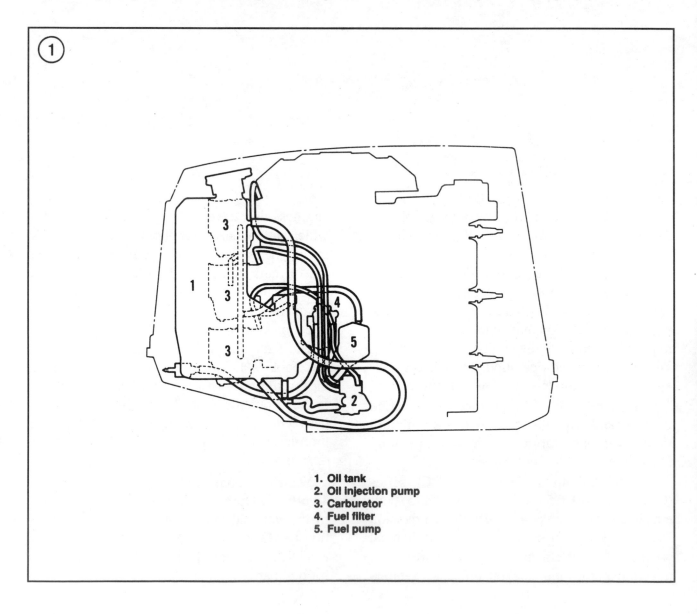

1. Oil tank
2. Oil injection pump
3. Carburetor
4. Fuel filter
5. Fuel pump

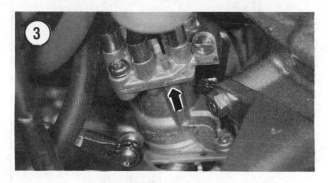

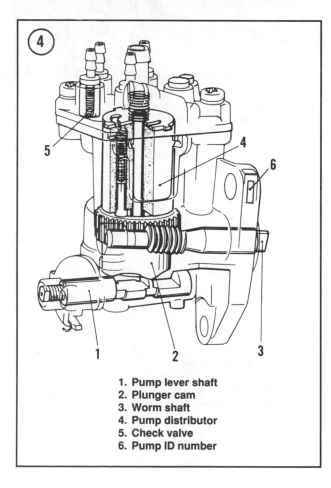

1. Pump lever shaft
2. Plunger cam
3. Worm shaft
4. Pump distributor
5. Check valve
6. Pump ID number

working on an L200, then refer to the 200 hp procedure.

SYSTEM COMPONENTS

The Yamaha oil injection system is a factory-installed standard feature. Models equipped with oil injection use a self-contained oil pump on the powerhead in addition to the fuel pump. **Figure 3** shows typical oil pump location, although there are minor differences among the various models covered in this book. The pump is connected to the throttle by a control rod. An oil tank or reservoir is mounted on the power head. The V-block models also have a remote reserve tank. When full, the tank(s) contains sufficient oil for approximately 5 hours of continuous wide-open throttle operation. A warning buzzer or a series of warning lights mounted on the lower cover or instrument panel and a warning buzzer located in the remote control box activates when the oil level becomes low.

OPERATION

The Precision Blend injection system supplies oil to the engine separately from the fuel. A drive gear on the crankshaft engages a driven gear on the oil pump shaft. This driven gear transmits crankshaft rotation through a series of reduction gears inside the pump, controlling the stroke of the pump plunger according to crankshaft speed (**Figure 4**) The plunger cam is designed to provide a 100:1 ratio with each full rotation of the crankshaft. Since the pump is mechanically linked to the throttle, it supplies the proper amount of oil according to engine speed and load.

NOTE
The oil injection pump is sealed at the factory and cannot be serviced. If defective, it must be replaced. Any attempt to disassemble the pump will void the factory warranty.

13

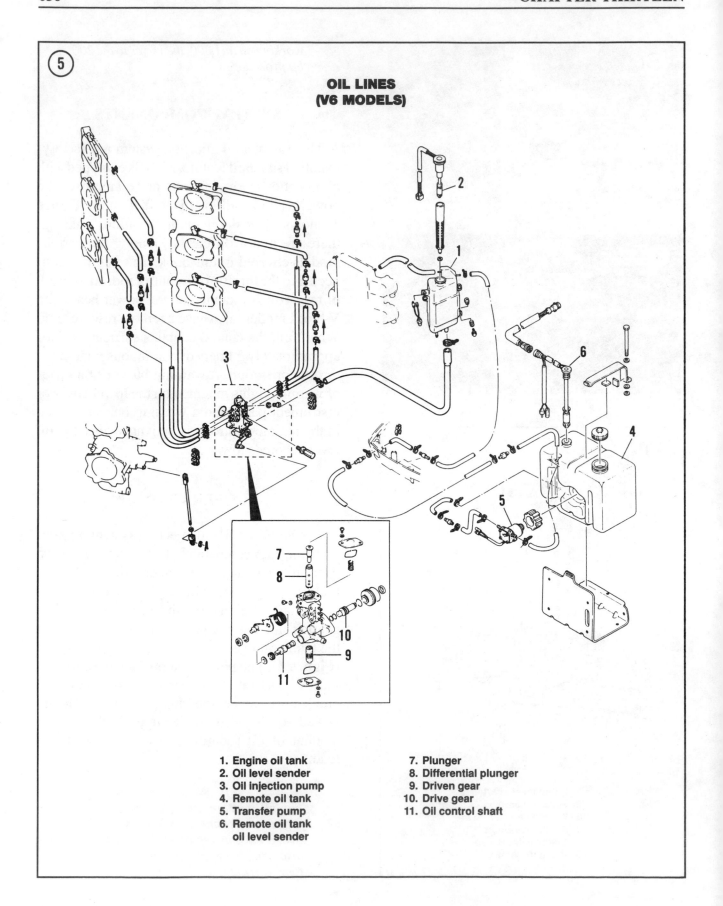

**OIL LINES
(V6 MODELS)**

1. Engine oil tank
2. Oil level sender
3. Oil injection pump
4. Remote oil tank
5. Transfer pump
6. Remote oil tank
   oil level sender
7. Plunger
8. Differential plunger
9. Driven gear
10. Drive gear
11. Oil control shaft

Oil travels to and from the oil pump through series of lines. **Figure 5** shows the system used on V-6 models; others are similar. A transparent hose connects to the outlet of each delivery hose which permits the user to check oil flow without removing a delivery hose.

Sensors in the integral and remote oil tanks are connected to the overheat warning buzzer in the remote control box and a series of 3 warning lamps mounted on the instrument panel.

Break-in Procedure

The first 10 hours of operation of a new or rebuilt engine should be with a 50:1 fuel/oil mixture in the fuel tank (see Chapter Four) *in addition* to the lubricant supplied by the injection pump.

Mark the oil level on the translucent oil tank mounted to the power head, then periodically check to make sure that the system is working (oil level diminishing) before switching over to plain gasoline at the end of the 10 hour break-in period. This applies both to outboard motors that have been overhauled and new engines out of the shipping box.

If returning a V-block model to service after several weeks (or more) of storage, make sure the remote oil tank contains a minimum of 5.3 qt. (5.0 l) of oil. If not, the oil feed pump chamber will not be filled and no oil will be delivered to the power head.

OIL LEVEL WARNING SYSTEM

On 25-90 hp models, the oil level warning system consists of an oil level gauge in the power head oil tank, one warning lamp and a warning buzzer on electric start models.

On all other models, the oil level warning systems consists of sensors in the power head integral oil tank and the remote oil tank, a control unit (except 225 hp), emergency switch, warning lamps and the remote control box warning buzz-

er. The control unit monitors signals from the oil level sensor(s).

On V-block models, the power head integral tank sensor also activates an oil feed pump when necessary. The oil feed pump supplies oil from the remote tank to refill the power head integral tank.

V-block Models Operation

The green light remains on during normal operation if the oil level in the tanks is satisfactory. If the green light does not come on when the engine is started, shut off the engine and check the oil level immediately.

If the level in the power head tank drops to about one-half quart (0.47 l), it sensor signals the control unit to activate the oil feed pump and transfer additional oil from the remote tank to the power head integral oil tank. If the remote oil tank level is too low to supply the power head integral oil tank, the yellow warning lamp lights.

Continued operation with the yellow light on without adding oil will cause the red light to activate, the warning buzzer to sound and a reduction in engine speed to approximately 2,000 rpm. At this time, you should shut the ignition switch OFF to stop the engine. Use the emergency switch to pump the oil remaining in the remote tank to the power head integral oil tank. Turn the ignition switch back ON, make sure the red light is off and restart the engine. This will allow you to reach port and refill the oil tanks. Failure to turn the ignition switch OFF will prevent engine speed from exceeding 2,000 rpm, even after the oil tanks have been refilled.

13

CAUTION
If the emergency switch is used as previously described, be sure to bleed the oil feed pump as outlined in this chapter when refilling the tank.

25-50 hp Models Operation

No light is illuminated during normal if the oil level in the tank is satisfactory.

If the level in the tank drops to 10 percent of capacity, the red lamp lights, the warning buzzer sounds (if so equipped) and the engine speed is reduced to approximately 2,000 rpm. At this time, you should shut the engine OFF, refill the tank and restart the engine. Failure to stop the engine will prevent it from exceeding 2,000 rpm even after the tank is filled.

60-250 hp Models Operation

The green light is illuminated during normal operation if the oil level in the tank is satisfactory. If the green light does not come on when the engine is started, check the oil level immediately.

If the level in the power head integral tank drops to about one-half quart (0.47 l), its sensor turns on the yellow lamp. If engine operation continues without adding oil, the red lamp will light, the warning buzzer sounds and the engine speed is reduced to approximately 2,000 rpm. At this time, you should shut the engine OFF, refill the power head integral tank and restart the engine. Failure to stop the engine will prevent it

from exceeding 2,000 rpm even after the tank is filled.

Thermo-Switch Overheat Protection

A thermo-switch is installed in the cylinder head and is connected to the warning lamp or to the warning buzzer to warn of an overheat condition. If the power head temperature exceeds the sending unit's specified value, the warning lamp will flash or the buzzer will sound continuously and the engine speed will automatically be reduced to approximately 2,000 rpm. Backing off on the throttle will shut the buzzer off as soon as the power head temperature drops to a specified value, unless a restricted engine water intake is causing the overheat condition. If a steady stream of water does not flow from the tell-tale or pilot hole (**Figure 6**) or if the warning lamps continues to flash or the buzzer continues sounding after 2 minutes, the engine should be shut OFF immediately to prevent power head damage.

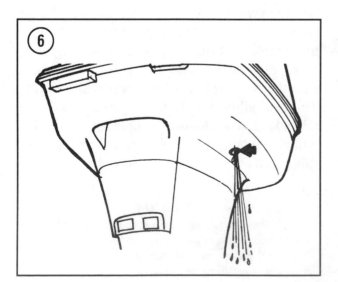

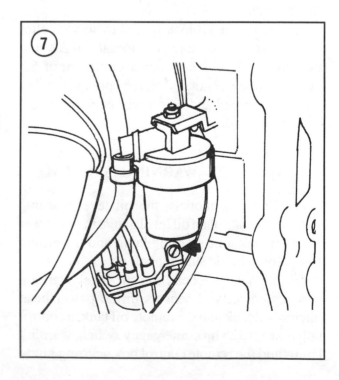

CAUTION
If the engine has overheated and the warning buzzer has sounded, retorque the cylinder head fasteners after the engine cools to minimize the possibility of power head damage from a blown head gasket.

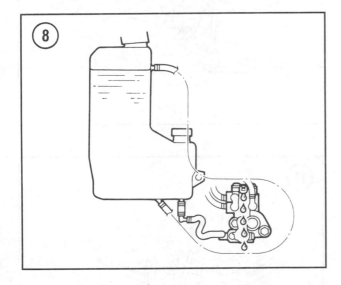

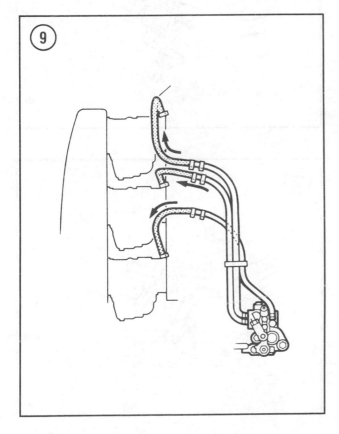

OIL INJECTION SYSTEM SERVICE

Power Head Oil Injection Pump Bleeding

Air generally enters the oil injection system during system service or a lengthy storage period. The oil injection system on 25-70 hp models is self-bleeding. However, on all other models, the system must be gravity-bled to remove any air present in the pump or oil lines.

90, 115 hp and 90° 130-225 hp V6 models

1. Remove the engine cover.
2. Remove the oil tank cap. If necessary, fill the oil tank with the recommended oil.
3. Make sure the outboard motor is in the upright position. If tilted in a trailering position, tilt it upright.
4. If the oil pump has been removed from the power head, fill the oil lines with the recommended oil before reconnecting them to the oil pump fittings.
5. Open the bleed screw on the oil injection pump 3-4 turns *counterclockwise* (**Figure 7**).
6. Wait several seconds, make sure oil is flowing through the bleed hole (**Figure 8**), then tighten the bleed screw securely.
7. Install the oil tank cap and tighten securely.
8. Start the engine and allow it to idle. Observe the oil lines and make sure the oil is flowing through the feed lines (**Figure 9**).
9. Shut the engine off and install the engine cover.

76° 225 and 250 hp V6 models

CAUTION
The engine should be operated with 50:1 fuel/oil mixture in the fuel tank during this procedure.

1. Remove the engine cover.

13

2. Remove the oil tank cap. If necessary, fill the oil tank with the recommended oil.

3. Make sure the outboard motor is in the upright position. If tilted in a trailering position, tilt it upright.

4. If the oil pump has been removed from the power head, fill the oil lines with the recommended oil before reconnecting them to the oil pump fittings.

5. Open the bleed screw on the oil injection pump 3-4 turns *counterclockwise* (**Figure 10**).

6. Wait several seconds, make sure oil is flowing through the bleed hole, then tighten the bleed screw securely.

7. Install the oil tank cap and tighten securely.

8. Remove the oil pump control rod from the oil pump (**Figure 11**).

9. Start the engine and allow it to idle.

10. With the engine running at idle speed, push the oil pump lever up to the full-open position (**Figure 12**).

11. Observe the oil lines and make sure oil is flowing through the feed lines (**Figure 13**).

12. Shut the engine off.

13. Reconnect the oil operating rod onto the oil pump.

14. Install the engine cover.

Oil Feed Pump Bleeding
(V-block Models Only)

1. Fill the remote oil tank with the recommended oil. Remote tank capacity is approximately 5.3 U.S. qt. (5.0 l).

2. Turn the main switch to the ON position.

> *NOTE*
> *In Step 3, the oil level indicators will be illuminated and the warning buzzer will sound.*

3. The oil feed pump in the remote oil tank will be activated for 180 seconds to supply oil from the remote oil tank to the power head integral oil tank.

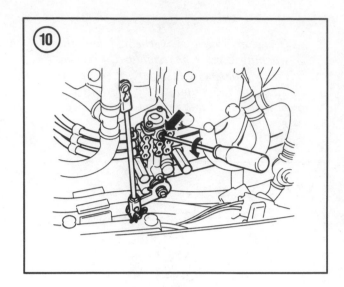

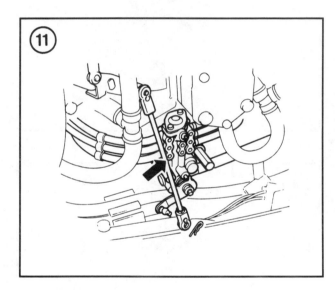

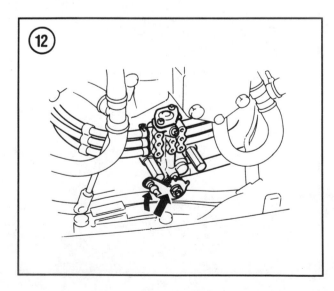

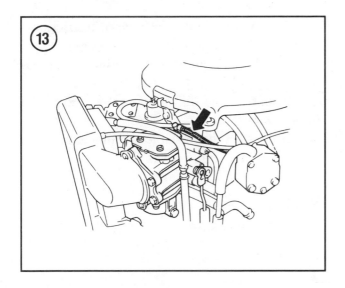

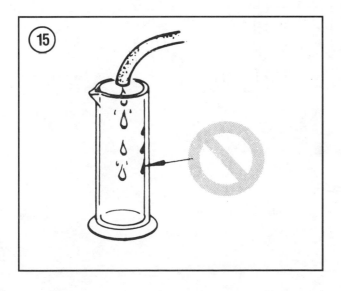

4. After 180 seconds have elapsed, the oil feed pump will stop operating. The oil level indicators should return to normal and the warning buzzer should stop. If they do not, the oil has not reached the required 14.9 oz. (440 ml) level in the power head integral oil tank. If this occurs, turn the main switch to OFF and then turn it again to the ON position to activate the oil feed pump again.

Oil Pump Discharge Adjustment

See *Oil Pump Link Adjustment* in Chapter Five.

Oil Pump Delivery Rate Test

CAUTION
The engine should be operated with a 50:1 fuel/oil mixture in the fuel tank during this procedure.

1. Start the engine and run at idle for 5 minutes or until it reaches normal operating temperature. Shut the engine off.
2. Remove the engine cover.
3. Install a tachometer according to its manufacturer's instructions.
4. Start the engine.

NOTE
Use a container with graduations of at least 0.1 cc to confirm that the specified amount of discharged oil is accurate.

5. Disconnect one of the oil pump injection lines from the intake manifold (**Figure 14**) and insert it into a suitable graduated container so that the oil will drip directly into the container, not on the side of the container (**Figure 15**).
6. Disconnect the oil pump control rod from the oil pump lever (**Figure 11**, typical).
7. Rotate the lever to the wide-open position (**Figure 12**, typical).
8. Run the engine at 1500 rpm for exactly 3 minutes, then reconnect the oil line to the intake manifold fitting.

13

9. Measure the amount of oil discharged at the end of 3 minute period. Refer to **Table 1** for oil discharge specifications.

10. Repeat Steps 5, 7 and 8 with each remaining oil injection line.

> *NOTE*
> *If the quantity of oil discharged varies substantially from that recommended in* **Table 1**, *repeat the test 2-3 times to ensure accurate results.*

11. If the oil discharged is not within the specification listed in **Table 1**, check the injection lines for possible kinks, leakage or restrictions. If none are found, replace the oil pump.

12. Shut the engine off and bleed the oil injection pump as described in this chapter.

13. Reconnect the oil pump control rod to the oil pump lever.

14. Disconnect the portable tachometer.

15. Install the engine cover.

Oil Pump Control Unit Troubleshooting

See Chapter Three.

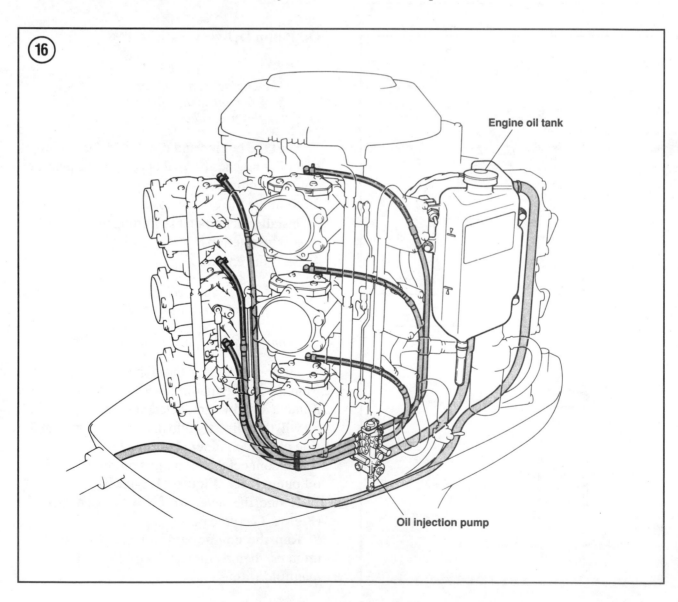

Engine oil tank

Oil injection pump

COMPONENT REPLACEMENT

Integral Power Head Oil Tank Removal/Installation

1. Remove the engine cover.

NOTE
If a clean container is not available in Step 2, pinch the end of the oil line during removal, then plug it with a suitable size bolt to prevent oil leakage and the entry of foreign matter.

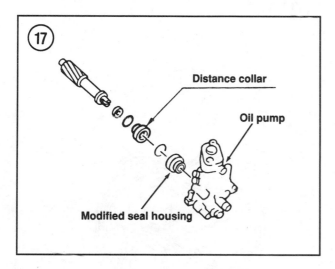

Distance collar

Oil pump

Modified seal housing

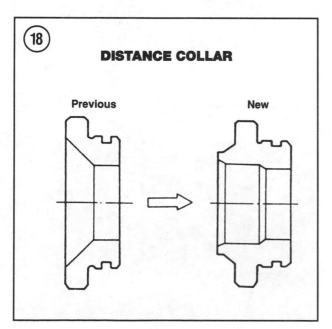

DISTANCE COLLAR

Previous

New

2. Place a clean shop cloth under the oil tank, then disconnect the line between the oil tank and the oil injection pump. Drain the contents of the oil tank into a suitable container.

3. Disconnect the oil sensor electrical leads.

4. Remove the bolts securing the tank to the power head. Remove the oil tank.

5. Installation is the reverse of removal. Refill the tank with Yamaha TC-W3 Two-Cycle Outboard motor oil. Bleed the oil pump as described in this chapter.

Oil Injection Pump Removal/Installation

CAUTION
Oil injection lines must be installed between the pump and the power head correctly and connected to the proper cylinder fitting on the intake manifold. Figure 16 shows a typical V6 engine oil line routing.

CAUTION
Yamaha has determined that there is a possible problem with the oil seal moving out of position on 1990 40-90 hp models. If removing the pump on these models, check the shape of the oil pump drive shaft distance collar (Figure 17). If the oil style distance collar is still in place, remove it and install the new design distance collar (Figure 18), part No. 6H1-13117-01-00.

1. Disconnect the battery negative cable.

2. Remove the engine cover.

3. Remove the oil tank as described in this chapter.

4. Place clean shop cloth under the oil injection pump to catch any oil that leaks out when the oil lines are disconnected or the pump removed.

NOTE
Prior to disconnecting the oil lines from the oil pump or the fittings on the intake manifold, label each line according to

13

the fitting in which it is connected. This will make installation easier.

5A. If the oil pump is to be replaced but the oil injection lines reused, disconnect the lines from the oil pump.

5B. If the oil pump and the injection lines will be reinstalled, disconnect the lines from the fittings on the intake manifold.

6. On 90° V6 models, remove the injection line retaining clamps from the power head (**Figure 19**).

7. Disconnect the control link from the oil pump (**Figure 20**, typical).

8. Remove the bolts securing the oil pump to the power head. Remove the oil pump.

9. Pull the driven gear from the power head.

10. Installation is the reverse of removal. Note the following:

    a. Align the slit in the oil pump driven gear with the tanks on the oil pump.

    b. If the oil lines were disconnected from the oil pump, refer to **Figures 21-27** for proper reconnection.

    c. Fill the oil injection lines with Yamaha TC-W3 Two-Cycle Outboard motor oil before connecting the to the intake manifold fittings.

    d. Connect the control link at the oil pump and adjust it as required. See Chapter Five.

    e. Carefully check all oil lines and connections for oil leakage before starting the engine.

    f. Bleed the oil pump as described in this chapter.

Oil Injection Pump Correct Part Number (V4 and V6 Models)

When replacing the oil pump on V4 and V6 models, be sure to install the correct part designed specifically for these years. The oil pump used on the older 1984-1989 models (not cov-

ered in this book) turn in one direction and the 1990 and later models (covered in this book) turn in the opposite direction. These oil pumps *cannot be interchanged*. If a 1984-1989 model oil pump is installed on a 1990 and later model it will *not* pump oil to the engine, resulting in costly engine failure.

The oil pump used on 1984-1989 models is marked with a -09 on the control lever (**Figure 28**). The 1990 and later models are marked with

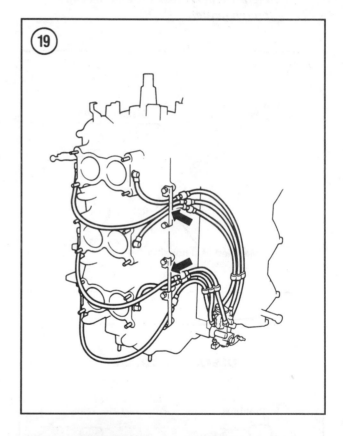

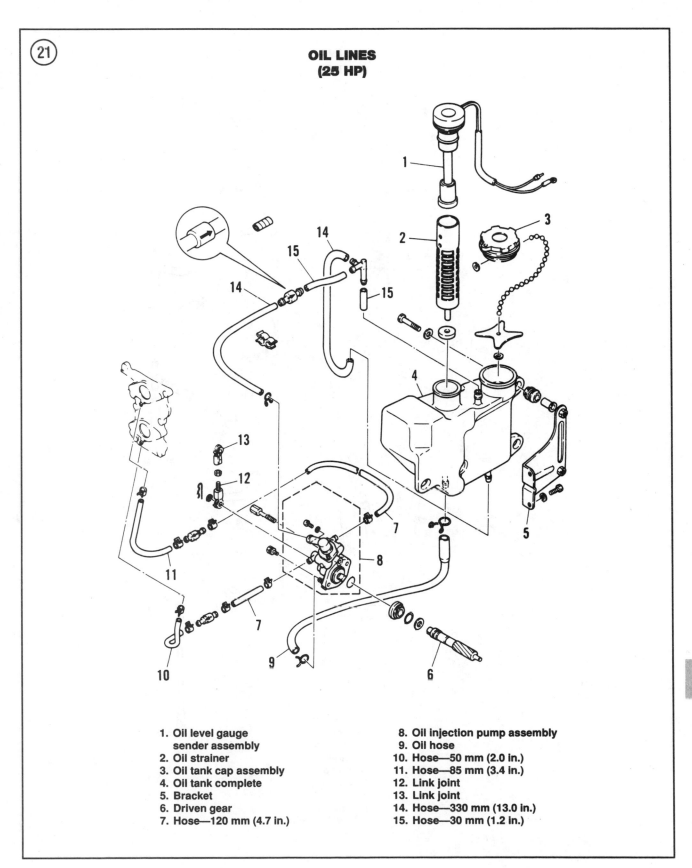

**OIL LINES
(25 HP)**

1. Oil level gauge
   sender assembly
2. Oil strainer
3. Oil tank cap assembly
4. Oil tank complete
5. Bracket
6. Driven gear
7. Hose—120 mm (4.7 in.)
8. Oil injection pump assembly
9. Oil hose
10. Hose—50 mm (2.0 in.)
11. Hose—85 mm (3.4 in.)
12. Link joint
13. Link joint
14. Hose—330 mm (13.0 in.)
15. Hose—30 mm (1.2 in.)

13

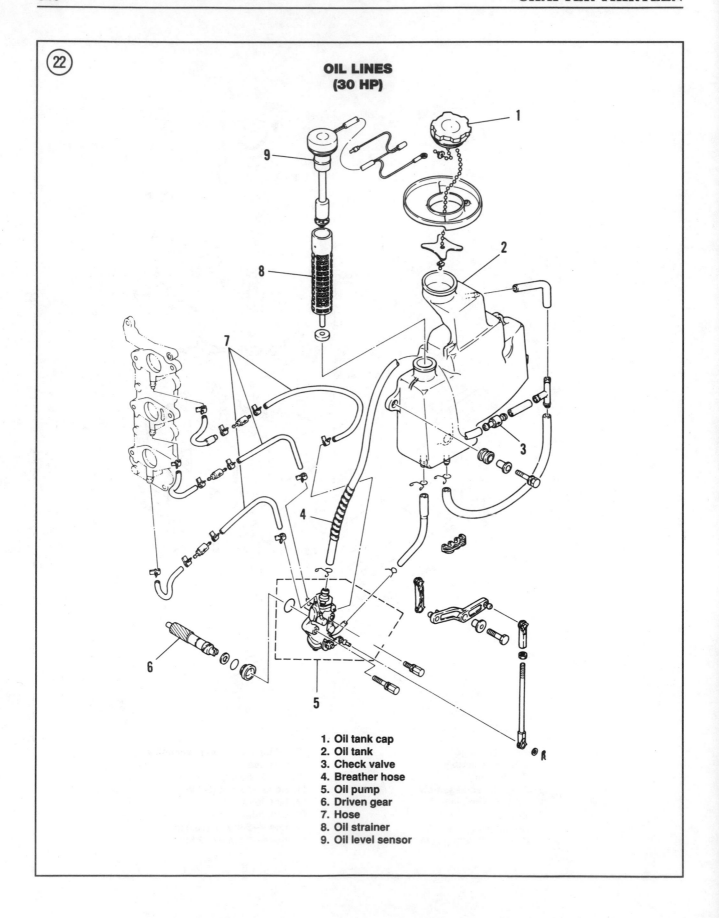

㉒

**OIL LINES
(30 HP)**

1. Oil tank cap
2. Oil tank
3. Check valve
4. Breather hose
5. Oil pump
6. Driven gear
7. Hose
8. Oil strainer
9. Oil level sensor

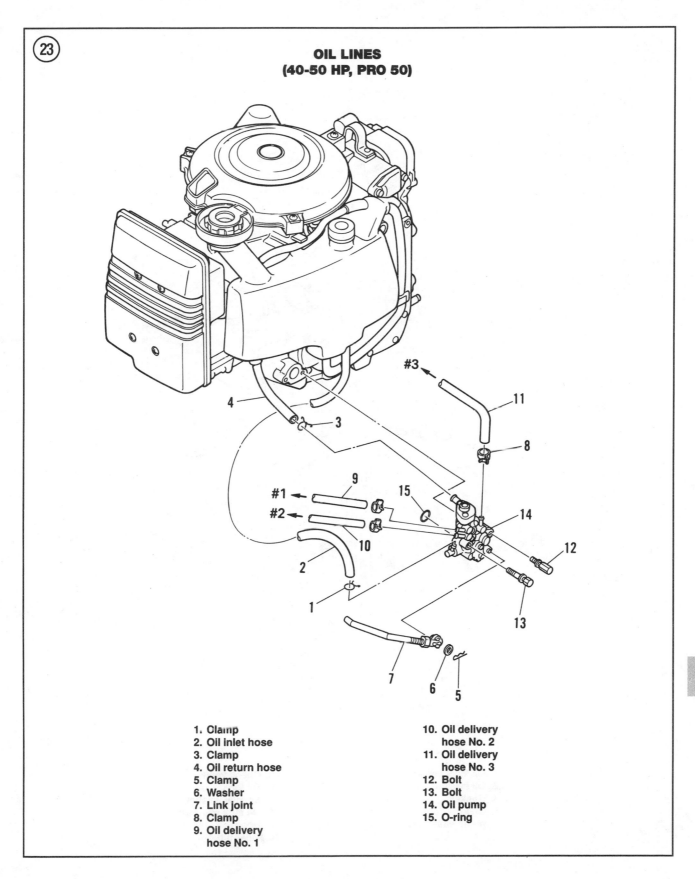

㉓

**OIL LINES
(40-50 HP, PRO 50)**

1. Clamp
2. Oil inlet hose
3. Clamp
4. Oil return hose
5. Clamp
6. Washer
7. Link joint
8. Clamp
9. Oil delivery
hose No. 1
10. Oil delivery
hose No. 2
11. Oil delivery
hose No. 3
12. Bolt
13. Bolt
14. Oil pump
15. O-ring

13

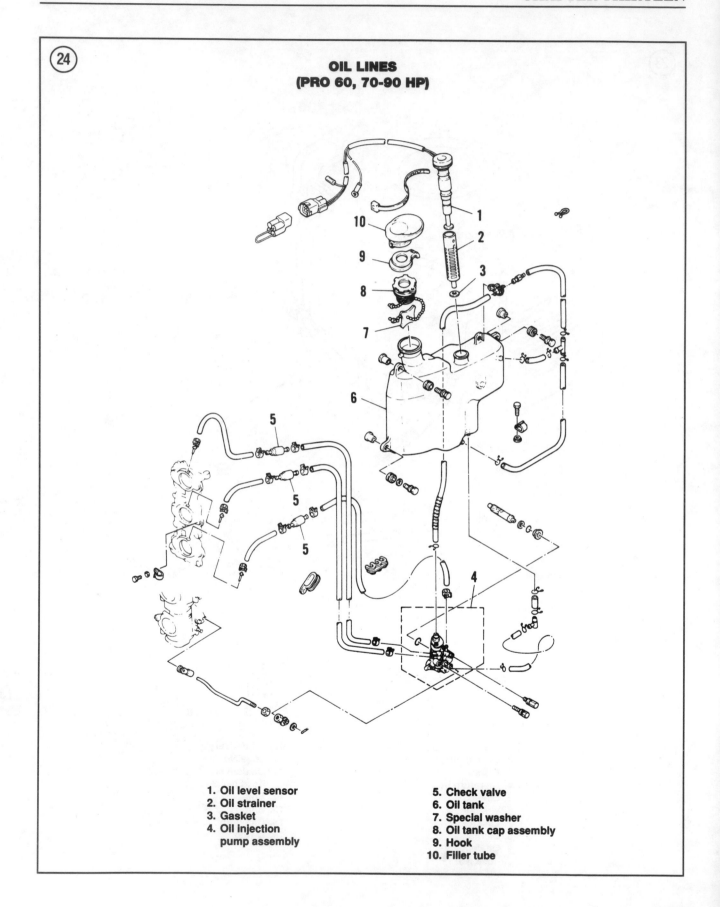

**OIL LINES
(PRO 60, 70-90 HP)**

1. Oil level sensor
2. Oil strainer
3. Gasket
4. Oil injection
   pump assembly
5. Check valve
6. Oil tank
7. Special washer
8. Oil tank cap assembly
9. Hook
10. Filler tube

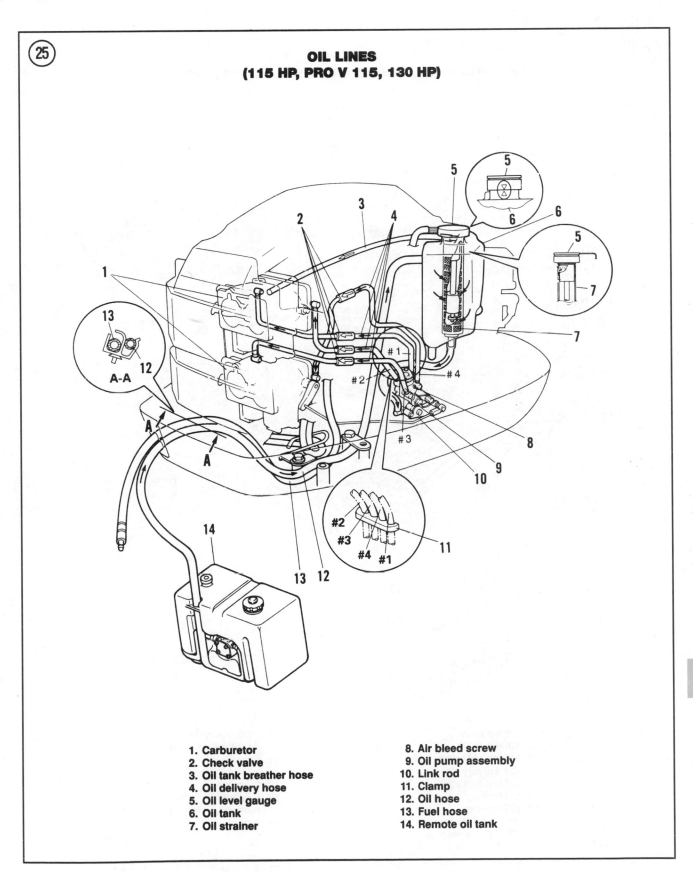

OIL LINES
(115 HP, PRO V 115, 130 HP)

1. Carburetor
2. Check valve
3. Oil tank breather hose
4. Oil delivery hose
5. Oil level gauge
6. Oil tank
7. Oil strainer
8. Air bleed screw
9. Oil pump assembly
10. Link rod
11. Clamp
12. Oil hose
13. Fuel hose
14. Remote oil tank

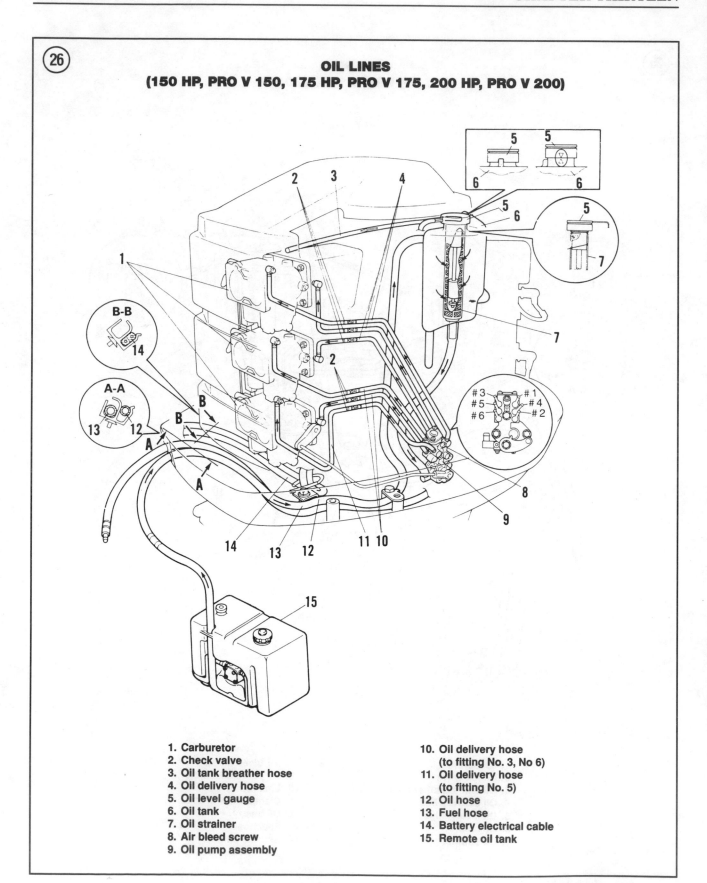

㉖

OIL LINES
(150 HP, PRO V 150, 175 HP, PRO V 175, 200 HP, PRO V 200)

1. Carburetor
2. Check valve
3. Oil tank breather hose
4. Oil delivery hose
5. Oil level gauge
6. Oil tank
7. Oil strainer
8. Air bleed screw
9. Oil pump assembly
10. Oil delivery hose
    (to fitting No. 3, No 6)
11. Oil delivery hose
    (to fitting No. 5)
12. Oil hose
13. Fuel hose
14. Battery electrical cable
15. Remote oil tank

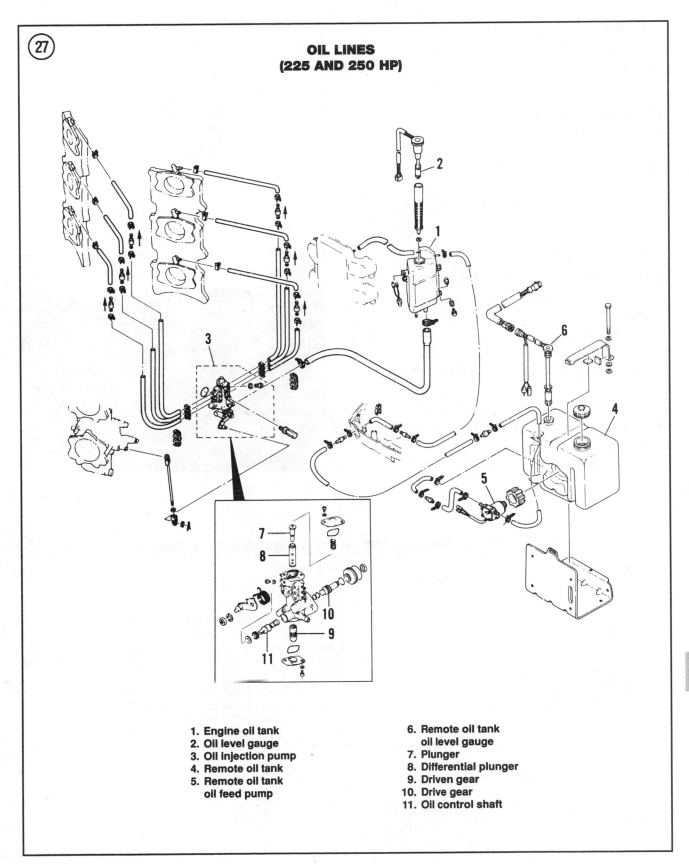

㉗ **OIL LINES
(225 AND 250 HP)**

1. **Engine oil tank**
2. **Oil level gauge**
3. **Oil injection pump**
4. **Remote oil tank**
5. **Remote oil tank
   oil feed pump**
6. **Remote oil tank
   oil level gauge**
7. **Plunger**
8. **Differential plunger**
9. **Driven gear**
10. **Drive gear**
11. **Oil control shaft**

13

a -00. Both oil pumps look identical, so check this number to make sure it is correct when purchasing a new oil pump.

Oil Pump Control Unit
(115 and 130 hp V4 Models)

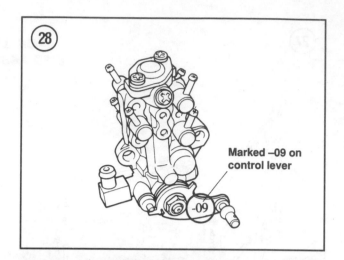

NOTE
On all V6 Models, the oil pump control unit is an integral part of the CDI unit. All other models are not equipped with an oil control unit.

The oil control unit receives signals from the oil tank sensor(s). It activates the warning lights and buzzer and reduces engine speed when necessary.

1. Disconnect the negative battery cable.
2. Remove the engine cover.
3. Disconnect the oil pump control unit electrical connector.
4. Remove the bolts securing the oil pump control unit and remove it from the power head (**Figure 29**).
5. Installation is the reverse of removal.

Table 1 OIL PUMP DELIVERY RATE (3 MINUTE TIME PERIOD)

Engine	Oil quantity
25 hp	0.7-0.9 cc (0.024-0.032 oz.) @ 1,500 rpm
30 hp	0.8-0.9 cc (0.021-0.029 oz.) @ 1,500 rpm
40, 50 hp, Pro 50	1.4-1.8 cc (0.047-0.061 oz.) @ 1,500 rpm
Pro 60, 70 hp	2.0-2.4 cc (0.067-0.081 oz.) @ 1,500 rpm
90 hp	2.8-3.4 cc (0.095-0.115 oz.) @ 1,500 rpm
115 hp	2.9-3.5 cc (0.098-0.118 oz.) @ 1,500 rpm
130 hp, L130	4.3-5.3 cc (0.145-0.179 oz.) @ 1,500 rpm
150 hp, L150, Pro V 150, 175 hp	2.6-3.2 cc (0.088-0.108 oz.) @ 1,500 rpm
Pro V 175, 200 hp, L200	3.1-3.7 cc (0.105-0.125 oz.) @ 1,500 rpm
Pro V 200, 225	4.3-5.3 cc (0.145-0.179 oz.) @ 1,500 rpm
76° V6	5.9-7.3 cc (0.199-0.247 oz.) @ 1,500 rpm

Chapter Fourteen

Yamaha 703 Remote Control Box

The Yamaha 703 remote control box is provided on all 40-250 hp electric start models and is available as an option on 6-30 hp models.

The 703 remote control box houses the ignition or main switch, emergency stop, choke, tilt or trim/tilt and neutral start switches and the overheat/oil warning buzzer. The remote control box is connected to the engine gear shift handle and magneto control lever by cables, allowing the operator to shift the engine and control the throttle at a point away from the engine (**Figure 1**).

This chapter covers disassembly and assembly of the 703 remote control box. Testing of the 703 switches is covered in Chapter Three.

NOTE
The "L" series models (counter rotation models) are included in all procedures. Unless there is a separate procedure designated for an "L" series model, re-

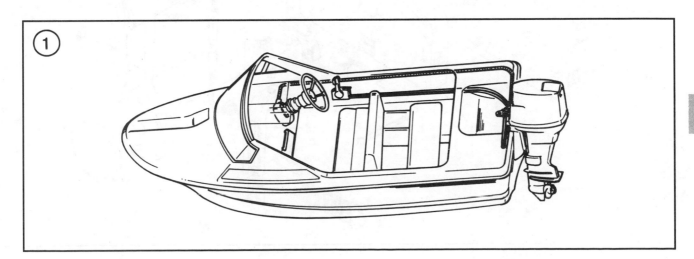

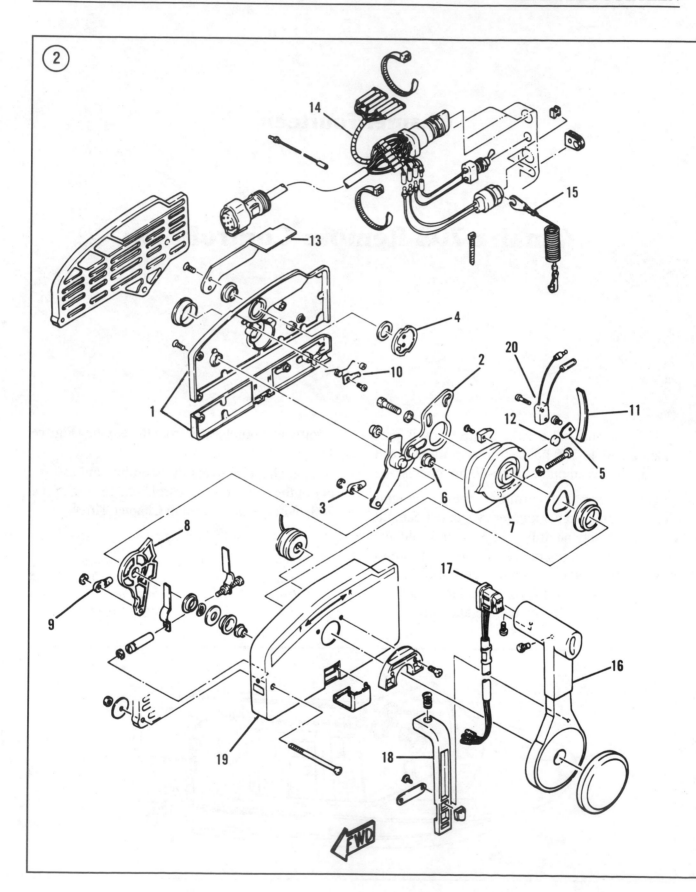

1. Bottom plates
2. Throttle arm
3. Throttle cable end
4. Free acceleration shaft
5. Retainer
6. Cam roller
7. Gear
8. Shift arm
9. Shift cable end
10. Detent roller
11. Leaf spring
12. Free acceleration roller
13. Free acceleration lever
14. Electrical wire harness and switch assembly
15. Lock plate
16. Control lever
17. Tilt or trim/tilt switch
18. Neutral position lever

fer to the procedure that relates to the same horsepower rating. If you are working on an L200, refer to the 200 hp procedure.

Disassembly/Assembly

Refer to **Figure 2** for this procedure.
1. Disconnect the electrical wire harness coupler and remove the remote control box from its mounting bracket.
2. Remove the cover from the lower side of the box (**Figure 3**).
3. Remove the screws securing the 2 back panels (**Figure 4**). Remove the panels.

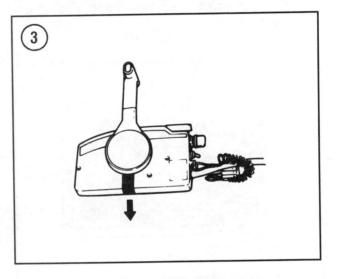

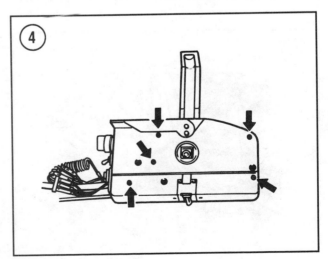

14

4. Disconnect the remote control cables at the throttle and shift arms (**Figure 5**).

5. Disconnect the power tilt or power trim/tilt switch leads, if so equipped.

6. Disconnect the electrical lead (**Figure 6**) and remove the warning buzzer.

7. Loosen the nuts securing the ignition, choke and emergency stop switches. Remove the switches.

8. Remove the neutral start switch.

9. Loosen the throttle friction screw (A, **Figure 7**). Pull out the throttle arm (B, **Figure 7**) and remove the bushing, cam roller and washer from the control box or throttle arm (**Figure 8**).

10. Remove the throttle friction screw circlip. Remove the throttle friction band and screw (**Figure 9**).

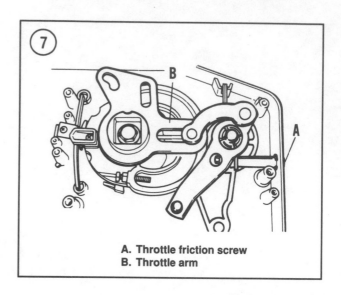

A. Throttle friction screw
B. Throttle arm

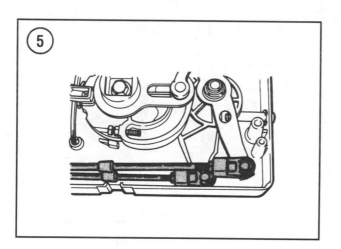

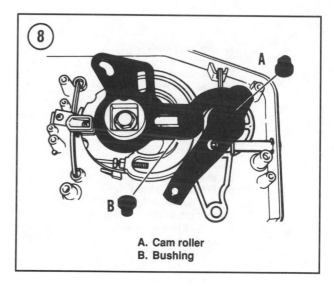

A. Cam roller
B. Bushing

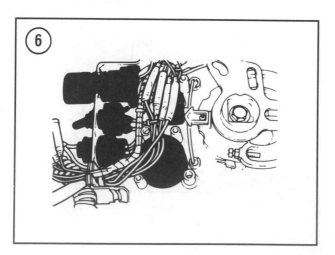

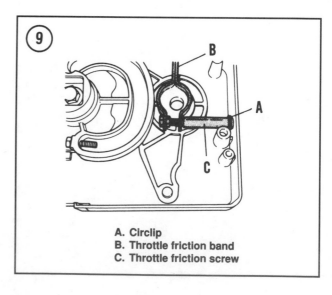

A. Circlip
B. Throttle friction band
C. Throttle friction screw

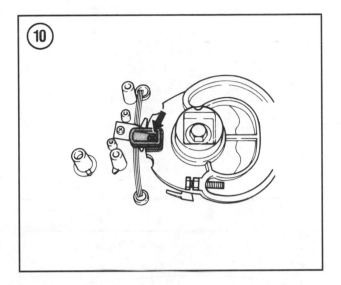

11. Remove the neutral switch operating arm (**Figure 10**) from the gear.

12. Remove the leaf springs and detent roller (**Figure 11**).

13. Loosen the center bolt until its head comes free of the gear, then tap the bolt with a plastic hammer and pull the control lever from the gear (**Figure 12**).

14. Remove the gear and control cam (**Figure 13**).

15. Remove the shift lever arm (**Figure 14**).

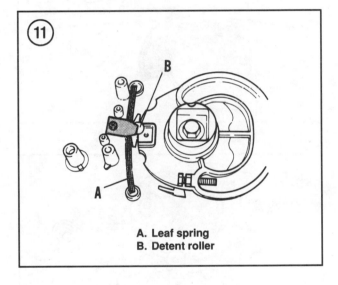

A. Leaf spring
B. Detent roller

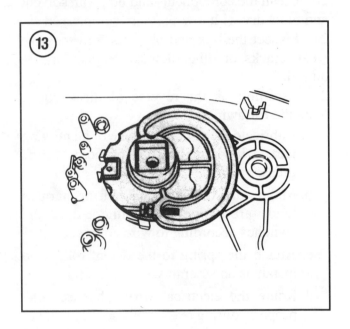

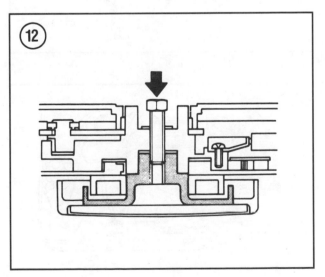

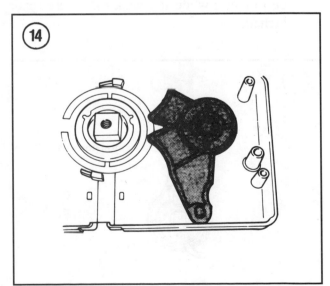

14

16. Remove the neutral position lever from the control lever (**Figure 15**). Remove the spring.

17. If equipped with a power tilt or power trim/tilt switch, remove the switch from the control lever as required (**Figure 16**).

18. Remove the neutral lock holder or position plate from the control box (**Figure 17**).

19. Carefully remove the retainer plate from the back cover to prevent the detent roller from flying out. Remove the detent roller and spring (**Figure 18**).

20. Clean the components and box with solvent and blow dry with low-pressure compressed air.

21. Inspect the box and all parts for excessive wear, cracks or other defects. Replace as required.

22. Assembly is the reverse of disassembly. Note the following:

    a. Lubricate the contact surface of all moving parts with Yamalube All-purpose Marine grease.

    b. Make sure the electrical wiring harness leads are properly reconnected to the switches according to wire color coding.

    c. Attach the spring to the detent roller and install as an assembly.

    d. Route the electrical wiring harness lead properly during reassembly so they will not be pinched when the back plates are reattached.

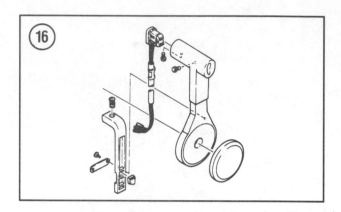

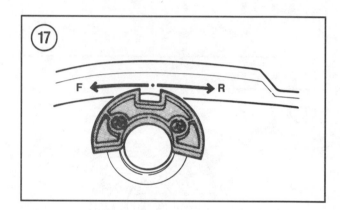

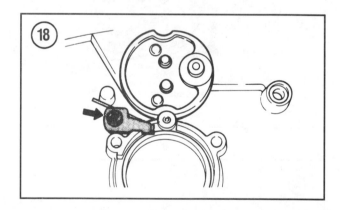

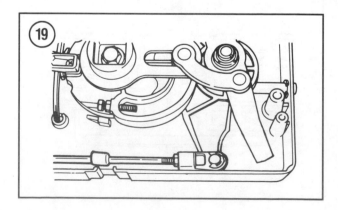

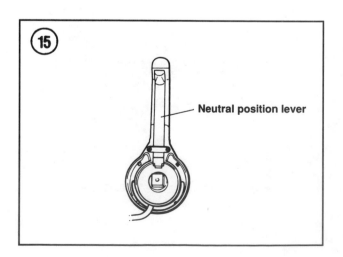

Neutral position lever

e. Fit the shift cable on the shift lever arm (**Figure 19**) and secure it with the circlip. Install the cable anchor spacer, then connect the throttle cable to the throttle lever arm (**Figure 5**) and secure it with the circlip.

f. After reinstalling the back plates, operate the control lever to make sure the cables work properly.

g. Once the control box is reassembled and reinstalled on the boat, operate the control lever several times to make sure that the mechanism shifts properly (**Figure 20**). The shift and throttle operation should follow the pattern shown in **Figure 21**. If shift or throttle adjustments are necessary, adjust the cable length at the engine shift lever or at the carburetor linkage.

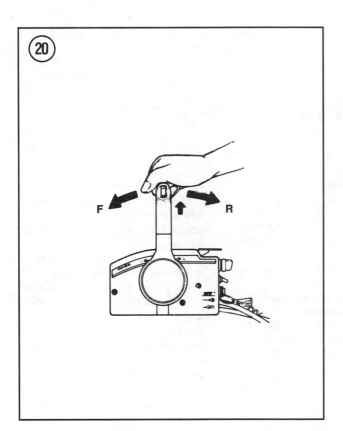

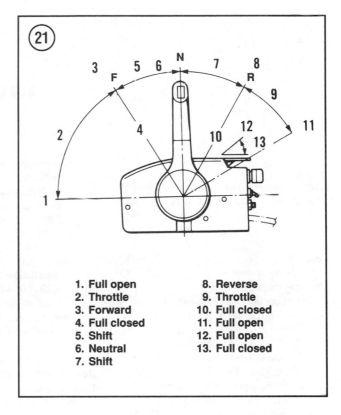

1. Full open
2. Throttle
3. Forward
4. Full closed
5. Shift
6. Neutral
7. Shift
8. Reverse
9. Throttle
10. Full closed
11. Full open
12. Full open
13. Full closed

Index

15

15

2 HP (1990-1994)

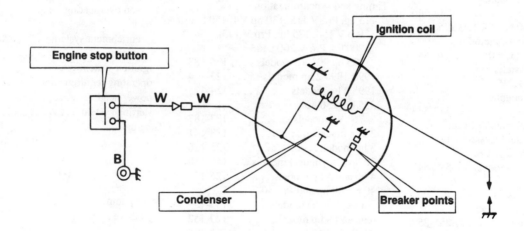

B : Black
W : White

2 HP (1995)

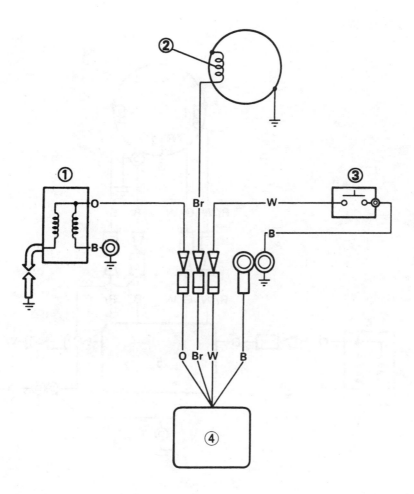

1. Ignition coil
2. Charge coil
3. Stop switch
4. CDI unit

B : Black
Br : Brown
O : Orange
W : White

3 HP

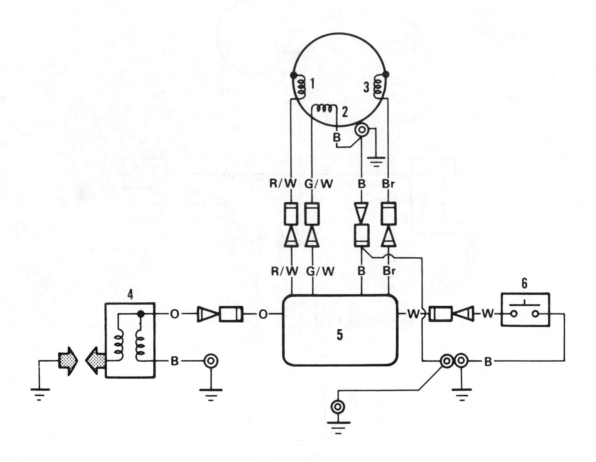

1. Pulser coil 1   B : Black
2. Pulser coil 2   Br : Brown
3. Charge coil   G : Green
4. Ignition coil   O : Orange
5. CDI unit   R : Red
6. Stop switch   W : White

4 AND 5 HP

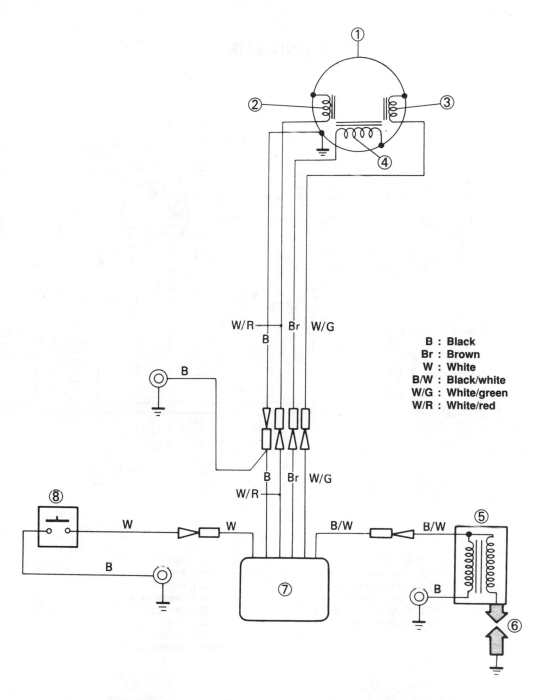

W/R — Br W/G
B

B : Black
Br : Brown
W : White
B/W : Black/white
W/G : White/green
W/R : White/red

B Br W/G
W/R

W ▷ W
B ◁

B/W ◁ B/W

B

1. CDI magneto
2. Pulser coil No. 1
   (high speed side)
3. Pulser coil No. 2
   (low speed side)

4. Charge coil
5. Ignition coil
6. Spark plug
7. CDI unit
8. Stop switch

6 AND 8 HP

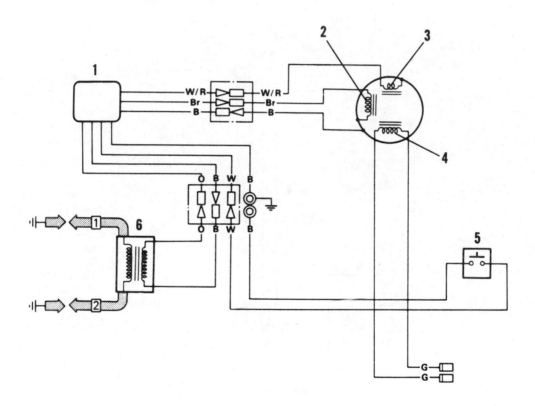

1. CDI unit
2. Charge coil
3. Pulser coil
4. Lighting coil
5. Engine stop switch
6. Ignition coil

B   : Black
Br : Brown
G   : Green
G/W : Green/white
O   : Orange
R   : Red
W   : White
W/R : White/red

9.9 AND 15 HP MANUAL START, TILLER HANDLE

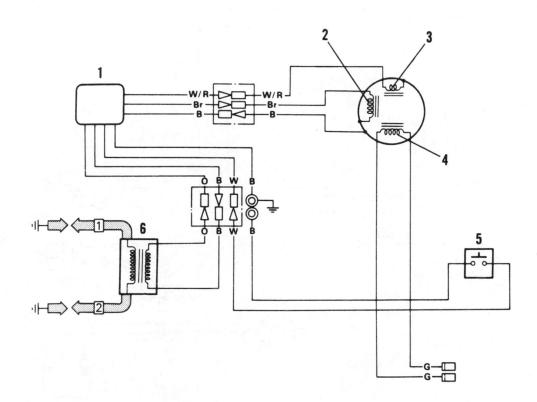

1. CDI unit
2. Charge coil
3. Pulser coil
4. Lighting coil
5. Engine stop switch
6. Ignition coil

B : Black
Br : Brown
G : Green
G/W : Green/white
O : Orange
R : Red
W : White
W/R : White/red

9.9 AND 15 HP ELECTRIC START, TILLER HANDLE

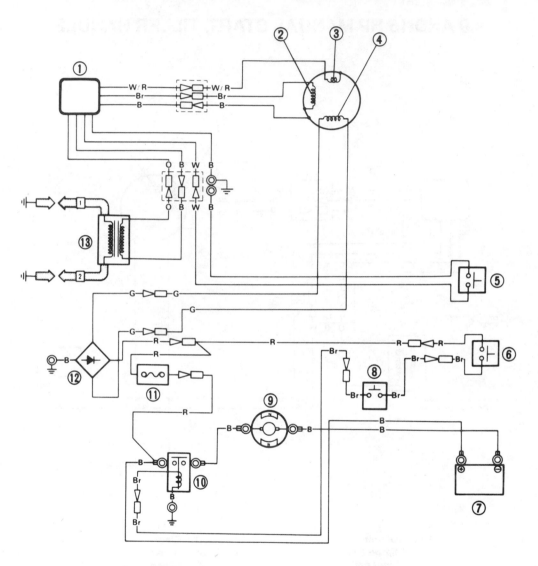

1. CDI unit
2. Charge coil
3. Pulser coil
4. Lighting coil
5. Engine stop switch
6. Starter switch
7. Battery
8. Neutral switch
9. Starter motor
10. Starter relay
11. Fuse
12. Rectifier
13. Ignition coil

B : Black
Br : Brown
G : Green
G/W : Green/white
O : Orange
R : Red
W : White
W/R : White/red

C25 ELECTRIC START, REMOTE CONTROL

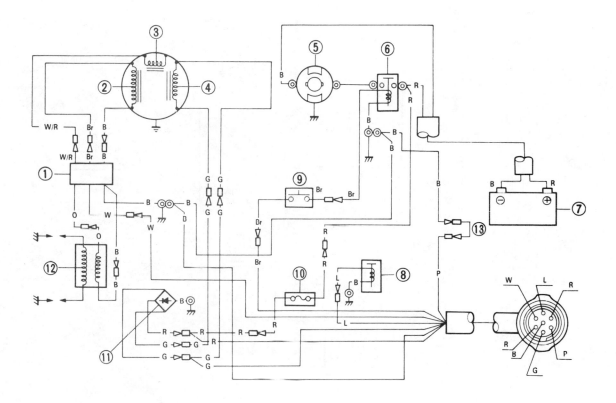

1. CDI unit	**B : Black**
2. Charge coil	**Br : Brown**
3. Pulser coil	**G : Green**
4. Lighting coil	**L : Blue**
5. Starter motor	**O : Orange**
6. Starter relay	**R : Red**
7. Battery	**W : White**
8. Choke solenoid	**W/R : White/red**
9. Neutral switch	
10. Fuse (20A)	
11. Rectifier	
12. Ignition coil	
13. Cover lead wire	

16

C25 ELECTRIC START, TILLER HANDLE

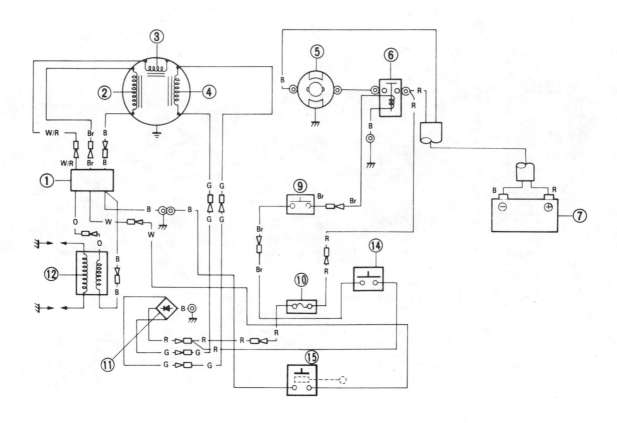

1. CDI unit
2. Charge coil
3. Pulser coil
4. Lighting coil
5. Starter motor
6. Starter relay
7. Battery
8. Choke solenoid
9. Neutral switch
10. Fuse (20A)
11. Rectifier
12. Ignition coil
13. Cover lead wire
14. Starter switch
15. Stop switch

B : Black
Br : Brown
G : Green
L : Blue
O : Orange
R : Red
W : White
W/R : White/red

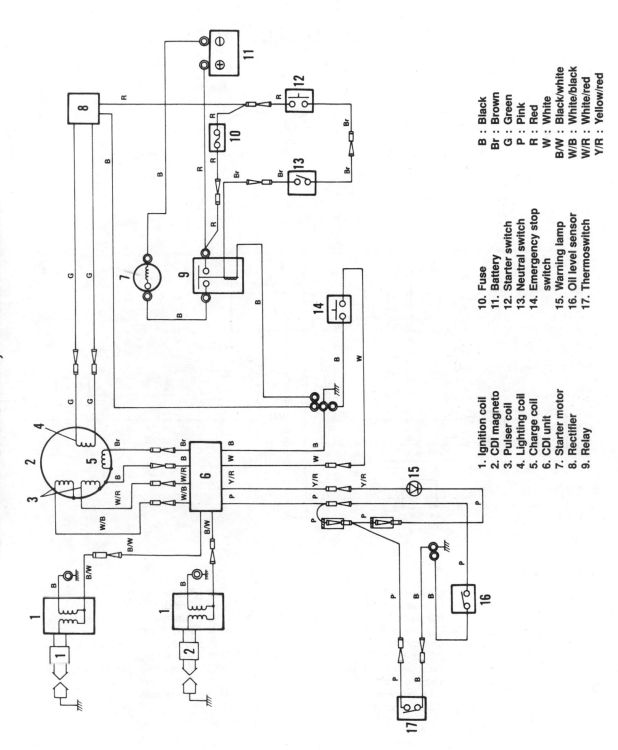

25 HP MANUAL START, TILLER HANDLE

| B : Black |
| Br : Brown |
| G : Green |
| P : Pink |
| R : Red |
| W : White |
| B/W : Black/white |
| W/B : White/black |
| W/R : White/red |
| Y/R : Yellow/red |

1. Ignition coil
2. CDI magneto
3. Pulser coil
4. Lighting coil
5. Charge coil
6. CDI unit
7. Starter motor
8. Rectifier
9. Relay
10. Fuse
11. Battery
12. Starter switch
13. Neutral switch
14. Emergency stop switch
15. Warning lamp
16. Oil level sensor
17. Thermoswitch

25 HP MANUAL START

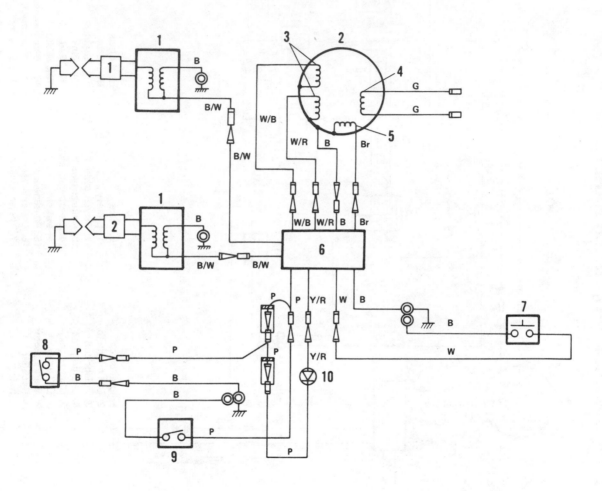

1. Ignition coil
2. CDI magneto
3. Pulser coil
4. Lighting coil
5. Charge coil
6. CDI unit
7. Emergency stop switch
8. Thermoswitch
9. Oil level sensor
10. Warning lamp

B : Black
Br : Brown
G : Green
P : Pink
W : White
B/W : Black/white
W/B : White/black
Y/R : Yellow/red
W/R : White/red

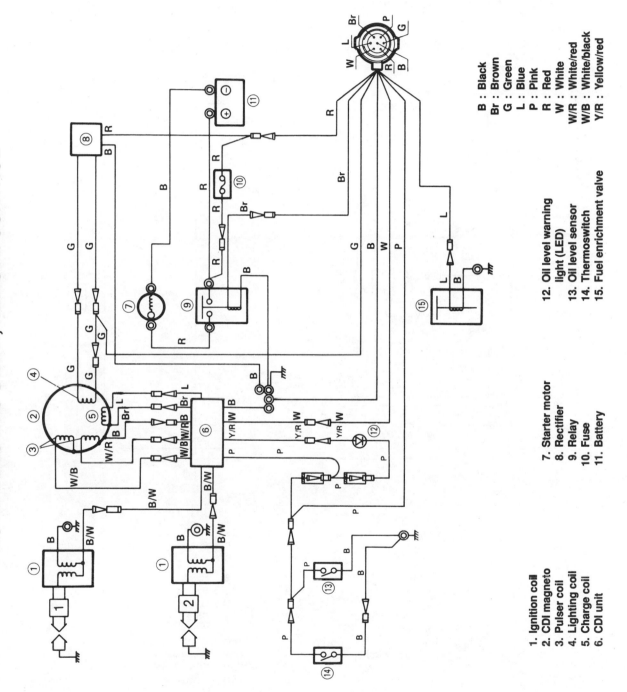

25 HP ELECTRIC START, REMOTE CONTROL

B : Black
Br : Brown
G : Green
L : Blue
P : Pink
R : Red
W : White
W/R : White/red
W/B : White/black
Y/R : Yellow/red

1. Ignition coil
2. CDI magneto
3. Pulser coil
4. Lighting coil
5. Charge coil
6. CDI unit

7. Starter motor
8. Rectifier
9. Relay
10. Fuse
11. Battery

12. Oil level warning light (LED)
13. Oil level sensor
14. Thermoswitch
15. Fuel enrichment valve

16

C30 MANUAL START, TILLER HANDLE 2-CYLINDER

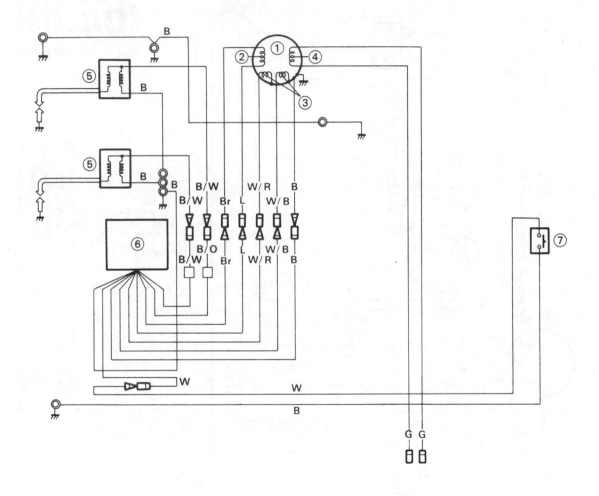

1. CDI magneto
2. Charge coil
3. Pulser coil
4. Lighting coil
5. Ignition coil
6. CDI unit
7. Engine stop switch

B : Black
Br : Brown
G : Green
L : Blue
W : White
B/O : Black/orange
B/W : Black/white
W/B : White/black
W/R : White/red

C30 ELECTRIC START, REMOTE CONTROL 2-CYLINDER

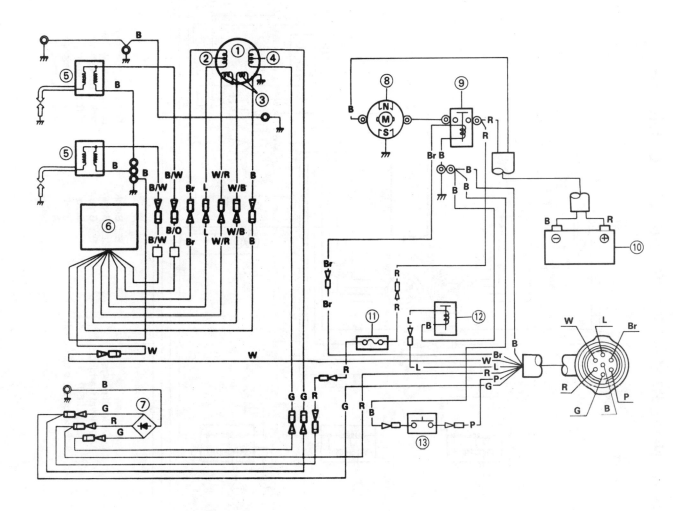

1. CDI magneto
2. Charge coil
3. Pulser coil
4. Lighting coil
5. Ignition coil
6. CDI unit
7. Rectifier
8. Starter motor
9. Starter relay
10. Battery
11. Fuse
12. Fuel enrichment solenoid
13. Thermoswitch

B : Black
Br : Brown
G : Green
L : Blue
P : Pink
R : Red
W : White
B/O : Black/orange
B/W : Black/white
W/B : White/black
W/R : White/red

16

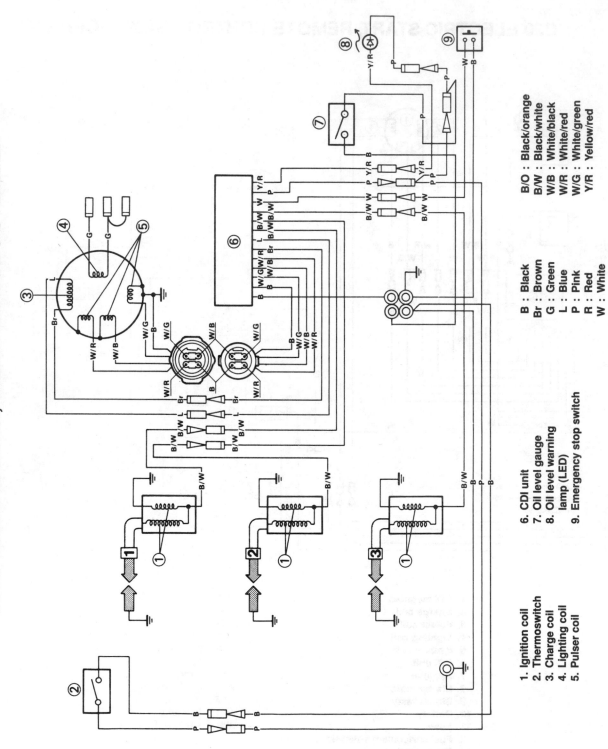

30 HP MANUAL START, TILLER HANDLE 3-CYLINDER

1. Ignition coil
2. Thermoswitch
3. Charge coil
4. Lighting coil
5. Pulser coil

6. CDI unit
7. Oil level gauge
8. Oil level warning lamp (LED)
9. Emergency stop switch

B :	Black
Br :	Brown
G :	Green
L :	Blue
P :	Pink
R :	Red
W :	White

B/O :	Black/orange
B/W :	Black/white
W/B :	White/black
W/R :	White/red
W/G :	White/green
Y/R :	Yellow/red

30 HP ELECTRIC START, TILLER HANDLE 3-CYLINDER

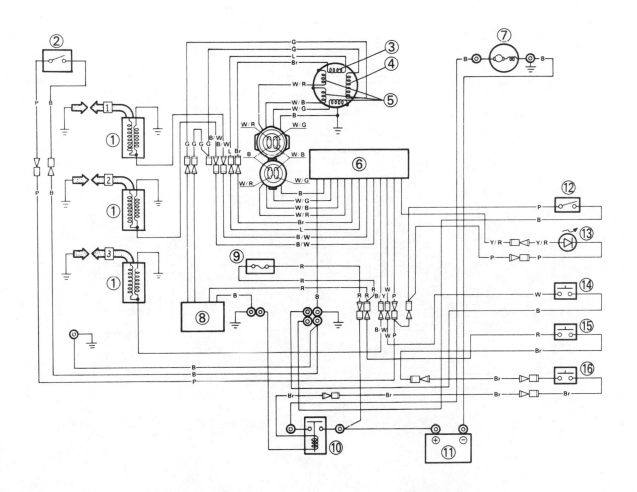

1. Ignition coil
2. Thermoswitch
3. Charge coil
4. Lighting coil
5. Pulser coil
6. CDI unit
7. Starter motor
8. Rectifier
9. Fuse (10A)
10. Starter relay
11. Battery
12. Oil level sensor
13. Oil level warning lamp (LED)1
14. Engine stop switch
15. Starter switch
16. Neutral switch

B : Black
Br : Brown
G : Green
L : Blue
P : Pink
R : Red
W : White
Y : Yellow
B/O : Black/orange
B/W : Black/white
W/B : White/black
W/R : White/red
W/G : White/green
Y/R : Yellow/red

30 HP ELECTRIC START, REMOTE CONTROL 3-CYLINDER

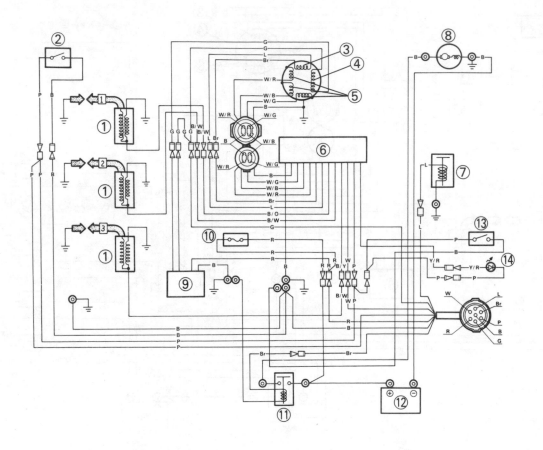

1. Ignition coil
2. Thermoswitch
3. Charge coil
4. Lighting coil
5. Pulser coil
6. CDI unit
7. Fuel enrichment valve
8. Starter motor
9. Rectifier
10. Fuse (10A)
11. Starter relay
12. Battery
13. Oil level sensor
14. Oil level warning lamp (LED)1

B : Black
Br : Brown
G : Green
L : Blue
O : Orange
P : Pink
R : Red
W : White
Y : Yellow
B/O : Black/orange
R/W : Black/white
W/B : White/black
W/R : White/red
W/G : White/green
Y/R : Yellow/red

C40 2-CYLINDER

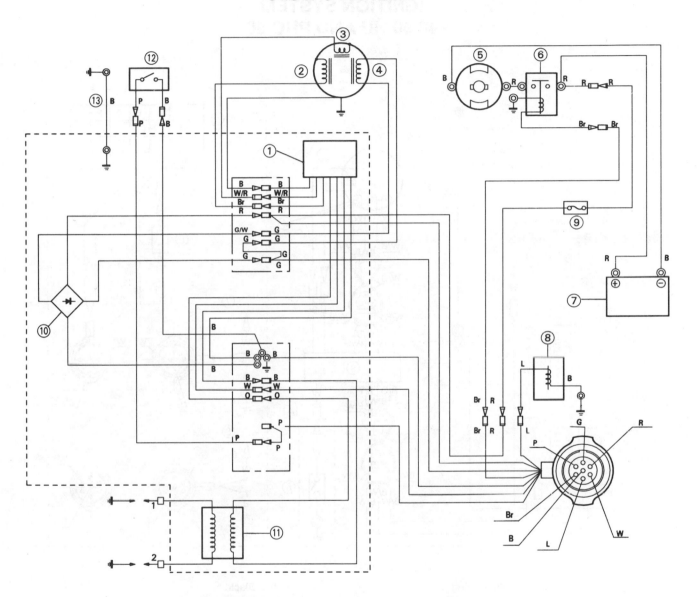

1. CDI unit
2. Charge coil
3. Pulser coil
4. Lighting coil
5. Starter motor
6. Starter relay
7. Battery
8. Choke solenoid
9. Fuse (10A)
10. Fuse (10A)
11. Ignition coil
12. Thermoswitch
13. Ground wire

B : Black
Br : Brown
G : Green
L : Blue
O : Orange
P : Pink
R : Red
W : White
G/W : Green/white
W/R : White/red

IGNITION SYSTEM
40-50 HP AND PRO 50

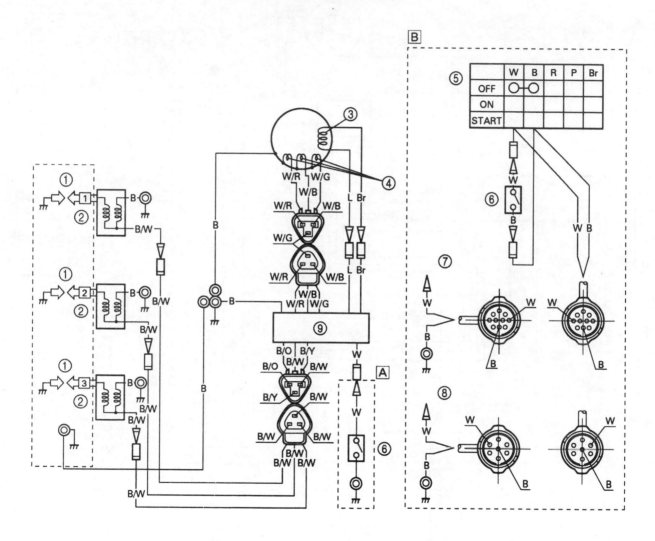

1. Spark plug
2. Ignition coil
3. Charge coil
4. Pulser coil
5. Main switch
6. Engine stop switch
7. 10-pin electrical connector
8. 7-pin electrical connector
9. CDI unit

A : Manual start models
B : Electric start models

B : Black
Br : Brown
L : Blue
W : White
B/O : Black/orange
B/W : Black/white
B/Y : Black/yellow
W/B : White/black
W/R : White/red
W/G : White/green

STARTING SYSTEM
40-50 HP AND PRO 50

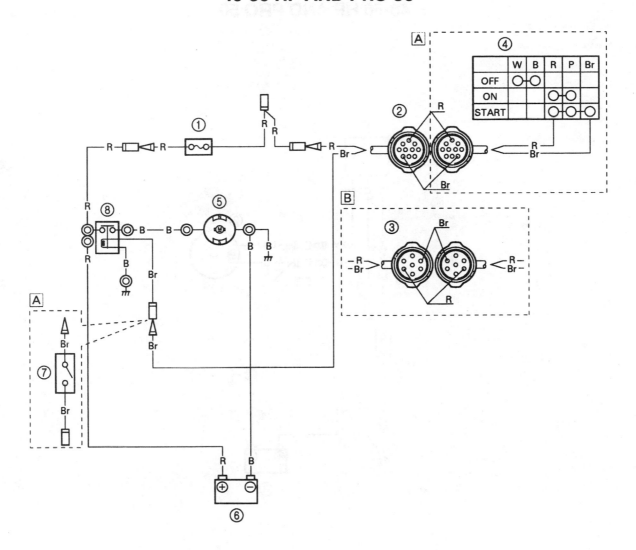

		W	B	R	P	Br
OFF		O—O				
ON				O—O		
START			O—O	O		O

1. Fuse
2. 10-pin electrical connector
3. 7-pin electrical connector
4. Main switch
5. Starter motor
6. Battery
7. Neutral switch
8. Starter relay

A : Except remote control models.
B : Remote control models.

B : Black
Br : Brown
R : Red

16

CHARGING SYSTEM
40-50 HP AND PRO 50

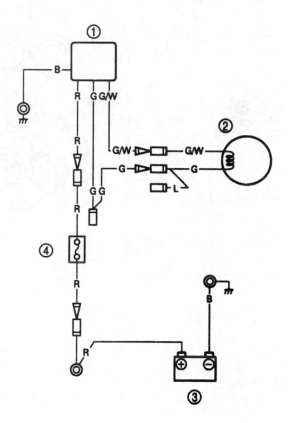

1. Rectifier/regulator
2. Lighting coil
3. Battery
4. Fuse

G : Green
G/W : Green/white
R : Red
B : Black

POWER TRIM AND TILT SYSTEM
40-50 HP AND PRO 50

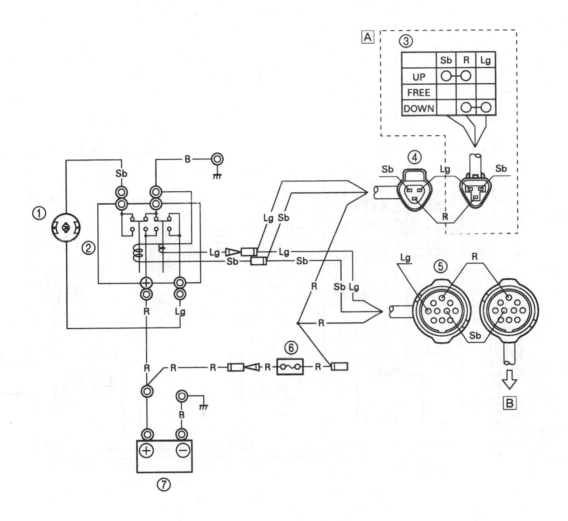

	Sb	R	Lg
UP	○—○		
FREE			
DOWN		○—○	

1. PTT motor
2. PTT relay
3. PTT switch
4. 3-pin electrical connector (black)
5. 10-pin electrical connector
6. Fuse
7. Battery

R : Red
LG : Light green
Sb : Sky blue
B : Black

A : Bottom cowl PTT switch model
B : To remote control

C55 ELECTIC START 2-CYLINDER

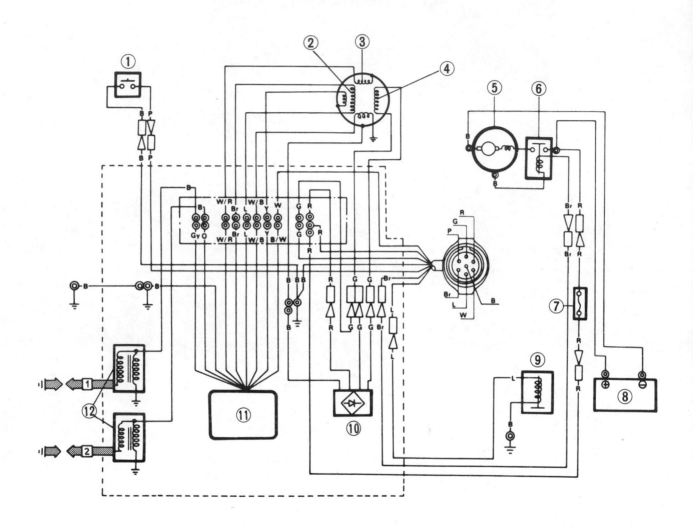

1. Thermoswitch	B : Black
2. Charge coil	Br : Brown
3. Pulser coil	G : Green
4. Lighting coil	Gy : Gray
5. Starter motor	L : Blue
6. Starter relay	O : Orange
7. Fuse (20A)	P : Pink
8. Battery	R : Red
9. Choke solenoid	Sb : Sky blue
10. Rectifier	W : White
11. CDI unit	Y : Yellow
12. Ignition coil	Lg : Light green
	W/R : White/red
	W/B : White/black
	B/W : Black/white

PRO 60 AND 70 HP

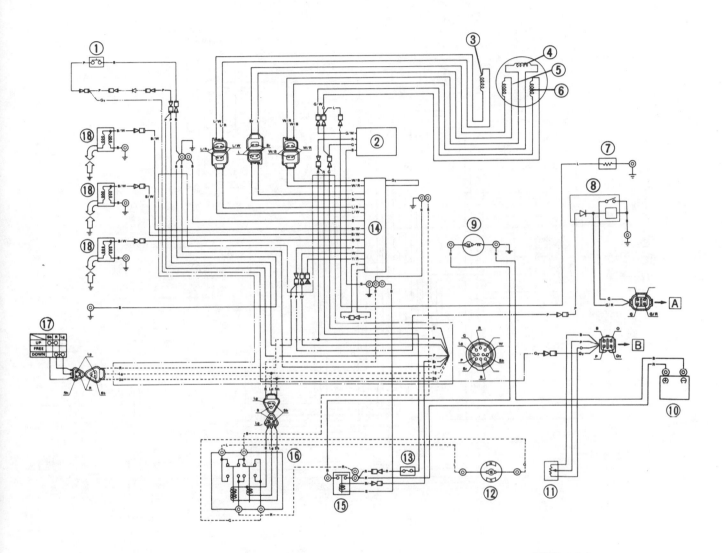

1. Thermoswitch
2. Rectifier/regulator
3. Crank position sensor
4. Pulser coil
5. Charge coil
6. Lighting coil
7. Electrothermal valve
8. Oil level sensor (oil injection models)
9. Starter motor
10. Battery
11. Trim sensor (PTT models)

12. Power trim and tilt motor (PTT models)
13. Fuse (20A)
14. CDI unit
15. Starter relay
16. Power trim and tilt relay (PTT models)
17. Power trim and tilt switch (PTT models)
18. Ignition coil
19. Oil warning lamp
A : To oil level gauge
B : To trim gauge

B : Black
Br : Brown
G : Green
Gy : Gray
L : Blue
O : Orange
P : Pink
R : Red
Sb : Sky blue
W : White

Y : Yellow
Lg : Light green
W/R : White/red
W/B : White/black
B/W : Black/white
L/R : Blue/red
L/W : Blue/white
G/W : Green/white
G/R : Green/red

16

90 HP

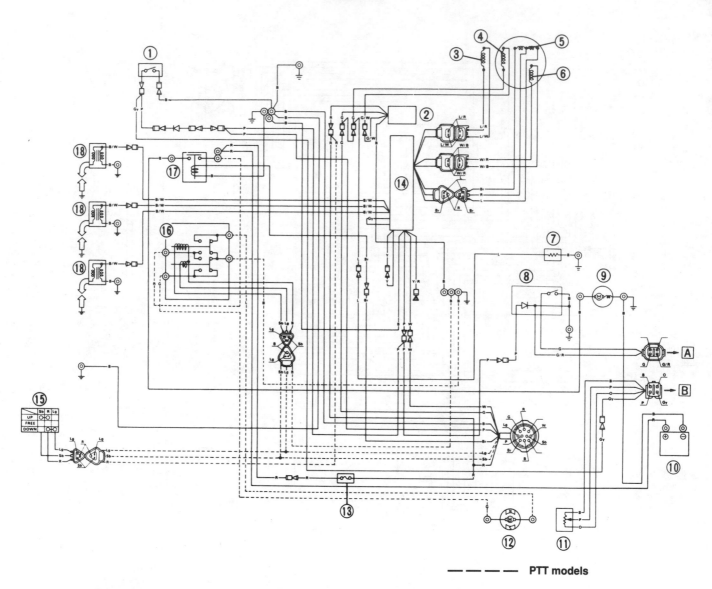

— — — — PTT models

1. Thermoswitch
2. Rectifier/regulator
3. Crank position sensor
4. Lighting coil
5. Charge coil
6. Pulser coil
7. Electrothermal valve
8. Oil level sensor
   (oil injection models)
9. Starter motor
10. Battery
11. Trim sensor
    (PTT models)

12. Power trim and tilt
    motor (PTT models)
13. Fuse (20A)
14. CDI unit
15. Power trim and tilt
    switch (PTT models)
16. Power trim and tilt
    relay (PTT models)
17. Starter relay
18. Ignition coil
 A : To oil level gauge
 B : To trim gauge

B : Black
Br : Brown
G : Green
Gy : Gray
L : Blue
O : Orange
P : Pink
R : Red
Sb : Sky blue
W : White

Y : Yellow
Lg : Light green
W/R : White/red
W/B : White/black
B/W : Black/white
L/R : Blue/red
L/W : Blue/white
G/W : Green/white
G/R : Green/red

C75 AND C85 ELECTRIC START

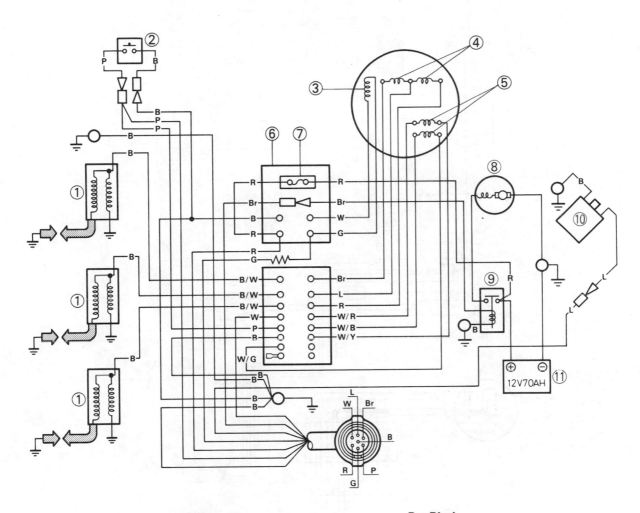

1. Ignition coil
2. Thermoswitch
3. Lighting coil
4. Charge coil
5. Pulser coil
6. Rectifier/regulator
7. Fuse
8. Starter motor
9. Starter relay
10. Choke solenoid
11. Battery

B : Black
Br : Brown
G : Green
Gy : Gray
L : Blue
O : Orange
P : Pink
R : Red
Sb : Sky blue
W : White
Y : Yellow
Lg : Light green
B/W : Black/white
W/G : White/green

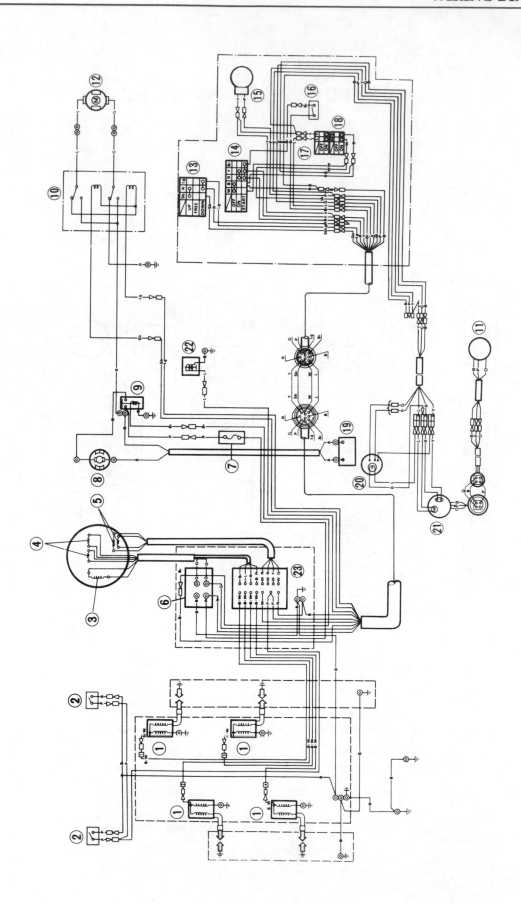

C115

1. Ignition coil
2. Thermoswitch
3. Lighting coil
4. Charge coil
5. Pulser coil
6. Rectifier/regulator
7. Fuse (20A)
8. Starter motor
9. Starter relay
10. Power trim and tilt relay
11. Trim sensor
12. Power trim and tilt motor
13. Power trim and tilt switch
14. Main switch
15. Overheat buzzer
16. Neutral switch
17. Choke switch lever
18. Engine stop switch
19. Battery
20. Tachometer (optional)
21. Trim meter
22. Choke solenoid
23. CDI unit

B : Black
Br : Brown
G : Green
Gy : Gray
L : Blue
O : Orange
P : Pink
R : Red
Sb : Sky blue
W : White
Y : Yellow
Lg : Light green
B/W : Black/white

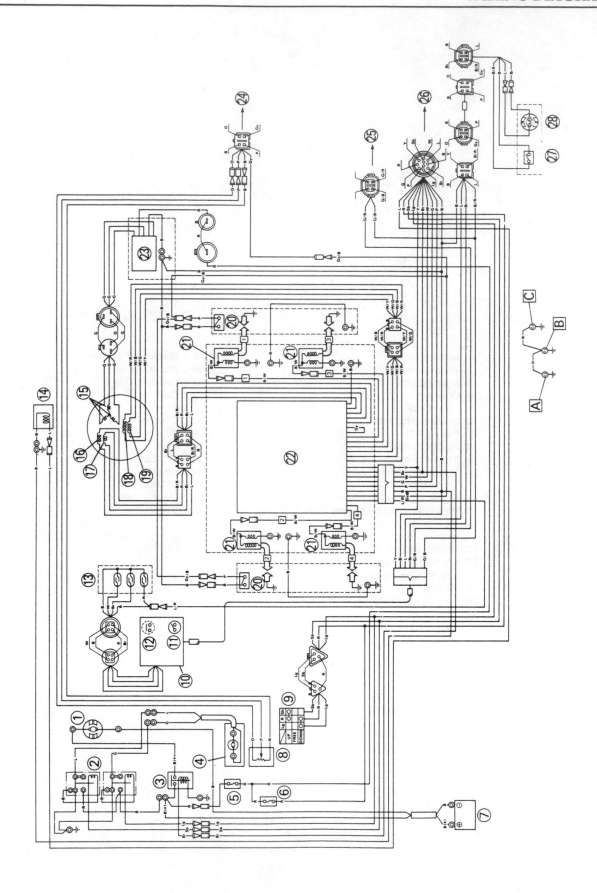

115 AND 130 HP
POWER TRIM/TILT, REMOTE CONTROL
(20 AND 25 IN. SHAFT)

1. Starter motor	B : Black
2. Power trim and tilt relay	Br : Brown
3. Starter relay	G : Green
4. Power trim and tilt motor	Gy : Gray
5. Fuse (30A)	L : Blue
6. Fuse (20A)	O : Orange
7. Battery	P : Pink
8. Trim sensor	R : Red
9. Trailer switch	Sb : Sky blue
10. Control unit	W : White
11. Emergency switch	Y : Yellow
12. Tilt switch	Lg : Light green
13. Oil level gauge (engine oil tank)	B/W : Black/white
14. Choke solenoid	B/R : Black/red
15. Lighting coil	L/R : Blue/red
16. Charge coil (high speed)	Gy/B : Gray/black
17. Charge coil (low speed)	G/B : Green/black
18. Pulser coil (No. 1, No. 3)	G/R : Green/red
19. Pulser coil (No. 2, No. 4)	W/Y : White/yellow
20. Thermoswitch	W/G : White/green
21. Ignition coil	W/B : White/black
22. CDI unit	W/R : White/red
23. Rectifier/regulator	
24. To trim meter	
25. To oil level meter	
26. To remote control or switch panel	
27. Oil level gauge (remote oil tank)	
28. Oil feed pump motor	

A : Ground to bottom cowling.
B : Ground to upper casing.
C : Ground to exhaust cover.

16

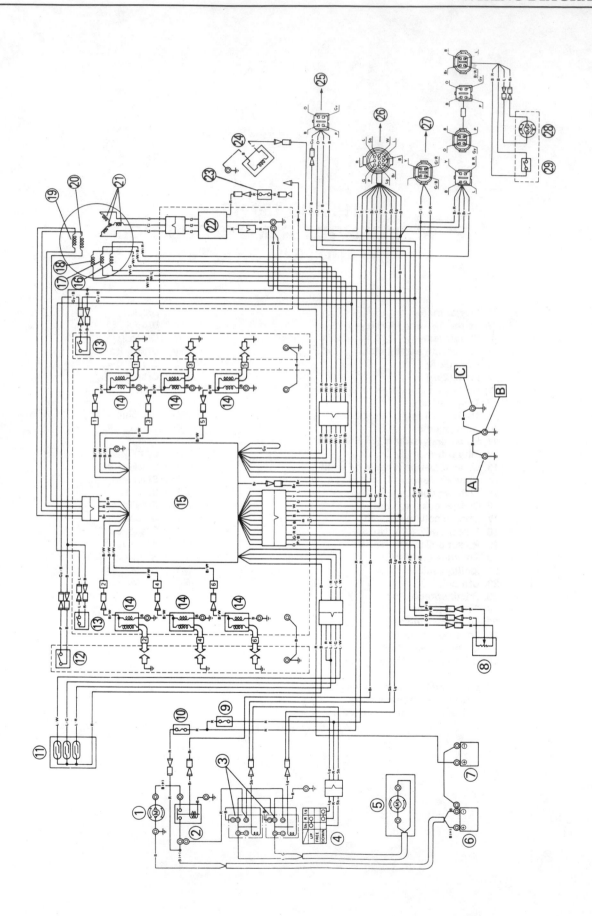

150, 175 AND 200 HP; L150 AND L200; PRO V 150, PRO V 175 AND PRO V 200

1. Starter motor
2. Starter relay
3. Power trim and tilt relay
4. Trailer switch
5. Power trim and tilt motor
6. Battery (for engine starting)
7. Battery (for accessory-option)
8. Trim sensor
9. Fuse (20A)
10. Fuse (30A)
11. Oil level gauge
    (engine oil tank)
12. Thermoswitch
13. Emergency switch
14. Ignition coil
15. CDI unit
16. Pulser coil (No. 1, No. 4)
17. Pulser coil (No. 2, No. 5)
18. Pulser coil (No. 3, No. 6)
19. Charge coil (low speed)
20. Charge coil (high speed)
21. Lighting coil
22. Rectifier/regulator
23. Fuse (30A)
24. Choke solenoid
25. To trim meter
26. To remote control or
    switch panel
27. To oil level meter
28. Oil feed pump motor
29. Oil level gauge
    (remote oil tank)

A : Ground to bottom cowling.
B : Ground to upper casing.
C : Ground to exhaust cover.

B : Black
Br : Brown
G : Green
Gy : Gray
L : Blue
O : Orange
P : Pink
R : Red
Sb : Sky blue
W : White
Y : Yellow
Lg : Light green
B/W : Black/white
B/R : Black/red
L/R : Blue/red
Gy/B : Gray/black
G/B : Green/black
G/R : Green/red
W/Y : White/yellow
W/G : White/green
W/B : White/black
W/R : White/red

16

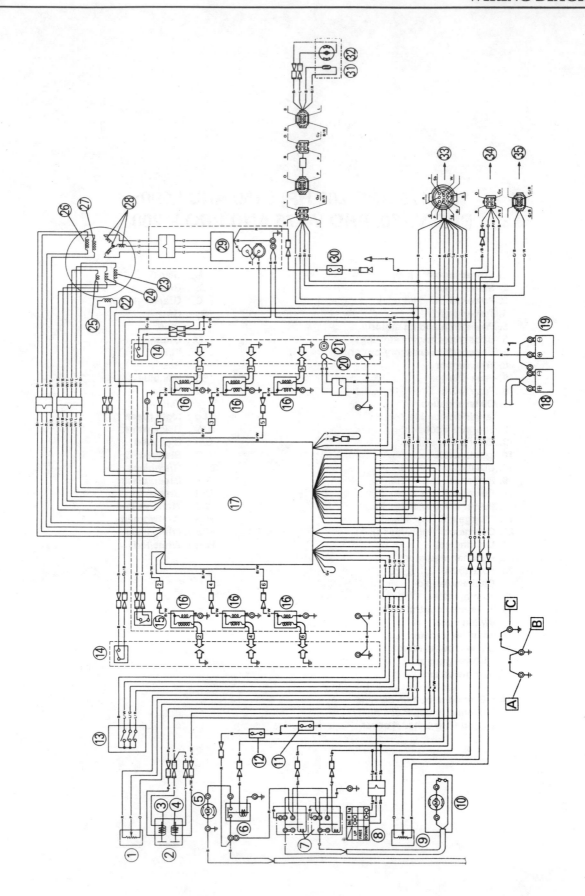

225 HP

1. Throttle position sensor
2. Prime starter
3. Valve A
4. Valve B
5. Starter motor
6. Starter relay
7. Power trim and tilt relay
8. Trailer switch
9. Trim sensor
10. Power trim and tilt motor
11. Fuse (20A)
12. Fuse (30A)
13. Oil level gauge (engine oil tank)
14. Thermoswitch
15. Emergency switch
16. Ignition coil
17. CDI unit
18. Battery (for engine starting)
19. Battery (for accessory-option)
20. Thermosensor
21. Knock sensor
22. Crank position sensor
23. Pulser coil (No. 3, No.6)
24. Pulser coil (No. 2, No.5)
25. Pulser coil (No. 1, No.4)
26. Charge coil (low speed)
27. Charge coil (high speed)
28. Lighting coil
29. Rectifier/regulator
30. Fuse (30A)
31. Oil level gauge (remote oil tank)
32. Oil feed pump motor
33. To remote control or switch panel
34. To trim meter
35. To oil level meter

A : Ground to bottom cowling.
B : Ground to upper casing.
C : Ground to exhaust cover.

B : Black
Br : Brown
G : Green
Gy : Gray
L : Blue
O : Orange
P : Pink
R : Red
Sb : Sky blue
W : White
Y : Yellow
Lg : Light green
B/W : Black/white
B/R : Black/red
L/R : Blue/red
Gy/B : Gray/black
G/B : Green/black
G/R : Green/red
W/Y : White/yellow
W/G : White/green
W/B : White/black
W/R : White/red

16

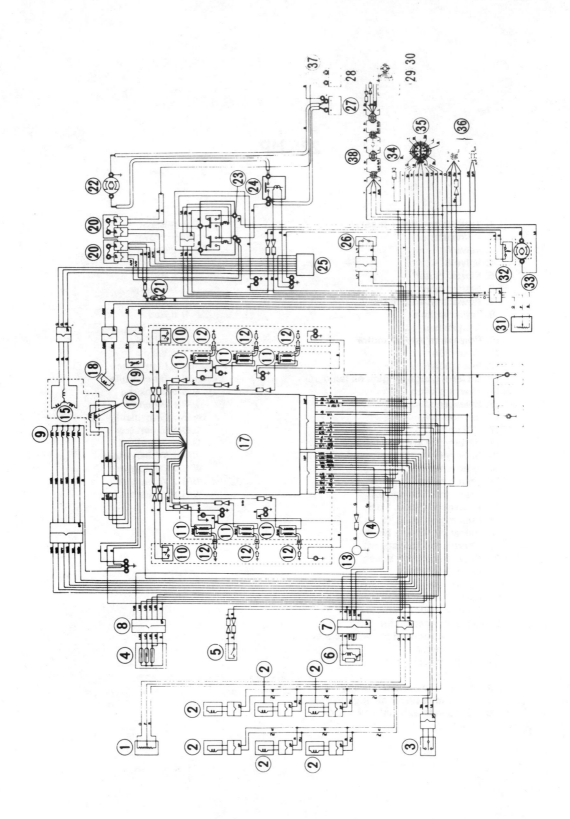

225 AND 250 HP;
L225 AND L250

1. Throttle valve angle sensor
2. Fuel enrichment solenoid valve
3. Power trim and tilt switch
4. Oil level gauge (engine oil tank)
5. Emergency switch
6. Electromagnetic fuel feed pump
7. Emergency connector
8. Diagnosis connector
9. Pulse coil assembly
10. Thermoswitch
11. Ignition coil
12. Spark plug
13. Knock sensor
14. Over-rev control stopping lead
15. Lighting coil assembly
16. Charging coil assembly
17. CDI unit
18. Crank position sensor
19. Thermo sensor
20. Fuse holder (80A)
21. Fuse holder (20A)
22. Starter motor
23. Power trim and tilt relay
24. Starter motor relay
25. Rectifier
26. Shift cut switch
27. Battery (for starter motor)
28. Battery (for accessory-option)
29. Oil level gauge (remote oil tank)
30. Oil feed pump
31. Trim angle sensor
32. Power trim and tilt
    motor thermoswitch
33. Power trim and tilt motor
34. To electromagnetic
    primer pump (option)
35. To remote control box
36. To digital meter
37. Negative lead
38. Extension wire lead (inner part)

B : Black
Br : Brown
G : Green
Gy : Gray
L : Blue
O : Orange
P : Pink
R : Red
Sb : Sky blue
W : White
Y : Yellow
Lg : Light green
B/W : Black/white
B/R : Black/red
L/R : Blue/red
Gy/B : Gray/black
G/B : Green/black
G/R : Green/red
W/Y : White/yellow
W/G : White/green
W/B : White/black
W/R : White/red

16

703 REMOTE CONTROL BOX

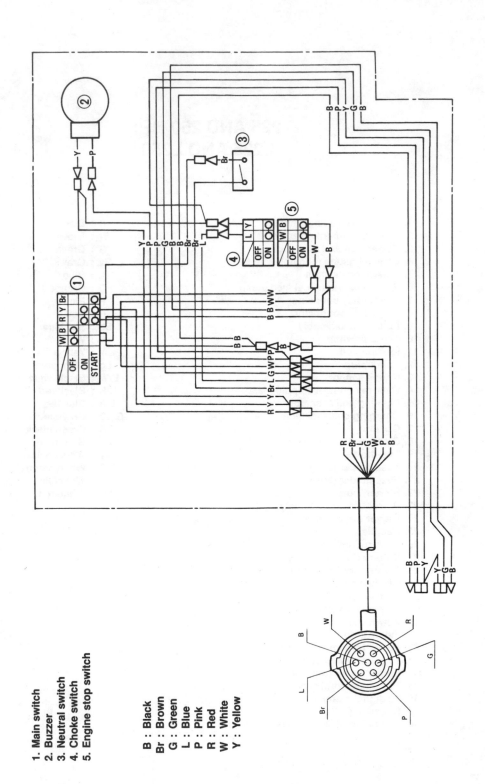

1. Main switch
2. Buzzer
3. Neutral switch
4. Choke switch
5. Engine stop switch

B : Black
Br : Brown
G : Green
L : Blue
P : Pink
R : Red
W : White
Y : Yellow

NOTES

NOTES

NOTES

MAINTENANCE LOG

Service Performed	Mileage Reading				
Oil change (example)	2,836	5,782	8,601		